THE
TWILIGHT WAR

THE
TWILIGHT WAR

The Secret History of America's Thirty-Year Conflict with Iran

DAVID CRIST

THE PENGUIN PRESS
New York
2012

THE PENGUIN PRESS
Published by the Penguin Group
Penguin Group (USA) Inc., 375 Hudson Street, New York, New York 10014, U.S.A. •
Penguin Group (Canada), 90 Eglinton Avenue East, Suite 700, Toronto, Ontario, M4P 2Y3
(a division of Pearson Penguin Canada Inc.) • Penguin Books Ltd, 80 Strand, London
WC2R 0RL, England • Penguin Ireland, 25 St. Stephen's Green, Dublin 2, Ireland (a division
of Penguin Books Ltd) • Penguin Books Australia Ltd, 250 Camberwell Road, Camberwell,
Victoria 3124, Australia (a division of Pearson Australia Group Pty Ltd) • Penguin Books
India Pvt Ltd, 11 Community Centre, Panchsheel Park, New Delhi—110 017, India •
Penguin Group (NZ), 67 Apollo Drive, Rosedale, Auckland 0632, New Zealand
(a division of Pearson New Zealand Ltd) • Penguin Books (South Africa) (Pty) Ltd,
24 Sturdee Avenue, Rosebank, Johannesburg 2196, South Africa

Penguin Books Ltd, Registered Offices:
80 Strand, London WC2R 0RL, England

First published in 2012 by The Penguin Press,
a member of Penguin Group (USA) Inc.

Library of Congress Cataloging-in-Publication Data

Crist, David.
The twilight war : the secret history of America's thirty-year conflict with Iran / David Crist.
p. cm.
Includes bibliographical references and index.
ISBN 978-1-59420-341-1
1. United States—Foreign relations—Iran.   2. Iran—Foreign relations—United States.
3. United States—Military relations—Iran.   4. Iran—Military relations—United States.
5. Espionage, American—History.   6. United States. Central Intelligence Agency.
7. Espionage, Iranian—History.   8. United States—Foreign relations—1981–1989.
9. United States—Foreign relations—1989–   I. Title.
E183.8.I55C75 2012
327.73055—dc23
2011050573
Printed in the United States of America
1   3   5   7   9   10   8   6   4   2

DESIGNED BY AMANDA DEWEY
MAPS BY JEFFREY L. WARD

For my family

CONTENTS

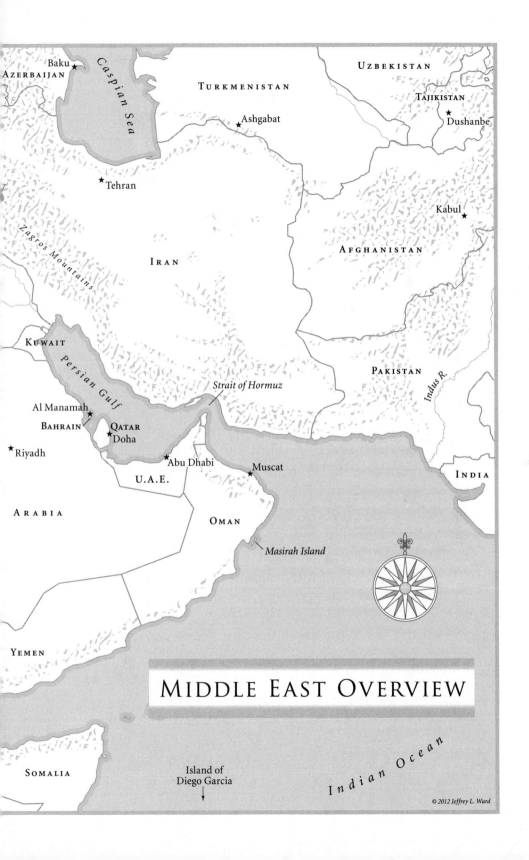

Baku
AZERBAIJAN
Caspian Sea
UZBEKISTAN
TURKMENISTAN
TAJIKISTAN
Ashgabat
Dushanbe
Tehran
Kabul
Zagros Mountains
IRAN
AFGHANISTAN
KUWAIT
PAKISTAN
Persian Gulf
Strait of Hormuz
Indus R.
Al Manamah
BAHRAIN
QATAR
Doha
Riyadh
Abu Dhabi
Muscat
INDIA
U.A.E.
ARABIA
OMAN
Masirah Island
YEMEN

MIDDLE EAST OVERVIEW

SOMALIA
Island of
Diego Garcia
Indian Ocean

© 2012 Jeffrey L. Ward

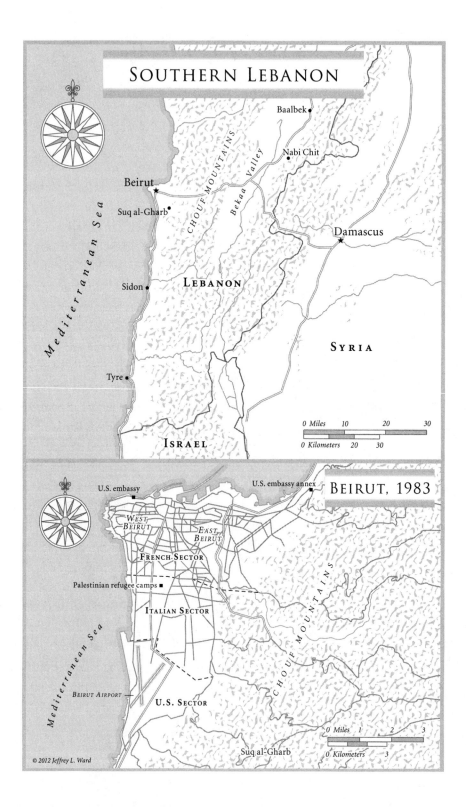

SOUTHERN LEBANON

Baalbek

Nabi Chit

CHOUF MOUNTAINS

Bekaa Valley

Beirut

Suq al-Gharb

Damascus

Sidon

LEBANON

Mediterranean Sea

SYRIA

Tyre

0 Miles 10 20 30

0 Kilometers 20 30

ISRAEL

BEIRUT, 1983

U.S. embassy

U.S. embassy annex

WEST BEIRUT

EAST BEIRUT

FRENCH SECTOR

Palestinian refugee camps

ITALIAN SECTOR

CHOUF MOUNTAINS

Mediterranean Sea

BEIRUT AIRPORT

U.S. SECTOR

0 Miles 1 2 3

0 Kilometers 3

Suq al-Gharb

© 2012 Jeffrey L. Ward

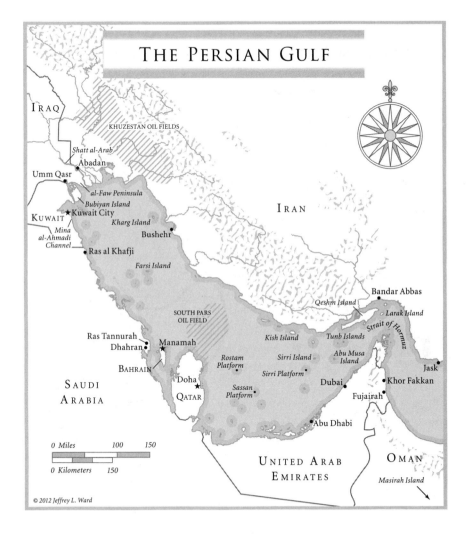

THE PERSIAN GULF

IRAQ

KHUZESTAN OIL FIELDS

Shatt al-Arab
Abadan

Umm Qasr

al-Faw Peninsula
Bubiyan Island

KUWAIT ★ Kuwait City

Mina
al-Ahmadi
Channel ● Ras al Khafji

Kharg Island
Bushehr

Farsi Island

IRAN

SOUTH PARS
OIL FIELD

Bandar Abbas

Qeshm Island
Larak Island

Ras Tannurah
Dhahran ●
Manamah

BAHRAIN

Doha
QATAR

Kish Island

Rostam
Platform

Sirri Island
Sirri Platform

Sassan
Platform

Tunb Islands

Abu Musa
Island

Strait of Hormuz

Jask

Dubai ●
Khor Fakkan

Fujairah ●

SAUDI
ARABIA

Abu Dhabi ●

OMAN

0 Miles   100   150

0 Kilometers   150

UNITED ARAB
EMIRATES

Masirah Island

© 2012 Jeffrey L. Ward

IRANIAN MOVEMENTS INTO IRAQ, 2003

TURKEY

SYRIA

Euphrates River

•Arbil

Tigris River

IRAN

Zagros Mountains

IRAQ

Baghdad ★

Mehran •

Al Kut •

Karbala •

An Numaniyah •

Tigris River

•Najaf

Al Ahmarah •

Euphrates River

Ahvaz •

JORDAN

SAUDI
ARABIA

Basra •

Shatt
al-Arab

al-Faw Peninsula

Umm Qasr •

0 Miles   50   100   150

0 Kilometers   150

KUWAIT

Persian
Gulf

© 2012 Jeffrey L. Ward

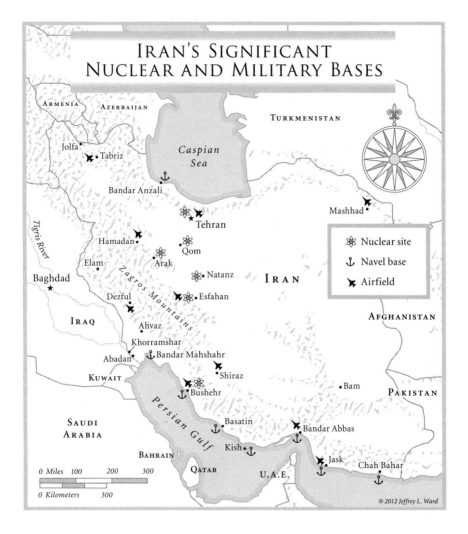

IRAN'S SIGNIFICANT NUCLEAR AND MILITARY BASES

ARMENIA
AZERBAIJAN
TURKMENISTAN

Jolfa
Tabriz

Caspian
Sea

Bandar Anzali

Mashhad

Tehran

Hamadan
Qom

Elam
Arak

Baghdad

Natanz

IRAN

Nuclear site
Naval base
Airfield

Esfahan

Dezful

AFGHANISTAN

IRAQ

Ahvaz

Khorramshar

Abadan
Bandar Mahshahr

KUWAIT

Shiraz

Bam
PAKISTAN

Bushehr

SAUDI
ARABIA

Persian Gulf

Basatin
Bandar Abbas

BAHRAIN
QATAR
Kish

0 Miles 100   200   300

Jask
Chah Bahar

0 Kilometers   300

U.A.E.

© 2012 Jeffrey L. Ward

PREFACE

Every day one fifth of the world's oil exports flow through the twenty-mile-wide Strait of Hormuz that links the Persian Gulf with the outside world. Since 1949 the U.S. Navy has patrolled this waterway, projecting American power and ensuring the continuous flow of the lifeblood of the world's economy. There are few areas regarding which the United States has more firmly committed its blood and treasure to safeguard its interests. In the past twenty-five years, the United States has fought three wars in the area: two in Iraq and one, the subject of this book, a still ongoing struggle against Iran.

This strategically vital body of water can be an uninviting place. When the wind kicks up, the blowing sand and dust create a haze that blurs the horizon and the muddy waters into one seamless brown tapestry. If you add in the tangled clusters of poisonous sea snakes and temperatures in excess of 120 degrees and humidity to match, there are few places that American servicemen and -women serve that are as inhospitable as the Persian Gulf.

The morning of April 4, 2003, broke better than many. A strong sea breeze and brilliant sunrise portended well for the day's mission. The American invasion of Iraq was two weeks old. As a major in the marines corps, I sat off the entrance to the Shatt al-Arab—a wide river formed by the confluence of the Tigris and Euphrates rivers, which serves as the border between Iran and Iraq. I was embarked on board one of the strangest ships in the navy's inventory: a giant catamaran. Built as a high-speed ferry, it had a cavernous interior of car ramps and was still replete with a bar and stadium seats for passengers to relax and enjoy cocktails. Sailors replaced the booze with cases of bottled water and juice, and a sophisticated command center occupied half of the lounge, with chairs and tables removed for banks of computers and a large screen that showed in blue, red, and green military symbols the real-time locations of every U.S., Iraqi, and Iranian ship and plane in the area. I happened to be one of the few marines assigned to the navy's elite SEALs. As a reservist, I had been recalled to active duty by Special Operations Command to deploy with this group under an energetic captain named Robert Harward. I had served under him the year before when special operations forces led the way into Afghanistan after 9/11 and hunted the Taliban and al-Qaeda, which were hiding out in caves and farms across the rugged southeastern parts of that harsh land. This time, our mission was to drop off four small, heavily armed boats to transit the Shatt al-Arab all the way up to the second-largest city in Iraq, the important port city of Basra. The point of the operation was to assert American freedom of navigation and to search for possible suicide boats that the navy worried would spring out of the inlets and repeat the disaster of the USS *Cole* a few years earlier.

This was not my first war in the Middle East. I spent eight months baking under the desert sun during the first war against Saddam Hussein in 1991. Then I had been assigned to a marine armor reconnaissance battalion under the command of a future general named Keith Holcomb. He had been a United Nations observer in south Lebanon, knew Arabic, and engrossed me with stories of the guerrilla war being waged by a Shia group called Hezbollah, or Party of God, against the modern Israeli army. The entire experience spurred my interest in the Middle East. After the war, I went back to graduate school for a doctorate in modern Middle East history during the decade-long lull between the two Iraqi conflicts.

I had more of an awareness than many of my military contemporaries of the tortured relations between the United States and Iran. During the 1980s, my father, a four-star marine general named George Crist, commanded U.S. Central Command—CENTCOM, as it's commonly abbreviated—with responsibility for all the American forces in the Middle East. At the time, the

Soviet Union dominated Washington's thinking and Europe, not the Middle East, was our army's most important theater. But my father and CENTCOM had been involved in a strange conflict with Iran, best described as a guerrilla war at sea, a struggle waged by covert naval mining from dhows and hit and run attacks against American convoys by a mosquito fleet of fast boats manned by aggressive Revolutionary Guards. The United States and Iran engaged in this quasi-war for nearly two years, culminating in the U.S. Navy's largest surface battle since the Second World War, all while the Pentagon worried more about fending off hordes of Soviet tanks on the plains of central Europe than Iran. However, over the past thirty years, the Persians and not the Russians proved to be the more enduring threat for the United States.

When I looked for a dissertation topic, I discovered this largely unknown secret war with Iran. I spent the next five years researching and writing the story of this first war with Iran and how it fit into the larger context of President Ronald Reagan's policy for the Middle East.

Iran, however, was not on my mind as dawn broke over the blue Gulf waters on the morning of April 4, 2003. Inside the command center of the catamaran turned warship, I watched as our four gunboats puttered north, into the Shatt al-Arab, threading carefully the divide between Iran and Iraq. Harward was worried about provoking Iran. He took pains to avoid a confrontation, placing a Farsi-speaking SEAL in the lead boat and ordering the small flotilla well within Iraqi territorial waters, so much so that they ran aground several times. We even erected a makeshift Iranian flag on one of the boats, which Harward felt would display our peaceful intentions. The Iranian Islamic Revolutionary Guard Corps responded by sending four small boats toward us at high speed, the largest being a fast Swedish-built Boghammer, which resembles a cigarette boat, outfitted with a twin-barrel machine gun on its bow. It was this same boat that had been the bane of the U.S. Navy during my father's time fifteen years earlier. With rooster tails of white water, the boats came barreling over to the Iraqi side of the waterway, surrounded us, and took the tarp off at least one multiple rocket launcher and pointed it directly at our lead boat. A major shootout with Iraq's powerful Persian neighbor appeared imminent. Suddenly, my research on Iran no longer seemed so academic.

What I did not know until later, while researching this book, was how little CENTCOM or the civilians in the Pentagon had bothered to consider

Iran when planning to remove Saddam Hussein. The incident with the Iranians off the Iraqi coast should have come as no surprise. This would not be the only oversight in what was one of the worst planned campaigns ever executed by the U.S. military. When the last U.S. troops withdrew in December 2011, nearly five hundred Americans had died at the hands of the Iranian-backed militias, and the nature of the democratically elected Iraqi government, achieved at the cost of so much American blood and treasure, had been brokered in Tehran.

The twilight hours hold special significance in warfare. Your eyes are not acclimated to the changing light, and normal body cycles make soldiers less alert. I had this drilled into me as an aspiring marine corps officer. As dusk approached following a day of trudging around the woods of Quantico, Virginia, the last hour spent struggling to dig a fighting hole through a maze of roots with a small folding shovel that was frustratingly inadequate for the task, a captain suddenly hollered, "Stand to!" As the setting sun cast long shadows across the forest, I dropped into my partially dug pit and pointed my rifle out into the brush and trees. "You are always most vulnerable to enemy attack during the periods of morning nautical twilight and evening nautical twilight," the instructor said, as part of a well-rehearsed lesson on tactics. "Dusk and dawn are transition periods," he continued, with matter-of-fact delivery.

In 1987, when I attended the Basic School, a six-month-long school mandatory for all newly minted marine second lieutenants, many officers and senior enlisted had served in Vietnam. The lessons of that conflict, where the Vietcong frequently struck during twilight hours, had been seared into the collective memory of the service. Although with current technology a modern military can attack even on moonless nights or at the peak of the midday sun, the idea remains a valid military tactic. In July 2008, one of the worst attacks inflicted on the U.S. Army occurred just as the first hint of light appeared in the eastern sky of Afghanistan, when the Taliban struck a remote outpost, killing and wounding thirty-six soldiers. While no one attacked us during the training exercise in Quantico, the point stuck with me.

Twilight is an accurate metaphor for the current state of affairs between the United States and Iran. With no diplomatic ties and only occasional meetings in dark corners of hotel bars and through shadowy intermediaries, neither side has an accurate view of the other. The United States lacks clarity about Iranian leaders and the complex structure of the Iranian government. Meanwhile, Iran grows increasingly isolated and ignorant about the United States. This gray zone is dangerous. The threat of miscalculation is great and the military consequences can be grave. For three decades, the two nations have been suspended between war and peace. At various times, relations have moved from the light of peace to the darkness of war. But in the end, 2012 still looks remarkably like 1979, with the two nations still at loggerheads.

Both countries bear some culpability for perpetuating this conflict. The Iranian Revolution was born from anti-Americanism. The leaders who spearheaded that movement thirty years ago remain in power and see little need to change their stance. Hard liners in Iran reject the status quo of American supremacy in the region. With each chant of "Death to America," they hope to reinvigorate the same fervor that swept them into power and tossed out an unpopular dictator, the shah of Iran, who had been imposed by the United States in a coup in 1953. While in this conflict the United States remains largely the good guy, it has not always been the perfect guy. Both Bush administrations dismissed Iranian goodwill gestures and refused to accept any dialogue that addressed Iran's legitimate security concerns. The United States supported Saddam Hussein and his Arab bankrollers in a bloody war against the Islamic Republic that killed several hundred thousand Iranian soldiers. The mantra of regime change remains a frequent slogan in many quarters in Washington. Unfortunately, Iran's response to these trespasses has invariably been to use the tools of the terrorist: an exploding car bomb on a crowded street or a plot to kill a diplomat in a popular Washington restaurant.

The research for this book, which included more than four hundred interviews, started in 1994 when I first traveled to the Tampa headquarters of CENTCOM to speak with officers charged with running this Iranian cold war from a worn, mazelike building at MacDill Air Force Base. I traveled to the backstreets of south Lebanon Shia neighborhoods and to the posh capitals of the Persian Gulf states interviewing Iranians and Arabs involved in the story. I went through my father's papers and then the first of many linear feet of other personal papers and official records.

While the focus of the book changed as time passed and history continued to unfold, the essence of the story has remained: the two countries have been engaged in a largely unknown quasi-war since the Iranian Revolution in 1979. Six different American presidents have faced a seemingly intractable foe in Tehran. Each had a defining event that pushed the two countries like a pinball back and forth between rapprochement and war. What I found myself involved in on that April morning in the northern Gulf was the latest chapter in the ongoing saga of this shadowy conflict.

This story continues to unfold. As of this writing, Iran has threatened to close the Strait of Hormuz, and the two countries seem headed to the dark side of military conflict over Iran's nuclear program. The saga is seemingly playing on an endless loop. After reading one recent memo outlining the Bush administration's policies toward building an Arab coalition against Iran, as I relayed to the marine deputy commander at CENTCOM, John Allen, I could have interchanged the memo for one that had been written twenty-five years earlier as his predecessor grappled with the same enduring challenge of Iran. Iran's quest for nuclear technology has heightened the stakes and the tension but it has not been a catalyst for the conflict.

I have tried to tell the most accurate and complete story I could of this three-decade-long conflict between Iran and the United States. The story begins with the seminal events of the Iranian Revolution that decisively turned the two countries from allies to adversaries and continues to the stories behind the headlines of today's newspaper. The ideas presented in this book are my own and do not represent the views of the Department of Defense or the U.S. government.

The experienced American diplomat Ryan Crocker said to me in an interview, "For Iran, there is no such thing as history; it is all still the present. We are the most ahistorical and they are the most historical" of nations. In telling this story, I hope to rectify this fact. It is a story in which I have been a participant, dispassionate scholar, and, most recently, an adviser to senior Defense Department officials. It is a war of the shadows, largely unknown, arguably the most important and least understood conflict in recent history. It is the twilight war.

One

"A Little King in Your Heart"

At two a.m. on January 4, 1979, the loud ringing of the secure telephone jolted U.S. Air Force General Robert "Dutch" Huyser awake and out of his warm bed in Stuttgart, Germany. The early-hour call did not come as a surprise to the fifty-four-year-old Huyser. During a crisis, you worked Washington hours. As the workday ended on the East Coast, it was common to receive a flurry of last-minute inquiries from the Pentagon, depriving you of sound sleep even if you did wear four stars.

Slightly overweight and with a round, rugose face, Dutch Huyser was a product of the air force's bomber community. During the Second World War, he flew four-engine B-29s over Japan, and in the early days of the Cold War, he piloted the same plane, only now loaded with an atomic bomb earmarked for the Soviet Union. As American aircraft technology advanced, so too did Huyser's career. He flew B-52 missions over North Vietnam and assumed his current job as the deputy commander of American forces in Europe in September 1975.

The week prior to his early morning phone call, Huyser had exchanged numerous calls with his boss, General Alexander Haig, and the new chairman of the Joint Chiefs of Staff and a longtime acquaintance, General David Jones, about traveling to Iran on a secret mission. Over the previous three years, Huyser had developed a cordial acquaintance with the shah of Iran, Mohammad Reza Pahlavi, one of America's most important allies in the Middle East. Now, with a popular revolution sweeping the country and the monarchy unraveling, Washington wanted a high-level military envoy to travel to Iran to work with the Iranian military, although to do exactly *what* remained unclear.

The modern American military has produced few generals as political as Al Haig. The onetime aide to the imperious General Douglas MacArthur had learned the battlefields of Washington as well as those of East Asia. Haig deplored the Carter administration's feeble response to the Iranian Revolution and argued for a more resolute show of U.S. support for the shah. But more important, Haig did not want his career tarnished by the debacle of the collapse of Iran. He deliberately tried to distance himself from the unfolding drama in Tehran. When General Jones suggested to Haig that Huyser was ideal to convey a message to the Iranian leadership, Haig, the supreme commander of Allied Forces Europe and Huyser's superior, vociferously opposed the idea.[1]

At two a.m., picking up the receiver, Dutch Huyser heard the brusque voice of his boss. "Dutch, we lost. You're going to Iran."[2]

When he took the oath of office on a cold, bright January 20, 1977, neither Iran nor the Persian Gulf was on President Jimmy Carter's mind. He knew of the importance of Middle Eastern oil, but rather than focusing on securing American access to this oil, the president concentrated his policy initiatives on the root cause: America's growing demand for imported fuel. The emerging energy crisis became an early mantra of his administration, and the president threw the entire weight of his office behind addressing the looming crisis, delivering his first salvo in a nationally televised address just two weeks after moving into the White House. Sitting in a wooden chair next to a roaring fire in the White House library, Carter wore a cardigan sweater and lectured his audience on the need for shared sacrifice regarding energy conservation.

Carter followed that with another prime-time address three months later. On the evening of April 18, 1977, television viewers expecting to see the popular family drama about austere life on the frontier, *Little House on the Prairie*, instead saw a somber president dressed in a dark suit. "Tonight," he began in a sharp tone, notwithstanding the lilt of his Southern inflection, "I want to have an unpleasant talk with you about a problem that is unprecedented in our history. With the exception of preventing war, this is the greatest challenge that our country will face during our lifetime." By the 1980s, the president warned, demand for crude oil would outstrip the world's reserves. Carter foretold dire consequences: closed factories, lost jobs, rampant inflation, and fierce international competition for scarce energy resources. "If we fail to act soon we will face an economic, social, and political crisis that will threaten our free institutions." The looming oil crisis, said Carter in one of the more memorable lines of his presidency, "is the moral equivalent of war."[3]

President Carter inherited a Persian Gulf policy forged entirely on the anvil of the Cold War. One of the first crises between the United States and the Soviet Union had occurred in that region in March 1946, when the Soviets refused to leave northern Iran following the end of World War II and then moved tanks menacingly toward the Iranian capital of Tehran.[4] When the United States forcefully objected, Moscow backed down, unwilling at that point to go to war.[5] For the next three decades, while the United States focused its resources on confronting Moscow in Central Europe, the United Kingdom served as the major military power in the Middle East protecting it from Soviet expansion. The British had a large military presence in the area, and the Gulf sheikdoms were still colonial dependencies. But in January 1968 Prime Minister Harold Wilson announced his cash-strapped British government's decision to withdraw all its armed forces and end 140 years of colonial occupation in the Persian Gulf. As the Union Jack lowered over the newly independent sheikdoms, the United States, bogged down in Vietnam, lacked the military resources to post to the Gulf.[6]

So in the early 1970s, President Richard Nixon devised a new economy-of-force plan, unofficially known as the twin pillars strategy. America's Persian Gulf security would rest on the two staunchly anticommunist powers in the region: Iran and Saudi Arabia. With Saudi oil money and its regional prestige as keeper of the holy cities of Mecca and Medina, coupled with Iran's military muscle, these two nations would serve as America's proxies to contain the Soviet Union. "The vacuum left by British withdrawal," Henry Kissinger wrote in his memoirs, "would be filled by a local power friendly to us." American security in the Persian Gulf now rested largely with the growing might of the shah's military.

The shah of Iran, Mohammad Reza Pahlavi, enthusiastically stepped into this role. Since his reinstatement on the throne, with the assistance of the Central Intelligence Agency (CIA), following a 1953 coup, the shah proved to be ambitious, expansionistic, and fervently anticommunist. He made it known throughout diplomatic circles that he sought Iran's ascendancy as the new regional power. Deftly playing on American fears of communism and fueled by petrodollars, which increased twenty-four-fold in the seven years from 1968 to 1975, the shah expanded the Iranian military to become the largest force in the Middle East.[7] The Ford and Nixon administrations sold some $12 billion in weapons to Iran, offering the Iranian despot the most advanced weapons, short of nuclear, in the American arsenal.

The shah was not shy about using his freshly acquired military might to encroach on his neighbors. In November 1971, following the final British pullout of forces from the Gulf and the scheduled independence of its former protectorates—the United Arab Emirates, Qatar, and Bahrain—the shah forcibly reasserted Iran's control of the contested Tunb Islands and the island of Abu Musa in the Persian Gulf. While small (Abu Musa is only twelve square kilometers), the islands are strategically located. Abu Musa, for example, sits astride the deepwater route leading into the western approaches to the Strait of Hormuz. Any oil tanker exiting or entering the Gulf must pass close by the island. The shah also backed Kurdish rebels in northern Iraq, as a result of which in 1975 then Iraqi vice president Saddam Hussein reluctantly signed the Algiers Accords, which established as the southern border between the two nations the midpoint—and not the Iranian bank—of the Shatt al-Arab, a strategic waterway between the two nations and an important entry for Iraq into the Persian Gulf.[8]

President Carter continued Nixon's twin pillars policy, though with less enthusiasm. He initially hoped to demilitarize the Persian Gulf. Carter floated the idea to Moscow of reducing the quantity of weapons sold to the third world, a strategy that would include a drastic reduction of American weapons sold to both Saudi Arabia and Iran.[9] The president then proposed a treaty to reduce naval forces in the Indian Ocean as the first step in what he hoped would lead to an accord on demilitarizing that body of water. Neither proposal went beyond perfunctory discussions. Moscow steadfastly refused to curtail arms shipments to buyers in the Middle East, all of whom happened to be among the Soviets' largest weapons clients.[10]

A fundamental split divided Carter's foreign policy team. The two principal antagonists were Carter's national security adviser and longtime Democratic foreign policy expert, a forty-nine-year-old Polish-born Cold War hawk named Zbigniew Brzezinski, and his sixty-year-old secretary of state, Cyrus Vance, who had served as secretary of the army and deputy secretary of defense in the two previous Democratic administrations. While the two advisers generally agreed with Carter's emphasis on human rights, they clashed on just about every other significant issue. The potential pitfalls associated with these two men and their rival philosophies in the same administration came as no surprise. Hamilton Jordan, Carter's youthful campaign manager, quipped during the transition: "If, after the inauguration, you find Cy Vance as secretary of state and Zbigniew Brzezinski as head of national security, then I would say we failed. And I'd quit." President Carter appointed both men, and Jordan remained as chief of staff.[11]

The two men also differed in their views of the Persian Gulf. Brzezinski advocated a more robust American military presence. He viewed Gulf oil as an Achilles' heel of the West in relation to the Soviet Union and stressed the need to retain unfettered access to Middle East oil. If oil resources became scarce, the next battle of the Cold War would be not for Berlin, but for Riyadh or Tehran. Secretary Vance wanted to downplay the role of the U.S. military in the Gulf. The secretary advanced the prevailing view within the State Department that the presence of U.S. forces in the Persian Gulf would be counterproductive. In an area with a long colonial legacy and deep suspicions of superpower motivations, better to keep U.S. forces beyond the horizon than to increase the military footprint in the region.[12]

The new secretary of defense's view lay somewhere in between. The forty-nine-year-old Harold Brown had earned his doctorate in physics at Columbia University at the remarkable age of twenty-two. A self-described impersonal and analytical man, he was a brilliant scientist and had arrived at the Pentagon as a member of Kennedy defense secretary Robert McNamara's "whiz kids." Brown had spent most of the 1960s earning the deserved reputation as a moderate and a realist, but when it came to the Middle East, Secretary Brown generally agreed with Brzezinski's more hawkish assessment of Soviet intentions. He shared Brzezinski's concern about Soviet dominance of the

Persian Gulf: "Soviet control of this area would make virtual vassals of much of both the industrialized and developing worlds."[13]

Despite this discord, the stakes remained low for Washington, as the shah appeared to be firmly in power and in America's pocket. In January 1977, the State Department's Bureau of Intelligence and Research produced an optimistic report that echoed the intelligence community's views of the shah's prospects for political survival: "Iran is likely to remain stable under the shah's leadership over the next several years. The prospects are good that Iran will have relatively clear sailing until at least the mid-1980s."[14] On a stopover in Tehran in December 1977, at the end of his first year in office, Carter reemphasized his support for the shah during a lavish New Year's Eve gala, noting that under the leadership of the shah, Iran "is an 'island of stability' in one of the more troubled areas."

But all was not as rosy as the U.S. intelligence community believed for the Pahlavi dynasty. In the early 1960s, the shah actively encouraged modernization and secularization. He forced land redistribution, especially of the vast holdings of Shia clerics, which struck at the heart of their wealth and power. The shah ordered state-owned businesses sold; the enfranchisement of women, including their ability to hold political office; and the removal of Islamic dogma from schools. The shah largely dismissed Islam as a backward force that impeded the formation of a new, modern Iran. The by-products of his brand of modernization were rapid social change and increased instability.[15] While Iran's newfound oil wealth remained in the hands of a small elite, rural unemployment grew, and the population of Tehran multiplied fivefold as peasants poured into the city in search of work.[16]

In 1975, the shah canceled elections and abolished the two nominally independent political parties in favor of a single party dedicated to the Pahlavi regime. Any pretense of a constitutional monarchy vanished. The opposition movement grew, as did the murmur of discontent in the streets of Tehran, stoked by thousands of underemployed students freshly educated in Western universities.

From the beginning, one of the most vocal opponents of the shah's designs was a religious scholar from Qom, Ayatollah Ruhollah Khomeini. Alarmed by Khomeini's unwavering vitriolic criticism of the secularization of society, the shah had ordered the sixty-year-old cleric imprisoned in 1963 and exiled the following year. Khomeini settled in the Shia holy city of Najaf, Iraq, where he continued his incessant monologues against the "corrupt" Pahlavi dynasty and its chief supporter, the United States. Khomeini remained revered by multitudes of Iranian people. He developed a mystical persona among both secularists and Islamists opposing the shah. Khomeini preferred to stay above the political fray, providing broad policy guidance and leaving the details to his key advisers. Many Western observers mistakenly viewed this leadership style as a sign that Khomeini intended to serve in the traditional role of a Shia imam: influential and powerful, but aloof from secular politics. Ayatollah Khomeini, however, had a clear view of where he wanted to take Iran, and it was not in the direction of either a Western democracy or a constitutional monarchy. He called for a purge of all corrupt influences and for the Islamization of Iranian society. Khomeini believed history had shown that the throne was not to be trusted; the monarchy needed to go. Ayatollah Khomeini intended to remake Iran into a new Islamic republic. The mosque would supplant the imperial throne.

The shah's power began to unravel in late 1977. Khomeini's eldest son died, likely of a heart attack, but Khomeini accused the shah and his secret police, Savak, of murdering him. A short time later, on January 7, 1978, an article published in a government newspaper ridiculed the ayatollah, questioning his religious credentials and even his sexual preference. Riots erupted in the religious city of Qom. In the resulting mayhem police shot several protesters; reports of the exact number killed varied from six to three hundred. The streets remained quiet for the next forty days in accordance with the Iranian custom of remembering the dead, but when the mourning period ended, on February 18, protests over the killings erupted in every major Iranian city. In Tabriz events turned violent, and the government sent in the army to quell the unrest, killing more than one hundred people. In a recurring pattern over the coming months, each of the events was followed by a period of mourning and then another clash between protesters and government security forces.

Attacks grew in intensity and violence, especially against targets seen as Western and decadent, such as liquor stores and movie theaters. In one of the most horrifying incidents, Khomeini supporters set fire to the Cinema Rex, a movie theater in a two-story commercial building in the port city of Abadan. Thick black smoke overwhelmed many patrons as fire spread quickly through the theater. More than four hundred people died, most of them incinerated while still sitting in their seats. In the Middle East, suspicions of conspiracy often supplant fact: despite the evidence against Khomeini's supporters, rumor spread in the Iranian streets that the government actually had started the fire to discredit the religious opposition.[17] The rumor turned many of those sitting on the fence decidedly against the shah and marked the beginning of the end of his quarter-century reign.[18]

The shah found himself in a difficult position. If he tried to crush the dissidents, he would face the wrath of the United States for his human rights abuses. If he allowed the protests to continue, it would encourage the opposition.[19] The shah did neither. On July 22, he met with the head of Savak to discuss policy regarding the demonstrators. The meeting adjourned with the shah clearly directing that the demonstrations should be quelled by force and authorizing the army to open fire.[20] But his directive was never implemented as the conscript army recoiled at opening fire on the populace. On August 19, less than a month later, the shah shifted course and released 711 political prisoners, most of whom immediately joined in the street protests.[21] A memorandum from the director of the CIA's office for the Near East, which was responsible for Iran, summed up the monarch's difficulties: "The shah's efforts to modernize Iran have unleashed unexpected if accurate strong forces of reaction that are not being contained by martial law or piecemeal concessions to the opposition."[22]

At the Iranian government's urging, and perhaps to forestall a similar uprising among its own majority Shia population, the Iraqi government ordered Khomeini out of the country in a forlorn attempt to isolate Khomeini from the Iranian populace.[23] Khomeini initially sought refuge in Kuwait, but the emir turned him away at the border. This rejection turned out to be fortuitous. Khomeini's close adviser Ebrahim Yazdi urged him to find refuge in a democratic country. Yazdi, who had lived in the United States, believed that a free press would facilitate the spread of Khomeini's message. So Ayatollah Khomeini moved into a house at Neauphle-le-Château in the Paris suburbs. There, unshackled by the Iraqi Baath Party's authoritarian restraints, he found a more free-flowing outlet in the sympathetic Western press for his revolutionary rhetoric. In the first few months, Ayatollah Khomeini conducted more than 450 interviews with the press as part of a sophisticated media campaign against the shah.[24]

The protests expanded. Supporters smuggled cassette tapes of Khomeini's talks back inside Iran. Technocrats, democratic reformers, communists, and disgruntled merchants all joined in the growing protests. Oil workers went on strike, and the violence reached a crescendo in early December, when hundreds of thousands of protesters took to the streets. Meanwhile, Khomeini approved sending small teams of supporters to Iraq, Syria, and Lebanon to begin training as guerrilla fighters for the long insurgency he expected to wage against his rival for control over Iran.[25]

The shah's troubles took official Washington by surprise. Initially, the American government did not even consider the religious aspect of the opposition. "There had never been an Islamic revolution before," observed the State Department desk officer for Iran at the time, Henry Precht.[26] Despite the fact that the American embassy in Tehran was the fifth largest in the world, few American diplomats had any sense of the sentiments in the streets. The shah effectively controlled the information available to the diplomats, and the State Department did not encourage Foreign Service officers to get out and talk to dissenters, especially religious leaders. As one political officer recalled, "I doubt if anybody in the embassy ever knew a mullah."[27]

The CIA devoted considerable resources to monitoring the Soviet Union and to tracking communists inside Iran. But the agency's intelligence-gathering effort had not been focused on recruiting spies within Iran. "After all," as one retired CIA operative sardonically observed, "we had the shah's secret police, Savak, to tell us what was going on."[28] The two intelligence agencies did cooperate on tracking down the Mujahideen-e Khalq (MEK), or People's Mujahideen of Iran, a leftist-Islamist hybrid sect which had conducted a series of terrorist killings of Americans in Iran, including the serious wounding of U.S. Air Force Brigadier General Harold Price in one of the first uses of an improvised explosive device in the Middle East. The CIA had developed biographical studies on key Iranian military and civilian leaders.[29] But for the most part, the CIA devoted its efforts to countering Soviet influence in the region.[30] In a self-assessment of its efforts in 1976, the spy agency reported that "generally speaking, reporting from the mission on most topics is very satisfactory."[31]

The American intelligence community committed one enormous oversight in not studying the shah himself. In 1974 Jean Bernard, a renowned French hematologist, secretly flew to Tehran to examine the Iranian monarch, who was suffering from an enlarged spleen. Dr. Bernard diagnosed the problem as a serious case of chronic lymphocytic leukemia and Waldenstrom's macroglobulinemia, a blood condition.[32] However, fearing that news of his ailment would leak, the shah steadfastly refused either to undergo additional tests or to begin cancer treatment. His ailment remained unknown to Washington, though rumors of the shah's ill health were commonplace in Tehran. The cancer left the shah increasingly listless and withdrawn. Meanwhile, Washington continued to support him, blissfully unaware that the man upon whom America relied to safeguard Persian Gulf oil was dying.

The troubles in Iran divided the Carter administration along familiar lines. Brzezinski wanted the shah to use force to crush the resistance. He believed the United States needed to express its unqualified support for the monarch, and he advocated dispatching an aircraft carrier to the Gulf of Oman as a show of support. Secretary of State Cyrus Vance cautioned, however, that the Iranians might interpret a movement of U.S. forces to the region as a precursor to invasion; the United States needed to assist Iran in a transition from autocracy to democracy.

The president himself remained torn, harboring private sympathy for the democratic reforms sought by the shah's opponents, while recognizing the grave strategic blow to the United States should the shah be overthrown. The president remained bothered by the shah's poor human rights record under which political dissidents were frequently imprisoned and tortured. But the Iranian leader had consistently supported both Israel and Carter's Camp David Accords, signed in September 1978 between Israel and Egypt, and his offer to assure Israel's fuel requirements had contributed to Israel's agreement to withdraw from the Sinai and relinquish control of the Abu Rudeis oil fields in western Sinai.

Carter agreed to send an aircraft carrier off the Iranian coast to demonstrate American resolve, and he dispatched his dutiful but bland deputy secretary of defense, Warren Christopher, who would later serve as secretary of state (1993–1997) under Bill Clinton, to meet with the Iranian ambassador in Washington and inform him of President Carter's unqualified support for the shah.[33] A week later President Carter penned a handwritten note to the shah: "Again, let me extend my best wishes to you as you continue your successful effort for the beneficial social and political reforms in Iran."[34]

The American ambassador in Tehran was an experienced Foreign Service officer named William Sullivan. Polished and well dressed, with a shock of white hair, Sullivan had served in two previous ambassadorial postings, including as ambassador to Laos at the height of the Vietnam War. He was no stranger to the dirty side of foreign policy and, while he was in Laos, had supported the CIA-led secret war against the North Vietnamese.

Sullivan agitated to open a dialogue with Khomeini. When the shah once told him that Khomeini supporters were "crypto-communists," Sullivan flatly rejected the notion. The influence of Shia Islam was stronger than any Western-imposed ideology, especially the secular communists, Sullivan countered.[35] Khomeini supporters held the real power behind the opposition movement and would serve as a natural bulwark against the communist groups, Sullivan thought. Any post-shah government would require Khomeini's support to facilitate an orderly transfer of power to a new democratic government, and the sooner Washington recognized this, Sullivan observed, the better for America's standing in the future Iran.[36]

Brzezinski rejected Sullivan's views of the situation in Tehran. It was not a choice between the shah and democracy, he told Sullivan: should the shah fall, Khomeini would inexorably move the new government toward theocracy. The national security adviser began backdoor conversations around Sullivan with hard-liners inside the Iranian government about a possible military takeover.[37] In an October 28, 1978, meeting at the White House with CIA Director Stansfield Turner, Brzezinski asked the CIA to look into developing information that could be used to undermine the opposition and strengthen the shah. Turner agreed, but he cautioned Brzezinski that many members of Congress looked upon the shah as so undemocratic that they would not tolerate a covert program designed to keep him in power.[38]

Turner responded a few days later. He believed the CIA could help keep the shah in power for the short run and this might provide breathing space for the Iranian government. But for the strategy to succeed, the shah needed to use "maximum force." And in the long run, CIA analysts cautioned, it would not solve the shah's problems. He needed to move more swiftly to establish a democratically elected civilian government.[39]

Undeterred, Brzezinski asked Sullivan about prospects for a successful military takeover if the shah was willing to use maximum force to crush the opposition. In a tense series of secure telephone conversations, Sullivan countered that a military takeover might be feasible, but every day that passed reduced the chances of a successful outcome. More important, Sullivan said, the cost to long-term American interests would be exceedingly high. Loss of life would be great, and this would scuttle any possibility of moving the country in the direction of democracy. Sullivan again advanced the idea of opening contacts with the opposition, which the national security adviser flatly rejected. Over the coming days, exchanges between the two men grew heated on the issue. They frequently shouted at each other, their arguments clearly audible in adjacent rooms.[40]

On September 8, 1978, a massive throng of demonstrators—largely unaware that the shah had declared martial law the day before—gathered in Jaleh Square in Tehran. When the army moved in, the demonstration turned violent and jittery soldiers opened fire. While the true number of Iranian civilians killed was less than one hundred, news quickly spread through the streets that thousands of peaceful demonstrators—including many women— had been cut down in the streets. Today this day is known in Iran as Black Friday. The carnage horrified both the shah and the demonstrators, giving pause to the latter to rethink their actions. But as senior CIA Iran analyst and Iranian military historian Steven Ward noted, "The government then mis-handled what possibly was one of its best opportunities to reassert control."[41] With the opposition reeling, the shah opted for reconciliation. He dismissed security officials, released imprisoned opponents and replaced them with some of his own Savak agents, and ordered the army to fire above the heads of the crowds. Rather than placating the revolutionaries, the shah's actions only emboldened them as he now appeared weak and irresolute.

A few days after Black Friday, President Carter called the shah and stressed continued American support as well as the importance of liberalization. The shah had it posted verbatim in the newspapers as a sign of American support. It backfired. To the Iranian population, it read as though the United States stood behind a government that had just shot down tens of thousands of unarmed civilians in Jaleh Square, fueling hatred of the shah and his chief supporter in Washington.[42]

To gain a better idea of what was going on in the streets of Tehran in early November 1978, Stanley Escudero arrived in Tehran. Fluent in Farsi, the thirty-five-year-old diplomat of Mexican ancestry from Daytona, Florida, had recently served for four years in the embassy. With dark hair and a dusky complexion, he could pass as a local—perhaps not from Tehran, he admitted, but from an outlying area such as Azerbaijan. His previous assignment to Iran in the early 1970s had not been a particularly career-enhancing tour of duty. Escudero had annoyed his State Department superiors in Foggy Bottom by questioning the long-term viability of the Pahlavi dynasty. While he had not predicted the shah's current difficulties, he openly questioned the viability of rule by the shah's son. This assessment was not what Henry Kissinger and the State Department had wanted to hear. Compounding his impropriety of straying off the policy reservation, Escudero had met repeatedly with the shah's opponents, especially religious leaders. "Iran was too important to the United States," he later said. "I believed we would be better advised to have relations with whoever ran Iran, be it the shah or the opposition. This was not popular in Washington."[43] Escudero, relegated to working in the then less prestigious Bureau of International Organization Affairs at State, seemed destined for a lackluster career. But the shah's troubles revived Escudero's standing. In fall 1978, Harold Saunders, the deputy assistant secretary for Near Eastern affairs, and Henry Precht, the country desk officer for Iran, each asked Escudero if he would be willing to go back to Tehran to assess the opposition and the shah's likelihood of survival.

Reluctant, Escudero answered, "You want me to go out and meet with the same people that got me into trouble in the first place, and tell you things that you know are not going to suit current policy?"

Saunders and Precht acknowledged that Escudero had been correct in his predictions regarding the shah. They added, "We don't have anyone else to send who stands a reasonable chance of survival." Escudero decided to accept their offer. "I was young and stupid," he said with a chuckle years later.[44]

Landing in Tehran, he set about going native and infiltrating the revolution. He donned Iranian clothes and cropped his beard close in a style common among Iranian men. To preserve his cover, he distanced himself from the embassy and traveled to its sprawling grounds only during darkness in order to provide updates to Ambassador Sullivan. He lived in apartments of trusted Iranian friends, moving frequently for his and their safety.

Escudero traveled to Qom and met with Ayatollah Sayed Shariat-Madari, an opponent of the shah, but less extreme than Khomeini and more favorably disposed to the United States. Posing as a journalist, Escudero met with religious leaders from Khomeini's camp to glean their views of the revolt, which confirmed both Brzezinski's views of Khomeini's true intentions and Sullivan's intuition about the importance of the ayatollah in the future of

Iran.[45] He discovered that the religious leadership played a prominent role in mounting antigovernment demonstrations. "The demonstrations were very organized," he observed. Wardens with armbands kept the crowd orderly, orchestrating their chants and keeping the mob unified. While the crowds were composed of a mixture of all the shah's detractors, the Islamic movement was the most organized and best funded. Khomeini supporters, such as a fluent English speaker named Mohammad Beheshti, the ayatollah's representative in Hamburg, Germany, played a pivotal role in orchestrating the protests.[46]

Masquerading now as a student, Escudero infiltrated the mobs protesting against the shah, where he blended in with the thousands of others, shouting "Death to the shah! Death to the shah!" and raising a fist in defiance as he joined the throngs confronting the Imperial Army. It was hazardous duty. Had the students or clergy discovered an American Foreign Service officer in their midst, vengeance would have been swift and deadly.

It soon became apparent to Escudero that the shah's days were numbered. His reports reinforced Sullivan's opinion of the inevitability of the monarch's overthrow. In numerous cables to both Vance and Brzezinski, the ambassador wrote that the only solution available was to push for a democratic government before the revolution spiraled out of control and it became impossible to save anything from the disaster looming before them.[47]

Supporting Escudero's reports, on December 12, 1978, veteran American diplomat and Middle East hand George Ball delivered a report on Iran to the president. Ball had worked Middle East issues for both the Nixon and Carter administrations, and he was instrumental in helping Nixon develop the twin pillars strategy. Echoing Sullivan's views, he stated bluntly that the shah needed to act immediately to effect the transition to a civil government and transfer all power, except that as commander of the armed forces. Otherwise, Ball predicted, "he will collapse."[48]

Carter reluctantly approved his first covert operation for Iran in a final stab at saving the shah. The president had a strong distaste for these actions, but had finally been convinced to try a small effort. The CIA began a very limited psychological operations campaign to highlight awareness of the Iranian communist Tudeh Party's support for Khomeini's return in a forlorn hope to rally anticommunists to support the shah and undercut the opposition movement. It failed and the CIA terminated it little more than a month later.[49] While

Iranian protesters accused the American embassy of being a "den of spies," a senior White House staffer wrote to Carter's national security adviser Zbigniew Brzezinski: "It is supremely ironic that we should stand accused of so much espionage out of our embassy in Tehran when we have done so little."[50]

As Christmas 1978 approached, pessimism reigned in both capitals—Washington and Tehran. Emblematically, President Carter ordered the lights turned off the national Christmas tree behind the White House on the Ellipse to save electricity. The only caroling heard at the U.S. embassy in Tehran, Sullivan wrote, came from "a rather scruffy crowd of teenagers marching by the embassy and chanting 'Yankee Go Home.'"[51]

On January 4, 1979, General Dutch Huyser arrived in the Iranian capital. As he drove through Tehran, he was shocked at the sight of the once vibrant city, now with stores shuttered and the streets empty of the usual bustling, chaotic traffic.

In view of Alexander Haig's vocal objections to his mission, an uneasy Huyser insisted that Defense Secretary Brown provide him with written instructions. When the message arrived just before his departure for Tehran, the directives were as ambiguous and muddled as was U.S. policy toward the crisis. Huyser was told to convey to the shah the president's continued support to the Iranian military as the critical link in the transition to a new stable government: "It is extremely important for the Iranian military to do all it can to remain strong and intact in order to help a responsible civilian government function effectively," the instructions said. "As the Iranian military move through this time of change, they should know that the U.S. military and the U.S. government, from the President down, remain strongly behind them."[52] Precisely what this message conveyed to the Iranian military remained a mystery to Huyser. Vance had intended it to inform the Iranian generals that the United States backed the transition to a democratic government. Brzezinski, however, intended for Huyser to give the green light to the Iranian military to stage a coup, declare martial law, and take over the government. The muddled language of Huyser's instructions represented a compromise between the two competing positions, but it left both the messenger and its intended audience utterly confused.

Huyser arrived at the embassy to meet with Ambassador Sullivan, the first of many such meetings over the ensuing month. "The shah is finished," the ambassador abruptly told Huyser. "The military has already decayed to the point they are incapable of doing anything." Ayatollah Khomeini and an Islamic government would be better than a military coup, and the sooner the United States began mending relations with the powerful clerical force, the better in the long term. But Carter had prohibited any discussions with Khomeini on the grounds that they might undermine the shah's tenuous authority. In response, Sullivan sent a combative message to Vance urging direct talks with Khomeini. "You should know that the president had made a gross and perhaps irretrievable mistake by failing to send an emissary to Paris to see Khomeini. I cannot understand the rationale for this unfortunate decision. I urge you immediately to join Harold Brown in this plea for sanity!"[53]

The next morning, January 11, both Huyser and Sullivan traveled across the city from the embassy to the shah's expansive palace to deliver the president's message of support and to discuss the Iranian leader's prospects. They found the shah looking haggard, dressed uncharacteristically in a dark suit rather than the military uniform he had worn exclusively since the crisis began. Clearly ill, he showed no vitality or strength to inspire confidence in his long-term political survival.

After a bit of small talk, the shah raised the prospect of leaving Iran on an "extended vacation." He hoped it would help calm the streets, apparently still dreaming that he might yet return to his throne after things calmed down. "When should I go?" he asked.

Sullivan immediately responded, "As soon as possible would probably be the best for all concerned." The shah agreed.

As the meeting concluded, General Huyser reminded the shah of a conversation the two men had had just five months earlier, at the outset of the shah's troubles. The shah had emphatically told the air force general that he would not lose control of power. "What happened, Your Majesty?" Huyser asked.

Mohammad Reza thought quietly for some time, glaring at Sullivan through his thick glasses. "Your commander-in-chief is different from me. I am a commander-in-chief who is actually in uniform and, as such, for me to give the orders that would have been necessary. . . ." He paused. "Could you as commander-in-chief give the order to kill your own people?"[54]

On January 16, 1979, the shah left Iran for Egypt on his "extended vacation." He never returned. Hundreds of thousands of jubilant Iranians celebrated until nightfall. As Huyser walked across the darkened embassy to the secure room for his evening talk with Washington, it was extraordinarily quiet, but, Huyser sensed, "there was a different feeling in the air."

Over the next month, General Huyser met repeatedly with Iranian military leaders. Huyser helped develop a series of military options to maintain order and ensure a smooth transition. The most extreme was Option C—a military coup designed to break any strikes and resistance, and to regain control over the country. When Huyser back-briefed this military option in a secure conference call with Brzezinski and Brown, the national security adviser latched onto it in congruence with his long-standing support of a military takeover to preserve a pro-American government. "The coup option needed to remain on the table," Brzezinski stressed. "Could the army execute it?"

"Yes," General Huyser responded, "as long as the army continued to hold together."

Whether they would open fire on the opposition remained an open question, however, as the conscripted soldiers had shown no stomach for killing fellow Iranians. Furthermore, the shah had maintained tight control over the military leadership and did not reward generals who showed much initiative.

On February 1, Ayatollah Khomeini returned by jet to Tehran. Some five million people poured into the streets to welcome him. At Huyser's urging, the Iranian military provided Khomeini with protection, escorts, and even a helicopter to travel about the city. It was a strange spectacle, as the shah's military leadership ordered honor guards and protection for the man they all despised.

On the night of February 9, Iranian television broadcast a rerun of Khomeini's return, inciting a group of low-ranking technical officers called Homafaran (the equivalent of warrant officers in the U.S. military) to protest openly against the shah at an air base in eastern Tehran that housed the Iranian air force's headquarters. The Homafaran clashed with a detachment of the shah's elite "Immortals" unit. The next morning, the Homafaran forced their way into an armory and began distributing weapons to other military defectors and leftist sympathizers. Pitched clashes between the rebels and the Iranian army soon broke out all over the city. Events culminated in a series of dramatic attacks on February 11, a day still celebrated in Iran as a national holiday called Islamic Revolution's Victory Day. A mob stormed the Supreme Staff headquarters—the Iranian version of the Pentagon—and soldiers mutinied and shot dead the army chief of staff outside his own headquarters building. By the end of the day, the remnants of the old regime had been swept away and nearly all Iran's senior military leadership were in jail.[55]

A week later, back in Stuttgart, Huyser casually spoke to Haig about the latter's retirement plans. An aide interrupted with an important phone call from Washington. Both Haig and Huyser picked up phones; on the other end of the line were the deputy secretary of defense, Charles Duncan, Brzezinski, and the chairman of the Joint Chiefs of Staff, General Jones. The men had just left a meeting at the White House in which the decision had been finally made to have European Command plan for military intervention in Iran. While the president had made no decision about executing such an operation, the U.S. Army's 82nd Airborne Division at Fort Bragg had been placed on alert. Would General Huyser, Jones asked, be willing to return to Tehran and conduct a military takeover?

Incredulous, Huyser privately wondered, "Why didn't they ask that question while I was in Tehran and the Iranian military was still intact?"

"Sir, I'll consider doing it," Huyser said, suppressing his growing anger, "but there would need to be unlimited funds. I would need to handpick ten to twelve U.S. generals and I'll need ten thousand of the best U.S. troops, because at this point, I have no idea how many Iranian troops I could count on. And finally, I must have undivided national support." There was silence on the other end of the phone.

After a long pause, Huyser resumed. "I don't think the people I am talking to are ready for that type of action, nor do I believe the American people would give their support. The answer is obvious—it's not feasible."

Brzezinski asked a few perfunctory questions, and Jones asked Haig if he had any comment. "Nope," Haig replied tersely. The conversation ended and so did any further talk of a coup or American military intervention.

While the new Islamic Republic wanted to retain the skilled officers to run the military, the government moved quickly to purge the Iranian armed forces of unreconstructed royalists. One of these was Commander Said Zanganeh. Of average height and balding but with a distinguished persona and strong bearing, Zanganeh had joined the Imperial Iranian Navy in 1964.[56] In 1977, less than two years before the revolution, Zanganeh became the first commanding officer of Iran's new flotilla of French-built missile boats, each armed with advanced American-made Harpoon antiship missiles, capable of striking a target ship sixty nautical miles away.[57]

After the revolution, Zanganeh was ordered to attend a mandatory assembly with a senior cleric. "You all have a little king in your heart, and we have to eliminate it," the cleric told the audience of officers. While this was not said in a menacing tone, his intent was clear.

A secular Muslim, Zanganeh had strongly supported the shah. He simply could not bring himself to work for a government he viewed as dominated by backward, uneducated clerics. After the shah's departure, he walked into the now empty office of the chief of naval operations and penned his resignation letter.

A few days later a cleric, recently appointed as a senior admiral, called Zanganeh into his office. "Why are you resigning? I've looked over your file and you have no political association with the shah or his crimes."

Zanganeh replied with a religious analogy he knew the cleric would understand. "I don't know Islam as well as you do, but I know that Ali was a great man. Nevertheless, if I were a married woman and Ali wanted to take me to bed, I still wouldn't let him."

The cleric signed his approval without ever taking his eyes off Zanganeh. The commander hastened out of the office, fully expecting a bullet in his head for his insolence. Fortunately, he left the building alive and left for the United States the following year.

The Carter administration wanted to continue normal diplomatic relations with the new Iranian government. The provisional Iranian government's first prime minister was handpicked by Ayatollah Khomeini: seventy-two-year-old Mehdi Bazargan. A devoted Muslim but also a secular democrat, he favored continued ties with the United States. While scaling back consular services, the American embassy in Tehran remained open, even after a six-hour takeover of the embassy grounds in February by leftist students overcome with revolutionary fervor. Ayatollah Khomeini immediately ordered the students out of the embassy, not wishing to hand such a propaganda victory to the Marxists, his growing rivals for power. But that takeover was a precursor of things to come.

When Sullivan stepped down as ambassador in March 1979, Carter nominated another experienced diplomat, Walter Cutler, as his replacement. But after the execution of a prominent Iranian-Jewish businessman who had close ties to the shah, and with a growing perception of an anti-Semitic attitude on the part of the new regime, New York senator Jacob Javits pushed through a resolution critical of the new Iranian government. This action sparked violent protests outside the twenty-seven-acre U.S. embassy compound, with the U.S. flag torn down and anti-American graffiti painted on the embassy walls. The State Department withdrew Cutler's name and, in June 1979, dispatched fifty-eight-year-old Bruce Laingen as the new chargé d'affaires and senior American diplomat in Iran. A naval officer in the Pacific during the Second World War, Laingen had been posted to Tehran once before, in 1953, arriving just after the United States engineered the coup that reinstalled the shah to power.

Laingen continued meeting with Iranian officials to try to normalize relations. One of his major headaches involved sorting the status of billions of dollars, worth of military hardware and spare parts in transit or sitting in American warehouses—weapons destined for Iran. Not surprisingly, Iran wanted the matériel, while Washington showed trepidation, weighing the merits of sending military supplies to a potential adversary against the prospects that this new Iran might still serve as an ally against the Soviets.

In a meeting with Laingen on August 11, Prime Minister Bazargan expressed the desirability of close cooperation between the two nations, but he stated that the U.S. government's support for the shah remained a strong impediment to friendship. Laingen replied that his government had no intention of trying to reinstall the shah on the throne. Bazargan greeted this assertion with skepticism.[58]

In June 1979 the Iranian deputy prime minister had traveled to Sweden and met with American officials. The U.S. delegation included one of the CIA's best Iranian specialists, fifty-year-old George Cave. Tall, thin, and with a quiet, reflective demeanor, Cave was fluent in Farsi and had served two tours in Iran, his first in 1958. The group met to discuss normalizing relations between the two countries. Over the next two months, these talks set a framework for more substantive talks in Tehran. The CIA dispatched Robert Ames, the national intelligence officer for the Near East, to Tehran, where he joined Laingen and other senior State Department officials in discussions about improving relations. Here they met repeatedly with a tough but cordial cleric, Ayatollah Mohammad Beheshti. Second only to Khomeini as the most powerful cleric in Iran and one of the main authors of the new constitution for the Islamic Republic in Iran, Beheshti was an important leader in the newly formed, shadowy Revolutionary Council. Established by Khomeini, the council was composed of mullahs and dedicated Islamists and served as the power behind the Bazargan mask. Beheshti had little love for the United States, but he supported the talks on normalization.

Throughout the autumn of 1979, U.S. negotiators continued their secret meetings, making slow headway toward patching up their differences. The last meeting occurred in Algiers on November 1, 1979, between U.S. national security adviser Brzezinski and Iranian prime minister Bazargan. Brzezinski told the Iranian delegation that the United States recognized the revolution and had no intention of trying to reinstall the shah. The talks ended abruptly, however. News of the meeting leaked, infuriating student radicals as no one in the Iranian leadership wanted to be seen negotiating with the Great Satan.

On October 23, 1979, Bruce Laingen was sitting at the breakfast table in the embassy residence when a marine guard brought him an urgent message. The cable stated that the U.S. government had decided to allow the shah into the country for cancer treatment and instructed Laingen to inform the Iranian government that the shah would be allowed in strictly for humanitarian purposes. The shah was deathly ill and his supporters in Congress lobbied President Carter to admit him. The president had reluctantly agreed.

Laingen knew that no one in the new Iranian government would believe this statement, and he raised strong objections back to headquarters. The situation in Iran remained precarious, and that country's population would greet with open hostility anything that smacked of renewed cooperation between the United States and the shah. This was a major blunder and neither Laingen nor the others at the State Department knowledgeable about Iran had any illusions about the likely Iranian response: they would overrun the embassy.

George Cave was in Paris when he received a cable asking him to return to Tehran to help Laingen explain to the Iranian government why the shah would be allowed to enter the United States. He phoned Laingen. "Bruce, I don't think there is much I can do to help you."

"Yeah," Laingen replied. "You'd just be one more body taken in the embassy."

"No one in Iran believed that the shah had gone to the United States for humanistic reasons," observed Mohsen Sazegara, a Western-educated engineer and early supporter of the revolution. "The United States backed the shah and would bring him back to power and overthrow the revolution. Everyone believed this in Iran." Rumor of the shah's cancer had circulated through the streets of Tehran for years. To the men in the new revolutionary government, Washington and its omnipresent intelligence apparatus had to know of the shah's illness. The sudden admittance of the shah to the United States appeared all the more nefarious, and Laingen's explanation sounded ludicrous.

Laingen and Cave's predictions became reality. The first massive demonstration against the United States took place on November 1. Some rocks were thrown, but little more transpired. On the night of November 3, Laingen attended a movie premier at Iran's foreign office for a new documentary on the revolution. Although its theme was anti-American, Laingen found the film interesting, chiefly due to its footage of mobs storming the U.S. embassy back in February. The next day Laingen was attending a meeting at the foreign office when reports came in about students trying to scale the walls of the U.S. embassy. He tried to drive back to the compound, but the embassy staff warned him to stay away; the situation was becoming too dangerous. Back at the Iranian foreign office, Laingen located a civilian phone and notified Washington of the deteriorating situation at the embassy.[59]

When news of a disturbance at the U.S. embassy in Tehran arrived at Alexander Haig's European Command headquarters in Patch Barracks, Germany, newly promoted Marine Corps Brigadier General George Crist hastened down to the operations center. As the deputy J-3, or operations officer, it was Crist's responsibility to track current events. He picked up an unsecured phone and called the embassy to find out what was going on. The phone rang a few times before it was answered by a man on the other end speaking Farsi. Crist asked him a question, only to discover that the man did not understand English.

"I need a Farsi speaker!" Crist hollered, sending officers at European Command headquarters scrambling to find someone in the building who could converse with the Iranian on the other end of the phone line. Of the hundreds of people in the headquarters, including the intelligence section, not one person could speak Farsi. After a few more minutes of incoherent discussion, the bemused Iranian student lost interest and hung up the telephone.[60]

A group of students representing Iran's universities had conspired to launch a coordinated takeover of the American embassy. Calling themselves Muslim Student Followers of the Imam's Line, they were inspired by recent statements by Khomeini railing against the United States. They decided to strike a blow against the Great Satan. While the shah's admittance into the United States served as the catalyst, planning for the move had been under way since September. Marine security guards failed to halt the mob with a prodigious use of tear gas. Laingen pleaded with Iranian security forces to send personnel to expel the students, but none materialized. In short order, embassy staff had been rounded up and paraded, bound and blindfolded, before a stunned world media.

Initially, the students had intended to hold the embassy for just a few hours. In some ways, it was the Iranian version of American student protests of the 1960s, in which protesters would occupy the president's office, smoke his cigars, make a few statements, and leave with self-congratulatory remarks about having stood up to the establishment.

But the embassy takeover acquired a life of its own. Foreign Minister Ebrahim Yazdi called Khomeini and received permission to go to the embassy and order the students out. But the ayatollah quickly reversed himself. He had no advance knowledge of the students' action, but the embassy takeover afforded him the chance to consolidate power and rally the public behind the Islamists at the expense of liberals and nationalists within the revolutionary movement, who Khomeini regarded as the chief rivals to his vision of an Islamic state. When Ayatollah Khomeini publicly endorsed the action, Bazargan, Yazdi, and other moderates resigned in protest the next day. This left the Revolutionary Council and the Islamists in sole power, and over the next year Khomeini supporters moved to expunge the remaining moderates and secularists from positions of authority.

For the next 444 days, fifty-two Americans, including Laingen, languished as hostages, held by Iranian student radicals. President Jimmy Carter froze Iranian financial assets, severed diplomatic relations, and tried through a variety of means to end the crisis peacefully. Carter took military action off the table as divisions emerged within the administration on how to handle the crisis. The national security adviser advocated the use of force, while Cyrus

Vance worried about the consequences of such an action on the hostages. For six months, Carter sided with Vance.

The strain of these challenges took a toll on President Carter. He reveled in policy details. He impressed the White House staff with his sheer capacity to read and retain the information in towering piles of paperwork. He returned lengthy memos with his handwritten comments on the last page, often replete with grammatical corrections. But this attention to minutia, especially the demands of attending to the hostage crisis, consumed Carter. He averaged five hours of sleep a night, arriving at the Oval Office at five thirty a.m. and regularly not leaving until midnight. He scaled back his daily jogging from five miles to three, frequently running around the White House grounds late at night. He grew increasingly and uncharacteristically testy and often snapped at his staff for no reason.

The United States tried repeatedly to negotiate with the Iranians, but to no avail. A State Department report summed up the challenges of negotiating with the Islamic Republic:

> It is clear that we are dealing with an outlook that differs fundamentally from our own, and a chaotic internal situation. Our character, our society are based on optimism—a long history of strength and success, the possibility of equality, the protection of institutions, enshrined in a constitution, the belief in our ability to control our own destiny. Iran, on the other hand, has a long and painful history of foreign invasions, occupations, and domination. Their outlook is a function of this history and the solace most Iranians have found in Shi'a Islam. They place a premium on survival. They are manipulative, fatalistic, suspicious, and xenophobic.

The U.S. military developed a series of plans, including imposing a naval blockade of Iran. A combative naval officer in the Office of the Chief of Naval Operations named James "Ace" Lyons, who was destined to play a significant role regarding Iran over the coming decade, formulated a plan to use marines backed by carrier air to seize the key Iranian island of Kharg, through which 95 percent of all Iranian oil flowed to awaiting tankers. The island was unguarded and relatively easily accessible by American amphibious forces. "You take Kharg," Lyons said, "and Iran can't export a single drop of oil."[61]

On March 20, 1980, following a meeting with Carter's principal foreign policy advisers at the White House, Deputy National Security Adviser David Aaron and Joint Chiefs chairman David Jones cleared the room of everyone but the small handful of individuals involved with military strategy. Aaron then asked about the blockade plan: "Would you just halt oil exports, or would you need to blockade all their ports as well? If the U.S. took such action, what would be Iran's response?"[62]

CIA Director Stansfield Turner answered Aaron's question. "To be effective, it would have to be a complete cutoff of all imports, including food. It would have a significant impact on Iran's economy within two weeks." But Japan would be hit hard, because that nation imported 10 percent of all its fuel from Iran. Turner added that the loss of oil on the world market and the ensuing crisis would drive oil prices up 15 to 30 percent.

In response to Aaron's second question, State Department representative David Newsom cautioned that a blockade would lead to a strong reaction in both Iran and the Islamic world, "which, in the worst case," he warned, "could lead the militants to start killing the hostages."

Turner rejected that dire prediction, however, believing that such action could strengthen the hand of the Iranian moderates. The meeting ended with no decision. In the end, President Carter rejected the blockade option unless the hostages were put on trial.

The only military plan Carter ever seriously considered was the rescue mission code-named Eagle Claw, using the newly formed elite Delta Force. General David Jones formed a new, compartmented planning cell within the Joint Staff's J-3 directorate to be known as Special Operations Directorate. Months of planning and training in the United States, Egypt, and Oman followed. In spring 1980 Carter authorized the operation.

On April 24, 1980, U.S. helicopters took off from the deck of a U.S. aircraft carrier with a cargo of elite U.S. forces intent on an eventual rendezvous with a network of supporters near Tehran, organized by the CIA, who would truck them into Tehran. Upon the rescue of the hostages, the entire group would gather at a stadium near the embassy, where helicopters would arrive and fly them all to freedom.

Following a series of helicopter mechanical failures, however, U.S. forces decided to abort the risky rescue mission. One helicopter had crashed into a four-engine C-130 during a refueling operation at a remote Iranian desert airstrip known as Desert One. Eight Americans died. After the failed hostage

Two

A NEW GRAND
STRATEGY

On a cold, crisp January evening in 1980, a caravan of black limousines and their police escorts pulled out of the south grounds of the White House. Following a six-minute drive down Pennsylvania Avenue, the presidential motorcade arrived at the U.S. Capitol, its brilliant white dome illuminated in the night sky. Within the hour, President Jimmy Carter would give his last State of the Union address before a joint session of Congress and a worldwide television audience.

Carter knew this would be an important speech. The day before, his close confidant and youthful chief of staff, Hamilton Jordan, had echoed this sentiment in a lengthy "eyes only" memo for the president: "In the next several months, you will shape, define, and execute a new American foreign policy that will not only set the tone for U.S.-Soviet relations for the next twenty years, but will largely determine whether or not our country will play an effective role as the leader of the Free World."[1]

Jordan's intent was to outline a strategy to salvage the president's political fortunes. American presidential elections occur every four years, regardless of national or international crises, and the calendar is not always convenient for the incumbent. This was an election year, and on that night, January 23,

1980, Carter faced mounting political problems. Iran still held captive fifty-two American hostages, and the U.S. economy was in recession. The preceding month, still another foreign policy imbroglio had landed on Carter's desk: the Soviet Union had rolled three mechanized divisions into the remote Central Asian country of Afghanistan to prop up the mountainous nation's fledgling communist government. This new crisis portended a grave Cold War confrontation between the superpowers. Domestically too Carter found himself challenged not only within his own party, by Massachusetts senator Edward Kennedy, but also by the likelihood of an even more formidable Republican opponent: either the former governor of California Ronald Reagan or the seasoned foreign policy hand George H. W. Bush.

President Carter took the podium shortly after nine p.m. It was one of the most truculent speeches ever given by the Georgian. "The 1980s have been born in turmoil, strife, and change," he began. "The region which is now threatened by Soviet troops in Afghanistan is of great strategic importance: It contains more than two-thirds of the world's exportable oil. . . . The Soviet Union is now attempting to consolidate a strategic position; therefore, that poses a grave threat to the free movement of Middle East oil."[2]

In the most important line of his terse thirty-minute speech, the president drew a line in the sand in the Persian Gulf: "Let our position be absolutely clear: An assault by any outside force to gain control of the Persian Gulf region will be regarded as an assault on the vital interests of the United States of America, and such an assault will be repelled by any means necessary, including military force."[3]

After months of vacillation and indecision in dealing with the Iranian hostage crisis, the American public and the press welcomed presidential resolve.[4] A *Time* magazine headline declared, "Carter Takes Charge." In Carter's first address on energy in the spring of 1977, he'd never mentioned the Persian Gulf. Now he was committing the United States to go to war to protect this foreign source of oil should the need arise. For a president who had come to power in the aftermath of Vietnam and prided himself on the fact that no American servicemen or -women had died in combat on his watch, it was a remarkable transformation. In what would become known as the Carter Doctrine, the president had established for the first time that the United States regarded Persian Gulf oil as vital to the nation's interests, worth spending American treasure and spilling blood to defend.[5]

———

Since the early days of the Carter administration, ideas for a new military strategy to defend Persian Gulf oil from the Soviet Union had flowed in and out of the minds of the president's foreign policy team. Shortly after taking office, Carter had called for a major across-the-board reassessment of American strategy in the Cold War. Noted Harvard political scientist Samuel Huntington had headed the review at the National Security Council, and he'd singled out the Persian Gulf as an area ripe for Soviet expansion, due chiefly to the tenuous character of the regimes governing in the region and the difficulty of projecting American power there. As a result of this review, on August 24, 1977, President Carter approved Presidential Directive 18, which directed the formation of a "deployable force of light divisions," a military organization that could be deployed quickly, on short notice, to any global hot spot, be it Korea or, in the minds of Brzezinski and Huntington, the Middle East.[6]

This concept was not new. It had become something of a policy mainstay with the Democratic Party's defense intelligentsia since the Kennedy administration. Faced with a similar concern and responding to Soviet-"inspired" wars in the third world, in 1961 Secretary of Defense Robert McNamara had directed the formation of a highly mobile force based within the United States capable of quickly reacting to any global crisis. To command this force, the Pentagon established U.S. Strike Command, headquartered in a new white-and-black-striped square building at MacDill Air Force Base, Tampa, Florida.[7] However, opposition by the navy and marine corps limited the command's effectiveness. The marine corps viewed itself as the nation's rapid reaction force, especially for military adventures short of major war, and parochially guarded this mission. The navy simply did not want any joint non-navy headquarters to control its ships.[8] President Nixon scrapped the idea and ordered Strike Command disestablished.[9]

Initially, Carter's idea for a rapid deployment force fared no better. Despite the president's proclamation, the idea languished in the bureaucratic netherworld, a victim of endless staff studies and overall disinterest within the halls of the Pentagon. Until the shah's overthrow, Pentagon planners continued to recommend relying on "regional coalitions," chiefly with Iran and Saudi Arabia, and selling more weapons to both nations to strengthen their military abilities.[10] With the nation still suffering from the post-Vietnam hangover, no one in Washington had much stomach for military adventurism in the developing world or for a command solely dedicated to that purpose.

The chairman of the Joint Chiefs, General David Jones, like Dutch Huyser, came from the strategic bomber community. The now fifty-seven-year-old South Dakota native and former B-29 pilot had once served as an aide to the controversial architect of the firebombing of Japanese cities, Curtis LeMay. As chief of staff of the air force, Jones had impressed President Carter, who'd selected Jones for the top military job in 1978. Jones and Carter shared a similar managerial style—a penchant for micromanagement.

Jones believed it was a mistake to divert military forces from the main Cold War game in Europe to the Middle East. "Unless Moscow invaded Iran," Jones told Defense Secretary Harold Brown after a formal briefing on the Middle East in September 1978, "the U.S. military combatant forces should not become involved in the minor contingencies."[11] In the absence of a crisis, there was no urgency to create the rapid deployment force, and the military dawdled. "It took a crisis to get a good idea the needed attention," Secretary Brown dryly observed. "The takeover by Khomeini had that effect."[12]

On December 2, 1978, Brzezinski sent a classified memo to President Carter laying out his concern that the Middle East was rapidly becoming an "arch of crisis." "There is no question in my mind that we are confronting the beginning of a major crisis, in some ways similar to the one in Europe in the later 40s," he wrote. If so, this would open up the region for the Soviets to exploit and posed a grave challenge to American security.[13]

Brzezinski's strategic view was clear and crisp. He excelled at distilling meetings down to the salient points, cutting off extraneous discussions, and moving recommendations quickly up to President Carter.[14] The national security adviser believed that the Middle East was now inexorably linked to the larger Cold War. He argued that fixating on Europe missed the real dynamic: Persian Gulf oil had become the Achilles' heel of the West. The Soviet Union could bring Europe to its knees simply by cutting off Middle East oil and turning off the tap that drove the economic engines of Western Europe and

Japan. With the United States perched on the precipice of political calamity as the Iranian Revolution unfolded on the streets of Tehran, Brzezinski proposed that the United States forge a new security framework for the Persian Gulf.

Brown backed Brzezinski's vision. He ordered Robert Komer, undersecretary of defense for policy and the third most senior civilian in the Pentagon, to conduct a complete review of the military plans for Iran and the Persian Gulf. A seasoned hand in Washington, Komer had nearly four decades of foreign policy experience. During the 1960s, simpatico with President Lyndon Johnson's Vietnam policies, Komer had headed the political side of the South Vietnamese pacification effort. The bespectacled Komer had a booming voice and a personality to match. During the Vietnam War, Komer had earned the apt nickname "Blowtorch Bob," bestowed by an exasperated Ambassador Henry Cabot Lodge, who said that "arguing with Mr. Komer was like having a flamethrower aimed at the seat of one's pants." Komer reported back to the secretary that the Joint Chiefs' planning was less than satisfactory; in fact, he told Brown privately, "it was very poor."[15]

It was not that the generals and admiral failed to grasp the importance of the Persian Gulf. However, the military was not eager to commit resources to the Middle East, and each service had its own rationale. As far as the army was concerned, the region diverted badly needed reserves from the Cold War's main game against the Soviets in Central Europe. In the aftermath of Vietnam, the U.S. Army had committed itself intellectually and fiscally to building conventional forces poised for a massive clash of tanks and artillery in Germany. With the large disparity in numbers between the U.S. and Soviet forces in Europe, the army's leadership deemed it imprudent to pull troops away from the Cold War's principal front. "U.S. forces engaged in defense of the Persian Gulf area will not be available for Europe, thus adding to the considerable risks entailed," the Joint Chiefs collectively wrote to Brown.[16] While the admirals shared some of their army brethren's concerns about diverting ships away from the main effort against the Soviets—in their case, in the Atlantic and Pacific Oceans—the Persian Gulf presented considerable challenges for the U.S. Navy. Although since 1949 the United States had maintained a small show-the-flag flotilla based in Bahrain called Middle East Force, the navy had little experience operating in this remote, torrid region. The Persian Gulf lay three thousand miles from the nearest naval base. The United

States had no port facilities or logistical infrastructure to support large-scale naval operations in the area.[17] Additionally, and not to be underestimated, the Islamic prohibition on alcohol and its tenet to separate the sexes made most ports of call in the region rather uninviting to American sailors.[18]

On January 9, 1979, Secretary Brown met with the five members of the Joint Chiefs of Staff—the chairman plus the head of each of the four services—in the "Tank," their conference room in the Pentagon's outer E ring. The room was just down the hall from the chairman's executive suite, along a long corridor lined with offices occupied by senior military leadership and the chairman's dining room. The name of the room dates back to the early days of the Joint Chiefs during World War II, when the newly formed body met in a basement room of the Public Health Service's building on Constitution Avenue. Participants entered the Tank by stepping down a set of stairs and then passing through a narrow archway, giving the impression that one was descending into a steel-hulled tank, rather than a government conference room.

Pressured by their political masters, the Joint Chiefs presented the defense secretary with a plan developed hastily by Alexander Haig's European Command. The idea was to dispatch U.S. troops to protect Saudi oil fields in the event of a Soviet move toward the Persian Gulf in the aftermath of the upheavals in Iran. Called Operational Plan 4230, it consisted of moving up to seven thousand men from the United States, with the first airborne troops arriving in as little as three days from their base at Fort Bragg, North Carolina. The plan was rudimentary at best. It required twenty days of preparation before they could even fly the first troops to Saudi Arabia. The Pentagon lacked both the aircraft and the ships to move quickly to the Gulf, and Washington had failed to lay the diplomatic groundwork with Arab countries that would be necessary to deploy American soldiers, even if Washington wanted to send them.

Brown traveled to the Middle East to assess the situation for himself. He found governments in the region on edge, nervous about the events transpiring in Iran and uncertain about the American commitment to their security. To try to assuage their fears, the Pentagon had recently deployed a squadron of F-15 aircraft to Saudi Arabia, in response to a Saudi request.[19] Nevertheless, an anxious Saudi government privately pressed Brown for more concrete defense assurances.[20]

Brown ordered the military to take some immediate steps to strengthen the U.S. military in the Gulf.[21] The Joint Chiefs answered with an imaginative scheme to conduct fifty-four separate military exercises. While many of these amounted to little more than sending a squadron of aircraft to Saudi Arabia or Oman to fly with their air forces for a week, or training on search and rescue techniques, or increasing routine naval deployments to the Gulf, it represented a significant increase in the U.S. military presence in the Gulf states. When staggered over the course of a year, these exercises were tantamount to a permanent presence of U.S. military forces within the Gulf's Arab countries, under the guise of exercises.[22]

As the administration struggled to develop a new strategy, once again serious fissures developed within Carter's foreign policy team. On March 1, 1979, the secretaries of defense and state met with the national security adviser for their weekly lunch date. The topic of the day was the Persian Gulf. Both Brzezinski and Brown favored an expansion of American bases in the area, which would serve to support a military force that could deploy rapidly to the Persian Gulf in the event of a Soviet move on Iran. But Secretary of State Cyrus Vance rejected this view. A more visible American military presence, he argued, would simply fuel anti-American sentiment, not just in Iran, but also throughout the Arab nations. The United States needed to demonstrate an interest in the welfare of the Gulf states, while at the same time keeping a low profile to avoid the perception of neocolonialism.

Two days later and one month to the day after Ayatollah Khomeini's return, Brzezinski tried to force a decision in a top secret paper to the president. The crisis in Iran presented the West with a grave challenge, one that could spin "dangerously out of control." When combined with the Soviet forces in Afghanistan that seemed poised to invade Pakistan or Iran, Brzezinski wrote, pro-Western Gulf Arabs lacked confidence in Washington's ability and willingness to protect them. Brzezinski proposed a complete strategic reorientation toward the Middle East. He called for a massive expansion of military bases in the region, with forces dedicated to intervene to counter Soviet aggression, and a permanent naval presence in the Persian Gulf.[23]

By the end of June 1979, the chief architects of Carter's foreign policy had sketched the outline of a new defense scheme for the Persian Gulf, called the Persian Gulf Security Framework. The strategy struck a balance between Brzezinski's and Vance's positions. The United States would strengthen its ties by means of bilateral agreements with pro-Western Gulf states. The agreements would provide the United States with access to military bases in and around the Gulf, and the United States would sell more weapons to Gulf

Arabs to enable them to shoulder a larger burden of the defense of their oil fields. The U.S. military would position itself around the periphery of the Persian Gulf, poised to intercede directly into either the Gulf or Iran in the event of a Soviet attack. This approach respected the sensitivities of the Arabs, who wanted to work with the United States but did not necessarily want large numbers of infidels in the midst of the Arab heartland. The United States agreed to keep this strategy "low-key" and squarely out of the press while working quietly with the Gulf states to build closer military ties.[24] The Defense Department focused on Oman, Somalia, Kenya, and Diego Garcia to establish their first bases. Saudi Arabia refused to allow any U.S. bases on its territory, but with a nod and a wink it secretly agreed to overbuild its airfields and military infrastructure with the tacit understanding that in the event of a real threat to the kingdom from Iran or the Soviets, the American military could use these facilities. After three years of haggling, the Pentagon would forge ahead to establish a rapid deployment force to serve as the principal intervention force for the Middle East.[25]

Great Britain gave permission for the use of its airfield on the tiny Indian Ocean island of Diego Garcia. The Pentagon spent nearly $600 million over the next four years to upgrade the airfield. The State Department reached an agreement with Oman for the use of four airfields and over the next three years spent well over $200 million to upgrade these bases for the U.S. Air Force and Navy.[26] One on the island of Masirah—a British Royal Air Force base since the 1930s—was particularly well situated for American requirements. The isolated island lay fifteen miles off the Omani coast in the Gulf of Oman, but sat near the Strait of Hormuz. Following the signing of a ten-year lease agreement between Washington and Muscat in 1979, the United States expanded the small runway and built a second one to accommodate combat aircraft. In addition, the Americans upgraded facilities and buildings, pre-positioning sites to accommodate twenty-six thousand troops. This base would serve as a staging base for the failed rescue operation in Iran in April 1980, and would remain a key American facility for the next two decades, including providing a base for yet another group of American special operations forces, those that went into Afghanistan in October 2001.

Egyptian president Anwar Sadat quietly consented to allow U.S. forces to use his military bases. Egypt would serve as the logistics rear for U.S. forces defending the Persian Gulf and would be an important transit point in deploying troops to the Persian Gulf. Komer dispatched his deputy undersecretary of defense for policy planning, Walter Slocombe, to look at the Egyptian facilities. At age forty, Slocombe already was an experienced hand in the Democratic defense establishment, and in the coming years he would go on to serve as the number three man in President Bill Clinton's Pentagon and would play a key role in the decision to disband the Iraqi army in May 2003 following the overthrow of Saddam Hussein.

After touring an airfield near Cairo, Slocombe headed down to a large, abandoned Egyptian military cantonment at Ras Banas, a peninsula jutting out into the Red Sea about three-quarters of the way down the Egyptian coast. Built before the 1973 Yom Kippur War with Israel, the facility included both a large runway and a port.[27] The base was perfect, Slocombe thought. It sat astride the Saudi Red Sea ports of Jeddah and Yanbu, and would easily serve as another means to get U.S. forces into Saudi Arabia should the Soviets seize the Strait of Hormuz. It sat out of range of Soviet aircraft, and it provided an excellent base for massive U.S. B-52 bombers as well as a mustering area for a U.S. Army headed to Iran. With improvements, it could serve as a staging base for an entire American division. More important, it lay nearly two hundred miles from the nearest city, permitting the base to be built in secret. Both Secretary Brown and General Jones liked Slocombe's idea. With congressional approval, the United States pumped more than $200 million over the next few years to upgrade the facilities, turning Ras Banas into a major hub for the U.S. military.[28]

The decision to establish a rapid deployment force touched off a contentious interservice squabble inside the Pentagon. No senior officer really wanted the new command, but if it was going to exist, every general or admiral wanted to control it as well as the money inevitably linked to the new mission. The army and air force proposed a three-star army general to command the rapid deployment force under the Tampa-based Readiness Command, the successor to Strike Command, whose responsibilities encompassed wartime deployment planning for army and air force units based in the United States. The army further added that it should be only a wartime headquarters, with the army-dominated European Command controlling operations in the Middle East during peacetime. Not surprisingly, the chief of naval operations, Admiral Thomas Hayward, took a different view. The rapid deployment force should be an independent force, he said, perhaps under the nominal control of

Readiness Command, but with direct access to the Joint Chiefs, who would oversee military planning for the Middle East. This, the naval services hoped, would take the rapid deployment force out from under the army's thumb and position it under the Pentagon, where the navy would have greater say in running the command. Chairman of the Joint Chiefs David Jones came down somewhere in the middle, generally supporting the air force and army, but with his penchant for micromanagement, he liked the idea of greater control over the rapid deployment force by him and the Joint Chiefs.

As the summer of 1979 waned and with the military still at loggerheads, President Carter grew exacerbated at the impasse. "Who is in charge? PACOM [Pacific Command]? EUCOM [European Command]? Or who?" the president asked Brown. The defense secretary tried to assure the president that they had made progress, but Carter would have none of it. The president scribbled in the margins of one of Brown's memos, "I don't see that any progress has actually been made."[29] Brown too grew weary of the endless haggling between the generals and admirals. "The rapid deployment force was to be an extension of military power," Brown wrote to Jones, "not an excuse to justify more forces or larger budgets."[30]

After months of debate, the Joint Chiefs forged a convoluted compromise. The new rapid deployment force would be a separate joint, or all-service, organization, under the command of a three-star general. The force would report to the Readiness Command and be colocated with it in Tampa. However, the command would maintain a separate liaison office in Washington to allow direct access for the command to the Joint Staff and the senior leadership at the Pentagon. While not perfect, this was good enough for Secretary Brown. Two weeks before the embassy takeover in Iran, he issued a memo to General Jones ordering the new command's founding by March 1, 1980. While primarily intended for the Persian Gulf and the Middle East, the new rapid deployment force would be called upon for "contingencies threatening American interests anywhere in the world."[31]

Tall, broad shouldered, and square jawed, Paul Xavier Kelley looked like a marine. His demeanor exuded an intense confidence. Born on Armistice Day in 1928, the fair-skinned redhead was both proud and defensive about his Irish heritage. Critics and supporters both agreed that P.X. could be emotional, and he frequently took professional criticism personally, especially if it implicated his beloved marine corps. He was a devoted family man; the only priority in his life higher than the marine corps was his wife and children. After a command in Vietnam, he served as military liaison to the Paris peace talks that ended American participation in the Vietnam War. This assignment gave Kelley his first strong dose of Washington politics and American diplomacy. The latter, at least, left him less than impressed, as he observed the shenanigans of President Nixon's secretary of state and national security adviser Henry Kissinger.[32]

On a Friday afternoon in the fall of 1979, P. X. Kelley received a phone call from General Jones's secretary asking if Kelley would meet with the chairman the next day at ten a.m. to interview as the first commander of the rapid deployment force.[33] The commandant of the U.S. Marine Corps had been lobbying hard to give the command to his service, and while Jones viewed this as a purely parochial move, the marine's argument resonated throughout the defense secretary's office.[34] On Saturday morning, as Kelley prepared to drive over to the Pentagon, the chairman's secretary called again to relay that Jones had been called to a meeting at the White House. She was not sure how long that meeting would last, but could Kelley please just stand by, and she would notify him when Jones returned?

"Well," Kelley answered, "that all depends. You see, I've promised my granddaughter that I would take her to see *Snow White and the Seven Dwarfs* this afternoon, and that is one appointment I can't miss."

Fortunately for both the granddaughter and Kelley's career, General Jones returned to his office at the Pentagon, and P.X. arrived around noon for an informal and affable meeting with the air force chairman. Dressed in his dark green service uniform with a panoply of ribbons on his left breast, Kelley looked as if he had come from central casting, and Jones quickly discovered that his mind matched his appearance. The chairman liked what he saw and offered command of the new rapid deployment force to the marine. As Kelley left the office, Jones said slyly, "General, enjoy *Snow White*." The chairman's secretary just grinned.

On March 1, 1980, the new command became a reality, now formally called the Rapid Deployment Joint Task Force (RDJTF) and located at Mac-Dill Air Force Base, a sprawling air base in Tampa, Florida. The base sits on a wide peninsula about five miles south from the tall buildings that dominate downtown Tampa. The sprawling air base of pine trees and palmettos is typical U.S. Air Force, replete with an eighteen-hole golf course, a marina, and a small but quaint beach, which looks out onto the placid Tampa Bay and affords a pleasant view of the cruise ships and merchants going in and out of Tampa. Established during World War II to train new bomber pilots, the base was featured in the 1955 film *Strategic Air Command*, an overt piece of air force propaganda starring Jimmy Stewart.

P. X. Kelley established his headquarters in a large, square, half-buried structure next to the runway on a remote corner of the base. Numbered Building 5201, it was better known as the "molehole." Accessible by a single mile-long road, the molehole had been built in the 1950s to serve as a ready room and command center for nuclear-armed bombers waiting for Armageddon. As of this writing, it houses the Special Operations Command that runs the secret wars in Afghanistan and the Middle East.

The new command took shape, despite the lethargy with the four services in filling its 250-man staff. The Soviet invasion of Afghanistan fostered a crisis atmosphere in the molehole, with officers routinely working sixteen-hour days. Less than two months after the command's formal commissioning, Kelley held the unit's first full-scale exercise in the mountains of Idaho. A modest effort compared to those that would follow, it involved flying in a single army battalion in a simulated defense of Pakistan against a Soviet invasion. This was the first of a demanding schedule of exercises across the Middle East, the largest of which would be Bright Star in November 1980, which involved sending some sixty-five hundred American troops for twenty days to the Egyptian desert in a biennial exercise that continues to this day.[35]

K elley's staff quickly began planning for World War III in Iran. They saw two possible Russian invasion plans. One would be a quick incursion designed to seize Iranian Azerbaijan, either to support a communist coup in Tehran or to forestall the Islamic Revolution from spreading to Moscow's own Muslim population. The second, more serious threat involved a full-scale invasion of Iran by fifteen to twenty-four divisions, with the objective of quickly seizing the Khuzestan oil fields in southwestern Iran as well as the vital choke point, the Strait of Hormuz, to cut off the oil flow to the West.[36] With Iran subjugated, as one U.S. war planner surmised, "The Soviets could undertake a subsequent offense operation against the Arab nations in the region." Soviet aircraft could destroy Saudi Arabian oil facilities and cut the flow of crude to the West. Red Army tanks would be poised to threaten Turkey and the southern flank of NATO. U.S. military planners worried that the Soviets might try a lightning attack, using airborne troops to seize the Strait of Hormuz, perhaps even parachuting down on the Saudi oil fields and conquering the kingdom in a coup de main.

These American fears had an air of absurdity. Even if Moscow committed all its army coupled with extensive support from regional surrogates such as Iraq and Syria, Moscow would face a monumental task in conquering Iran, let alone the entire Middle East. The idea that the Red Army could sustain hundreds of thousands of soldiers with bullets, beans, and benzene over a thousand-mile-long supply route that ran over Iran's formidable Zagros Mountains seems ridiculous in hindsight, especially in light of its military's poor performance in Afghanistan. But in the panic that gripped Washington following the Soviet invasion into Afghanistan, no one in either political party questioned the reality of their anxiety, especially in an election year and in an administration already lambasted for being soft on defense.

Kelley's war plans for Iran hinged on support from the Gulf Arabs.[37] American troops and airplanes would muster in Saudi Arabia, Oman, and Bahrain, both to safeguard their oil facilities and to serve as a staging base for a subsequent move directly into Iran. The U.S. Marines, backed up by naval carrier airplanes, would storm the beaches around Bandar Abbas, seizing the port and airfield and securing the Strait of Hormuz and Kharg Island, the latter location from which 96 percent of Iran's oil exports flowed.[38] Once the sea-lanes into the Persian Gulf were secure, three U.S. Army divisions would seize the northern Gulf port of Bushehr and then move inland to take the strategically positioned Iranian city of Shiraz at the foothills of the Zagros, and block Soviet forces moving south through the mountains, safeguarding both the Khuzestan oil fields and the Persian Gulf.[39] Depending on what happened in Europe at the same time, as many as two hundred thousand servicemen and -women were allocated to the Iran invasion.[40]

Time became the critical watchword for American planners. The Defense Intelligence Agency, or DIA, estimated that it could provide only seven days' advance notice of a limited incursion, and perhaps three weeks' warning for a full-scale invasion. But the United States could muster only about thirty-five thousand army airborne soldiers and marines to the Gulf within the first three weeks, and planners both in Tampa and at the Pentagon predicted it would take thirty days to move any sizable number of combat forces to the

Gulf. Under the best of conditions, time was not on Kelley's side in the race for Iran.[41]

However, Kelley had an ace in his deck of cards to buy time and halt the Soviet advance into Iran: nuclear weapons. The United States never shied away from planning to use nuclear weapons to defend Persian Gulf oil. Washington did hesitate to nuke the Soviet Union proper out of concern that such a move would lead to a full-scale nuclear war, one U.S. planners in 1982 surmised would kill 50 to 75 percent of the U.S. population. But Soviet troops inside Iran were seen as fair game. If the Red Army were poised to win the race for the Strait of Hormuz, tactical nuclear weapons would be the force of choice to stop them.[42]

The United States started from a distinct disadvantage in the nuclear balance in the Middle East. The Soviets arrayed a massive arsenal of strategic weapons toward the Persian Gulf, capable of devastating the area's military bases, ports, and refineries and oil fields. Embedded within their armor and mechanized divisions were 152 tactical mobile rockets designed to carry nuclear warheads, as well as nearly 300 nuclear artillery shells. Larger ballistic missiles based in the southern Soviet Caucasus could easily reach any corner of the Middle East. Backing this arsenal were 283 aircraft capable of dropping nuclear bombs with a destructive power that dwarfed Hiroshima. U.S. intelligence detected nuclear storage bunkers at four Soviet airfields alone just to support an invasion of Iran.

In December 1980, Undersecretary Komer released a study on the potential use of nuclear weapons to defend the Persian Gulf. The first objective remained, Komer said, to deter Soviet aggression in Iran. But if deterrence failed, the use of nuclear weapons would signal to Moscow the American resolve to defend the Gulf. Komer approved three options for employing nuclear weapons against the Soviets in Iran. The first two options used nuclear weapons only within Iran, with the objective to block Soviet forces by destroying the mountain passes on the Iran-Soviet border and the Zagros Mountains, which would impede Moscow's movements southward toward the Gulf. If Soviet troops were already in Iran, American bombers would hit Soviet rear echelon units entering Iran, while the U.S. Army's tactical artillery nukes would devastate frontline ground forces attacking U.S. forces. The third option expanded American nuclear attacks to bases and nuclear missile sites in the southern Soviet Union, striking Soviet nuclear headquarters, logistics bases, and conventional forces. The goal, a Pentagon plan summarized, would be to destroy Moscow's ability to "sustain military operations in Iran."

Komer's preference for nuclear weapons in Iran was, in the best Dr. Strangeloveian speak, known as the "passive option." U.S. Special Forces would detonate nuclear devices in key mountain passes, tunnels, and roads into western Iran from the Soviet Union. The resulting nuclear detonation would collapse mountains and spawn avalanches, and thus prevent Soviet tanks from moving into Iran. Because time was the Achilles' heel of the U.S. rapid deployment force, Komer's study noted, "Closing the passes in front of the initial invasion would significantly impede a Red Army advance, and, if the Soviets did not respond in kind, could provide additional time for the U.S. to deploy forces." Furthermore, it had the added advantage of not directly targeting Soviet troops, which otherwise might lead to rapid escalation in a nuclear war. The Pentagon allocated over twenty atomic demolition munitions for this task in Iran. Popularly referred to as "manpack nukes," they had been in the U.S. inventory since the 1950s. Each device weighed less than 163 pounds and easily could be parachuted or clandestinely smuggled in by a small special forces team. The small nukes were to be buried and set with a variable yield, which could create either a relatively small explosion to destroy a large tunnel or a massive detonation to collapse an entire mountain pass.[43]

The one downside, Komer noted, was that this strategy necessitated the first use of nuclear weapons. This preemptive use of nuclear weapons "bears the risk of uncontrolled escalation," he wrote. Even with the "passive option," the Soviets might respond in kind and obliterate the ports of Bushehr and Bandar Abbas to deny them to arriving American forces. But neither the Joint Chiefs nor Komer viewed this response as particularly bad. In the harsh calculations of the Cold War, Komer wrote, "the net effect could be, at least in the short-term, to produce a militarily neutral situation with respect to U.S.-USSR ground forces." If neither side could get into Iran, the United States would still achieve its goal of safeguarding the oil fields. No one reflected on how the Iranians might view such a scenario.

The political winds did not blow in President Jimmy Carter's favor in November 1980. The voters tossed the Democrats out in a hurricane that came in the form of Ronald Reagan, who won forty-four of the fifty states in an electoral landslide. Implementing the Carter Doctrine would fall to his successor. But Carter's State of the Union speech on that cold January night had put into motion an important new American strategy for the Middle East. After floundering through one Middle East crisis after another, in his final year in office President Carter's fractured foreign policy team finally coalesced around a new plan to defend Middle East oil.

In his last month in office, Carter continued to modify his Middle East strategy. On January 7, the president signed a secret directive staking out the American policy of freedom of navigation in the Persian Gulf. Specifically, Carter authorized the Pentagon to use force to prevent Iran from closing the Strait of Hormuz to oil exports. Just five days before leaving office, Carter signed his last directive laying out Brzezinski's Persian Gulf security framework. Written largely for the new administration, it encapsulated the decisions hashed out over the previous year. Carter had set down a marker: the United States would use force to prevent Iran from hindering the free flow of oil from the Persian Gulf.[44] The U.S. government moved to develop closer military ties with the pro-Western Arab states ringing Iran and reached tacit agreements to facilitate the operations of America's new military limb designed specifically to intervene in the Middle East. The first military plans had been refined to combat the Soviets. While Reagan's supporters touted the dawn of a new, firmer stance against the Soviet Union in the Cold War, in fact it had been Jimmy Carter who laid the foundation for American grand strategy for the next decade.[45]

Three

BARBED-WIRE BOB

On January 20, 1981, the day Ronald Wilson Reagan became the fortieth president of the United States, Jimmy Carter spent much of his last morning in office finalizing the release of the American hostages in Iran. It was a bittersweet day for Carter; the new president had already taken the oath by the time the hostages departed Tehran airport for their flight to Algeria and freedom.

At sixty-nine, Reagan was the oldest man ever elected president. Despite the creases of age showing in his long face, he was as energetic and vernal as his jet-black hair indicated. Perennially upbeat, he rarely displayed anger. The new commander in chief had a strong sense of right and wrong. Reagan famously avoided the intricacies of policy particulars. Instead, he provided an unwavering broad world vision: the moral righteousness of the free world's confrontation with an expansionistic evil Soviet empire.

Reagan hated personal confrontations, sought to avoid face-to-face disagreements, and tended to defer unpleasant decisions, especially if they involved his longtime acquaintances serving in the administration. While this made for genial staff meetings, it also resulted in important national security sessions adjourning without anyone having the foggiest idea of what the president had actually decided.

At first appearance, the new president stood in stark contrast to his predecessor. Carter came across as a scolding headmaster; Reagan appeared win-
some. Where Carter delved into the nuances of policy, Reagan remained
a generalist, aloof from the sausage making. Carter had a clear view of the
way forward in the Middle East with the Arab-Israeli peace process and the
rapid deployment force; Reagan came to office with no firm convictions.
Carter had been slow to recognize the threat posed by Soviet adventurism in
the Middle East; Reagan came to the Oval Office determined to confront
Soviet expansion.

U.S. Marine Corps commandant General Robert Barrow liked the new
president. A tall, courtly Southern gentleman from Louisiana, Barrow had
won the Navy Cross, the nation's second highest military medal, as a company commander during the epic retreat from the Chosin Reservoir in Korea.
Although he had considerable respect for the intellect of Defense Secretary
Harold Brown, Barrow harbored misgivings about many of Carter's defense
policies, which he thought had left America weak and vulnerable to the
Soviet Union. The yearlong trauma of the hostage crisis and the debacle of
the failed rescue mission only added to Barrow's melancholy. Reagan's campaign promise to increase defense spending came as a welcome balm, soothing the anxieties of Barrow and many of his fellow generals.

During the marine commandant's first meeting with Reagan on the
reviewing stand during the inaugural parade, a military formation carrying
the American flag passed by. The president turned to Barrow and asked if it
would be okay if he returned their salute even though he was a civilian.[1]

"Yes, sir. You're the commander in chief, Mr. President," Barrow answered
in his Louisiana drawl. Reagan did so, establishing a precedent that continues
to this day.

The political appointees who comprised the new Republican administration arrived distrustful of any holdover from the Carter years. During the
transition, they showed little interest in being briefed on Carter's defense initiatives and displayed open disdain for anyone who had gone along with Carter's perceived weak-kneed policies against Iran and the Soviet Union. The
chairman of the Joint Chiefs of Staff, General David Jones, bore the brunt of
the new civilian team's disrespect. The Republicans believed he had been too
willing to go along with Carter's policies, such as giving up American control
over the Panama Canal and cuts in defense programs such as the B-1 bomber.
President Reagan considered firing Jones, who still had a year left in his term

as chairman. But the president decided against it, concerned that it would set a bad precedent. Reagan's solution was simply to cut the chairman out of any serious deliberations until he could appoint a general more to his liking. For the first year of his presidency, Reagan refused to go to the Pentagon and meet with the Joint Chiefs. It was an exceptional snub, and one that left no illusions in Washington about what the new administration thought of those in uniform who had worked for Carter's Defense Department. It had no less a political impact on the military than if Reagan had replaced Jones.[2]

In June 1982, David Jones retired on schedule, and Reagan appointed Army General John "Jack" Vessey as the new senior military adviser. Unpretentious, Vessey was a muddy-boots soldier. He had risen through the ranks, having received a battlefield commission at the bloody battle of Anzio in Italy during the Second World War. Lean with graying hair, the new chairman was a religious man. Contemporaries never viewed Vessey as an intellect, but he was respected within the military and had the deserved reputation as being both honest and apolitical, both traits that appealed to President Reagan. For Vessey, war was not an academic exercise. Having experienced combat up close in three wars, he remained reticent about risking young men's lives. Military force, Vessey believed, should be the option of last resort.

While they were loath to admit it, the Reagan foreign policy team continued many of Carter's Persian Gulf defense policies. Early in the administration, the Joint Staff produced a new study on additional construction for U.S. forces from Morocco to Somalia that reflected Carter's conclusions. Secretary of Defense Caspar Weinberger liked it, and the Reagan administration pushed through an additional $700 million for base construction in the Middle East to support the rapid deployment force.[3]

On September 30, 1981, Reagan's national security team met in the Cabinet Room, next to the Oval Office, to finalize a decision directive for the president's signature outlining the administration's approach toward Iran. The release of the hostages had not led to improved relations between Tehran and Washington. That would depend, National Security Adviser Richard Allen wrote to the secretary of defense, on "Iran's willingness to demonstrate by specific action its restored respect for international law and civilized usage."[4] This new policy document reiterated the importance of preventing Soviet domination of Iran's oil and laid out steps to increase intelligence gathering inside Iran, prevent the expansion of the Islamic Revolution, and cultivate pro-Western moderates within the Iranian government.[5] These remained the cornerstones of American policy toward Iran for the next eight years of Reagan's presidency.

Caspar Weinberger, the new secretary of defense, was a slight, impeccably dressed, affable bulldog. The California native was a close political and personal friend of Reagan's as well as a Republican stalwart, having served as President Nixon's budget director and secretary of health, education, and welfare. Unlike his immediate predecessors as defense secretary, "Cap," as most within the Reagan White House called him, had seen war. He'd served in the Pacific during the Second World War as an infantry officer and later as an intelligence officer on MacArthur's staff. Weinberger's brief military service affected his outlook in his new role.

When Weinberger arrived in his Pentagon office on the third-floor outer E ring, he immediately removed a large formal portrait of dour-looking James Forrestal, the first secretary of defense, who'd suffered from depression and committed suicide by throwing himself out a top window in the imposing tower at Bethesda Naval Hospital. Weinberger replaced it with a more uplifting four-hundred-year-old Titian painting of a Catholic cardinal bestowing his beneficence upon an abbot, a colorful piece that the new secretary found soothing. Two bronze busts adorned his expansive office, one of Weinberger's wartime boss Douglas MacArthur, and the other of an infantryman. "I also wanted to make it clear that our administration was not worried about being too militaristic," Weinberger later wrote.[6]

In policy, Weinberger was a cautious man. He viewed military force as a last resort and not a first. "He liked to have the power, but did not really want to use it," remarked noted military historian Steven Rearden. Weinberger's philosophy was best summed up in a speech he gave at a luncheon held November 28, 1984, at the National Press Club, just down the street from the White House. In what became known as the Weinberger Doctrine, the defense secretary outlined a series of criteria for committing the U.S. military to combat: only for vital national interests, with clearly defined goals for victory, and only if supported by the American people.

This view reflected the beliefs of those the secretary surrounded himself with, especially his two most important confidants, his senior military assistant, Major General Colin Powell, and Deputy Assistant Secretary of Defense Richard Armitage.[7]

Powell had impressed Weinberger from when he'd briefly served under him as a White House Fellow during the Ford administration. Powell was easy to like. He displayed many of the best traits of an army leader: smart, precise in his verbiage, with an infectious smile and a good sense of humor. Powell inspired loyalty and respect from superiors and subordinates alike. But Colin Powell could never be described as a muddy-boots soldier. The consummate political general and Beltway insider, he stood in sharp contrast to Chairman of the Joint Chiefs John Vessey. Powell had first arrived in Washington as a midgrade officer in September 1969, and with the exception of obligatory short command tours needed to check the box for promotion, he'd never left. By the time he took the job as Weinberger's senior military assistant, he'd already had nearly a decade under his belt of working the corridors of the Pentagon, including the same billet as military assistant for the number two man in the Defense Department during the Carter administration.

In many ways Richard Armitage was an anomaly in Washington. In a city of smooth politicians, lobbyists, and lawyers, Armitage had been formed from a different mold. A former navy officer, he'd served multiple tours in Vietnam. An avid weight lifter, he trekked every day down to the Pentagon Officers Athletic Club, or POAC, a dingy maze that sufficed as the Pentagon's gym. Here Armitage, then in his forties, routinely bench-pressed more weight than most of the far younger servicemen. Direct, blunt, and unpretentious in manner, balding and barrel-chested, he resembled Uncle Fester on the TV show *The Addams Family*, with the exception of his bright blue eyes that revealed a quick mind and an unlimited reservoir of energy. He was a close confidant of Weinberger's and arguably the most influential man in the Pentagon. "If you wanted something done," said one four-star general at the time, "you went through Rich."

On his first day as the new defense secretary, Weinberger found a letter on his desk from General Volney Warner. The army general had drafted a series of recommendations intended to pull under Warner's command both Paul X. Kelley's rapid deployment headquarters and the elite counterterrorism headquarters known as Joint Special Operations Command at Fort Bragg.[8] Weinberger had followed the contorted history of the rapid deployment force. He found the idea of a major land war in Iran unrealistic and sided with those who believed that what the military needed was not an interventionist force for the Middle East, but a deterrent capability. However, he faced the same dilemma as Secretary Brown: the military remained hopelessly divided on how to deal with Iran and the Middle East.

Weinberger's brief military experience had taught him about the dangers of unit boundaries, the problems presented where two friendly units came together. "I had seen some of the difficulties where boundaries of command came together," Weinberger said. "The enemy tried to exploit these seams between our units." In the Middle East, Weinberger noted, you had just such a boundary between two massive four-star commands—European Command and Pacific Command—running through the most volatile region in the world. In Weinberger's mind, the rapid deployment force only compounded the problem about who was really in charge in the event of a war in the Middle East. "We need one man in charge over the whole area," Weinberger thought. The letter from Warner spurred him to action.

In early April 1981, Weinberger met in the Tank with the Joint Chiefs to discuss the future of the rapid deployment force. Not one of the five flag officers present supported retaining the organization. "Operations in the Persian Gulf would extend the two fleets enormously," Weinberger recalled of the chief of naval operations' views.[9] Caspar Weinberger brushed aside the opinions of both the Joint Chiefs and Volney Warner and sided with P. X. Kelley. The secretary ordered the rapid deployment force into a new four-star headquarters. This would be a new unified command, as the Pentagon termed it, and would control all U.S. military forces, regardless of service, throughout the Middle East.

The defense secretary's decision only added to the polemical discussions by the five gray-haired gentlemen in the Tank. They wrangled over what units to assign to the command and which countries should be included (Egypt and Israel being the major bones of contention). Even the name of the new four-star headquarters occupied a staggering amount of mental energy on the part of the Pentagon's leadership. One suggestion was Crescent Command. Someone else proposed Commander in Chief, Middle East, Africa, Southwest Asia, shorted to the acronym CINCMEAFSWA. Kelley's replacement at the rapid deployment force, Lieutenant General Robert Kingston, recommended the name United States Central Command, as it had a ring of significance. However, the Joint Chiefs did not like this name, as it was unclear to them what the command was central in relation to. They countered with Southwest Asia Command. But others within the bureaucracy objected to this on the grounds that it sounded too much like an interventionist force, which of course was the command's raison d'être. At one point, one of Weinberger's military assistants wrote to the secretary, "I did hear someone mention WEINLUCCICOM but I don't understand what the letters stand for."[10] And so it continued, month after month.

Gentle prodding by the president finally broke the gridlock. Ronald Reagan understood the havoc Iran wreaked upon his predecessor, and the president took an unusually keen interest in the formation of a military command for the Middle East. "I endorse it with enthusiasm," Reagan wrote to Weinberger upon hearing of his decision to form a four-star Middle East headquarters: "I have long felt that the importance of this region is such that we need the optimal command arrangements possible, and this means a separate command. I approve your decision and I look forward to the specifics of your implementation plan." When a year had passed with no new command established, the president sent a polite yet firm reminder to Weinberger to update him on the specifics of the new command. The president put the Pentagon on notice to get on with business.[11] It worked.

The Pentagon quickly finalized the details of the new Middle East command in spite of a last-minute effort by the navy to kill the initiative backed by the head of the powerful Senate Appropriations Committee, Alaska senator Ted Stevens.[12] Weinberger approved standing up U.S. Central Command, or CENTCOM, as the military abbreviated it. CENTCOM's area of responsibility spanned nineteen countries, from Egypt in the west to Pakistan in the east to Kenya in the south. Most of the forces assigned came from those already under the rapid deployment force, with both the army and air force establishing subordinate headquarters to support CENTCOM. The army reactivated the famed Third Army to command its divisions for the Middle East, which General George Patton had commanded in Western Europe as the spearhead of American armored forces in Europe during the Second World War.[13] In order to smooth the concerns by General Barrow over control of CENTCOM, General Vessey implemented a tacit agreement that CENTCOM's commander would alternate between the army and the marines. The understanding held for the next twenty years, until 2003, when pressures related to the troubled U.S. occupation in Iraq led to successive army commanders.

Weinberger's decision ended General Volney Warner's career. He turned down another major command in Europe and wrote to Weinberger that since "I no longer enjoy the support and confidence of the Joint Chiefs of Staff, request that I be relieved of my duties." Weinberger concurred. An embittered Volney Warner penned a five-page letter to President Reagan blasting Weinberger's decision and the parochial and ineffectual Joint Chiefs.[14] Warner refused a retirement parade. Instead, he and some close comrades parachuted from a plane at Fort Bragg, where a keg of beer awaited the skydivers in the landing zone. "It was the way I wanted to go, with a few friends and a few beers."[15]

The decision to form CENTCOM received a warm reception from the pro-Western Arabs. Just after sunset on the afternoon of December 16, 1982, Prince Bandar bin Sultan, the affable and shrewd Saudi ambassador to Washington, arrived in Weinberger's office to relay a message from the Saudi monarch. "King Fahd was one hundred percent in support of the newly created U.S. Central Command and saw it as a good move, one that sent the right signal to the Soviets," the prince said. CENTCOM made Moscow very uneasy, Bandar added, mentioning that the Soviets had tried to convince Saudi Arabia that this was merely an American vehicle to take over the region. The king rejected this argument and stood firmly behind American goals in the Persian Gulf, Bandar told the secretary.

In typical Saudi style, however, Bandar ended the meeting with a straightforward pronouncement that his government would have to makepublic statements distancing itself from CENTCOM, but Weinberger should not pay any attention to those statements. Weinberger understood and nodded in agreement, and the meeting adjourned with a hearty laugh as the two men reflected on the duplicity that permeated the Middle East.[16]

The one notable Middle East country unhappy with America's new defense scheme was Washington's most stalwart ally in the region, Israel. The Jewish state worried about the ramifications of an American military command dedicated solely to the support of the Arabs, and hoped that closer military ties would strengthen the relationship between the two countries. Israel pushed forcefully for inclusion in the American defense plans for the Middle East. Knowing full well the hawkish Cold War views of the new civilian leaders in Washington, the Israeli government emphasized the Soviet hand in the Arab-Israeli conflict. Just a month after the inauguration, the Israeli foreign minister showed up in a Pentagon conference room to meet with Secretary Weinberger. Yitzhak Shamir repeatedly stressed to Weinberger that the Soviet Union created most of the region's instability. "The PLO is a terrorist organization that works directly for the Soviet Union,"

Shamir said forcefully, if not entirely truthfully, to Weinberger during one of their first meetings. Prime Minister Menachem Begin would repeat this mantra in his first meeting with Reagan in the Oval Office. He saw little difference between Soviet client states in the Middle East and those of the Warsaw Pact in Europe. He offered the use of Israeli air bases and ports, even going so far as to commit the Israeli air force to fly for the U.S. military over the Persian Gulf. In return, he wanted the United States to essentially scrap its recent agreements with Arabs supporting the rapid deployment force. Begin singled out Iraq as the key enemy for Israel, and by inference the United States, due to its large conventional military and budding nuclear program. That Israel's anxiety over the military might of Iraq had little to do with the Cold War was omitted from the talking points, but the prime minister's forceful advocacy for Israel as a Cold War asset to Washington affected American officials.[17]

Alexander Haig, now secretary of state in the Reagan administration, never needed convincing; he already viewed the Middle East through a Cold War lens and was an ardent supporter of Israel. Both he and Reagan believed that Israel should be included in CENTCOM, an opinion initially shared by Weinberger too.

However, both the Joint Chiefs and the civilians in the Defense Department swayed Weinberger to recommend against it. The Joint Chiefs believed that Israel lay too far from the Persian Gulf and that including Israel would jeopardize the important basing agreements with the Arab nations.[18] The senior civilian responsible for military issues apart from the Soviet Union was a marine Vietnam veteran, Bing West. He warned Weinberger that Reagan was under the undue influence of a pro-Israeli staffer on the National Security Council, or NSC, and that this was why he wanted the Jewish state included in CENTCOM.

This insinuation greatly irritated Weinberger. "He's the president," the secretary responded to West. "Whose advice he consulted before making a decision is irrelevant."

After meeting with the Joint Chiefs in the Tank on May 25, 1982, however, Weinberger reversed his position and wrote to Reagan recommending excluding Israel, Lebanon, and Syria from the new Middle East command out of deference to Arab sensibilities. "I do not entirely share this view, but we can always change it if need be," Weinberger wrote.[19]

The replacement for P. X. Kelley and the first commander of CENTCOM was Robert "Barbed-Wire Bob" Kingston. Tall and thin, with a stern demeanor and explosive temper, Kingston was all about the business of war. "He had a gaze that said, 'Don't fuck with me,'" remarked Jay Hines, the longtime civilian historian at CENTCOM. He'd earned his moniker when he strung concertina wire around his command post to keep soldiers from walking on the grass. While no great strategic thinker, Kingston was a warrior, gifted with the natural ability to lead men in combat. As a young lieutenant during the Korean War, he'd led a hundred-man force up to the frozen bank of the Yalu River on the Chinese border and had repeatedly distinguished himself during the American army's chaotic flight south following the Chinese intervention in November 1950.

Kingston had a long association with the CIA. After his first tour in Korea, he moved over to a joint military-CIA paramilitary organization that infiltrated South Korean agents into the north and conducted raids from submarines, blowing up trains and bridges deep behind North Korean lines. Kingston was one of the few Americans to go ashore with the Korean operatives on sabotage missions. "At the time, I thought it was great fun," Kingston later said.[20] After Korea, Kingston became one of the few military officers to be run through the CIA's case officers' course, which trained CIA officers to handle foreign agents. In the spring of 1967 Kingston took command of OP-34, a highly sensitive mission that sent teams of South Vietnamese agents into North Vietnam to try to organize an insurgency against the communist government. Begun by the CIA in the early 1960s, the military took over responsibility in 1964.

Shortly after his arrival, Kingston suspected the entire operation had been compromised. Of the five hundred agents dropped into the north, all had been killed or turned out to be double agents working for the communists. Kingston gave the bad news to his boss, Colonel John Singlaub—himself a legendary former Office of Strategic Services (OSS) agent who had parachuted into France before D-Day—in his usual blunt manner: "What do you want to tell Ho Chi Minh? Your teams are double agents and I can send Ho the message through them."[21]

Kingston maintained his CIA contacts after arriving in Tampa as the new commander. He became a frequent visitor to its headquarters in Langley,

Virginia.[22] Kingston had a knack for obtaining raw CIA intelligence outside of the normal channels. This provided Kingston with unique information not normally available to a four-star general, and it eventually caught the attention of Deputy CIA Director Robert Gates, who ordered this back channel closed. Gates directed that only approved intelligence documents be given to CENTCOM, through the conventional channel of the Defense Intelligence Agency.[23]

The plan Kingston inherited from Kelley to defend Iran from the Soviets rested on the Zagros Mountains strategy. Now labeled Operations Plan (OPLAN) 1004, this rested on long-standing Cold War fears of a Soviet invasion of Iran that would threaten Western access to Middle East oil. It called for the deployment of four U.S. divisions and three aircraft carriers, first to secure the sea-lanes out of the Persian Gulf, and then to land troops at Bandar Abbas at the Strait of Hormuz as well as at the northern end of the Gulf near Abadan. From there, the Americans would advance northeast into the Persian interior, intent on establishing a defense line along the Zagros, a massive, jagged mountain range with many peaks in excess of ten thousand feet stretching from northeastern Iraq near Kurdistan then southeast and ending near the Strait of Hormuz.

As Kingston looked at revising the Iran plan, the one glaring weakness was how the Islamic Republic would react to a crisis between the superpowers. If the Soviet Union unilaterally invaded Iran, perhaps to support a pro-Soviet coup, Kingston concluded that Khomeini might set aside his hatred for the United States and cooperate with the U.S. military. A cooperative or at least passive Iran would immensely improve the U.S. military's chances of success. CENTCOM hoped to work with the Iranian military and use it to defend the Khuzestan oil fields in southwestern Iran, which might alleviate Iranian concerns that the United States just wanted to seize the country's oil.[24]

In August 1983, however, the intelligence agencies reassessed their assumptions about Iran's placidity should the U.S. military arrive ostensibly to protect them against the communists. Iran, DIA analysts concluded, disliked the Americans as much as it did the Soviets and would be likely to resist both with equal vigor. A CIA assessment came to the same conclusion, noting that the Iranian government worried about a secret desire by the superpowers to repeat World War II and divide Iran: "Fear of superpower collusion to divide Iran into separate spheres of influence has been infused in the Iranian people by Khomeini and his clerical infrastructure." If the Soviets staged a coup and installed a puppet government, as they had in Afghanistan, CENTCOM's intervention would encounter stiff resistance. Iran would be convinced that Washington and Moscow were colluding to overthrow the Islamic Republic. CENTCOM would have to fight its way into Iran even before locking horns with the Red Army.[25]

Kingston revised his plans to reflect this reality. The U.S. military would now wait until after the Soviets first crossed the border into Iran. With the bulk of the Iranian army moving north to meet the Red Army, this would allow the marines and soldiers to seize the ports of Bushehr and Bandar Abbas without much opposition. More important, by waiting until Moscow struck first, CENTCOM planners surmised, the Iranians would be far more willing to cooperate with the U.S. military to counter an invasion by the communists.[26]

Kingston's extensive background in covert operations was reflected in his belief that CENTCOM needed to develop an underground organization in Iran. If the proper arrangements could be made with the Iranian military, Kingston hoped to grease the skids for arrival of American troops and help organize Iranian resistance to the Soviets. Kingston looked to NATO plans as the model. In the event of war in Central Europe, the Pentagon intended to insert small teams of special forces behind the Soviet lines in Eastern Europe to execute direct action missions, blowing up bridges and attacking important targets deep in the enemy rear, and to conduct unconventional warfare operations, which entailed working with anti-Soviet guerrilla forces to foment a revolution within these less than enthusiastic members of the Warsaw Pact.[27] To support this plan, the U.S. Army had secretly hidden caches of weapons and explosives throughout Eastern Europe.

Kingston developed an aggressive special operations forces plan for Iran. He formed a new, close-hold headquarters in Tampa called the Joint Unconventional Warfare Task Force, commanded by an army brigadier general. It would control the large contingent of several thousand Army Special Forces, Navy SEALs, and air force planes and helicopters that would conduct clandestine operations in Iran. The U.S. Army's 5th Special Forces Group, specially trained for the Middle East with linguists in Farsi and Arabic, would fly in and establish its headquarters at Seeb, Oman. Its three battalions would then be dispatched to Turkey, Pakistan, and Saudi Arabia.[28] Even before hostilities began, they would secretly fly into Iran and deploy near the mountain passes in its northwestern regions along the likely avenues of invasion for Soviet troops. There they would destroy select roads, bridges, and rail lines to hinder the Soviet advance. Meanwhile, other soldiers would make contact with Iranian resistance forces and begin to organize a guerrilla army behind the Russian lines.

Should Iran resist the Americans, Navy SEALs would quickly seize the important ports of Bandar Abbas and Bushehr and kill the defenders before they had time to organize any coherent defense. U.S. Marines or elite Army Rangers would then be hastily flown in to secure the port, a critical link in the support of the larger follow-on force of tank divisions.

Located in an unobtrusive compound outside of Washington, D.C., was one of the most closely guarded "black" units in the U.S. Army: the Intelligence Support Activity (ISA). Established in March 1981, ISA owed its creation to the Iranian hostage crisis and the subsequent failed rescue mission. The new organization would serve as a fusion group for tactical human, signals, and electronic intelligence to support special forces units. ISA's first years were marked by some highly questionable actions. It provided financial and intelligence support for former Army Special Forces lieutenant colonel, and later fringe presidential candidate, James "Bo" Gritz in his fantastical schemes to rescue American prisoners of war supposedly left in Laos after the Vietnam War. In response, in 1982 Deputy Secretary Frank Carlucci temporarily suspended all ISA operations, noting in a memo for the undersecretary of defense for policy, Fred Iklé, that he found the organization's excesses "disturbing in the extreme." The next year Weinberger issued a new charter for ISA, placing it under tight reins under a command in Fort Bragg, and the organization soon put its past behind it, developing into one of the premier units in the U.S. military. By 1987, ISA, under the command of Colonel John Lackey III, swelled to nearly four hundred people, with distinct clandestine operations, signal collection, and communications squadrons.[29]

In 1983 Lieutenant General William Odom, the senior army intelligence officer, or G-2, tasked ISA with developing conduits and recruiting agents in Iran to support CENTCOM. Thin and with horn-rimmed glasses, Odom was a scholar-soldier. An expert on the Soviet Union with master's and doctorate degrees from Columbia University, he'd risen to prominence as the military assistant to Carter's national security adviser, Zbigniew Brzezinski. Odom thought that what Kingston needed were Iranian agents at a lower level who could actually help get U.S. troops into Iran—agents with detailed knowledge of roads who could tell you, for example, how much weight a specific bridge could hold.

"I'd like to have taxicab companies, trucking companies, hotel managers," Odom said later, "recruits at a lower level but someone who could meet you at the airport and get forces quickly into the country." With the support of the chief of staff of the army, General Shy Meyer, Odom elevated the priority level for human intelligence in Iran for ISA so it was second in priority only to spying against the Soviets in Europe.[30]

Working closely with the small group of officers under Kingston in Tampa, ISA formed two special detachments focused on Iran. Detachment E operated undercover out of the nine-story I.G. Farben building in Frankfurt, West Germany. The 1930s structure housed the U.S. Army's V Corps headquarters as well as the military's counterintelligence and clandestine operations for Europe and the Middle East. That detachment targeted exile and resistance groups within Iran, and soon expanded to establish another office in Pakistan from which it controlled operations and agents inside Iran proper.[31] Detachment L, in the United States, worked out in the open to cultivate former Iranian military officers who would contact old friends and colleagues still in Iran who could obtain firsthand information on the state of the Iranian military.

ISA was less successful in cultivating the disparate ethnic and separatist groups within Iran, especially the Kurds in the northwestern regions. Odom believed they would be a natural ally for the United States and might even provide an alternative safe haven for U.S. Special Operations Forces. "We had access to the Kurds," one U.S. Army intelligence officer later said, "but neither the Turks nor the Iraqis wanted the U.S. to stir up any separatist movements with the Kurds—unless they controlled it—for fear it might spread to their own countries."

Odom's staff dusted off an old defense plan, code-named Armish-Maag, that the 10th Special Forces Group had developed for the shah to defend Iran from a Soviet invasion. It contained detailed targeting data on the tunnels and the mountain passes leading into northern Iran from Soviet Azerbaijan. The shah's army had used this information to pre-position materials to destroy bridges and tunnels. One of the Iranians now working for ISA confirmed that the explosives had been removed, but the predrilled holes along bridge pilings and tunnel entrances remained. Armed with this information, Army Special Forces would only have to replace the explosives so as to quickly close many of the important roads needed by the Soviet Union to invade Iran. It saved years in research, an army analyst later acknowledged.

However, ISA drew the ire of the CIA. The CIA had legal responsibility for all recruitment of agents during peacetime and viewed the ISA officers as amateurs. Howard Hart, an experienced CIA operative who'd organized the initial effort to arm the mujahideen in Afghanistan and later ran the CIA's Special Activities Division, which controlled all the paramilitary forces, believed that the military lacked the subtlety for sensitive operations. "The military men are patriots, but in general when it comes to paramilitary operations and spying, they are well-intentioned amateurs. When the military sends someone undercover into Iran disguised as a Middle East businessman, they seem to look like a guy pretending to be a businessman. When CIA sends one in, he is a Middle Eastern businessman."[32] At the time, the U.S. military's view of the CIA was just as jaded. A senior U.S. military officer who spent two decades working with the CIA used a common military acronym related to commanders or headquarters, C2, which stands for "command and control," when he noted that in the CIA, C2 stands for "control and credit."

Even though ISA had to coordinate all its operations with Langley, the CIA viewed the military unit as a liability that was intruding on its turf. Odom knew that Langley wanted ISA shut down, and some of his officers accused CIA of distorting ISA's problems and of leaking the damaging information to Congress in 1982 that had nearly led to the organization's disbandment. According to Odom, the CIA undermined the Pentagon's Iranian operation. The CIA station chief in Pakistan invited the ISA army officer in charge of Iranian operations to a diplomatic cocktail party in Islamabad. He made a point of staying close to the officer and loudly proclaimed that the two men worked together. As the station chief operated out in the open, the officer's public association with him destroyed his cover and forced him to leave the country. His departure halted the army's recruitment in Pakistan. This petty move by the CIA infuriated senior officials within the Pentagon, Weinberger included.[33]

The Reagan administration came to office convinced that the machinations of Soviet adventurism caused most of America's national security problems.[34] The Arab-Israeli confrontation was seen largely through the prism of the Cold War: the American-backed Israelis were pitted against the

Soviet client states of Syria and the Palestine Liberation Organization. Kingston and ISA had developed a clandestine spy organization in Iran whose mission focused solely on confronting the Soviet Union and not the Islamic Republic. This unitarian view downplayed both historical and regional causes behind the steady stream of conflicts that had dominated the region since the Second World War. The Iranian Revolution did not fit neatly into ISA's worldview, to put it mildly. Only slowly did Washington replace this myopic view and begin to realize that Iran itself, and not the Soviet Union, represented the real challenge to American control over the Persian Gulf.

Four

A DEN OF SPIES

William Casey was sixty-eight when Ronald Reagan appointed him to run America's principal spy organization. The new director of central intelligence did not radiate a James Bond aura; in fact, he resembled a superannuated college professor. He shuffled more than walked; bald, with pronounced jowls, the once tall New Yorker was now stooped with age. He mumbled, at times to the point of incoherence, a trait that seemed to worsen when he testified before Congress, an institution he generally disdained. His clothes were rumpled and flecks of food stained his jacket and tie, complementing a heavy coat of white dandruff. Eating across from William Casey, contemporaries noted, was not for the fainthearted.

Despite his visible aging, Casey retained a keen mind. A voracious reader and astute student of history, he roamed Washington's bookstores for material, especially on the Soviet Union, often buying stacks of books in a single outing. During briefings, he often appeared comatose, slumped back in his stuffed chair with only a sliver of his eyes visible through his drooping eyelids. Then, suddenly, Casey would spring to life, firing off a rapid series of probing questions.

Casey had a distinguished career both in and out of government. He had served as the intelligence chief for Europe with the Office of Strategic Services (the precursor to the CIA) during World War II, as a corporate lawyer after the war, then as head of the Securities and Exchange Commission under President Nixon. A staunch Republican, he was Reagan's campaign manager for the 1980 election and aspired to become secretary of state. When that post went to Alexander Haig, Casey eagerly accepted the job as CIA director, determined to reinvigorate the clandestine wing of the agency, which he believed had been gutted by congressional investigations and poor leadership during the 1970s.

Casey, who displayed a gift for organization and planning, seemed an ideal choice to head the CIA. "The man had a natural bent for what the Germans call *fingerspitzengefühl*, a feel for the clandestine," recalled Richard Helms, Casey's roommate in London during the war and later CIA director.[1] In 1944, Casey had been sent to Paris to reinvigorate efforts to insert agents into Germany. "The place had gone slack. There was no sense of purpose," said fellow OSS officer Walter Lord, who worked for Casey and later wrote the acclaimed novel about the Titanic *A Night to Remember*. Casey soon gained the admiration of Lord and other subordinates. "He was blunt and impatient," observed Lord, "but he knew exactly what to ask."[2] Casey energized the headquarters and initiated some of the riskiest missions of the war. Disguised as foreign laborers, more than one hundred agents were air-dropped into Germany, both to spy and to determine the location of key industrial sites for Allied bombers. Remarkably, sixty-two of the agents ended up reporting information back to Casey, and only 5 percent were lost.[3]

As director, Casey had little interest or inclination in running the CIA bureaucracy. "He was going to run the clandestine service," said Robert Gates, who ran the Directorate of Intelligence—the analysis wing of the CIA—for nearly four years under Casey and later served as CIA director himself, as well as secretary of defense under Presidents George W. Bush and Barack Obama. "I don't think he would have recognized the CIA organization chart in the first several years he was there, if his life depended on it."[4]

Casey viewed the world's crises through the lens of the Cold War. An avowed anticommunist and unrelenting opponent of the Soviet Union, he became an important advocate within the administration for paramilitary actions in Central America and for the arming of the mujahideen resistance in Afghanistan to fight the Red Army. To the CIA director, the Soviet invasion of Afghanistan fit into a long-standing desire of the Russian empire to have a warm-water port, only now this dovetailed into controlling Middle East oil. He cared little about the regional conflicts or their long-term consequences, except in terms of how they affected the balance of power in the East-West rivalry.

One senior CIA officer who worked the Middle East recalled having dinner with the director in 1986. The conversation turned to the long-term American strategy for Afghanistan after the Soviets had been driven out of the country. "What are we going to do after we win?" the officer asked Casey.

"We're not going to do a goddamn thing! Once we get the Russians out, we're finished," Casey responded, smacking his hands together to emphasize the point. That focus on the Soviets would blind the United States to other perils.

Casey did not see Iran as an intrinsic threat. The Iranian Revolution had been significant, he believed, chiefly because it eliminated America's defender of Persian Gulf oil against Soviet expansion. Casey downplayed the importance of the Islamist movement behind Khomeini. Instead, he worried about Moscow exploiting the shah's overthrow and turning Iran into another Soviet proxy. He understood the danger posed by Iranian terrorism, and the 1985 seizure of William Buckley, the CIA station chief in Lebanon, by Iranian surrogates would weigh heavily on him. But Casey believed the long-term solution was to bring Iran back into the anti-Soviet fold. In his mind, the CIA needed to cultivate political moderates and pro-Western reformers in Tehran. Agents were needed inside the Iranian government to favorably influence and counter its anti-American stance.

In the first couple of years after the revolution, Casey had a legitimate reason to worry about a communist takeover in Iran. The pro-Moscow Tudeh Party openly challenged Khomeini's rule, waging an urban insurgency against the Islamic Republic. In July 1981 it bombed the Iranian parliament, killing the prime minister and seriously injuring future supreme leader Ayatollah Ali Khamenei, who lost partial use of his right arm when a bomb concealed in a tape recorder exploded beside him. Casey saw the hidden hand of Moscow behind Iran's leftist opposition and believed that if the party succeeded in overthrowing the mullahs' rule, it could lead to Iran's becoming a Soviet client state like Cuba.

In 1983 a Soviet defector presented William Casey the means to strike a fatal blow to the communist movement in Iran. In the fall of 1982, a senior KGB officer who had been stationed in Tehran, Vladimir Kuzichkin, had defected to Great Britain, reportedly carrying with him a treasure trove of documents on Soviet spy operations. London's overseas intelligence organ, MI6, shared this information with its CIA colleagues, who put together a long list of dozens of Soviet spies and pro-Moscow Tudeh Party members in Iran. Casey ordered this roster surreptitiously passed on to Tehran through Iranian exiles. Iranian security forces promptly rounded up and executed scores of suspected communists and socialists. And so, with a little help from the CIA, the Islamic Republic eviscerated its domestic opposition.[5]

Within the CIA's headquarters in Langley, Virginia, intelligence officers had differing opinions about their director's views of Iran and the prospects of influencing the regime. The Soviet analysts at Langley tended to share Casey's alarmist view, but those in the Near East Division remained skeptical. In August and September 1983, the CIA's Near East Division produced two intelligence assessments on Soviet-Iranian relations, concluding that the Soviet efforts to court the Islamic Republic had failed, aggravated by Iran's support of the mujahideen in Afghanistan. Subsequent CIA reports came to the same conclusion, adding that the Tudeh Party had ceased to exist. But Casey remained unconvinced, grasping at a 1985 draft report that concluded that the Soviets could gain influence through arms sales to an Iran desperate for weapons in its war with Iraq.[6]

"No one doubted the importance of Iran," observed George Cave, one of the agency's principal experts on Iran. "If you want stability in the Middle East, you need to have some sort of meaningful relationship with Iran." However, neither Cave nor the other CIA officers working in Langley believed the Islamic regime would be wooed by Moscow. Khomeini's hatred of the United States was eclipsed only by his contempt for atheism and communism. The Iranian cleric's vitriolic Friday sermons were aimed as much at Moscow as at Washington.

"There were reformers in Tehran," noted retired CIA official Jack Devine, who had worked the Iran desk during the mid-1980s, "but they were all by-products of the revolution. Their arguments were about economic reform and not political."[7]

When Casey assumed the CIA directorship, the American espionage effort in Iran was in shambles. The CIA station in Tehran had been one of the agency's largest in the world during the shah's reign. What remained of the CIA's spy operation had evaporated with the students' takeover of the American embassy, with the CIA station chief among its hostages. Casey was determined to revive human spying within Iran. It was one of the most strategically important countries in the Middle East, yet the CIA knew next to nothing about what was happening there. Even such mundane matters as annual crop yields eluded U.S. intelligence officials. If the Iranian government was leaning toward Moscow, Casey wanted to know about it and position American agents there in hopes of drawing Iran back to the United States' side of the Cold War.

The CIA's mission in Iran became an early subject of discussion within the Reagan administration. Expanding the number of human spies there was an obvious requirement. Shortly after taking office, Reagan signed a presidential finding—an authorization of a covert operation required by law—approving a renewed effort to build a spy network in Iran.

The administration had less certainty about the wisdom of actually trying to overthrow the regime. On March 9, 1981, the NSC principals, with no aides or note takers, met in the White House Situation Room for a closely held deliberation on possible covert actions against Iran. The select assemblage agreed to search for a group that "we can support [in] destabilizing Iran," according to a handwritten note kept by one of the attendees. Exactly which group to throw America's weight behind, however, eluded the attendees. They contemplated aiding the Kurds, but quickly rejected that out of fear of angering an important NATO ally, Turkey. Casey recommended looking at exile groups headed by former Iranian military officers and other separatist movements, such as the one in Baluchistan.

On September 30, Reagan's foreign policy doyens met for another meeting on Iran in the White House Cabinet Room. Chaired by the national security adviser, Richard Allen, they finalized a National Security Decision Directive on Iran for Reagan's signature. The men agreed on two key policy goals: preventing Soviet domination of Iran, and keeping the Iranian Revolution from spreading across the Middle East. The key, they believed, was pulling Iran back into the American Cold War camp. This would not be easy. The United States' ability to subvert the Iranian government was negligible; a CIA coup à la 1953 had little chance of success and would only fuel more anti-Americanism, to the advantage of Moscow. Nevertheless, they believed there were actions the U.S. government could take to influence the Islamic Republic: expanding Voice of America broadcasts, working with allies who had more influence within the Iranian government, and seeking out moderates within the Iranian government. The goal would be to cultivate pro-American military personnel and civilians who could steer the Iranian policies away from the Soviet Union and moderate the regime's anti-American opinions. Casey's officers would try to reach out to "forces in Iran favoring a more moderate government," as one memo described it.[8]

A day or two later, President Reagan signed an executive order directing the CIA to begin an important wide-ranging operation called the Iranian Covert Action Program. Its objective was to moderate Iranian behavior toward the United States and to undercut the expansion of the Iranian Revolution. Intelligence officers began looking for Iranians inside and outside the country who favored better relations with the United States and who were positioned to influence key government officials. The CIA launched a broad influence campaign. The Voice of America stepped up its Farsi broadcasts to blunt anti-American propaganda in the Iranian media. Working through Pakistan, the CIA promoted greater ties between Iran and the mujahideen fighting the Red Army in Afghanistan, with the goal of highlighting the Soviet threat and the shared objectives between Washington and Tehran in seeing the Soviets defeated. The CIA began indirectly passing intelligence to Tehran via the Swiss and Algerian governments that highlighted Soviet designs on Iran and stressed Washington's support for Iran's territorial integrity.

The administration remained divided on armed subversion inside Iran. The Iranian Covert Action Program signed by President Reagan prohibited providing weapons for either exiles or internal dissidents. But in 1982, when the program came up for its annual review, the Reagan administration debated the wisdom of this prohibition. "If the United States was really serious about countering the Iranian threat, why not arm the Islamic Republic's opposition?" said Charles Cogan, the CIA's chief for Near East and South Asia, during a meeting at the White House in 1982. "The basic issue is whether the present regime in Iran is in U.S. interests."

Robert McFarlane, the deputy national security adviser, believed the United States should explore more extreme measures to overthrow the Iranian regime. In a September 10, 1982, memo, he wrote, "It is difficult to come to a judgment on the issue without altering the 'halfway house' finding: that is, lift the restriction against providing lethal weapons to the Iranian opposition. This having been done, we could explore with the Iranian opposition and with friendly governments there of possibly creating disturbances within Iran."

Caspar Weinberger concurred. The defense secretary frequently voiced the need to look at a more ambitious program to replace, or at least significantly undermine, the Islamic Republic. Arming an opposition movement might not lead to an overthrow of Khomeini, but forcing Iran to battle a fifth column might sap the revolutionary energy that otherwise would be directed outward toward friendly Arab governments.

Casey agreed with Weinberger. Supporting an Iranian insurgency was no different than what he was already doing with the Contras in Nicaragua and the mujahideen in Afghanistan. "An enhanced covert action program against Iran would provide reassurance to the Saudis and others of our serious interest in containing Iran," wrote an NSC staffer in laying out for Casey and Weinberger the pros of a more aggressive paramilitary operation against Iran.

On July 13, 1982, President Reagan concurred with a recommendation by his national security team for the CIA to explore building an armed opposition against Iran. Feelers were sent out via intelligence circles to both Saudi Arabia and Oman about building an insurgency within Iran, including funneling arms for the insurgents through the two countries in order to distance Washington from the operation. A joint military-CIA team traveled to Oman to look at a proposed base for the guerrilla army on the Musandam Peninsula, the jut of land that the Strait of Hormuz wraps around. During intelligence exchanges with Baghdad, the CIA floated the idea to the Iraqis of working together to subvert the Iranian government. Not surprisingly, Saddam Hussein eagerly embraced the idea.

However, in the end Reagan never approved fomenting an armed counterrevolution within Iran. "The downside always outweighed the gain," said McFarlane.[9] The CIA eventually concluded that no armed group could seriously challenge the regime. The State Department consistently voiced concern that it would only fuel even greater anti-Americanism and destroy any hope of reconciliation, a view shared by many CIA analysts. After months of debate and discussions about building an insurgency in Iran, the idea died the death of inaction.

Building a spy network in Iran would not be an easy proposition. Iran was, in the parlance of the spy business, a "denied country." With no American embassy to provide cover for CIA officers or to serve as a base of operations, the agency would have to infiltrate Iran from outside the country. The

CIA established a new office to run its Iranian operations inside one wing of the I.G. Farben building in Frankfurt, the same headquarters housing ISA, the U.S. Army's V Corps, and the military's regional clandestine operations. It also quietly served as the main support base for CIA operations in Europe, Africa, and the Middle East. Langley called its new unit "Tehfran," an amalgam of Tehran and Frankfurt. Germany provided reliable cover for the operation; after 1979, many Iranian exiles had settled there. Bonn maintained diplomatic relations with Tehran, and Iranians often traveled to Frankfurt. The CIA could easily bring recruits to the city for screening and training, as well as for the occasional rendezvous between handlers and agents.[10]

"Tehfran" began the painstaking process of recruiting agents. As Turkey did not require a visa for Iranian citizens, it served as a corridor for those trying to escape the repression under the ayatollah. Ankara and Istanbul swelled with Persian expatriates looking to obtain visas to travel to Europe or the United States.

Turkey quickly took center stage in the spy contest between Washington and Tehran. The CIA used the American consulate in Istanbul as a recruiting center for Tehfran, with an intelligence officer assigned to identify potential Iranians for recruitment. The grounds around the consulate became a favorite recruiting locale for American intelligence officers.

"It was a heavy workload," recalled Philip Giraldi, who worked in the Istanbul consulate and ran its Iranian operations from 1986 to 1989. Sifting through the stacks of visa applications for those in the military or with political connections, he conducted around twenty interviews each week, with one or two showing promise. "Of these, one every couple of months we would actually go after and pitch. And the pitches were frequently successful."[11]

The CIA found fertile ground among Iranian military officers. Many had attended schools in the United States and had close friends in the U.S. military. The navy and air force were the most pro-American, and Giraldi himself recruited three senior air force officers, including a brigadier general. CIA case officers across Europe were on the watch for important Iranians, people "needing a favor with information we could use," as one retired CIA employee put it. Operating under diplomatic cover and using fictitious first names, the CIA encouraged their recruits' sympathies for the United States or their abhorrence of communism. If that failed, the Americans used coercion to obtain cooperation, dangling a coveted visa to the United States for a recruit's family in return for spying for Langley. This proved one of the most effective means employed by the CIA to obtain cooperation.[12]

One of those recruited by Giraldi in September 1986 was a prominent air force colonel, Masoud Babaii, who'd flown to Istanbul with his family to request a visa for the United States. Babaii spoke good English, having graduated from pilot training in Texas. He openly cooperated with Giraldi during his interview and volunteered detailed information about the status of the Iranian air force and the war with Iraq. "He was one of the nicest guys you'd ever want to meet," Giraldi recalled. The CIA brought in a Farsi speaker to make the pitch to work for the Americans. Babaii agreed to go back to Iran for several years in return for a guaranteed visa for him and his family.[13]

One of the naval officers who accepted the American pitch was Captain Touradj Riahi. Highly regarded by fellow Iranian officers, Riahi rose rapidly to command a squadron of American-made minesweeping helicopters. Fluent in English, fair skinned with light brown hair and a matching mustache, Captain Riahi, like many secular officers, felt no affinity for the new religious government. He was fond of the United States and had relatives in Hawaii. Aspects of the Western lifestyle embraced by Riahi were not acceptable under Ayatollah Khomeini's rule. The captain made wine in his basement. He and his wife entertained and played cards as the alcohol flowed freely, with even his daughter allowed to sample occasionally.[14]

In the winter of 1985, Captain Riahi traveled to Ankara, Turkey, seeking a U.S. visa for his son to live with an aunt in Hawaii. This was not an easy proposition for an Iranian military officer. But his son was two years away from mandatory military service, and Captain Riahi wished to save him from becoming one more martyr in the war with Iraq. Five years of war and revolution had brought only ruin, he believed. While he remained an ardent nationalist, he felt growing disdain for the governing clergy, whom he thought were intent on taking Iran back from modernity. While it was painful to send his son away, Riahi believed the United States offered him and his family the best future.

Captain Riahi made his way to the sprawling American embassy off a bustling divided highway named Ataturk Boulevard. He submitted passport photos and filled out a detailed visa application. A few days later, he interviewed with an American Foreign Service officer and at one point met with an embassy employee who introduced himself only as "Parker." Pleasant and nondescript, Parker offered to cut through the red tape and speedily stamp his son's visa request. It could be done quickly enough through the West German embassy, he told the Iranian captain. In return, though, Parker wanted information on the Iranian military.

Captain Riahi agreed to Parker's terms out of both pragmatism and idealism. "He was a good man but naive when it came to the harsh reality of espionage," a close friend, Commander Said Zanganeh, recalled later. "He thought they [CIA] would take care of him."[15]

Using a false passport, Riahi flew with a CIA officer to Frankfurt, Germany, where he underwent a standard lie detector test to ensure he was not a double agent for Iranian intelligence. While his son's visa was being arranged, the CIA trained him on how to communicate with his handlers. Thus Captain Riahi officially became a U.S. intelligence agent, or, as an Iranian commentator later put it, one of those "who had sold their faith and honor for the CIA's deceptive glamour."[16]

The CIA recruited at least five naval officers.[17] One of the agency's most valuable trophies was a close friend of Riahi's, Commodore Kanoush Hakimi, who'd played a key role in negotiating many of Iran's sensitive arms agreements. His major success had been the purchase of powerful Chinese Silkworm antiship missiles that would enable Iran to control the Strait of Hormuz by threatening ships navigating this choke point for the world's oil.[18]

In addition to the military officers, the CIA recruited a diverse group of civilians. This included a lawyer in the Iranian foreign ministry, local government officials, an engineer employed at a chemical factory—all with access to the broad range of information needed by American intelligence.[19] The CIA even managed to penetrate Iran's elite Revolutionary Guard. Among those recruited from the Revolutionary Guard, divisions existed, despite their overt loyalty to the state. Some were young idealists who'd joined the revolution and then rebelled against the oppressive republic that emerged. Others simply wanted a better life in America.

One of those recruited was a Revolutionary Guard official known by his pseudonym, Reza Kahlili. From an upper-middle-class family, he had attended school in California, where an aunt lived. He'd joined the guard with some friends out of youthful enthusiasm. While one friend went on to a senior position in the guard's intelligence unit, Kahlili served in a propaganda unit, which prized his English-language skills.

His disillusionment had occurred after a visit to Evin Prison. While he witnessed repeated beatings of political prisoners or their family members, the most repugnant act he viewed was the deliberate rape of two women before their execution. Their crimes were little more than being related to the wrong person. But according to religious belief, virgins could go to heaven despite their crimes. The head of the Revolutionary Court, Ayatollah Mohammad Gilani, ordered the guards to rape the two women to deprive them of any chance of salvation.[20] Repulsed, Kahlili flew back to California to visit his aunt. After briefly contemplating defecting, he decided to contact the FBI and offer his services and information. They passed him on to the CIA, which after the usual polygraph and background checks formally brought him into the agency's stable of agents.

Analysts back in Washington generated a laundry list of questions for these agents: How was the Revolutionary Guard Corps organized, and what were its military tactics? Who were the rising religious leaders? What were people worried about domestically? What was the political situation in Kurdistan and other provinces?[21]

In Frankfurt, Tehfran employed several means of communicating with its agents inside Iran. A few agents received specialized equipment that allowed for encrypted burst transmissions to be sent over regular phone lines back to Tehfran. For Kahlili and others, they purchased standard shortwave radios on the black market and, at predetermined times, listened for Morse-coded messages that came across the airwaves as blocks of numbers. A separately provided paper cipher translated those numbers into individual letters.[22]

The CIA's prime means of communicating with agents was an old trick, dating back a century: invisible ink. Its various formulas remained some of the oldest secrets held at the National Archives, with some not declassified until 2011.[23] The Iranian spies would respond using more-or-less-invisible (MLI) writing tools—plastic pens and other items coated with a special chemical that left a hidden residue that could be retrieved by applying the proper solution. Kahlili used specially treated writing paper. On the front, he would write innocuous letters to fictitious friends in Frankfurt. On the back, using a special MLI pencil, he wrote his message, which remained invisible until the CIA officer in Tehran washed the paper with a special solution.[24] Hundreds of these letters traveled between Iran and Germany—one air force officer admitted to sending 110 letters himself back to Tehfran.[25]

The spy network produced a mixed bag of rumor and fact. None of the recruited spies was senior enough to influence the regime or shed much light on Iran's position toward the superpowers, as Casey had hoped. They frequently reported erroneous information.[26] One agent told his American handlers that Iran had provided helicopters to Hezbollah, the Lebanese militant group, and intended to arm it with missiles. To confirm the report, the CIA consulted all its Iranian sources, including debriefing an Iranian pilot who had recently defected to Iraq. In the end, intelligence officials concluded that the report was false, based on little more than barroom gossip picked up in the Iranian officers' club.

But the agents did provide useful information that helped Washington undermine Iran's military adventures. One agent tipped off the CIA to an attempt by Iran to purchase French-made Exocet antiship missiles, allowing the State Department to intervene and scuttle the sale. An aircraft mechanic for the Iranian air force provided important diagrams of the large Iranian air base near Bushehr. Others helped identify key Iranian naval and air force targets for the U.S. military, including the location of important command and control facilities used by the Revolutionary Guard.

In addition to recruiting spies, the Iranian Covert Action Plan authorized the CIA to cultivate Iranian exile groups. The anti-Khomeini movement began shortly after the shah's overthrow. As early as August 1979, CIA sources had begun reporting efforts by former Iranian military officers to organize an external opposition to the clerics in Tehran. One of the first gatherings had occurred in London, led by former Iranian air force general Hassan Toufanian, an impressive man whom General Huyser referred to as "a human dynamo, running on 110 percent." He'd brought together in a London hotel former Imperial Iranian officers from across Europe and the United States to plot and discuss ways to overthrow the Khomeini regime. The Iranian government learned of this meeting following the U.S. embassy takeover, when students pieced the strips of the shredded message that described Toufanian's gathering in London back together.[27]

The CIA paid millions of dollars each year to several expatriate organizations believed to have access into the Iranian leadership. A favorite of Casey's was the group headed by Rear Admiral Ahmad Madani, based in Germany. The son of a prominent clerical Shiite family, Madani had been a strong supporter of the revolution and was its first defense minister before falling out of favor with the Islamists. He still maintained strong contacts within the Iranian military.[28]

According to an account by author Kenneth Timmerman, in January 1983 Casey and White House deputy chief of staff Michael Deaver met with the shah's oldest son, Cyrus Reza Pahlavi, at the Chevy Chase Club outside of Washington, D.C. The twenty-two-year-old Reza launched into a monologue about the weakness of the Islamic government, its growing economic crisis, and the opportunity this presented to reestablish the monarchy. "The people of Iran will carry His Majesty to Tehran on their shoulders!" an aide added.

The shah's son proposed that the agency help him fund a network of former Iranian intelligence agents to gather information inside Iran as part of a scheme to return him to power. It was pure fantasy; the young shah had no support within Iran. But it offered what Casey and the administration wanted to hear. Despite the widespread disdain for the Pahlavi family within Iran, Casey agreed to pay a monthly stipend to support the junior shah's efforts.[29]

As part of the campaign against the Iranian regime, the CIA secretly financed an Egyptian radio station that broadcast four hours of anti-Khomeini propaganda daily into Iran. The station ran stories designed to highlight the problems of Khomeini's rule, from food shortages to the brutal excesses of the Revolutionary Guard.[30] The agency supported a television broadcast into Iran by Reza that managed to disrupt two channels for precisely eleven minutes on September 5, 1986—an amount of time, said one cynical retired CIA operative, that was synonymous with the young man's abilities.

The exiles proved to have limited utility, and CIA officials viewed them with considerable suspicion. "Exiles operate on rumint," said retired operative Jack Devine, using an unofficial acronym for rumor and intelligence. "They're often penetrated by double agents, or working their own agenda, which does not necessarily meet the U.S. objectives. They are never the pathway back to power. But they are always out there and can usually find an audience."

The longtime Iran operative George Cave became disenchanted early with the opposition groups. In July 1980, a cadre of high-ranking air force officers had hatched a plan to decapitate the entire revolutionary government by bombing key government and military sites in Tehran, starting with Khomeini's home. The commander of the Iranian air force, Major General Saeed

Mahdiyoun, was to spearhead the effort inside Iran. The son of a wealthy Tabriz merchant and reputedly one of the air force's best pilots, he quietly assembled several dozen F-4 aircraft at a large fighter base, Nojeh, near Tehran. Under the cover of darkness, three aircraft would bomb Khomeini's home, hitting every building in the compound with a massive ordnance of 750-pound bombs, cluster bombs, and precision-guided weapons. In quick succession other jets would strike the prime minister's and the president's residences, army barracks, and the headquarters of the Revolutionary Guard. With Khomeini dead, Shapour Bakhtiar would enter the country from Iraq at the head of a force of exiles. He would join forces with disaffected elements within the army to overthrow the Islamic Republic. The Nojeh coup, as it became known, involved much of the expatriate community. Admiral Madani in Germany provided funding.

Yet neither Bakhtiar nor any other coup leaders disclosed the plan's details to the CIA, perhaps to avoid revealing Saddam Hussein's complicity. During a meeting with Cave in Paris, Bakhtiar asked the CIA to provide helicopters to move his operatives "inside of and around Iran." When Cave pressed for specifics—when, where, why, how many men—Bakhtiar remained evasive. Shortly before the attack was to begin, someone inside the expatriate community tipped off the Iranian embassy in Paris. The Iranian government moved quickly, rounding up hundreds of people. General Mahdiyoun, the air force commander, was forced to confess before a videotaped kangaroo court. He was found guilty, and his executioners gouged out one eye before riddling his body with bullets.

"The exiles refused to cooperate with each other," Cave said with irritation, looking back on the disparate groups trying to overthrow Ayatollah Khomeini. "They all wanted to be in charge." He used to joke that "every Iranian male is born with a chip in his brain that periodically broadcasts: 'I am the leader of the Iranian people.'"

William Casey and the CIA had another Iran-obsessed client: the U.S. Department of Defense. In the summer of 1981, General Kingston revised CENTCOM's plans to respond to a Soviet invasion of Iran. A key element of General Kingston's new scheme would involve deployment of clandestine special forces teams to organize a guerrilla army and to conduct sabotage behind the Russian front lines. But the military needed the CIA to develop an indigenous support organization inside Iran. Existing legal mandates authorized only the CIA to conduct covert paramilitary operations in peacetime (i.e., any mission intended to conceal American involvement and permit plausible deniability by Washington). In theory, the CIA would build the foundation of an indigenous paramilitary network in peacetime, which the much larger U.S. Army Special Forces—better known as Green Berets due to their unique headgear—would exploit during wartime.[31] But the CIA's paramilitary operations had to be coordinated with Kingston. The agency's schemes needed to be synchronized with the military war plans to make sure the two were not working at cross-purposes.

In the spring of 1982 the CIA and Defense Department began working on a combined plan for Iran. With Kingston's extensive experience with the CIA, he persuaded the defense secretary to agree to fund a CIA operation to build a covert paramilitary network within Iran. This would serve as the foundation upon which Kingston's special forces could conduct their insurgency against the Red Army.[32] Casey eagerly supported the agreement. It offered one more avenue to develop new contacts in Iran—and with Defense Department money.

Iran required a major commitment by the CIA. The spy agency had to build a fifth column within Iran designed to undermine any "Vichy-type governments" installed by Moscow, as one Defense Department memo described it. The CIA needed to recruit the Iranians who would greet American parachutists arriving in the middle of the night. The agency had to provide the military information on roads, bridges, and airfields, establish mustering stations for arriving American troops, conduct sabotage, and rescue pilots who were shot down.

To manage the paramilitary effort in Iran, the CIA created a new organization—given the nonsensical cover name "BQ Tug"—inside the Tehfran cell at Frankfurt. Langley chose a former Army Special Forces officer—described by former CIA officer Reuel Gerecht as "earthy but likable"—to run the their mission. He worked closely with a small cadre of military officers at the Central Command headquarters in Tampa, who identified specific targets for the Iranian agents to destroy and airfields the U.S. military wanted to use to support the Pentagon's war plan.

With a few million dollars from the Pentagon, BQ Tug recruited more than half a dozen teams, four to six men each. The teams included Iranian military officers, a smattering of senior enlisted men, and peasants from villages the U.S. military considered strategically positioned. Much of the recruiting was conducted in Iranian Azerbaijan in northwestern Iran and astride the border with the Soviet Union.[33] Some of the Iranian agents' only responsibility was to keep watch on the Soviet forces across the border or to monitor important border towns such as Jolfa, where all imports and exports from Iran to the Soviet Union traveled across a major highway and railway line.[34] The CIA tried to bring team leaders out for a polygraph and some training. Several recruits later claimed they were flown to Oman for specialized weapons and explosives training.

The CIA's pitch to each recruit downplayed his employment by the United States and emphasized the necessity of defending Iran from atheists and anti-Islamic communists. They were serving their country by helping the United States defend Iran against communism.

A typical recruit was Muhammad Zanif-Yeganeh, a housing department employee in northern Iran. He later claimed that a friend already on the CIA payroll had enticed him to travel to Turkey on the pretense of buying crystal to sell on the black market. He later described being approached by an American Farsi speaker who asked him about working with the United States to help protect Iran from a Russian attack. With five hundred dollars a month as added incentive, he agreed. He surveyed a remote poultry farm as a potential landing zone for U.S. forces and sent a detailed map of the area back to Frankfurt.[35] The farm owner was also recruited and added to Yeganeh's team, and the two men identified other landing zones for helicopters.

At one point the CIA considered using these agents to conduct covert attacks against the Khomeini regime. One proposal was to use the BQ Tug agents to bomb sensitive Iranian military sites such as command and control centers in Tehran or the port of Bushehr—"the bomb in the Hitler bunker," as one retired CIA officer described it. At the Pentagon's request, the CIA looked into using them to attack launch sites for the new Chinese antiship missiles around the Strait of Hormuz in 1987. However, none of these proposals materialized.

"Agents are funny people," observed Howard Hart, a longtime CIA officer. "Few are willing to make that leap of actually putting bombs or attacking their own country. They will give you chapter and verse and GPS coordinates for sensitive sites, but it's a huge leap to actually blow it up themselves."[36]

Despite Casey's support, many inside the CIA viewed BQ Tug as a waste of time. The operations directorate did not always assign the best officers to BQ Tug. Its liaison in the headquarters at Langley was a CIA officer who had recently filed a disability lawsuit against the agency over his supposed chronic back pain, which he eventually won, forcing the CIA to buy him a special chair to sit in until his retirement.

On one occasion, the deputy chief of Tehfran, a former military officer, flew into Turkey with eight fake Iranian passports for operatives who were scheduled to go back into Iran on a collection mission. "He was a klutz," Philip Giraldi recalled. "He could screw anything up." After issuing the phony documents, the Tehfran deputy collected the real passports of the Iranian agents, stuffed them in his coat, and headed to the airport to fly back to Frankfurt. When he went through the metal detector, two pens in his shirt pocket set off the metal detector, and he was ordered to empty out his pockets. The Turkish security guards found the bundle of passports and arrested him. When the Tehfran deputy chief did not arrive back in Frankfurt, Giraldi was sent out looking for him. When Giraldi arrived at the deputy's hotel, Turkish police arrested him too. As Giraldi was an embassy employee with a diplomatic passport, the Turks released him. But it required considerable effort, involving some favors with Turkish intelligence, to get Tehfran's deputy released.

"Its mission was a joke; no one took it seriously," said one CIA officer. "The Soviets were not likely to invade Iran. If they did, these half dozen teams would have the effect of a gnat hitting a truck." More important, the Iranian regime was decidedly hostile to the United States and no one could say what Ayatollah Khomeini's reaction would be to the arrival of U.S. Special Forces inside Iran. As another CIA officer observed: "We now had a plan to defend those who don't want to be defended against those who are not going to attack."

While the United States recruited spies and paid exile groups, the agents of Iran's Ministry of Intelligence and Security (MOIS) did not remain idle. From the days of the shah and Savak, the Iranians excelled at counterintelligence. The new Iranian intelligence service was formed in August 1984 by combining several smaller intelligence groups that sprang up after the revolution. Surprisingly, considering the hatred Khomeini's backers had for the shah's secret police, MOIS employed a large number of former Savak officers—perhaps one-third of those working for MOIS had worked for the shah. They proved equally as formidable in addressing security threats for the Islamic Republic as they had for the royal regime.

Iran received some assistance from other spy services eager to undermine the CIA. Despite the Islamic Republic's disdain for communism, common purpose overcame ideology when the MOIS developed cooperative relationships with both East German and Romanian intelligence services.[37] The Romanians provided new technology and trained the Iranians on spy craft. The East Germans conducted surveillance of Tehran's activities in Frankfurt, providing important pieces to fill in the American spy puzzle.

The MOIS external security directorate tracked dissident groups. It created small hit teams, blending in with Iranians traveling to Turkey, to assassinate critics of the Islamic regime. Moving from Istanbul to Western Europe, the teams carried out dozens of beatings, stabbings, bombings, and other acts of intimidation and murder. In August 1991, for example, three Iranian men talked their way past a French guard and into the house of the shah's last prime minister, Shapour Bakhtiar. They then killed him and his secretary with a kitchen knife. U.S. intelligence attributed more than eighty killings to MOIS agents between 1980 and 1995, the date of the last known Iranian assassination. Few MOIS officers were apprehended; they typically left only a body, say, on a Paris sidewalk, with a bullet in the back of the head as testimony to their handiwork.

Unfortunately for the CIA, many of MOIS's victims were prospective American recruits. The MOIS staked out the U.S. embassies that were trying to enlist Iranian citizens and were not shy about killing suspected American collaborators. Philip Giraldi frankly admitted that "the Iranians in particular were very good and often were able to identify and assassinate our agents. These were people who were providing information to the U.S. embassy and CIA station in Ankara."[38]

On a few occasions, the Iranians tried to run double agents to Tehran. Reuel Gerecht, a large, gregarious Farsi speaker who replaced Giraldi at the consulate in Istanbul, uncovered two MOIS agents during his interviews with visa applicants. Both men seemed too eager to offer their services and information about the Iranian government.

Iran soon uncovered Casey's spy ring. According to former Iran minister of intelligence and security Mohammad Reyshahri, in July 1985 the MOIS was alerted when the CIA tried to recruit a midlevel government official in Iranian Azerbaijan for BQ Tug.[39] Unfortunately, the United States approached the wrong guy. Rather than cooperate, he immediately alerted MOIS to the

CIA recruitment drive. Then the Iranians rolled up two CIA agents working in the Iranian foreign ministry. One had foolishly kept all the coded messages received over the radio from his CIA handler in his house. The MOIS discovered these as well as his codebooks and his radio.

The MOIS was nothing but patient. For the next few years, its counterintelligence officers painstakingly unraveled the CIA's spy network. It recruited its own spies within the Iranian military to keep watch on senior officers who might be susceptible to the CIA's pitch. Junior officers were encouraged to spy on senior officers. For Captain Riahi, the MOIS recruited a first lieutenant and fellow pilot to monitor his movements. Aware of a possible compromise, Reza Kahlili's case officer instructed him to change his codes. He and the others did, and continued to relay information back to Tehfran as Langley remained ignorant of the calamity that would befall them. Meanwhile the MOIS watched and waited.[40]

Five

A Fig Leaf of Neutrality

Heading east toward Iran from the compact squalor of Iraq's second-largest city, Basra, the specter of an old battlefield fills the barren landscape. Clearly discernable on either side of the bumpy, dusty road choked with trucks, dilapidated taxis, and donkey carts are miles of trenches crisscrossing the desert, stretching off in all directions to the horizon. Endless rows of U-shaped earthen berms and large triangular fighting positions are slowly eroding, the tanks that once occupied them long since removed for other wars or stripped for scrap metal by the local villagers. Craters large and small pockmark the desert moonscape. Rain and wind frequently reveal the bleached bones of hastily buried soldiers, some still wearing boots and pieces of now indistinguishable uniforms, their sculls broken and cracked by bullets and hot metal. Twenty years after the fighting ended, unexploded ordnance littering the desert floor regularly takes the lives of civilians who stray off the roads and beaten paths.

These scenes testify to one of the bloodiest wars since World War II: the eight-year slaughter of the Iran-Iraq War. When it mercifully ended in August 1988, neither side had achieved very much: the border was unchanged, no territory had been gained, and both Saddam Hussein and Ayatollah Khomeini remained in power, safely seated in their respective capitals. But well over a million men had given the full measure of devotion, with perhaps four times that number permanently maimed. It was a war of incompetence, two lumbering giants repeatedly hammering each other with the clubs of modern firepower, killing thousands with each swing but achieving little. Institutional constraints hamstrung both countries, preventing any learning curve of more than a gentle glide slope. The Iraqi leader, Saddam Hussein, a military neophyte, frowned upon commanders who showed either initiative or too much battlefield prowess. Iran's once mighty military had been gutted by the revolution. Instead of using tanks, infantry, and aircraft in a combined arms doctrine of a modern military, Khomeini and the revolutionary commanders believed élan and revolutionary zeal in the form of human wave assaults could overcome rows of Iraqi tanks and artillery laid hub to hub.

While the war achieved little militarily, it had a pronounced effect on the region. Iran spent its revolutionary fervor, leaving the country isolated, with a profound sense of grievance and insecurity. The war ushered in Iraq's military supremacy and two decades of wars between Saddam Hussein and the West. It left the Gulf Arabs deeply suspicious of Iran. For the United States, heightened fear of an Iranian threat to Washington's control over Middle East oil led to an unlikely alliance with Iraq that Washington would soon regret.

Saddam Hussein was both pragmatic and paranoid. The descendant of Sunni shepherds from the town of Tikrit north of Baghdad, the dark-haired, mustached Hussein had risen through the ranks of the socialist Baath Party initially as an enforcer, before he ascended to the presidency in 1979. While he advocated secularism and Western socialist ideals such as universal education and women's suffrage, his true focus was political survival and personal aggrandizement. Saddam Hussein's political savvy was combined with ruthless suspicion. Anyone who appeared too capable might find himself imprisoned or executed. "Saddam was always wary of intelligent people," said Ali Hassan al-Majid, better known as "Chemical Ali" for his role in gassing hundreds of Kurdish civilians in 1988 to crush a perceived hazard to Saddam's rule.[1]

The Iraqi leader soon found himself in the crosshairs of the Iranian Revolution. Ayatollah Khomeini had not forgotten that Saddam Hussein had ordered his expulsion from Iraq at the behest of the shah. The supreme leader held Saddam and his secular Baathist Party in contempt. Khomeini publicly criticized the Iraqi regime as "corruptors of the true faith" and openly called for Iraq's majority Shia population to revolt. The ayatollah emphasized the unity of all Muslims, rejecting traditional Western concepts of nation-states and national identity. The *umma*, or community, was the sole basis for Islamic politics, and the Prophet's concept of a united Islamic nation drove the Iranian revolutionary vision. "We will export our revolution throughout the world . . . until the calls 'There is no god but God and Muhammad is the messenger of God' are echoed all over the world," said the supreme leader during one of many similar-themed Friday sermons.

Khomeini's words were matched by actions. Iran began backing Kurdish separatists in northern Iraq. Iranian agent provocateurs infiltrated Iraq, providing weapons and training to Shia opposition groups. Iran increased support for the Iraqi Shia militant group Islamic Dawa Party, which included a number of future leaders of Iraq, including prime ministers Ibrahim al-Jaafari and Nouri al-Maliki. Shortly after the shah's overthrow, the Dawa Party moved its headquarters to Tehran and escalated its guerrilla operations against Baathist rule in Iraq. In April 1980 alone, Iranian-backed terrorists assassinated twenty Iraqi officials and narrowly missed killing Iraq's deputy prime minister and close confidant of the Iraqi leader, Tariq Aziz.[2] In response, spurred privately by Saudi Arabia, which was deeply concerned that the Iranian Revolution would stir up Shia passions in its own eastern provinces, Baghdad clamped down by arresting prominent religious leaders, expelling thousands of Shia, and threatening to support an insurgency in the Arab populace of southern Iran. Tension grew along the border, and military skirmishes became common. In response to one Iranian infiltration, on December 14, 1979, Iraqi troops moved five kilometers into Iran before withdrawing under the umbrella of a massive artillery barrage that rained shells down all along Iran's southern border. By the summer of 1980 Iran and Iraq seemed poised for war.[3]

Saddam Hussein viewed the Iranian Revolution as both an existential threat and an opportunity. To Saddam Hussein, Iran looked weak. The Iranian Revolution had consumed much of the officer corps of the shah's once vaunted army and unleashed long-standing tensions between the Persian majority and Iran's ethnic minorities, such as the Kurds in the north and the Baluchis in the south. The Iraqi leader wanted to abrogate the 1975 Algiers Accords with Iran; imposed by the shah, it had established the border between the two nations at the center of the Shatt al-Arab, giving Tehran control of half of Baghdad's only outlet to the Persian Gulf. Also, Saddam Hussein cast his eye on the Iranian province of Khuzestan, directly across the border near Basra. Under its sands were most of the Iranian oil reserves, and with a majority Arab population, Saddam Hussein calculated they would welcome his "liberation" of them from Persian control. The Iraqi records captured after the American invasion in 2003 are replete with such megalomaniac ideas. Saddam Hussein believed that Egyptian president Anwar Sadat's peace treaty with Israel abrogated Egypt's leadership of the Arab people, and that this mantle now fell on Iraq's shoulders. He envisioned himself taking up the mantle as the new leader of the Arab people. Saddam Hussein saw himself as the new Saladin, believing it was his destiny to unite the Arab people in a great crusade to retake Jerusalem with the ultimate goal of becoming the new caliphate.

In October 1979, one month before Iranian students stormed the U.S. embassy, CIA officer George Cave flew back to Tehran carrying with him some highly sensitive intelligence that he hoped would impress the new Iranian government as to American sincerity. He met with the minister of foreign affairs, Ebrahim Yazdi, a pragmatic moderate whom Cave had known for a number of years.

"The Iraqis are planning to invade Iran," Cave said simply. U.S. intelligence had strong evidence, including communications intercepts, and before leaving Washington Cave had seen satellite imagery of the Iraqi army rehearsing crossing the Shatt al-Arab. While he did not mention this visual evidence to Yazdi, he relayed the CIA's anticipation of an Iraqi attack the following year.

Cave told Yazdi about a CIA-operated signals intelligence collection station located at Ilam, near the Iraq border and parallel to Baghdad. Beginning in 1973 and using the code word Ibex, the agency built this base at the request of the shah; its sole purpose had been to eavesdrop on Iraq. Four specially configured Iranian C-130 airplanes collected Iraqi communications, downloading the intercepts to the ground station, where they would be translated and analyzed. "The general who ran it is still in Iran," Cave urged. "You need to reactivate it to find out what Iraq is up to."[4]

But with a wave of the hand, Yazdi dismissed Cave's advice. He replied in Farsi, "They wouldn't dare!" Iran's dismissal of the CIA's warning could have proven fatal for the fledgling Islamic Republic—had their antagonist not been Saddam Hussein.

During a news conference at the end of the first American war with Iraq, in 1991, the brusque, imposing General H. Norman Schwarzkopf famously said of Saddam Hussein's military acumen: "He is neither a strategist nor is he schooled in the operational arts, nor is he a tactician, nor is he a general, nor is he a soldier. Other than that he's a great military man." Nothing reveals the truth of this statement more than Iraq's dysfunctional attack on Iran.

On September 22, 1980, Iraq tried to duplicate the successful Israeli attack during the 1967 war by leading its ground invasion in its opening gambit with a massive air attack on Iran's airfields and destroying Iran's air force. But Iraq's effort proved a poor imitation, and only three planes were destroyed on the ground. The Iranian pilots responded with surprising vigor. In a series of dogfights in the opening week of the war, their American training and equipment proved superior in the blue skies over southern Mesopotamia. Had it not been for the shortage of spare parts and pilots that soon curtailed the number of Iranian sorties, the Iraqi invasion might have ended before it began. A delusional Saddam Hussein suspected that Israeli pilots had really been conducting these effective attacks.

Nine Iraqi divisions lumbered across the border into central and southern Iran. It was an anti-blitzkrieg. Despite only sporadic Iranian resistance, the Iraqi army moved glacially. Frequently orders came from the high command in Baghdad straight down to division commanders, bypassing the intermediary corps headquarters. Operating in the dark, with no planned military objectives, and not wishing to question Saddam Hussein's methods, senior Iraqi commanders did nothing. Units advanced a few kilometers and stopped; they dug in and awaited further orders from Baghdad.

Saddam's timid attack permitted Iran to send reinforcements unhindered to the front and forced Iraq to fight in a wide-open, coverless wasteland. While it required weeks for the disorganized Iranian military to muster enough forces to blunt the Iraqi armor divisions, the halting pace of Baghdad's invasion gave Tehran the luxury of time. The Iraqis succeeded in capturing only one important city in Khuzestan: the port city of Khorramshahr—now called Arabistan by Saddam Hussein—which fell after four weeks of house-to-house fighting at the cost of six thousand Iraqi casualties.

Iran saw the hand of the United States behind Iraq's aggression. Just as Iranians believed that the shah had been admitted into the United States to plot a countercoup rather than for humanitarian reasons, the prevailing view on the streets of Tehran was that Iraq would not have attacked without the permission of the American superpower. The two nations had colluded to overturn the revolution. Iranian leaders believed their suspicions were confirmed when news leaked that the last prime minister under the shah, Shapour Bakhtiar, had joined the Iraqis and entered the occupied part of Iran. "It was believed that Bakhtiar would seek to establish a separate government in the region, which would be recognized by the United States and others, igniting a civil war inside Iran."[5]

While the United States frequently receives the credit or the blame for much of what transpires in the Middle East, Washington's hidden hand was not behind the Iraqi attack. "The U.S. government was taken by surprise when the attack occurred in the magnitude that it did," said Gary Sick, who worked the Persian Gulf desk for Brzezinski at the White House.[6] Carter steadfastly refused Brzezinski's urgings to consider more serious military options to pressure Khomeini to release the hostages.[7] The last thing the White House wanted was a massive regional war and another crisis in the Middle East instigated by the paranoid megalomaniac ruler in Baghdad.[8]

Ayatollah Khomeini also saw an opportunity in the onset of war. Steven Ward, a senior Iranian analyst at the CIA, observed that Iraq's invasion of Iran proved to be a "godsend" to the new Islamic Republic. "The Iraqi aggression ensured the clerical regime's survival by reviving the public's nationalism and diverting attention from the country's slide into tyranny."[9] Ayatollah Khomeini frequently said this too, boasting that the Iraqi threat afforded the Islamic Republic the chance to rally the public behind the regime and the excuse needed to purge domestic opponents, such as the powerful communist Tudeh Party. Just as the takeover of the American embassy allowed Khomeini to purge the liberal opposition from the government, Saddam Hussein's overt aggression provided a similar excuse to expunge the communists and consolidate power around the mullahs. While it plunged Iran into a virtual civil war, by 1983 Khomeini had succeeded in breaking the Tudeh Party, with the death toll tallying into the thousands.

The Iranian army struggled to roll back the Iraqi assault. Perhaps half the entire Iranian military had deserted or been purged since the revolution, including many of the skilled officers. In January 1981 clerical leaders, who knew much more about the Koran than about Clausewitz, goaded a reluctant army into conducting its first major counterattack. Iran committed most of its armor reserve—some three hundred tanks—in a massive attack during the winter rainy season. The Iranian tanks became bogged down in the muck and mire and tried to slug it out at close range against dug-in Iraqi T-62 tanks. Despite generally outfighting their Iraqi opponents, nearly two-thirds of Iran's irreplaceable tanks were left as smoking hulks in front of Iraqi trenches.[10] The failure of the attack by the armored forces left the professional soldiers discredited. So the same amateurs who'd ordered the army's failed attack turned to their own newly created organization, the Revolutionary Guard.

M ohsen Sazegara had been an early supporter of Ayatollah Khomeini. Short with bright blue eyes that expressed a keen intellect, Mohsen attended school in Tehran and the Illinois Institute of Technology in Chicago. He was studying to be an electrical engineer when he decided to travel to Iraq to work for the ayatollah in his bid to overthrow the shah. Although he was Shiite, the draw of Khomeini had been less religious and more youthful idealism. Like many other well-educated Iranian students, Sazegara had been swept up in the Persian equivalent of the student rebellions that had gripped Western campuses during the 1960s. "It was a blend of newfound religious identity and Marxism," he noted.

Sazegara proved to be a good analyst and accompanied Khomeini to Paris, where he helped translate Western stories and coordinate the sophisticated public relations campaign in the Western media that demonized the shah and moderated Khomeini's image. When Khomeini returned triumphantly to Tehran, Sazegara accompanied him, descending from the jet just ahead of the ayatollah.

Security became a major preoccupation in the early months of the new Islamic Republic. The new government felt under siege. Weapons looted from the military armories during the chaotic death throes of the shah's rule were everywhere and had found their way into the hands of communists and Kurdish separatists, the latter using the newly acquired hardware to increase attacks against the weakened central government in Tehran. The loyalty of the military remained questionable. Sunni rebels in Turkmenistan along the border with the Soviet Union had approached Moscow about supporting an independence movement and were given its promise of aid if they showed the military capacity to hold a sizable area. The new regime obsessed about an American-led coup to reinstall the shah, even an invasion by the United States, perhaps using a trumped-up border conflict with Turkey as an excuse for a NATO attack. "Everyone believed that the United States wanted to overthrow the revolution and reinstall the shah," said Sazegara. "It was a universal truth as far as we were concerned."[11]

Sazegara and others began working on the idea of a people's army to defend the revolution. Stealing a page from the Marxist playbook, they wanted to build a military organization filled by volunteers from the masses to combat their plethora of foreign and domestic enemies. Sazegara wrote the first draft charter for the people's army, an idealistic organization that had no officers and whose directives stemmed from popular consensus, under the supervision of a five-member board chaired by an ayatollah reporting to Khomeini. On April 4, 1979, a group of students, including Sazegara, met with Ayatollah Khomeini at his home in Qom to brief him on the proposed military organization. Khomeini did not look at them, but sat quietly with his hands folded, listening intently. When they finished, Khomeini looked up and flashed a very rare smile. "Yes. This is a very good idea. I have worried about an American coup."

Sazegara soon discovered that two other similar Revolutionary Guard units had sprung up. One was headed by the son of the powerful liberal-leaning Ayatollah Hussein Ali Montazeri and was located in an old military barracks. The other group was in the west of Tehran, formed by former political prisoners, a major in the shah's Immortals guard, and several members of the shah's household who had secretly spied for Khomeini. After several meetings, both of these fledgling military groups merged with Sazegara's group.

In May 1979 the people's army became a reality. Officially it became known as the Army of the Guardians of the Islamic Revolution, or Sepah-e Pasdaran in Farsi. In English it has been simply labeled the Revolutionary Guard. The guard established its headquarters in a brand-new building in Tehran, which had been recently built to allow the shah's secret police, Savak, to monitor domestic phone conversations. The building was empty and its only damage during the revolution had been some broken windows.

With furniture and telephones installed, Sazegara invited Mostafa Chamran over to the new headquarters to brief him on the new group. A brilliant professor of engineering, Chamran had taught at Berkeley and worked at

NASA's Jet Propulsion Laboratory. He was widely respected in Iranian academic circles as the only student at the University of Tehran to get a 100 percent on his thermodynamics test under Mehdi Bazargan, the school's toughest instructor who would also become the first prime minister of the revolutionary government. But in the 1970s, Chamran had found religion. He'd turned his back on science, grew his beard, and replaced his slide rule with a Kalashnikov. He traveled to Lebanon—then in the midst of its sectarian civil war—where he established the military wing of the main Shia militia. Sazegara believed Chamran was a logical choice to lead this new people's army.

"That's fantastic!" Chamran replied when he saw what was being conceived. "But you need military-trained leadership." As the idea of an officerless corps quickly fell away as unworkable, Chamran brought a small group of Iranians back from Lebanon to begin training the first cadre of two hundred officers, all of whom were chosen for their ideological commitment to Khomeini. These combatants were joined by others with military experience, including the future head of the Revolutionary Guard, Mohsen Rezai, who had fought with the MEK before falling out over its emphasis of Marx over Muhammad.[12] In a strange twist, a number of former intelligence officers from the shah's military offered their tradecraft to aid the Revolutionary Guard in rooting out state enemies. Reporting only to Khomeini, the guard quickly grew into the thousands.

Over the next year both Chamran and Sazegara moved on to other jobs in the new government, but the organization they'd helped create continued to evolve. As the defense minister, Chamran streamlined command of the guard and ensured clerical supervision at every level of command. The Revolutionary Guard cut its teeth fighting the various separatist movements and as a gendarmerie for internal security. It became the key tool for consolidating power in the hands of the Islamic Republic, with many of the country's future leaders emerging from its ranks.

The Iraqi war forced a transformation in the Revolutionary Guard. Rather than counterinsurgency, the Revolutionary Guard found itself embroiled in a major conventional war. Drawing recruits from the large, poor Shia population through the strong appeal of religious fervor, not to mention better pay and benefits, their ranks swelled to more than a quarter million frontline soldiers. Disdain for the regular Iranian army prevented any merger, and the Revolutionary Guard emerged as a separate, parallel army that soon surpassed the army if not in numbers, then certainly in clout. It was backed by the popular pro-Khomeini militia force called the Basij, Farsi for "mobilization." More than six hundred thousand strong, Basij provided a steady stream of replacements for the Revolutionary Guard.

In April 1981 the Revolutionary Guard spearheaded an attack using human wave assaults led by young, often unarmed Basij men who unwittingly cleared the Iraqi minefields with their own bodies. Despite horrific losses, these untrained conscripts of the Revolutionary Guard overran the Iraqi defenders, capturing frontline trenches before their attack stalled due to shortages in supply and mechanized forces to exploit the breakthrough. Chamran himself died a martyr's death in these early attacks, killed by an Iraqi mortar round while leading a group of Basij militia.

The Iranians touted this victory as a new way of Islamic warfare. Revolutionary zeal supplanted traditional military competency as the key to victory. Faith in God and a commitment to spread the revolution would overcome Western weapons, tactics, and training. The human cost was immaterial, even encouraged in a society that prized martyrdom. The sprawling Behesht-e Zahra cemetery in southwest Tehran soon filled with graves—adorned with photos and personal mementos—of thousands of young men.

But these human wave assaults proved effective. One Iraqi officer who witnessed them has never forgotten the image of nearly a dozen Revolutionary Guardsmen riding atop a tank firing rocket-propelled grenades as they headed toward his position. Even after their tank had been knocked out, the survivors, some on fire, jumped off and continued to run toward the Iraqi troops until they were finally cut down in a hail of machine-gun fire at the foot of the Iraqi trench. "It unnerved our troops and many ran," he dryly commented, before adding that he wished he had such dedicated soldiers. Over time, the Revolutionary Guard operations became more sophisticated as military necessity forced amateurism to give way to a modicum of professionalism. The Revolutionary Guard grew adept at probing the Iraqi lines, finding weakly defended positions and gaps between Iraqi units. Then, under the cover of darkness, massed Basij and Revolutionary Guard forces infiltrated behind the Iraqi lines, repeatedly opening gaping holes in the Iraqi defenses.

With Ayatollah Khomeini's approval, the army began promoting officers favored by the Revolutionary Guard. As these like-minded men assumed leadership positions in the army, it fostered a better working relationship between the two separate forces. Now army tanks and infantry backed by artillery began exploiting the guard's nocturnal infiltration operations. While Iran struggled to sustain its offensives—each attack required weeks of amassing ammunition and supplies—over months it chipped away at Saddam's army, slowly driving them out of Iran and, by the summer of 1982, back into the outskirts of Iraq's second-largest city, Basra.

A divided Iranian leadership debated its next steps in the war. No one advocated accepting the cease-fire suddenly offered by Saddam Hussein. Ayatollah Khomeini's son Ahmed Khomeini, as well as the chief of staff of the army, pressed for an aggressive offensive to take Basra, overthrow Saddam Hussein, and establish an Islamic state within Iraq. But president and future supreme leader Seyed Ali Khamenei, foreign minister Ali Akbar Velayati, and the pragmatic speaker of the parliament and head of the armed forces, Ali Akbar Hashemi Rafsanjani, were less sanguine about invading Iraq proper. They argued for seeking punitive reparations and ending Saddam Hussein's ability to threaten the revolution. The chief of the general staff, General Zahir Nejad, opposed the invasion because he feared that the international community would see Iran as the antagonist and not the victim of aggression. Ayatollah Khomeini lay somewhere in between the two views. He deeply wanted to overthrow the Baathist regime and spread the Islamic Revolution, but he shared General Nejad's concerns about Iran being perceived as the aggressor. The supreme leader preferred to achieve Saddam Hussein's ouster without an invasion of Iraq.

The debate came to a head in a pivotal meeting of the powerful Supreme Defense Council, Iran's equivalent of the National Security Council, in June 1982. Both Velayati and Khamenei remained opposed to invading Iraq, but Rafsanjani had come around to support the idea, and he and other hawks argued that Basra could be taken. That spring, Iranian intelligence agents had fanned out throughout southern Iraq and Kuwait; they reported back that the Shia population was receptive to Iran's revolutionary message and ripe for revolt. This would cause a chain reaction and lead to the overthrow of Saddam Hussein, and perhaps even of the pro-Western emir in Kuwait. The final decision fell to Ayatollah Khomeini. Despite his own personal reservations, he sided with the hawks and agreed to a robust attack to take Basra and end the Baath regime. Once the supreme leader had made his decision, he never looked back. In the coming years he consistently called for a war until victory. It would take another six years of slaughter before he changed his mind.

On June 21, Ayatollah Khomeini publicly proclaimed that the "road to Jerusalem ran through Karbala." He enunciated a grandiose vision of a Shia crescent stretching across the Middle East. The divided Supreme Defense Council rallied behind the decision. With revolutionary fervor and a sense of divine victory awaiting its army, Iran pressed forward into Iraq, intent on capturing Basra, bringing down the Baath regime, and installing a pro-Iranian Shia Islamic government. "War! War until victory!" became the chant in the streets of Tehran.[13]

With Iran poised for a major attack on Basra, alarm bells sounded in the White House. "It appears Iran will invade Iraq in the next few days," National Security Adviser William Clark wrote to President Reagan. "Given the past performance of the Iraqi army," Clark added, "it seems likely that Iran eventually will succeed in accomplishing its military objectives." This, Clark warned the president, could succeed in bringing down Saddam Hussein, posing a direct threat to Kuwait and Saudi Arabia and grave danger to American interests in the region. "Our principal objective," Clark wrote, "is to bring an end to the war before Iran can assume hegemony in the region."

At five p.m. on July 12, 1982, Clark convened a meeting of President Ronald Reagan's senior foreign policy team in the White House Situation Room. The mood was somber as the men seated themselves around the wooden table in the small, windowless conference room. The first briefing, by an intelligence officer, did little to improve the mood. The Defense Intelligence Agency officer expected the Iranians to attack Basra within the next twenty-four to forty-eight hours, and while the fighting would be heavy, the agency predicted the Iranians would take the city. The chairman of the Joint Chiefs of Staff, General Vessey, cringed when the analyst described the incompetent disposition of the Iraqi army. Rather than using natural barriers, such as defending behind rivers, the Iraqi units sat in front of them, with the nearest armor reserves capable of blunting the Iranian attacks more than four days away from the critical front at Basra.

From the outset the Reagan administration took a pro-Iraqi stance. The United States and Iraq had severed diplomatic relations after the 1967 Arab-Israeli War and had had a testy relationship for the interceding fifteen years. Now, however, the two countries shared contempt for the new Islamic Republic of Iran, and Washington saw the war as an opportunity to wean Iraq from its chief arms supplier, the Soviet Union. "Closer ties with Iraq would benefit the U.S. and could shift Iraq into opposition against Iran and Syria," Assistant Secretary of Defense Bing West wrote to Secretary Caspar Weinberger in a memo laying out the pros and cons of closer military ties to Iraq.[14] In spring and summer of 1981, a string of senior American diplomats arrived in Iraq for meetings with a close confidant of Saddam Hussein, a powerful Christian Baath Party insider named Tariq Aziz.[15] Over occasional glasses of whiskey from Aziz's well-apportioned walk-in liquor cellar, the two nations gradually moved toward normalization of diplomatic relations.

But the chief catalyst for America's tilt toward Iraq was the drubbing of the Iraqi army at the hands of Iran's Revolutionary Guard. The crisis in the marsh and sand around Basra galvanized the White House that hot Washington July. A crisis mood prevailed as the United States awoke to Iran as the main threat to American hegemony over the Persian Gulf. An air force lieutenant colonel taking notes summed up the opinions after one meeting: "Although there is limited room for maneuver in our policy, it is definitely in U.S. interests to keep the Iraqi government from becoming pro-Iranian."[16] The United States needed to protect moderate Arab states from Iranian aggression and to safeguard Middle East oil. But the challenge, as Washington viewed it, was to support the Iraqis without alienating Iran and pushing it into the Soviet camp.

Nevertheless, that summer a consensus emerged among Reagan's frequently fractious inner circle to support Iraq. With Jordan and Saudi Arabia lobbying for Baghdad, the United States threw its support behind Saddam Hussein.[17] Reagan concurred. He signed a top secret security directive instructing the government to take all measures short of direct military aid to prevent Iraq from losing to Iran.[18]

Not everyone within the bowels of the U.S. foreign policy establishment agreed with the tilt toward Iraq. William Taft in the Defense Department disagreed with the cooperative arrangement, believing that Iraq was little better than Iran. The State Department's directorate for Near Eastern affairs, including its director for regional affairs, Philip Wilcox, and his boss, Deputy Assistant Secretary of State James Placke, both were uneasy about siding with Iraq as it might close the door on any chance for normalization with Iran.[19] They were joined by a concoction of Cold War hawks, such as Paul Wolfowitz at the State Department and Richard Perle at the Defense Department, who opposed supporting Iraq because they believed that Saddam Hussein posed a greater danger. Perle expressed particular concern about transferring American computer technology to Iraq, fearing it could wind up in the hands of the Soviet Union.

The senior leadership at the White House, the Pentagon, and the State Department, however, tended to see Iraq as the lesser of two evils. Saddam Hussein could provide stability in the region and serve as a bulwark against Iran. Iraq was more independent and perhaps could be wooed away from Moscow. The legacy of the Iranian hostage crisis resonated within the debate. Secretary of Defense Caspar Weinberger despised the Iranian regime and never forgave it for taking over the U.S. embassy. He favored most any plan that would make trouble for the Islamic Republic of Iran.[20] "There was no great love for Saddam Hussein," said Richard Armitage. "Neither side was a good guy. It's a pity the war could not have lasted forever."[21]

The debate was not settled overnight. However, over the course of the next two years, as the war dragged on and Iraqi fortunes on the battlefield ebbed more than flowed, President Reagan consistently sided with those supporting closer relations with Saddam Hussein. Despite Washington's discomfort with Iraq's human rights abuses and liberal use of chemical weapons, the United States gradually moved to a position that a senior State Department official labeled a "fig leaf of neutrality" in the Iran-Iraq War.

After the July 12 White House meeting, the United States moved to reassure its Gulf allies. The Gulf Arabs had good reason to worry about the wrath of Iran, and many privately supported the Iraqi invasion. In the brief pan-Sunni euphoria that followed the Iraqi attack, Oman, Saudi Arabia, and the United Arab Emirates allowed nearly one hundred Iraqi aircraft to stage at their air bases for a planned massive strike on Bandar Abbas.[22] Alarmed, Washington pressured them to seek withdrawal of the Iraqi planes and to avert starting a much wider, much more dangerous Middle East war. Saudi Arabia, however, secretly allowed Iraqi aircraft to "hot-pit" refuel at its bases as they returned from attacking Iranian oil tankers near the Strait of Hormuz.

The United States tried to reassure a skittish Saudi government. Reagan sent a personal letter to King Fahd of Saudi Arabia expressing America's concerns about an Iranian victory, offering "our readiness to cooperate in the defense of the kingdom." Under the innocuous name of European Liaison Force One (ELF-One), the United States dispatched to Riyadh four E-3 AWACS (airborne warning and control system) aircraft accompanied by air-to-air refueling tankers.[23] This modified Boeing 707 aircraft mounted a large saucer-shaped radar dome capable of detecting Iranian aircraft more than four hundred nautical miles away. They served as the linchpin in an elaborate American-designed Saudi air defense system arrayed against Iran. The Saudis kept aloft American-built F-15 fighters ready to intercept any Iranian jet detected by the AWACS. American technicians manned a communications network throughout the kingdom that linked the American AWACS to the Royal Saudi Air Force. An operations center manned by the U.S. Air Force at the King Abdul Aziz Air Base near Dhahran comprised radar and communications equipment that received the AWACS data.[24]

The Saudi government worried about the fallout within the Muslim world should it be openly revealed that the keeper of the two holiest sites in Islam allowed a de facto permanent American military presence within the kingdom. So the Americans tried to keep a low profile. Once a week a U.S. Air Force C-141 cargo jet arrived, off-loading supplies and new airmen dressed in civilian clothes and traveling on temporary duty orders ranging from 21 to 179 days. They were quietly billeted in local hotels. The bulk of Americans in Riyadh stayed at the al-Yamamah Hotel, an unremarkable but well-appointed building most notable for a seventy-pound marble ball in the large center lobby. Each day, Saudi buses transported the Americans from their comfortable barracks to the nearby Saudi air base.[25] This routine remained unchanged for the next six years as thousands of American airmen quietly rotated through Saudi Arabia, all under the public radar and all without any formal agreement between the two nations.

Washington extended commodities credit guarantees to purchase American agricultural products to prop up Baghdad's economy.[26] A windfall for American farmers, this totaled $345 million in exports in 1983, increasing to $652 million a couple of years later.[27] This also freed up hundreds of millions of dollars for the Iraqis to use to purchase military hardware. Vice President George Bush intervened with a Yale classmate, William Draper, who headed the federal government's Export-Import Bank, which extends credit to purchase American goods, to overrule his own staff and extend to Baghdad nearly $500 million to finance a new Iraqi oil pipeline to Jordan to be built by the U.S. company Bechtel. As Bush wrote to his friend Draper, "Eximbank could play a critical role in our efforts in the region."[28]

In December 1983 Reagan dispatched Donald Rumsfeld to Baghdad. The president had appointed the former defense secretary and Republican stalwart as his special Middle East envoy with a portfolio that included dealing with the myriad problems confronting the United States, from Middle East peace to Iraq's war with Iran. A tenacious bureaucratic infighter, Rumsfeld was both smart and complex; he could be both charming and acerbic. After several months of diplomatic groundwork, Rumsfeld arrived in Baghdad on December 19, 1983, carrying an amicable letter from President Reagan for Saddam Hussein. He had an impromptu meeting with Tariq Aziz in which over the course of two and a half hours they discussed all the fault lines of the region. Aziz, fluent in English, could be equally as glib as Rumsfeld, and the two men largely agreed on a shared view between the two nations, especially in curbing Iran's power.

"The U.S. has no interest in an Iranian victory," Rumsfeld told Aziz. "To the contrary. We would not want Iran's influence expanded at the expense of Iraq." As Rumsfeld wrote afterward, "I thought we had areas of common interest, particularly the security and stability in the Gulf which had been jeopardized as a result of the Iranian revolution."[29]

The next day Rumsfeld met with Saddam Hussein for ninety minutes. It was the highest-level meeting between the two states in nearly twenty years. Saddam showed up in an army uniform, wearing the epaulets of a field marshal and a pistol on his hip. Iraqi television captured the two men's prolonged handshake, much to Donald Rumsfeld's later chagrin when it became a much ballyhooed video on the Internet following the U.S. overthrow of the same Iraqi leader when Rumsfeld was secretary of defense in 2003. Saddam was pleased with the warm tone of Reagan's letter, telling Rumsfeld that it indicated a deep and serious understanding of the implications and dangers of the war and of an Iranian victory. "Having a whole generation of Iraqis and Americans grow up without understanding each other had negative implications and could lead to mix-ups," Hussein stated. Rumsfeld agreed, saying that despite differences between the United States and Iraq, the two countries shared a common view, especially regarding stability in the Persian Gulf and curbing Iran. Rumsfeld expressed qualified American support to prevent Iraq's defeat and pledged to try to curb the arms flow to Iran that perpetuated its military offensives. While the meeting between Rumsfeld and Hussein ended without any grand bargain, it reaffirmed American support for

Iraq's war against Iran and set the two nations on the path to full diplomatic relations, which formally occurred with the exchange of ambassadors in November 1984.[30]

I f the Foreign Service can produce muddy-boots diplomats, Robert Oakley, the lean, drawn former naval intelligence officer, was certainly one of that rare breed. By 1984 Oakley had already had nearly thirty years of foreign policy experience, having served a tour on the NSC and ambassadorial postings to Zaire and Somalia, and he had seen his share of war, including Vietnam. Like most of his colleagues, Oakley viewed Iran as the major menace to American interests. While far from enamored with Saddam Hussein, Oakley believed an Iranian victory would spell catastrophe for the United States and its Arab allies.

Oakley headed an NSC-led interagency group to coordinate support for Iraq. Meeting in the Old Executive Office Building next to the White House's West Wing, representatives from State, Defense, CIA, and the Treasury Department examined the latest intelligence on the battlefront and looked for ways to provide the best assistance to the Iraqi military and to solicit support from other countries for Iraq.

While the United States refused to provide direct military support, Washington strongly encouraged other countries to do so. Oakley's team looked at the military requirements of Saddam Hussein and tried to match up donor countries to meet those needs. In one case, South Korea provided 155-mm artillery shells for long-range artillery pieces provided by South Africa. The U.S. government discreetly approached both the French and the Italians to sell more equipment to Iraq. President Reagan personally supported the initiative, lobbying the Italian prime minister to supply Iraq with arms during an Oval Office meeting. Both countries obliged. For Paris, it was a lucrative business, with 40 percent of all its arms sales going to Iraq during the first half of the 1980s. This included a massive contract for 130 combat aircraft.[31] The French sold the Iraqis five advanced Super Étendards to carry the Exocet antiship missile. This provided Iraq the means to effectively hit Iranian oil tankers throughout the Gulf. The aircraft arrived with a team of French advisers who instructed the Iraqis on everything from maintenance to tactics against Iran.

Oakley's group elicited commitments from both the Egyptian and the Jordanian governments to provide even more assistance; both countries sent military advisers to Iraq.[32] Egyptian president Hosni Mubarak sent thousands of "volunteers" to the country, who joined a brigade from North Yemen fighting in the trenches alongside the Iraqis. Jordan agreed to serve as an intermediary for American-made radars capable of detecting incoming Iranian missiles. Washington provided the radars to Jordan, which then sent them on to Baghdad. The United States and Egypt reached a secret agreement whereby Cairo would sell off its older, surplus Soviet-built equipment and, in return, Washington would backfill Mubarak's military with more advanced, American-made weapons. Over the course of the war, Egypt sold over a billion dollars' worth of military equipment to Iraq.[33]

Oakley took a liberal view of providing nonmilitary assistance to Iraq. The United States sold communications equipment, sixty Hughes helicopters (the same make as those used by U.S. Army Special Forces), as well as two thousand heavy trucks themselves worth $234 million. Iraq impressed all of this matériel into its army. To help justify the truck sale, the State Department used twisted logic, stating that, as Iraq was on the defense in the war, it "is now unlikely to use the trucks to contribute significantly to the destabilization of the region."[34]

To complement the arms for Iraq, the United States worked to cut off a similar flow to Iran. To feed its military needs, Iran purchased $2 billion worth of weapons, munitions, and spare parts every year. It was a lucrative trade; any country who could fulfill that need stood to make huge profits. Overt and illicit weapons flowed into Iran from all over the globe in an underground arms trade. Iranian agents met in Frankfurt and Lisbon with shady arms dealers intent on profiting by providing American spare parts to Tehran. Israel and countries in Europe and Asia all clandestinely sold compatible apparatus for Iran's American-made hardware. Between 1983 and 1985, Spain alone sold $280 million worth of spare artillery tubes, ammunition, and small arms. In the same period, 28 percent of Portugal's entire arms exports went to Iran, including the illegal transfer of as many as four thousand U.S.-made TOW missiles. Belgium and other NATO allies refurbished Iranian F-4 aircraft engines.[35]

In order to curtail weapons flowing to Iran, in the spring of 1983 the United States initiated Operation Staunch, spearheaded by Richard Fairbanks. Having succeeded in taking Iraq off the terrorism watch list, the State Department now declared Iran to be a state supporter of terrorism. This permitted the U.S. government to impose export sanctions against Iran, which prohibited the export of any American-made weapons to Tehran. Fairbanks knew it would be impossible to halt all arms sales to Iran, but he concentrated on stopping the sale of sophisticated equipment, such as radars and aircraft parts.[36] He issued two or three démarches every month to European and Asian nations to pressure them to halt these exports. Ambassadors in Europe and Asia were instructed to "preach" the virtues of Operation Staunch: the dangers of providing armaments to Iran that perpetuated the war.

The U.S. military supported Fairbanks's diplomatic campaign too. Senior officers at CENTCOM traveled across the Middle East with instructions to convince their counterparts to agree with the arms embargo and to forge a united effort to curtail selling any equipment that could aid the Iranian military.[37]

The United States obtained South Korea's consent to refrain from selling aircraft parts and intervened with Italy to halt the transfer of Boeing Chinook helicopters. Great Britain agreed to clamp down on its companies selling equipment that had military applications. This constant anti-Iranian drumbeat by U.S. diplomats eventually forged widespread consensus in both Europe and the Middle East as to the culpability of Iran in perpetuating the Gulf conflict. Tehran found itself increasingly isolated and on the diplomatic defense for its unwillingness to accept a cease-fire. In late 1981 Reagan signed a secret finding that allowed the Central Intelligence Agency to pass Iraq intelligence by way of third countries. CIA officers began giving their Jordanian counterparts at the General Intelligence Department low-level intelligence on Iranian troop dispositions intending for it to be passed on to Iraq. Saddam Hussein took interest in this information ostensibly coming from Jordan. He reviewed it personally before giving it to his own military intelligence personnel. Whether Hussein knew the information had come directly from the United States is not clear, but a senior Iraqi army intelligence general, Wafiq al-Samarrai, later explained, "I was sure Jordan was not capable of getting such information."[38] Saudi Arabia provided another venue for the CIA to pass nonattributable information to Saddam Hussein. Like Jordan, the CIA had a long-standing relationship with the Saudi General Intelligence Directorate, al-Mukhabarat Al-A'amah. Saudi Arabia was only too willing to pass on similar information, sharing a view of Iran similar to that of its Sunni allies in Baghdad.

With the Iranian victories in 1982, Reagan authorized the CIA to increase its intelligence support for Iraq. In June 1982 a three-man team, headed by a fifty-year-old American who introduced himself as "Thomson," arrived in Baghdad for several days of lengthy meetings with the head of Iraqi military intelligence and the Iraqi intelligence service, known as the Mukhabarat. "We are here to help you and are willing to provide you with more information which will help you in your war against Iran," said Thomson in his opening remarks with the Iraqis.

The two sides exchanged views on the Iranian military, and both sides agreed on the need for better intelligence to counter the Iranian attacks around Basra. Thomson said that the CIA was willing to provide regular information on Iranian troop movements in order to prevent further Iranian advances. At the close of the conference, Thomson gave the Iraqis detailed drawings based on American overhead images of Iranian military troop locations arrayed east of Basra in southwestern Iran. At the end, Saddam Hussein thanked the Americans and gave his approval for the expanded intelligence cooperation.

As the United States had no embassy in or formal diplomatic relations with Iraq until 1984, both sides agreed to establish an unofficial station in Baghdad headed by a senior CIA officer who would serve as a liaison between the two countries.[39] To support this, the CIA established a small Iraqi intelligence cell within the Near East Division of the operations directorate, which comprised a mixture of veterans and brand-new officers, many of whom went on to form the next generation of American Middle East spies. Here they compiled satellite images of the battlefront and intercepts of Iranian communications and distilled these into sanitized documents that would neither compromise the sources nor divulge capabilities. Langley passed on to the Iraqis this distilled information in documents outlining Iranian unit locations and depots and summaries of where American intelligence believed Iran intended to attack next. The CIA passed on selected information regarding the capabilities of the U.S.-manufactured equipment operated by Tehran, especially on the F-14 and F-4 aircraft that made up the heart of the Iranian air force.

Clair George, who headed the agency's clandestine arm, closely supervised the intelligence sharing. To this consummate professional spy, the true importance of maintaining these intelligence exchanges with Iraq was to recruit new Iraqi agents from among the senior ranks of its military and intelligence services. Except when Basra appeared threatened, George ordered a steady dribble of relatively insignificant information passed on to Baghdad—enough to keep his intelligence officers talking and coercing Iraqi officers, but not enough to really impact the fighting. "The CIA gave them chickenfeed," observed the head of the DIA's Middle East operations, Walter Patrick Lang.[40]

In general, however, the CIA remained lukewarm about the policy tilt toward Iraq. "It was a horrible mistake," said Kenneth Pollack, an influential Middle East expert who was a rising star within the CIA's analytical directorate in the 1980s. "My fellow analysts and I were warning at the time that Hussein was a very nasty character."[41] Pollack was not alone in rejecting the view that Hussein was the lesser of two evils.

Despite Saddam Hussein's outward pleasure with the CIA information, the Iraqis were very suspicious about the intelligence passed by the Americans. "They thought maybe we were trying to mislead them in some way," said the CIA's George Cave. However, the Iraqis became converts in February 1984. Having spent two years conducting futile human frontal assaults on the Iraqi defenses around Basra, Iran secretly amassed more than a quarter of a million men for a surprise attack north of the city in the seemingly impregnable seven-hundred-square-mile Hawizeh marshes. Using a flotilla of improvised boats and barges, the Iranians made their way through waist-deep stagnant black water, establishing fighting postings on the natural islets of grass and marsh reeds as well as on several man-made islands that supported oil drilling. The terrain played to Iran's advantage in light infantry, and its audacity caught the Iraqis completely by surprise. Iranian troops nearly seized a narrow causeway over which the major road between Basra and Baghdad traversed. If Iran cut this vital roadway, Basra and its one million inhabitants would have been severed from Baghdad's control.

Alarmed, the CIA rushed new imagery of these Iranian forces to Baghdad. The agency strongly advised the Iraqis to seal this breach before the Iranians could exploit their breakthrough. The Iraqis mustered superior armor and artillery and counterattacked in one of the largest and most savage battles of the war. Iraqi shells rained deadly nerve gas while electric power lines were diverted into the swamp, electrocuting many of the Iranian defenders. After two months of fighting, Iran held on to a few toeholds of mosquito-infested swamp islets, but more than twenty thousand Iranians died in their failed bid to cut the road.[42]

When full diplomatic relations were established in 1984, the CIA opened a full-scale station in Baghdad supervised by a station chief under the direct supervision of the operations directorate.[43] On paper the CIA station chief met formally on fourteen separate occasions with senior Iraqi officials over the next few years, but in reality it was much more a continuous ongoing relationship. The CIA relayed classified data obtained from Saudi and ELF-One AWACS on Iranian aircraft operations and passed the latest imagery of Iranian units directly to Baghdad, where the station chief was authorized to show a slightly altered version to the Iraqis. The Iraqi generals were free to study the imagery, taking notes and keeping drawings provided by CIA analysts. While the Iraqis would check the CIA's photographs with satellite imagery they received from the French too, nevertheless this presented the Iraqi generals with an unprecedented view into the lay of the Iranian military, as well as American intelligence capabilities.

Six

SHARON'S GRAND DESIGN

Modern Lebanon sprang from a touch of European colonialism and a dash of Middle Eastern haggling. After the First World War, the French carved out the country from the old Ottoman Empire and granted the rump state independence in 1943. However, they structured Lebanon's government into a Gordian knot. Maronite Christians, Sunnis, Shias, Druzes, and more than a dozen other confessions shared power in an arrangement that allocated every significant job in the government based upon the populace's religious affiliation as determined by a 1932 census—the last ever taken in the country. In this antediluvian text, the Christians made up the majority population, and thus were permanently allotted the powerful presidency and head of the armed forces. The next largest group, the Sunnis, were given the less powerful prime minister's slot, while the Shia received the weak speakership of the parliament. This arrangement stumbled along for the next three decades, and Lebanon prospered. The business acumen of the population transcended their political divisions. According to one tale, when a Lebanese schoolboy was asked by his teacher, "How much is two and two?" he replied, "Am I buying or selling?"[1]

Beneath this veneer of harmony, however, Lebanon was held together with chewing gum and baling wire. As the population demographics changed, the power-sharing arrangement reflected less and less the realities within the country. The establishment of Israel strained this delicate balance as two hundred thousand disenfranchised Palestinian refugees arrived in southern Lebanon. The Shia community of southern Lebanon, viewed as backward hicks by their Christian and Sunni countrymen, had been relegated to minor cabinet posts devoid of real power, but they were the fastest-growing sect within the country, soon making up a third of the population. The facade of unity finally shattered in the 1970s. Several thousand Palestine Liberation Organization (PLO) fighters led by the charismatic Palestinian nationalist Yasser Arafat arrived in Lebanon after being forcefully expelled from Jordan. In Lebanon, Arafat established a de facto state with a separate army and parallel government in the Palestinian refugee camps in West Beirut and southern Lebanon. They repeatedly launched attacks into northern Israel, with the poor Shia of south Lebanon bearing much of the brunt of the massive and sometimes indiscriminate Israeli reprisals. The Shia populace bitterly resented Arafat and the PLO, as did the ruling Maronite Christians, who viewed them as a threat to their hold on power.

The powder keg finally exploded in April 1976, following a failed assassination attempt by the PLO on Pierre Gemayel, the leader of the right-wing Christian Phalange, as he left church. Gemayel's brutish foot soldiers retaliated by ambushing a bus, killing twenty-seven Palestinian civilians. Lebanon soon split apart along confessional seams in an orgy of slaughters and reprisals. Syria moved troops into Lebanon as peacekeepers, with the scheming Syrian president Hafez al-Assad obtaining a mandate from the Arab League that enabled him to occupy two-thirds of the country. By the time Ronald Reagan took the oath of office, Lebanon was a country in name only. Perhaps one hundred thousand people had died in the six-year civil war. Warring factions divided the country: West Beirut and southern Lebanon were governed by the PLO, left-wing Sunni, and the Shia Amal Party; East Beirut was run by competing Christians; the hills surrounding the city were occupied by Christians and Druze; and the Syrian army controlled the north and west Lebanon with troops entrenched in West Beirut.

In July 1981, an especially bloody exchange between the PLO and Israel left more than five hundred dead and threatened to expand into a wider war with Syria. Secretary of Defense Caspar Weinberger feared this would erode Arab support for the newly announced CENTCOM, so Reagan dispatched the skilled American negotiator Philip Habib to broker a cease-fire. Habib, a Lebanese American who grew up in a Jewish neighborhood in Brooklyn, succeeded in getting both the PLO and Israel to agree to a cease-fire in Lebanon. Yet it remained an uneasy peace, and was not popular with many in the right-wing Likud government of Israeli prime minister Menachem Begin, especially his defense minister, Ariel Sharon.

In a 2002 statement to reporters, President George W. Bush famously described Ariel Sharon as "a man of peace," a description at odds with the Israeli leader's actions over fifty years.[2] In fact, Ariel Sharon was a warrior. He'd joined a paramilitary unit as a teenager, and he eventually rose to senior command, launching Israel's daring attack across to the west bank of the Suez Canal during the October 1973 war. At times ruthless, he earned the nickname "The Bulldozer" due to his girth and style. Like a hussar of an earlier era, Sharon showed a flare for both brilliance and recklessness.

Sharon and Begin longed for an opportunity to destroy the PLO. "Begin viewed Arafat as little more than Hitler," said retired senior DIA analyst Jeff White, who worked Lebanon for the chairman of the Joint Chiefs of Staff. Sharon unilaterally expanded the Lebanon cease-fire to include any attack against a Jew worldwide, arguing that the PLO and Beirut remained the nexus of all terrorism and so it all ultimately went back to their culpability.

Ariel Sharon formulated a plan to solve the Lebanese problem in one great sweep of Israeli armor. Since 1975, Israel had been developing a close military relationship with the Maronite Christians, providing them with arms and equipment. Sharon proposed a combined attack to destroy both the PLO and the Syrians. The vaunted Israeli Defense Forces would drive to Beirut, destroying Arafat's meager force and, along the way, smashing the Syrian army too. With these two troublemakers out of the way, Bashir Gemayel would assume the presidency and then recognize Israel. In one stroke, Lebanon would move from an Israeli liability to an asset.[3] In January 1982, Sharon secretly flew to Beirut to meet with Gemayel and his father, Pierre, to consummate the deal.

The Phalange leader embraced Sharon's scheme. The Israelis would conduct the major combat operations against the PLO and the Syrians, but the Christians would do the dirty work of cleaning the PLO remnants off the streets and out of the buildings of West Beirut, a mission Sharon was not eager for the casualty-averse Israeli army to undertake.

Both Begin and Sharon worked to garner U.S. support for their plan. Appreciating the Cold War myopia of the American superpower, they repeatedly stressed to Reagan and other senior officials the Soviet hand behind Syria and the PLO and the important role Israel could play in defeating these clients of Moscow. In February 1982, Israel provided Weinberger with an overview of the proposed operation, which called for occupation of almost half of Lebanon.

An Israeli invasion of Lebanon alarmed most of official Washington. The CIA feared it could trigger a Soviet intervention. Bing West at Defense argued that military action would not solve Israel's long-term problem. "Palestinian nationalism to say nothing of Arab nationalism or Islamic fundamentalism will not die with the PLO infrastructure," he wrote Weinberger. The defense secretary was even more strident, recommending to Reagan that the United States dissuade the Israelis by threatening to withhold further weapons sales.[4]

The professional diplomats at the State Department shared this view. "The primary effort should be directed toward deterring the Israeli action, but concurrently we must cut our losses by clearly dissociating the United States before the fact from any action Israel may take in Lebanon," wrote L. Paul Bremer, then a senior official in the secretary of state's office.[5]

But Bremer's boss, Alexander Haig, who'd graduated from senior general in Europe to secretary of state, did not agree. A staunch supporter of the Jewish state, he viewed the Arab-Israeli crisis in Cold War terms, pitting the American proxy against the Soviet-backed Arabs. Neither the historic roots of the conflict nor the sectarian milieu that fostered the Lebanese Civil War entered into Haig's calculations. Lebanon was a Cold War battleground, and he saw Israeli victory entirely in that light. Critics later accused Haig of privately giving the Israelis a green light for their attack. But Haig always denied the charge, and the documentary evidence supports his view. During a meeting with Israeli general Uri Sagi, Haig repeatedly cautioned that an unprovoked Israeli attack would have "grave" implications for U.S.-Israeli relations.[6] Nonetheless, Haig clearly favored a robust Israeli attack on the PLO, if based on a legitimate provocation.

Following one meeting between Sharon and Haig, the American secretary of state enthusiastically pointed to a map of Lebanon and said, "You see, if they have to go in, their plan would be to link up the group here in the south with the Christians up here."

The normally reticent diplomat Morris Draper blurted out, "For Christ's sake, Mr. Secretary, there's a million and a half Muslims between them, and at least a million of them are Shia!" This fact came as a surprise to Al Haig.[7]

Sharon got his casus belli on June 4, 1982, when the Israeli ambassador in London was shot and seriously wounded. The fact that the culprits were from Abu Nidal's splinter organization and bitterly opposed to Arafat made no difference. Two days later, on Sunday morning, June 6, Israeli troops poured into Lebanon in three giant columns swiftly moving north.

Israeli officials reassured the United States that they had no intention of advancing to Beirut or starting a war with Syria. Prime Minister Begin personally assured President Reagan that his army would not move more than forty kilometers into Lebanon—just far enough to drive the PLO away from rocket range of northern Israel. Israel's ambassador told Weinberger a similar story.[8] On June 9, after meeting with Begin, Philip Habib flew to Damascus to assure President al-Assad that Israel had no interest in a war with Syria. But the Israelis' words failed to match their army's actions. While Habib was still talking with al-Assad, Sharon ordered an attack on Syrian air-to-air missile sites in the Bekaa Valley. The unprepared and outclassed Syrian air force rose to challenge the Israeli jets. In a massive daylong dogfight the Jewish pilots decimated the Syrians, knocking eighty-two jets out of the sky without a single loss of their own. A dismayed Habib cabled back to Haig, "I am astounded and dismayed by what happened today. The prime minister of Israel really sent me off on a wild goose chase."[9]

The Soviet premier sent Reagan a message via the hotline between Washington and Moscow warning that the Israeli attack created an "extremely dangerous situation." He warned that it risked a wider war between the superpowers. Alarmed, Reagan called for a cease-fire to take effect the next day at six a.m. local (Lebanese) time. The president then sent a warning to the Israeli prime minister: "Menachem, Israel's refusal to agree to this cease-fire would aggravate what is already a great threat to world peace and place a permanent stain on a relationship I truly treasure. Sincerely, Ron."[10]

Begin accepted the American cease-fire in name, but he refused to halt the army's advance northward, calling it a "rolling" cease-fire. "Show us in the president's message where it says 'in place'?" Begin demanded of Habib following the latter's arrival in Tel Aviv from Damascus, having secured al-Assad's backing for the cease-fire.

"What are you talking about?!" an incredulous Phil Habib asked the prime minister during a tense meeting. "A cease-fire is a cease-fire in place!"[11]

Begin finally agreed to the cease-fire, but not before Sharon drove one column into Syrian-controlled Lebanon, where the forces manhandled an armor division that had been moved to try to block the Israeli advance. In just eight days, the Israelis linked up with Gemayel's forces, trapping in West Beirut not only the PLO, but Syrian military personnel. The Israelis imposed a blockade and began shelling the PLO-controlled West Beirut in an intense bombardment that on one day rained a thousand hundred-pound artillery shells down on a densely packed area of only six square miles.

The wanton carnage and the Israeli deception about the true scope of their war aims raised the ire of President Reagan. CIA Director William Casey recommended cutting off intelligence support to Israel, which Weinberger supported. Richard Armitage suggested the United States should consider suspending "normal" diplomatic relations and push for a Security Council resolution condemning the Israeli attack. When Begin came to Washington on June 21, the president chastised the prime minister for Israel's actions.

Haig harbored no such desire to rein in the Israelis. With Yasser Arafat cornered, he shared Sharon's impulse to kill the quarry. "By God," said a furious Al Haig after Reagan's dressing-down of the Israeli prime minister, "I'm going to tell Begin to go into Be-rut and finish the job."[12] Haig countered that the United States needed to support Israel, force the Syrians out, and help Gemayel form a new government in Lebanon. The secretary advocated deploying a large peacekeeping force of perhaps fourteen thousand men to help prop up the new Phalange government.[13] "The quick Israeli victory posed an opportunity to strengthen our position," he wrote to Reagan.

Weinberger and General John Vessey steadfastly opposed sending any American peacekeepers into the boiling cauldron of Lebanon. "Any introduction of U.S. forces without an agreement would put U.S. lives at risk in a possible continuous low-level warfare from every extremist faction in the area." Both feared it could lead to greater Iranian or Syrian involvement.

The haughty secretary of state chafed at both the Defense Department's views and their meddling in Lebanon policy. His personal relationships quickly deteriorated within the administration, including with the White House staff. On June 25, the thin-skinned Al Haig resigned, citing differences on foreign policy. While Reagan actually leaned toward Haig's views at the time, he was not sorry to see the imperious general go. Writing in his diary, Reagan noted, "Actually the only disagreement was over whether I made policy or the secretary of state did."[14]

The president replaced Haig with a former combat marine and

Republican stalwart, George P. Shultz. The new secretary of state shared many of Haig's views on the Middle East, but had a less prickly persona. Smart, serious, and composed, he was slow to anger, but when he did get angry, his eyes narrowed conspicuously as his voice grew stern. In bureaucratic infighting, Shultz proved stubborn, every bit the equal of the mule Caspar Weinberger, and the two men were soon at loggerheads on a host of policy questions, including Lebanon.

Habib brokered an agreement to evacuate the PLO. Arafat and his five thousand PLO fighters left for Tunisia, embarked on Western ships, as U.S. Marines and French and Italian peacekeepers deployed around Beirut to provide a buffer between the antagonists until the PLO's departure. It was not an easy sell to the Israelis, requiring another threatening communiqué from Reagan to Begin to bring it about: "There must be an end to the unnecessary bloodshed particularly among innocent civilians. I insist upon a cease-fire now and until the PLO have left Beirut. The relationship between our two nations is at stake."[15]

Neither Weinberger nor Vessey supported the Habib plan. "By putting U.S. forces between the PLO and the Israelis we might as well be pouring burning gasoline on an already difficult situation rather than putting oil on troubled waters," General Vessey wrote to the defense secretary.

With Arafat gone, the peacekeeping troops were withdrawn, but the situation around Beirut remained tense. Sharon champed at the bit to get into West Beirut, and he remained convinced that many PLO fighters had stayed behind in the city and in the Palestinian refugee camps south of Beirut. While Arafat had escaped his noose, Sharon's grand design to remake Lebanon appeared within reach. Only American intransigence prevented him from seeing it to completion.

Despite the president's anger at Begin, to bring stability back to Lebanon, the Reagan administration plan largely parroted Sharon's scheme. Washington would prop up the Lebanese government by strengthening its army, traditionally the least sectarian organization within the country. As the Lebanese military capacity increased, it would gradually expand its control outside of Beirut. And the man the United States backed as the new Lebanese president was none other than Bashir Gemayel.

Although he espoused national unity and an end to the civil war, Gemayel operated more as Tony Soprano than as Abraham Lincoln. Gemayel ordered the killing of his chief Christian rival, Tony Frangieh. His Phalange militia had the reputation as the executor of some of the worst atrocities of the civil war. "Bashir, when he wasn't murdering people, was a likable man," recalled American ambassador to Lebanon Robert Dillon. "He had great boyish charm."[16]

"A murderous thug" is how one retired CIA officer who worked Lebanon during the early 1980s described the Lebanese president. Nevertheless, Reagan threw his support behind him.

This decision immediately alienated many Lebanese Shia. Up to this point, American diplomats had a good rapport with this growing population in Lebanon. An experienced Middle East hand, Nathaniel Howell recalled traveling throughout their squalid neighborhoods, listening to their concerns and offering American goodwill. His actions typify those of American diplomats even during the dark days of the civil war. But the Israeli invasion severely strained these ties, and the bargain with the Phalange leader Gemayel ended them.

At four p.m. on Tuesday, September 14, 1982, Bashir Gemayel arrived at the Phalange headquarters in East Beirut to give a speech to his followers. Looking on was a twenty-six-year-old Maronite Lebanese, Habib Shartouni, a member of the Syrian Socialist Nationalist Party. Motivated by President al-Assad's desire for revenge against Israel, Shartouni waited until he believed the Phalange leader had arrived at the podium, then went to a nearby rooftop and pressed a button, remotely detonating a powerful bomb he had previously planted in his sister's apartment directly above the meeting room.[17] Gemayel died in a flash of cordite and crumbling concrete, along with twenty-six other senior Phalange members.

Sharon now had his excuse. The Israeli army occupied West Beirut. Sharon met with Phalange commanders atop a five-story building that served as an Israeli forward command post located a few hundred meters from the Palestinian refugee camp of Shatila.[18] They agreed for the Phalange fighters to move into that camp as well as another nearby Palestinian camp, Sabra, in order to root out the Palestinian fighters Sharon thought remained. Over the next two days, under the apathetic eyes of the Israeli military, the Phalange fighters exacted revenge. Rather than eradicating PLO soldiers, it was a slaughter of the innocents. The Phalange methodically moved through the two camps executing between eight hundred and two thousand civilians—elderly, women, and children—in one of the worst acts of terrorism committed in the modern Middle East.[19] The resulting international outcry led to the dismissal of Ariel Sharon.

Shocked by the massacre, on September 29, Reagan sent the marines back into Beirut as part of a force of British, French, and Italian peacekeepers. Their mission was a nebulous tasking called "presence." The State Department's director of political-military affairs, Jonathan Howe, best defined this as "to support the government of Lebanon and the Lebanese armed forces by their presence. That presence provides the Lebanese government clear evidence of international concern for Lebanon and an element of needed stability and confidence which reinforces its pursuit of national recognition."[20] Overall, the American plan remained the same. The marines would provide the Lebanese government with reassurance and the breathing space needed to rebuild its army, which would allow it to gradually reassert its control over the entire country. The United States now threw its support for Lebanese president behind Bashir's younger brother, Amin Gemayel, a man who lacked the brains and gravitas of his older sibling.[21]

The U.S. Marines undertook their vague presence mission with their customary vigor. Based around the airport, they conducted patrols to maintain visibility among the Lebanese population. Prudent defensive precautions such as entrenchments, earthen berms, and antivehicle ditches were openly discouraged by senior generals and admirals as they would isolate and reduce the marines' visibility. For the first six months, the marines got along reasonably well with all the warring factions, including the Shia populace around the airport, who provided a number of tips about impending threats to the Americans.

The foundation for the American plan to save Lebanon rested on a canard. Despite its reputation as an organization inclusive to all the country's faiths, the Lebanese army suffered the same factional malaise that plagued the entire country. The rank and file retained more loyalty to their respective religious camps than to the national army. The officer corps was dominated by Maronite Christians. Amin Gemayel's actions only compounded the divides. He used the armed forces' intelligence service to focus on Muslim opponents and formed an army special force to attack his opponents. He formed a new army brigade that comprised only members of his own Phalange militia. In December 1982, he appointed Ibrahim Tannous as the army's senior general. While the newly arrived marines viewed Tannous as nonpartisan, he had a long history of involvement with the Phalange Party and had been Bashir Gemayel's chief military adviser. While Tannous did try to build a multiconfessional force, his pro-Israeli sentiment alienated many factions in the country. As one retired CIA officer stationed in Lebanon during the time observed, "We went out of our way to distinguish between the government of Lebanon and the Christians/Phalange, but it was a distinction without a difference, certainly as far as the Muslims were concerned."[22]

As the United States strengthened the Lebanese army, it chipped away at the perception of American neutrality. When the Lebanese army decided to strike at Shia and Druze militias as part of their inkblot expansion of control around Beirut, its artillery supported the attack from positions inside the U.S. Marine Corps perimeter at the airport. Marines manning joint checkpoints with Lebanese soldiers immediately found themselves the targets of those resisting Gemayel.[23] In a press conference, their powerful leader, Walid Jumblatt, said as much: "The mere fact that they [the marines] are providing the Lebanese factional army with logistical support, expertise, and training is enough to consider them enemies."[24]

Secretary Shultz's peace initiative compounded this neutrality gap. He shuttled among Israel, Syria, and Lebanon trying to reach an agreement to get both Israel and Syria to withdraw their forces and to get Lebanon to accept peace with the Jewish state. But the senior American diplomat never broadened his talks to include national reconciliation and excluded major sectional factions, especially the Shia and Druze. He managed to get Gemayel to agree to a largely Israeli-dictated peace settlement on May 17, 1983. However, it quickly foundered when the Syrians refused to withdraw their forces, which was a precondition for the Israeli pullout.[25] News of the secret deal between Israel and the Lebanese government confirmed the perception in the squalid refugee camps and back alleys of Beirut that the Lebanese government was little more than a tool for the Christians and Israelis. As Weinberger noted, "If the LAF [Lebanese armed forces] is seen to be operating . . . as an instrument of the Maronite Christian Faction no amount of U.S. support can develop the consensus needed for a sovereign nation."[26]

In the spring of 1983, the newly arrived marine commander at the airport, Colonel Timothy Geraghty, found himself in the middle of his government's dichotomous policy. A decorated Vietnam veteran with a characteristic marine "high and tight" haircut and ramrod bearing, he understood the danger his troops faced in Lebanon. Geraghty's mission remained presence and visibility, while at the same time providing support to the Lebanese armed forces. Although his forces were arrayed in static positions in the flat lowland around the airport, erecting berms and ditches was seen as incompatible with his peacekeeping mission. The increasing support by the Americans for the Lebanese army made marines the obvious target of those opposing Amin Gemayel.[27] In retrospect, as Geraghty observed, "Conducting a comprehensive training program for the Lebanese armed forces while simultaneously participating in a peacekeeping mission is inherently contradictory."[28]

Nevertheless, the marines clung to the illusion of nonalignment. "Our commitment here is really a peacekeeping role," Geraghty told a marine corps historian in May 1983. "It is highly political with the diplomatic side and the political side overshadowing the tactical side." He eschewed using force and continued to have his men carry unloaded rifles, worried more about accidental discharges than the Druze or Shia. This was especially true after one freakish accident when a marine's rifle inadvertently discharged and the bullet struck the legs of two Lebanese soldiers jogging together along the perimeter road around the airport.[29]

As the United States became associated with one faction of the civil war, shells increasingly fell around the airport. The marines maintained restraint, but they no longer jogged; instead, the nation's premier warriors dug more bunkers and filled more sandbags, adopting a molelike existence, not venturing out unless in extremis.[30]

Despite the deteriorating situation, Secretary Shultz continued to advocate for the marines to stay in Lebanon. "They are an important deterrent, a symbol of the international backing behind the legitimate government of Lebanon," said Shultz before the House Committee on Foreign Affairs. "To remove the marines would put both the government and what we are trying to achieve in jeopardy."[31]

In response to Geraghty's plight, the Joint Chiefs did nothing. No one in Washington thought to change the restrictive rules of engagement that governed Geraghty's actions, and during months of discussions in the Tank about arming the Lebanese army, the impact of this policy on the safety of the marines at the airport rarely came up for discussion. The steady stream of generals and Pentagon civilians who visited Geraghty's headquarters, just off the main road to the airport terminal, recognized the marines' vulnerability, but remained committed to the existing course. The Pentagon briefly considered sending in another thousand-man marine battalion, which would have allowed the marines to expand their perimeter, giving them some breathing room, but neither Weinberger nor Vessey wanted to expand the ground commitment.[32] While the Joint Chiefs, including the new marine corps commandant, P. X. Kelley, recommended avoiding becoming involved in the growing intramural fighting, they also offered no change in the marine peacekeeping mission or its defense posture.[33]

But Geraghty did not help his position. On one occasion, when Vessey was out of town, acting chairman Admiral James Watkins personally called Geraghty asking for his assessment. "Was there anything he would like to do differently or anything else he needed? Did he need a change in mission?" Geraghty answered no to each inquiry from Watkins.[34]

In late July of 1983, Deputy National Security Adviser Robert "Bud" McFarlane arrived in Beirut as the new presidential envoy, replacing Philip Habib. The forty-six-year-old Naval Academy graduate and retired marine corps lieutenant colonel had a promising career as an artillery officer, with two tours in Vietnam before becoming the first marine White House Fellow and then military assistant to Henry Kissinger during the heady days of the China opening. Like many other military officers, once exposed to the White House and the exhilaration of Washington, he found it hard to go back to the dull chores of the barracks.

McFarlane soon fleeted up to be Reagan's third national security adviser in as many years. Yet he did not exude confidence to his contemporaries. He spoke with a ponderous, monotone voice. McFarlane's melancholy demeanor reinforced this opinion. Although cordial, he appeared tormented and gripped by self-doubt. The two administration potentates—Weinberger and Shultz—questioned the depth of his foreign policy pedigree. "McFarlane is a man of evident limitations," summed up the dismissive defense secretary.[35]

The Cold War guided much of McFarlane's understanding of the conflict. Settling in at the American ambassador's residence in East Beirut, he saw the Syrian hand, and by extension the Soviet Union's, behind much of the opposition to the Lebanese government. The fact that Syria's support for the Druze had more to do with local power politics, and not any wider agenda by Moscow, did not affect his calculations. McFarlane immediately wanted to expand the American military mission to prop up the fledgling Lebanese army. He called for another battalion in order to expand the marines' control into the strategic hills west of the airport and proposed embedding American advisers into the Lebanese army.[36]

Geraghty opposed this overt shift from neutrality to combatant. When sophisticated army radar arrived to help the marines to detect incoming shells, McFarlane wanted these to support the Lebanese army. Both Geraghty and his senior commander, Vice Admiral Edward Martin, expressed serious reservations about this mission creep. Martin, an experienced combat pilot who'd spent six years as a prisoner in North Vietnam, replied with a prescient message: "The finely balanced position of neutrality with regard to the various factions is in jeopardy, and should one of the factions believe that this info is assisting a rival in targeting their weapons, the U.S. Multinational Force will become a target for their frustrations."[37]

As Martin predicted, as U.S. support increased for the Lebanese army against the Druze and Shia, marine casualties mounted. In just a little more than a month, from August 4 to September 7, 1983, four marines died and twenty-eight were wounded, more than three times the casualties suffered during the entire previous ten months of the marines' deployment to Lebanon.[38]

The situation came to a head in September 1983. With casualties mounting, the Israelis unilaterally pulled their tanks out of the Chouf Mountains to a more defensible line to the south. This created a power vacuum in the strategic hills overlooking Beirut. Militias of all stripes—Christian, Druze, and Shia—moved into the void. A three-thousand-man force of Gemayel's Phalange won the footrace, only to be clobbered by Walid Jumblatt's Druze forces, backed by Syrian artillery. General Tannous ordered the Lebanese army into the fray to reassert Lebanese government control and also to protect the routed Phalange.[39] He committed his best unit, the 8th Brigade, a multiconfessional unit (although its officers were majority Christian) trained by American special forces and under the command of an indecisive and panicky Francophile general named Michel Aoun. Fighting raged around the strategic hamlet of Suq al-Gharb. Before the war, this had been a pleasant vacation spot, nestled in pine trees with bucolic vistas of the city and harbor below. Now it was a strategic locale, and whoever controlled it threatened Christian East Beirut.

Increasingly hysterical reports from Aoun alarmed both McFarlane and his senior military adviser, a cool, slow-talking Tennessean, Brigadier General Carl Stiner of the special forces, who had been sent by the chairman as his representative to the Lebanese army. McFarlane sent a cable back to the White House urging a prompt American military response and expanding the marines' mission to combat. There are "enormous strategic stakes for the U.S. and the western world in the eastern Mediterranean . . . that would certainly justify the possible use of military power," wrote McFarlane.

The next night, Druze forces hit the 8th Brigade from the south and east. Tannous turned to Stiner for help. The special forces general liked the Lebanese general.[40] Stiner approached McFarlane about providing military support for Aoun's hard-pressed brigade.

On Sunday morning, from the library of the U.S. ambassador's residence, McFarlane wrote a cable that has become famous in the chronicles of American foreign policy. It is known as "the sky is falling" memo: "This is an action message. A second attack against the same Lebanese Armed Forces unit is expected this evening. Ammunition and morale are low and raise the serious possibility that the enemy brigade, which enjoys greater strength and unlimited fire support and resupply, will break through and penetrate the Beirut perimeter." McFarlane continued in dramatic fashion: "Tonight we could be in enemy lines."

McFarlane laid the blame on Syrian and now Iranian mischief. He couched the issue as an epic struggle of the Cold War. If Suq al-Gharb fell, then Lebanon would succumb to the Soviet client in Damascus. The United States needed to commit its airpower immediately or risk losing a major battle against the communists. As veteran CBS News Pentagon correspondent David Martin astutely noted in his 1988 book on the Reagan administration and terrorism: "It was a message perfectly tuned to the ear of a President who boasted that not one inch of territory had been lost to the communists on his watch."[41]

Weinberger remained dubious of McFarlane and his dire predictions. After reading the cable, he called down to the National Military Command Center (NMCC) to get his own intelligence update. The brigadier general on watch told the secretary that DIA's own assessment did not "read it as badly as McFarlane." The 8th Brigade had actually repulsed the attack.[42]

At six p.m., senior officials gathered in the White House Situation Room to discuss what to do about the remote town of Suq al-Gharb, upon which

American prestige now rested. With Shultz backing McFarlane's view and at loggerheads with Weinberger, the two men decided on a compromise. They shifted the entire decision of using force down to Colonel Geraghty. They would leave it up to the marine commander to decide if they should support the Lebanese army. Later that evening, President Reagan signed an order to that effect: "The dominant terrain in the vicinity of Suq al Gharb is vital to the safety of U.S. personnel. As a consequence, if the U.S. ground commander determines it is in danger of falling as a result of attack involving non-Lebanese forces and if requested by host government, appropriate U.S. military assistance is authorized."[43]

Initially, Geraghty resisted McFarlane's plan. The colonel knew that his marines would pay the price for America directly intervening at Suq al-Gharb. As tempers flared, the hard-nosed marine exchanged heated words with Stiner over the wisdom of a direct American involvement in the war. When Stiner proposed embedding a small team of marines with the 8th Brigade to direct American air and naval fire, Geraghty fired back: "I firmly believe that this is in direct violation of my mission."[44] During one of these passionate exchanges with Stiner, Geraghty yelled, "General, don't you realize we'll pay the price down here? We'll get slaughtered!"[45]

Amid this crisis, Geraghty received a phone call from Washington. He was on his way to a meeting with General Tannous when his staff called him back to headquarters. Someone using an unknown call sign—Silver Screen Six—wanted to speak to the marine. On the other end of the line was Ronald Reagan.

"Tell the marines that the entire nation is proud of you and the outstanding job you are doing against difficult odds," the president said in his usual upbeat manner.

Geraghty, who liked the Republican president, thanked Reagan and ended the call with the U.S. Marines' motto: "Semper fi, Mr. President."[46]

While it was a typically kind gesture by Reagan, he might have better served the marines had he bothered to correct his administration's feeble, drifting Lebanon policy. While the United States rushed spare parts and ammunition to support the 8th Brigade's fight in the hills around Beirut, the administration continued to deny active involvement in the civil war. Uncertain about using force, Reagan had passed the buck to a hard-pressed colonel to decide the wisdom of escalation.

On September 19, a massive artillery bombardment hit Suq al-Gharb and Phalange militia targets around Beirut. Druze infantry and armor then struck the venerable 8th Brigade, with some Palestinians joining in the fighting for good measure. With General Tannous pleading for help and signals intelligence detecting Syrian and Iranian support for the attackers, Geraghty finally relented to McFarlane and Stiner. Four U.S. warships lobbed about three hundred seventy-pound explosive shells down on the Druze artillery and a column of tanks. This firepower blunted the attack.

"The firing we did in support of the Lebanese army up at Suq al-Gharb clearly changed our role in my opinion," Geraghty said. "That moved us across the neutrality line." The toll to Geraghty's marines for straying across the line and becoming embroiled in the civil war would be much higher than anyone had predicted.[47]

Seven

A SPECTACULAR
ACTION

I n the dark hours of a summer day in 1982, a four-engine Iran Air 707 landed in Damascus. About two dozen Revolutionary Guards walked down the metal stairs and were greeted by the Iranian ambassador, Hojjat ol-Eslam Ali Akbar Mohtashemi. Operating on specific instructions from Iran's foreign ministry, Mohtashemi spirited the guardsmen across the border into Lebanon, where they established a headquarters in some vacant houses and a hotel just outside of the magnificent Roman ruins at Baalbek, home to three of the largest surviving temples to Jupiter, Venus, and Bacchus.

The approval for this clandestine effort had been worked out during an earlier meeting between senior officials in Damascus. The Iranian delegation included not only Mohtashemi but the minister of defense and the head of the Revolutionary Guard, Mohsen Rezai. The twenty-eight-year-old guard commander was a pragmatic zealot. An economics student and doctoral candidate, he had never attended school in the West. He was ruthless and powerful, a trusted servant for both Khomeini and his successor, Ayatollah Khamenei. It was Rezai who transformed the Revolutionary Guard from a ragtag military into a sword for the Islamic Republic.[1]

The meeting came at a critical juncture in Iran's war with Iraq. Ayatollah Khomeini had just made the fateful decision to invade Iraq and depose

Saddam Hussein. In carrying forward the war to spread his religious revolution, the Israeli invasion afforded a new opportunity to spread his message among a sympatric Shia populace and to strike directly at the hated Jewish occupier of Jerusalem.

Initially, Syrian president Hafez al-Assad refused to allow many Revolutionary Guardsmen to transit his country. Khomeini's revolution held little appeal to the secularist-socialist despot. After the outbreak of the Iran-Iraq War, al-Assad did permit some Iranian military into Damascus in order to make his hated Baathist rival Saddam Hussein's life uncomfortable with the possibility of an Iranian military threat on Iraq's western border. But when Sharon instigated the fight with the Syrian army during Israel's invasion of Lebanon, a bitter and revengeful al-Assad decided to open the floodgates for Khomeini's bearded foot soldiers to strike back at Sharon.

These two dozen men became the vanguard of eight hundred Iranian Revolutionary Guards sent to this base in the fertile eastern Lebanese valley.[2] Under the protective umbrella of the Syrian army, they soon moved into more permanent billeting at Baalbek, taking over a Lebanese army base, the Sheik Abdullah Barracks. With a mission not unlike that of the American Green Berets, they came bearing military, political, and humanitarian assistance to the downtrodden Lebanese Shia, all the while spreading Iran's revolutionary message in the Levant. Within three years, this Iranian delegation united several disparate Shia fighters into the Islamic Republic's biggest foreign policy success: Hezbollah, or the Party of God. Over the next coming years, these fighters morphed from a small guerrilla band into a major political party in Lebanon, one whose military wing eclipsed that of the Lebanese army. They staved off the region's most powerful military—Israel—in two wars, and in one precise bombing inflicted the largest tactical defeat on the U.S. military since the Korean War.

As it did many young Shia boys growing up in southern Beirut, the Lebanese Civil War shaped Sayeed Ali's future occupation.[3] The son of a poor father who worked at the airport for an Eastern European airline, he was only seven when the war began. As a young teenager, Sayeed Ali longed to fight as he and his friends played army with real AK-47 assault rifles. He wanted the adventure of combat as he saw older kids joining the Amal militia commanded by a secularist named Nabih Berri. He too joined Amal, playing trumpet in their marching band until he was old enough to exchange his horn for a rifle. He and his friends would gather together, but rather than kicking a football around the sandlot, they drove to the daily firefight and took potshots at either the Phalange or the Palestinians. Sayeed Ali then worked as a bodyguard for the prominent cleric Sheik Mohammad Mehdi Shamseddine. Shamseddine was moderate by Lebanese Civil War standards. While he shared al-Sadr's views of Israel, he preached civil disobedience against the Israelis, as well as Christian-Muslim reconciliation. "There is no Lebanon without its Christians, and there is no Lebanon without its Muslims," he once said.

An Iranian-born Lebanese cleric, Musa al-Sadr influenced his political environment. He pressed for increased Shia power in Lebanon as well as waging war on Israel to free the occupied lands. "Israel is an utter evil" was a frequent al-Sadr slogan.[4] The cleric's disappearance in 1978 during a trip to Libya galvanized large swaths of the Shia population into backing his Amal movement.

The Shia communities of Iran and Lebanon had a long, entwined history, with ties going back some four hundred years. Families intermarried. Lebanese imams attended the same seminaries in Qom or Najaf. The Iranian Revolution excited many Lebanese Shia. Khomeini provided a beacon, a new way forward for the downtrodden masses in southern Lebanon. A few Iranians had fought in Lebanon during the civil war, most prominently Mostafa Chamran, one of the founders of the Revolutionary Guard. A steady trickle of religiously motivated Iranians attended the mosques in Beirut to proselytize, trying to plant the seeds of Khomeini's revolution. "There were always Iranians around, praying in the mosques and offering support to us," Sayeed Ali recalled.

In Sharon's zeal to destroy the PLO, he remained wholly ignorant of the Lebanese Shia population that stood in his army's path. Happy to be rid of the PLO, many Shia greeted the Israeli soldiers warmly, showering them with fistfuls of perfumed rice and flowers. This hospitality quickly changed, however. The Israeli army's liberal use of firepower and its frequent tactic of recon by fire in which tanks fired at anything that might remotely be a threat—a parked car or a house that overlooked its positions—killed many civilians. Operating in an alien culture, the ill-prepared Israelis adopted a heavy hand in their occupation, angering many Shia and opening the door even wider for Iran's message of resistance.[5] Had Sharon and Begin not blundered into

invading Lebanon, "I don't know whether something called Hezbollah would
have been born. I doubt it," said the organization's secretary general, Hassan
Nasrallah.[6]

As more Revolutionary Guardsmen arrived, they began making their
way into the Shia slums of southern Beirut. They served as both social welfare agents and military advisers. They funded schools and organized basic
services such as trash collection and sewage systems. The Iranians attended
local mosques and after Friday prayers gave speeches extolling Ayatollah
Khomeini and the natural ties between the Shia of Iran and Lebanon. The
Iranian agents repeatedly linked the Israeli transgressions with Israel's chief
benefactor, the United States, arguing that the two worked in consort against
both Muslims and the Iranian Revolution.

Many of the future leaders of the Iranian military earned their spurs as
part of the initial vanguard of guardsmen in Lebanon. This included the
future Iranian defense minister, Ahmad Vahidi, who served as a military
adviser and later formed an intelligence unit that eventually morphed into
the Revolutionary Guard's elite clandestine paramilitary special forces unit,
the Quds Force.

Iran established a formal chain of command for its operatives in Lebanon.
Orders were relayed from the Iranian foreign minister in Tehran to the
embassy in Syria, where Ambassador Mohtashemi would relay it by radio or
courier to the Revolutionary Guards in the Bekaa. Iranian cargo jets regularly landed at the Damascus airport, off-loading pallets of arms and munitions that were trucked to Lebanon.

Iran's embassy in Lebanon served as another link in the guards' opera-
tions. One of the chargés d'affaires, Kamal Majid, had been one of the stu-
dent instigators who took over the U.S. embassy in 1979. A lifelong
Revolutionary Guard officer, he later served as the Iranian ambassador to
Sudan, where he oversaw a similar paramilitary effort designed to expand
Iran's influence along the Red Sea.[7] The military attaché, Colonel Ahmad
Motevaselian, gave tactical direction to the early guard operations in Beirut.
The Tehran native operated under diplomatic cover and served as a key con-
duit between the Shia community in West Beirut and the Revolutionary
Guard at Baalbek. A popular, charismatic commander, he played an impor-
tant role in cultivating disenchanted Lebanese Amal fighters.

The Israeli invasion divided the main Shia Amal militia, headed by

Nabih Berri. Members disagreed sharply over how much they should oppose or cooperate with the Israelis as well as over the role of Iran in the Shia organization. Berri rejected the Iranian overtures. He continued to see his movement as Lebanese and would not countenance taking directives from Tehran. But many of the young fighters embraced a more politically active Islam. Even if Israel had not invaded, these young devotees of Khomeini would likely have broken away from Berri, but Israel's actions galvanized those calling for jihad and advocating the establishment of an Islamic state in Lebanon.[8] The Revolutionary Guard helped sow this discontent by criticizing Amal's military prowess and offering both training and equipment to improve Shia fighting abilities.[9]

These emerging cracks finally split Amal apart during a tense meeting one evening at Shamseddine's house south of the airport. Nabih Berri had participated in an American-led effort to end the Israeli siege of West Beirut. He justified this decision as an effort to spare further injury to the Shia population that found itself caught in the crossfire between the Israelis and the PLO. When Berri arrived at Shamseddine's home, a heated argument ensued over the future of the Amal movement. Young hotheads accused Berri of compromising the Shia cause by striking a bargain with the American and Israeli foe. At the end of the night, many young fighters walked away from Berri's leadership. This included Sayeed Ali, who had been guarding Shamseddine's house.

Disenchanted, Sayeed Ali moved back into his parents' house in south Beirut and idled away in search of excitement. A friend of his, Mohammed Khodor, whose brother drove for a rising young cleric named Hassan Nasrallah, invited him over to his house along with about thirty other neighborhood friends. The Iranians had assigned Khodor to recruit and build a cell in his neighborhood. He told them about the Iranian plans and how they were going to spearhead the resistance against the Israeli occupiers. He explained Imam Khomeini's teachings and stressed both the importance of Islam in one's life and resistance to the beguiling Great Satan. While some rejected his pitch, the majority liked what they heard. This included Sayeed Ali. "It sounded interesting, and I was young and dumb," he said later.

By 1984, American intelligence estimated that eight hundred Iranian guardsmen operated in Lebanon. Despite the numbers, Iran remained cautious about having the Revolutionary Guard engage in actually fighting, leaving that chore to their Lebanese allies. Instead, they brought Shia fighters to their camps in the Bekaa Valley, where the Revolutionary Guard ran an organized boot camp at which they supervised the training curriculum. While Sheik Abdullah Barracks served as Iran's headquarters, they established three other military training camps. There Lebanese were taught the basic skills of marksmanship and explosives. In subsequent courses, the soldiers received more sophisticated training on how to destroy enemy tanks.

The Revolutionary Guard displayed considerable flexibility to train the new recruits. With many of the recruits young students, the Iranians held the classes during breaks in the school schedule, and the Revolutionary Guard tried to accommodate by holding classes in Beirut for those who did not have enough time between classes to travel all the way to the Bekaa. Sayeed Ali attended a technical school where he was studying the unlikely discipline of interior decorating. He attended one of the camps about an hour away from Baalbek during his summer break.

Political and religious lessons broke up the martial regime. Through Arabic translators, Iranian speakers extolled Khomeini or lectured on religious subjects. Hassan Nasrallah frequently came as a guest lecturer, giving rousing talks touting the righteousness of their struggle. Sayeed Ali became friends with Nasrallah and went to his house frequently. "He was very charismatic and good at telling jokes; he was always smiling and laughing," Sayeed Ali recalled.

In addition to Sayeed Ali, Iran recruited another more important fallen Nabih Berri supporter, a Lebanese chemistry teacher turned revolutionary named Hussein al-Musawi. After the cantankerous meeting at Shamseddine's home, al-Musawi had formed his own breakaway group called Islamic Amal. Young and idealistic like Sayeed Ali, al-Musawi was an ardent supporter of the Ayatollah Khomeini, publicly proclaiming, "We are the children of Iran." After breaking with Berri, al-Musawi fled to his village in the Bekaa Valley to establish his coterie. According to retired CIA officer Robert Baer, al-Musawi spearheaded the takeover of the Sheik Abdullah Barracks, inviting the guards to use it as their base.[10]

Acceptance of Iran in Lebanon received a boost when the prominent cleric Ayatollah Sheik Sayed Muhammad Hussein Fadlallah backed the Revolutionary Guard's mission. A scholar of considerable renown and a prolific writer on Islam, he settled in Beirut's southern suburbs, where he brought together under his control a number of humanitarian organizations that provided basic services to the Shia slums. His power increased when the Iraqi government expelled dozens of Lebanese theology students in a crackdown on Shia radicalism. Many of these flocked to Fadlallah and served as his core supporters.[11]

Fadlallah welcomed the Iranian Revolution and openly endorsed Ayatollah Khomeini's Shia activism. "It empowered the Shia and gave strength to them," he said. After the Israeli invasion, Fadlallah was a principal motivator for the Shia resistance, and his rhetorical jabs at the U.S. government frequently carried the same vitriol as Khomeini's.

After Israel's invasion, an Iranian delegation came to Fadlallah's compound in south Beirut to meet with the ayatollah. The Iranians wanted him to lead their Lebanese operations. Many of Iran's early supporters prayed in his mosque and had been inspired by him.[12] But Sheik Fadlallah refused. His religious training stemmed from Najaf, not Qom. While he embraced Khomeini's view of political Islam, he had no intention of being subservient to Iran. They were Arabs, not Persians, and the Lebanese struggle should be run by Lebanese, he believed.[13]

Sheik Fadlallah's intransigence in opposing Iranian leadership of the Shia resistance caused considerable tension with the Revolutionary Guard. He carried too much gravitas to purge, so the Iranians maintained an uneasy association with him. But American intelligence failed to notice these important distinctions and divides. For years cables from the embassy in Beirut continued to refer to Fadlallah as "Hezbollah's spiritual adviser," a characterization that both Hezbollah and Fadlallah emphatically denied.[14]

The Iranian-backed resistance to Israel and the United States began spastically. Factions launched uncoordinated and feeble attacks against the Israeli army around Beirut and in south Lebanon. "We fired a lot of ammunition and many men were killed or wounded without achieving very much," Sayeed Ali remarked about the early operations.

But they struck their first major blow against the Israelis on November 11, 1982. At seven in the morning, seventeen-year-old Ahmed Qassir, a native of the small village of Deir Qanun al-Nahr just ten miles from the Lebanese city of Tyre, plowed his car into a seven-story building that served as a major headquarters for the Israeli army in southern Lebanon. Qassir had lost several family members during a 1978 Israeli incursion into southern Lebanon and he wanted revenge. The car bomb, packed with explosives and cylindrical gas canisters, leveled the building. It blew one Israeli soldier out of the fifth floor; miraculously, a chair and a refrigerator landed around his head and formed a protective cocoon that saved him from the tons of steel and concrete that descended on top of him.[15] Seventy-five other Israeli soldiers were not so fortunate, including many of Israel's elite internal security force, Shin Beit, as well as fourteen Arabs who were being interrogated. Israel declared a day of mourning for those killed, and the attack remains one of the worst suicide attacks the country ever suffered.[16]

Israel remained oblivious to this new force their invasion had unleashed. In the chaos of Lebanon, their early attacks, as one Hezbollah founder recalled, were like "a scuffle of camels in the desert."[17] An unknown group, Armed Struggle Organization, claimed responsibility for the attack.[18] Hezbollah later claimed the bombing in Tyre as its first "martyrdom" operation. To avoid retribution by Israel against the driver's family, the group refrained from announcing the details until 1985, and then only after Israelis had pulled back from Tyre. That same year, Iranian supporters erected a memorial in the bomber's village, and the family personally received from Ayatollah Khomeini a portrait of the imam embossed with the emblem of the Islamic Republic.[19]

This also marked the first use of what would be the hallmark of Hezbollah military success: the suicide bomber. Car bombs were commonplace in Lebanon during the civil war. But the pro-Iranian Shia put a unique spin on this Lebanese tradition by putting a human behind the wheel. The unique tenets of this branch of Islam emphasized martyrdom, and Iran found no shortage of drivers willing to exchange their lives for the cause and eternal glory. While Israel and the United States condemned these as acts of terrorism, in truth the attacks were not terrorism. The founders of Hezbollah had devised the poor man's smart bomb and aimed it at their opponents' ill-prepared military. "If Hezbollah had GPS-guided bombs dropped from thirty thousand feet, they would not need martyrs," said one Lebanese with ties to the organization.

Initially, the pro-Iranian Shia militias remained a fractured movement. "Everyone wanted to be in charge," Sayeed Ali recalled. Iran supported multiple groups, including Hussein al-Musawi's Islamic Amal, as well as other Lebanese splinter groups. A 1984 American intelligence report provided to Defense Secretary Caspar Weinberger listed ten different Iranian-backed Lebanese militias. This included the Dawa Party of Lebanon, a counterpart to the Iranian-sponsored Dawa Parties in Iraq and the Persian Gulf countries. The Dawa Party was further subdivided into two semi-independent wings: a political front called the Muslim Student Union, and a military arm, the Jundallah (Soldiers of God). Even Islamic Amal had a subgroup called the Hussein Suicide Squad, whom al-Musawi recruited to execute his martyrdom operations. All told, they had fewer than one thousand fighters, but as the U.S. intelligence report acknowledged, they commanded widespread support among the Shia population.[20]

The true giant in the burgeoning Shia resistance was a man of only twenty, Imad Mugniyah. Born near Tyre in July 1962, the oldest of four children, Imad was remembered by friends as a bright boy with academic potential. He attended Beirut University for one year before dropping out to fight in the Lebanese Civil War as a soldier in Yasser Arafat's elite unit, Force 19. Young and strong with a dark beard and serious persona, he possessed the natural gift of a combat leader. He was well spoken and wholly committed to Islam's struggle against Israel. In fact, Sayeed Ali recalled, he spoke of nothing else. "Imad Mugniyah was a masterful organizer and operator. Few of his lieutenants were as capable," said former CIA director of operations Charles Allen.[21]

The Israeli invasion inspired Mugniyah too. In July 1982, he took a taxi to Baalbek and met with an Iranian Revolutionary Guard officer and ethnic Arab named Sheik Hussein.[22] Mugniyah liked the pitch and threw all his considerable energy into his own organization, the Islamic Jihad Organization. Mugniyah appealed to the Iranians. His connections with Arafat and numerous Shia leaders made him the indispensable man. He opened the door for Iranian influence in Lebanon in ways no outsider could.[23]

To Iran, Mugniyah became more than an ally; he served as a partner. Iran commissioned him an officer in the Revolutionary Guard and many of his Iranian comrades genuinely mourned his death when a car bomb in Damascus sent him on into the afterworld in 2008. As Hezbollah's chief military commander for over two decades, Mugniyah took on a mythical persona. Israel and the United States seemed to attribute every guerrilla attack or act of terrorism to him, and his hand guided many even in his tender years. Few knew him; he hid his true identity even from his only son, Mustafa. The head of Hamas's operations in Lebanon, Osama Hamdan, met him masquerading as a stone salesman.[24]

Iran tried to morph these disparate supporters into a cohesive force. It formed the Council of Lebanon, a five-member committee of senior Lebanese and Iranian clerics to coordinate the religious, political, and military activities of the radical pro-Iranian Shia groups. The Revolutionary Guard centralized all military training at Baalbek. On June 27, 1983, the two main groups—al-Musawi's Islamic Amal and Mugniyah's Islamic Jihad Organization—were both placed under the direct control of Iranian officers. By 1984, American intelligence began reporting a new umbrella name for the pro-Iranian militias: Hezbollah, or Party of God.

Iran's growing role in Lebanon did not escape the attention of the United States. The head of America's top eavesdropping agency, the National Security Agency, William Odom, made a swing through the Middle East in early April 1983, which included a stop in Beirut to talk to the CIA station chief and the marines at the airport. A gunnery sergeant assigned to small signal collection from the marines' radio reconnaissance company gave Odom some of the communications they had intercepted between Sheik Abdullah Barracks and the Iranian consulate in Beirut. "The Iranian presence was growing," Odom recalled of these messages. "They were actually struggling to find enough Arabic speakers to meet their requirements."[25]

Odom did not share the Reagan administration's optimism about Lebanon. He came away from Beirut deeply disturbed. The rising attacks on the marines and the growing influence of Iran among the Shia population did not bode well for America, he thought. "The mere fact that terrorists have made attempts against the Marines is a bad sign to come," he wrote to Army Chief of Staff Edward Meyer upon his return to Washington.[26]

Just days after Odom's visit, on April 17, 1983, a green Mercedes swerved in and out of the congested Beirut traffic, barely missing a dump truck and a mother and her two children. The driver accelerated, then quickly turned up a driveway, passing nonplussed guards, and headed straight toward the front of the seven-story American embassy. The car jumped up the front stoop and smashed into the front door of the lobby and exploded.[27] The blast sheered off the entire front of the building, vaporizing eleven Lebanese bodyguards and their leader, Sergeant First Class Terry Gilden of the U.S. Army Special Forces, who happened to be milling about under the front portico waiting to take the ambassador to an appointment.[28] Marines arrived from the airport to provide security for rescue workers digging through the rubble to recover the dead and wounded. The final tally stood at sixty-three dead, including seventeen Americans.[29] Most alarming, the bomber had cleaned out America's entire spy operation within Lebanon. Seven of those killed had been CIA employees, including the chief of station, his deputy, and the head of all the agency's Middle East operations, Robert Ames, who happened to be visiting the embassy and having an ill-timed lunch meeting with the CIA's staff when the bomb went off. Few intelligence officers knew as much about the Middle East as did Ames. Both William Casey and the White House held him in high regard. "If there ever was someone irreplaceable, it was Bob," said one retired CIA agent who knew Ames well.

Odom's NSA pored over intercepted communications trying to find the culprits. A few nuggets between the Iranian foreign ministry and its embassies in Beirut and Damascus had indicated a vague goal of striking at American interests in Lebanon. While highly circumstantial, NSA analysts concluded it could only have referred to the embassy attack.[30] Odom agreed. "It seemed the logical conclusion."

The CIA rushed a new batch of case officers to the embassy. This included one of the few Arabic-speaking women, deploying to Beirut on her first assignment with the agency. The new chief of station was a thin, glum-looking case officer with limited field experience who had spent much of his career in headquarters, William Buckley. Casey had pressured the reticent Buckley into taking the assignment. The director liked Buckley, and the bench of senior CIA officers with Middle East expertise was not that deep. The marine officers had a mixed view of him. Colonel Geraghty thought highly of him, and the two developed a good rapport, but many junior officers found the CIA officer conceited. Buckley did have one serious flaw for an intelligence officer: he could not remember people's names. As an aide-mémoire, he kept a list of all the CIA officers who worked for him in his shirt pocket.

In early August 1983, the marines went on full alert after intercepted radio communications and a Shia human source both confirmed an imminent attack by militias loyal to Iran.[31] As the fighting intensified around Suq al-Gharb, marines repeatedly intercepted tactical discussions in Farsi. To help translate, one of the five Persian linguists in the entire marine corps arrived in Lebanon to help decipher the chatter.

Robert McFarlane reported Iran's involvement back to the White House on September 9. The attacks on Aoun's 8th Brigade, he said, were not the work of Lebanese, but of a nefarious combination of Iranian and Syrian forces.

The United States could not stand by while these countries sent in troops to interfere and oppose the legitimate Lebanese government. McFarlane noticed the irony in his stand. The United States too stood guilty of much the same offense: an outside country with military forces backing one faction in the civil war.

While hardly the external invasion McFarlane perceived, the Syrian army did provide an umbrella for the polyglot of opponents of the Phalange-backed government. Druze, Shia, and Palestinians all battled General Aoun's forces in the hills around Suq al-Gharb. The Revolutionary Guard lurked in the background, offering advice for their allies. With the United States actively aiding the Lebanese army, the visible symbol of the U.S. military, the U.S. Marines, found themselves the target of all those opposing Gemayel and the Israelis.

In Ayatollah Khomeini's mind, America continued to spearhead the assault against the revolution. If America aided Iraq, he saw no reason why American marines in Lebanon should be immune from retaliation. It was all intertwined, each a battle in the larger struggle between the Islamic Republic and the United States: righteousness versus wickedness. While the Druze shelled the marines, the Iranian militia turned to their poor man's precision-guided weapon.

On September 1, 1983, a Revolutionary Guard officer met with Hussein al-Musawi at Sheik Abdullah Barracks. Al-Musawi wanted to blow something up—"special targets," as he phrased it. He remained undecided about just exactly what should be destroyed, but he leaned toward Christian Phalange sites in East Beirut. The Iranian dutifully reported this back to Ambassador Mohtashemi in Damascus, who in turn relayed it back to Tehran. As the fighting raged around Suq al-Gharb, and McFarlane and Stiner pressed Geraghty for air strikes, al-Musawi approached the Iranians again. This time he wanted help in obtaining an eye-popping thirty tons of TNT and plastic explosives.

This got Mohtashemi's attention. He asked al-Musawi to come to Damascus and explain what he intended to do with all that lethality. On September 22, an al-Musawi relative, Sayed, and the brother of the head of the Hussein Suicide Squad, Abu Haydan Musawi, drove to the Syrian capital and met with the ambassador in his office at the Iranian embassy. The Lebanese explained that while they had no specific target in mind, they wanted to undertake a dramatic attack against their enemies—the Americans, the Phalange, or the Lebanese army.

Mohtashemi listened intently. "Yes, you should certainly concentrate your operations as much as possible on the U.S. forces, Phalange, or the Lebanese army," he replied. Then the Iranian ambassador offered up a suggestion: "You should undertake an extraordinary operation against the U.S. Marines."

Sayed liked the idea. It had not occurred to him, but a blow against the marines would undermine the entire American and Israeli designs in Lebanon. Mohtashemi instructed him to make sure that he coordinated his actions with Hezbollah, which meant Imad Mugniyah.

"Perhaps when this great mission is over, we could come to Iran," Sayed asked excitedly. "Maybe we could even meet with Ayatollah Khomeini?"[32]

"You would be most welcome," Mohtashemi said, rising to shake Sayed's hand as he bid him good luck. "But the Iranian government cannot officially invite you. It is best we keep our distance publicly."

Two days later, Ambassador Mohtashemi called Tehran and reported his meeting to the Iranian foreign minister. Al-Musawi's proposal was debated by the senior official and Ayatollah Khomeini likely gave final approval for the attack.

The word came back to Mohtashemi approving "a spectacular action against the U.S. Marines."

On October 18, Abu Haydan Musawi and twenty members of the Hussein Suicide Squad arrived in Beirut from Baalbek. Iran failed to provide enough explosives, so Abu Haydan Musawi met with a Palestinian contact about obtaining four thousand more pounds of explosives. The day following, three trucks showed up in front of the Islamic Amal office in Beirut loaded with his requisition. This amount of explosives far exceeded what could be packed inside a Lebanese car bomb, and the Musawi clan seemed ready to make good on its promise of a spectacular show.

A few days later, Mohtashemi made a telephone call to Baalbek. Speaking with a Revolutionary Guard officer, he passed on the order to proceed with the attack. In addition to the marines, however, he wanted the French peacekeepers attacked too. France had just sold Iraq advanced attack aircraft, the Super Étendards, and even deployed a military team to train and provide tactical advice to the Iraqi pilots. The government in Iran took a dim view of this abrogation of France's neutrality, and French troops in Lebanon were now fair game. Islamic Amal agreed, in part because French aircraft had recently bombed Muslim forces in response to mortar attacks on their troops.

The Hussein Suicide Squad outfitted at least two trucks with thousands of pounds of explosives and tanks of compressed gas to enhance the destructive power of the bomb. The detonators were connected near the steering wheel for easy access by drivers, enabling them to ignite their cargo even if wounded.

The likely man chosen for the attack on the marines was a familiar acquaintance of Sayeed Ali's, Assi Zeineddine. His parents lived two buildings down from his, close enough that he could throw a rock to their apartment window from his balcony. Unlike Sayeed Ali, Zeineddine came from wealth. His father owned a string of small businesses and rental apartments. In school, Sayeed Ali recalled Zeineddine as a loud teenager with a funny, sarcastic sense of humor. How he was chosen remains unclear. Sayeed Ali does not recall that he was that much more devout than any of the other young men who joined Hezbollah. But as planning began for the martyrdom operations, Zeineddine's handlers ensured that he stayed segregated from the other soldiers.[33]

American intelligence picked up on the conversations between the Iranian embassy in Damascus and the home office in Tehran. On September 27, the NSA issued a message that outlined the impending attack, a message that included the Iranian ambassador's own damning words of "take a spectacular action against the U.S. Marines." Unfortunately, the message never made it outside of a very limited intelligence channel, and those who did not have a "need to know" included Colonel Geraghty and those up the marine's chain of command. On October 25, the director of naval intelligence raced up to the office of the chief of naval operations carrying the late September NSA message that outlined the impending attack. Unfortunately, this happened to be two days after the Hussein Suicide Squad had carried out its mission.[34]

It began as a typical Beirut morning. The sunrise dawned bright and beautiful. Since it was Sunday, the marines surrounding the airport had a more leisurely day scheduled. They remained a bit longer in their sleeping bags, grabbing an extra half hour of rest, and the normal six a.m. staff meeting at the battalion headquarters had been canceled. The day before, on October 22, 1983, a country-western band had entertained the marines and pizza had been flown in from a navy ship off the Lebanese coast. The marines occupied three buildings just off the main four-lane road leading to the Beirut airport terminal. The band played in front of the large four-story building that housed the infantry battalion headquarters. Elevated off the ground floor by large columns, with an open atrium, the building had originally held the office for the Lebanese aviation administration. Now a bombed-out shell, the large plate-glass windows that had adorned the upper floors had been replaced by plastic sheets and plywood and reinforced by thousands of sandbags. But the concrete and steel structure remained solid and provided a modicum of protection against gunfire and mortars, and the senior marine commander, Colonel Timothy Geraghty, agreed to allow his subordinate battalion to concentrate his large administrative support unit in this one structure. Now some 350 marines slept in its dusty rooms beneath a large overhanging roof that protected them from the rain and the Mediterranean sun.

The previous night, stray bullets had impacted the concert side of the building and a few rockets landed close by. The marines went to a higher level of alert, but it was a quiet night for a country in the middle of a civil war. And, undeterred, one marine went for a jog that morning, earning a rebuke from the sergeant of the guard, Steven Russell.

Around five in the morning on October 23, a yellow Mercedes stake-bed truck with no lights on pulled into the large open public parking lot south of the headquarters building and just east of the main thoroughfare to the Beirut airport terminal. A single three-foot-high fence of circular concertina wire separated the parking lot and the city at large from the battalion headquarters building. The truck circled once and then left. Lance Corporal Eddie DiFranco noticed it from his guard post, but these trucks were common enough around the airport that he paid it no further attention and did not believe it warranted reporting to Sergeant Russell. An hour later, another sentry noticed a white Mercedes car drive by. The driver reached across the passenger seat and snapped a photograph of the marine compound.

At 6:22 a.m., DiFranco heard the sound of a revving engine. He looked over to the parking lot just as a speeding yellow Mercedes truck swerved abruptly and crashed through the concertina wire fence, accelerating as it headed directly toward the battalion headquarters seventy yards away. To avoid accidental discharges, Colonel Geraghty had forbidden the sentries from carrying loaded rifles. Realizing what was about to occur, DiFranco struggled to unsling his rifle from his shoulder and load a magazine into his M-16. There just wasn't time. The large truck barreled past him; the driver, a

Caucasian with a bushy mustache and his hands gripping the steering wheel, looked down at DiFranco with a wild smile across his face. The truck went through an open gate in a chain-link fence and through an eight-foot gap between two large black sewer pipes placed on the ground.[35]

In his small sandbagged booth at the entrance to the headquarters building, Sergeant Russell had his back turned, talking with the wayward jogger and with the static hiss of multiple radios next to his ear. He heard a crackling or popping sound as the truck ran over the concertina wire. When he heard the growing noise of a loud diesel engine, he turned around to see the front of a large truck headed straight for him.[36]

Russell ran through the open courtyard, repeatedly yelling: "Hit the deck! Hit the deck!" He glanced over his shoulder just as the yellow Mercedes smashed through his guard shack, scattering sandbags and wood into the lobby. The truck came to rest in the middle of the atrium, its front windshield smashed in. For several long seconds everything was quiet. Still running and telling marines to "get down," Russell looked back at the truck to see a bright orange-yellow flash at the front of the vehicle as the equivalent of twenty thousand pounds of high explosives, enhanced by canisters of flammable gas, detonated.[37] A massive wave of heat and the powerful concussion blew him fifteen feet into the air, searing his flesh and twisting him around like a rag doll.

The explosion traveled straight up the open center of the building, forming an inverted V shape in the roof as it forced the entire building up off its foundation. The structure then collapsed in on itself like an accordion, reducing all four floors to a single level in a massive mushroom cloud visible across the city. The FBI later determined the type of explosives used when residue was found on a piece of underwear—all that remained of a marine who happened to be exercising in a small gym near where the truck stopped.[38]

A few lucky marines survived. Some sleeping on the roof managed to stay alive by riding down on top of the collapsing building. The battalion commander, Lieutenant Colonel Howard Gerlach, was blown out of his office and came to on the ground next to the heap of rubble that had been his headquarters. A fine powder of gray dust of pulverized concrete covered everything. Chunks of human flesh were scattered around the marine compound. One body, still in its sleeping bag, had been tossed into a tree. One marine rescuer nearly threw up when his boot kicked something spongy.[39] He looked down to see a severed hand, palm up with a wedding ring still on its finger. Paper—letters, technical manuals, pornography—slowly rained down around the ruins as the dazed survivors and Lebanese rescuers struggled to pull the injured from the rubble.

Geraghty was in his second-floor office a short distance away, just across a wooded outcrop. The blast blew out all the windows of his building, sending fragments flying about the offices. He rushed downstairs and went around behind his headquarters. He looked in the direction of his subordinate battalion's headquarters. As the fog of dust and debris cleared, Geraghty saw that the entire building had disappeared. He immediately got on a secure phone and called the Sixth Fleet commander. Losses were going to be heavy, he advised.[40]

Simultaneously, another truck bomb hit the nearby French military headquarters. The French paratroopers had only recently moved into a nine-story headquarters building along the seaside in West Beirut, which they'd hoped would afford better protection. French sentries opened fire on the approaching truck, perhaps wounding the driver before his deadly cargo detonated.[41] In that one morning, 241 American servicemen and 58 French paratroopers died. For the U.S. Marine Corps, it was the worst loss of life in a single day since Iwo Jima in 1945.

After October 23, no one ever again saw Assi Zeineddine. His family refused to talk about their son's whereabouts or his involvement. But within his close-knit neighborhood, no one doubted who had caused the explosions that rocked Beirut that Sunday morning. His parents suddenly traveled frequently to Iran, where officials treated them as honored guests. This included an audience with Ayatollah Khomeini.

Eight

THE AMERICAN HAMLET

A t two in the morning of October 23, 1983, Robert McFarlane's secure phone rang. On the other end, a military officer in the White House Situation Room passed on news of the attack on the marines in Beirut to the new national security adviser. Reagan, George Shultz, and Robert McFarlane were in Augusta, Georgia, with the president staying at the Eisenhower cottage on the grounds of the venerable country club that is home to the Masters golf tournament. Reagan intended for this to be a relaxing weekend away from Washington. It had been anything but. The night before, he had stayed up late discussing a military intervention in the tiny Caribbean nation of Grenada. Even his golf outing had been disrupted at the sixteenth hole when a deranged man took several hostages in the clubhouse and demanded to speak with the president. Reagan obliged, only to have the man hang up on him. Fortunately, the drama ended with the man apprehended and no one injured.

McFarlane dressed and went over to the Eisenhower cottage, where the president greeted him dressed in his pajamas, covered in a bathrobe, and wearing open-toed slippers. McFarlane went over the scant details. First reports confirmed at least seventy marines killed and another hundred wounded. These numbers would certainly rise, he told both the president and

Shultz. The president looked shocked and then angry. "Those sons of bitches. Let's find a way to go after them."[1] The presidential entourage packed up and immediately flew back to Washington.

At nine the next morning, Reagan met with his senior advisers in the Situation Room. Caspar Weinberger gave a quick update. "A truck drove into the building kamikaze style. Casualties were now 111 dead and 115 wounded; these numbers would certainly rise." Secretary Weinberger continued explaining that another truck hit the French; their losses stood then at 75 killed and wounded.[2]

"The Iranians probably were behind it," added CIA Deputy Director John McMahon, who was filling in for William Casey. "They had bombed the embassy in April."

"Can't we do anything to Iran?" queried the president.

Shultz responded, "We need a big intelligence effort to find out who was behind it."

But Weinberger cautioned that they needed to make sure of the right target before they started bombing. "It might make us all feel better," he said, "but that would not punish those responsible." He then recommended again that the marines be withdrawn to ships offshore to reduce their vulnerability.

Shultz strongly objected. "To withdraw now would undermine our entire policy," he argued. "It would be disastrous for American prestige." He recommended a new presidential-led diplomatic effort for Lebanon.

The president and his advisers reconvened back in the Situation Room in the White House basement at four p.m. This time, McMahon produced hard evidence of Iranian culpability. Someone had called a news agency in Beirut claiming that the attack had been conducted by an Amal splinter group with close ties to Iran, headed by Hussein al-Musawi, McMahon said. He then offered a detailed narrative of the timeline leading up to the attack, provided to the CIA by a Lebanese security official with close ties to al-Musawi. His information was impressive, detailing their movements from Baalbek to Beirut and their preparations for the attack. The agent had even witnessed three pickup trucks loaded with explosives in front of al-Musawi's office in south Beirut. McMahon continued by laying out for the president a string of communications intercepts from Iran to its embassy in Damascus directing it to "destroy U.S. targets." All pointed to direct Iranian involvement with al-Musawi. McMahon closed his brief by adding that French intelligence sources reported that the Iranians had evacuated their Beirut consulate immediately after the bombing, anticipating a reprisal attack. McMahon's information was as close to conclusive evidence as you were ever going to find in the murky world of intelligence.

"We need to show resolve," Shultz stated empathically after McMahon's presentation. "We need to take action against those who committed this atrocity and strengthen the Lebanese government."

Weinberger again cautioned that they should not take military action just for revenge. "It must be directed at those who perpetrated the act," he countered.

After listening to the two antagonists squabble, Reagan told the Joint Chiefs to plan for a retaliatory air strike. Clearly moved by the enormity of the calamity, the president added, "We must show that the cause was worth dying for." Reagan directed Marine Commandant P. X. Kelley to go to Beirut to see what further steps needed to be taken to protect the marines. As Kelley got up from the table to leave the Situation Room, Reagan put his arm around the general's broad shoulders and said warmly, "Vaya con Dios—Go with God."[3]

With 241 American servicemen dead, military retaliation should have been a foregone conclusion. But sharp divisions emerged within the administration on this issue from that first meeting in the White House. McFarlane had wanted military intervention even before the attack. Now he and his deputy, Vice Admiral John Poindexter, pressed for military action. Ronald Reagan clearly favored a response. In a nationally televised address on October 27, he looked into the camera and told the nation: "We have strong circumstantial evidence that the attack on the marines was directed by terrorists who used the same method to destroy our embassy in Beirut. Those who directed this atrocity must be dealt justice, and they will be."[4] The next day, he minced no words in his written order to Secretary Weinberger and the military: "Subject to reasonable confirmation of the locations of suitable targets used by elements responsible for the October 23 bombing; attack those targets decisively, if possible, in coordination with the French."[5]

But across the river at the Pentagon, those charged with carrying out the president's order were less enthusiastic about using force. Both Weinberger and General John Vessey had opposed the deployment of the marines, and now with Lebanon deteriorating and no diplomatic solution forthcoming, they wanted the marines out of the quagmire. Vessey, a decorated soldier who'd come up through the ranks as an enlisted man, had seen his share of killing, and he had little use for McFarlane, who seemed overeager to drag the United States into the Lebanese war. Weinberger agreed. "It is easy to kill people, and that might make some people feel good, but military force must have a purpose, to achieve some end," Weinberger said in 1994. "We never had the fidelity on who perpetrated that horrendous act."[6]

"Weinberger and Vessey were charter members of the Vietnam never again club," recalled Poindexter. "It was not just Lebanon; they opposed *every* military operation during that time. Cap wanted a strong military, but never wanted to use it." Both Poindexter and McFarlane objected to the numerous excuses offered by Weinberger and Vessey: there was no smoking gun; Sheik Abdullah Barracks sat too close to some of the most important Roman ruins, and they might get hit by mistake; if they used cruise missiles one might be a dud and then fall into Syrian hands and compromise its highly classified guidance system. "There was always a reason why we should not do something," recalled Poindexter.[7]

While Vessey unenthusiastically prepared a military plan for reprisal, an admiral within the U.S. Navy pressed forward with his own bombing scheme for Lebanon. The developer of this secretive plan was the imaginative surface warfare officer Vice Admiral James "Ace" Lyons. Stout, with thinning hair, Lyons lacked tact and voiced his opinions frequently and stridently, especially when dealing with superiors he viewed as fools. Lyons wanted to clobber Baalbek. He had been handed the NSA intercept that linked Iran to the attack on the marines just two days after the bombing. "If there ever was a 24-karat gold document, this was it," he said later. "This was not something from the third cousin of the fourth wife of Muhammad the taxicab driver."[8]

A few days after the bombing, Lyons went out to Langley and had lunch with CIA Deputy Director John McMahon and the head intelligence analyst, Robert Gates. Lyons had developed surreptitious relationships with Casey and Poindexter at the National Security Council. Both men shared Lyons's in-your-face approach to dealing with the Soviet military, and the navy admiral was certainly not part of the "Vietnam never again" crowd.

That afternoon, the CIA passed to Lyons the intelligence it had amassed that clearly linked Iranian agents at Sheik Abdullah Barracks with those who'd attacked the marines. "Whatever I give you," one of the men told Lyons, "you can't give it to the Joint Staff, because I don't want to read about it in the *Post*." That suited Lyons just fine, as he had no intention of working through Vessey or the Joint Staff.

In his offices in the Pentagon, Lyons developed a navy-only plan. Eight aircraft bombers would pulverize Sheik Abdullah Barracks. As Lyons suspected the Soviets had broken the navy's communications code (which they had, thanks to the Walker spy ring), he had his plan hand couriered out to a naval task force off Lebanon. In doing so, Lyons bypassed the normal chain of command, which ran through Army General Bernie Rodgers at European Command and his deputy who handled Lebanon operations, Air Force General Richard Lawson.

In the deep blue waters off the coast of Lebanon, Rear Admiral Jerry O. Tuttle commanded the carrier battle group poised to strike back at al-Musawi and Iran. In his naval carrier, Tuttle won the deserved reputation as an aggressive, imaginative, and profane commander. He referred to himself as "S.L.U.F.—short little ugly fucker."[9] He was also smart and brought computers into the navy's command system, including implementing the first global position locator that displayed every ship's location in near real time, called JOTS, which stood for joint operational tactical system, but everyone in the service simply called it "Jerry O. Tuttle's system." Tuttle refined Lyons's plan, adding a few more planes as insurance. As his pilots went into high alert planning the attack, Tuttle's boss in Stuttgart remained unaware of the unilateral action, although Lyons claimed to have sent a briefing team to talk with Lawson.

With his plan in the hands of Tuttle, the chief of naval operations, Admiral Jim Watkins, told Lyons to go down and brief General Vessey. The chairman was livid at Lyons's end run around Rodgers and ordered Lyons to turn over all the information he'd received from the CIA to the Joint Staff and the DIA.

"I can't do that because of the agreement I made with CIA," Lyons replied. This response did not go over well with Vessey or, later, Weinberger.

On Sunday, November 6, General Vessey appeared on *Meet the Press*. When pushed about who had been behind the attack and his view on retaliation, the chairman demurred despite knowing that the intelligence reports pointed to Iran and its Lebanese allies. "I really don't know who did it. I wish I did," he told *New York Times* correspondent Richard Halloran. On retaliation, he refused to be pinned down about any plans for it, other than to say,

"When American servicemen are killed and killed in any numbers, my gut reaction is to retaliate."[10]

The next day, Reagan met again with Vessey and other senior officers about a military response. The president was leaving the following day for a week in Asia, and they needed to decide whether to strike before or after his return. Vessey briefed the president that European Command, the unified command that had responsibility for Lebanon, had developed a list of sixteen targets, all demonstrably hostile to the multinational force. This included every actor but the Christians: Iranian, Syrian, Druze, Palestinian, and Shia. The targets included Baalbek and several other Iranian surrogate bases, referred to by Weinberger on the three-by-five sheets of paper that he scribbled his notes on as "Syrian terrorist camps." The president seemed convinced by the evidence about who had attacked the marines and French paratroopers, but he agreed to meet again the next day just before boarding the plane.

That afternoon, a flurry of calls ensued among all the principals: McFarlane called Weinberger advocating bombing now; Vessey called Weinberger expressing doubts about the intelligence linking Baalbek with the perpetrators; Weinberger told McMahon at the CIA about the chairman's concerns. The CIA had no reservations about who had been behind the attack.

On November 8, Reagan met yet again with his advisers before leaving for Asia. Gathering in the Red Room of the White House, both Vessey and Weinberger suggested they hold off until the president returned, which would allow them to collect more information on Baalbek. Reagan agreed to take up the issue upon his return from Japan and South Korea. But the president seemed perplexed by Weinberger's reticence. After giving a farewell speech in the East Room, Reagan turned to the secretary. "Cap, I thought you were planning on bombing the camp?" There is no record of Weinberger's response.

With the president gone, meetings continued in Washington on the retaliatory strike. Vessey updated the proposed targets in the Bekaa Valley and agreed to cooperate with the French military on any reprisals. Weinberger continued to balk at any reprisal: "Need better intelligence on enemy targets," he wrote in his notes after one White House meeting.

This mantra continued after Reagan returned on November 14. The military was ready, Vessey told the president, but it risked losing aircraft to Syrian antiaircraft batteries, and retaliating against them risked expanding the conflict, with the marines at the airport likely to bear the brunt of Syrian retaliation. Weinberger again pressed that they needed better intelligence before attacking. Once again any strike was placed on hold. "We have some additional intelligence," Reagan wrote in his diary, "but still not enough to order a strike."

The next day, Reagan met again with his military advisers. This time, the gruff CIA director, William Casey, tried to undercut Weinberger's hand-wringing by presenting strong evidence of the role of Sheik Abdullah Bar-racks as a base for the planning and the attack on the marines. He also linked the operatives with another nearby base in the Bekaa Valley three miles from the Syrian border at the town of Nabi Chit. Weinberger responded by adding a new wrinkle: there might be some Lebanese army soldiers still at Sheik Abdullah Barracks. They needed to make certain they were gone before bombing.

While Reagan's gut reaction had been a military strike, now Vessey and Weinberger's qualms came out of the president's mouth. He told the assem-blage that he wanted to make sure that they could link the target directly to those responsible. A mistake could exacerbate the Lebanese crisis. Once again, nothing was decided; Casey agreed to look again at the CIA's sources and brief them again the next day.

That evening the Israelis rendered one target moot when its aircraft pounded the Shia base at Nabi Chit. Begin had no reservations about its links to those who had attacked them. Less than two weeks earlier, a green Chevrolet truck driven by a twenty-year-old Shia had crashed through the main gate of the Israeli headquarters in Tyre. "He looked like a nice boy," said one Israeli soldier on duty near the entrance. Unlike the American marines, the Israeli sentries had loaded weapons; they opened fire, wounding the driver. He detonated eight hundred to one thousand pounds of explosives, collapsing the building and killing thirty-nine soldiers. For the third time in less than two weeks, the Islamic Amal and its deadly Hussein Suicide Squad had used the ultimate precision-guided weapon to deal a deadly blow to its enemies. Unlike Washington, Israel did not deliberate endlessly on the wis-dom of responding. Four warplanes swooped down on the base at Nabi Chit. They bombed three buildings in the training camp and a nearby ammuni-tion dump. Perhaps thirty Shia fighters died, with fifty more injured, includ-ing five Iranian advisers.[11] Hussein al-Musawi nearly found himself in this statistic. He had left the camp just two days earlier to see his parents in Beirut.

A routine rotation of aircraft carriers in the eastern Mediterranean meant that Tuttle now had two of these mighty symbols of American military power with more than 150 planes to avenge the marines. Tuttle expanded his plan, now using twelve attack aircraft to bomb Sheik Abdullah Barracks and two other bases, supported by electric jammers and fighter interceptors. On November 15, his French counterpart, who commanded the much smaller carrier *Clemenceau*, flew over to see him, carrying a letter authorizing him to conduct a joint strike with the Americans. Tuttle agreed, and the two staffs developed a plan to divide up the targets around Baalbek, with the heavier load falling to the more capable American aviators. The French wanted to carry out the attack in forty-eight hours, on November 17. Tuttle wished the United States showed the same bloodlust for revenge as the Israelis, but he cautioned the French admiral that he had yet to receive any order to attack. His hands were tied until the Pentagon cleared his pilots hot.

On November 16, Reagan and his advisers reconvened in the Oval Office. After going over intelligence about the Israeli air attack, Casey rebuffed Weinberger's concerns about Sheik Abdullah Barracks. Since the marine barracks bombing, the CIA had doubled its staff at the Beirut embassy to twenty-two. They now had a source within the compound, and he confirmed it was an exclusively Iranian military site with no civilians. Casey recommended hitting it. Weinberger still remained unconvinced.

What President Reagan decided that day remains mired in controversy. McFarlane left the Oval Office convinced that the president had authorized the attack in conjunction with the French. He later regretted not getting the order in writing, but he had no doubt about the president's intentions agreeing with Casey's and McFarlane's recommendation. But Weinberger recalled the meeting ending differently; he received no such directive from Reagan. His note from that meeting confirms his recollection: "Concluded we should get more intelligence."[12] It was not the first time people had left a meeting with the president uncertain of how Reagan had ruled. Reagan hated personal confrontations, and passions were growing heated with each delay in the air strikes.

What is known is that, later that day, Vessey met with Weinberger and said that "they were going final with the Lebanon targets," meaning that the U.S. military was ready to strike. The defense secretary also received a call from his French counterpart, who expressed Paris's eagerness to conduct a joint attack with the Americans. If Reagan did order the attack and Weinberger wanted it reversed, the defense secretary never spoke with the president after the NSC meeting to express his reservations.[13] Despite the advance readiness of the U.S. military, no execute order for Admiral Tuttle ever left the Pentagon.

Early the next morning, November 17, McFarlane called the National Military Command Center to find out how the air attack had gone, which he assumed had been carried out at first light in Lebanon. "The secretary ordered a stand-down," the military officer on the other end said.

McFarlane was livid. He called Weinberger and asked, "Why didn't they execute the attack?" According to McFarlane, the defense secretary replied, "I did not think the time was right to strike." After Reagan arrived in the Oval Office, McFarlane walked in and told the president that Secretary Weinberger had not ordered the attack. Reagan was visibly angry, McFarlane recalled. He pounded his fist on the massive oak desk.

"You need to do something, Mr. President. You can't have a cabinet official disregarding your orders!" McFarlane added empathically.

As Weinberger headed to the Pentagon that morning, his military assistant, Major General Colin Powell, called him in his car, letting him know French defense minister Charles Hernu wanted to talk to him immediately regarding the air strike in Lebanon. When he arrived at his office, Weinberger conferred with General Vessey, who told the secretary that the French intended to strike within an hour, but the original plan called for a joint U.S.-French strike. Without U.S. aircraft, they could hit only two targets at Baalbek.

Weinberger then called Hernu in Paris. The French minister said his forces were ready to strike. "We could delay for sixty-five minutes," he said, "if the Americans wanted to join us." According to Weinberger's notes of the conversation, the secretary answered, "The president has not made a decision; he is still considering it." Weinberger said that he had no orders from the president to launch the American portion of the joint operation. "Unfortunately, it is a bit too late for us to join you in this one," he added, wishing the French good luck.[14]

Weinberger called McFarlane and told him about his conversation with Hernu and the impending French attack. Hoping to salvage the joint attack, McFarlane immediately sent a message to the French that the United States still "might join them in an attack, but they could not do it that morning." There was just not enough time, he said.

But France would not delay its air attack. Without any American support, fourteen Super Étendard fighter jets took off from the aircraft carrier *Clemenceau*. They swooped over the Sheik Abdullah Barracks with the afternoon sun at their backs. Aiming for the headquarters building of Islamic Amal militia leader Hussein al-Musawi, they dropped a few bombs and fired some rockets, most of which landed in the town of Baalbek or hit harmlessly in the hillsides. The French attack was an abject failure, and the Parisian press pounced on President François Mitterrand for the anemic military response. Privately, the French government fumed at their supposed ally's refusal to respond to the attack on the multinational force.[15]

"The French never forgave us for not backing them in the attack," recalled John Poindexter. They believed the United States had betrayed them by pulling out of the joint attack. Weinberger's refusal to commit was seen as an act of betrayal to an ally. The French exacted their revenge three years later. In April 1986, intelligence implicated Libya's Moammar Gaddafi in the bombing of a disco in Berlin that killed two American servicemen. It was now Paris's turn to thwart an American air strike. They refused to allow American warplanes taking off from England to overfly its airspace, forcing a seventeen-hour round-trip flight around Europe. While the American public expressed outrage at France's action, no one except a handful in the government realized the reason behind their refusal to cooperate.

In the end, President Reagan did nothing. Weinberger sent a memo to the commander in chief that in light of the French and Israeli air strikes on Baalbek, there was no reason for the United States to do its own attack. McFarlane strenuously disagreed, but Reagan sided with Weinberger. Dutifully, McFarlane wrote to Weinberger of the president's decision on November 22: "We should discontinue current plans and associated readiness to execute preemptive attacks in response to the October 23 tragedy." Despite his repeated public statements promising to punish those who had perpetrated the attack, Reagan had quietly decided to do nothing in response to an attack that killed more servicemen in a single day than any other since the Second World War.

Reagan ordered one Pyrrhic air strike unrelated to the barracks bombing. It turned into a fiasco. Syria launched a missile at a U.S. reconnaissance plane that overflew its military positions in eastern Lebanon. This time Vessey made sure there was no "navy-only" plan and that European Command ran the military operation. The command in Stuttgart assigned thirteen separate targets to Tuttle, requiring nearly forty aircraft from both carriers to carry out the reprisal. Tuttle had intended to launch the strike so the planes would arrive over the positions at high noon and the sun would be in the face of the Syrian gunners and the visibility would allow for easy identification. At five in the morning, an aide woke Tuttle, informing him that a message arrived instructing him to hit the Syrians at seven thirty a.m., only two and a half hours away.

"It is not possible," he told his fleet commander. "It will take four hours just to get the ammo on the planes. I need a delay of at least two hours."

Tuttle's request went back to General Lawson at European Command, who twice asked the Joint Staff for a delay. It was denied. Why remains unclear, but apparently Vessey had made a remark to the defense attachés from Britain, France, and Italy about a first-light strike at seven thirty a.m. This became set in stone as far as the operations officer within the Joint Staff was concerned, even though Vessey had never intended this.

Planes and pilots were hastily sent aloft. Only twenty-eight of the planned thirty-eight jets were launched, and only one had its full bomb load. Syrian gunners shot down two aircraft. One two-seater A-6 piloted by twenty-six-year-old Mark Lange was shot as it dove down from two thousand feet. "I remember the plane being jostled," said Lange's weapons officer, Lieutenant Robert Goodman, "and instead of looking at the sky, I was looking at the ground." Both pilots ejected just before hitting the ground, but Lange's chute failed to deploy and he died of his injuries shortly after being captured by Syrian troops. Goodman survived with three broken ribs and was taken to Damascus and held in a basement cell watching old John Wayne movies and the TV comedy *Gimme a Break!*[16] To the embarrassment of the administration, the preacher-turned-negotiator Jesse Jackson traveled to Damascus and secured the pilot's release. It led to an awkward ceremony at the Rose Garden with Reagan welcoming Goodman and thanking Democratic presidential hopeful Jesse Jackson.

Tension grew between Weinberger and McFarlane and the two men wrote dueling memos to the president. The national security adviser bitterly resented Weinberger's refusal to respond to the attack on the marines and remained unwilling to admit that the U.S. policy he advocated in Lebanon had failed. McFarlane wrote to Reagan urging him to stay the course in

Beirut. "There has been progress, and the trends suggest more progress is in the offing," he said about the growing strength of the Lebanese army. "That said," McFarlane added, "the U.S. cannot yield to state-sponsored terrorism."[17]

Weinberger countered in his memos that the presence mission assigned to the marines had been flawed and had led to the disaster. It was impossible to be passive peacekeepers in the midst of a civil war. In light of the size of the bomb, more bunkers and trenching would not "prevent continuing significant attrition to the force," Weinberger wrote to Reagan. The political situation had deteriorated to the point where he and the chairman again urgently recommended pulling out the marines.[18]

In early 1984, the facade of a multiconfessional Lebanese government and army collapsed. After fighting between the pro-Iranian militias and the Lebanese army, Sheik Fadlallah issued a fatwa for the Shia to leave the army. Overnight, one entire Lebanese brigade defected. Within days the army shattered along sectarian lines. America's effort to rebuild Lebanon in a way pleasing to Washington lay in ruins. With a presidential election looming, the Reagan administration cut its losses, and on February 26, 1984, the last marines withdrew from the airport to their ships off the coast.

One marine lieutenant, caked with dirt from months living in the mud of his bunker, looked down at the city below as he flew out on a helicopter and thought of those he knew who he had seen dead and mangled in the rubble of his battalion headquarters. "For all the sacrifice," he thought to himself, "I hope we accomplished something." In the end, 269 marines, sailors, and soldiers had died; Lebanon remained unchanged.

Although the marines had left, the infighting within the administration continued. The animosity boiled over during an early morning breakfast meeting on April 5, attended by McFarlane, Shultz, and Noel Koch, a senior civilian at Defense. Koch made a statement that the United States used the term "terrorism" very selectively: "When our friends engaged in this behavior it was always diplomatically inconvenient to refer to it as state-supported terrorism." The problem, he added, was not Iran, but that the United States backed one faction in the war. "If we retaliate against Iran with overt military forces, we will provide what Iran will see as cause for a justified counter-retaliation."

A visibly angry Shultz, his eyes squinting, looked straight at Koch. "I couldn't disagree more. We could not permit what happened in Beirut to go unpunished." He accused Koch of being a statistician. "The unpleasant truth is that the bombings in Lebanon changed the Middle East by creating a public reaction which forced the withdrawal of the marines from Lebanon." Our lack of will would only encourage Iran and other terrorists, he added.

The Israelis provided some bit of revenge to the United States and the killing of the marines. In 1984, they mailed a book of Shia holy places to Iran's ambassador in Syria. When Ali Akbar Mohtashemi opened the package, it exploded, blowing off several fingers and part of one hand.[19]

I f the United States was in retreat, Iran and its Lebanese allies were on the offensive. The string of vehicle-borne suicide bombings against the West had succeeded beyond their expectations. Israel was reeling, and the American and European forces were out of Lebanon. In September 1984, they struck again at the American embassy annex in the Christian suburbs of East Beirut. The six-story building had just been completed and was protected by a low wall surrounding the building and serpentine barriers erected along the main road leading to the entrance. U.S. Marines had been providing security around its perimeter, but, under pressure from the Pentagon to reduce the military footprint in Lebanon, this duty had recently been handed over to contract Lebanese except for the normal small contingent of embassy marines guarding the building itself.

Shia militants in nearby hills surveyed the embassy building. With Tehran's approval, relayed again through its ambassador in Damascus, they built near Sheik Abdullah Barracks a mock-up using barrels to outline the streets leading to the annex. The bomber repeatedly rehearsed his approach, each time increasing his speed through the zigzag barriers. On September 20, he drove the real route. As he approached the annex, he pressed on the accelerator. As two contract guards opened fire, he swerved in and out of the barricades designed to halt him and detonated his bomb outside the wall, only twenty feet from the annex's north corridor. Two American servicemen working at their desks died instantly as part of the building collapsed. The blast slightly injured the American ambassador.[20] For the second time in as many years, the Iranian-backed militia had devastated the U.S. diplomatic mission in Lebanon.[21]

After being woken with the news of the attack, Reagan flew on to political rallies in Iowa and Michigan. When asked by a student about this latest attack in Lebanon, Reagan disingenuously blamed his predecessor and the "near destruction of our intelligence capability" during Carter's presidency. Fortunately for the president, no one asked about his own culpability for the disastrous foreign policy regarding Lebanon.[22]

Two days later, Reagan met with his staff in the Situation Room. McFarlane and Poindexter brought images taken by a spy satellite over Baalbek. The picture revealed an odd racetrack, with barrels arranged in a distinct pattern and tire tracks around each where a driver had repeatedly taken each turn at high speed. An observant analyst had married that image up with the approach to the embassy annex; the two overlapped exactly. Again intelligence placed the occupants at Baalbek at the center of an attack against the United States.[23]

The discussions fell along now familiar lines. Weinberger and Vessey expressed caution. Innocent family members of the fighters lived there, they said. Meanwhile McFarlane and Shultz pressed for military action. Casey chimed in that his information showed no women or children at Sheik Abdullah Barracks, but he could not be certain that three American hostages held by pro-Iranian Lebanese were not at those barracks. The president said he did not object to military response, provided it actually prevented future attacks, but he worried that the attack would be seen as revenge, as if that were somehow beneath the dignity of the United States. McFarlane countered that the only way you were going to dissuade future attacks was by punishing those responsible.

President Reagan again erred on the side of caution. After telling Shultz to issue a stern message to Syria for its tacit support of the terrorists, the president spent the rest of the day drafting a speech to be given at the United Nations and planning for an upcoming meeting with the Soviet foreign minister.[24]

Secretary of State Shultz became increasingly vocal at the lack of a willingness to respond to direct attacks on the United States. He agreed with McFarlane that striking back would cause Iran and Syria to think twice about repeating their terrorist undertakings. On October 25, Shultz gave a public speech in New York in which he cautioned, "We may never have the kind of evidence that can stand up in an American court of law, but we cannot allow ourselves to become the Hamlet of nations, worrying endlessly over whether and how to respond." Speaking before a predominantly Jewish audience, Shultz praised the Israeli way of "swift and sure measures" against terrorists. As the *New York Times* reported, "Mr. Shultz, almost alone of senior officials, has been waging virtually a one-man campaign since last spring for a policy of force toward terrorists."[25]

In the end, Reagan became the American Hamlet. The debate over responding to terrorist attacks continued week after week in the White House until, eventually, the attacks faded from the public's memory. While Reagan basked in his electoral landslide that November, his indecision and misguided Lebanon policy had been the policy equivalent of a fighter dropping his guard, and Iran landed a blow squarely on the Gipper's chin. None of this had been preordained. A shortsighted Israeli policy and American Cold War naïveté opened the door for Iran in Lebanon. Israel's myopic obsession with destroying the Palestinian resistance spawned a far more dangerous enemy, while an American government equally fixated on halting Soviet influence in the Middle East had led to misguided meddling in a Lebanese quarrel that Washington barely understood. In the process, Hezbollah's success emboldened Iran on the value of terrorism and the poor man's precision weapon—the truck bomb—as instruments for successfully beating a superpower.

I n the meantime, Lebanon spawned a new crisis, one that would nearly consume the Reagan administration. On July 4, 1982, Iran's military attaché, Revolutionary Guard officer Colonel Ahmad Motevaselian, and two other Iranian diplomats were returning to Beirut when Christian Phalange soldiers stopped them at a checkpoint in the seaside town of Borbara, thirty miles north of the capital. The militia pulled the three men from their car; it was the last anyone ever saw of them. The Phalange executed all of them shortly after their abduction. The taking of the Iranian diplomats, including their senior Revolutionary Guard commander, infuriated Tehran.[26] In response, Iran ordered the taking of their own hostages, hoping to use them as barter. On July 19, 1982, masked gunmen kidnapped the acting president of the American University of Beirut, David Dodge, as he strode on his customary afternoon walk. A longtime resident of Beirut and the great-grandson of the founder of the university, Dodge had been born in Beirut and lived for years in Lebanon, including service in the region during the Second World War. Dodge was bound and taken to Damascus, where an Iranian aircraft flew him to a prison near Tehran. American intelligence intercepted the Iranian communications about Dodge's transfer to Iran, and the international outcry about the abduction and Iran's complicity in his kidnapping forced his release exactly one year later. The Dodge kidnapping had been a major blunder by the Revolutionary Guard. By taking Dodge to Iran, it implicated the Iranian government and exposed its operations in Lebanon. The guard made a calculated decision: they would provide resources and tradecraft training, but hostage taking would be left to the Lebanese. The Iranian government needed to stay out of the limelight and not be directly tied to the abductions.[27]

Hostage taking was a time-honored tradition in the Levant, with every party engaging in it. And in the 1980s, taking Westerners became the fad for Iran's surrogates. The arrest of the Dawa Party members in Kuwait and hundreds of Shia held in Israeli prisons launched a wave of hostage taking to serve as barters for their release. In 1984, two Americans and a French citizen were snatched off the streets. This included a professor at American University and CNN bureau chief Jeremy Levin. Over the course of the next few years, the hostage-taking frenzy snatched nearly a hundred foreigners off the Lebanese streets, chiefly persons from America (twenty-five in all) and Europe.

Iran's biggest prize occurred on March 16, 1984. CIA station chief William Buckley had been personally sent to Beirut by William Casey to rebuild the agency's operations following the April 1983 embassy bombing. But he failed to heed those who wisely cautioned him about varying his daily routine for his own safety. As he left home at his regular time, a group led by Imad Mugniyah overpowered him and stuffed him in the trunk of an old Renault. A marine operating a signal collection station in the embassy tracked Buckley's abductors as they drugged and spirited him out of Beirut in a coffin. In Buckley's pocket, his abductors discovered a sheet of paper listing every CIA officer in the country, and the exposure of all its operatives led to yet another neutering of American intelligence in Lebanon.

Where Mugniyah took Buckley remains unknown. At the time, some in U.S. intelligence believed he had been flown to Iran for interrogation. CIA operative Bob Baer wrote that he and many other hostages had been taken to a building at Sheik Abdullah Barracks identified by a wooden sign as "married officers' quarters." Unlike the other hostages, Buckley was savagely beaten by his captors. They forced him to write a lengthy manuscript about his spy activities. To the Iranians' great annoyance, his Lebanese captors allowed him to die of pneumonia in June or July 1985. When news of his death reached one senior guard commander, Ali Saleh Shamkhani, he reportedly flew into a rage, screaming at his subordinates at a meeting in Tehran of the senseless death of such a valuable hostage. He apparently ordered a doctor sent to Lebanon to look after the well-being of other sick hostages.[28]

The kidnappings were not very organized. Once started, the craze took on a life of its own, as anyone who knew of an American could gather some friends and snatch him. After Buckley's death, Imad Mugniyah played a key role in trying to get all the hostages under one central control. One of the hostage takers, a man named Farouk, owned several car dealerships. While traveling south to Sidon to beat up a dealer who had not paid him his money, Mugniyah intercepted his car, and the two men got out on the side to talk. Mugniyah ordered Farouk to turn his two hostages over, much to Farouk's annoyance.

Mugniyah also played a major role in Hezbollah's infamous hijacking of a TWA Boeing 727 en route from Athens to Rome, which had been intended to secure the release of the Dawa members in Kuwait. During two tense weeks in June 1985, the drama unfolded in Beirut. The two hijackers, Mohammed Ali Hamadi and Hasan Izz al-Din, brutally beat a U.S. Navy diver, Robert Stethem, who happened to be on the flight and traveling with his military ID card. They then shot him and dumped his body on the Beirut airport tarmac.

Sayeed Ali did not know about the hijacking in advance, but when he heard of the TWA jet in Beirut, he joined other Hezbollah members in guarding the plane and passengers in case of a U.S. rescue mission. Amal leader Nabih Berri interceded and took control of the passengers and crew, demanding for their exchange Lebanese prisoners being held in Israel, some of whom were also being held as bargaining chips.[29] The speaker of the Iranian parliament, Hashemi Rafsanjani, was flying back from Libya and stopped in Damascus to meet with al-Assad. Rafsanjani had been critical of taking the jetliner. In a meeting that included Iran's ever present ambassador Mohtashemi, they struck the deal to release the remaining TWA hostages in exchange for prisoners held in Israel. By the end of June, Israel released 766 Lebanese prisoners, and all the 150-odd hostages on the plane came home— all except Seaman Stethem.

In January 1985, Casey had asked Charles Allen to be the national intelligence officer for counterterrorism. Tall and thin, with a terse, businesslike persona, the self-described workaholic had been running a still sensitive program at the Pentagon. While there, he had witnessed firsthand the growing strength of Hezbollah. What impressed him was the sheer number of weapons flowing to Hezbollah fighters from Tehran via the Damascus airport. Weekly scheduled flights of large Russian-made Il-76s arrived in the Syrian capital, where they were unloaded and moved via truck to the Bekaa Valley. "It was a very different organization than any other terrorist organization the U.S. faced," Allen said.

The fate of the Western hostages weighed heavily on Reagan. "He was an extraordinarily kind man," Allen observed. "The plight of the hostages and their families appealed to him emotionally. He became obsessed with releasing the Lebanese hostages, to the point that it distorted his aperture by concern for their welfare."[30]

Allen focused on both penetrating Hezbollah and developing intelligence to support a military rescue mission. West Beirut was effectively a denied area for the CIA, and though they tried to get some sources into it, they were never able to really penetrate Hezbollah, settling instead for sources with secondhand access. After a meeting at the White House, Reagan signed a presidential finding to create a Lebanese counterterrorist team run by the army's intelligence organization. Robert Oakley, then the State Department's coordinator for counterterrorism, and the CIA's head of the directorate of operations, Clair George, supported the idea as a means of countering the Shia militants who had attacked the marines and the embassy. "We wanted to be sure that the Lebanese team was properly trained and disciplined; we certainly did not want another 'loose cannon' roaming the streets of Beirut," Oakley later said. The agency's paramilitary special activities branch headed the effort, but found the group wanting, and it never materialized into a useful agent for the CIA.[31]

In 1986, Casey and his deputy, Robert Gates, asked Allen to head up the agency's hostage-location task force, which he did for the next fourteen months. Allen sent officers and agents and other collection means across the Green Line into West Beirut trying to find the hostages. Working with Carl Stiner and Delta, they developed a support network within Lebanon and

Cyprus to undertake a rescue mission. But the military wanted its own guys to have eyes on the target and did not trust the tactical judgment of either a CIA officer or one of the agency's Lebanese agents. However, the likelihood of getting a military officer covertly near Sheik Abdullah Barracks or West Beirut was nearly zero, severely limiting any chances of undertaking a rescue. Stiner's men assembled a few times in Cyprus on an intelligence tip about the whereabouts of one of the hostages, but the information never seemed firm and a frustrated group of special forces and SEALs never got a chance to ply their craft and exact some revenge.

At various points either the CIA or the Israeli Mossad tried to even the score. One of their prime targets was Imad Mugniyah. On one occasion, the CIA suspected him to be in Paris. Casey proposed kidnapping him off the streets without telling the French. Robert Oakley heard about the CIA's idea from an FBI associate. He immediately went to see Shultz in his seventh-floor office to raise his objection. How could the United States criticize others for kidnapping and engage in the same conduct? This unilateral action would destroy our cooperation with the French on other terrorism or sensitive issues, Oakley told the secretary.[32]

As Oakley made his case, Bud McFarlane called Shultz. "The president has approved Director of Central Intelligence Casey's recommendation to kidnap Mugniyah off the streets of Paris," McFarlane said. That started a three-day running battle in the White House Situation Room, with Justice, FBI, and Oakley objecting, but McFarlane and the CIA concurring. The debate ended when the report turned out to be spurious.

Two weeks later, another Mugniyah sighting placed him again in Paris. The United States reported this to the French. Casey dispatched Duane "Dewey" Clarridge—heading the CIA's European Division—to coordinate with Paris on apprehending him. French police raided a hotel room in which the CIA believed he was staying. Instead of a twenty-five-year-old Lebanese terrorist, they found a fifty-year-old Spanish tourist. However, a French intelligence officer passed to Clarridge a photo of the wanted man taken in the airport on his way back to Beirut.[33]

CIA Director Casey placed Sheik Fadlallah in his crosshairs. Accounts differ on how Casey decided to remove the Lebanese. But Christian Phalange members trained and equipped by the United States parked a car packed full of explosives near Sheik Fadlallah's home and the mosque where he preached. On March 5, 1985, it exploded just as Friday services let out. Eighty people

Nine

SLEEPY HOLLOW

On Sunday morning, May 13, 1984, the Kuwaiti oil tanker *Umm Casbah*, heading south out of the Persian Gulf. Lumbered low in the water, her holds were filled with a load of refined petroleum for the United Kingdom. An Iranian reconnaissance plane relayed the tanker's location back to an air base near Bushehr. An hour later, an Iranian F-4E painted in a desert-camouflaged scheme of light and dark brown swaths took off with its characteristic deafening roar and trail of black smoke. It took less than fifteen minutes for the two-seat jet to cover the distance across the Gulf. The Iranian electronic warfare officer looked into a small video screen and put the crosshairs squarely on the eighty-thousand-ton tanker; he launched two small Maverick missiles, which had been designed to destroy tanks, not supertankers. The missiles hit the tanker squarely amidships, starting a small fire that the crew quickly extinguished. The next day, Iranian aircraft struck again with another missile, this time inflicting real damage, blowing a five-meter hole in the side of another Kuwaiti tanker, *Bahrah*. Two days later, Iran added Saudi Arabia to its target list. Iranian missiles hit the Saudi tanker *Yanbu Pride* while she sat anchored at the oil loading facility of Ras Tannurah. The Iranian pilot then swooped in low, strafing the hapless tanker with its machine gun.[1] Over the next seven months, Iran struck fifteen more Gulf Arab ships.

These attacks marked a major escalation in the Iran-Iraq War. The ensuing tanker war, as it became known, threatened to consume the entire Persian Gulf and curtail the flow of precious oil from the Middle East. Over the next four years, Iran and Iraq attacked more than five hundred ships, with the tonnage lost or damaged equally half that lost in the Atlantic during the Second World War.[2] For the United States, the tanker war turned the simmering tensions between Tehran and Washington into a very real shooting war.

Saddam Hussein started the tanker war. Shortly after the outbreak of war, both sides declared war exclusion zones in which neutral shipping would risk attack. Iran issued a "Notice to Mariners" declaring a wartime exclusion zone running from twelve to sixty nautical miles from the Iranian coastline. Ships not bound for Iranian ports were ordered by Tehran to remain outside this zone. Iran's stated purpose was to ensure the safety of neutral shipping, but its true motive was to allow Iranian naval and air forces free rein through half the Persian Gulf, providing it the ability to attack shipping bound for Iraq or its supporters. But in effect it provided Iraq with a "free fire zone," for only ships bound for an Iranian port would sail in the Iranian exclusion zone.[3] Any ship in Iran's exclusion zone was fair game, and Iraqi pilots took full advantage of it. With the land war bogged down in the trenches outside Basra, in February 1984 Iraqi aircraft escalated their attacks against Iranian oil exports, pounding Iranian shipping in the free fire zone near Kharg Island and Bushehr.[4]

Iraq made use of recently provided French jets and training. In early October 1983, France leased five Super Étendards to Iraq. Designed to fire the Exocet antiship missile, they served as the Iraqi frontline attack planes against Iranian shipping until France delivered the more advanced F-1 fighters in 1985. While this overt military support from Paris made its peacekeepers targets for suicide bombings in Beirut, it gave Saddam's air force an unmatched capability to hit oil tankers leaving Iran's main oil terminal at Kharg Island. Iraqi pilots in their sleek French jets took off from Iraqi airfields and hugged the Kuwaiti and Saudi coastline, frequently flying through both countries' airspace with their tacit concurrence. When they flew past the small Iranian island of Farsi, just south of the Saudi-Kuwaiti border, the Iraqis turned east toward Kharg and the Iranian exclusion zone—a maneuver known as the Farsi hook. Then they unleashed their missiles on the first blip appearing on the radar screens before hightailing it back to Iraq to avoid being attacked by a wayward Iranian jet.

In a three-month span, from February through April 1984, Iraqi aircraft sank or heavily damaged as many as sixteen ships. This included some friendly fire when an Iraqi Exocet missile struck the Saudi-owned tanker *Safina al-Arab*, which was carrying 340,000 tons of Iranian crude destined for France. The ship erupted in a massive fireball, rendering it a total loss and killing one of the crew.[5]

Iran did not respond immediately to these Iraqi provocations. Despite later accusations by the United States that Iran spread the war throughout the Gulf, Iran never wanted the tanker war. With Iraq exporting most of its oil through pipelines to Turkey, there were only a few Iraqi-bound tankers to attack, and as the chief quarry in the tanker war, Tehran constantly pushed for a cease-fire to the shipping attacks.[6]

After weighing its options and making vacuous threats about closing down the Strait of Hormuz, the Iranian government decided on a different strategy: to strike at the supporters of the Iraqi war machine, Saudi Arabia and Kuwait. And so on Sunday morning, May 13, the *Umm Casbah* became the first casualty of Iran's reprisals. Lacking the French connection and under a tight American arms embargo, the aging Iranian fleet of American twin-seat F-4s bombed and strafed ships in the northern Gulf, in much more restrained tit-for-tat strikes responding to the incessant Iraqi attacks on Kharg Island.

Even though Iraq had started the tanker war, the Gulf Arabs pointed the finger of blame at Iran. On May 21, 1984, they requested a meeting of the United Nations Security Council to address Iran's attacks and the issue of freedom of navigation in the Gulf. On June 1, 1984, the UN passed Resolution 552, which called upon all states to respect the right of freedom of navigation and warned Tehran that if it did not comply, the UN would "consider effective measures."[7] Iran responded with indignation at the selective rebuke of the world's governing body, which ignored Iraq's role in spreading the war beyond the land.

Saudi Arabia responded to the Iranian attacks by establishing a no-fly zone in the northern Gulf called the Fahd Line, named after the Saudi king. This line extended well into the Gulf, encompassing all the Saudi offshore oil fields. The Saudi government warned Iran that it would challenge any air incursions across this line and suggested that it would use force should an Iranian jet cross this line to attack Saudi shipping. Behind the scenes, the American air force provided the backbone for the Fahd Line. American AWACS based in Dhahran provided air surveillance, while U.S. air-to-air tankers refueled Saudi F-15 fighters patrolling the Fahd Line.

On June 5, an American AWACS detected two Iranian F-4 jets crossing the Fahd Line and vectored in two Saudi fighters, one of which had an American flight instructor in the rear seat. The Iranians ignored two warnings to turn back, and instead radioed back to their base asking for instructions. Encouraged by the American in the backseat of the cockpit, the tentative Saudi pilots each "pickled" off a heat-seeking missile. One struck home, turning an Iranian aircraft into a fireball and sending its two occupants down to the ocean below.

Both sides scrambled nearly sixty aircraft, and it looked as though a major dogfight was about to ensue over the Persian Gulf. However, Iran backed down first. The Iranian wing commander recalled his aircraft, avoiding a major confrontation that neither side particularly desired.[8] While the Saudi defense minister was furious over his air force's aggressive action against Iran, fearing it would lead to an escalation of attacks on Saudi shipping, Iran learned a different lesson.[9] Never again would the Iranians send their planes to challenge the Fahd Line or use their scarce aviation resources to attack shipping in the northern Gulf. This unusual display of Saudi fortitude effectively eliminated the Iranian air threat. "Resolution prevailed against the Iranian bully!" remarked the Saudi ambassador, Prince Bandar, to Caspar Weinberger.

In Washington, the tanker war caused more frantic meetings in the White House Situation Room. All agreed on the need to support Iraq and to strengthen the military capabilities of the Gulf Cooperation Council, but beyond that, the deep policy rifts exposed during the Lebanon crisis carried over to these new discussions about the tanker war.

Both Robert McFarlane and George Shultz believed Tehran would use the Iraqi attacks as a rationale to expand its terrorist operations to destabilize the Gulf Arab countries, and that it was looking to conduct another spectacular attack against the U.S. military, perhaps by using a suicide plane against a warship in the Persian Gulf. Shultz still chafed about the lack of an American military response to the marine barracks bombing. He stressed to Weinberger during one of their weekly breakfast meetings that the United States could not let terrorism go unpunished; this would only lead to attacks at home and against our allies. McFarlane went beyond the secretary of state, suggesting during one White House meeting that the United States should consider a preemptive strike against Iran.

Weinberger viewed this saber rattling with incredulity.[10] He quarreled with McFarlane in several meetings in June and July, arguing that this would just draw the United States into the larger Iran-Iraq War. The defense secretary could be a tenacious fighter, and he stymied the interagency deliberations with point papers and sheer stubbornness during meetings.[11]

Weinberger's underlings took a different tack to temper McFarlane's and Shultz's martial ideas. They raised the continuing concerns about long-term alienation of Iran. The number three man in the Pentagon, deputy for policy Fred Iklé, cautioned that military action against Iran would neither hinder its terrorist operations nor achieve much more than Iraq could do. In his early sixties with graying hair, Iklé came to prominence primarily for his writings on nuclear and strategic warfare. A staunch Cold War hawk, he often proposed covert action against the Soviets in Afghanistan.[12] However, when it came to Iran, he took the line of reconciliation. "The most important midterm issue is the Soviet rule [sic, role] in a post-Khomeini Iran. By maneuvering ourselves into a deeper confrontation with Iran now, we will make it easier for the Soviets to establish themselves."[13]

Other civilians in the Pentagon agreed. The United States needed to plan to eventually "reestablish ties with, hopefully, a moderate Iran in the post-Khomeini period," wrote Deputy Assistant Secretary of Defense Sandra Charles, echoing her boss Iklé's views.[14] While Weinberger couldn't have cared less about reestablishing any rapport with the Islamic Republic, the argument did resonate with William Casey and Bud McFarlane, and eventually with Ronald Reagan.

President Reagan eventually signed two directives to respond to the tanker war. He reiterated the American goal of preventing an Iranian victory. He rejected any military attack on Iran, but ordered American forces to be ready to respond immediately should Iran attack an American merchant ship or try to halt the free flow of oil through the Strait of Hormuz.[15] Additionally,

Reagan authorized the transfer of four hundred Stinger missiles as part of a major upgrade for Saudi Arabia's air defense, and he offered more military aid to the Gulf Arabs.

Administration officials then fanned out in the region to reassure the Arabs. The president's envoy, Donald Rumsfeld, made a swing through the Gulf Arab capitals, promoting closer defense ties with Washington and encouraging the Arabs to develop contingency plans with CENTCOM, bringing promises of new arms. As deputy national security adviser, John Poindexter led an interagency team to Saudi Arabia, where they found Saudi officials in a blustering, bellicose mood and unhappy that Reagan had not taken a harder line. "The king would not stand for appeasement with Iran," one Saudi official told him. "We intend to strike back if Iran escalates their attacks on our tankers!" Yet when Poindexter pressed Saudi Arabia for a public show of support for the United States against Iran, perhaps allowing U.S. forces to use Saudi bases, the king balked. Despite the Iranian attacks, the Gulf states remained reluctant to allow American boots on their ground.[16] They encouraged the United States to take action against Iran, but in the event of war, America's Gulf Arab partners would remain firmly on the sidelines.

Privately, Reagan harbored reservations about such open-ended aid to these feckless friends. When McFarlane placed the proposal for more helicopters and artillery for Kuwait on the president's desk, the Gipper read it and looked up. "Bud, the current interests of the Kuwaiti government in working with us are at best transitory," he said. Incredulous, he added, "The United States is increasingly responsible for the defense of a country that openly criticizes our policy."

On November 23, 1985, General Robert Kingston turned over the reins of CENTCOM to Marine General George B. Crist. Slim with dark hair, the son of a naval officer, Crist attended Villanova University, the same school as General P. X. Kelley. Kelley, now the marine commandant, pushed Weinberger and General John Vessey to appoint Crist to be the first marine to ever command a major, theater-unified command. The original agreement for CENTCOM called for alternating marine and army commanders; it was now the corps' time. Crist's experience outside of the confines of the smallest service made him a strong candidate. He had unprecedented joint experience: as an aide to the president in the 1950s, as assistant to the chairman during the Vietnam War, as deputy operations officer for Europe during the Iranian hostage crisis, and most recently as vice director of the Joint Staff during Lebanon and Grenada crises. Kelley knew that both the defense secretary and the chairman thought highly of Crist, having seen him in action daily as the vice director.

In the mid-1980s, CENTCOM was anything but the center of the American military universe. The Middle East remained a backwater, and officers on the fast track avoided going to the Tampa headquarters that many within the military called "Sleepy Hollow." With the military's focus on a war with the Soviets in Europe, few wanted to go to a tertiary theater such as the Middle East. CENTCOM had more officers retiring than moving on to other assignments. When Major General Samuel Swart of the air force—the new J-3, or operations officer—came to Tampa in 1986, a good friend of his wrote him a note jokingly saying, "From all work to no work."[17]

General Crist focused on putting together a better staff for his 751-person headquarters. He brought in a new chief of staff from the army, Major General Donald Penzler. Experienced working in large European army headquarters and recently as the deputy chief of staff at the army's Training and Education Command, he had served with Crist on the Joint Staff from 1981 to 1983, and Crist requested that he come down to be his chief of staff. Penzler was tough, discreet, and loyal. He initiated "Operation Slash," a program designed to get rid of deadweight and bring new, energetic officers to the staff. His first goal was forcing the retirement of a senior colonel who was running his own side business in town.[18]

Crist faced the challenges of two major wars. Shortly after he took over as chief of staff at CENTCOM, the Soviet military began a massive new operation in Afghanistan. Unbeknownst to U.S. intelligence at the time, the newly installed Soviet leader, Mikhail Gorbachev, decided to unleash the Soviet military in a last attempt to win the war. Elite special forces, Spetsnaz troops, backed by a hundred frontline attack aircraft, relentlessly pursued the guerrillas. The Soviets dramatically increased their attacks into Pakistan proper. In 1986 alone, the Soviets conducted more than 880 air and ground incursions, attacking guerrilla bases and destroying supply depots.[19] The Soviet military formed a new, high-level Southern Theater of Military Operations command, stationing a very experienced general, the former chief of staff of the Soviet forces in East Germany, as its new commander.

Crist agreed with the prevailing assessment of the Soviet desire to secure warm-water ports and Middle East oil.[20] An analysis group inside the intelligence directorate produced a monograph that portrayed two hundred years of gradual, unrelenting Russian expansion south into the Caucasus. The study stated that the Soviet invasion of Afghanistan was one more manifestation of this trend. "In any event," Crist wrote to the chairman, "it is instructive to recall that the Soviets have occupied Iran four times in the Twentieth Century alone."[21]

But the marine knew that in the event of a general war against the Soviets, CENTCOM would become a backwater theater. CENTCOM would never send any ground troops into Iran. In the event of a major war with Moscow, forces allocated to his command to deploy to Iran, such as the 82nd Airborne Division, were also slated to go to the main front in Europe. "The plans were unrealistic," Crist said later, "but you had to keep them for defense funding as all the resources were tied to Soviet war plans and the reason for CENTCOM's being."[22]

But it would be the expanding Iran-Iraq War that soon eclipsed Cold War worries as the CENTCOM commander's chief anxiety. In February 1986, Iran amassed over one hundred thousand men in what both U.S. and Iraqi intelligence officials meeting in Baghdad believed would be another major frontal assault on Basra. Instead, on the night of February 10, amid a pouring rainstorm, Iranian Revolutionary Guardsmen loaded up in small boats and rafts and crossed the mouth of the Shatt al-Arab and easily captured the al-Faw Peninsula, a muddy finger of land that served as Iraq's oil terminus for all its crude exports from the Persian Gulf. The Iranians quickly reinforced their foothold, and some thirty thousand soldiers pushed up the two small roads running north to Iraq's only port, Umm Qasr, and the city of Basra. A humiliated Saddam Hussein immediately ordered the peninsula recaptured. The Iraqi army threw three of its best divisions into an inept, piecemeal attack that the dogged Iranian defenders easily drove back, inflicting some eight thousand casualties.[23] Iran's lack of trucks or tanks for its foot soldiers, as well as poor logistics, prevented its victory at al-Faw from becoming the southern gateway to Basra, and this front bogged down into another war of the trenches. But the Iranian gains rattled every Arab state in the Middle East, none more so than Kuwait and Saudi Arabia.

———

The tanker war took another dangerous turn. Iran announced an expanded blockade of Iraq. The Iranian navy would confiscate any military cargo destined for Iraq, including cargo transferred through a third country like Kuwait or Saudi Arabia. The Iranian navy began enforcing this decree by challenging ships entering the Strait of Hormuz, asking for their nationality and last and next ports of call. Any vessel destined for Kuwait was stopped, and a boarding party of Iranian sailors would come aboard to check the ship's manifest and open any suspicious containers. Any ship found carrying suspicious cargo was diverted to Bandar Abbas, where Iranian authorities would conduct a detailed search of the cargo holds, seizing any military hardware.[24] In the first eight months, sixty-six ships were stopped and searched by the Iranian navy—a small fraction of the ships that entered the Gulf, but enough to make everyone, especially those assisting Iraq, very nervous.[25]

Around eleven a.m. on January 12, 1986, the six-hundred-foot-long American Lines ship *President Taylor* steamed twenty-four miles off the coast of the United Arab Emirates. Bound for the port of Fujairah with a small load of cotton, the ship was intended to pick up a load of bagged food for CARE and Catholic Relief Services before heading off for India. A small Iranian patrol boat came alongside the U.S.-flagged ship and, over the radio, demanded, "Heave to."

The *President Taylor*'s captain, Robert Reimann, tried to protest. "We are in international waters. You have no right to stop us," he replied.

The Iranian boat trained its main gun on the defenseless merchant, and an Iranian voice over the radio politely insisted that the ship "stop her engines." Reimann had little choice but to comply.

The Iranians dropped a small rubber Zodiac boat into the undulating seas and, in short order, seven Iranians, including two officers, boarded the *President Taylor*, taking control of the ship's radio and its forty-three crewmen. They asked Captain Reimann to produce his manifest. He did so, and after examining it and looking into a couple of containers, the Iranians expressed their satisfaction, telling the American master they only wanted to verify that the ship was not carrying contraband bound for Iraq. In less than an hour, the seven Iranians had departed, leaving the *President Taylor* to make her way on to Fujairah.[26]

The problem for the United States, as a Pentagon spokesman acknowledged the day after the incident, was that Iran had every right under international law to search ships suspected of carrying war matériel to Iraq. The United States faced the age-old problem of a neutral's ability to engage in commerce and the right of a belligerent to maintain a naval blockade. But with Weinberger's utter disdain for Iran and this incident occurring only three months after the Palestinian hijacking of the Italian cruise ship *Achille Lauro*, in which an elderly American, Leon Klinghoffer, had been shot in his wheelchair and dumped over the side, the Reagan administration was in no mood to risk another such hostage crisis from a country with a track record of taking Americans hostage.

On February 1, the State Department sent a tersely worded cautionary message to the Iranian government through the Swiss embassy in Tehran: "Irrespective of the legal issues involved, the visit and search of U.S. flag vessels by armed Iranian forces during a period of heightened tension and regional conflict could lead to a confrontation between U.S. and Iranian military units, which neither nation desires."[27]

"If this continues," wrote General Vessey to Secretary Weinberger, "escalation of the current conflict appears inevitable."[28]

Weinberger ordered the navy to prevent any further boardings of an American merchant.[29] U.S. warships would now position themselves within visual range of any U.S.-flagged merchant ship transiting the Gulf, poised to interdict any approaching Iranian vessel. Should an Iranian warship try to stop a U.S. merchant, an American naval officer would go over to the merchant and check for any military equipment for Iraq. Assuming the ship carried no contraband, the U.S. naval officer would inform the Iranian captain of this fact. Since the United States did not provide Iraq directly with arms, it was inconceivable that any ship flying the Stars and Stripes would be guilty of carrying war matériel, but if they were, the U.S. Navy on-scene commander would divert the merchant to a neutral port and then allow the Iranians on board to remove any prohibited items under the supervision of the U.S. Navy.[30] Under no circumstances, however, would any U.S. merchant be diverted to an Iranian port.[31] If the Iranians persisted in trying to board after the U.S. Navy had certified the absence of contraband, Poindexter wrote to Weinberger, the "on-scene commander will use whatever means may be appropriate, including measured military force, to forestall any such attempt."

Shortly after the *President Taylor* incident, Crist formulated a plan to attack Iran should the country try to interfere with neutral shipping. CENT-COM planners drew up a top secret operation called Invoke Resolve that entailed massive air strikes on Iranian naval forces at Bandar Abbas. On February 7, 1986, Crist provided an overview of it in the Tank before the chairman of the Joint Chiefs of Staff and the secretary of defense. U.S. Navy aircraft from the carrier in the Gulf of Oman would strike an important air defense headquarters outside the Persian Gulf near the small port town of Jask just before dawn, before flying at a low level to the Persian Gulf to destroy the Iranian surface-to-air Hawk missiles that ringed Bandar Abbas, as well as the Bandar Abbas International Airport, which, in addition to being a commercial airport, was the main southern airfield for the Iranian air force. Simultaneously, fourteen B-52s from Guam, supported by nearly fifty air-refueling tankers and an array of sophisticated reconnaissance planes and electronic warfare aircraft, would launch precision-guided cruise missiles that would lead, knocking out hard-to-reach targets such as the 1st Naval District headquarters building, which sat uncomfortably close to a hospital. Then nine of the massive four-engine aircraft—each capable of carrying sixty thousand pounds of bombs—would pummel the Bandar Abbas Naval Base. Operating in groups of three, each could saturate an area one and a half miles long by a mile wide with hot shrapnel and raw explosive power.[32] Should Iran try to retaliate and escalate the conflict, the United States was prepared to conduct further air strikes and drop air-delivered mines in Bandar Abbas Harbor, which would effectively close it down for all military or civilian vessels.[33]

Over the long term, General Crist thought that the only way for his Sleepy Hollow headquarters to counter either the Russians or the Iranians lay in building military ties with the Gulf Arabs. In the spring of 1986, just four months into command, General Crist wrote a lengthy letter to Secretary Weinberger laying out his thinking: "A premium has to be placed on coalition warfare. Our friends and allies have to assume a share of the responsibility for the defense of the region."[34] With Egypt, this already existed, but the Persian Gulf remained the key shortfall and the Gulf Cooperation Council was hardly a credible military alliance.

Crist proposed developing separate bilateral military-to-military defense arrangements with each of the Gulf countries, with Crist's staff synchronizing them into one combined force that could augment the U.S. military. "At a minimum," he wrote to Chairman Crowe, "it offers the opportunity to open doors in countries that have largely been off-limits to the U.S. military."

Crist and Penzler flew to Washington to brief Weinberger on the idea, intending to concentrate on the three countries that offered the most promise: Saudi Arabia, Bahrain, and Kuwait. The Pentagon leadership liked the idea and authorized Crist to go forward. Crist then ran it by Richard Murphy, who headed the State Department's Near Eastern Affairs Bureau. He too thought it had merit, and with Secretary Shultz's concurrence, instructions went out to the embassies in the Gulf to assist in the CENTCOM planning effort.

At first glance, Jeremiah Pearson belied the appearance of a warrior-diplomat. With a large round head and dowdy appearance, "he looked like a big sack," one senior officer remarked. A pilot, he took on the persona of dumb fighter jock. But his bright blue eyes revealed a considerable intellect. With a degree in aeronautical engineering, he joined the marine corps in 1960, earning his wings as a marine corps pilot and distinguishing himself in Vietnam. Later he became a test pilot and was selected for the astronaut program. Four months after being promoted to brigadier general, in April 1986 he and his wife drove down in the stifling summer heat to Tampa, Florida, where Pearson assumed the job of CENTCOM's forward headquarters commander and inspector general. Pearson arrived somewhat unsure of his duties and of his new boss, the CENTCOM commander. He had never served in a joint billet, and General Crist had a reputation within the marine corps for not liking aviators. But the marine corps commandant, General Paul Kelley, had called to give Pearson a strong recommendation, and after meeting with Pearson in his office at MacDill Air Force Base, Crist liked what he saw in the quiet, self-confident young brigadier general enough to give him the chance to test his mettle.

Pearson spearheaded CENTCOM's bilateral military planning with the Gulf Arabs, code-named New Splendor. He established a small planning cell within the headquarters that reported directly to General Crist. By both coincidence and design it was largely composed of marines. Pearson flew out nearly every week to the Gulf, traveling to each country, building trust through hours of sitting around talking and sipping cups of hypersweet tea. To pass the time on the nineteen-hour flights from Tampa to the Gulf, Pearson checked out Arab-language tapes from the Defense Language Institute and discovered he had an aptitude for the difficult language. Pearson soon commanded a conversational knowledge of Arabic—a novelty for military officers at CENTCOM—which greatly enhanced his standing with his Arab counterparts. "At least," Pearson chuckled, "it kept me from getting ripped off in the souk."[35]

The Gulf Arabs had a healthy distrust of the United States. All questioned Washington's ability to keep their cooperation confidential and out of the *New York Times*. Some leaders viewed CENTCOM as an American interventionist force, whose mission was only to advance U.S. goals in the area.[36] All repeatedly asked Pearson, "Can we rely on Washington if Iran attacks us?"

To help Pearson, Crist shared classified intelligence briefings about the Iran-Iraq War with the Gulf states. "It was one of the tools we used to build trust and cooperation and to get them thinking about their security," said the CENTCOM intelligence director, Brigadier General Cloyd Pfister of the army.[37] Not surprisingly, this proved very popular with regional leaders, and military intelligence officers, and the CIA traveled with Pearson to provide regular sanitized updates on Iran based upon sources that only a superpower had access to.

Pearson's meetings gradually moved from government buildings to the private homes of senior leaders. With the consultation of Murphy's Bureau of Near Eastern Affairs at the State Department, with whom Pearson spoke regularly, the conversations turned from the mundane to the substantive.[38] Privately, the Gulf leaders all conveyed their concerns about Iranian intentions and the calamity that would befall their regimes if Tehran defeated Iraq. They accused Iran of trying to establish a Shia crescent across the Arab world, stretching from Lebanon, across Iraq, and down through the "Arabian" Gulf, as they preferred to call the body of water. Bahrain and Saudi Arabia, with their sizable Shia populations, voiced these concerns the loudest. Bahrain's ruler, Sheik Isa, loathed the Iranians, whom he viewed as arrogant and intent on stirring up discontent among his Shia subjects. The powerful Saudi defense minister, Prince Sultan, echoed similar warnings to Pearson. The United States and Saudi Arabia, he stressed, needed to support Saddam Hussein because he provided a buffer against Iran, and they needed to be ready to use military force. "They were all scared shitless of the Iranians," Pearson succinctly summarized.

In June 1987, New Splendor achieved its first success with an agreement with Bahrain to defend the tiny emirate against Iranian attack. After lengthy meetings at the Bahrain Defense Force headquarters in Manama with defense minister Sheik Hamad bin Isa al-Khalifa and chief of staff of the armed forces Major General Abdullah bin Salman al-Khalifa, the United States agreed to provide F-16s and other aircraft to jam Iranian communications and weapons systems in the event of an Iranian attack. To support the U.S. military, Sheik Khalifa promised to build a hardened command bunker near Manama (with the United States installing the communications suite) and a new airfield in the southern tip of the country especially for the U.S. military.[39]

Pearson obtained a similar agreement with Kuwait. Unlike Bahrain, Kuwait's border sat astride the key front of the Iran-Iraq War, and with the capture of al-Faw, the rumble of artillery fire rattled the windows of the American ambassador's residence in Kuwait City. With the government's open support of Baghdad, the emir worried that the Iranian military might try to outflank the Iraqi defenders by simply going through Kuwait. Pearson agreed that the U.S. government would enhance the Kuwait air defense system by selling them Hawk air defense missiles to be stationed around Kuwait City.

Saudi Arabia proved the most difficult. A steady stream of diplomats and generals held labored negotiations with the Saudi delegation, headed by the strong-willed chief of staff of the Saudi Arabian air force, Lieutenant General Ahmad al-Buhairi, under the oversight of the powerful defense minister, Prince Sultan. They explored possible Iranian threats to the kingdom, including a large-scale ground attack by Iran and an Iranian air attack on Saudi oil facilities and oil tankers.[40] At Weinberger's urging, Crist repeatedly tried to get the Saudis to agree to permit pre-positioned American equipment and to allow access to Saudi air bases for U.S. combat aircraft. Each time, the Saudis politely changed the subject. While they made headway in solidifying the American AWACS integration into the Saudi air defense scheme and defense of the Fahd Line, the Saudis had little enthusiasm for anything formal. As Penzler recalled, they wanted to keep talking just in case Iran did attack and they needed American help, but otherwise preferred to keep CENTCOM at a distance. "It was just too much to ask of the Saudis before the Iraqi invasion of Kuwait," said General Russell Violett, who enjoyed a close relationship with the Saudi royal family.[41]

In October 1985, Admiral William Crowe replaced Vessey as the chairman of the Joint Chiefs of Staff and the nation's top military man. A balding, bulbous Oklahoman, Crowe had risen through the ranks through his political acumen, not because he was a warrior. With a doctorate in political science from Princeton, Crowe held a series of strategy and policy positions inside the Beltway, beginning with an early posting as an assistant to President Eisenhower's naval aide. The one notable exception was in 1970, when he volunteered to serve as a senior adviser to the South Vietnamese riverine forces. His experience fighting the Vietcong in small patrol boats in the brown-water tributaries of the Mekong Delta left a significant impact on Crowe's views of war. "I did not have a traditional naval officer's view, but one more akin to the army or marines, shaped by fighting a guerrilla war," Crowe would later reflect.[42] In the 1970s, Crowe also served as commander of the small show-the-flag Middle East Force based in Bahrain. A purely diplomatic assignment, it had afforded Crowe insight into the political dynamics of the Persian Gulf and the Arab governments.

As the United States discussed Iran strategy, in 1986 Congress forced sweeping legislation down on a hidebound Pentagon. Officially called the Defense Reorganization Act, it was widely referred to by the names of its two sponsors, Barry Goldwater and William Nichols. Sam Nunn and Les Aspin, among others, looked into how best to integrate the separate services into a more effective joint war-fighting force. The need was real. Interservice rivalry plagued the Pentagon. Each branch independently procured and developed its own hardware. Key systems, such as air force and navy air defense radars, could not share data; radios were not compatible. Even such common items as wrenches differed from service to service. Over the objections of Secretary Weinberger and the service chiefs, Goldwater-Nichols passed, marking the first major restructuring of the Department of Defense since 1947. The legislation elevated the chairman of the Joint Chiefs of Staff as the principal military adviser to the president, rather than the corporate body composed of the chairman and the four service chiefs. It clearly delineated the military chain of command as running from the president to the secretary of defense to the unified four-star commanders in chief, or CINCs (pronounced "sinks"), such as Crist at CENTCOM, and provided the CINCs wide latitude to organize and employ the forces of all four services in their theaters. This effectively cut out all the service heads from any operational decisions and limited them to training and equipping their forces. The days of the chief of naval operations actually controlling the fleet had ended.[43]

Crowe's first response to this new law was to issue a personal message to the unified commanders that he advocated a go-slow approach to this new policy. Crowe chose not to exercise his new authorities, but continued to defer

Ten

ARMS FOR THE
AYATOLLAH

On the morning of June 18, 1985, Major General Colin Powell, the senior military assistant to Defense Secretary Caspar Weinberger, sat at his desk in the plush, expansive defense secretary's suite on the outside ring of the third floor of the Pentagon. A number of classified documents were stacked in Powell's in-box for Weinberger, the most sensitive delivered by couriers using locked pouches. One document immediately caught Powell's eye—a top secret "eyes only" draft National Security Decision Directive from the White House. These directives were some of the most important documents produced by the government. Intended for the president's signature, they laid out U.S. foreign policy and served as principal guides to focus the entire U.S. government. The cover letter was signed by National Security Adviser Bud McFarlane and entitled "U.S. Policy Toward Iran."

What McFarlane proposed was a drastic change in American policy toward Iran. "Dynamic political evolution is taking place inside Iran," McFarlane began. "Instability caused by the pressures of the Iran-Iraq War, economic deterioration and regime infighting create the potential for major changes in Iran. The Soviet Union is better positioned than the United States to exploit and benefit from any power struggle that results in changes in the Iranian regime." The future presented a picture of growing unrest that gave Moscow a golden opportunity to exploit the turbulence. The strategic buffer provided by Iran protecting Persian Gulf oil would be gone, effectively opening up the entire region to Soviet control. It was a dire prediction and a grave strategic threat to the West if the United States did not develop a new strategy.

Rather than containing Iran as Weinberger advocated, the national security adviser proposed détente. McFarlane recommended using allies to sell Iran weapons as a means of undercutting Soviet leverage and in the process currying favor with "moderate" elements within the regime. This could pull Iran back into the Western fold and array it against the Soviet Union.

Since this was well above Powell's pay grade, he dutifully sent the document in to Weinberger, writing on a small white buck slip with his letterhead, "SECDEF, This came in 'Eyes Only' for you. After you have seen recommend I pass to Rich Armitage for his analysis."

Cap Weinberger was appalled. He had never forgiven the current regime in Tehran for seizing the U.S. embassy and holding the hostages for 444 days—an event he viewed as a national humiliation. "The only moderates are in the grave," he thought. Now this man in the White House is trying to say we approach them in the spirit of forgiveness and based on the assumption there were some sort of fanciful pragmatists around Khomeini? "It was nonsense."[1] Weinberger sent the document back to Powell, scrawling across his military assistant's white paper, "This is almost too absurd to comment on. By all means pass it on to Rich, but the assumption here is: 1) Iran is about to fall, and 2) we can deal with them on a rational basis. It's like asking Gaddafi to Washington for a cozy chat."

Armitage had the same reaction to the draft directive as his boss. "Bullshit," he said, cutting to the quick.

What no one realized in June 1985 was that McFarlane's proposal would embark the United States on a foreign policy path that would lead to the biggest scandal of the Reagan administration, Iran-Contra. Profits from secret arms sales to Iran were siphoned off to fund pro-American guerrillas fighting the leftist government of Nicaragua. Three government investigations with multiple indictments followed before the independent counsel finally wrapped up the last one in 1993, after a last-minute string of pardons by outgoing president George H. W. Bush ended the affair. In reality, Iran-Contra was actually two separate issues: one the attempt by the Reagan administration to resupply anticommunist guerrillas in Nicaragua, and the other the sale of weapons to Iran in the vain hope of releasing seven American hostages being held by Hezbollah as a precursor to renewed diplomatic relations with the Islamic Republic. The two efforts merged in the White House under a self-righteous marine lieutenant colonel named Oliver North.

O n the afternoon of July 3, 1985, David Kimche, the director general of the Israeli foreign ministry and a close friend to Israeli prime minister Shimon Peres, stopped by Bud McFarlane's office in the West Wing just down the hall from the Oval Office. After the usual pleasantries about the hot, humid Washington weather, Kimche asked to talk to McFarlane alone. McFarlane respected the Oxford-educated Kimche, who had a distinguished career with the Israeli intelligence service, Mossad. The two men had worked together two years before during the U.S. intervention in Beirut, and McFarlane found him highly intelligent and a kindred spirit on their views of the Middle East.[2] When the other staff left the room, Kimche said, "You know, Mike Ledeen came and asked us whether we had any judgments about an Iranian opposition movement. We told them we do."

Michael Ledeen was a loquacious, self-appointed Middle East expert whom the National Security Council kept on retainer. He frequently vacationed in Israel and had developed good contacts with senior government officials there. In early May 1985, Ledeen flew to Israel and met for nearly an hour with Peres. The Israeli prime minister expressed some displeasure with Israel's intelligence on Iran and advocated that the two nations work together to improve both countries' knowledge of Iran. Ledeen enthusiastically relayed this back to McFarlane.

"A year or so ago," Kimche said, "we began talking with Iranians who are disaffected. We believe we have made contact with people who are both willing and able, over time and with support, to change the government."

Kimche described an Iran close to collapse, with internal dissent rising. But the pro-Western moderates inside the government needed outside support, especially from the United States. To show their bona fides, they offered to release the American hostages in Lebanon, likely in exchange for some military equipment. "They are confident they can do this," Kimche ended. It seemed almost too good to be true—a potential opening with Iranian moderates who could possibly steer Iran back toward the United States, in addition to the release of the Lebanon hostages.

McFarlane mentioned Kimche's proposal to President Reagan a few days later. "Gosh, that's great news!" Reagan responded. He instructed McFarlane to explore the matter further.

Kimche's proposal was nothing new. The Israeli ambassador to Washington, Moshe Arens, had suggested a similar plan to use weapons to influence the Iranian government in October 1982. The Iran-Iraq War had put the two allies on opposite sides of the conflict. Despite Iran's support for Hezbollah, Israel viewed Saddam Hussein's Iraq as the greater of the two enemies. The Israeli government strongly opposed the Reagan administration's effort to secretly support Iraq and allow third-party countries to provide weapons. During the days of the shah, Israel and Iran had good relations, and many senior Israelis still harbored ideas of Iran's being a natural ally against their common Arab foe. Israel repeatedly lobbied Reagan administration officials to endorse its arms-selling scheme as a means to improve relations with Iran.[3]

In the summer of 1985, agents working on behalf of the United States surreptitiously shipping arms to the Nicaraguan resistance stumbled on a warehouse in Lisbon, Portugal, with Israeli weapons headed for Iran. When confronted, a senior Israeli replied that they had not technically violated the ban on weapons to Iran because the arms were being shipped by a private company, with each aircraft dropping off arms also returning with Iranian Jews. The Israeli government permitted this because it would build credibility with moderate elements in the Iranian military that might grow strong enough to establish a more reasonable Iranian government.[4] Now Kimche approached McFarlane to propose this same idea.[5]

Israel's contact within the Iranian regime was Manucher Ghorbanifar. Born in Iran in the early 1940s, this self-described export-import businessman made a comfortable living by peddling his services to various intelligence agencies, including the shah's Savak and Israel's Mossad. Short, stocky, with thinning hair and a round face, he had a forceful personality and the manner of a polished used-car salesman.

In 1984, he approached a U.S. Army intelligence officer working in the Middle East, who in turn passed him off to the CIA's Tehfran operation in Frankfurt. Ghorbanifar claimed he had information about the recent kidnapping of William Buckley, the Beirut CIA station chief, and even more important, knowledge of a plot to assassinate candidates in the upcoming American presidential election. The CIA administered a polygraph to Ghorbanifar. He failed on every significant question. In June, the CIA station in Frankfurt administered another lie detector test to Ghorbanifar, but he failed that one too. Langley concluded he could not be trusted and issued a "burn notice," which notified all U.S. intelligence agencies to avoid using Ghorbanifar as an intelligence asset.[6]

On Thursday, July 11, Ledeen met for lunch with Adolph "Al" Schwimmer, an Israeli arms merchant and adviser to Prime Minister Peres. Schwimmer told Ledeen that Ghorbanifar had access to the highest levels of government in Tehran, including senior cleric and reputed moderate Ayatollah Hassan Karoubi. In exchange for the seven hostages in Lebanon, Ghorbanifar proposed that the United States allow Israel to sell Iran around a hundred TOW antitank missiles. The swap of armaments for hostages would lead to improved relations with Khomeini's regime. Ledeen liked the idea, writing McFarlane that the TOW missiles were part of that process, "a demonstration of good faith and a sample of what would happen if Iran agreed to a rapprochement with us."[7] As the proposal came from the most senior level of the Israeli government, McFarlane did not look at the recommendations with too critical an eye. One hundred antitank missiles, he thought, certainly would not change the balance of power in the Iran-Iraq War, and if it secured the Lebanese hostages and provided an opening with moderates in the regime, McFarlane believed the gains outweighed any risks.[8]

President Reagan was supine in a bed at Bethesda Naval Hospital, just outside Washington in suburban Maryland, recovering from the removal of a cancerous polyp in his colon. McFarlane went up to the president's room. Reagan sat up in his bed, tired but in good spirits. After discussing some new issues on arms control with the Soviets, McFarlane laid out the Israeli proposal. Reagan brightened at the prospect of releasing the hostages and said he understood why Iranians would want to overthrow Khomeini. Reagan encouraged his national security adviser to continue pursuing the Israeli opening.[9]

Next, Kimche flew to Washington and met with McFarlane. Was the United States going to sell Iran the weapons? If not, Kimche pressed, "What if we [the Israelis] provide the weapons?" This passed the cost off to Washington but avoided placing the Americans in the awkward position of directly providing weapons to Iran. If Israel did this, Kimche wanted assurances that the United States would backfill their stock of TOW missiles.

With Reagan back in the White House recuperating from his surgery, on the morning of August 6 he met with his senior advisers in the second-floor residence. The assemblage sat at the far west end of the long main hallway in a comfortable, yellow-painted sitting room, beneath a large half-moon window overlooking the press office and the long white portico leading to the West Wing and Oval Office. Reagan, dressed in his bathrobe, presided over the meeting, sitting on a red flowery-patterned chair. McFarlane opened with a rundown on his meeting with Kimche and the Israeli offer to ship the TOWs in lieu of the United States, provided "we" backfill their missiles.

Weinberger immediately opposed the idea. "I don't think it's legal." He went on, "Even if a third party shipped the missiles, it still requires notification of Congress." As far as an opening for Iran, he said, "Nothing indicates that there has been any slight change in the virulently anti-Western, anti-American attitude of those in charge of Iran." He added ominously, "It would open us up to blackmail by any one of those who knew."[10]

Shultz and Weinberger detested each other and were often at loggerheads over policy, but in this instance they found common cause. Shultz agreed with Weinberger's conclusions. After carefully examining the idea, he concluded it would seriously undermine our public diplomacy to isolate Iran, and despite the pronouncements of this being a precursor to an opening with Iran, it looked to Shultz like a straight-out arms-for-hostages deal.

While Bill Casey did not attend that meeting, he was the one man who supported McFarlane. The CIA director shared similar concerns about Soviet influence in Iran and the prospects for wooing Iran with weapons. On May 17, 1985, CIA national intelligence officer Graham Fuller reinforced this view in a memo to Casey suggesting that the Iranian arms embargo might work against U.S. interests by moving the Iranians, who were desperately seeking arms on the world market to carry on their war with Iraq, toward a closer relationship with the Soviet Union.

To Casey, what the national security adviser proposed simply rehashed the CIA's current tasking from the 1981 presidential finding, which required him to build conduits inside Iran to influence the regime. After four years, access still plagued his agency. While they had developed their spy network in the country, it remained primarily composed of midgrade military officers and bureaucrats. They did not penetrate the veil of secrecy that surrounded the Islamic Republic. The true decision makers around Khomeini remained elusive. If the Israelis thought they had some new contacts that might help the CIA fulfill this mission, Casey supported them. Casey also worried about the fate of William Buckley, the CIA station chief held hostage by Hezbollah, whom he had encouraged to go to Lebanon in the wake of the 1983 embassy bombing. That spring, reports began filtering back to the agency that the Iranians were torturing Buckley.[11] If the Israelis thought that Ghorbanifar might succeed in freeing Buckley, why not give it a try?

President Reagan did not make a decision that morning but called McFarlane into the Oval Office several days later. As McFarlane later described it, "The President brooded quietly for a few moments. He pressed his fingertips tighter reflexively and stared at the carpet. Finally he looked up: 'Well, I've thought about it, and I want to go ahead with it. I think that's the right thing to do.' "[12]

The idea of an opening to Iran had long appealed to the perennially optimistic president. During his first term, Reagan signed three letters on White House stationery, each delivered by a different country's foreign minister, to the Iranian government, urging them to improve relations with the United States.[13] While he had received no response, he believed the two religious countries remained natural allies against the Soviets, with a common cause in Afghanistan. The plight of the seven American hostages bothered Reagan. A naturally compassionate man, Reagan frequently let his heart, rather than his brain, govern his decisions.

"The president always talked about the hostages, and at times it seemed that it was his greatest priority," Poindexter said later. "But the two dovetailed together. We would have tried reaching out to the Iranians even if we did not have the hostages."[14]

On August 20, 1985, an Israeli-chartered 707 aircraft landed in Tehran with a pallet load of ninety-six U.S.-made TOW missiles. No hostages emerged from Lebanon. Ghorbanifar, who accompanied the shipment to Iran, claimed that Revolutionary Guards had seized the missiles on the tarmac and absconded with them; the weapons had failed to reach the desired moderates. During a contentious meeting in Europe, Ghorbanifar explained that the United States needed to send the second batch of four hundred TOWs in order to gain the release of *one* hostage. After a phone call between Reagan and McFarlane, Reagan agreed to ship the second batch of missiles.

Early on the morning of September 15, another Israeli-chartered aircraft landed in the northwestern Iranian city of Tabriz loaded with 408 missiles. This time, Ghorbanifar came through. The Iranians offered to release one hostage, and the United States could decide which one. McFarlane and Casey wanted Buckley, but through Ghorbanifar the Iranians relayed that Buckley was "too ill" to be released. Buckley had, in fact, been dead for nearly three months. McFarlane then requested Reverend Benjamin Weir, in part because his family had been outspoken critics of the administration's attempts to free the hostages. Thus far, 504 TOW missiles had yielded one hostage.

In anticipation of the possible hostage release, the Joint Staff began working on a contingency plan to secure the released Americans in Beirut and safely transport them out to Cyprus and back to the States. The nuts and bolts of working out the details within the National Security Council fell to forty-two-year-old Marine Lieutenant Colonel Oliver North. Charismatic and energetic, North was a decorated and respected Vietnam veteran. He arrived at the White House in 1981 as one of several military officers assigned to an unadorned room on the third floor of the Old Executive Office Building adjacent to the West Wing. North would likely have gone on to a successful military career, but the excitement and power of his NSC position seduced him, and he extended his tour at the White House, now in its fifth year. North, as the CIA's Robert Gates noted, had the deserved reputation as the "go-to guy to get things done."

Ghorbanifar lied about a great many things, but the Israelis knew he had real access to senior officials in the Iranian government who desperately wanted American weapons. All of Iran's military equipment had come from the United States. After six years of war and an American-led arms embargo, chronic shortages existed in the stocks of munitions and spare parts needed to keep its war machine operating. With Iraq's superiority in airplanes and tanks, missiles to counter these were especially important. While the Iranian government remained committed to winning the war and spreading the revolution, splits developed within the government between pragmatists and purists over approaching the West, including the United States, for the needed military hardware. A confidant of Ayatollah Khomeini's, speaker of the Iranian parliament Hashemi Rafsanjani, led the realist camp. A corrupt but skilled political survivor who would later enrich himself by cornering Iran's pistachio exports, he had commanded the army earlier in the war. He had no qualms about trading with the Great Satan in order to win the war. If that led to improved relations, so be it. Prime Minister Mir-Hossein

Mousavi supported Rafsanjani. An architect before the revolution, the stern Mousavi came more from the leftist body of the Islamist movement. He shared Rafsanjani's views and advocated working with the Israelis, although he seemed guided more by the pressing needs of war than any opening with the West.

On the other side of the divide sat the appointed successor to the supreme leader, Ayatollah Hussein Ali Montazeri. A liberal by Iranian standards, the learned theologian from Qom staunchly supported the revolution, but he believed in a more liberal government, one in which an Islamist jurist presided in a multiparty limited democracy. He later clashed with Khomeini over the heavy-handed tactics used to suppress opponents, especially the mass executions ordered by Khomeini in 1988. But in spite of his democratic persona, he had no interest in any rapprochement with the United States. He maintained his own armed militia, headed by the brother of his son-in-law, Mehdi Hashemi. A thuggish dogmatist, Hashemi had served time in jail during the shah's rule for killing prostitutes and homosexuals. He remained totally dedicated to Montazeri and worked to export the revolution to Lebanon through Hezbollah.

Ayatollah Khomeini learned of the secret dealings with the Americans and Israelis after the shipment of the second batch of TOW missiles. He sided with the pragmatic Rafsanjani. What McFarlane had missed and Ghorbanifar had obfuscated was that a "moderate" wing never existed in Iran. Every faction leader knew of the dealings, and the supreme leader endorsed them. For Khomeini, it was never about a strategic opening but rather about beating Iraq and spreading the revolution. He had no compunction about turning America's own weapons on their maker.

Enticed, the Iranian pushed for more arms. Ghorbanifar's shopping list included advanced air-to-air missiles, Harpoon antiship missiles, and an improved variant of the American-made Hawk antiaircraft missile, which he falsely claimed Iran needed to counter Soviet Bear bombers that repeatedly violated Iranian airspace. It was the type of argument that might appeal to the Cold War hawks in the administration.[15] To sweeten the pot for the Americans, Ghorbanifar introduced Ledeen to Hassan Karoubi, whom Ghorbanifar claimed to be the leader of the "middle way," as he termed the supposed moderate faction within the Iranian government.[16] Karoubi claimed to be a close adviser to the supreme leader, spending three days a week at Khomeini's home.[17] He was the type of senior official that McFarlane hoped to contact. While McFarlane balked at selling some of the more sophisticated weapons, Reagan authorized eighty Hawk antiaircraft missiles to be sent to Iran via Israel.

On the evening of November 22, Duane Clarridge awoke to a call from Oliver North. "Look, I've got a problem, and it involves Portugal. I need to see you right away." North and Clarridge were friends, occasionally meeting for a drink at a bar called Charley's Place in McLean, Virginia.[18] A few hours after the phone call, the two men met at Clarridge's office at CIA headquarters. North explained that he needed Clarridge's assistance in facilitating an Israeli delivery of oil drilling equipment to Iran. In truth, the plane was carrying the Hawk missiles. It was to land in Portugal, where the missiles would be transferred to another, neutral aircraft before being flown to Tehran. But Israel had sent the aircraft without obtaining landing rights, and the Portuguese government suspected the plane carried more than oil drilling equipment and prohibited the aircraft from landing in Lisbon.

To avoid Portugal, Clarridge ordered aircraft from a CIA proprietary company, St. Lucia Airlines, to fly the missiles directly from Israel to Tehran. The plane, flown by a West German pilot, landed in Tehran in the wee hours of November 25. On the tarmac to meet the jet was no less than Prime Minister Mousavi. The smaller CIA aircraft could carry only eighteen missiles, and the Israelis had sent an antiquated version replete with Hebrew markings and the Star of David stenciled on each missile. Mousavi went ballistic. He called Ghorbanifar, who in turn called Ledeen. Near hysterical, Ghorbanifar yelled repeatedly that the United States had cheated them. The Hawk debacle should have ended the entire Iran arms affair. Instead, it only convinced those who supported it of the need for the United States to take a more direct role in the arms transfers.

On Saturday, November 30, 1985, President Reagan had finished pruning a large walnut tree in the front yard of his ranch in California, when a letter addressed for his eyes only arrived. Bud McFarlane was tendering his resignation, stating the long-standing Washington rationale of wanting to spend more time with his family. In announcing McFarlane's departure to the press five days later, on December 4, President Reagan quipped prophetically: "I should warn you that I'll probably be calling on you from time to time for your wise counsel and advice."[19] Reagan announced that McFarlane's deputy,

Navy Vice Admiral John Poindexter, would be the new national security adviser, the fourth man to hold the position thus far in his administration. Poindexter was unquestionably brilliant. He'd graduated first in his class at Annapolis before going on to earn a doctorate in nuclear physics from Caltech in 1964. An incessant pipe smoker, he displayed a quiet and reflective demeanor. But Weinberger believed Poindexter was out of his element as national security adviser: "He possessed no strong credentials in foreign policy." Poindexter had done an effective job at managing the NSC staff, however, and had proven to be a loyal subject to the White House. He also shared his good friend Bill Casey's disdain for congressional meddling in foreign affairs.

Poindexter and Reagan had discussed the Israeli arms-transfer debacle in November. Both agreed that the Israelis had fouled up the shipment. The solution would be for the United States to take a more active role. On the morning of December 7, both Pearl Harbor Day and the day of the annual Army-Navy game, Reagan met again with McFarlane, Shultz, Weinberger, Poindexter, and CIA Deputy Director John McMahon, filling in for Casey, who was in New York being treated for cancer. The meeting degenerated into a remarkably freewheeling exchange between the president, Shultz, and Weinberger. Shultz made an impassioned argument against dealing with terrorists. "We need to put this operation aside," he said. "The operation should be stopped. We are signaling to Iran that they can kidnap for profit."

Reagan turned to Caspar Weinberger. "What do you think?"

"Are you really interested in my opinion?" the defense secretary responded, knowing full well that the president knew he had opposed the idea from the outset.

"Yes," Reagan replied, without amplification.

Weinberger echoed Shultz's comments and proceeded to blast continuing the Iranian contacts. The Iranian regime remained viscerally anti-American. "This will undermine Operation Staunch and our entire effort to contain Iran. We will lose all credibility with our allies. There are legal problems here, Mr. President, in addition to the policy problems. It violates the Arms Export Control Act, even if done through the Israelis. It violates our arms embargo against Iran. It is illegal."[20]

Frustrated by Weinberger and Shultz's strenuous objections, Reagan replied, "Well, the American people will never forgive me if big, strong President Reagan passed up a chance to free the hostages over this legal question."

"Then, Mr. President, visiting hours are on Thursday," Weinberger responded sardonically.

Reagan vacillated. Weinberger's handwritten notes taken during the meeting reflect that the president believed any weapons would go to moderate elements within Iran and not to the Revolutionary Guard. At the end of the meeting, Weinberger believed his rare cooperation with Shultz had carried the day with the president. Upon his return to the Pentagon, his military adviser, Colin Powell, came in and asked how it went. Weinberger replied with a slight grin, "I believe the baby has been strangled in its cradle."

But Reagan remained reluctant to give up on what appeared to him to be the only thread of hope to secure the release of the hostages. Despite all the broken promises, the arms deals had secured the release of one of those held in Beirut; Reagan simply could not bring himself to admit there was little the United States could do to influence Hezbollah.[21]

"No one outside of the White House believed that there were moderate Iranians we could work with," Poindexter recalled. "My view, and I think the president agreed with me, was that we should try." Bill Casey concurred. "It's risky," he told the president, "but most things worth doing are."

Rather than strangling the Iran baby, the NSC under Poindexter gave it new life. On January 17, 1986, Reagan signed a new finding of covert action. It tasked the CIA with taking charge of the arms-transfer effort. The goal remained unchanged. Reagan wanted to strengthen moderate elements within the Iranian government "by demonstrating their ability to obtain requisite resources to defend their country against Iraq and intervention by the Soviet Union."[22] Rather than use Israeli weapons, the United States would sell the TOWs or Hawks directly to Iran through the Israelis, who in turn would transfer them to Ghorbanifar's intermediaries in Tehran.[23]

The CIA director brought in retired Air Force Major General Richard Secord to help facilitate the transfer of American weapons to Iran. An arms peddler, Secord was also providing weapons to the Contras for both Casey and North. The release of the hostages was listed as a tangential benefit in the finding, but this aspect remained paramount in Reagan's mind. As the president noted in his diary about signing the finding prior to heading to Bethesda for a physical: "Only thing waiting was NSC wanting decisions on our effort to get our five hostages out of Lebanon. Involves selling TOW anti-tank missiles to Iran. I gave a go ahead."[24]

Ghorbanifar relayed a new request from his contacts in Tehran. The

Iranians wanted intelligence about Iraq. McMahon had gone over to the White House to see Poindexter and voice his strong objection to providing Iran with any intelligence. "Providing defense missiles was one thing," McMahon argued, "but when we provide intelligence on the Iraqi order of battle, we are giving the Iranians the wherewithal for offense action." This could cause the Iranians to win the war, with "cataclysmic results" for the United States. Poindexter did not dispute this, but countered that it was an opportunity that should be explored, adding, "A map of Iraqi order of battle is perishable anyway."

That afternoon, North met with the CIA's Robert Gates, John McMahon, and Tom Twetten to discuss what type of intelligence to provide Iran. Gates called over a secure phone to Charles Allen, an experienced CIA officer assigned as the national intelligence officer for counterterrorism, requesting that he work with some analysts in the Near East Division to put together some limited intelligence for Iran. The request, Gates stated, was coming from the White House, but he emphasized to Allen to make sure that the intelligence provided "would give no significant advantage to the Iranian military."[25]

The next day, Allen handed Gates a map laying out the disposition of Iraqi forces along the Iranian border, including the locations of Iraqi division headquarters and key military installations.[26] To try to mitigate the damage, it showed details of one Iraqi division's front line in central Iraq, well away from the decisive southern front near Basra. A few days later, it was passed to Ghorbanifar and then into the hands of the Iranian military, who used the windfall to launch a night attack that drove the Iraqi forces back a mile and a half. Iraq had to commit its corps armored reserves to restore the front line, which it managed to accomplish but at the cost of over one thousand casualties.[27] Iran was also given the complete order of battle of Iraqi ground and air forces, the information coming from the unwitting Defense Intelligence Agency.[28]

The CIA's rank and file distrusted Ghorbanifar. Charlie Allen met with Ghorbanifar at Ledeen's home on January 13 to ascertain the Iranian's true knowledge of the Iranian government. Allen concluded that the Iranian businessman was a "cheat and a crook."[29] This feeling was shared by the head of the Iran desk, Jack Devine, who requested another polygraph. Ghorbanifar failed again on thirteen of fifteen key questions regarding his access and the accuracy of his statements about the Iranian government. But the

CIA director remained committed to the enterprise. Ghorbanifar might be exaggerating his influence within the Iranian government, but if he could provide any credible access to the government, it was worth the risk. "Well, maybe this is a con man's con man," Casey countered. And with that the operation went forward.[30]

With the president's finding, an unhappy Weinberger directed Powell to work with the army to transfer four thousand TOW missiles to the CIA. Powell coordinated the delivery with the vice chief of staff of the army, General Maxwell Thurman.[31] On February 15, an unassuming white aircraft with "Southern Air Transport" adorning its fuselage picked up the first batch of five hundred TOW missiles at Kelly Air Force Base, near San Antonio, Texas, and flew them to Israel. There, a ground crew transferred the TOWs to an Israeli plane for the final leg to Iran, arriving on February 17. Ten days later, a second installment of five hundred TOWs arrived at the joint military-civilian airport at Bandar Abbas. Despite one thousand missiles sold to Iran, not one hostage emerged from the back alleys of Beirut.

North and Poindexter, however, remained optimistic. On February 25, Ghorbanifar arranged a meeting at the Sheraton Hotel in Frankfurt between North and an adviser from Prime Minister Mousavi's office, Mohsen Kangar-lou, accompanied by an Iranian Revolutionary Guard officer, Ali Samii, and two senior Iranian military intelligence officers. Two days of talks ensued, with the Americans pushing for the release of the hostages and a very suspicious Kangarlou advocating for the United States to provide Iran advanced air-to-air missiles for its fleet of F-14 fighters. North gave the Iranians the CIA-produced map of Iraqi units positioned along the central front and repeatedly tried to impress upon them the threat posed to their country by the Soviet Union, hoping it would strengthen the possible cooperation between the United States and Iran in the Cold War. The meeting adjourned with both sides agreeing to another high-level meeting on the Iranian Persian Gulf island of Kish.

North sent an upbeat e-mail to McFarlane's home classified computer: "While all this could be so much smoke, I believe that we may well be on the verge of a major breakthrough—not on the hostages/terrorism but on the relationship as a whole."[32]

"Roger Ollie," McFarlane replied to North's e-mail. "Well done—if the world only knew how many times you have kept a semblance of integrity and gumption to U.S. policy, they would make you Secretary of State."

Nothing in this tortuous affair developed as planned. The meeting at Kish never materialized. Now Ghorbanifar demanded an array of even more weapons be sent to Iran. This included 240 different spare-part items for Hawk missiles, air-to-air missiles, and sophisticated Harpoon antiship missiles. North accepted this request and worked out a convoluted scheme whereby money, hostages, and weapons would be exchanged in a series of sequential operations, but this too failed to move beyond discussions.

Casey decided to augment North and assigned the CIA's elder Iran analyst, George Cave, to the Iran initiative in March 1986. Casey had argued that they needed an experienced operations officer fluent in Farsi. Cave held a dim view of Ghorbanifar, having witnessed his failed polygraph test in January, and was incredulous that the Israelis had vouched for him.

Cave flew to Paris and met with Ghorbanifar and the new Israeli interlocutor, Amiram Nir. In his mid-thirties, good-looking with thick curly black hair, Nir briefly served as a military correspondent on Israeli television before casting his political lot with the Labor Party. In 1984, Peres elevated him to adviser on counterterrorism. In this capacity, he worked closely with Oliver North during the *Achille Lauro* hijacking and, in the fall of 1985, played a supporting role for Kimche in working with Washington on selling weapons to Iran. Nir's role would be to keep the Americans using Ghorbanifar.

Cave pulled Nir aside and asked, "Have you fully vetted Ghorbanifar?"

"Yes, he's trustworthy," Nir answered, but Cave remained unconvinced.

Knowledge of both the presidential covert action finding and the subsequent arms shipments remained tightly held by the NSC and the CIA. Worried that the NSA might uncover the details of the arms transfers, Oliver North wanted access to any intercepted communications limited, and ordered the agency's director, William Odom, to exclude both Shultz and Weinberger. To North's annoyance, Odom refused. "I work for the defense secretary and the president, not Bill Casey or Ollie North," the stubborn Odom replied. He had the pertinent intercepts hand carried to Powell. "Weinberger knew of each transfer within a few days by the signals intercepts."[33]

Odom considered offering the same information to Secretary Shultz, but the secretary of state refused. He vigorously opposed the arms deals, and the less he knew, the happier and better Shultz felt. But his department certainly knew of the gist of the dealings. Assistant Secretary of Defense Armitage spoke daily to his counterpart at State, Arnold Raphel, about the significant developments from the intelligence reports on the secret dealings with Iran.[34]

Odom thought the entire idea was foolhardy. In Weinberger's office one afternoon, the two men discussed the arms-for-hostages operation. "You know this is going to leak, and I hate to say it, but it is going to cause a great crisis," said Odom. "Why don't you go over and convince the president to call it off. There is no chance it will succeed."

"Bill, I've tried," a frustrated Weinberger replied. "He just can't be convinced."

Chairman of the Joint Chiefs of Staff William Crowe remained the one man in the dark on the shenanigans. He accidentally discovered the affair in July 1986. His executive assistant, Lieutenant General John Moellering, had attended an NSC meeting in which North let slip a reference to Iranian arms sales. After the meeting, he and Rich Armitage drove back to the Pentagon together.

"What was that reference to Iran and arms?" Moellering asked.

"You don't know what they've concocted? When we get back, come up to my office and I'll fill you in."

Moellering promptly told Crowe, who confronted Weinberger.

"I was against it," shrugged Weinberger, "but the decision had been made and the president wasn't going to change his mind. I saw no point in bringing you in."[35]

In April, Ghorbanifar appeared to achieve a breakthrough. He returned from Iran and proposed a meeting in Tehran with senior Iranian officials, including a meeting with the speaker of the Iranian parliament, Rafsanjani, and Prime Minister Mousavi as part of a final exchange of weapons for the hostages. Initially, Cave and North were to fly first to Tehran with Ghorbanifar to lay the groundwork for the larger meeting with McFarlane. Ghorbanifar offered use of a Lear jet and a house to stay in in Tehran. But Poindexter overruled this as too risky, perhaps fearing news would leak before McFarlane's more important meeting.[36]

North sent a memo to Poindexter: "I believe we have succeeded. Thank God—he answers prayers."[37]

At eight thirty in the morning on May 25, 1986, an unmarked Israeli aircraft piloted by the CIA touched down at the airport in Tehran. The U.S.

delegation consisted of Bud McFarlane, Oliver North, George Cave, NSC staff member Howard Teicher, Israeli Amiram Nir (pretending to be an American), and a CIA communicator who provided secure communications for the entourage back to Poindexter in Washington. Their plane carried one pallet of Hawk missile parts, with another aircraft filled with twelve more pallets standing by in Israel to be sent the minute the hostages were released. An Iranian airport guard ushered the group into a VIP lounge. Here they waited for someone to appear, content to make polite small talk with the Iranian base commander, who entertained them with an air show using some of his F-4s, having recently received a shipment of spare parts from the West.

In fact, the U.S. visit caught the Iranians completely by surprise. Despite the agreement and having relayed the day of McFarlane's arrival, the Iranians did not really think the Americans would come. When the Revolutionary Guard heard of this strange delegation's appearance in Tehran, they sent men over to the old U.S. embassy to examine the personnel files. They scanned them and could find no one named McFarlane or North, but did see a George Cave. So they agreed to meet with the Americans.[38]

More than an hour later, Ghorbanifar appeared with Kangarlou in tow, both men looking harried. Ghorbanifar made an excuse about the Americans arriving early and escorted them to several old cars that would serve as their humble motorcade. They drove to the old Hilton Hotel—now called Independence Hotel—where the Revolutionary Guard had hastily cleared the entire top floor for the unexpected American delegation. A secure message transmitted to the White House regarding their arrival stated, "We have been treated politely, though heavily escorted by Revolutionary Guard types who are also physically and technically surveilling our rooms."[39]

The first meeting began at five p.m. Three Iranians arrived, none of whom appeared to be either polished or senior officials. The Iranians opened with a litany of grievances and American transgressions. Regardless, McFarlane put that aside and began with rehearsed remarks designed to get the negotiations moving.

President Reagan had asked him to do what was necessary to find common ground for discussions in the future, to try to find common ground for cooperation, McFarlane told the Iranians. The United States had no desire to reverse the Iranian Revolution and was willing to work with the government.

Very quickly, however, it became apparent that the two sides were operating from completely different views on what had been agreed to. The

United States expected the hostages to be released immediately, and before any more Hawk missile parts arrived. The Iranians thought that the United States intended to provide them a vast array of weapons and spare parts, with the hostages to be released at a later date. It became apparent to Cave that Ghorbanifar had promised the Iranians much more in the way of weapons than the United States would ever agree to. Ghorbanifar had lied to both sides.

In a message sent to Poindexter, McFarlane relayed his view of the Iranian government: "It might be best for us to try to picture what it would be like if after a nuclear attack, a surviving tailor became vice president; a recent grad student became secretary of state; and a bookie became the interlocutor for all discourse with foreign countries. While the principals are a cut above this level of qualification, the incompetence of the Iranian government to do business requires a rethinking on our part of why there have been so many frustrating failures to deliver on their part."[40]

When McFarlane threatened to leave, the Iranians promised him a meeting with an official of greater stature. A short time later, a member of the parliament and a senior political adviser to Rafsanjani, Hadi Najafabadi, arrived on the fifteenth floor of the old Hilton Hotel to meet with the Americans. A short, bearded man, Najafabadi immediately impressed the delegation. A mullah who had taken off his turban, he was several cuts above the other Iranians: confident, Western educated, cultured, and able to converse in excellent English.

McFarlane repeated why they were in Iran and his hopes that this would create the beginning of a renewed friendship and a strategic opening between the two nations. He stressed the threat of the Soviet Union to Iran. He told them that the United States knew about a planned Soviet invasion and that the Soviets had already conducted two rehearsals. The United States had a high-level source, a Soviet major general named Vladimir, who confirmed the Soviet intentions. This was pure fabrication, concocted on the plane ride over, but it drove home the theme the United States wanted to leave with the Iranians: that Moscow, not Washington, posed the greater risk to Iranian security.

McFarlane handed over to Najafabadi a slickly produced packet of intelligence developed by the CIA on Soviet forces arrayed along the Iranian border. He then informed the Iranian that the Soviets had recently told their rival, Saddam Hussein, that they would do everything in their power to keep Iraq from losing the war. McFarlane conveniently left out that American public diplomacy was doing the same thing for Iraq.

Najafabadi agreed with McFarlane's assessment of the Soviet threat. He also impressed upon his American counterpart the risk his own government took in meeting with the Americans. It all looked hopeful. McFarlane cabled Poindexter with a slightly optimistic message: "Have finally reached a competent Iranian official. . . . We are on the way to something that can become a truly strategic gain for us at the expense of the Soviets. But it is going to be painfully slow."[41]

Najafabadi added new conditions set by Hezbollah for the hostages' release. This included Israeli evacuation of the Golan Heights, monetary compensation, and release of seventeen Shiite prisoners who had been arrested for participation in a massive series of bombings in Kuwait in July 1983. The American delegation convened out on a balcony to avoid the presumed microphones in the hotel rooms. No one could be sure whether the Iranians were simply trying to extract more concessions or had difficulties controlling their surrogates. McFarlane stuck to his instructions from Poindexter. He insisted on the hostages' release first and no new preconditions.[42]

On Tuesday, May 27, talks continued. The two sides wrangled over sending the Hawk spare parts immediately or an immediate release of the hostages. Late in the afternoon, a conciliatory Najafabadi arrived bearing "good news." The Lebanese captives had dropped all their demands except release of their colleagues in Kuwait. He then pleaded for the United States to immediately send the spare parts to Iran. The Americans could not deliver on this, but drafted a proposed statement they hoped would satisfy the Iranians, saying the United States would "work to achieve a release and fair treatment for Shiites held in confinement." It did not, but talks continued well into the next morning. They were like two parties haggling in the bazaar. McFarlane threatened to leave if all the hostages were not returned, and Najafabadi and the other Iranians offered two hostages immediately in return for more missile spare parts. After a phone call with Poindexter around one thirty in the morning, McFarlane gave the Iranians until four a.m. to free all the hostages. If they did, an aircraft carrying the remainder of the Hawk spare parts would arrive in Tehran at ten a.m. If not, the U.S. delegation would leave. The Iranians balked, pleading for more time; McFarlane gave them until six thirty. When no hostages emerged, the U.S. delegation ate breakfast and packed up to go to the airport.

A visibly exhausted Najafabadi again asked for more time. "The hostages are not in our control."

"You have our position," McFarlane replied. "When you can meet it, let me know."

Privately, the Americans worried the Iranians might try to hold them hostage, but the real threat came from opponents of the talks within the regime. News spread of the arrival of McFarlane and the Americans. Not everyone liked it. Mehdi Hashemi organized a mob to go and get the Americans. At about eight a.m., his mob of vigilantes formed and began moving toward the hotel. Kangarlou came into the hotel and yelled at Cave, "Get everyone up. You need to leave immediately!" The Iranians brought three nondescript jalopies and they drove McFarlane's group by backstreets to the military side of the airport. Had Hashemi succeeded, Reagan would have had his own hostage crisis.

Just as Cave boarded the aircraft, a senior Revolutionary Guard intelligence officer, Feridoun Mehdi-Nejat, approached Cave and begged him to stay a few more days. The two intelligence officers had warmed to each other during the three days of talks. "Let's stay in touch," he told Cave. Cave nodded in agreement.

As he prepared to board the plane, McFarlane told one of the Iranians that this was the fourth time they had failed to honor an agreement. "Our lack of trust will endure for a long time. An important opportunity has been lost." With that the cabin door closed and the four-engine 707 taxied down the runway, taking off at 8:55 a.m.

President Reagan followed the McFarlane mission closely. After being informed of the failure of the mission, President Reagan wrote in his diary, "It seems the rug merchants and the Hisballah [sic] would only agree to 2 hostages. Bud told them to shove it, went to the airport and left for Tel Aviv. This was a heartbreaking disappointment for all of us."[43]

The failure of the meeting in Tehran should have ended the affair. McFarlane recommended as much to Reagan when he back-briefed the president upon his return to Washington. Reagan refused to concede defeat. Ghorbanifar and Nir continued to encourage the policy, and they found a willing accomplice in North, who zealously continued to work the scheme.

On July 26, Hezbollah released Father Lawrence Jenco, the director of Catholic Relief in Lebanon, after 564 days in harsh captivity. Ghorbanifar had promised the Iranians the remaining twelve pallets of Hawk missile parts when they ordered Jenco's release. For William Casey, this validated Ghorbanifar. "It is indisputable," he wrote, "that the Iranian connection actually worked this time." Casey attributed this success to Nir sitting on Ghorbanifar. Casey, while not pleased with the deal Ghorbanifar had arranged, recommended continuing with the arms deliveries as a means of securing the release of more hostages. Absent from the director's arguments was any mention of the strategic opening to counter the Soviet Union that he had so firmly advocated since the spring of 1985.[44]

Jenco carried with him a videotape from another hostage, David Jacobsen, criticizing Reagan for not doing enough to free the hostages. Reagan took this personally; he anguished over the hostages' plight and bristled at the accusation that he or his administration was not doing enough to secure their release. On July 29, Reagan called Father Jenco to convey his regards, extending him an invitation to visit the White House, which he did in what Reagan called "an emotional experience" on August 4. Moved by Father Jenco, Reagan approved sending the remaining twelve pallets of Hawk missile parts to Iran. They arrived from Israel on August 4. The entire operation had now degenerated into purely an arms-for-hostages arrangement.

Poindexter believed the United States needed a new conduit into the Iranian government. Frustrated, he wanted a second channel to cut out Nir, the Israelis, and Ghorbanifar. Poindexter authorized North to seek a new opening shortly after the Tehran meeting. After considerable effort by North's team, they met with Ali Hashemi Bahramani, a nephew of Hashemi Rafsanjani and a Revolutionary Guard officer with a distinguished combat record against Iraq. Bahramani was smart and well versed in Western politics and Middle Eastern affairs. He advocated better relations with the West and showed his desires by frequently visiting Europe. On August 25, Bahramani met in Brussels with Secord and an Iranian expatriate working with Secord, Albert Hakim. This second channel was not well received in Israel, but the nephew of Rafsanjani promised better access to the Iranian regime, without all the double-talk of Ghorbanifar.

On September 19, Bahramani and two Revolutionary Guard officers, including Feridoun Mehdi-Nejat, whom Cave had met with McFarlane in Tehran, arrived in Washington for an extraordinary meeting with the Americans. The supreme leader had personally approved Bahramani's visit, and it required considerable effort on the American side, with North coordinating with both the FBI and the CIA to get the Iranian delegation into the United

States. But on that day, the nephew of the Iranian speaker sat in Ollie North's office in the Old Executive Office Building next to the White House.

Two days of talks followed. The two sides found common ground on a number of issues. Bahramani echoed American concerns about the Soviet Union and offered a captured Soviet-built T-72 tank to examine. His government wanted strategic cooperation with the United States, he said, and he proposed forming a joint committee between the two nations to resolve their differences.[45] The first task set for the joint committee would be to work out establishing commercial arrangements. After this was in effect, perhaps six months later, the two nations would reestablish diplomatic representation. Bahramani proposed ways the two nations could support the mujahideen in Afghanistan. He offered to establish a base inside Iran to facilitate the flow of American weapons to the mujahideen. One of the senior Revolutionary Guard officers stunned Cave. One day he said he was pleased that the Americans had started to provide advanced Stinger missiles to the mujahideen, since Iran had just acquired ten of them from their own sources in the mujahideen, later determined to be Ismail Khan.

Bahramani brought a laundry list of weapons and parts. This included the ever popular Hawk missile parts and ten thousand rounds of advanced, extended-range artillery ammunition for their U.S.-manufactured howitzers. North reassured Bahramani that they could ship much of this as soon as the hostage issue was resolved. While the Iranian demurred on achieving their release, both sides generally agreed to the premise of a tit-for-tat exchange of hostages and weapons.

North provided the Iranians with a CIA-prepared annotated map, replete with talking points discussing the general location of Iraqi forces behind the front lines, as well as some additional information on Soviet forces. But rather than give them anything based upon imagery, the units were placed on a commercially available, fifteen-year-old map of Iraq.

George Cave and the younger Bahramani developed a friendly rapport. During one meeting with Cave, Bahramani laid three letters on the table in front of Cave, each a copy of one of the letters signed by Reagan urging better relations. "Did you really send these letters?"

"Yes," Cave answered, surprised that the Iranians apparently did not realize their authenticity.

Bahramani then asked Cave for American assistance in bringing about a cease-fire with Iraq, before adding that they wanted to launch one last offensive to take Basra.

"Well, what are you going to do if you take Basra?" Cave asked.

"Of course we will declare an independent Shia state for Iraq with Basra as the capital!" he answered without hesitation. "He was too young and naive to realize he was saying too much," Cave later chuckled.

After the first day of talks, North gave the Iranians a private tour of the West Wing. The group wandered across the street from the Old Executive Office Building and into the side entrance to the White House proper. They walked past the hallway leading down to the White House Situation Room and up to the next floor, past the Cabinet Room and the Roosevelt Room. There Bahramani and his two Revolutionary Guard companions gazed into the Oval Office, prevented from entering this American sanctum only by a felt rope.

Both North and Cave thought the meetings had gone well. North wrote to Poindexter, "We appear to be in contact with the highest levels of the Iranian government." North exuberantly compared Reagan with Theodore Roosevelt, who received the Nobel Peace Prize for ending the Russo-Japanese War in 1905. "Anybody for RR [Ronald Reagan] getting the same prize?"[46]

When the Iranians left, Cave went to Poindexter's office. The CIA veteran believed Bahramani to be earnest in his desire for better relations. "I think we will get two or three hostages out," he reported. Cave thought that this channel might just lead to the diplomatic breakthrough the president craved.

Talks continued in October. Once again, they broke down into a series of exchanges: five hundred TOW missiles for one hostage. Then the United States would approach the Kuwaitis about releasing at least some of the seventeen Iranian-backed terrorists held in their jail for the bombings in 1983. Then another five hundred TOWs would be sent to Iran, followed by at least one more hostage. Then the United States would consider sending artillery ammunition and provide more intelligence on Iraq, with Iran promising to do its "utmost to secure the release of the remaining hostages."[47] On October 28, 1986, the first batch of five hundred TOW missiles arrived in Iran. Five days later, the Lebanese released hostage David Jacobsen.[48]

In September and October, three more Americans were kidnapped in rapid succession—likely to replace the ones released—off the streets of Beirut: Frank Reed, Joseph Cicippio, and Edward Tracy. More than a year of providing weapons to Iran had yielded three hostages released, and three hostages taken—a net gain of zero with the terrorists in Lebanon.

The day after Jacobsen's release, the Lebanese magazine *al-Shiraa* ran a story about McFarlane's secret mission to Tehran. While inaccurate in several important details—such as the date of the meeting—it exposed the back-channel meetings between Iran and the United States. Cave suspected Ghorbanifar had leaked it, since he remained friendly with all the political rivals in Tehran. But the clear culprit was Ayatollah Montazeri. In October, authorities had arrested Mehdi Hashemi for kidnapping a Syrian diplomat. In retaliation, his supporters leaked the details of the secret dealings to embarrass Khomeini.

The next day, Rafsanjani admitted the McFarlane visit during a speech marking the seventh anniversary of the takeover of the U.S. embassy in Tehran. He revealed that the Americans brought a "key-shaped cake to be a key to resumed relations," adding, "but the kids were hungry and ate the cake."[49] As Weinberger had warned over a year earlier, the Iran arms sales had leaked, starting a feeding frenzy in the media.

The Reagan administration initially denied and obfuscated. On November 6, during an immigration reform bill signing in the Roosevelt Room just across the hallway from the Oval Office, a reporter asked, "Mr. President, do we have a deal going with Iran of some sort?" Reagan responded with the first of several misleading statements: "No comment." Then he cautioned the press about engaging in speculation "on a story that came out of the Middle East, and that to us has no foundation—all of that is making it more difficult for us in our effort to get the other hostages free."[50]

On November 10, Reagan met with his senior foreign policy team in the Oval Office to discuss the Iranian arms revelations and what they should tell the public. It would be the first airing of the details of the arms deals and the first senior-level meeting on the topic in nearly a year. Despite the grave looks around the room, President Reagan characteristically tried to keep the mood light; he and Vice President Bush exchanged some reasonably raunchy jokes. The meeting began with Poindexter providing an overview of the last year, the presidential finding signed in January and the arms sales that had ensued. Both Weinberger and Shultz expressed surprise upon hearing of both the presidential finding and the extent of the arms transactions with the Iranians. "I did not know of that," Shultz pointedly told Poindexter. In the case of the secretary of state, it was a true statement, but Weinberger knew about most of the details from the NSA intercepts provided by General Odom. Shultz lambasted the entire Iranian overture: "The Israelis sucked us up into their operation so we could not object to their sales to Iran," he said, then adding, "It is the responsibility of the government to look after its citizens, but once you do a deal for hostages, you expose everyone to future capture."[51]

Reagan remained in denial. "We did not do any trading with the enemy for our hostages. The old bastard [Khomeini] will be gone someday, and we want better leverage with the new government. Actually," Reagan added, "the captors do not benefit at all. We buy the support and the opportunity to persuade the Iranians."

Neither Reagan nor Poindexter wanted to reveal all the details, as it would only hinder the release of more hostages and endanger those in Iran who had cooperated with the operation. Weinberger cautioned that "we have given the Israelis and the Iranians the opportunity to blackmail us by reporting selectively bits and pieces of the total story."

At 8:01 p.m. on November 13, President Reagan addressed the nation from the Oval Office in a prime-time speech. "Good evening," he began. "I know you've been reading, seeing, and hearing a lot of stories in the past several days attributed to Danish sailors, unnamed observers . . . and especially unnamed government officials of my administration. Well, you're going to hear the facts from a White House source, and you know my name."

An indignant Reagan continued, "The charge has been made that the United States has shipped weapons to Iran as ransom payment for the release of American hostages in Lebanon, undercut its allies, and secretly violated American policy against trafficking with terrorists. These charges are utterly false." He laid out in broad terms the transactions with the Iranians, focusing solely on their role as a strategic initiative with Iran to end the Iran-Iraq War and as part of a larger containment strategy against the Soviets. He had authorized sending McFarlane to Iran when negotiations appeared promising, comparing this trip to Kissinger's secret trip to China as part of that diplomatic opening. The president bristled at the rumors that the United States had provided "boatloads or planeloads" full of American weapons to Iran to spare the hostages. Reagan admitted, though, that the United States had provided a small amount of "defensive" weapons, but these modest deliveries, taken together, could easily fit into a single cargo plane.

At best, Reagan told the American public half-truths. An underpinning of the entire overture with Iran centered on hostages, most especially with the president. While Casey and McFarlane saw it through the lens of a strategic influence in Tehran, Reagan's private discussions and personal diary myopically viewed the negotiations as an effort to free the hostages, with the by-product being better relations with the mullahs. In the last six months of the North-led effort, it had degenerated into a purely arms-for-hostages deal, personally approved by President Reagan. Whether the president deliberately lied or was merely self-delusional remains debatable, but the United States had not only negotiated with a declared terrorist regime, but sold senior officers of the military arm of the Islamic Revolution—the Revolutionary Guard—planeloads of advanced weapons that could easily be used for offensive action. They had even provided them a tour of the White House.

The ramifications of the arms-for-hostages affair were not confined to Washington. The supreme leader's handpicked successor, Ayatollah Montazeri, stridently opposed any dealings with the United States. He publicly called for the execution of all those who had met with the Americans. Since Khomeini had sanctioned those activities, he defended their actions as a necessity based upon the pressing needs of the war. The two religious leaders exchanged a series of letters in which their disagreement aired before the Iranian public. Khomeini removed Montazeri as his successor and ordered the execution of Mehdi Hashemi and several of his followers, despite pleas for clemency by Montazeri.

With the covert opening fully exposed, Reagan ordered the State Department to take charge of any new talks with the Iranians. Charles Dunbar, a Foreign Service officer ignorant of any of the previous discussions with the Iranians, joined George Cave to meet with Feridoun Mehdi-Nejat on December 13 in Frankfurt. Dunbar stuck to his instructions. The strategic concerns regarding the Soviet Union that had led to the arms transfers remained unchanged. However, there would be no further arms transfers and no normalization of relations while Iran continued to countenance hostage taking and supported terrorism. Mehdi-Nejat tried to ingratiate himself to the Americans. Iran remained committed to continuing the strategic opening. He pressed for the United States to abide by earlier discussions regarding providing more weapons and advocating for the release of the Dawa terrorists held in Kuwait in exchange for Iran using its influence to get hostages released. The two parties had finally reached an impasse.[52]

Dunbar returned to the States; Cave stayed in Europe to visit his grandchildren. On December 14, Cave received a call in his hotel room. On the other end was Mehdi-Nejat. He urgently wanted to meet with Cave the next morning. Cave agreed, as the two men had become friendly over the past year.

Mehdi-Nejat said he had talked with his superiors (although Cave suspected he'd spoken to a senior Iranian in Frankfurt). "Tehran is most anxious to push forward and is interested in how fast the State Department can draw up a plan." The United States had promised TOW missiles, intelligence, and cooperation in getting rid of Saddam Hussein, Mehdi-Nejat argued. He urged Cave to check back with Washington again, since it had reneged on these commitments.

Despite his long-standing objections, Secretary Shultz did not want to end the Iranian channel. Mehdi-Nejat had consulted with Rafsanjani, and there were some indications that the Iranian foreign minister was interested in working through this conduit. Shultz did not want the CIA involved, so he ordered Cave off the detail. Dunbar planned to meet with Mehdi-Nejat again in Geneva on December 27, to again reiterate that the channel remained open to pass messages, but the days of providing arms and intelligence were over.[53]

On December 19, Odom dutifully brought Weinberger the intercepts related to the meeting and the State Department's secret contacts. Weinberger was livid. He immediately sent a nasty memo to the White House: "I had assumed that we were finished with that entire Iranian episode and so testified to Congressional Committees during last week. I was astounded, therefore, to learn after my testimony, that the United States 'negotiators' were still meeting with the same Iranians." Angry at Shultz for not telling him about the meetings, he wrote, "I would very much have appreciated an opportunity to present to the President arguments as to why we should not continue dealing with these channels in Iran."[54]

Shultz backpedaled and objected to Weinberger's hostile tone. But the defense secretary had finally succeeded in killing the Iranian weapons-for-hostages baby.

In popular lore, the Iranian arms dealings have been portrayed as rogue policy pursued by the national security staff due to an inattentive president. In truth, the arms-to-Iran initiative continued a five-year-long strategy, one deeply rooted in Cold War fears of revolutionary Iran falling under the Soviet sphere. While the U.S. government publicly tried to isolate Iran,

Reagan ordered the CIA to surreptitiously develop contacts within the Iranian government in a quiet attempt to steer Iran back to the West. Its chief architects—Robert McFarlane, John Poindexter, and William Casey—viewed providing weapons as just another means to find a pragmatic faction to work with inside the Iranian government. As Poindexter wrote in an op-ed piece in the *Wall Street Journal* at the height of the scandal, he firmly believed that cultivating such a group, over time, would break down the deep mutual suspicion that permeated both sides. Iran again might serve as a bulwark against Soviet expansionism. In the process, it would help release the American hostages in Lebanon and curb Iranian terrorism. Reagan agreed, scribbling on a copy for Poindexter, "Great. RR."[55] Instead, it degraded into a swap of weapons for hostages, a political scandal. Public officials in both Washington and Iran had been badly burned by the revelations. The real legacy of the Iranian arms affair was to scuttle any hope of rapprochement for the next two decades.

Eleven

A RING ON THE AMERICAN FINGER

I t was the nadir of the nadir," commented Richard Armitage about Christmas 1986. The Iran-Contra revelations threatened to unravel the Reagan presidency.

The other shoe had dropped on the Iranian arms dealings. Beginning with the very first shipment of TOW missiles, both the Israelis and Americans had overcharged the Iranians. A bill charged to Iran called for $10,000 per missile, when the actual cost to the Defense Department was closer to $3,500. This quickly accumulated into millions of dollars of surplus of non-appropriated funds, Iranian money. Rather than turn it over to the U.S. Treasury, Oliver North funneled it with General Secord into buying arms to support the U.S.-backed rebels in Nicaragua, a scheme he later termed, "a neat idea." This treaded on illegality, and Congress was revving up for hearings that spring, dragging senior officials, including John Poindexter and Oliver North, before the cameras in hearings that promised to be as electrifying as the Watergate hearings a decade earlier.

A presidential commission looking into the matter, headed by Republican stalwart former Tennessee senator John Tower, mildly criticized Reagan for his detached leadership style and for allowing the National Security

Council to conduct operations and not just coordinate policy. The Tower report concluded that the president had traded arms for hostages. Reagan, like Claude Rains in *Casablanca*, professed "shock" to the affair even though he had been instrumental in the policy from the outset.

The strain of the scandal caused backbiting and open hostility within the administration. Secretary George Shultz took the rare action of going on television and publicly criticizing the president for trading arms to the ayatollah. This angered the First Lady, Nancy Reagan. She confided to the affable Saudi ambassador, Prince Bandar, that Shultz should go for being "disloyal to the president."[1] Reagan refused to take his wife's advice and fire his secretary of state, although the two continued to verbally spar during following meetings in the White House Situation Room over the wisdom of the entire enterprise. Reagan, despite the growing scandal, continued to believe it had been a worthwhile endeavor.[2]

The scandal caused a major housecleaning in the White House. Poindexter resigned and Frank Carlucci came in as the new national security adviser, with Weinberger's former military aide, Colin Powell, going over to the White House as his deputy. Robert Oakley joined them, reluctantly accepting the Middle East portfolio. Over at the CIA, William Casey suffered a massive stroke in December and remained in his hospital deathbed, and after a failed effort to confirm Robert Gates as his replacement, FBI director William Webster accepted the assignment heading the spy agency.

News of Washington's secret dealings with Iran caused a crisis of confidence in the Middle East. "While we were sending high-level intelligence briefers to see the king of Saudi Arabia and the emir of Kuwait to warn them about the dangers they faced should Iran defeat Iraq, it turns out we were sending weapons to Iran. You can imagine the reaction," said Peter Burleigh, who headed the Office of Northern Gulf Affairs at the State Department. "They had not expected us to do that!"[3]

The Organization of Islamic Cooperation held its annual meeting in Kuwait in January 1987. Amid the noise of the artillery rounds of the Iran-Iraq War, members debated the real policy of the United States in the region and American treachery. While Washington had publicly pressured countries not to sell Tehran weapons, it had secretly engaged in precisely that. Saudi officials who'd suspected the U.S. arms transfers had repeatedly been reassured that no such secret actions were under way. News of this duplicitous policy shook the confidence of moderate Arabs in the good faith of the U.S. government and called into question American reliability against Iran. Few believed the Reagan administration's excuse that it was a rogue operation from the White House basement.[4]

"America is a vastly successful conspiratorial power," remarked veteran Middle East diplomat Richard Murphy about the Arab view of the United States. "The Gulf states are pretty damn cynical, very much wedded to the idea that nations have interests and not affections, and if we saw it in our interest to play with Iran, we'll play with Iran. But it made them nervous."[5]

L eaders in the area were suspicious of us because of Iran-Contra," remarked Sandra Charles, who headed Middle East policy in the Pentagon under Armitage. When intelligence reports showed that Iran was positioning Hawk antiaircraft missiles—the same type sold by North and company to Iran—on the disputed island of Abu Musa, the defense minister of the United Arab Emirates responded to Charles during one meeting, "Great to know the missiles that you provided them are now a threat to your own forces. A fine mess you got yourselves into."[6]

Carlucci and Powell revamped Operation Staunch. President Reagan formally designated Secretary of State Shultz as the lead for coordinating a new interagency effort to halt weapons flowing to Iran. He assigned the task to the undersecretary for security assistance, former congressman from Illinois Edward Derwinski, who formed an Operation Staunch committee composed of representatives from across the government, including the intelligence agencies. It met every two weeks in the Old Executive Office Building, where it went over the latest open and sensitive intelligence reports about weapons destined for Iran and developed a coordinated government-wide response to cancel any sales. The new Operation Staunch immediately had success, especially in Europe. Munitions sales by Western Europe to Iran dropped dramatically, from $1 billion in 1986 to less than $200 million in the first half of 1987, and only four NATO nations sold arms to Iran, a drop from twenty-three the year before. At the end of that year, the United Kingdom ordered Iran to close its weapons procurement office in London through which Tehran purchased an estimated 70 percent of its weapons.[7]

While the State Department pursued Operation Staunch, the Pentagon fell back on the ongoing military-to-military contacts to mitigate the political damage. "The military-to-military ties through CENTCOM were a source of comfort to them and showed constancy in the relationship," remarked Richard Murphy. In one instance, while Richard Armitage was being flailed by Jordan's King Hussein over the inconsistencies in American policy toward Iran, CENTCOM and Jordanian officers were in the next room planning an exercise as though nothing had happened."[8] The CENTCOM commander noted this too, after a swing through the region. "For the short run, our military cooperation has survived the shock intact and is in a position to provide some cushioning for other elements of our relationships in the region," General George Crist wrote to Weinberger.[9]

While scandal consumed the politicians in Washington, the tanker war escalated dramatically. Iraqi aircraft struck sixty-five ships flying flags from various nations transiting to Iranian ports. Saudi Arabia allowed Iraqi Mirages to refuel at their air bases, permitting them to extend their range to the Strait of Hormuz. The Iraqis added long-range bombers newly purchased from Moscow. These lumbering four-engine planes, called Badgers, carried a powerful punch—Chinese-made cruise missiles packing a warhead with three times the explosive power of an Exocet.[10]

The Gulf Arabs increased their assistance to Iraq. Saudi Arabia paid to improve Iraqi oil pipelines running through Turkey. Kuwait and Saudi Arabia provided Iraq with as much as $1 billion in assistance each month, and Kuwait's contribution alone amounted to some $13 billion by 1987.[11] Kuwait opened the door for military aid flowing to Iraq. In one week alone, in December 1986, an unprecedented seven Soviet arms carriers arrived in Kuwait and delivered more than three battalions of T-72 tanks, plus advanced MiG-29 aircraft.[12]

After seven years of war and revolution, Iran's conventional military capabilities to respond had greatly diminished. A combination of spare-parts shortages and combat losses had reduced its air force, according to DIA estimates, to no more than a few dozen operational aircraft, and most of these were committed to the Iraqi front. Following the downing of their F-4 by the Saudis, the Iranians used Italian-made helicopters outfitted with small missiles to attack shipping and shifted operations to the central-southern Gulf, where they operated from the island of Abu Musa and the Sirri oil platform. They hit eighteen ships in 1986 before the lack of spare parts halted flight operations.[13]

The burden of waging Iran's campaign fell to the vestiges of the shah's once impressive navy. After the revolution, clerics assumed senior positions to monitor the loyalty of the service, leading to an exodus of officers to the National Iranian Tanker Company or into exile. With the outbreak of war with Iraq, the government tried to retain the officers needed to operate aircraft and ships, often successfully appealing to their nationalist sentiments. Others remained driven less by the tug of country than by family or the need for a paycheck. Among these were professional, American-trained officers who rose in rank and took the helm of a depleted navy in its first major war against Saddam Hussein.

By 1986, the Islamic Republic of Iran's navy comprised fifteen thousand men and eighteen warships. But spare-parts shortages and losses reduced the combatant ships by half, and at any one time, only one or two ships of the Iranian fleet were at sea. Iran had only one functioning Harpoon antiship missile, placed on the missile boat *Joshan*, and for years tracking this single missile became a minor fixation at the Office of Naval Intelligence.[14] The bulk of the Iranian operations fell to the four small British-built frigates, each armed with small "Sea Killer" antiship missiles and a 4.5-inch rapid-fire gun.

The Iranian leadership held the regular navy in some disdain; it suspected the officer corps of harboring sympathies for their old friends in the U.S. Navy and rightly questioned their overall loyalty to the Islamic Republic. The navy had produced few martyrs, and the Revolutionary Guard believed the force lacked the proper dedication and aggressiveness. In July 1985, Revolutionary Guardsmen manning small powerboats executed their first naval operation, seizing the Kuwaiti freighter *al-Muharraq*. With no other resources to expand their naval operations, the Iranian Revolutionary Guard Corps Navy, as their naval arm was labeled, grew quickly, and by early 1987 it became the primary means of attacking shipping.

While the Iranian navy comprised a professional, Western-trained force, the Revolutionary Guard consisted of amateur officers who made up for their lack of training with enthusiasm. The guard's rank and file was a blend of dedicated revolutionaries and impressed conscripts. One Revolutionary Guard sailor happened to be a deserter from the army who went to Bushehr to visit a friend serving in the navy. The Revolutionary Guards scooped him off the street, and twenty-four hours later he found himself manning a machine gun on a small boat in the middle of the Persian Gulf.

The backbone of this fleet was an improvised fleet of several hundred small boats, a mix of Boston Whaler–type boats and fast speedboats. If one could picture a swarm of bass-fishing boats armed with rocket launchers and machine guns attacking a tanker the length of three football fields, this gives an idea of what this new menace in the Gulf resembled. This mosquito fleet lacked the firepower to sink an oil tanker, but it could inflict serious damage and kill crewmen.

In 1984, over American objections, the Swedish government allowed nearly forty Boghammers, labeled as "cabin cruisers," to be sold to Iran. The Revolutionary Guard impressed every boat.[15] Forty-one feet long and powered by twin Volvo engines, they could reach speeds of forty-five knots. Armed with 107-mm rockets, RPG-7s, and 12.7-mm machine guns, they became the backbone of the guard naval flotilla.

The Revolutionary Guard's navy used simple procedures to attack ships. Operating in groups of three to five boats, they approached close to their intended victim, then sprinted ahead of the tanker and simply waited for the ship to go by and raked its bridge and superstructure with automatic weapons and rocket-propelled grenades. Later, they developed more sophisticated tactics. They would approach a ship at high speed from opposite directions, spraying the ship with gunfire in repeated, coordinated passing attacks. Their first attack occurred in April 1987, with forty-two other vessels meeting a similar fate that year.[16] On September 16, 1987, a significant event occurred that was a precursor to changing Iranian tactics. For the first time in Gulf war history, a speedboat was used to attack a Kuwaiti tanker, the *al-Funtas*, in an unprecedented night attack. This took away the safe haven of night transit.

The guard operated from the same bases as the Iranian navy, particularly Bandar Abbas and Bushehr. However, the Revolutionary Guard maintained a parallel, but independent, command. Both the regular navy and the Revolutionary Guard were (and still are) divided into four district commands. Each had the same designation, so the 1st Naval District in Bandar Abbas or the 2nd in Bushehr was the same headquarters name for the navy and the Revolutionary Guard. But other than the title, the two commands operated independently. In 1987, the Iranians attempted to form a joint headquarters to coordinate Revolutionary Guard and regular naval operations, but this effort failed when the Revolutionary Guard refused to cooperate and subjugate their operations under a single command.

The relationship between the Revolutionary Guard and the Iranian navy was poor. Privately, many professional Iranian naval officers held the Revolutionary Guard in contempt, viewing them as arrogant and undisciplined. The Revolutionary Guard saw the navy as too conservative and still harboring sympathies for its former ally, the U.S. Navy. The two factions exchanged gunfire on several occasions, including one incident between an Iranian navy helicopter and a Revolutionary Guard small boat near one of the oil platforms. But the Revolutionary Guard rapidly became the more powerful. In one case, the guard forced the commander of the Iranian navy to resign when he opposed their seizure of a Kuwaiti freighter.

At times, neither force showed great discipline. Individual commanders disregarded orders from their respective district headquarters. In July 1987, Hashemi Rafsanjani assured Japan's foreign minister that Iran would not attack Japanese shipping in the Gulf. But independent-minded Revolutionary Guard officers subsequently attacked two Japanese tankers.[17] The captain of the navy frigate *Sabalan*, Lieutenant Commander Abdollah Manavi, who later rose to vice admiral and head of naval operations, earned the reputation of being a rogue commander. A zealot, on numerous occasions he ignored orders from 1st Naval District in Bandar Abbas not to fire on specific merchant ships. Manavi acknowledged receipt of the order and then opened fire on the hapless tanker. He deliberately aimed at the bridge and living quarters to kill as many of the crew as possible. For this, Captain Manavi earned the apt nickname "Captain Nasty."

In order to find the tankers to attack, Iran relied on a few American-made P-3 surveillance planes and Iranian C-130s—several outfitted with signals intelligence collection equipment provided by the CIA before the fall of the shah. This equipment proved useful in monitoring ship radio communications, ascertaining port destinations, and relaying information down to the naval district.

The key link in the Iranian monitoring scheme was the Iranian-held islands and oil platforms in the Persian Gulf, which sat astride the tanker routes. Under the command of the regular Iranian navy, these locales served as both command and control sites and as forward operating bases. They became staging bases, initially for helicopters and later for Revolutionary Guard small boats. They provided an important communications link between the land-based headquarters and naval forces operating in the Gulf some one hundred to two hundred miles away. With the exception of Farsi Island, which reported back to 2nd Naval District in Bushehr, all of the platforms and island bases reported back to the larger 1st Naval District command in Bandar Abbas.

In February 1986, the 1st Naval District headquarters published a detailed operations order for tracking and monitoring prospective targets, including U.S. Navy warships. The command divided the southern Gulf and the Strait of Hormuz into eastern and western zones and formed subordinate headquarters on Larak, Abu Musa, and Sirik Post (just outside the Gulf at the entrance to the Strait of Hormuz). These subordinates reported directly back to Bandar Abbas over a common radio network to notify the Iranian command of any "suspicious" vessels. Additionally, the navy stationed four men on each platform. Operating undercover as employees of the National Iranian Oil Company, it was their mission to monitor all ships passing their respective platforms and to relay this information back to Bandar Abbas.[18] If the district commander determined one should be attacked, the order would be relayed to any one of the platforms or islands along the ship's projected path, and naval vessels or Revolutionary Guard small boats would sally forth. More than one-third of all Iranian attacks on shipping occurred within fifty nautical miles of the three key platforms of Sirri, Rostam, and Sassan.[19]

While the Iranian navy ran the operations on the platforms, the Revolutionary Guard small boats required them for staging bases as they could not operate for any length of time out in the open water. On any given day, Revolutionary Guard small boats clustered around each platform, using the navy's radios to relay messages back to the Revolutionary Guard headquarters.

The guard and the regular navy escalated their strikes on Saudi and Kuwaiti vessels, attacking forty-one tankers, most of them in the central Gulf and off the coast of the United Arab Emirates (UAE), including one tanker waiting to take on crude in Dubai itself.[20] Beginning in September 1986, they shifted their fury to the vulnerable Kuwait. Of Iran's next thirty-one attacks, twenty-eight were directed at Kuwaiti tankers.[21] Lloyd's of London increased the insurance premium fivefold for ships bound to Kuwait.[22] Tankers tried to make the run to Kuwait at night, hoping to avoid the Iranian navy.[23] Iran ratcheted up the pressure by sending in saboteurs, who blew up two of Kuwait's main crude oil manifolds.

Kuwait was not a particularly sympathetic victim. An accident of

Better days: President Jimmy Carter meets with America's stalwart ally the shah of Iran at the White House in 1977. *(Carter Library)*

American diplomats and marines are paraded before the news media after pro-Khomeini students stormed the U.S. embassy in Tehran, November 4, 1979. *(Associated Press)*

President Carter (*left*) confers with his national security adviser, Zbigniew Brzezinski (*center*), and Secretary of State Cyrus Vance (*right*) near the White House Rose Garden. Carter's advisers were deeply divided on how to respond to the Iranian Revolution with Brzezinski advocating for an Iranian military coup and Vance supporting a transition to democracy. (*Associated Press*)

Ayatollah Ruhollah Khomeini waves to a massive, enthusiastic crowd shortly after his return to Iran from exile following the overthrow of the shah, February 1979. (*Getty Images*)

Marine general Paul X. Kelley (seen here as the marine corps commandant in 1986) commanded the first U.S. multiservice military command dedicated to the Middle East. Kelley pushed for a permanent American military command to defend the Persian Gulf, which was a controversial decision within the Pentagon. (*Department of Defense*)

The battalion headquarters building for the marines in Beirut, Lebanon, in the spring of 1983. While the marines tried to remain neutral in the Lebanese civil war, the Reagan administration's support for the Christian-dominated government made them targets of the Iranian-backed Shia militias. *(U.S. Marine Corps)*

Sunday morning, October 23, 1983: a massive mushroom cloud rises above south Beirut after a suicide bomber rammed a truck packed with explosives into the marine battalion headquarters. *(U.S. Marine Corps)*

Aftermath: rescuers dig for survivors amid the rubble of the battalion headquarters in Beirut. The death toll of American servicemen was 241. *(U.S. Marine Corps)*

President Ronald Reagan (*left*) meets with his national security team to discuss retaliation after the bombing of the marines in Beirut. *Foreground:* Vice President George H. W. Bush; *seated to Reagan's left:* Secretary of State George Shultz; *standing right:* Secretary of Defense Caspar Weinberger. (*Reagan Library*)

Deputy National Security Adviser John Poindexter urged retaliation for the bombing of the marine barracks in Lebanon. But despite its public pronouncements, the Reagan administration never responded militarily to the marines' worst day since Iwo Jima in 1945. (*Associated Press*)

Maverick admiral James "Ace" Lyons (*left*) greets Defense Secretary Caspar Weinberger (*right*) in Hawaii on June 18, 1987. Lyons used the occasion to push for his own secret plan to wage war on Iran. (*James Lyons*)

CIA director William Casey arrives at Capitol Hill on December 11, 1986, to answer questions regarding selling weapons to Iran in an attempt to develop ties with moderates in the Iranian government. Casey saw Iran through the lens of the Cold War and worked to rebuild CIA operations inside Iran. (*Associated Press*)

Chairman of the Joint Chiefs, Admiral William Crowe, briefs Reagan and his national security advisers in the White House Situation Room on the plan to protect Kuwaiti oil tankers from Iranian attack. The administration saw this as an opportunity to undo the damage of the Iranian arms sales and deploy military forces into the volatile Persian Gulf. (*Reagan Library*)

The USS *Stark* burns after being accidently hit by two Iraqi missiles, killing thirty-seven sailors. *(Department of Defense)*

A U.S. naval convoy of Kuwaiti tankers transits the Persian Gulf in the summer 1987. As a key supporter of Iraq in its war against Iran, Kuwait became the target of Iranian reprisal attacks. *(Department of Defense)*

The commander of U.S. Central Command, General George Crist, USMC (*left*), talks with Navy lieutenant Paul Hillenbrand about operations against Iranian attack boats. The marine general commanded all U.S. forces in the Middle East during two tense years of a quasi-war with Iran. (*Paul Hillenbrand*)

SEALs storm the Iranian ship *Iran Ajr*. In one of the biggest intelligence coups in recent history, American special operations forces attacked the Iranian ship while it was laying mines aimed at sinking U.S. warships. (*Department of Defense*)

The crew of an American patrol boat rescues Iranian Revolutionary Guard sailors from the *Iran Ajr*. They had abandoned their ship the night before after being strafed by U.S. Army helicopters, September 22, 1987. *(Department of Defense)*

To defeat swarms of Iranian small boats, the U.S. military developed an imaginative solution by converting the large oil construction barge *Hercules* into a floating base for navy patrol boats, elite SEALs, and army special forces helicopters. Its timely deployment in October 1987 blunted a large Iranian naval attack on Saudi Arabia. *(U.S. Special Operations Command)*

geography placed its tiny population atop one of the world's largest oil reserves. The country owed its entire existence to Great Britain. The once great colonial power had carved out the protectorate, and after independence in 1961 sent seven thousand soldiers and marines to prevent Iraq, which claimed with some basis that Kuwait historically was part of it, from gobbling up the new nation. Kuwait imported tens of thousands of better-educated Palestinians to run its bureaucracy and develop its oil industry, but refused to enfranchise their Arab brothers and held them in fearful contempt.

During the Cold War, Kuwait tried to play the United States and the Soviet Union off each other for its own advantage. It was the only Gulf state to maintain full diplomatic relations with the Soviets, a constant thorn in the side of U.S.-Kuwaiti relations.[24] Despite Kuwait's diplomatic balancing acts, it remained a defenseless state surrounded by wolves. The constant artillery fire rattling the windows of Kuwait City served as a reminder to the ruling al-Sabah family of their vulnerability. Kuwait feared the Iranians, but threw its support behind the duplicitous Saddam Hussein, who coveted Kuwait and refused to resolve their long-standing border dispute. While Kuwait kept the United States at arm's length so as not to anger its Persian neighbor, in the end it looked to the United States for its survival.

"The Kuwaitis pretend neutrality, but when they put their money down, they put it on the West," observed the State Department's political adviser to CENTCOM and later ambassador to Kuwait, Nathaniel Howell.[25]

The Kuwaiti oil minister Sheik Ali Khalifa grew increasingly concerned by Iranian attacks on his tankers. With a mustache and soft features, Ali Khalifa looked more like an international businessman than an Arab Bedouin. Within the ruling family, he was seen as smart, with a good business sense, which is why the ruling emir, Sheik Jabir al-Sabah, appointed him to run Kuwait's most important commercial venture. At twenty-nine, he took over running the Kuwait Oil Company, helping transform it into a global concern, including installing four thousand gas stations in Europe.[26]

In the summer of 1986, Ali Khalifa and the other senior members of the al-Sabah family discussed how to respond to Iran's attacks. Unlike Tehran's terrorist attacks, these went to the heart of Kuwait's economy. They briefly considered using Kuwait's small navy to protect their ships, but defense minister Sheik Salem al-Sabah countered that Iran would simply attack their patrol boats and thus draw them into the Iran-Iraq War. Ali Khalifa agreed. Only the protection offered by a superpower would deter Iran, he felt.[27]

The real question that weighed on the minds of Kuwaiti leaders was whether they could trust the United States. If the tanker war grew worse, would Washington cut and run as it had in Beirut two years earlier, leaving tiny Kuwait to deal with Iran's wrath? Ali Khalifa decided to test the American waters.

On December 10, the American embassy in Kuwait City received an unusual inquiry from the Kuwait Oil Company asking about the requirements for registering ships in the United States.[28] Edward Gnehm at State, later ambassador to the country, was asked whether any reflagged tankers would then receive "U.S. Navy protection."[29] The same day, the manager of fleet development for the Kuwait Oil Tanker Company, Tim Stafford, telexed the U.S. Coast Guard requesting guidance on the possible reflagging of four of Kuwait's liquid petroleum gas carriers, currently registered in France, under the American flag.

The coast guard responded to Tim Stafford with a mind-numbing list of regulations, from the number of fire extinguishers needed on board to pollution control requirements. Any tanker the Kuwait Oil Tanker Company wanted to register under the U.S. flag must: 1) have a U.S. citizen as the ship's master; 2) have at least 75 percent of the crew be American citizens; 3) be owned by a U.S. company or a corporation where the majority of the board members were American citizens; and 4) be liable for use by the U.S. military during a war.[30]

But Sheik Ali Khalifa had hedged his policy and quietly approached Washington's adversary. He met with the Soviet ambassador about registering some ships under the hammer and sickle. Moscow responded immediately and favorably with no concerns about fire extinguishers or corporations. The next day, Khalifa telephoned the American ambassador, Anthony Quainton, to brief him on a Soviet offer to transport all of Kuwait's oil using either Soviet tankers or Kuwaiti ships under the Soviet flag. "Would the United States be willing to match the Soviet commitment by reflagging some or all of Kuwait's tankers?" he politely asked. "It smacked a little bit of blackmail," recalled the national security adviser, Frank Carlucci.[31]

Sheik Ali Khalifa's call set in motion yet one more debate within an administration still struggling with its Middle East foreign policy in the wake of Iran-Contra. While the basic tenets of containing Soviet and Iranian expansion were never questioned, there were divisions about whether this unexpected Kuwaiti overture helped these goals. In a private memo for senior officials, Shultz summed up his views: "It is not the role of the United States to take the lead in protecting neutral shipping in the Gulf."[32] Overall, the State Department remained hesitant about rushing in and accepting the Kuwaiti request. It appeared to be little more than a blatant attempt to pressure the United States into saving Kuwait's economy with very little in return.[33]

Once again, Weinberger clashed with Shultz. The United States had a request for assistance in an area vital to American security, Weinberger argued, and this presented a grand opportunity to develop the closer military ties needed for U.S. security—what the New Splendor effort envisioned. Inaction risked undermining the U.S. position in the Persian Gulf and would open the Persian Gulf door to the Soviets.[34] As to the legalities of reflagging, the secretary of defense asserted that whether the ships were under U.S. registry or not was immaterial. If we decided to safeguard Kuwaiti ships, he asserted, we could do it because it was in our interests and served to ensure our principle of freedom of the seas. "There wasn't the slightest question about propriety of the request and the purpose of our helping them," Weinberger said of his position. "It was in international waters, we and everyone needed the oil, so why not do it?"[35]

Although Weinberger later said the Iran-Contra debacle had not influenced his decision, Richard Armitage and Robert Oakley on the NSC staff both viewed the Kuwaiti request through the lens of the scandal. "This presented a golden opportunity to assist the moderate Arabs and restore U.S. reliability after Iran-Contra, having devastated them by lying," said Armitage.[36] Oakley agreed, adding that the U.S. policy was in tatters and the fear of an Iranian victory was serious.[37] Sheik Ali Khalifa's request offered Washington the opportunity to clearly demonstrate American support for our allies in the Gulf and to show which side we were on regarding Iran.[38]

Winter soon gave way to spring with still no firm American commitment to Kuwait.

Finally a frustrated Kuwait dropped a bombshell. Sheik Abdul Fattah al-Bader of the Kuwait Oil Tanker Company announced to startled American diplomats that Kuwait and the Soviet Union had reached an agreement to reflag five tankers, to be manned entirely by Soviet crews and escorted by three

Soviet warships between Khor Fakkan, UAE, and Kuwait.[39] The Kuwaiti government still wanted to proceed with registering six ships with the Americans, but the Soviets had been much more responsive. The entire process would take just one week, as opposed to twenty weeks with the U.S. Coast Guard.

This news created consternation on the third floor of the Pentagon. Sandy Charles, director for Middle Eastern affairs, drafted a memo for Weinberger for his weekly breakfast meeting the next morning with Carlucci and Shultz.[40] She recommended that the United States offer to protect all eleven of the tankers in question—including the five offered to Moscow—regardless of coast guard paperwork or even if they flew the Stars and Stripes.[41]

The next morning, Weinberger broke the logjam. The United States risked an expanded Soviet military presence in the Gulf if it failed to act. We cannot sit by and allow the Iranians to intimidate Kuwait, he said. While Carlucci concurred, Shultz remained unconvinced. After an hour of debating, Weinberger called the president directly. Reagan agreed to protect all eleven Kuwaiti tankers.[42]

Weinberger immediately sent a letter to the Kuwaiti defense minister, Sheik Salem al-Sabah:

> The President believes continued attacks on non-belligerent shipping, coupled with the Iranian Silkworm threat, pose a serious threat to our mutual security interests. The President has asked me to convey to you his readiness to provide protection for these eleven tankers, currently under Kuwaiti registry. We would be prepared to provide this protection to Kuwait's vessels whether or not Kuwait sought to register them under the U.S. flag.[43]

The U.S. government immediately pressed Kuwait to renege on its deal with the Soviets. But now Sheik Salem and the Kuwaitis had the upper hand. After berating the Americans for their foot-dragging and their overly complicated bureaucracy, Salem added that he resented their request for the Kuwaitis to alter their policy decisions. After all, he said, "Kuwait is a sovereign country."

As far as reneging on their deal with the Soviets, he said, "Where there is a will, there is a way." But Sheik Salem then cautioned, "In England, once a man had proposed to a woman, he could not back out, and this was the situation between Kuwait and Moscow."

The American deputy consul, James Hooper, deftly countered, "It was not official until the man put a ring on the woman's finger. Had Kuwait put a ring on the Russian finger?"[44]

"Let us say that our hand is reaching toward their hand," Sheik Salem slyly replied, "but the ring has not yet been placed on the Russian finger."

On March 9, Ali Khalifa telephoned Crist in Tampa after a meeting with Crown Prince Saad. The Kuwaiti government had agreed not to take the Russian bride. It accepted the U.S. offer to protect all eleven Kuwaiti tankers. Kuwait had slipped the ring onto the American finger.[45]

Chairman of the Joint Chiefs of Staff William Crowe arrived in Bahrain for scheduled meetings with the emir and the commander of Middle East Force, Rear Admiral Harold Bernsen, prior to going to Kuwait to consummate the agreement. After landing, Crowe learned that Khalifa had not been entirely honest. Kuwait still intended to charter three Soviet tankers to carry some of its crude oil. The revelation blindsided Crowe.[46]

"Should we just rescind the offer and let Kuwait fend for itself against Iran? Let Kuwait make the best deal it can with the Soviets?" Crowe asked Bernsen. The chairman generally supported the reflagging idea, but privately shared many of Shultz's concerns. He was also not an admirer of Kuwait's aloof stance toward the United States and had little sympathy for its straddling the fence between the superpowers.

"I think it's too late, sir," said Bernsen. "Backtracking now would seriously undermine American credibility with the other GCC countries."[47] When an angry Crowe finally calmed down, he agreed with Bernsen. There was little the United States could do except move forward and try to mitigate the Soviet's newfound prominence in the Persian Gulf.[48]

Kuwait had deftly manipulated both superpowers into providing protection against Iran. Kuwait had agreed to put the ring on the American finger, while leaving the door open for its Russian mistress.

With the political decision made, CENTCOM ramped up its plans to protect the eleven Kuwaiti tankers. Around six p.m. on Friday, March 6, Crist called his operations officer, Air Force Major General Samuel Swart, to get the "board of directors together," as the commander called his key staff officers.[49] At their meeting two hours later, Crist informed them of the proposed reflagging operation, which had been given the randomly selected name "Private Jewels." Washington's guidance to Crist had been to "minimize the risk to American lives" but still be prepared to launch retaliatory strikes on Iran within ninety-six hours.

Several shortfalls plagued CENTCOM for the upcoming convoy operation. Not only did it have no off-the-shelf plan, but Crist had no senior navy subordinate command to run what would certainly be a naval mission.[50] Lieutenant General Robert Kingston tried and failed to get the navy to stand up a Fifth Fleet for CENTCOM, and now Crist's sea service component consisted of a frocked rear admiral in Hawaii who handled budgets and paperwork. The heavy lifting of the operation fell to the small Persian Gulf flotilla, Middle East Force. Established in 1949, it consisted of a flagship and a few destroyers based out of Bahrain in an old British naval facility.[51] The navy never intended this to be anything more than a small show-the-flag naval force. In the event of a Middle East conflict, the four-star commander in Hawaii's Pacific Fleet would roll in and take over. The establishment of a joint military command legally responsible for the Middle East had not changed the U.S. Navy's scheme. CENTCOM could fight the land battle in Iran, but the Pacific Fleet would control the warships, perhaps in support of CENTCOM, but ultimately unilaterally and irrespective of the wishes of the commander in Tampa.

The commander of Middle East Force was not the type of admiral the institution would have chosen for such an important operation. Rear Admiral Harold Bernsen had graduated from Dartmouth, not the Naval Academy; an aviator but no "Top Gun" fighter jock, he had flown decidedly unglamorous airborne warning surveillance prop planes. Still, Bernsen knew the Persian Gulf. He had commanded the Middle East flagship, USS *La Salle*, at the outbreak of the Iran-Iraq War, and had recently served as Crist's senior planning officer at CENTCOM, where he'd earned Crist's respect. What Bernsen lacked in naval career gravitas, he made up for with political acumen. With a calm, measured persona that appealed to Gulf leaders, Bernsen understood the Arabs as few other military officers did. He was a smart and unorthodox thinker in the most conservative of the services. A skilled envoy, he forged a strong bond with the emirs and kings of the Gulf. This was a mission that would be political as much as military. While he never enjoyed the confidence of the navy hierarchy, especially the chief of naval operations, Admiral Carlisle Trost, Bernsen proved to be a perfect choice. Bernsen's operations officer, Captain David Grieve, arrived in Tampa to assist CENTCOM's planning. Working late into the night over the next few days, they hashed out a concept for the upcoming escort operation.

On March 13, General Crist briefed the chiefs in the Tank on their plan. Crist envisioned an expansion of the basic regime already under way since the boarding of the *President Taylor.* One or two U.S. warships would accompany the tankers along a six-hundred-mile route running from Khor Fakkan just outside the Gulf to Kuwait Harbor. CENTCOM requested two additional ships (bringing the Middle East Force total to eight) to protect the tankers and maintain communications links with air force AWACS in Saudi Arabia and the carrier well out in the Gulf of Oman.[52]

On Sunday, March 22, Bernsen's staff met for the first time with Kuwaiti oil officials and embassy representatives to talk about the escort plan. Bernsen did not have the ships to run a continual shuttle, but two or three ships could be gathered together at either end and then escorted the entire six-hundred-mile route. This slowed oil deliveries, al-Bader said, but he had little choice but to agree to the American plan. They quickly agreed on several southern Gulf routes for the convoys that avoided the Iranian exclusion zone, and Kuwait agreed to allow an American naval officer to be stationed in the Kuwait Oil Tanker Company headquarters to serve as a liaison officer. Armed with a satellite telephone, he would coordinate the tankers' schedules with Middle East Force. Additionally, al-Bader agreed to allow an officer to be stationed on board each tanker during the convoy. Kuwait agreed to purchase short-range walkie-talkies for these officers to communicate with the escorting warships. Their job would be to advise the tanker captains on military matters and to serve as coordinators between the civilian masters and the convoy commander.

Tehran greeted news of the Kuwaiti escort arrangement with characteristic vitriol. President Khamenei said Kuwait's request for U.S. protection "dishonored the region" and warned that Kuwait City and its oil facilities lay within range of Iranian forces. "Iran has not yet used its capabilities to bring pressure on Kuwait," said the Iranian president and future supreme leader on April 27.[53]

In addition to its diminutive navy, Iran had other military options. In August 1986, an Iranian naval officer, Commodore Kanoush Hakimi, traveled to China to negotiate a secret deal to purchase the powerful Chinese-built

Silkworm antiship cruise missiles. While guided by a relatively unsophisticated radar, these potato-shaped missiles packed a thousand-pound warhead capable of seriously damaging any supertanker or sinking any American warship. The Chinese agreed to sell twelve launchers and as many as one hundred missiles, and soon more Iranians arrived for training on the new weapon.[54]

American intelligence learned immediately of the sale. Hakimi happened to be on the CIA's payroll. Additionally, the British spy service, MI6, may have had an agent working the case. An Iranian arms merchant, Jamshid Hashemi, claimed to have negotiated the $452 million deal during ten chaotic rounds of haggling in China in 1985–1986. During that period, he worked for British intelligence, meeting with his Persian-speaking handler, "Michael," once a week in London.[55] The British government passed his information along to the CIA.

In a Pentagon meeting, Weinberger confronted his Chinese counterpart, who simply denied sending the missiles to Iran. "We've got satellites photographing the first shipment leaving China and off-loading at Bandar Abbas," replied the incredulous defense secretary.[56]

By January 1987, Iran had one Silkworm battery active and had announced the fact by sending a missile in the direction of Kuwait Harbor just before the meeting of the Organization of Islamic Cooperation. Iran began construction of a series of ten concrete Silkworm missile launchers ringing the Strait of Hormuz. The CIA and CENTCOM viewed this as a major new threat to Gulf shipping and to U.S. warships. Iran now had the means to seriously impede oil exports, as one Silkworm—with a range of fifty nautical miles—could turn a four-hundred-thousand-ton supertanker into so much scrap metal. Iran now had the means to control the Strait of Hormuz and to attack any ship entering or leaving.[57]

The chairman of the Joint Chiefs made obtaining one of the missiles for dissection a top priority for the Defense Intelligence Agency, which it succeeded in doing in the spring of 1987 with the aid of another intelligence service.

Regardless of Khamenei's bluster and his new Silkworm missiles, neither Bernsen nor Crist believed Iran would force a fight. "It appears unlikely that Iran will intentionally attack a U.S. combatant or a Kuwaiti flag tanker under U.S. escort," Crist's lengthy operational estimate stated. The CENTCOM plan emphasized deterrence over fighting. The Iranians would not risk U.S. retaliation. The carrier in the Arabian Sea provided the necessary muscle for a credible deterrence, and the Iranian military knew full well the capabilities of the U.S. military.[58] The risks posed in the upcoming operation seemed minimal. However, in the month after the Khamenei threat the hazards of the tanker war suddenly became very real. Once again, Saddam Hussein provided a wake-up call.

Twelve

THE WAKE-UP CALL

A t eight a.m. on May 17, 1987, the USS *Stark* steamed out of Manama, Bahrain, and gradually disappeared over the horizon, heading north out into the opaque blue of the Persian Gulf. Commanded by a forty-three-year-old Pennsylvanian with twenty years of commissioned service, Captain Glenn R. Brindel, the *Stark* was in a class of ships originally conceived as an inexpensive escort ship for Atlantic convoys during World War III. With a sleek hull and a boxy superstructure, she was armed with a little bit of everything, from antiship and surface-to-air missiles to a 20-mm chain gun; the latter, resembling a white R2-D2 from *Star Wars*, was called a close-in weapons system, or CIWS (pronounced "sea-whiz"), capable of firing three thousand rounds per minute and designed to shoot down incoming missiles. With a crew of 221 men, the *Stark* and her sister ships would provide the shield to protect Kuwait from Iran.

The *Stark*'s assigned station sat on the edge of the tanker war's killing zone. Serving as a radar picket for Middle East Force, the frigate headed for the north-central Persian Gulf, some fifty miles off the Iranian coast and a mere twenty miles outside the Iranian exclusion zone. The area just north of there had seen some 340 Iraqi air and missile attacks on Iranian shipping, sinking or damaging forty ships.[1] Recently, Iraq had begun striking Iran-bound ships farther south, flying directly over the areas where American ships operated.[2] Three days before the *Stark* sailed, an Exocet hit a Panamanian tanker just sixty miles from the *Stark*'s intended position. That same day the American destroyer *Coontz* nearly opened fire on an Iraqi pilot who failed to heed warnings and closed to within ten miles of the warship before abruptly turning away when he detected an audible buzz in his headset from the *Coontz*'s weapons control radar.[3] That evening, Middle East Force sent out an intelligence advisory to its ships stating that the Iraqis had conducted ship attack profiles in the central Gulf and that they expected this trend to continue for the next two weeks.

Brindel was well aware of the Iraqi threat. The day after the *Coontz* incident, Harold Bernsen went pleasure sailing with the *Stark*'s commander.[4] Bernsen mentioned the previous day's incident near where the *Stark* would be operating, and he asked Brindel to attend an intelligence briefing the following day that would go over the recent Iraqi attack profiles in the central Gulf as well as the rules for using force. The Iraqis flew fast and low along the west coast of the Gulf near Saudi Arabia, then quickly did the Farsi hook and turned east into the Gulf, at which point they would turn on their search radar and look for a target in the Iranian exclusion zone.[5] Frequently they fired at the first target they illuminated, with no attempt to visually identify the vessel. Bernsen instructed Brindel to make this information known to his officers so that there would be no uncertainty of the danger posed by the reckless Iraqi pilots.[6]

This was not the first time Captain Brindel heard the rules of engagement for the Persian Gulf. When his ship arrived in the Middle East, Captain David Grieve and Bernsen's intelligence officer, Commander Robert Brown, met the ship in Djibouti.[7] Brown emphasized that "the probability of deliberate attack on U.S. warships was low, but that indiscriminate attack in the Persian Gulf was a significant danger."[8] Grieve went through two formal documents governing the use of force and stressed that it was the responsibility of each captain to "take all possible measures and precautions to protect his unit."[9] The rules of engagement allowed any ship to engage an aircraft displaying hostile intent. This included such overt acts as locking on to the U.S. vessel with fire control radar or flying toward them in an attack profile. Iraqi aircraft were unpredictable and should always be regarded as potentially hostile.[10] Grieve left the *Stark*'s officers with a final thought: "We do not want, nor intend to absorb, a first attack."

As the *Stark* headed out into the danger zone, the atmosphere on board remained strangely lax. Bernsen's sagacity failed to alter Brindel's attitude, and the ship continued to operate as if it were cruising off the home port of Mayport, Florida, and not in the middle of a shooting war.[11]

The ship's executive officer was focused on an upcoming administrative inspection of the ship's propulsion plant. Inside the heart of the *Stark*, in the close spaces of the combat information center, where the glow from an array of screens and combat sensors illuminated the darkened confined space, none of the officers knew what defense state the ship should be in, nor did they seem to appreciate the threat posed by either Iran or Iraq.[12] Just that morning, Iraqi jets had conducted separate Exocet missile attacks on two large Iranian shuttle tankers, the *Aquamarine* and *Zeus*. Brindel had combined two billets—those of the watch officer and the weapons control officer. This effectively meant that no one was manning the critical weapons control officer station. None of the weapons were manned; the .50-caliber machine guns had no ammo loaded, and their crew was lying on the deck, perhaps asleep. The ship's defenses, designed to detect and defeat incoming missiles, were turned off.

At 7:55 p.m., the American AWACS flying out of Saudi Arabia picked up an Iraqi Mirage taking off from an air base near Basra flying south in the classic profile to attack Iranian shipping. This track was downloaded in real time to the U.S. warships—including the *Stark*—providing a continuous update on the Mirage's whereabouts, which due to interoperability problems between the navy and air force systems showed up on the navy radar screens as a "friendly" symbol aircraft.[13] Additionally, the destroyer *Coontz*, now pier-side at Manama, updated the Iraqi aircraft's position every five minutes over a secure radio telephone transmission to all warships, including the *Stark*.[14]

Captain Brindel walked into the combat information center fifteen minutes after the first sighting. The senior watch officer, Lieutenant Basil Moncrief, told his skipper about the Iraqi aircraft, noting that it had just gone "feet wet" and crossed out over the waters of the Persian Gulf. Brindel directed Moncrief to keep a close watch on the Iraqi aircraft and departed, apparently giving it little more thought as he worried about the upcoming engine inspection. It had become routine for U.S. warships north of Bahrain to go to general quarters as a precaution when an Iraqi aircraft was over the Gulf, but there was no thought of this on the *Stark* that night.[15]

Despite Brindel's instructions at the outset to keep a close eye on the Iraqi Mirage, none of the nine men in the combat center seemed very concerned. Even as the AWACS reported that the Iraqi jet had made the Farsi hook and was now headed east on a course that would come within eleven miles of the *Stark*'s position, one of the two fire control technicians who manned the radar and CIWS left to make an extended "head" call and was absent for the next twenty minutes.

The *Stark*'s own radar picked up the Mirage at seventy nautical miles and closing at the quick rate of six miles a minute. The radar operator told Moncrief that the Iraqi's projected path would take it to within four nautical miles of the *Stark*. Moncrief remained unconcerned, even when the ship's sensors detected the search radar emissions from the Mirage. A minute later, with the Iraqi aircraft now only forty-three miles away, one of the watch standers, Petty Officer Bobby Duncan, asked Moncrief if they should broadcast the standard warning as prescribed in the rules of engagement. "No, wait," the lieutenant replied, believing the Iraqi either would turn away or was too far out to hear the U.S. voice warning. Instead, Moncrief had them fill out a required administrative report on the incident.

Back in Bahrain, an officer on the flagship monitoring the situation grew concerned and called the *Stark* to make sure that they were aware of the fast-approaching Mirage.

"Affirmative . . . Evaluated Iraqi F-1. . . bearing 269, range 27 nautical miles, over," Moncrief answered. The *Stark*'s executive officer, Lieutenant Commander Raymond Gajan, arrived, having spent the last half hour in Brindel's cabin discussing the engine inspection. Detecting no sense of urgency, he contented himself to talk about routine administrative issues with Moncrief, paying little attention to an Iraqi jet coming in fast and low on their ship. At seven minutes past nine, the Iraqi pilot fired off his first missile, from only twenty-two miles away.[16]

As the Iraqi missile streaked undetected to the *Stark*, Moncrief finally noticed that the Mirage's course would take it directly over his ship. He finally ordered Duncan to broadcast a warning to the Iraqi F-1: "Unknown aircraft, this is U.S. Navy warship on your 076 at 12 miles. Request you identify yourself and state your intentions, over." There was no response from the Iraqi pilot, who then launched his second missile.

This time, the *Stark* detected his radar, which came in the form of an unmistakable, high-pitched tone easily heard throughout the combat center.[17] As Gajan looked on passively, an alarmed Moncrief ordered a second warning broadcast to the aircraft and sent a sailor topside to arm the chaff dispensers, which threw up a cloud of aluminum strips designed to confuse incoming missiles. After some confusion about which radar to use, Moncrief ordered the *Stark*'s own fire radar to lock on to the aircraft. He did so reluctantly, apparently worrying that this might be misinterpreted by the Iraqi aircraft as a hostile act. About this time a second missile radar was heard emanating from the F-1. Inexplicably, no one thought to activate the CIWS, the ship's best defense against an incoming missile, or even to sound general quarters.

Two minutes after the first missile was fired, a lookout on the *Stark* spotted a bright flash just off the port bow, with a "little blue dot coming from the center of that flash." He yelled into his headset, "Missile inbound!" But it was too late.

The first Exocet hit the port side of the ship. Entering through one berthing area, the missile traveled on into the chief petty officers' compartment. The warhead did not explode, but doused the interior with burning fuel. As many as twenty-eight men were instantly incinerated by the conflagration. Within the ship, sailors heard a muffled explosion. Captain Brindel, who happened to be in the bathroom at the time, rushed up to the bridge.

A tense voice came over the ship's internal speakers: "Missile inbound!" The metallic *clang-clang* sounding general quarters rang throughout the ship just as the second missile struck, eight feet from the first; its 330-pound warhead exploded, blowing apart metal and flesh, sending shrapnel through bulkheads, and creating a large gaping hole in the side of the ship.[18]

The *Stark* immediately filled with a thick, acrid smoke. Those trapped within the impact area donned their emergency escape breathing devices— basically a hood with about fifteen minutes' air supply—and stumbled in the dark trying to get through jammed hatches and past dangling live electrical wires. Six men either jumped or fell from the gaping hole down into the waters of the Gulf. A quick-thinking sailor on deck threw two of them life preservers after hearing calls for help. Men tried in vain to reach sailors trapped in their bunks, screaming for help before being overcome by smoke and fire.

Admiral Bernsen was in the wardroom of the Middle East Force's flagship, the USS *La Salle*, hosting a farewell dinner for a departing officer, with the guest of honor being the U.S. ambassador to Bahrain, Sam Zackem. The watch officer came down to the wardroom and asked Bernsen to come to the command center. Soon other staff officers followed suit, leaving Ambassador Zackem wondering what could possibly be going on. About five minutes passed, and Zackem decided to go and see for himself.

There he met a visibly shaken Bernsen. "Mr. Ambassador, the *Stark* was hit."[19] Zackem was stunned. Just the day before, he recalled, he had watched the *Stark*'s crew defeat the *La Salle*'s in volleyball, and Captain Brindel had given him a case of Coors beer.

Bernsen immediately ordered additional ships to come to the *Stark*'s assistance, and the *La Salle* made preparations to get under way and head north to take charge of the rescue effort. The crew dispatched one of their helicopters, named the "Desert Duck," carrying additional oxygen tanks, firefighting equipment, and a corpsman. Meanwhile, Ambassador Zackem phoned the crown prince of Bahrain and received permission to use that country's hospitals to treat the most seriously injured sailors. Bahrain emptied its main burn unit in anticipation of a large number of casualties, and two severely burned sailors arrived before being flown on with other sailors to the U.S. military's own burn unit at Brooke Army Medical Center in San Antonio, Texas.[20]

Back on the *Stark* the fire spread quickly. Within an hour, it had burned through two decks, consuming the combat information center and the galley and threatening the forward missile magazine. Brindel ordered it flooded. The heat was intense, melting protective fire masks and even fusing two keys in the pocket of Lieutenant William Conklin. Fire parties on the forecastle, led by Lieutenants Moncrief and Conklin, directed their hoses on the fires coming increasingly close to the magazine, as the heat from the fire peeled the paint off the base of the missile launcher.[21]

Their efforts, and the arrival of a civilian salvage tug with additional hoses, staved off disaster, but the large amount of water being poured on the fire caused a significant list that now threatened to capsize the ship. Brindel and Gajan conferred and agreed to punch holes in the side of the ship to allow the excess water to drain out.[22] One more crisis was averted.

The next day, a Bahraini helicopter rescued four of the six men who had gone overboard, while a fifth and the severely burned body of the sixth sailor were recovered by a U.S. warship. The five survivors had spent a taxing night in the open sea dodging sharks and sea snakes.

Even the Iranians tried to help. They sent two helicopters to assist in search and rescue. Although they were professionally competent, Bernsen gave them a search area well away from the *Stark*.

Word of the *Stark* disaster spread quickly through Washington. The National Military Command Center notified Armitage, who phoned Weinberger. "The USS *Stark* was hit by Iraqi missiles, probably an accident." The defense secretary relayed the message to the national security adviser, Frank Carlucci. Within an hour after the first missile hit, the president knew of the tragedy half a world away. "A beautiful day," Reagan penned in his diary, "until I got a call from Frank [Carlucci]."[23]

General Crist was in Pennsylvania to receive an honorary doctorate from his alma mater, Villanova University. Crist had recently stopped smoking, and other than craving cigarettes, he enjoyed his visit, which included a speech before newly commissioned marine lieutenants from the school's navy ROTC program. He arrived back in Tampa that evening to be met on the tarmac by a senior officer, Brigadier General Wayne Schramm, along with other staff.

"That's nice," he thought. "My staff has come out to welcome me back after receiving my honorarium." But when he got into the car, he learned about the *Stark*. It would be another five years before Crist tried again to stop smoking.[24]

After twelve hours the crew had finally extinguished the fire. The grisly task to find and remove the dead began. The final toll: thirty-seven sailors dead.

Crist ordered Rear Admiral Grant Sharp to conduct an investigation. Arriving in the Gulf, Sharp and his party formally began the investigation on May 26 aboard the *La Salle*, with the hulk of the *Stark* nearby and with the distinct smell of the fire hanging in the air. While crediting Captain Brindel and his officers and crew (including Gajan and Moncrief) with heroism and skill in fighting the fire and saving their ship,[25] Sharp's report was a scathing indictment on the complete lack of preparedness aboard the *Stark*: "The Commanding officer failed to provide combat oriented leadership, allowing *Stark*'s anti–air warfare readiness to disintegrate to the point that his CIC [combat information center] team was unable to defend the ship."[26]

Meanwhile, another investigative team arrived in Baghdad. Headed by a navy admiral, it included senior intelligence expert Pat Lang, who ran the Iraq operations for the Defense Intelligence Agency. Flying into Baghdad, the Americans were greeted by two separate caravans of Iraqi officials, one from the intelligence service and the other from the foreign ministry, who ushered the delegation off to the al-Rashid Hotel in downtown Baghdad. Saddam Hussein was nervous about America's response to the attack, worrying that the United States would turn against Iraq, cutting off the intelligence sharing or even pulling its support for the money and weapons flowing to his war machine. The next day, Lang and the other Americans met with the head of Iraqi air force intelligence, Sabur Abdul Aziz al-Douri. He had commanded a Republican Guard division and was known to Lang: "Al-Douri was one of these guys that light came in and none came out; he was a tough little bastard and not a guy to fool with."

This Iraqi general explained how they divided the Iranian exclusion zone into hunting boxes. Their pilots would be assigned a box, and their orders were to attack the first maritime target they detected. General al-Douri denied that they had targeted the American ship and accused the *Stark* of having strayed inside the Iranian exclusion zone.[27] The navy officers with Lang strongly denied this and accused the Iraqi pilot of being trigger-happy. Iraq refused to allow the Americans to interview the actual pilot. But Lang, fluent in Arabic, noticed a young major in the room who seemed to be answering queries about the attack from his fellow Iraqis. "They brought the pilot, but just did not want *us* to know about him." The Americans impressed on al-Douri that it was in their interest to be apologetic, especially with the United States providing them intelligence.[28] The Iraqi government agreed to pay $27 million in compensation to those killed.

When the Americans left, Saddam Hussein's anxious mood transformed into mocking contempt. "If someone had attacked my ship, I would have bombed the airfield the plane came from!" the Iraqi dictator told senior aides in a meeting.

The *Stark* attack ignited another firestorm in Washington over the Reagan administration's Persian Gulf policies. The Reagan administration believed it was now even more imperative to continue with the reflagging.

The consequences of an American pullout after the *Stark* would have been disastrous to U.S. interests, especially following on the heels of Beirut.[29]

Before the *Stark*, few within Congress showed any interest in attending Pentagon briefings about the Kuwaiti tanker operation. Now with the photographs of thirty-seven coffins in a hangar in Dover, Delaware, on the cover of every major newsmagazine, they suddenly held a flurry of contentious hearings divided largely along partisan lines supporting or opposing the idea of U.S. protection for shipping in the Gulf.[30] It did not help the Reagan administration that the political waters were already churned with the concurrent Iran-Contra hearings. Detractors denounced the undertaking on the floor of the House of Representatives, fearing it would draw the United States into another Vietnam, and insisted on the applicability of the War Powers Act, which required the president to get congressional approval for continuing any operation over sixty days.

The United States pressed forward with the reflagging operation in the wake of the attack on the *Stark* and despite congressional skepticism. Reagan resolutely defended his decision. "Mark this point well: the use of the vital sea-lanes of the Persian Gulf will not be dictated by the Iranians. These lanes will not be allowed to come under the control of the Soviet Union."[31]

Outside the public view, the entire national security apparatus focused on the ability of Crist and Bernsen to avoid another such debacle. Six days after the *Stark* tragedy, on May 22, Crist flew to Washington for a series of meetings capped off by a meeting at the White House. An emotional Ronald Reagan had flown down to Jacksonville, Florida, for a memorial service for those killed on the *Stark*, but before leaving he'd given Carlucci instructions to make sure that the rules of engagement were broad enough and that the U.S. military had all the forces it needed to protect the Kuwaiti ships. General Robert Herres relayed this to Crist in a message for his eyes only and reported that the commander in chief had privately told the secretary that he wanted a "much more proactive stance."[32] With presidential interest, keeping the status quo was not an acceptable course of action. In a meeting in his office before driving over to the White House, Weinberger asked Crist point-blank if he had the forces to conduct the mission; if not, the secretary said, "you should ask for it."

In the National Security Council meeting that afternoon, Crowe cautioned that he could not guarantee that there would be no further casualties, but that Iran's actions had been very circumspect. Iran knew we could hit its military or economic targets at will from our carrier. It is unlikely that Iran would try to challenge the U.S. convoys, Crowe told Carlucci.[33] Both Weinberger and Crowe pressed to liberalize the rules of engagement to avoid another such incident. Carlucci agreed, and said the president wanted to make sure that U.S. forces had everything they needed to complete their mission. He told Weinberger and Crowe to come back "urgent basis" on whether Crist needed more forces to carry out the escort operation.[34]

In a message that evening back-briefing Bernsen, Crist relayed the tone of the afternoon meeting in the White House Situation Room: "The heat is very hot in the kitchen."[35]

Bernsen did not think any modifications were needed to the rules governing use of force. The problem was the *Stark*, not the document. But the political realities in Washington demanded change. "We are on notice," Crist responded to Bernsen. "We can't afford a second hit. We shoot first. The captain is authorized, in fact required, to shoot if it is clear to the commanding officer that his ship has been placed at risk."[36]

The following day, Bernsen responded with some new rules. Any aircraft would be warned off at fifty nautical miles from any warship. Captains would be prepared to engage at twenty-five miles, or just outside the effective range of an Exocet missile.

On June 8, Weinberger approved these changes. The new rules stressed the captain's ultimate responsibility for defending his ship against an attack or a threat that demonstrated hostile intent, such as laying mines or using its weapons radar.[37] U.S. ships or planes were still prohibited from entering into Iranian or Iraqi territorial waters or airspace, including the declared exclusion zones. The only exception was that if U.S. forces were attacked from these areas, they could pursue into them, but only if the hostile force continued to pose an imminent threat to the safety of the American plane or ship. The minute the threat ended, they had to withdraw immediately unless approved by the Joint Chiefs.[38]

Meanwhile, the operational name for the convoys, Private Jewels, struck some as dirty, and with the operation being reexamined in a new light, the Pentagon changed the operational name to one that had a better ring to it: Earnest Will.

On May 27, Central Command forwarded its revived escort plan. While simple, it had a number of moving parts. The Middle East Force would herd together one to three tankers off either Kuwait or Oman and then proceed along a southern Gulf route with each convoy guarded by two or three U.S. warships staying within four thousand yards of the tankers. Additional navy vessels would be stationed at both entrances to the Strait of Hormuz, just outside the range of the Iranian Silkworm missiles. Another warship would be stationed in the northern Gulf to maintain the communications link with the Saudi-based AWACS. At twenty knots, it would take two days to transit, either inbound to Kuwait or outbound loaded with oil.[39]

If Iran tried to interfere, the carrier in the Gulf of Oman would be poised to strike. As a precaution, Crist ordered air force fighters to be ready to fly to Saudi Arabia and Oman. CENTCOM updated the Iran strike plans to include ten different targets for cruise missiles hitting naval and air defense sites around Iranian bases at Bandar Abbas, Jask, and Bushehr.[40]

The U.S. Navy had recently pulled four battleships out of mothballs. The chief of naval operations wanted to send one, the USS *Missouri*, to the Gulf to replace the aircraft carrier. The power of these World War II dreadnoughts captivated military planners in Tampa. Armed with nine 16-inch guns that each fired a shell weighing as much as a Volkswagen Beetle. They were now augmented with advanced Tomahawk cruise missiles but remained the quintessential symbol of American gunboat diplomacy. The battleship could single-handedly destroy every Iranian military facility in the southern Persian Gulf. While its cruise missiles destroyed naval air force headquarters at Bandar Abbas, the "Mighty Mo," protected by a fourteen-inch-thick belt of armor, would steam up into the strait and its guns would pound the Silkworm missile batteries into oblivion. A study produced by the Johns Hopkins University Applied Physics Laboratory concluded that the battleship could take eleven Silkworm missiles before being put out of action, and there were not enough missiles in the entire Iranian inventory to sink the forty-five-thousand-ton battlewagon. Suicide planes were even less of a problem. The *Missouri* had absorbed two off Okinawa in 1945 and escaped with little more than its paint scraped.[41] On June 12, the Joint Chiefs met in the Tank and agreed to send the battleship, supported by two cruisers and three destroyers, to the Gulf. Although the convoy operation would already be under way, this lethal task group would arrive in the Gulf by the end of August.

Another group of officers under CENTCOM arrived in Baghdad to hash out a secret arrangement between the U.S. Navy and the Iraqi air force. The two countries came to a formal agreement that amounted to a series of electronic nods and winks that permitted Iraqi planes to continue to pound Iran's tankers and avoid running into the U.S. Navy. When Iraqi aircraft went "feet wet," as aviators term flying over water, the pilot announced his presence to any U.S. warship by turning on his radar for a couple of minutes. The American AWACS plane flying out of Saudi Arabia would contact the Iraqi over a certain radio frequency provided every month to Iraqis by the U.S. military attaché in Baghdad.[42] The Iraqi pilot would reply using a predetermined call sign, again provided by the U.S. military, and the AWACS would pass on the location of all the U.S. ships in the northern Gulf.[43] There were draconian measures if the Iraqi pilot failed to adhere to this protocol, including being shot down if he came within thirty nautical miles of a U.S. ship without contacting the Americans.[44]

Initially this clandestine arrangement worked well. "I believe our initial understanding with representatives of Iraq has significantly reduced the risk of engagement of our forces," Crowe told Weinberger.[45] The two nations refined these procedures over the coming months, improving the coordination between Iraqi planes and the navy ships.[46] When Iraqi pilots made the Farsi hook, they were to relay this information and their new course to the Americans. Then, using a series of brevity codes agreed to by both countries, the Iraqis would pass information on their intended Iranian target and whether all the planes were going to hit the same or multiple sites. The communications between the United States and Iraq became sophisticated enough that U.S. controllers could steer Iraqi planes around navy warships.[47] Over the course of the next three months, further talks in Baghdad between the two nations refined their cooperative procedures. Middle East Force provided advance details of American ship movements to Iraq. During talks with the chief of operations for the Iraqi air force, Major General Salim Sultan, the United States helped Iraq refine its flight patterns to enable the Americans to better monitor the Iraqis' positions and still allow them to attack Iranian shipping. The only disagreement came when a U.S. Air Force colonel tried to get Iraq to refrain from attacking ships too far south in the Gulf. Salim responded, "If Saddam Hussein dictated the target, they must fly it." Since the Iraqi leader liked to pick targets, self-preservation prevented him from agreeing to avoid any part of the Gulf to attack.

The United States considered developing a similar arrangement with the Iranians, but it never went past a few discussions around a conference table in the Pentagon. Admiral Crowe had no interest in talking with Iran. As he told Weinberger in his endorsement of the Sharp Report on the *Stark*, "There has been no indication that the Government of Iran has any interest in the rational discussion of any relevant matters, including deconfliction procedures."[48]

Instead, the Iranians listened in on this steady stream of radio communications between the Americans and the Iraqis. Already aware of the ongoing intelligence sharing, this only reconfirmed their view of military collusion between their enemies. If the U.S. Navy and the Iraqi air force were cooperating, that made Bernsen's ships legitimate targets in the eyes of the Iranian leadership. The *Stark* had unintentionally served as a wake-up call for the Revolutionary Guard too.

I f secret deals had brought the Arabs on board with the American reflagging scheme, serious cracks emerged within the military branch most responsible for executing the plan, the U.S. Navy. The real problem for the men wearing uniforms of dark blue and gold braid was that the times were a-changing and the conservative sea service was clinging to the past. Both modern warfare and the Goldwater-Nichols Act forced interoperability among the four services. The navy had largely worked alone, without paying too much attention to the army or air force. But Congress had tipped the balance of power to the four-star joint unified commanders with passage of Goldwater-Nichols, and the days of army- or navy-only military operations were over. The green and blue uniforms had been morphed into purple, as joint command billets are informally called.

In the coming years, the United States forged a far more effective military by merging the sum of its parts, but the reflagging operation occurred during the middle of these growing pains. It required a generational change in the officer corps, with the old officers replaced by those who had grown up in the new system. But in 1987, "the prospect of a Marine commanding an almost exclusively navy mission was deeply disturbing to many in the naval community," Crowe wrote in his memoirs. And Crist's military plans for Iran, which included air force AWACS and combat jets supporting navy ships, had ruffled the admirals' feathers.[49]

The one thing the two men agreed on was that Iran would not risk war by challenging the escort operations. Iran had no reason, it seemed, to fight the United States too. A CENTCOM intelligence paper reflected the prevailing view within the American intelligence community: "The primary threat to the U.S. convoys is another accidental attack like the *Stark*. It appears unlikely that Iran will intentionally attack a U.S. combatant or a Kuwait owned tanker under U.S. escort."[50] CENTCOM did not consider the Iranian navy or aircraft a major threat, but the Silkworm missiles purchased from China were a different story. One site was active and another eight were near completion around the Strait of Hormuz. Intelligence sources indicated that the control of these missiles was highly centralized and that any decision to attack would have been made at the highest levels of the Iranian government: Ayatollah Khomeini.[51]

In June 1987, the U.S. State Department relayed a stern warning to Tehran via the Swiss embassy against using Silkworm missiles. The United States would view their use as a serious matter, and Washington would respond with massive force against military and economic sites. Iran never responded to the U.S. démarche, but despite all the hostility between the two nations over the coming year, Iran never fired a single Silkworm missile from its sites around the Strait of Hormuz.

Iran did have some mines, but no one in Tampa or Washington gave it too much thought. On Friday, June 26, less than a month before the first convoy, a DIA analyst briefed a group of senior three-stars in the Tank about the Iranian mine threat. The intelligence officer concluded his thirty-minute presentation: "We do not believe that Iran poses a major mine threat to the Gulf shipping at this time. Although the Iranians are capable of small scale mine laying . . . we estimate that they do not have the capability to lay and maintain systematic minefields. The threat is primarily psychological."

The analyst added that the Iranians lacked the training and expertise to lay mines and did not possess any proper minelayer. "Although small combatants or merchant ships could be modified for mine laying operations, no modification efforts have been noted." As far as the use of small dhows was concerned: "The unsophisticated nature of these platforms wholly limit[s] them to small scale, imprecise mine operations."[52]

Unfortunately, leaders in Tehran did not read the American intelligence assessments. Iranian ingenuity and resourcefulness had an ugly surprise awaiting both CENTCOM and the U.S. Navy.

Thirteen

THE INVISIBLE
HAND OF GOD

On the morning of July 6, 1984, the small cargo ship *Ghat* left Libya on its way to the Eritrean port of Assab. The round-trip journey through the Suez Canal normally took eight days, but nothing about this trip was routine. Instead of the usual cargo of foodstuffs and crated goods, *Ghat* carried advanced Soviet-made naval mines designed to detonate in response to the mere sound of a passing ship. Rather than her normal civilian crew, Libyan sailors, including the commander of Moammar Gaddafi's mine force, manned the pilothouse. Once in the Red Sea, the sailors lowered the stern ramp and hastily rolled the mines off into the water, where they settled on the silted seafloor. The improvised minelayer sowed its destructive seeds around two important choke points at either end of the Red Sea: first at the north end of the Gulf of Suez, just before the Suez Canal, and then at the south end around the narrow strait of Bab el Mandeb, where one of the busiest shipping routes in the world narrowed to a mere twenty miles.

It did not take long for the Libyans' handiwork to bring results. On the evening of July 9, an explosion rocked the Soviet-flagged cargo ship *Knud Jespersen* just outside the Suez Canal. The Egyptian government kept the news of this incident quiet, not wishing to alarm the merchants who used the canal and provided a main source of revenue for Cairo. This proved impossible when there was a spate of ships hitting mines outside the canal and at the far end of the Red Sea around Bab el Mandeb.[1]

The August Red Sea mining became an international whodunit as newspapers speculated about whose hand was behind this terrorist attack against the world's commerce. Egypt blamed Iran. Officials in Tehran had publicly boasted about using mines to close down the Strait of Hormuz as a means of punishing Gulf nations supporting Iraq. Egyptian warships began boarding Iranian ships transiting the Suez Canal, looking for the culprit.[2] The Saudi government agreed. With the annual hajj about to begin, Riyadh thought Iran intended to embarrass the kingdom by mining the two Red Sea ports of Jeddah and Yanbu, where tens of thousands of white-clad pilgrims arrived. If one of those liners were to strike a mine, the loss of life would be horrific. American intelligence organizations remained skeptical, however, and an Office of Naval Intelligence report doubted Iran's involvement. Its navy had few mines and no ships to drop those it did possess. Communications intercepts soon revealed Moammar Gaddafi's culpability.

The U.S. Navy joined an international naval flotilla to clear the mines.[3] At nine p.m. on August 6, Secretary of Defense Caspar Weinberger signed a deployment order, and by midnight, transport aircraft were taking off from Norfolk, Virginia, carrying large RH-53D minesweeping helicopters plus two hundred personnel, all headed for Egypt.[4] Once there, the crew assembled the helicopter rotors and flew them out to the amphibious ship USS *Shreveport* and the flagship of Middle East Force, USS *La Salle*, to begin sweeping for the remaining presents left by the Libyan leader.[5] Bitter memories remained from the recent debacle in Beirut, and the Italians and French refused to participate in any military arrangement with the United States. Paris had no desire to work with the American navy, publicly stating that it wanted no part of any American "crusade" in the Red Sea.[6]

Looking for mines was painstakingly slow. Sonar scanned along the ocean floor, with divers or remote-operation vehicles investigating suspicious objects. The Red Sea was littered with years of discarded items—old oil drums, pipes, coffee cans, automobiles, and mines left over from both the Second World War and the more recent Arab-Israeli wars. The American helicopters had the additional unpopular task of sweeping in front of the Saudi king's yacht when King Fahd took an ill-timed fourteen-mile day cruise from Jeddah.

The mines of August eventually claimed sixteen ships. Only one mine was ever found; an explosives diver defused its charge, and the serial number 99501 indicated it was one of hundreds of similar coastal mines sold to Libya by the Soviet Union. During a seminar on the operation at the Naval Institute in Annapolis, Maryland, naval expert Scott Truver observed, "The threat of terrorist mining of important sea areas is real, rather easily carried out, and should be expected to increase."[7] One country took this lesson to heart: Iran.

The shah's navy had never paid much attention to naval mines. It had one plan on its books, written in 1970, that called for laying V-shaped minefields near the Strait of Hormuz, arrayed to halt shipping through the strait while still permitting its own tankers to get through. But before the revolution, the Iranian navy had carried out only one mine-laying exercise. The war with Iraq spurred interest in naval mines by the new Islamic Republic of Iran. In 1981, Iran purchased a small number of unsophisticated moored contact mines from North Korea: the small Myam mine, with only a 44-pound explosive charge, and the much larger M-08. Both were based upon ancient technology. The latter had been patterned after a 1908—that is, pre–First World War—Russian-designed mine. Shaped like a large black ball attached to a cradle that served as its anchor, it packed a potent 250-pound explosive charge, but required a ship to physically hit one of its pronounced horns, which ignited a chemical charge to set off the mine. Neither mine could be used in deep water, such as the Strait of Hormuz, but both could easily be laid throughout much of the shallower Arab side of the Persian Gulf.

The Revolutionary Guard paid close attention to the Red Sea mining. Tehran and Tripoli had friendly military relations and, on at least one occasion, the Iranian embassy arranged for a Revolutionary Guard officer to travel to Tripoli to talk with the Libyan commander who'd carried out the mining operation. The plausible deniability afforded by naval mines appealed to the Iranian leadership. Libya had suffered no consequences for its flagrant mining of international waters. Libyan involvement remained murky; unless they were caught in the act, it was difficult to prove who had laid the mines. Naval mines seemed the perfect, low-risk means of striking back at the Gulf Arabs.

The Revolutionary Guard commander, Mohsen Rezai, formed a small group of eight officers to look into developing this capability for Iran. In late

1984, the team met at the National Defense Industries Organization in Tehran to try to reverse engineer some North Korean mines in order to produce an Iranian variant, while Libya provided a newer Soviet variant for comparison. The team constructed a large water tank filled with salt water near Tehran to test drop their mine and work out the many challenges of dropping the anchor correctly to get the mine to deploy at the correct depth. Over the next year, engineers conducted four tests, which included an explosives test of the mine's charge in the Iranian desert. Poor engineering plagued the design team. The detonation horns proved unreliable, the anchors repeatedly failed, and the designers could not get the mines to set for a specific depth. Mines failed to deploy or went too high, leaving them bobbing on the surface. By mid-1985, however, the design team had sufficiently overcome most of these problems to begin production. In July, the first Iranian-designated SADAF-01 (Myam) and SADAF-02 (M-08) mines began rolling out of an ammunition plant north of Tehran. At least twenty-two mines were produced each week. The Iranians hoped to produce three thousand such mines, and started stockpiling them near Bandar Abbas and 155 miles north at the large Saidabad naval ammunition depot at Sirjan. Meanwhile, regular Iranian naval forces confiscated four fishing vessels at Bushehr and modified each with a stern ramp. While dressed as fishermen to disguise their mission, they repeatedly practiced rolling dummy mines off the dhows.

In March 1986, the elite Special Boat Service of the Iranian marines, a holdover from the shah's military, carried out Iran's first mining operations in the shallow waters off Iraq in support of the country's various offensives to take Basra. Joined by Revolutionary Guards in small boats, they repeatedly slipped in close to the main Iraqi port of Umm Qasr to mine its channel and effectively shut down shipping to Iraq's major Persian Gulf port.[8]

Iran developed a military plan called the Ghadir, named for an early Shia battle, to fight the American navy. Approved in 1984, it became Iran's main plan to retaliate against an American attack. The Revolutionary Guard and the regular navy would form four surface groups, each comprising a destroyer or frigate supported by a number of guard small boats and logistics vessels converted into minelayers, and move quickly under the cover of air and artillery to lay three large minefields west of the Strait of Hormuz. The objective was to deny any tanker traffic from passing through the strait, except those headed to Iran, which would safely use several routes deliberately left open through the minefields. Once this mission had been completed, the four task forces would attack U.S. Navy ships within reach.

On paper, the Ghadir plan looked impressive and indicated significant cooperation between the regular military and the guard. In reality, the Iranian military never displayed any semblance of such coordinated efforts, due largely to animosity between the Revolutionary Guard and the regular Iranian navy. Any joint command to control naval forces never evolved beyond paper. However, when American special operations forces uncovered the Ghadir plan in 1987, the audacity of Iran's mining ambitions impressed the U.S. military. In two short years, it had gone from a saltwater tank in the desert to the conceivable ability to lay hundreds of mines and halt Gulf oil exports.

In May, Iran decided to try out some of its newly minted mines on Kuwait in hopes of intimidating the emir into reversing his decision to reflag his tankers with the Americans.[9] Two large Iranian dhows left Bushehr, mingling with the normal fishing and smuggling trade. They dropped fourteen mines in two parallel lines radiating off one of the channel's navigation buoys.[10] The mines were carefully spaced thirty meters apart. So as not to interfere with their own fishing and smuggling trade, the Iranians made sure to set the mines' depth to at least ten feet, well below the depth of a dhow but shallow enough to damage a large oil tanker.

On the same day the *Stark* met misfortune, the sixty-eight-thousand-ton Soviet tanker *Marshal Chuykov* entered the main deep-water entrance to Kuwait, Mina al-Ahmadi, to take on a load of Kuwaiti crude. Two miles east of the two navigation buoys that marked the channel's entrance, a massive explosion rocked the tanker, blowing an eight-by-six-meter hole in her starboard side, which required extensive repairs at the dry-dock facilities in Dubai. Over the next month, three more ships hit mines, all within three-quarters of a mile of where the *Chuykov* had met misfortune. "We have potentially a serious situation here," CENTCOM commander George Crist told Joint Chiefs chairman William Crowe.[11]

The American ambassador to Kuwait, Anthony Quainton, asked the Kuwaitis to undertake a more assertive military surveillance to prevent additional mines from being laid. But the Kuwaitis lacked both the hardware and the fortitude to counter this challenge from Iran, and their initial reaction was to try to hire someone to do the job for them. They also looked into leasing Dutch minesweepers. As the Iranian mines threatened the entire forthcoming convoy operation, Washington offered to remove them, which pleased the emir, so long as it did not bring too many Americans into his country.

The United States quietly dispatched an eighteen-man team with twenty tons of equipment to take care of the mines.[12] Arriving on June 22, they quickly set to work operating from a Kuwaiti tug at the entrance to the Mina al-Ahmadi channel. Three days later, their sonar picked up a mine on a shallow reef in a hundred feet of water—its round explosive case was floating just ten feet below the surface. Divers defused it and flew it back to the United States for analysis. The United Kingdom had its own sources and had acquired a list of serial numbers of mines manufactured in Iran. When the British compared their list with the number stenciled in white lettering on the side of the mine found by the Americans, the number matched up perfectly in the correct sequence.

Over the next month, nine more mines were discovered and destroyed by navy divers.[13] Carefully laid to cover the channel, they were clearly not the result of haphazard mining by a few dhows, but a carefully planned attack on Kuwaiti shipping. Remarkably, when faced with an obvious Iranian military attack against Kuwait using naval mines, no one in either Tampa or Washington bothered to change the assumptions guiding the American convoy operations. Bernsen, Crist, and Crowe continued to believe that Iran would never dare to take such an overt action against the United States. Faith in the deterrent effect of the carrier and American firepower clouded every level of American thinking. CENTCOM took the modest step of requesting that a helicopter minesweeping squadron in Norfolk be placed on standby for the Persian Gulf. Some officers speculated that Iran might attack the convoys with suicide boats or conduct terrorist attacks against the Middle East Force, and additional marine security forces arrived to protect the Middle East Force headquarters in Bahrain. But no one wanted to believe that Tehran would mine beyond Kuwait Harbor, despite a growing body of intelligence that warned of more mining in the Gulf. The navy leadership pressured both Crowe and Weinberger to minimize the forces for Earnest Will, and this contributed to the complacency that gripped U.S. military leadership regarding Iran's reaction to the United States protecting one of Iraq's chief supporters. Saudi minesweepers arrived on scene, and as the date for the first convoy

approached, the combined presence of Saudi and Kuwaiti vessels backed by
U.S. expertise seemed adequate to deal with any further Iranian actions
against shipping. Satisfied, Bernsen even recommended sending home some
of the eighteen men, so as not to aggravate Kuwaiti sensitivities.

The Iranian leadership worried about attacking the Americans directly.
With their mining of Kuwait Harbor having failed to change the
Kuwaiti emir's mind about working with the Americans, a heated debate
emerged within the Supreme Defense Council, Iran's national security decision-making body. Senior officers in the regular Iranian military urged caution. They had spent much of their careers working with Americans and
knew firsthand the destructive power the United States could bring down on
Iran. But Revolutionary Guard commander Major General Mohsen Rezai
dismissed their concerns. He believed the navy and air force officers still harbored an affinity for the Americans and were too enamored of technology. He
pressed for a direct confrontation with the Americans and urged attacking
U.S. warships.

"The Americans cannot take casualties. Vietnam and Beirut showed
that," he told his colleagues during one meeting in Tehran in June. "Any
losses and the Americans will flee the Gulf!" Rezai and other guard generals—
whose military experience was limited to fighting against the anemic Iraqi
army—largely dismissed the importance of American airpower. We have
been able to contend with the Western-backed Iraqi air force for seven years;
we can contend with the American bombers too, they argued.

The ever pragmatic Hashemi Rafsanjani came down in the middle. Pressuring Kuwait into withdrawing support for Iraq was a necessity for an Iranian victory, and the American convoys only propped up Saddam Hussein, he
stated. But American pilots were far better than Iraqi pilots; he pointed out
that the Americans had been able to drop a bomb right down on Gaddafi's
house during the air attack against Libya in April 1986. The Americans
could do the same to the supreme leader's home. Naval mines, however,
appealed to Rafsanjani. Covert mining against the Americans could inflict
the losses needed to drive them out of the Gulf, but still lessened the likelihood of a massive American reprisal. Rather than attack them directly as
Rezai advocated, how about surreptitiously mining the paths of the American ships? The final decision rested with Ayatollah Khomeini. In early July,

the supreme leader sided with Rafsanjani, over the vocal objections of Rezai. He ordered a secret mining campaign against the forthcoming American convoys, but no overt attack on any U.S. warship.

American intelligence knew nothing of the debate going on in Tehran. Instead, the chatter warned of an Iranian terrorist attack against Bernsen's headquarters in Bahrain. Weinberger ordered U.S. personnel to avoid public venues and restrict themselves to their homes or work, and he detached additional marines to guard the base.[14]

The U.S. military made preparations for the first Kuwaiti convoy. In order to meet the legal requirement of American ownership, the Kuwait Oil Tanker Company established a dummy company in Dover, Delaware— Chesapeake Shipping Inc.—and intended to reregister all eleven ships between mid-June and the end of August. Coast guard inspectors arrived in Kuwait to ensure the ships met U.S. safety regulations; many of the requirements were waived.[15] Although most of the crew remained foreign nationals, Kuwait hired new American masters from the Gleneagle Ship Management Company in Houston. One of the first to report was a retired navy captain, Frank Seitz, Jr. He took over the largest ship and the first to be reflagged, the sixth-largest tanker in the world, the four-hundred-thousand-ton *al-Rekkah*, now renamed the *Bridgeton*.[16]

In the first two weeks of July, General Crist traveled twice to Washington to brief the chiefs and Weinberger in the Tank.[17] Bahrain had agreed to combined air strikes should Iran attack the island in retaliation for its support of the United States. Kuwait remained more reticent, despite the United States escorting their convoys, and would permit American combat planes in the emirate only in the event of an Iranian invasion. Should this occur, Crist expected the emir to request American combat forces.

Crowe and Weinberger drove to Capitol Hill to brief congressional leaders on the classified details of the operation. Immediately after the hearing, the chairman of the House Armed Services Committee, Les Aspin, held a press conference and proceeded to describe all the sensitive details of the operation, including the number of ships and even Saudi Arabia's AWACS support.[18] The next morning, the *Washington Post* printed even more details, including the specifics of sensitive overflight agreements with the emirates.

Both Weinberger and Crowe were livid both at Aspin and about the damaging leak.

A defensive Aspin phoned Crowe. "If it was a classified briefing, why wasn't I told? No one ever told me it was a classified briefing."[19]

"I assumed you knew it was all classified. All ships' schedules are classified," replied a disbelieving chairman.

"No one ever told me it was classified," Aspin persisted. "I think I was set up!" Weinberger would later mockingly refer to Aspin's gaffe as "Les's lips sink ships."

On July 21, 1987, a flag-raising ceremony occurred on the fantail of the thousand-foot-long *Bridgeton*. In the sprawling Oman anchorage of Khor Fakkan, as dozens of ships sat waiting to transit the strait, a small gathering of Kuwaiti officials and military officers looked on as Ambassador Quainton hoisted the Stars and Stripes up the flagpole, where a strong breeze snapped it to attention in the hot, muggy summer air.[20] The flag had been provided by a congressman from Kentucky, who had wanted to raise it himself, but in deference to Kuwaiti sensitivities and to keep this low-key, Quainton decided to do the honor himself.[21]

Concerned that the leaks had tipped Iran to the start of the first convoy, Bernsen took additional precautions to remain distant from the other ships at anchorage. The U.S. warships manned their weapons in case Iran attempted to attack the convoy while anchored. Bernsen conferred with Crist that evening as to U.S. military response options in case Iran tried its own version of Pearl Harbor.[22]

The anxious night passed uneventfully. With no sign of Iranians lurking off Oman, the next morning the first Earnest Will convoy headed for the Strait of Hormuz. Escorted by two American cruisers and a smaller frigate, it comprised two reflagged ships, the massive tanker *Bridgeton* and a smaller, liquefied-gas carrier, *Gas Prince*.

The first ten hours of the two-day transit was seen as the most dangerous period. The convoy would be at its most vulnerable while within easy range of the Iranian Silkworm missiles ringing the strait, so CENTCOM orchestrated a complex ballet in the skies above the ships consisting of navy and air force surveillance planes, aerial refueling tankers, and fighters. A four-engine

P-3 code-named Reef Point and secretly staged on the Omani island of Masirah used advanced optics to look in on the Iranian missile sites. Fighters and bombers from the carrier two hundred miles out in the Gulf of Oman kept an overhead vigil, maintained aloft by airborne pit stops provided by three large air force refueling planes based on the small Indian Ocean island of Diego Garcia.[23] The air force launched a sleek black SR-71 Blackbird reconnaissance jet from halfway around the world. Taking off from Kadena, Okinawa, it was supported by no less than fifteen tanker jets stationed along the route. The Blackbird cut its way across the Strait of Hormuz and the Persian Gulf, flying at Mach 3 and on the edge of space at eighty thousand feet. Heavy cloud cover nearly scuttled the mission, but the skies cleared as the Blackbird arrived over the strait. Once it had taken its photos and its sensors had collected data on the Iranian missiles, the two pilots—Majors Mike Smith and Doug Soifer—did a wide, lazy turn over the northern Gulf before heading back to the other side of the globe at an estimated cost of $1 million for the exhausting eleven-hour mission.[24] None of these aircraft saw anything unusual, and Bernsen gave the go-ahead for the convoy to proceed.

For the next ten hours, both Crowe and Crist stayed in their respective command centers in Washington and Tampa, linked by an open secure telephone. Crist provided regular updates to the chairman, all the while sucking down one Carlton cigarette after another. The only tense moment came when the radar of one of the escorts, the USS *Kidd*, picked up an unidentified helicopter closing on the convoy. The warship fired a warning flare, and the helicopter abruptly turned away. It turned out to be carrying nothing more dangerous than the fourth estate: a team of reporters and photographers.

Having entered the Gulf without incident, everyone relaxed until the convoy approached the next danger area, a base for Revolutionary Guard small boats around the Iranian island of Abu Musa. Again, the Iranian forces appeared apathetic, and the convoy continued northward. The only bellicosity came from Iranian radio. "If the big shots in Washington think they can make the Islamic Republic bow to their oppressive policies by military display and threats, much more bitter consequences than the experiences of Lebanon or Vietnam await them."[25]

Despite the supreme leader's directive, Revolutionary Guard commander General Rezai still wanted to attack the convoy. On his own authority, he ordered the small boats at Farsi to attack the convoy when it passed Farsi Island on the night of July 23. However, someone in the Revolutionary Guard tipped off Ayatollah Khomeini, who immediately reined in his overeager commander, ordering him to keep with the agreed mining operation and avoid a direct fight with the American navy.

Now a chastised Rezai abided by his orders. A small lighter left Farsi and headed due west some twenty miles until it found a prominent navigation buoy called Middle Shoals, and then it turned north along the tanker route for another ten miles. Here the tanker traffic narrowed as it turned to skirt around the Iranian-declared war exclusion zone. A special unit of the Revolutionary Guard, which had spent several weeks practicing for this mission, laid a string of nine mines, each five hundred yards apart, and then hastened back to Farsi.

Just after sunset on July 23, American communications intercepts detected two fiberglass boats coming out of Farsi Island. Bernsen's intelligence officer, Commander Howell Conway Ziegler, came to Bernsen's stateroom on the *La Salle* and the two compared notes about what this development meant. The Iranian actions and a summary of the Revolutionary Guard's chatter all seemed to indicate that Iran planned to attack the convoy with speedboats as it passed Farsi. Ironically, American intelligence had discovered Rezai's aborted unauthorized attack but completely missed the actually mining operation that followed.

After reporting this back to Crist, Bernsen ordered the convoy to take a different route to avoid the main channel into Kuwait and to slow its speed in order to pass Farsi Island the next morning, as daylight would permit better targeting of the attacking small boats.[26]

At first light, Bernsen ordered a helicopter aloft to scout ahead of the convoy, and with the cruiser USS *Fox* in the van, the convoy proceeded past the menacing Iranian island without sighting a single attack boat or even a fishing dhow. Back in the Pentagon, Crowe greeted this news with relief. He called Weinberger and reported that the worst appeared to be over. The convoy was headed for Kuwait, and he expected to turn over the two tankers to their navy that afternoon. From the bridge of the *Bridgeton*, breakfast trays could be seen being passed to the crew on watch, down along the three-football-field-long deck of the supertanker.

Suddenly the master, Captain Seitz, heard a metallic clank. An undulating shock wave rippled down the length of the ship as if someone had taken the edge of a rug and whipped it rapidly. When the wave reached the bridge, "it felt like a five-hundred-ton hammer hit," Seitz recalled. The impact sent trays full of bacon and eggs flying as the men held on to keep from being thrown to the ground. "There wasn't much question that we had hit a mine."[27] The mine had blown a fifty-square-meter hole in the side of the mammoth tanker. The *Bridgeton* slowed but, despite the damage, did not stop. Its cavernous empty hold could easily accommodate the flooding compartments. The much smaller U.S. warships, however, would not be so lucky if they hit a mine. They quickly scrabbled to take refuge behind the large tanker, the guards protected by their charge as they sheepishly traveled in the wake of the *Bridgeton* to avoid hitting additional mines.

In the early morning hours, news of the *Bridgeton* mining rippled through the U.S. government as quickly as it had through the hull of the supertanker. Crist, who was monitoring the operation from his command center in Tampa, "literally came out of his chair" when he heard the news, one witness recalled. The duty officer in the National Military Command Center phoned a sleeping Admiral Crowe at his quarters at Fort Myer, notifying him of the *Bridgeton*'s plight. Crowe took an unusual action for the nation's senior military officer: he picked up the phone and called straight down to Bernsen on his flagship in the Gulf. Crowe liked Bernsen. The two had met in Germany, and the chairman had been impressed by Bernsen's grasp of Gulf politics and the complexities of the Kuwaiti convoy mission. Crowe had even endorsed Bernsen's membership in the New York Yacht Club, and frequently called him directly, often without Crist's knowledge.[28]

"What the hell's going on?" Crowe asked tersely.

Bernsen filled him in on the details. The *Bridgeton* had hit a mine. There were no casualties, and the convoy was continuing up to Kuwait at half speed.[29] Crowe summoned his driver, immediately threw on his uniform, and headed for the Pentagon.

When the convoy had safely reached Kuwait, Bernsen sat at his desk in his stateroom. "It is a new ballgame and we are not playing games," he thought. Bernsen penned a message for his boss in Tampa. "The events of this morning represent a distinct and serious change in Iranian policy vis à vis U.S. military interests in the Persian Gulf. There is no question that Iranian Forces specifically targeted the escort transit group and placed mines in the water with the intent to damage/sink as many ships as possible." That the *Bridgeton* was the only victim was due entirely to the luck of the draw. Iran had made the calculation that either the United States would not retaliate or Iran could survive a strike similar to that inflicted on Libya, he said, referring to the U.S. bombing the year before in response to Gaddafi's bombing of a disco in Berlin.[30] But Bernsen cautioned against the knee-jerk air strike. The Iranian population was war-weary, and any attack on their mainland would serve to help rally the population behind the government. "We don't need martyrs in Bandar Abbas."

That afternoon, Bernsen and Crist held a long phone call to discuss the way forward. Although neither man had expected such an audacious move by Iran, both agreed on the need to avoid dragging the United States into a war with the country. They mulled over other ways to respond, including a naval blockade or even mining Bandar Abbas. The first priority, however, was clearing out the mines. Crist ordered a halt to further convoys until they could get new forces in to support Bernsen's Middle East Force.

The Iranian leaders gloated at news of the *Bridgeton*'s misfortune. They publicly attributed the mines' sudden appearance to divine intervention, the work of the invisible hand of God. The day after the *Bridgeton* mining, the speaker of Iran's parliament, Hashemi Rafsanjani, praised those responsible as "God's angels that descend and do what is necessary."[31] Prime Minister Mir-Hossein Mousavi added, "The U.S. schemes were foiled by invisible hands. It was proved how vulnerable the Americans are despite their huge and unprecedented military operation in the Persian Gulf to escort Kuwaiti tankers."[32] After the mission, the Revolutionary Guard commandos who'd laid the mines each reportedly received a gold watch, given by General Rezai and the chief of the Iranian navy, as a reward for their heroism.

The mining had caught the Pentagon embarrassingly unprepared. That morning, a scheduled meeting with the president and his principals on Vietnam POWs went by the side as they talked about how to respond to Iran. The false assumption that Iran would not mine outside of Kuwait's channel had been based more on the American desire to keep force levels small than on any credible intelligence. Considerably more ships would be needed, especially minesweepers. The most powerful navy in the world had been attacked by speedboats dropping mines, and the convoys could not resume until the mine hazard was addressed.

Reagan set a circumspect tone at the opening: "Let's take our time and determine what happened before taking any action," the president said.

Crowe opened with a quick update. It was clear the *Bridgeton* had struck a mine. While the intelligence community had yet to conclusively prove Iranian culpability, the admiral had no doubt about who'd laid the mines. The chairman then gave a rundown on American countermine capabilities. The helicopters of Helicopter Mine Countermeasures Squadron 14 (HM-14), which had been on seventy-two-hour standby, would be the most immediate solution, but they were expensive and needed an air base to operate from; otherwise, a ship would have to be brought up into the Gulf to serve as a platform for the helicopters.[33] To address the long-term requirement, Crowe said, we would need minesweeping ships in the Gulf.

The first course would be to ask the Saudis for help in clearing the mines. The kingdom had four American-made minesweepers built during the 1970s, although they operated more as patrol boats than as mine hunters. Crowe offered to work with Prince Bandar, although he had little regard for the Saudis' training and little faith in any real cooperation.[34]

The next day, Crowe called Bandar. Despite their differing backgrounds, the admiral from Oklahoma and the wealthy Saudi fighter pilot had developed a close relationship. The two men spoke several times a week, and soon every day. Both were politically savvy, and they shared hawkish views on Iran. Bandar often dropped by Crowe's office unannounced, and the chairman frequently cleared his calendar to make way for the young prince, who had a deserved reputation as the consummate Washington insider.

"We really need your help. We need your minesweepers to clear the convoy route," Crowe said, his serious inflection revealing the gravity of the crisis.

"We are looking at the best way forward," Bandar answered. "The problem is people around here don't know how to keep their mouths shut. We don't want our assistance advertised in the papers. Could you send someone to my home to talk about this?" Crowe immediately dispatched a general to Bandar's home to go over the requirements.

Three days later Bandar called back and said his father, Prince Sultan, who served as the defense minister, had agreed to sweep the main Kuwaiti channel down to where the *Bridgeton* had met misfortune. Bandar's optimism failed to imprint on the Saudi lethargy, however. Crist soon called Crowe to report that no one had seen a Saudi sweeper, and in fact the Saudi navy had just let all its captains go on three weeks' leave.

Frustrated, Crowe called Bandar and asked about recalling the captains. Another day passed before Bandar responded with the news that his father had ordered the captains back and that they would sweep for mines every day. True to his word, that afternoon the first Saudi sweeper appeared in the Gulf. In what became a familiar pattern over the coming days, the ship steamed around for a few hours and stayed well away from Farsi Island and any Iranian mines.

The Europeans proved even more unaccommodating. At the request of Weinberger, Secretary of State Shultz sent letters to the governments of Britain, France, the Netherlands, and Germany requesting mine-clearing vessels, hoping to "portray a multinational commitment against the illegal mining of international waters."[35] In less than a week, all the European allies had turned down the secretary of state's request for assistance in what they viewed as a unilateral American military action to support Iraq. Only the French offered a counterproposal. Paris proposed selling the Americans two of its own mine hunters, manned by nonuniformed French sailors until American crews could be trained to take their place. The U.S. Navy had little interest in buying French ships, so Crowe tried to get the Kuwaitis to lease the two vessels for their navy. Neither Kuwait nor France showed any interest in that arrangement.

At ten a.m. on July 27, Crowe met in his office with Admiral Carlisle Trost, the chief of naval operations, and operations officer Vice Admiral Hank Mustin. Sitting around a small round table, they discussed their options for dealing with Iranian mines. Neither man had much enthusiasm for the convoy mission, especially Mustin, who vocally opposed both the operation and CENTCOM's control over navy ships.

"Why haven't the Saudis or the Europeans taken the mine-clearing mission?" Trost asked.

"The secretary is pushing forward on that," Crowe answered, "but we need to get our own assets over there now. The political pressure is growing to get the convoys restarted ASAP, and Secretary Weinberger is growing impatient."

Everyone agreed that the quickest response would be to fly the HM-14 helicopters over and marry them up with a ship, and the best candidate was the eight-hundred-man amphibious ship USS *Guadalcanal.* Essentially a small aircraft carrier, she was currently off the coast of Kenya loaded with marines headed for an exercise in Somalia. Long term, the United States needed to send its own minesweeping ships, all currently based on the East and West Coasts and manned by reservists.

Crowe then updated Weinberger. Anything in the American inventory that could sweep a mine and could be loaded on a plane or ship was headed for the Gulf: eight helicopters from HM-14 could be in the Gulf in early August and would operate from the *Guadalcanal*; four small eighty-ton mine-sweeping boats located in Charleston, South Carolina, and designed to sweep mines around U.S. harbors would be loaded onto the amphibious ship USS *Raleigh* and arrive in early September. Six larger minesweepers could be readied, but they would not arrive until November.

The timing of the Gulf fiasco could not have been worse for the Reagan administration. The Iran-Contra congressional hearings playing live on television reached their zenith. Oliver North and John Poindexter had testified, with Weinberger next on the docket. Even as he admitted to shredding documents, lying, and breaking the law, North emerged as something of a folk hero, a "Mr. Smith Goes to Washington" marine. As *Newsweek* reported, "North took the Hill with a mixture of straight-arrow toughness, flag-wrapped piety and macho swagger."[36] After his testimony, Reagan sent him a message: "Good Job."

Poindexter took the fall. The navy admiral never strayed from his Buddha-like composure. During questioning, he frequently pulled out his Zippo lighter to reignite his pipe, a technique that allowed him a few extra seconds to compose his thoughts.

Poindexter remained unshakable in his testimony that he believed Reagan would have supported the initiative, but that he'd deliberately kept him in the dark in order to shield the president from such a controversial policy.[37]

Meanwhile, the clamor opposing the convoy mission grew not only within Congress but inside the administration. The chief cheerleader for the opposition was the newly installed secretary of the navy, James Webb. The youthful new secretary was a Naval Academy classmate of Ollie North's, and the two forceful personalities had engaged in an intramural boxing match that grew famous as the two men rose in prominence. Webb had received the Navy Cross—the second highest award—as a junior officer before turning his talent to writing and penning a popular novel about Vietnam, *Fields of Fire*. He frequently offered up his opinion as an armchair general, although his expertise was that of a company-grade officer. He served three years as an assistant secretary, and Weinberger liked him. In 1987, when the current head of the navy, John Lehman, stepped down, the defense secretary recommended to Reagan that Webb replace him. Weinberger soon regretted the decision and repeatedly clashed with headstrong Webb over defense budgets and American policy.

"How will we know when we've won?" Webb asked Weinberger skeptically during one meeting in May. "What is victory? Why are we getting involved in the middle of a war in the Persian Gulf?"

"Every time we successfully sail a convoy through the Gulf we have asserted our right to freedom of navigation and that is a victory," Weinberger answered.

Webb's comments irritated the secretary. "We have the most powerful navy in the world and we can't keep oil flowing against an enemy armed only with Boston Whalers and a few ancient mines?" he asked in disbelief one afternoon. Publicly, Webb came around to support the convoy operation, but privately, he compared the open-ended operation to another Vietnam.

Instead, Bernsen proposed putting together a makeshift minesweeper. He told Crist they could outfit a civilian tug with minesweeping gear. It would travel ahead of the convoys, streaming V-shaped paravanes with serrated cables that would cut loose any Iranian mines. The mines would float to the surface and be easily destroyed by gunfire. He just needed to find a vessel with a large open space at its stern.

The day after the *Bridgeton* mining, Bernsen picked up the phone and called Fattah al-Bader, the head of the Kuwait Oil Tanker Company. As they were on an unsecured commercial phone, Bernsen talked around the issue, explaining that he was looking for an oil service craft with a large aft deck on which to "rig some things."[38] Al-Bader replied that he had two vessels that might work, two oceangoing tugs named *Hunter* and *Striker*, currently at Khor Fakkan. The next day, Bernsen flew to Kuwait to discuss the idea.[39] Al-Bader questioned Bernsen about the safety of the two tugs. While they were registered in Liberia, the crew worked for him. "What if they hit a mine?"

"That would be unlikely," Bernsen replied. "The Iranian mines are all set below the two tugs' twelve-foot draft."

The idea that the U.S. Navy had to depend on two tugs seemed laughable inside the Pentagon, had it not been for the seriousness of the problem. Experts viewed it as a political stunt, a deterrent at best, designed to look as though we had done something to address Iran's mining. Even if the two tugs cut a mine, it would still be impossible for one of the massive tankers following behind to either stop or turn fast enough to avoid the now floating mine.

Even more alarming, as evidence soon showed, due either to incompetence or to poor design, the Iranian mines laid off Farsi Island sat anywhere from the surface to the bottom of the ocean. The two tugs had as much chance of striking a mine as had the *Bridgeton*.[40] Nevertheless, Crowe decided there was no real alternative in the short run.

On July 28, the chairman ordered the deployment of minesweeping kits from a warehouse in Norfolk along with the eight sailors needed to operate the equipment. The two tugs arrived at the small Basrec shipyard in Bahrain, where, under the direction of British expatriate managers, crews worked around the clock welding additional deck plates and adding a crane that would be needed for *Hunter*'s and *Striker*'s unusual new mission. A quick shakedown followed, and the system worked satisfactorily. Moving side by side, the two tugs could clear a lane 270 yards wide—more than wide enough to allow the safe passage of the largest of the reflagged tankers with some safety margin on each side. Those operating these two tugs knew the hazardous nature of their new duty. In addition to the four-man American augmentees, each tug had a small polyglot crew from Sri Lanka and Pakistan, all under the command of a British expatriate. Their sole job would be to sweep before the convoys. Should any mine be laid at less than the ship's twelve-foot draft, they would become human minesweepers. Shortly before the first convoy, Bernsen recalled being asked by a rather nervous tug captain, "Do you think this is very safe?" Bernsen's reply did little to reassure him: "I hope the Kuwait Oil Tanker Company is paying you double for this, because I think you deserve it."[41]

Lieutenant Commander Frank DeMasi had been watching the television news of the *Bridgeton*. "You know, XO," he said to his number two, Ken Merrick, one afternoon while the two sat drinking coffee in the small captain's cabin of the minesweeper *Inflict*, "we are going to the Persian Gulf." Like other skippers in the minesweeping force, the fifteen-year navy veteran and Pennsylvania native had an aura of self-assurance.

"Sir, we're thirty-five-year-olds; we've got a reserve crew," Merrick replied. "No way are they ever going to send us to war!" Most in the navy would have agreed with him.[42]

In the massive buildup to a six-hundred-ship navy, minesweepers—or mine countermeasures, as they're more properly called—remained stagnant, left to the Europeans for defense of NATO. The United States had nineteen aged wooden-hulled ships in two squadrons based in Charleston, South Carolina, and Seattle, Washington. Designated *Aggressive*-class ocean minesweepers or MSOs (minesweeper ocean), most of these belonged to the reserves, with fully one-third of their seventy-five-man crews weekend warriors. Their training for the last twenty years had consisted of sailing around one weekend a month and two weeks a year. The West Coast–based vessels avoided operating at night as the massive Douglas firs loggers left drifting in the water of Puget Sound would leave a large hole in the waterline of their small wooden-plank hulls.[43]

It had been thirty-six years since the navy last faced an enemy using naval mines on the open sea, when North Korea (with Soviet advisers) had embarrassingly thwarted a U.S. landing off Wonsan Harbor in 1951.[44] The fleet commander at the time, Rear Admiral Allan Smith, summed up his frustrations in a letter to the chief of naval operations that remained apropos four decades later: "We have lost control of the seas to a nation without a navy, using pre–World War I weapons, laid by vessels utilized at the time of the birth of Christ."[45]

Despite their pugnacious names—*Conquest, Fearless, Inflict*—they were awkward little vessels at the end of their useful lives. With a high octagonal superstructure, they looked more like large fishing lure as they bobbed like corks to and fro in the large swells of the open seas. About half the fleet still had engines manufactured by the defunct Packard Company, which made finding spare parts more of a challenge with each passing year. None had been outfitted with new remotely operated vehicles—common in the European navies—that allowed them to examine a suspected mine from a safe distance. Instead, with the Americans, a diver had to physically swim up and examine every suspicious contact, a slow and potentially lethal undertaking.[46] In an otherwise steel-hull fleet, to reduce the magnetic signature that could set off advanced electromagnetic-influence mines, naval engineers had constructed the MSOs out of wood. Other than the two-hundred-year-old frigate USS *Constitution*, these were the last wooden ships in the American navy.

But DeMasi's hunch proved correct. The idea of sending these small, aging man-of-wars to the far-off Persian Gulf came up just after the *Bridgeton* incident. On July 25, Crowe called the Pacific Fleet commander Ace Lyons: "We are looking at possibly sending some MSOs," Crowe told the admiral. Lyons had already anticipated this. "We are getting them ready now, but we need to lean on the Saudis and the French." When the Saudis proved unable and the Europeans unwilling, the news spread quickly that some of the MSOs were headed for war.[47]

The navy settled on sending six MSO minesweepers, with three coming from each coast.[48] The main problem would be how to get them the nine thousand miles to the Gulf. The navy brass decided to tow them. A larger ship on each coast was detailed to pull them along by running a cable to each minesweeper. This enhanced tow allowed the minesweepers to use just half of their engines, while still maintaining a respectable speed of thirty knots. Departing in the first week of September, like a mother duck with three ducklings following behind, they would make a six-week trip to the far side of the world, where the East and West Coast ships would finally meet up in Bahrain.[49]

A nineteenth-century adage refers to seafarers as "wooden ships and iron men." The journey across the two oceans in cramped 170-foot ships conjured up that saying in the minds of twentieth-century sailors. The old MSOs produced enough freshwater for just two daily twenty-minute sets. Showers became an assembly line. One man jumped into one of the three stalls, wetted down, and then stepped out to lather himself while the next man in the queue hopped in. Fresh food ran scarce, and the daily meal often consisted of Spam or canned ravioli. The ships rolled in such an unorthodox manner in the ocean swells that many sailors took to carrying "barf bags." Both flotillas had close calls. Across the Atlantic, the *Illusive*'s rudder stuck hard left and crossed the towline of the *Fearless*, dragging them together before the line could be thrown off. In the Pacific, two MSOs collided while being towed, and one had to be sent back to Subic Bay for repairs.[50]

With every resource in the limited American minesweeping arsenal on its way to the Gulf, Bernsen remained optimistic that the conflict would not expand. Iran had not laid any more mines, and that appeared promising. Bernsen suspected Iran would confine its mining campaign to the northern Gulf, where shipping would be destined only for Kuwait. "The fact that the central and southern Gulf have not been mined probably reflects Iran's conscious unwillingness to expose ships not in trade with Kuwait to this type of threat," he wrote in a message in early August.[51]

The Iranian leadership saw the situation quite differently. Khomeini's gamble with the "invisible hand" had worked. An emboldened Revolutionary Guard now clamored to lay more mines against the Great Satan. And unlike

Bernsen's prediction, anywhere they saw an American ship would be fair game. While the United States rushed to send helicopters and ships to the Gulf, on August 1 the Iranian ambassador in Tripoli met with Gaddafi. Their collaboration on naval mines had been a tremendous success, and now the Iranian government accepted an offer for even more military aid.

"There is a strong likelihood of a direct confrontation with the U.S. because of the American president's intentions and our firm resolve to respond," Iran's ambassador in Tripoli told the Libyan leader. "We have put the first stage behind us with sea mining, and as you saw, the first oil tanker did strike a mine."

Looking on from his headquarters in Honolulu, Ace Lyons fumed. Iran had deliberately targeted the United States and mined international waters in a clear breach of international law. Yet Washington had done nothing in response to this naked aggression. Although Crist and CENTCOM ran the operation, Lyons, as the Pacific Fleet commander, still controlled all the ships outside the Gulf, including the aircraft carrier when its planes were not protecting Crist's convoys. And Ace Lyons had been working on his own secret plan to deal with the Iranians. His boss, Ron Hays, would never support it, but Lyons had the chairman's ear. All that was needed was a window of opportunity.

Fourteen

A WINDOW OF
OPPORTUNITY

T he chairman would like you to call him," said Captain Kevin Healy
to his boss, Admiral James "Ace" Lyons, during a short break between
meetings. The executive officer did not consider the request by Admiral William Crowe anything remarkable. Since the crisis had begun with the
Bridgeton, Crowe spoke daily to his longtime acquaintance in Hawaii. The
chairman wanted new ideas on how to respond to the Iranian mining.

Lyons served as a useful coadjutor to Crowe. Since Lyons worked for
Crowe in the 1970s, Crowe had tapped Lyons, looking for ideas on fighting
the Soviets and for ways to get things done, frequently outside of the normal
channels. "Ace Lyons had a great mind," Crowe said years later. "He loved
imaginative and unorthodox solutions."[1] For Crowe, Lyons was a man who
could get things done militarily in a way the more politically minded Crowe
never could, all the while offering the chairman plausible deniability if things
turned out ugly.

Lyons picked up the phone as Healy went to his desk to listen in on
another line. "Any ideas?" Crowe asked. "You've got access to me directly if
you need to pass any information."

Lyons always had a suggestion. "A window of opportunity is coming up
later this month." There would be two carriers turning over outside the Gulf

and the battleship *Missouri* would arrive in the Middle East. "We may well be in a position to exert a considerable amount of power against the Iranians," Lyons told Crowe. "Keep it very, very quiet."

The prospect of drubbing the Iranians appealed to Crowe. He had been privately advocating seizing Farsi Island with special operations forces, but Colin Powell as deputy national security adviser did not support such an aggressive move. But these were the type of ideas he liked from Lyons. "Okay," Crowe answered. "Work out a code word and you say whatever it is and you go."

"Write me a letter," Crowe directed, asking for Lyons's thoughts about striking back at Iran.

Ace Lyons already had an Iran war plan, appropriately called Operation Window of Opportunity. Beginning in late 1986, he'd designed a top secret plan outside of the normal military channels. Without General Crist's knowledge at CENTCOM, Lyons crafted a U.S. Navy–only operation comprising two days of punishing attacks on Iranian military sites all along the Iranian coast—from Chah Bahar outside the Gulf working up to Bushehr. Convinced that Iran could not stand up to a sustained American attack and that military force might bring down the regime, Lyons planned to hit dozens of Iranian military units, including headquarters, airports, ports, and missile sites—all pummeled by the combined firepower of two aircraft carriers and the World War II battlewagon USS *Missouri*, lobbing salvos of two-thousand-pound shells. But Lyons did not stop with destroying Iran's military. The second day of his grand design targeted Iran's economy by destroying its oil storage at Kharg Island, Iran's only gasoline refinery, and its major harbors. U.S. jets would destroy Iranian docks, and mines would be laid to close the large Iranian ports of Bushehr and Bandar Abbas. "Mining of Bandar Abbas and Bushehr and destruction of the port facilities essentially eliminates Iranian capacity to receive refined petroleum products and essential war matériel," Lyons noted. The admiral even intended to reduce the two partially completed light water reactors at Bushehr to concrete rubble and twisted rebar.[2]

Lyons had been pushing this idea for months. A month before the first convoy, in June 1987, Ace Lyons had briefed the secretary of defense on his idea. On June 18, Caspar Weinberger and Richard Armitage stopped in Honolulu on a swing through Asia, and Lyons saw an opportunity to get his plan to take down the Khomeini regime in front of the Reagan administration. At three p.m., Weinberger paid an office call on Lyons. With the two men sitting around a table, and Armitage and Lyons's executive officer Kevin Healy in the background, the bulldog admiral pulled out his Iran plan and leaned forward in his chair.

"Mr. Secretary, we have an opportunity," he began. On August 26, the carrier *Ranger* would be relieving the *Constellation* on station in the Gulf of Oman, giving a brief overlap when two of the battle groups would be available. Additionally, the Joint Chiefs had just decided to send the battleship *Missouri* and five more warships to the Gulf about the same time. Lyons then pulled out his fourteen-page Window of Opportunity plan. There had never been so much firepower available near the Persian Gulf, he added. "We can cut 70 percent of their imports and exports. The objective of these strikes is to facilitate freedom of navigation and apply pressure to Iran to enter into serious negotiations to end the Iran-Iraq War."

Weinberger listened politely but took no notes. Weinberger had no intention of bombing Iran without a provocation or of getting the United States mired in a war and alienating many Gulf allies. He viewed Lyons as an activist, and this performance was in perfect keeping with Ace's personality, trying to take advantage of his visit in order to get his agenda pushed to the top. Several times the defense secretary tried to get out of his chair, but Lyons kept gesticulating forward to keep him seated. After an hour, Weinberger left without comment. Armitage just shook his head. "It was typical bullshit from Ace. The secretary had no intention of starting a war with Iran."[3]

Undaunted, Lyons pitched his plan to any senior official who came to Hawaii. When Secretary of the Navy James Webb swung through, Lyons received a more positive response. Lyons did not think much of the thirty-something secretary, but he offered to keep him informed of his other thoughts and views. Webb gave him the green light: "If you ever need to speak with me, call me directly." Lyons interpreted the message as a clear sign not to worry about the chain of command.[4]

Not that Ace Lyons had ever worried too much about the formalities of obtaining his boss's permission. His relationship was strained with his senior at Pacific Command, Admiral Ronald Hays, and naval operations chief Admiral Carl Trost had grown alarmed at some of Lyons's antics designed to intimidate the Soviets, especially some provocative mock air attacks directed at the Soviet forces at Petropavlovsk. He feared Lyons intended to start a war with the Soviets. "Ace had no concept of a chain of command if it did not fit his needs. He was making U.S. policy and setting the means to execute that policy without any guidance from those above. I think guys like that are dangerous," Trost said.[5]

Now, following Crowe's solicitation for ideas, Lyons composed a letter for Crowe. On August 11 he sent a six-page document typed on Lyons's four-star stationery, offering many suggestions for the chairman on how to run the Persian Gulf operation. "I have come to the conclusion," he began, "that no amount of ships and aircraft will deter Iran as long as its leaders believe we will not respond to isolated attacks."

He advocated using his Window of Opportunity plan. Lyons included an updated version that added the *Missouri*'s 16-inch guns pulverizing the Silkworm sites ringing the Strait of Hormuz and marines from the 13th Marine Expeditionary Unit storming the beaches to seize the small but strategically placed island of Abu Musa. Lyons stressed for the chairman, "Our response needs to be vigorous and decisive. Half measures and gradualism will not do if we are to ever get their attention," he wrote in the opening paragraph of the plan.[6] Lyons suggested to Crowe that the best time for the strike would be August 29, when the battleship, two carriers, and a marine amphibious force would all be near the Gulf. "We will not have a similar opportunity for some time," he wrote.[7]

Since Lyons distrusted the security of normal communications channels, he dispatched his lawyer, Captain Morris Sinor, to hand carry the letter plus the latest version of his Window of Opportunity plan back to Washington and drop it off in Crowe's office at the Pentagon. Despite Lyons's general disdain for navy lawyers, he trusted Sinor, and his long-suffering lawyer had a reciprocal respect for his boss: "Admiral Lyons could be rude, crude, and arrogant, but he was the most brilliant naval officer I ever met."[8] Sinor dutifully complied, leaving the classified package with Crowe's executive officer and fellow navy captain Joseph Strasser.

Crowe called Lyons the next day after reading his letter. "That is a lot to ask of the U.S. government and the president," Crowe said.

With the Iran-Contra congressional hearings in full vigor and the Reagan administration being raked over the coals every night on the evening news, Lyons responded, "Bill, it's going to save the president."[9] The chairman kept the letter and Lyons's plan in his files, but never shared it with either Crist or Trost.

Crowe and Lyons did, however, conspire on slipping the large amphibious ship USS *Guadalcanal* past the Iranian Silkworm missiles around the Strait of Hormuz and into the Gulf, where it would be used to support helicopters clearing Iranian mines.

"Do you have any thoughts as to how she should go through?" Crowe inquired, then adding, "We don't want any messages."

"I will work out the details and only you will know," an enthusiastic Lyons answered. "We can't tell anyone or it will leak."

"Okay," said the chairman. That same day Lyons formulated a scheme to disguise the nineteen-thousand-ton ship as a freighter by rigging lights to mimic that of a commercial ship rather than a warship carrying navy and marine helicopters.

Lyons worried about press leaks, believing many stemmed from inside the Pentagon, so he devised another ruse to fool the U.S. military. He issued a false message that the *Guadalcanal* had electrical problems and would be delayed four days before heading to the Persian Gulf. Lyons called the scheme Operation Slipper, and the only men privy to the fact that the message was false were Crowe and the Seventh Fleet commander, Vice Admiral Paul David Miller. Two days later, Lyons updated Crowe on Slipper. "It will transit the straits on the night of the fourteenth. It will look like a container ship going through," he told Crowe's assistant, a colorless toady, Vice Admiral Jonathan Howe. "Keep this information with the chairman and yourself," Lyons added. "Don't let anyone else know—don't need a lot of questions out of Tampa."[10]

Operation Slipper fooled the American generals and admirals. The *Guadalcanal* sailed under strict radio silence with its lights and camouflage netting configured to make it appear to be a large cargo ship. All the while CENT-COM, the Joint Staff, and Crowe's own operations deputy briefed both the chairman of the Joint Chiefs and Weinberger every morning that the electrical problems were delaying the *Guadalcanal*'s departure. The two four-stars in charge of the Middle East and the Indian Ocean remained oblivious too. Unaware of Crowe and Lyons's machinations, Crist and his counterpart at PACOM, Ron Hays, worked on their own protection scheme for the *Guadalcanal*. Crist suspected something was amiss when he learned that the *Guadalcanal* had left Diego Garcia, and he queried Crowe. The night before the *Guadalcanal* was due to transit the Strait of Hormuz, Crowe had his assistant call Lyons asking to let the CENTCOM commander in on the deception plan.

"Okay," Lyons answered. "He can tell Crist only. You know, no one at CINCPAC [i.e., Admiral Hays] knows. Make sure the chairman understands."

"Okay—he knows," Howe responded.

The *Guadalcanal* passed through the Strait of Hormuz on the night of August 14 without incident. As they normally did, the Iranian navy hailed the unidentified ship (the *Guadalcanal*'s bridge watch refused to respond), but the Iranian military showed little interest in the oddly configured container ship. While there is no evidence that Iran ever considered attacking such a high-visibility ship, Lyons remained pleased. "We slipped it right past them!"

The ramifications of the self-deceit reverberated around the most senior levels of the Pentagon. Unwitting to the chairman's role, Crist viewed it as more of Ace Lyons's meddling in his command. When Ron Hays learned of the *Guadalcanal*'s unexpected arrival in Bahrain, the normally composed admiral was livid. He immediately called Lyons.

"Don't talk to me. Crowe was the one who ordered it," Lyons dismissively told Hays.

Hays could not believe that Crowe would have gone behind his back; he called the chairman and complained about Lyons's "cutting him out." Crowe sympathized but never let on that he had directed Ace's machinations.[11]

As the Americans engaged in tomfoolery, the vitriolic warnings from Tehran increased. "They had better leave the region; otherwise we shall strike them so hard they will regret what they have done," said Iranian president Ali Khamenei. The United States took the rhetoric seriously.[12] The Central Intelligence Agency issued an intelligence alert warning that Iran would likely conduct more mine attacks to stop the Kuwaiti convoy operation.

Sheik Abdul Fattah al-Bader, the chairman of the Kuwait Oil Tanker Company, pressed Bernsen to get the reflagged ship *Gas Prince* and its load of liquid petroleum gas to sail due to important contractual obligations. Bernsen cautioned against this move. While he did not share this with al-Bader, American intelligence had solid evidence of an Iranian spy inside al-Bader's company. This agent had tipped off the Revolutionary Guard to the *Bridgeton* convoy and would do the same again. Until they had some minesweeping capability, another convoy seemed too risky.

Reluctantly, Bernsen bowed to al-Bader's needs and hastened a convoy out of Kuwait—the same day as Khamenei's threat. Two U.S. warships rendezvoused with the *Gas Prince* and escorted the ship south, hugging the Saudi coastline as they passed Farsi Island and with the Saudi military both sweeping ahead for mines and providing two F-15 fighters for cover. To throw off the Iranians, the navy liaison officer in Kuwait passed a false convoy route to the Kuwait Oil Tanker Company, with the convoy commander telling the master of the *Gas Prince* the real route only after they had set sail from Kuwait. To avoid Iranian mines, the convoy cut across the Iranian exclusion zone, with Iraq notified beforehand to avoid another attack like that on the *Stark*.

The United States saw threats everywhere. An Iranian four-engine P-3 approached to within twenty-five miles before the USS *Klakring*, on picket duty in the central Gulf, locked on to the aircraft with its fire control radar, sending the P-3 heading off swiftly in the opposite direction.[13] An Iranian frigate shadowed the Americans. As the weather cleared, Iranian small boats appeared on the horizon and approached to within a few miles of the convoy, close enough to conduct suicide or surprise attacks, one admiral later wrote. Eight Iranian warships were under way—the bulk of Iran's operational fleet.

U.S. fears seemed justified when the USS *Kidd* detected a Silkworm targeting radar, perhaps a precursor to launching one of its thousand-pound missiles. A U.S. electronics jet from the carrier *Constellation* immediately jammed the Iranian radar. The phones lit up between Washington, Tampa, and Middle East Force as the United States braced for a possible Iranian attack. The carrier strike group commander, a gruff, aggressive, decorated combat veteran aptly named Lyle Bull, ordered additional aircraft launched, ready for a strike against the Iranian missile sites. As tense minutes passed, however, Iran launched no missiles and the radar emissions ended. The U.S. convoy steamed safely without incident into the open waters of the Indian Ocean.

To Lyons and his simpatico strike group commander, Rear Admiral Bull, the Iranian actions demonstrated hostile intent and the United States should respond with force if they tried it again. Bernsen viewed it as far less menacing, more akin to Tehran tweaking the American nose.[14]

On August 4, the Iranian Revolutionary Guard began a weeklong exercise under the dour name "Martyrdom" in the Strait of Hormuz. Tehran radio repeatedly warned ships and aircraft to "avoid approaching the area of the maneuvers," adding, "The Islamic Republic of Iran will not be held responsible for the danger to these planes and ships that approach, due to the use of missiles and shells."

Even more alarming had been Iran's instigation of an uprising during the annual hajj. As punishment for Saudi Arabia's support to the United States and Iraq, Ayatollah Khomeini ordered the Revolutionary Guard to start an uprising in Mecca during the July 1987 hajj. Hundreds of guardsmen began quietly flying into Saudi Arabia disguised as pilgrims. They carried guns and knives stashed on board the Iran Air jets. The plan called for a massive, choreographed demonstration against Saudi Arabia and the United States, designed both to embarrass the king and to create turmoil inside his kingdom.[15]

Reza Kahlili was still working as part of William Casey's spies run out of the CIA station in Frankfurt. One of Kahlili's friends came up to him excited at having been picked to participate in an operation of such importance. "Everything is in place and the Saudi monarch is going down," he told Kahlili, adding, "These Arabs are the servants of America, and they will pay big this time." Writing on the back of his specially treated paper, Kahlili wrote a hidden message back to the CIA: "Thousands of Guards have been sent as pilgrims and flown by Iran Air. The plan is to incite the Muslims for a demonstration condemning American and Israeli policies. They intend to escalate the demonstration to an uprising against the Saudi kingdom."[16]

The CIA tipped off Saudi authorities, who interdicted most of the guardsmen and their weapons. When the orchestrated uprising occurred on August 1, the Saudi security forces were poised and ready. When the first Iranian pulled out a weapon, the Saudis opened fire with automatic weapons, cutting down 275 Iranians, both Revolutionary Guards and innocent pilgrims. That afternoon the ever bellicose Prince Bandar called Crowe: "They call us wimps yet we shot down their plane [the F-4 downed in 1984] and now killed about three hundred Iranians! The Iranian problem," Bandar added, "is going to get worse."[17]

Crowe and Crist conversed on the afternoon of August 7. A number of intelligence reports had raised concern about Iranian intentions. The Office of Naval Intelligence had just issued a dire threat alert predicting that within the next seven to ten days Iran would take "combat action against U.S. interests in the Persian Gulf."[18] Crowe emphasized to Crist the growing concern in Washington about neither starting a war nor repeating the *Stark* incident. It was a political tightrope, he said, which fell to individual ship commanders to straddle.[19]

Both Bandar and the intelligence predictions proved correct. Iran's real purpose behind the Martyrdom exercise soon showed itself. Amid all the publicity surrounding their swaggering exercise, the Iranian ship *Charak*, normally used for resupply operations, sailed from Bandar Abbas, broke away from the exercise, and headed for the anchorage at Khor Fakkan, the major port supporting all the shipping entering the Gulf and the assembly location for the *Bridgeton* convoy. On either August 8 or 9, the *Charak* laid a string of sixteen large M-08 mines in the middle of the tanker anchorage and then scurried back to Iran.

This time Iran would not catch either Bernsen or American intelligence off guard. As Bernsen prepared to restart the convoys, his intelligence officer, Commander Ziegler, came in with an NSA intercept, a tantalizing snippet of a Revolutionary Guard conversation that indicated that the next mining operation would be at "a place where things gather." Where this referred to, Ziegler added, remained unclear and had caused considerable consternation within the intelligence community. The DIA and the CIA believed the Iranians intended to mine Kuwait Harbor. Bernsen sat down and pored over a chart with Ziegler and his operations boss, David Grieve. Everyone but Bernsen focused only on targets inside the Gulf, but Bernsen came to a different conclusion: "It could only mean the anchorage of Khor Fakkan."[20]

Bernsen immediately called Crist. "I think Khor Fakkan is their target, and I want to delay the next convoy for twenty-four hours and form it up well to the south of where we planned."[21]

Crist remained skeptical. His own J-2 intelligence section agreed with the DIA and CIA. But the CENTCOM commander was not going to overrule Bernsen. "Hal, if you believe it is best to alter the convoy's schedule, then do it."[22]

On August 10, Bernsen's actions were vindicated. The tanker *Texaco Caribbean* had just pulled into Khor Fakkan to anchor overnight before heading to Amsterdam with a load of Iranian crude. Suddenly, a powerful explosion rocked the tanker, as a mine ripped a four-meter hole in the ship, spilling some 2.5 million barrels of crude.[23] The irony of this was not lost on the Americans: the victim of Iran's mines had been a ship carrying its own oil. But the laughing stopped five days later when the mining turned deadly. The small UAE supply vessel *Anita* was making her rounds servicing anchored ships when she hit another mine. The 250-pound charge reduced the *Anita* to splinters, instantly killing six men, including the British master.[24]

That mining incident, off Fujairah, UAE, backfired on Iran. Instead of intimidating the West, this blatant mining of international waters galvanized European support for mine-clearing operations in the Gulf. Less than two weeks after rejecting an American request to send minesweepers, the United Kingdom, France, Belgium, and the Netherlands all dispatched countermine vessels to the Persian Gulf. The UK sent four minesweepers plus support ships and began conducting its own escort operations for British-registered vessels. Belgium and the Netherlands sent a combined force that included a support ship and two minesweepers, commanded by a grizzled old commodore who had been in the Red Sea clearing Libyan mines. The following month, the Italians joined the U.S. effort by sending three frigates and three minesweepers to assist in keeping the Gulf open. France went even further, dispatching three minesweepers and one of its two carriers, the *Clemenceau*, to the Persian Gulf.[25]

While this transformed the mine clearing into a multinational effort, it did not translate into a coalition against Iran. While direct military-to-military cooperation was quite close with sharing of intelligence on Iran, the governments remained careful not to publicly ally themselves with the U.S. effort. There was no joint command, and the coordination of the mine-clearing effort was done on an ad hoc basis by weekly meetings in the Gulf between naval officers. Despite DOD and State Department efforts for a unified approach to countering Iranian mines, the other countries had their own specific economic interests in the region, which did not always coincide with Washington's. The British and French arrived first in October. They quickly cleared fourteen mines off Fujairah and found two anchors—all that remained of the mines that had hit the *Anita* and the *Texaco Caribbean*.[26]

The French aircraft carrier did help the Americans. After the Khor Fakkan mining, the French minister of defense privately told Weinberger that his country would consider a joint air strike on Iran should the mining continue. Paris still wanted to settle the score from the Beirut bombings four years earlier. Crist dispatched Bernsen to talk to the French admiral when the *Clemenceau* stopped in Djibouti. The two nations agreed to joint training between their carriers, and the Americans shared some of their Invoke Resolve Iranian war plans with the French. Commander Ziegler came away convinced that in the event of a war, France would stand with Middle East Force.[27]

Rafsanjani became the public face for Iran's response to the mining of Fujairah. He blamed the United States for backing Iraq and creating the crisis. "Iran has announced time and again that its operations in the Persian Gulf are retaliatory. If those responsible for creating the insecurity were prevented from doing so, all problems would now have been solved."[28] In a revealing speech at Friday prayers at Tehran University on August 21, Rafsanjani offered Iranian minesweepers to aid the international effort while casting the blame for the mining on the United States. "It is the situation in the United States that forces Americans to embark on adventurism in far corners of the world," he said. The Iranian laid the blame on the need to shore up the administration's popularity in the aftermath of the Iranian arms-sales scandal, which Rafsanjani called "McFarlane's disgrace." Rafsanjani failed to mention his own significant involvement in that incident, which he said revealed America's "rotten nature."

While laying the blame for the mines on Iraq or the United States, Rafsanjani bragged, "If we intended to plant mines, well, oh God, it is quite a different story . . . this is fully within our means. You can send twenty-seven or twenty-eight ships to the Gulf," he continued. "Each one of these vessels is a target for us. There used to be four targets, now there are twenty-seven."[29]

In response to the mining, the United States sent a tame démarche to Iran via the Swiss embassy. It reassured the Iranians of American neutrality while asserting the right to freedom of navigation and to protect U.S.-flagged vessels. The United States called on Iran to accept a cease-fire with Iraq and to refrain from laying additional mines as the "U.S. government would consider this an extremely dangerous escalation and a direct military threat." Iran never responded to the U.S. letter and took it as more hollow words.[30] They had laid three strings of mines aimed squarely at the United States and the superpower had replied with a tepid warning.

Iran answered the démarche by laying more mines. Another Revolutionary Guard vessel operating from Farsi Island dropped a string of smaller Myam mines about twelve miles south of the *Bridgeton* field, where the convoy route took a turn to wind around the Iranian exclusion zone. The Iranian vessel set its stern on the light at the small Saudi island of Karan and simply headed back toward Farsi, dropping one off the stern every three hundred yards. The targets of these mines were not the convoys but the American minesweepers that would have to move through this stretch on their way north to clear the *Bridgeton* field. The Iranians set the mines for a much shallower depth.[31]

With *Hunter* and *Striker* ready and having dodged the Khor Fakkan mining, on August 8 the United States began its first major convoy since the *Bridgeton* attack. Tensions remained high in Washington as Crowe phoned Crist for hourly updates, and the CENTCOM commander spent the better part of three days in his own command center monitoring the convoy's progress, sleeping occasionally on a cot in his office. When the convoy entered the Strait of Hormuz and into the range of the Silkworm missiles, Crowe entered the maze of the National Military Command Center, taking a seat in a small conference room where a brigadier general sat twenty-four hours a day as the senior watch officer, just off a large open area where action officers tracked events from around the globe. Crowe monitored the ships' movement, poised to immediately contact either Weinberger or Carlucci in the White House Situation Room should the Iranians decide to attack the convoy.[32]

A 107-foot-long black SR-71 flew a sweep along the length of the Gulf photographing the Silkworm sites, then up north to photograph Iranian Revolutionary Guard boats at Farsi, Bushehr, and Kharg Island. To turn around, the high-flying jet flew over both Kuwait and Saudi Arabia, with Prince Bandar getting the king's permission to cut over the northeast section of the kingdom. As the SR-71 passed Bandar Abbas, the State Department sent out a flash message warning the American embassies in Baghdad, Riyadh, and Kuwait of the flight. The aircraft cut across Iranian waters before heading west over Kuwait and Saudi Arabia, then turned with a loud sonic boom that rattled the Kuwait capital.[33]

Lyons looked to provoke a fight with Iran. He had Rear Admiral Lyle Bull on the carrier USS *Constellation* aggressively push his F-14 fighters in toward Bandar Abbas. Several times they intentionally flew into Iranian airspace, either to intimidate Iran or to provoke the war Lyons wanted.[34] About two hours before the convoy entered the strait, a U.S. Navy P-3 prop aircraft took off from the air base on the Omani island of Masirah. With their exceptional electro-optical surveillance systems, CENTCOM viewed the P-3 flights as a key component in monitoring Iranian Silkworm sites. As the plane headed around the strait just outside Iranian airspace and flew into the Gulf, what appeared to be an Iranian F-4 took off from Bandar Abbas and closed in on the tail of the P-3. Fearing the F-4 would fire on the helpless P-3, two F-14s were vectored in to engage the Iranian jet. The two large swing-wing American fighters dove down onto the Iranian aircraft. The lead American fired off one air-to-air missile that promptly malfunctioned. So the F-14s launched another missile each, both of which sailed wide when the pilots hastily pulled the trigger without a proper fix on the Iranian boogie. The F-4 banked hard and headed back to the air base at Bandar Abbas. The U.S. aircraft decided not to pursue.[35]

Instead of inciting Iran, the air engagement brought the simmering Crist-Lyons feud to a full boil. The following day, after a closer examination of the Hawkeye's tapes and signals information collected by the NSA, Bernsen and Crist concluded the Iranian aircraft was not an F-4, but a much larger and slower four-engine C-130 used by the Iranians for maritime surveillance. After going over the evidence, both agreed that the Iranian aircraft had not been headed toward the P-3 and likely never even knew the U.S. plane was there. In a "personal for" message for senior military leaders, without mentioning Lyons by name, Crist cautioned on the need "to guard against" starting an unintentional war with the Iranians. He viewed Lyons's actions as reckless and risking escalation of the low-grade conflict into a full-scale war that neither side wanted.[36]

When Crist called Lyle Bull asking for clarification on the incident, he was met with insolence. Bull's carrier had just left the designated station to support Earnest Will and CENTCOM, so he technically fell back under PACOM and Lyons's control. The gruff rear admiral and supporter of Lyons cheerfully told the marine four-star general, "I don't have to answer your questions. I don't work for you now."[37]

General Crist turned bright red with anger. "Who does that son of a bitch think he is!" He called Crowe to complain, and the chairman promised to look into it. Meanwhile, Crowe continued his sidebar dealings with Lyons. When news inevitably leaked out and CNN reported the incident two days later, Lyons suggested to Crowe, "Tell them we fired a warning shot at the Iranians." Crowe liked the idea and reported it as such.[38]

General Crist had had enough of Lyons, Bull, and the navy. Few senior officers had his joint expertise, and he even kept a copy of the Goldwater-Nichols legislation in his top desk drawer as a reference. The act had been designed to fix just this sort of service parochialism. It gave him the legal authority to run military operations in his area, and if Crowe would not enforce the law, he would bring the issue to a culmination.

As the operation expanded to include a battleship, an aircraft carrier, and nearly thirty warships, and the prospect grew of a military action against Iran, Earnest Will surpassed the realm of a single one-star admiral in Bahrain to control. On August 10, Crowe met privately with Trost in his office to discuss command and control for the Persian Gulf. The chairman did not invite Crist, even though it directly impacted his forces. The chief of naval operations agreed to get back quickly with a recommendation for Crowe, which he did the next day. Drafted by his operations officer, Vice Admiral Hank Mustin, it largely concurred with Lyons's views and recommended giving the mission to an existing navy command.

General Crist challenged the process with his own recommendation. He proposed forming a new headquarters: a joint task force to command all the military forces involved in Earnest Will. The aircraft carrier or battleship outside the Gulf, as well as air force AWACS planes in Saudi Arabia and Bernsen's Middle East Force, would all belong to this one commander, who in turn would report back only to General Crist in Tampa. "The entire command structure was based upon nod of the head and handshake deals," Crist said in an interview in 1988. "It violated everything I knew about unity of command." If Iran decided to escalate, Crist added, there needed to be a way to coordinate the individual services. "What I wanted was to create one command for the whole force and integrate all our resources under one commander served by a staff composed of members from all services." There would not be another incident where a carrier commander supporting the convoys would say he did not work for the CENTCOM commander.[39]

While technically Crist had the authority to establish this command himself, the idea would be too contentious to implement unilaterally. He ran the idea past Armitage to make sure he had Weinberger's support, and on August 13, the day Crowe told Crist about Lyons's deception with the *Guadalcanal*, the CENTCOM commander sent a formal message proposing the task force idea to Crowe. Based upon the provisions of the newly enacted Goldwater-Nichols Act, the joint task force would control all forces taking part in Earnest Will regardless of service and location inside or outside the Gulf. Crist proposed a navy admiral as the commander, since the navy had the preponderance of the forces assigned, but his deputy would be an air force brigadier general, as that service's planes would be crucial for any larger attacks against Iran.[40] While forming this type of command is routine today—in fact the norm for military operations—in 1987 it challenged conventions, and the thought of an air force general riding around on a navy ship seemed surreal.

The next day Weinberger and the Joint Chiefs met in the Tank to discuss Crist's proposal. With Weinberger already behind the idea, the chiefs and Crowe swiftly agreed to Crist's recommendation.[41] Their only input was to downgrade the rank of the commander from three stars to two.

But Lyons still held out hope that Crowe would give him the go-ahead to conduct his Window of Opportunity plan. On August 17, he flew out to the *Constellation*. Lyons carried the latest version of his Iran war plan to personally pass to Lyle Bull. When the *Constellation* and *Ranger* turned over on August 28, the former would steam southeast into the Indian Ocean as if headed back to her home port in the Pacific. A few days later, on September 3, the *Missouri* would arrive, at which time Lyons would secretly order Bull's carrier battle group back to the north Arabian Sea. Lyons's forces would be in place for a major military action, with Iran being none the wiser. No doubt it was a clever means to clandestinely build forces under the noses of the Iranian military, but in doing so, Lyons never consulted either of the two unified commanders sanctioned by law to make such decisions—Hays and Crist. The chairman of the Joint Chiefs had encouraged Lyons, but he'd kept that to himself and never informed the defense secretary, who had more than passing interest in whether the United States attacked another country.

That evening, Lyons met with Bull and a cocksure redhead named Anthony Less, the incoming *Ranger* battle group commander. They were joined by Rear Admiral Dennis Brooks, who had been selected as the new joint task force commander, a man Lyons held in disdain.[42] Brooks had just returned from Bahrain and his first meeting with Bernsen and Crist, and Lyons ordered him to back-brief him on what Crist had said to Brooks. Everything Denny said irritated Lyons. Crist had given Brooks specific instructions that he would work only for Crist and was not to have any contact with Lyons. Brooks opined that he might get a third star out of the assignment and suggested he needed a staff of 120 people. "You are lucky to have one star," Lyons thought as he heard Brooks talk about cutting him out of the operation.

But what really set off Lyons was a passing reference by Brooks to the Window of Opportunity plan. Lyons immediately halted the discussion and threw both Bull and Less out of the stateroom to chew out Brooks in private for divulging his top secret plan.

Less had no idea what Brooks was talking about, so he met privately with one of Lyons's aides, whom he'd known for many years.

"What is this all about?" Less asked when they were alone in a darkened passageway.

"It is extremely sensitive, but Admiral Lyons is preparing to attack Iran using your carrier, the *Connie*, and the *Missouri* once she arrives."

"Holy shit," a stunned Less answered, realizing the magnitude of what Lyons had concocted.

Ace Lyons's fertile mind had still other ideas for Iran. While on board the *Connie*, he called the commander of the Pacific submarine force, Rear Admiral James Reynolds. "Look at getting the best guy in WesPac [Western Pacific] and load him out with the best combination of torpedoes and mines. The idea," Lyons continued, "is to send a sub into the Gulf to seed key Iranian areas, to have them think it's their own mines, and if possible torpedo a few of their ships. Take a look at the channels around Larak Island. Don't discuss this with anybody," Lyons sternly cautioned. "It will have to be covert."

Two days later Reynolds called back to Lyons. "The Los Angeles attack sub USS *Honolulu* is due in Subic Bay on the nineteenth and could be loaded out with mines and on station by August thirtieth." Reynolds cautioned about the mining scheme, worried that the Gulf was too shallow for the sub mining.

Lyons knew he would have to get Crowe's authority to do this, but the timing for the sub's arrival would be perfect as an added weapon for Window of Opportunity.

Satisfied that all was progressing, Lyons flew back to Hawaii. He stopped in Guam for the night—long enough to phone Trost to voice his concerns about Brooks. "This cabal between Hays and Crist is essentially cutting me from the pattern," Lyons complained, before lambasting the decision to select Brooks. "I can't tell you how disappointed I was to put Brooks into this job. We need to watch this very carefully. We don't want the navy and this country embarrassed," he told the naval operations chief.

Trost did not disagree with everything Lyons said. He too thought it was unwise to cut out the expertise of the Pacific Fleet. But he found it strange to refer to two theater commanders doing their job as a cabal. He also held a higher opinion of Brooks.

Lyons continued to wait for the word from Crowe. As time ticked down, he began to think that once again the United States did not have the balls to deal with Iran. On August 27, he called Crowe, who was at Fort Leavenworth attending a meeting of the theater commanders. Lyons spoke to Captain Strasser, Crowe's executive officer. Lyons inquired, "Do I need to talk to the chairman about the Window of Opportunity plan?"

Although Crowe had encouraged Lyons's plan, he'd never told Lyons it was going to happen. Instead, Strasser spoke for the chairman: "Absent another provocation, no one here has the stomach for that."

With Crowe's unwillingness to press for attacking Iran, the window of opportunity envisioned by Lyons closed. The carriers rotated out and Lyle Bull headed back to the West Coast. "We blew a golden opportunity to clobber the Iranians while the threat was manageable, perhaps even bring down the regime," Lyons lamented years later.

But Ace Lyons's anomalistic behavior had finally reached the breaking point with his boss, Ron Hays. Ace had repeatedly kept Hays in the dark about his actions and plans—the *Guadalcanal*, using a sub to sink Iranian ships, or pushing to execute the Window of Opportunity plan—frustrating the genial admiral in Honolulu.

Hays wrote a letter to Weinberger: it was either Ace or him, and if Lyons did not go, then Hays would retire. The letter arrived in Armitage's box; he quickly pulled it and called Hays. "You better not send that letter in," Armitage said. "First, we don't want this all over the building, and second, if the secretary does not agree to fire Ace, then you have to retire."

The two men agreed to shred Hays's letter and quietly approach Weinberger in private. Armitage arranged a phone call between the two men. After explaining all of Lyons's maneuverings, Weinberger agreed with Hays. Lyons needed to be fired, and the secretary wanted him retired as a two-star, not as a customary four-star rank.

After talking with Webb, Weinberger called Trost, who was on vacation at his home in Virginia Beach. "I want Lyons to retire immediately, and he can go as a two-star." Trost agreed—he had no love for Lyons—but he suggested they offer to retire him as a four-star if Lyons would go quietly.

Trost also knew of another hammer to use against Ace. A chief petty officer on Lyons's plane had lodged a complaint on the waste and fraud hotline. While Ace was out on the *Constellation*, he had allowed his marine fleet force commander, Lieutenant General Dwayne Gray, to use his aircraft to fly back to the mainland for a speech. Lyons had included a piece of furniture for his daughter in Norfolk to be loaded onto the plane. The plan was for his daughter to pick it up where the plane landed with Gray, but Gray, trying to help out his boss, asked the pilot if he had a reason to go on to Norfolk. When the pilot said, "Sure," Gray sent the plane along and the pilot dropped the furniture off with Lyons's daughter—all without Lyons's knowledge. The complaint alleged Lyons had misused government aircraft.

At eight forty on the morning of September 4, Lyons was sitting at his large desk in Hawaii, the same one used by Admiral Nimitz during the Second World War. Trost called and requested a clear line. Lyons's executive officer, Kevin Healy, dutifully hung up his phone.

"I don't know anything about this," Trost dishonestly began, "but I've been told to tell you that you have violated the chain of command and they want your retirement by October first. We need your answer by tomorrow." There would be no further discussions.

A few hours later, Lyons finally got ahold of Crowe. "Bill, what the hell is all this crap?" Crowe, who had just spoken to Ron Hays, responded, "Hays thinks you went around him. I never told you not to keep your superiors informed. Besides, you're in trouble with the secretary of the navy for misuse of your aircraft."

"What the fuck are you talking about? I've never misused my airplane."

"You sent an aircraft on to Norfolk on personal business," Crowe responded.

"I don't even know what you are talking about," Lyons answered incredulously. "And you told me not to send any messages or tell anyone about what we were doing."

"I never said not to keep the chain of command informed," the chairman said disingenuously. "But you still have got a lot of friends back here in Washington."

Lyons was stunned. He could not believe that Crowe had knifed him in the back by not defending him in Washington. "Well, from where I sit, that is pretty hard to see. How come I was not given my day in court to come back and defend myself?"

"We thought it was best to handle it this way. But when this all blows over, I want you to come and see me and we can talk, because there are a lot of things we can do," Crowe added, as if this were a minor change of assignments. Crowe could not afford to have Lyons come forward and expose his private dealings with the chairman, especially since Crowe had deliberately avoided the chain of command that Lyons now stood accused of circumventing. Crowe remained silent. For political expediency, Lyons would take the fall. The chairman never mentioned any of his private conversations with Lyons to either Weinberger or Trost. Ace Lyons never spoke to Crowe again.

Lyons agreed to submit his retirement papers. But he refused to expose Crowe's duplicity. When asked why, Lyons answered, "I spent forty years serving in the navy. I was not going to be a part of tearing it down."[43]

On October 1, Lyons thanked his staff in a brief retirement ceremony on the deck of the cruiser *Antietam*. "The old surface warrior is gone . . . that's all I can say now," Lyons said shortly before leaving.[44]

Amazingly, Crowe had the chutzpah to send Lyons a flattering personal message that praised his skill and creativity: "I greatly value your friendship and the wise counsel you have provided me during our frequent association. You leave a void that will be difficult to fill. Warmest regards, Bill."[45]

"Fuck you," Lyons muttered when he read it.

Lyons retired to his home in McLean, Virginia, but his troubles only grew. The long knives were out for the maverick admiral, with Trost leading the way. Agents from the Naval Criminal Investigative Service hounded Lyons. For the next year, they staked out his house, watching who came and went, and launched a series of investigations. While agents tried to get other officers to swear that Lyons had used his government plane to fly his dogs around to exclusive dog shows, others confiscated classified papers he'd sent back to the Naval Historical Center's archives in Washington. He and his wife collected antiques, and rumors spread that Lyons had used his aircraft to ferry them for his wife's business. Although his wife never sold antiques, investigators spent hours digging into that unsupported accusation. Lyons was then accused of spiriting away from Pacific Command highly classified papers that should not have left the command safes. Trost wanted to press charges, but he could not get the navy secretary to agree. "What they confiscated," Lyons said later, "were papers that were embarrassing to them—that's what they wanted." The vice chief of naval operations, Huntington Hardisty, offered quarters during his transition. Lyons refused, but asked for his two stewards to remain to help him with his move. No one could recall this, and Lyons had to reimburse the government for the cost of the airfare for the two enlisted men. "It was purely vindictive," Lyons's lawyer, Morris Sinor, said. After more than a year, the new secretary of the navy, William Ball, finally ordered the harassment to cease.

While Lyons was out of the way, CENTCOM's troubles with the navy remained. News articles appeared in the *San Diego Union*, a paper with a strong source within the navy hierarchy, that the mining of the *Bridgeton* had resulted from a lack of proper naval planning at the Tampa headquarters. Anonymous admirals warned that "more mistakes could cost American lives."

Not only had Crist finally cut out Lyons and the Pacific Fleet, but navy brass was aghast at his plan for dealing with the Iranians. Rather than view the conflict as a traditional naval fight, Crist approached it as an insurgency, a guerrilla war at sea. His approach was more akin to Vietnam or Iraq after 2007. It would be a low-tech fight where small boats and helicopters had more impact than multibillion-dollar cruisers.

Crowe publicly supported Crist. "These criticisms [of Crist] are just plain wrong," he said during a trip to California. But behind the walls of the Pentagon, a duplicitous chairman had the long knives after Crist too.

Fifteen

THE NIGHT STALKERS

While the military brass feuded, the onus for defeating Iran bore down squarely on the shoulders of Hal Bernsen and his tiny thirteen-man staff on board their aging white-painted command ship. Staying up late into the evening talking with a few key officers, Bernsen rethought his plan. Clearly the Iranian leadership had not been awed by the power of the U.S. Navy and had risked war by targeting the first U.S. convoy.[1] With the horse out of the barn, military intelligence analysts now fed him a steady stream of possible future Iranian Revolutionary Guard attacks.[2]

One of Bernsen's principal discussants was his controversial intelligence officer, Commander Howell Conway Ziegler. One retired officer described him as "a mad genius—true on both accounts," while others called him a "whirling dervish." His mind worked fast and ginned up unorthodox solutions to equally unusual problems. A common refrain said about him by many of those interviewed was: "He would come up with ten solutions to a problem; nine would be bullshit, but that tenth would be brilliant." Ziegler's role in Middle East Force went beyond his intelligence duties. Shortly after the *Bridgeton* mining, Bernsen dispatched him to Djibouti to negotiate with the French about increasing their support for the escort operation. Ziegler inserted himself into operational decisions, perturbing many who believed he was in over his head and earning him the unflattering nickname "Conway Twitty."[3] But it would be his analysis that unraveled the Revolutionary Guard operations. More important, Bernsen and his operations staff respected and trusted him, convinced that his out-of-the-box thinking was what was required to address the Iranian threat.

"So what is the threat, then?" Bernsen asked Ziegler reflectively one evening. The "threat is essentially an unconventional one." The Iranians were unlike any adversary the U.S. Navy had fought. They posed a low-tech threat of mines and hit-and-run attacks with speedboats outfitted with recoilless rifles and inaccurate but lethal rocket launchers. They operated more akin to the Vietcong than to the Japanese. Their Silkworm missiles did pose a risk, but Iran was not likely to cross that line, he surmised, knowing full well that it would mean a massive U.S. retaliation that would destroy Iran's navy and air force.[4] "They already had their hands full with Iraq," Bernsen remarked.

Over the next couple of days Bernsen, Ziegler, and his operations officer brainstormed how to deal with the Iranian threat in late night staff meetings on board the *La Salle* and in lengthy phone calls with General George Crist, who was eight hours behind at CENTCOM in Tampa. Bernsen developed a robust surveillance regime to watch the Iranians. It seemed unrealistic to have a presence over the entire five-hundred-mile length of the Gulf, so he targeted the shallow choke points near Farsi or Abu Musa that presented the best locations to lay mines targeted against the American convoys, based largely on a picture of the Iranian operations being painted by Ziegler. He divided the five-hundred-mile Persian Gulf into roughly eight patrol zones in which U.S. warships would be more or less permanently stationed.[5] In the unlikely event the few Iranian aircraft decided to venture out, one cruiser was stationed in the middle and one outside the Gulf linked to the air force AWACS in Saudi Arabia. But defeating the Iranian mines or hit-and-run attacks would not be done by large warships or bombers. In Bernsen's mind, helicopters and some sort of smaller patrol boats would be needed to control the vast space of the Persian Gulf.[6]

The northern part of the Gulf near Farsi Island presented the greatest obstacle. Here, the shallow water forced shipping into a narrow corridor of deep water that passed too close for comfort to the Iranian stronghold of Farsi Island; the Revolutionary Guard dominated the hundred-mile stretch from Kuwait to the island. The Iranian air force did not pose a serious risk, contenting itself with fending off its Iraqi counterpart and protecting Iranian oil tankers. Iranian mines or spillover from the Iran-Iraq War raging just to the north made CENTCOM very reluctant to risk sending two hundred sailors and a billion-dollar ship into an area that many in Tampa and out in the Gulf began referring to as "Indian Country."[7] But unless the United States maintained some sort of permanent presence to prevent the Iranians from mining at their leisure, Earnest Will would be short-lived. Bernsen had to find a way to check the Comanches.

Ziegler passed Bernsen a report that profoundly affected the admiral's thinking. A quick analysis of the damage to the *Bridgeton* by American naval engineers and the Office of Naval Intelligence indicated that the mine had been set to float about twenty feet below the surface of the water. While this reinforced the threat to a U.S. Navy warship (a frigate draws some twenty-six feet), it did not preclude using a smaller draft vessel such as a patrol boat. "Those boats," Bernsen surmised, "could maneuver with fair confidence throughout the area, without the danger of striking a submerged, tethered mine."

Bernsen had no idea what kind of patrol boats the U.S. military possessed, so he and his operations officer, Captain David Grieve, simply opened the ship's copy of *Jane's Fighting Ships* to see what types of patrol boats the navy had in its inventory. As they flipped through the pages, the options available looked slim; only three boats appeared to have any applicability. One was the small thirty-two-foot fiberglass patrol boat riverine (PBR), designed originally for the rivers of Vietnam. Its recent claim to fame had been serving as the centerpiece in the movie *Apocalypse Now*. Relegated to the reserves, with a crew of five, the PBR was air transportable, but wholly incapable of operating in anything but the calmest of seas. Also in the inventory was the small, sleek Naval Special Warfare boat called Seafox. Made of radar-absorbent material, it might be useful for clandestine operations against the Iranians. Slightly more promising was the sixty-five-foot fiberglass Mark III patrol boat. Built in the early 1970s based on Vietnam requirements and experiences, it had a range of 450 miles and could achieve speeds of up to thirty knots. It included an enclosed cockpit and cabin to shelter its ten-man crew from the weather. The Mark III had never been designed to operate in the open seas, and lacked such creature comforts as showers, but it did pack a punch with a 40-mm cannon forward and a 20-mm machine gun aft, not counting heavy machine guns and automatic grenade launchers. These just might work, Bernsen thought.

All this led to the next logical question: "Where do you base them?" Small boats are not self-sufficient; they require a base for refueling, crew rest, and shelter in the event of foul weather. The Persian Gulf infamously kicks up some surprisingly large waves. Kuwait or Saudi Arabia might be willing to allow a small U.S. base, but both lay too far from the shipping channel to adequately support a round-the-clock operation. "What we needed," Bernsen thought, "was some kind of sea-based platform from which the small boats, helicopters, or whatever else we wanted could operate."[8]

As Bernsen mulled over the barge idea, he called the head of the Kuwait Oil Tanker Company, Fattah al-Bader. Talking around the issue over the open phone line, he asked al-Bader if he had some ships that could accommodate a helicopter. The Kuwaiti mentioned that Bernsen could use two self-propelled barges owned by the Kuwaiti coast guard, which resembled ferry boats without any passenger areas and were topped with a large flight deck for helicopters. As neither was being used and, more important for the bottom line–minded Kuwaitis, both had already been paid for, Kuwait was more than happy to let the Americans use them. Bernsen flew up to Kuwait and toured the two vessels. Unfortunately, they could accommodate only about forty people and perhaps one or two helicopters—not nearly large enough. "What I need is something that we can move, holds two hundred people, can support helicopters, and we could tie boats alongside."

"Well," al-Bader answered, "you go find it and we'll pay for it."[9]

Over the past several years Bernsen had become friendly with an American businessman from Houston who owned a company based out of Sarjah, UAE, that leased oil service boats. With a quick mind and a slow Southern drawl, he knew the Gulf as few other Americans did.[10]

Bernsen decided to call him. "This is a nonconversation, but I'm looking for some boats that I can put some helicopters on that can hold about two hundred people."

The man from Houston called back in a couple of hours. "I've spoken to a friend of mine at Brown and Root." This was the Halliburton subsidiary that maintained extensive dealings throughout the Persian Gulf, including with the Iranians, supporting the oil industry. "They have two oil construction barges that are not being used sitting right there in Bahrain. One of them is named the *Hercules*. There is a Brown and Root office about a mile from where your ship is tied up. Why don't you go over and talk to him; I've already made the arrangements with Brown and Root's Middle East representative."

Bernsen hopped in his car and drove to the Brown and Root office and met with the company's senior representative, a British national named John Rahtz. He confirmed that there were two barges owned by Brown and Root tied up right in Bahrain that might fit the American need: *Hercules* and *Wimbrown VII*. After showing Bernsen the blueprints, they went down to the small shipyard where the two barges sat moored.

At first glance both appeared in terrible shape. Their exteriors were covered by rust and peeling paint, and the decks were piled high with rusting equipment and cables. "They look like crap," Bernsen said to Rahtz. But when the two went on board and took a tour, it became apparent that both barges were in sound shape, *Hercules* a bit more so. *Hercules* was the larger of the two. One of the largest oil barges in the world at 400 by 140 feet, flat and wide, it had been designed for the construction of offshore oil platforms and laying underwater pipelines. On one end sat a large, white, elevated helicopter landing pad complete with a small control tower. At the other end, sitting atop a large cylindrical pedestal, sat a rectangular mount, painted red and orange, that connected to a massive crane 50 feet plus tall. Emblazoned at the back end of the crane in large black letters on a fading yellow background was the word "Clyde." Its 250-foot-long boom towered above the entire barge, giving *Hercules* an unmistakably lopsided appearance. In between was a large, flat open space perfect for helicopters and storing small patrol boats. Below the main deck, *Hercules* had berthing for 160 men, in addition to a large galley, cafeteria, even a theater or recreation room adorned with blue curtains. For potential operations in the mine-strewn area near Farsi, it had the added advantage of being double hulled, surrounded by a floodable tank that would provide excellent protection against a mine strike.

The *Wimbrown* was smaller, only 250 feet long with a beam of 70 feet. Designed as a jack-up barge, it was equipped with removable extendable legs, whereby the entire barge could be lifted up by air jacks to provide a stable work platform. It had a small helicopter platform on one end, adjacent to a large, elevated modular office building aloft of the main deck.[11] It did not have a built-in crane like Clyde, substituting a much smaller tracked commercial variant. It had extensive berthing facilities, capable of housing nearly one hundred more than *Hercules.* Each had a relatively shallow draft that would make them less susceptible to a mine strike. Each barge was anchored by a four-point mooring system and could be moved only by tugs, a procedure that required two hours to get under way and moved the barges at a ponderous four knots per hour.[12] With some cleaning, scrapping, and a new coat of paint, these two just might work, Bernsen said.

Bernsen shot out a flash message to General Crist laying out his thoughts:

> In my view, to be successful in the northern Gulf we must establish an intensive patrol operation to prevent the Iranians from laying mines, sweep those few mines that may be placed in the water despite our patrol efforts, and third, protect the reflagged tankers from Iranian small boat attack while transiting the northern Gulf. I believe we can achieve the desired results with a mix of relatively small patrol craft, boats, and helos.

Rather than using regular naval vessels, the area could be better patrolled by a mixture of attack helicopters and small boats augmented by Navy SEALs and U.S. Marines.[13]

General Crist liked the idea. "What the Iranians were doing reminded me of Vietnam. They planted mines and roadside bombs all along our key roads and line of supply. It seemed to me they were doing the same thing, only on the water," Crist said in a 1988 interview. The CENTCOM commander coined an expression for the unusual fight in which the Americans now found themselves involved: "a guerrilla war at sea." He forwarded Bernsen's plan to both Chairman Crowe and Admiral Ronald Hays in a message for their eyes only.

Crowe also immediately grasped Bernsen's sea base scheme. His tour in the Mekong Delta during Vietnam had acquainted him with a similar idea called Sea Float, in which the navy had constructed a floating base by connecting numerous pontoon barges together south of the Mekong Delta. It served as a forward support base for riverine patrol boats in an attempt to undermine the Vietcong guerrillas moving along the Cua Lon River. The chairman immediately threw his support behind it. After a meeting between Crowe and Caspar Weinberger on July 31, the secretary of defense approved the deployment of all the patrol boats requested by Bernsen, including eight

Mark III patrol boats, with four coming from Special Boat Squadron 2 in Norfolk, Virginia, and the other four from Special Boat Squadron 1 at Coronado, California.[14]

Bernsen assigned two new officers to turn it into reality. On August 11 Commander Richard Flanagan arrived from California. A SEAL, he commanded Special Boat Squadron 1, which comprised all the U.S. patrol boats on the West Coast.[15] Flanagan had cut his teeth as a junior officer in the waterways of the Mekong Delta and knew Sea Float.[16] The day after Flanagan's arrival, Captain Frank Lugo arrived in Bahrain. Commissioned in 1953, Lugo had an impressive résumé of both operational and command billets. A competent, experienced staff officer, he'd recently served as the operations officer for Second Fleet and was slated to start training in preparation for assuming command of a new cruiser on the West Coast. Lugo's name came up for consideration as he was in between assignments and was well respected by the navy hierarchy, including Chief of Naval Operations Trost and his operations deputy, Vice Admiral Hank Mustin.[17]

Secrecy about the barges remained paramount. Crist intended to limit those within the military who even knew of the idea to a handful, and had sent the message outlining his concept via a special communications channel under the code name Privy Seal. To prevent Iranian mine laying and small-boat attacks upon U.S. shipping along a hundred-mile route from the Mina al-Ahmadi channel off Kuwait to an area south of Farsi Island, CENTCOM proposed deploying two barges, or mobile sea bases as they were officially designated, in the water astride the convoy route, with each covering a fifty-mile stretch.[18] Each mobile sea base would serve as a home base for four sixty-five-foot patrol boats and army special operations helicopters. If the Iranians tried to attack the barges directly, each would be protected by a force of SEALs and marines armed with automatic grenade launchers, heavy machine guns, antitank missiles, and Stinger antiaircraft missiles. In all, each mobile sea base would have a complement of about 140 men.[19]

Meanwhile, Iran increased the pressure on Kuwait. It launched three Silkworm missiles at Kuwait's key oil terminal at Mina al-Ahmadi. While all landed harmlessly to the south near some beachside villas at Mina Abdullah, it was a stark reminder to Kuwait about antagonizing its northern neighbor. In response, Kuwait expelled five Iranian diplomats suspected of being covert agents.[20]

Paul Evancoe looked like a poster boy for the elite Navy SEALs. A natural leader, tall, fit, with dark hair and a matching mustache, he had a reputation as an aggressive—some thought reckless—officer. He'd served as an enlisted man in Vietnam, rose through the ranks, and was now commander of Special Boat Unit 20 in Norfolk. During the reception party after taking over his new command, the flash message arrived giving him just forty-eight hours to load his four boats and sixty-seven officers and men onto the amphibious ship USS *Raleigh* and head for the Persian Gulf. While Evancoe remained for a couple of weeks in Norfolk to scrounge more spare parts and get two smaller Seafox boats flown to Bahrain, his executive officer, Lieutenant Peter Wikul, took charge of the boats heading over on the *Raleigh*. Wikul shared many of the personality traits of his boss; while short and solid, he was aggressive and hyper. He had been burned badly while serving as an observer in Lebanon when he rushed into a tent to save a man when a propane heater exploded.[21]

Wikul and the boats arrived in the Gulf at the end of August, and a week later he conducted his first patrol north of Farsi Island prior to the next Earnest Will convoy. It turned out to be an arduous 530-mile, five-day mission. While a frigate to the south provided his men showers and hot meals, the constant pounding in the small fiberglass boats left the men and boats bruised and battered.

The Pentagon struggled to meet Bernsen's requirements for helicopters. The navy primarily used its helicopters for antisubmarine missions and did not want to turn them into gunships. The marines had attack helicopters already on the *Guadalcanal*, but their pilots lacked the skills to fly at night, when the Iranians conducted most of their mining.[22]

Crowe had been briefed on an elite army aviation unit named Task Force 160 (TF-160), the "Night Stalkers," located at the sprawling army base at Fort Campbell, Kentucky, home to the 101st Airborne Division. The Night Stalkers had been formed in October 1981, following the disastrous Iranian hostage rescue effort; their sole mission was to provide helicopter support to special operations forces.[23] They operated a variety of specially configured helicopters, one of which was a modified McDonnell Douglas 530 helicopter, popularly referred to within TF-160 as "Little Bird." Crewed by two, it had a speed of 120 knots and a range of one hundred miles; these small, jelly bean–shaped helicopters were highly maneuverable, easily deployable, and exceptionally quiet. The 530's specially configured blades produced a subdued *whir* sound rather than the loud *thump, thump* of most helicopters. As one SEAL observed, "At night you could just about see the aircraft's outline before ever hearing its rotors turning." These craft were designed to operate exclusively at night; their pilots had hundreds of hours of flying time using night-vision goggles.[24] The helos came in two variants: an attack version outfitted with a 7.62-mm minigun on one side and a 2.75-inch rocket pod with explosive and dartlike fléchette rounds on the other. At three thousand rounds a minute, the minigun cut through a target more like a chain saw than a machine gun. The helicopters operated in threes, with one command and control version, which came with a forward-looking infrared radar (FLIR) and videotape system, and two attack birds.[25]

A future four-star general and commander of all U.S. Special Operations Forces, Major Bryan "Doug" Brown flew to Tampa to brief Crist on his unit's abilities. At thirty-eight, Brown had already spent twenty years in the army, having enlisted as a private in 1967 and soon thereafter earning the coveted green beret of the Army Special Forces. He subsequently obtained his commission before going off to flight school and Vietnam, where he earned a Distinguished Flying Cross. He already had a deserved reputation as a smart, competent officer who was going places in the army.

General Crist was not overly enamored with special operations forces, a view commonly shared by many infantry officers who had fought in Vietnam. They viewed the Green Berets—as well as the SEALs—as aggressive to the point of reckless, "snake eaters" who needed to be carefully watched. Brown arrived on a typically oppressive hot Tampa summer day and found the marine commander combative. Crist commented that he was not sure that his unit's helicopters had enough firepower or missiles to contend with the Iranian small boats. "He did not think we could actually do the mission," Brown recalled. But the army aviator stood his ground. "Sir, there are some people who can fire rockets and some who can't, and we are the guys who can!"[26]

Privately, Crist was pleased with the briefing and jotted down a list of the Night Stalkers' abilities in his black notebook. Behind the scenes, the CENTCOM chief of staff, Major General Don Penzler, who had knowledge of TF-160 from an army assignment, liked the idea of using the army. He

worked with both the army staff in Washington and his own in Tampa pushing the unit's deployment and did much to get over the lower-level opposition
within the military to this unorthodox marriage between the army and
the navy.[27]

On August 4, a single C-5 transport aircraft lumbered into the sky from
Fort Campbell. Its secret cargo comprised six Little Birds, plus thirty-nine
men and five pallets of equipment. They arrived at the Bahraini airport in
the pitch darkness of the early morning hours of August 5 and immediately
taxied for the small U.S. Navy hangar located at the airport. The Bahrainis
reluctantly agreed to allow the helicopters to transit through, provided they
were gone by daylight and the pallets with ammunition and weapons were
ambiguously packaged and marked so as to obscure their contents.[28]

Brown and the others were greeted by an air force major dressed in an
Arab robe and headdress—a sheik outfit or latter-day Lawrence of Arabia is
how one remembered it—in a weak attempt at a disguise. The plan to cover
their movement, he explained, would be to follow a Bahraini helicopter out of
the airfield. "We'll call the tower and you just keep your lights out and follow
us out. We'll go ten miles out and turn around, and you head to the *La Salle*."
In an hour the army crew had all six helicopters assembled. They took off,
following close to the Bahraini helo, and landed on board the *La Salle*.

The next day they met with Bernsen and his operations staff. The capabilities of TF-160 were a closely guarded secret within the U.S. military, and
neither Bernsen nor his staff had any real idea of what these helicopters could
do. They initially proposed using them to fly in daylight in front of the convoys looking for mines. Brown respectfully dissented. "Sir, we'll do whatever
you want us to do, but that is a waste of a tremendous asset. We're night
fighters!" They had been brought over by CENTCOM with the intent of
using them to hunt suspected Iranian small boats or minelayers, not to fly in
the daytime looking for mines in front of the convoy—any standard helicopter could do that. Bernsen quickly grasped the idea, and in two days he had
one detachment embarked on the USS *Jarrett* for the next Earnest Will
convoy.

To support Bernsen, CENTCOM's senior intelligence officer, Brigadier
General Cloyd Pfister, asked for more intelligence out in the Gulf. After
discussions with National Security Adviser Frank Carlucci and President

Reagan, on September 9 Weinberger approved a covert national intelligence effort as part of a closely held operation to support Earnest Will, under the unusually named banner of Operation Pollen Count. It involved sending specially configured National Security Agency intelligence teams to the Gulf.[29] Traveling with some small communications vans, they were mobile enough to be positioned far forward, in fact on individual navy destroyers and frigates patrolling the Gulf. Their purpose was twofold: one, to provide much better capability to eavesdrop on Iranian military communications; and two, to tap into the vast array of U.S. signals intelligence.[30] This allowed national intelligence to be piped directly down to the tactical forces who could use it most and, conceivably, allow them to respond quickly to any time-sensitive intelligence gleaned back at NSA's home in Fort Meade, Maryland. Wearing nondescript green and blue overalls, they joined a growing array of similar "black" units, from the five-man marine radio reconnaissance detachment to the army's elite unit under U.S. Special Operations Command (SOCOM), the Intelligence Support Activity.[31] As one intelligence analyst later said, "It was a host of 'spooky' cats and dogs wandering around the Gulf, all in sanitized uniforms."[32]

While Middle East Force implemented its new surveillance regime, CENTCOM looked to refine a new set of covert plans to deal with the Iranians. Shortly after the *Bridgeton* mining, the Joint Chiefs of Staff directed a review of the Invoke Resolve plans. As part of this, CENTCOM started looking to develop alternatives designed to "take the Iranian eyes out," as Crist described it. Specifically, his concept was to capture key Iranian islands in the Gulf such as Farsi, Abu Musa, Sirri, or the Tunbs. The last three of these were still contested by the UAE, having been occupied and de facto incorporated into Iran by the shah. After feeling out the Gulf Cooperation Council states, Crist concluded that taking them would cause little outrage on the Arab side of the Gulf and would not cause the same dramatic escalation in the minds of Tehran as a more direct attack on the Iranian mainland, such as Bandar Abbas or Qeshm Island. Seizing these Iranian outposts in the Persian Gulf would eliminate their key operating bases and would effectively drive their navy and Revolutionary Guards from the Gulf, push them back into their ports, and eliminate Iran's ability to project any military power into the Gulf proper that could threaten tanker traffic.

This was an important consideration, especially in the minds of the White House and the secretary of defense. Both Weinberger and Richard

Armitage supported Crist's strategy. Weinberger had no intention of getting the United States involved in a major war with Iran or of committing the United States to an incursion onto the Iranian mainland. With the Soviet Union still a threat in Europe and the Far East, the United States simply lacked the forces to commit to the expansive landmass of Iran to achieve anything decisive or conclusive. Echoing these sentiments, Richard Armitage knew that, however unpopular the Khomeini regime might be, the Iranians were a proud, nationalistic people, and he feared that such an overt attack would likely rally the populace behind the mullahs and actually strengthen support for the regime. Equally important in Armitage's mind was that any serious escalation in the conflict would likely result in Tehran's unleashing its terrorist surrogates on the West. Foremost was Hezbollah, which would likely step up the attacks on Israel from south Lebanon. Further, the Iranians had a sophisticated terrorist network in Europe, and the CIA concluded they would likely try to use it if the United States attacked Iran proper. The key, therefore, in Weinberger's and Armitage's minds, was to walk a delicate balance by waging a limited war against Iran to achieve the U.S. objectives of freedom of navigation and protection of the Kuwaiti tankers and by applying enough pressure to contain Iranian ambitions in the Gulf without escalating the conflict.

In addition to these overt plans against Iran, CENTCOM asked for assistance in developing clandestine options should President Reagan decide to strike back with Washington's own "invisible hand" against the Iranians. The work of developing the "black" plans fell to the newly established Special Operations Command, located only a few hundred yards from CENTCOM's headquarters at MacDill Air Force Base. As the head of a new command looking for a mission, the SOCOM commander, General James Lindsay, actively supported the development of various plans against Iran. He ordered a special compartmented planning cell to support General Crist, which included a legendary special forces officer, Colonel Wayne Long. Working closely with another similar special planning cell within the CENTCOM J-3, headed by army artillery officer Colonel James "Gunner" Laws, they developed a number of options, and in late July and August these moved from conference room discussions to written concept plans.

One of the more popular ideas was to take out the suspected mine-laying vessels in the harbors of Bushehr and Bandar Abbas. U.S. intelligence had narrowed down the possible ships to a relatively few supply or small amphibious ships, refined more with satellite or signals intelligence. The concept envisioned a small team of frogmen dropped off by a U.S. ship or submarine in international waters. Using a SEAL delivery vehicle—a small, fast, open-water submersible—they would stealthily move into an Iranian harbor traveling just under the surface, leaving no wake or visible trace of their presence. Then they would navigate to the targeted ships and plant timed explosives on the bottoms of their hulls. Once the SEALs were safely away, the charges would ignite, sending the minelayers to the bottom of the Gulf. With no evidence that the United States was to blame, there would be plausible deniability for Washington. A high-risk venture to be sure, it was relegated in the opinions of the president and his senior military advisers to an option of last resort. As one senior officer described, "It certainly would give Tehran a taste of their own medicine."

Other plans concocted by this cell were far less surreptitious. They looked at using SEALs to conduct a series of hit-and-run raids on the Iranian Silkworm sites as well as on the Iranian islands, the latter backed by extensive naval gunfire and U.S. aircraft. SEAL planners in the Gulf and back in Tampa were less than enthusiastic about these options. Both were very risky, and the islands were so small and heavily defended that it was difficult to merely conduct a raid without just taking the whole island. This required a greater ground force than that possessed by Naval Special Warfare and necessitated bringing in a more robust force of combat marines. To deal with Silkworm sites on Qeshm Island, they devised a plan to insert up to two Ranger battalions by U.S. Air Force MH-53 helicopters launched from Masirah Island, Oman, to physically destroy the sites in a short-duration, high-intensity, direct action operation. "It never got to the rehearsal stage," Wayne Long later said, "but we had worked up all the plans in case it needed to be done."[33]

Some of the more curious schemes devised by Long tried to exploit perceived divisions within Iran to provide cover for American covert operations. One involved using Iranian exiles, with American special operations forces' assistance, to infiltrate Iran and blow up some of the Silkworm missile sites around the Strait of Hormuz. Another hoped to take advantage of the growing tension detected by U.S. intelligence between the fanatical Revolutionary Guard and the regular, U.S.-trained Iranian navy and air force. The two were not in a happy marriage; distrust between the two prevailed. One comprised enthusiastic, untrained ideologues, while the other was more professional and slightly more reticent. They maintained separate chains of command, with the Revolutionary Guard being virtually independent, often not even reporting back to Tehran about its operations activities. On several occasions the differences between the two forces escalated to exchanges of gunfire. Colonel Long hoped to take advantage of this discord, providing U.S. deniability while exacerbating the tensions between the regular military and the Revolutionary Guard. He had an American Huey helicopter—a common fixture in the Iranian military—repainted in a brown and tan color scheme and including the Iranian national insignia, a green, white, and red circular emblem painted on the tail boom. Piloted by a TF-160 native Farsi-speaking warrant officer, this bogus Iranian helicopter would approach one of the oil platforms commonly used by the Revolutionary Guard for its attacks on Gulf shipping, such as Sirri or Rostam. After hailing the platform's occupants to lull them into mistakenly believing it was a friendly helicopter, it would approach close before opening fire with a barrage of machine-gun and rocket fire. With luck, this would knock the platform out of commission, with the blame falling on disgruntled units in the Iranian military. To Long's irritation, President Reagan never approved the operation.[34]

Everything seemed to be going exceedingly well," Bernsen said in an oral history interview, "[until] the whole operation almost came to a grinding halt"[35] when CENTCOM's formal plan for the mobile sea bases hit the Joint Staff and the four services ignited a bureaucratic hullabaloo. The entire navy leadership and its obsequious supporter, U.S. Marine Corps commandant General Alfred Gray, clamored to kill the concept. Secretary of the Navy James Webb refused to pay for anything related to the program. The opponents argued that the mobile sea base was not really mobile and lacked any protection against aircraft or inbound missiles. The mobile sea bases, therefore, were little more than an enticement dangled before Iran, with three hundred Americans laid helpless before an Iranian missile and air onslaught. Critics objected to a SEAL commanding it and could not envision how this polyglot of marines, sailors, and special forces could be integrated into a cohesive unit. In an age when service parochialism reigned supreme, few wearing the uniform could accept this level of joint interoperability by the armed forces.[36]

Over the next week memos, messages, and secure phone calls poured into CENTCOM and the chairman's office from every senior navy command, all opposing the idea. "This needlessly risks the lives of American service-men," wrote one admiral. The Atlantic commander, Admiral Lee Baggett, Jr., thought the idea crazy and told both Crowe and Crist so during an annual meeting of the four-star commanders at Fort Leavenworth: "This is a floating Beirut Barracks!"

One of the most scathing messages originated from Major General Royal Moore, Jr., a dark-haired, square-jawed marine and brash, cocky fighter pilot. As Admiral Ronald Hays's operations officer at Pacific Command, upon hear-ing of the sea base idea, he picked up the phone and called his counterpart at CENTCOM, Major General Samuel Swart of the air force, strongly objecting to this "half-baked, seat of the pants" idea that was "going to get people killed."[37]

The hostility to the sea bases only compounded Crist's problems inside the Pentagon. Crowe had the CENTCOM commander come to Washington to defend the size of the joint task force before the Joint Chiefs in the Tank. For two hours the chiefs picked apart his planned headquarters, the onslaught led by Trost and Al Gray. The ninety-six men Crist wanted seemed way too many, so without much analysis as to what each man would do, the chiefs summarily pared it down by about half, to fifty-two. In the process, they picked apart Crist's joint headquarters and the entire surveillance plan. They flatly rejected many of Crist's ideas, such as a subordinate special operations task force to run all the special operations and the mobile sea bases. Gray questioned having an air force deputy. "If the admiral gets killed, you're going to have an air force guy running navy ships," he said disdainfully. "If we have to worry about the admiral getting killed," Crist thought, shaking his head, "we've got bigger problems than one easy-to-replace admiral."

Having helped instigate the bloodletting, Crowe finally ended it. "We need to support George and make sure he's got what he needs." The chair-man backed the scaled-down joint headquarters and the new scheme to com-bat the Iranian maritime guerrillas.

Senior naval officers now pushed to fire Crist. Who orchestrated it re-mains unclear, but the vice chief of naval operations, Admiral Huntington Hardisty, and Ace Lyons both had their fingerprints on the effort.[38] The crazy idea of these mobile sea bases was the last straw in a series of decisions made by Crist that undermined the navy's operational independence and they viewed as lacking sound military judgment. Bowing to their pressure, Crowe raised the issue with Weinberger on two separate occasions. "We may need to replace

Crist," Crowe said in an afternoon meeting with the defense secretary. "He has lost the confidence of the navy." And just two days before he presided over Ace Lyons's demise, Crowe recommended replacing Crist with Tom Morgan, the deputy marine commandant. Weinberger's response is not recorded, but his close confidant, Rich Armitage, recalled, "The navy behaved very badly throughout the entire operation. It was more likely that the navy had lost the secretary's confidence." Crist stayed, and Crowe never again raised the subject.[39]

Unaware of Crowe's discussions about replacing him, Crist caved to the pressure and convened a three-day mobile sea base conference at his head-quarters at MacDill Air Force Base. On the morning of September 9, the assembled officers gathered in the main auditorium on the second floor of the main headquarters building, just down the hall from Crist's office. Senior officers and representatives came from all over the Departments of the Navy and Defense, most wearing navy blue and intending to kill the scheme.[40] Lugo explained the overall concept: "Two barges will be positioned along a hundred-mile stretch in the northern Gulf to cover this strategic choke point. Each mobile sea base would be responsible for maintaining control over a fifty-mile 'alley' along the convoy route, or SLOC." This offered a no-cost alternative to risking several navy combatants. The combination of helicopters, small boats, and defensive fire on the barges themselves was more than capable of dealing with any Iranian threat. They intended to move the mobile sea bases randomly every few days among the Saudi islands and oil platforms that dotted the northern Gulf to reduce the likelihood of Iranians being able to target the sea bases.[41]

The officers listened skeptically but attentively, occasionally asking questions. When queried about Iranians possibly trying to board the barges, Lugo responded that those assigned would carry 9-mm pistols, M-16s, various machine guns, and hand grenades, and they would be able to "repel boarders." This led to the under-the-breath sarcastic comment by one flag officer: "Are you going to issue them cutlasses too?"[42]

The conference did little to change the opinions of those opposed to it, which remained the majority of the attendees.[43] The day after the conference, Royal Moore sent a personal message to Crist's senior planning officer, Rear Admiral William Fogarty: "Bill, as you know, I developed serious misgivings over the mobile sea base concept. As a result of what I saw and heard, it is my assessment that the concept is so severely flawed that it should be dropped."[44]

Admiral Crowe had endorsed the mobile sea bases since their conception, but even his own operations directorate within the Joint Staff recommended against the venture.[45]

While Crist had the legal authority to implement the mobile sea base plan and he intended to drive forward with deploying the barges, with the entire naval services rising in opposition, the issue found itself elevated to Weinberger's desk. The opposition to the barges threatened to kill the mobile sea bases, and even Rich Armitage, a staunch supporter of both Crist and the barge idea, worried that the opposition might be too much to overcome.

On September 17, Crowe arrived in Bahrain. He spent the next two days touring several U.S. ships and getting a ride on a Mark III patrol boat. He went on board the barge *Hercules* and talked to SEALs about their planned operations and the scheme envisioned for the barges' defense. After this and several lengthy meetings with Bernsen, he sent a message back to Crist and Weinberger that effectively put an end at least to the overt bashing by the navy of the mobile sea bases. After praising Hal Bernsen, Crowe went on to say about the barges, "I am aware that there are many naysayers as far as the barges are concerned, but I came away from my tour feeling more comfortable with them than I had previously been." The barges were a "good-sense" alternative and should go forward.[46] Weinberger agreed.

Lieutenant Abdul Fouladvand had an easy command. Commissioned just after the shah's departure in 1979, the thin twenty-eight-year-old with thick dark hair commanded a 176-foot-long logistics ship named the *Rakhsh* before the revolution, now called the *Iran Ajr*. Painted hazy gray, Fouladvand's ship had a bow ramp and a large open deck for loading bulk cargo. At her stern rose the superstructure housing the bridge and quarters for a crew of around twenty. The war had passed by his tiny ship. For the past few years, he had contented himself with short runs from Bandar Abbas to resupply the Iranian military on Abu Musa Island and the oil platforms. But the hardships of the war had led Fouladvand to hoard supplies. He filled his cabin with foodstuffs, including Iranian-produced aspirin that turned out to be a placebo. Neither hygiene nor maintenance had been high on the young captain's priorities. The Japanese had built the *Iran Ajr* in the same year as Fouladvand's commissioning, but it already displayed severe rust and peeling paint.

It had never been cleaned: grease and dirt permeated every compartment and cabin. The one head on board no longer worked, but this had not stopped the crew from continuing to relieve themselves there. Human feces overflowed the toilet, and crewmen had tracked the remnants all around the deck.

Bandar Abbas was a relatively small town of only twelve thousand people in the mid-1980s. It was Iran's principal southern port and the region's leading commercial center. Within the large concrete breakwaters sat two distinct areas: a commercial area and a naval section in a port shaped something like an L, with the Iranian naval base occupying the short horizontal axis. In August 1987, Fouladvand received orders to dock over at the commercial side of the Bandar Abbas port, and the *Iran Ajr* tied up to one of the T-shaped piers, intermingled with commercial ships. A large warehouse sat next to the wharf. Inside, the Revolutionary Guard stored dozens of large, black, cylindrical mines, staged for quick loading on board the minelayer. The mines remained there for more than a month, until an Iranian agent in Bahrain tipped off the Revolutionary Guard to the ship's schedule and Tehran made the quick decision to try to mine this target of opportunity.

In mid-September, two Revolutionary Guard officers with an accompanying small team arrived and took over Fouladvand's ship. Commander Parvis Farshchian led this special group. A sixteen-year veteran, Farshchian was fluent in English and a staunch Islamic ideologue. His deputy was the cool and collected forty-two-year-old Farhad Ibrahimi. A twenty-year veteran of the Iranian marines, he had joined the Revolutionary Guard, where he put his special forces training to work leading a number of commando attacks against the Iraqis. An impressive man who spoke flawless English, Ibrahimi liked to flaunt his wealth and authority by wearing a very expensive Rolex diving watch.[47] Farshchian ordered eighteen mines pulled out from the warehouse and quickly loaded onto the ship's open deck, intermingling them with oil drums and covering them with a heavy tarp to try to conceal his illicit cargo. The crew welded a metal gangplank to the deck, dangling out over the ship's starboard side. The Iranians had decided to launch another mining attack. Emboldened by their earlier successes, this time they would target Bernsen directly. Farshchian intended to mine the main channel into Bahrain and the American naval base. By happenstance, the *La Salle* intended to conduct a gunnery exercise in the exact area Farshchian planned to lay his eighteen mines.[48]

The *Iran Ajr*'s crew did not welcome the new arrivals. The Revolutionary Guard displayed a haughty attitude toward their less dedicated comrades. They ate and slept separately and rarely mingled. In truth, some of the regular navy sailors hated the Islamic Republic. One enlisted man confided that he would gladly have defected had he not been the sole provider for his aging mother.

The *Iran Ajr* quietly departed Bandar Abbas on September 20. The 1st Naval District gave Farshchian strict instructions to report his position every hour. He dutifully did, signing off each message as "commander of special mission unit *Iran Ajr*."[49] As a cover story, Farshchian disguised his operation as a routine transit to the northern port of Bushehr. For a covert operation, the Iranians took this too far. At least eight Iranian soldiers hopped on board the ship looking for a quick trip to visit family and friends around Bushehr. After stopping overnight at the Rostam oil platform for final approval orders, the *Iran Ajr* continued north. On the evening of September 21, the ship diverted off her route, heading west toward Bahrain.

American intelligence nearly missed the *Iran Ajr*. Spy satellites actually photographed mines sitting on the dock next to her and a sister ship on August 16, 1987, but this image somehow got lost and never made it out to Bernsen in the Gulf. Three days before she'd left Bandar Abbas, an intelligence advisory stated: "Do not estimate Iran will deploy mines during next week." The first Ziegler knew of this impending attack was after the *Iran Ajr* had set sail; a string of intercepts started flowing into his small, secure facility on the *La Salle*, all from a ship calling itself a special mission unit and reporting back in flash messages to its headquarters every hour. Ziegler began tracking her movements, and when the ship stopped at the Revolutionary Guard–manned oil platform of Rostam and one communiqué mentioned an operation for eleven p.m. the next night, he went in to tell Bernsen. The Middle East Force commander ordered the USS *Jarrett* to investigate. The American frigate had three of the army Little Birds embarked.[50]

At ten p.m., the three small jelly bean–shaped helos took off from the fantail into a moonless night. Within forty minutes they had closed to within two hundred yards of the Iranian ship, carefully remaining upwind in order to minimize the chances of being heard. As the American pilots looked on, just before the magic hour of eleven o'clock, Farshchian ordered the ship's navigation lights turned off. Ibrahimi had six Iranians pull back the heavy tarp covering the mines and oil drums. He began methodically fusing the black spherical objects arranged on top of the flat open deck. With a stop-watch to set the mine intervals, he ordered the 253-pound explosive charge rolled down the small gangplank and into the ocean below. An army pilot watching them calmly reported that they were pushing "minelike objects" over the side.[51]

Bernsen and his operations deputy had been listening in to the reports from their command center on the *La Salle*. Bernsen was actually across the room on a secure phone talking with Crist, who happened to be out in the Gulf of Oman meeting with Denny Brooks, as the new joint task force had formally stood up the day the *Iran Ajr* left port. When Bernsen heard "mine-like object," he told Grieve, "Take them under fire."

An uncertain Grieve responded, "Sir, only minelike."

"Bullshit!" Bernsen answered. "They're mines!"[52]

Two Little Birds came in low and fast. While one strafed the deck with his minigun with nearly two thousand bullets, the other unleashed a hail of machine-gun fire and explosive rockets into the bridge and stern. One Iranian sailor who happened to be dumping trash caught the full force of one rocket in his face, cleaving off half his head, sending brains and bloody goo across the deck. A propane tank explosion killed another sailor near the engine.[53] The two helicopters broke hard right, and then came back around for another strafing run, showering the bridge and deck with bullets and fléchette rockets filled with tiny darts. They returned to the *Jarrett* to quickly rearm, leaving the *Iran Ajr* on fire and dead in the water.

When the helicopters returned about fifteen minutes later, incredibly, they found the ship under way and Ibrahimi's men pushing more mines over the side. The American helos came in again with two more strafing runs. One Iranian pushing a mine died instantly, while another was knocked overboard and disappeared into the black sea. The fusillade caught Farshchian: a bullet passed through his side and another blew off part of his hand; a fléchette ripped open his side, exposing his pelvic bone. An explosion knocked Ibrahimi to the metal deck, badly bruising his face. This time, the Iranians had had enough, and Lieutenant Fouladvand yelled, "Abandon ship!"

A dozen men jumped over the side, while ten more took to an inflatable life raft, bringing along the grievously wounded Farshchian. Others made their flight in an inflatable Zodiac speedboat. When one of the army helicopters approached and dropped down to a hover, an Ira-nian jumped up and made what the pilot later described as a "threatening gesture." As the helicopter flew alongside the boat, one of the army pilots pulled out a subma-chine gun from his holster, took aim, and blew the man away.[54]

Within thirty minutes, news of the firefight had arrived in the Pentagon. Crowe quickly held a short meeting with Weinberger, before heading to the maze of the National Military Command Center in a guarded area just down the hall from his second-floor office, where he spent the next eight hours monitoring the crisis. After informing the White House and key members of Congress, Weinberger authorized seizing the Iranian ship.

This order made National Security Adviser Frank Carlucci and his dep-uty, Colin Powell, nervous. Powell spoke with Weinberger. "The president has been informed," the army general said, "yet we do not want to risk Amer-ican lives by seizing the ship. We want to keep it contained and get them to surrender." Then he added, "But you can shoot if they offer resistance." Nei-ther Weinberger nor Crowe thought that directive made much sense, and it took nearly an hour before Carlucci finally informed Weinberger that the president had agreed they should seize the ship, but should avoid any unnec-essary risk to U.S. personnel.[55]

Lieutenant Commander Marc Thomas had been happily sleeping in his stateroom on the *Guadalcanal* when news of the firefight with the *Iran Ajr* interrupted his slumber around midnight. With his dark skin, Thomas could have easily been confused for an Arab rather than an elite Navy SEAL. His bright eyes, infectious smile, and easygoing demeanor made him popular with both senior officers and the fifteen men in his platoon. He had originally been a part of Gordon Keiser's marine amphibious unit, which the marine colonel had successfully lobbied to keep on board the ship in Diego Garcia. Now Bernsen wanted the SEALs' special skills to seize the stricken minelayer. Thomas rousted his men, and they donned their war-fighting kit and flew over to the *La Salle*. There Thomas found Bernsen's staff hastily trying to put together a plan to seize the *Iran Ajr* and round up the Iranian sailors scattered about the mine-strewn water. Thomas proposed simultaneous assault fast-roping down onto the ship from helicopters while marines assaulted from rubber boats.[56]

But Bernsen had just spoken with Crowe. Reflecting the nervousness in Washington, the chairman passed on that Bernsen could seize the boat only if it looked as though there was no armed opposition on board. To avoid running into mines and to be able to see any armed Iranians, Bernsen told Crowe and Crist that he would take the *Iran Ajr* the next morning, just after sunrise.[57] The SEALs would use one of the *La Salle's* logistics boats to storm the ship in broad daylight. Two U.S. Marine Cobra attack helicopters and Paul Evancoe's patrol boats would provide backup in case they got in trouble.[58]

At first light on September 22, the *La Salle* flooded its well deck; then Thomas boarded the landing boat and puttered toward the drifting Iranian ship in the bright blue daylight. With the SEALs crouched around the gunwales, the coxswain pulled alongside with a metal clang, turning his engines hard to keep his boat pressed against the side of the Iranian ship. "One hand grenade could kill us all," Thomas thought as he and his platoon scrambled up the side, moving swiftly to seize the bridge and engine room. They then methodically searched the ship, looking for saboteurs hiding in closets. But other than finding three bodies, the ship was empty.[59]

The SEALs discovered a treasure trove of intelligence. In their haste, the Iranians had tossed their radio crypto over the side, but had left reams of messages and decoded teletype. SEALs found the entire secret Ghadir mining plan to close the Strait of Hormuz; it was a remarkable bit of carelessness by the Iranian navy. They found a map detailing all of Iran's covert mining operations. Reams of messages contained details of their oil platforms' role in coordinating attacks and Iranian command and control procedures. The United States learned about Iranian eavesdropping on the radio bridge transmissions of the escorted tankers. One SEAL noticed a piece of paper sticking out of the foul-smelling toilet. He reluctantly stuck his gloved hand down and pulled it out, to discover an important codebook that some crewman had tried to hastily conceal.[60]

Among the documents, the Americans found poignant reminders of the humans they had just attacked. On one of the corpses, a marine Farsi interrogator found a photograph of a smiling ten-year-old boy—the same age as his own son.[61]

As Thomas cleared the ship, Evancoe and Wikul's two patrol boats suddenly appeared off the starboard side. In their haste to leave Bahrain, the boat with their only secure radio had run aground. They had no idea what frequency Thomas's forces used, and they could not raise the *La Salle*. Undaunted, they pressed on, planning their own assault on the *Iran Ajr*, determined to kill anyone remaining, unaware that Thomas's SEALs had already boarded.[62]

Evancoe spied a dark-skinned man carrying a rifle and immediately ordered all the guns trained on him. Thomas always thought Evancoe overly aggressive, and this action got his attention. "Okay, Paul, please don't shoot me!"

Wikul commanded the lead boat and ordered his men to hold their fire pending his order. When he rounded the other side of the *Iran Ajr*, he saw the *La Salle*'s boat. "My heart almost came out of my mouth. I nearly shot my friend."[63]

With disaster averted, Evancoe and Wikul turned their attention to picking up the survivors. Their two boats closed on a tented circular bright orange life raft. Unsure of what awaited them, Wikul pointed a shotgun at the Iranians and motioned for them to put their hands in the air. All immediately complied. One by one, each swam over to Wikul's boat. The Americans bound them, covered their eyes with gray duct tape, and stacked them unceremoniously facedown on the abrasive nonskid deck. When a SEAL discovered a pistol on one, he punched him unconscious and tossed the weapon overboard.

One man remained inside the raft: Commander Farshchian. Wikul grabbed a pistol, swam over, and climbed onto the life raft bobbing nearby. Unsure of the Iranian's intentions, Wikul started frisking him for a weapon and his finger inadvertently went inside a gaping wound in the Iranian's side. Farshchian screamed out in agony. Reflexively, Wikul pressed his gun to Farshchian before realizing it had not been a precursor to the Iranian blowing himself up. As he transferred Farshchian over to the American boat, the Iranian looked at Wikul and said in perfect English, "I still have four of my men in the water; would you please rescue them?" Even Wikul was impressed. "It's hard not to respect a guy who, despite his own wounds, his first words were for the welfare of his men."[64] The final tally: five Iranians dead and twenty-six captured, with several in the same bad shape as Farshchian.

The capture of the *Iran Ajr* was one of the biggest American intelligence coups in modern history. The invisible hand of God proved to be made out of Iranian flesh and spilled blood. That afternoon both Crist and Bernsen visited the Iranian vessel. They brought along photographers, and the next day newspapers around the globe carried front-page photographs of nine mines sitting on the *Iran Ajr*'s open deck.

Iran denied that the ship had been carrying mines. Speaking before the United Nations, President Ali Khamenei called the American charges a "pack of lies," and an Iranian spokesman said the ship had only carried food-stuffs.[65]

As the Iranian prisoners were being repatriated through Oman—all wearing newly provided USS *La Salle* T-shirts—Weinberger flew out to the Gulf and inspected the ship.[66] There a gleeful secretary told the assembled reporters that the capture was "not just a smoking gun, but a blazing gun." With the evidence obvious as to this ship's real mission, and public commendations coming even from the Soviet Union, Weinberger smiled, pointed to the mines sitting on the deck, and said: "That's the biggest load of groceries I've ever seen!"[67]

Weinberger ordered the *Iran Ajr* sunk. To make a point, a U.S. warship towed the minelayer well inside the Iranian-declared exclusion zone. Paul Evancoe rigged explosives and blew out the ship's bottom. She quickly sank, leaving only an oil slick and a few of the oil drums that had unsuccessfully tried to hide her deadly cargo.[68]

The Iranians immediately halted all mining operations. Embarrassed and exposed, with the world condemning them, Ayatollah Khomeini agreed to draw back the invisible hand. But Iran had hardly caved to American pressure. In Tehran during the Friday prayers after the seizure of the *Iran Ajr*, President Ali Khamenei told the gathering that "we will respond to America's wicked acts in the Persian Gulf." The Iranians were about to turn up the burner and make the Gulf a great deal warmer for the Americans.

Sixteen

A Very Close Call

When Admiral William Crowe read the top secret CIA memo, he immediately realized the magnitude of the crisis. The United States verged on the brink of war in the Middle East. Iran planned to conduct a massive naval attack on Saudi Arabia with the objective of crippling Saudi oil production, the late September 1987 report stated bluntly. Over the past month, American intelligence had reported an unusual congregation of small boats manned by fervent Revolutionary Guard sailors in the northern Persian Gulf, and recent satellite images confirmed boats being moved by truck from southern Iran.[1] But Iran's intentions eluded the Pentagon; analysts suspected it was only a military exercise. This new report, however, described in detail the numbers of Iranian boats and their targets in Saudi Arabia, and even predicted the time for the attack: within seventy-two hours. Crowe held the outline for Tehran's entire war plan.

"How good is your source for this?" Crowe asked the CIA officer.

"He is a recent recruit, a navy captain well placed within the Iranian military. He has proven reliable in the past," the officer replied.

After quickly checking with the deputy national security adviser, Colin Powell, at the White House, Crowe dismissed the CIA officer and swiveled around in his chair, picked up the secure telephone on the credenza behind his imposing wooden desk, and punched the autodial for the Saudi ambassador to Washington, Prince Bandar bin Sultan. Their relationship remained strong with Bandar helping to arrange financial support for the CIA's secret wars in Afghanistan and Central America, and he had recently hosted a meeting at his Potomac River home between the CIA and Iraqi officials about sharing satellite intelligence of Iran.[2]

That afternoon the two men met in Crowe's office. "We have a tip-off from a source of an impending attack on your oil facilities," Crowe began. "The Iranians are deliberately flooding their radios with false information, so we don't know the exact day, but likely October second. You need to give them a warm welcome."[3]

"I told you the Iranians were building up for something," Bandar replied, referring to a conversation between the two men earlier. "If pushed, we will respond forcefully." He grew visibly angry as he continued. "We will bomb their oil facilities! Our military plans are doable; we will hit Iranian oil facilities on Kharg Island and their port of Bushehr with ten Tornado aircraft! I just need to know," Bandar added, "will you support us?"

In July 1987, Iran had tried to instigate an uprising in Mecca during the annual hajj. Dozens of Revolutionary Guard soldiers had secretly arrived in the holy city armed with rifles and explosives. One of William Casey's CIA recruits in the Revolutionary Guard, Reza Kahlili, had tipped off the agency to the Iranian scheme. The CIA passed it to Saudi security, which moved forcefully against the Iranians, killing 275 Iranian demonstrators, including some hapless civilians. The commander of the Revolutionary Guard, Major General Mohsen Rezai, advocated retaliation. The truculent former electrical engineer had long advocated an attack on Saudi Arabia or American forces in the Gulf, and he had nearly succeeded in doing so on the night of the first convoy, until he was reined in by the supreme leader. This time, Ayatollah Khomeini agreed with Rezai. Kuwait and Saudi Arabia needed to be taught a lesson.

Captain Touradj Riahi served in a plum billet as head of the navy plans division in Tehran. He worked closely with a Revolutionary Guard officer and former colleague in the old shah's navy to write a plan to strike back at Saudi Arabia, fittingly named Operation Hajj. The plan showed a rare level of cooperation between the Revolutionary Guard and the Iranian navy. The Iranians would amass dozens of guard small boats at Bushehr and Kharg Island in the northern Gulf. With a Revolutionary Guard officer in charge, embarked on one of the smaller navy missile boats serving as his flagship, this mosquito swarm of a fleet would be split into three flotillas. Under the cover of darkness, they would move en masse across the Gulf and then attack different Saudi and Kuwaiti oil facilities around al-Khafji with rockets and machine guns. One group would land commandos in Saudi Arabia to destroy a vital oil pumping station, perhaps even one of the Saudi desalination plants, which provided much of the desert kingdom's freshwater.

On September 30, 1987, General Rezai arrived at the Persian Gulf port of Bushehr. To control Operation Hajj, the Iranians had established a makeshift headquarters in an old dormitory building next to the jetty at Bushehr. Captain Riahi came down from Tehran to serve as the senior naval officer, with the head of the Revolutionary Guard, General Rezai himself, supervising the operation. Using the diversion of their well-publicized "Martyrdom" military exercise around the Strait of Hormuz, the Iranians quietly began pulling a number of the small Boston Whaler–type gunboats out of the water and loading them on flatbed trucks. They covered the boats with tarps to conceal their nature from prying eyes and passing American satellites. Over a period of several weeks, the Revolutionary Guard drove an untold number of boats up to Bushehr and quietly amassed at least four dozen small boats and one missile patrol boat in the northern Gulf.

After the *Iran Ajr* sinking, the Iranian commander decided to also establish a blocking force to interdict any American reinforcements moving up from Bahrain. He would park a few boats astride the shipping channel, and they would carry a nasty surprise. In case the army Little Birds helicopters showed again, the Revolutionary Guard brought along a Stinger missile, the most sophisticated American handheld antiaircraft system. Only recently the U.S. government had decided to allow the CIA to provide these to the Afghan mujahideen fighting the Soviets, and the Stingers had helped turn the tide of the war against Moscow. Without the agency's knowledge, Ismail Khan, a powerful Afghan warlord friendly to Iran, had spirited ten of these missiles to the Iranian military. Now Iran gleefully intended to turn America's own weapons back on the Great Satan. As the day of the attack approached, senior officials from Tehran arrived to witness the operation, joining a cadre of army and navy officers.

Within the CIA, Captain Riahi was a prized agent. He had repeatedly proven his worth by a steady stream of timely and accurate information about the Iranian military. He now found himself as the senior naval officer in the most significant Iranian military operation of the entire war. At considerable risk, Riahi managed to quickly get the details of the Iranian attack back to his handler at Tehfran. How he passed this is not clear. He may have relayed it through a German-speaking man in Tehran simply known as "the Austrian." While the CIA had a spy effort against Iran in Vienna (Austria was one of the other countries where Iranians could obtain a visa to the United States), his true nationality remains ambiguous. This mystery man emerged from the shadows on one occasion: he turned up one evening for a party at Captain Riahi's home and was introduced as the man who'd helped obtain his son's visa.[4]

Alerted to the threat, CENTCOM started monitoring the massing of small boats near Bushehr. On September 26, the DIA reported up to thirty-three small boats alone at the port. Four days later, U.S. intelligence detected as many as seventy Revolutionary Guard boats arrayed along a forty-five-mile-long front.[5] This alert brought Bandar into Crowe's office that afternoon.

On October 1, General George Crist, who was in the region, called Crowe to update him about a conversation with senior Saudi military officials. If Iran attacked, the Saudis would allow U.S. attack helicopters and surveillance aircraft into the kingdom. Crist wanted to send three U.S. Navy P-3 turboprop planes immediately to Saudi Arabia, as their excellent surface search radar would be invaluable for detecting the Iranian boats. Crowe contacted Bandar and relayed the request, adding that these were "nonoffensive" planes. Prince Bandar immediately called his father, the defense minister, in Riyadh and obtained his permission for the deployment of the P-3s to the King Abdul Aziz Air Base at Dhahran. Crist assigned his chief of staff, Don Penzler, to coordinate the details with the Saudi military.[6] The next day, Crowe, Crist, Armitage, and Bandar (accompanied by a Saudi major general) gathered for a hastily arranged conference in the chairman's office. Bandar appeared nervous and agitated but struck a defiant tone. His government, however, was clearly worried and wanted reassurances of American support if Iran attacked. The P-3s were on the way, Crowe said, due in Dhahran in three days, and Crist offered to deploy attack helicopters or fighter jets if the Saudis asked.

That evening, October 2, an American AWACS radar plane out of Saudi Arabia patrolled the northern Gulf. Designed to detect airborne targets, on that night it used its radar to look for any movement on the surface of the water. Suddenly, it picked up forty-five small blips moving rapidly toward the Saudi-Kuwait border and the al-Khafji oil facility. The expected attack appeared under way, and the pilot sounded the general alarm. Saudi Arabia scrambled F-15 fighters. Harold Bernsen at Middle East Force ordered the two frigates carrying the army Little Birds plus the helicopter carrier *Guadalcanal* with the marine attack helicopters north at maximum speed to intercept the Iranian horde.[7]

When the host of American and Saudi ships and planes arrived, they found no Iranian fleet, just a few odd fishing dhows plying the waters. The next day the American P-3s began flying, and they too saw nothing unusual. After a week of intelligence warnings, the Iranian forces had simply disappeared.

Saudi generals then accused the Americans of making up the entire attack story. Penzler received an earful from the skeptical commander of the Saudi land forces, General Yusef Rasid, who accused him of being part of an elaborate hoax to get U.S. military forces inside his country. Others pointed out that it had been a stormy night; perhaps the AWACS had picked up nothing more than wavelets?[8]

In truth, Mohsen Rezai had had every intention of attacking Saudi Arabia that night. The dark moonless night and rough seas had combined to turn his attack into a fiasco. The missile boat serving as the command ship became disoriented. She veered well off course, heading in the wrong direction. The high seas swamped one of the small boats and tossed and scattered the others all over the northern Gulf.[9] Undaunted, the Revolutionary Guard commander ordered another attempt for the following week. This time, Captain Riahi could not get the message out to his American handlers at Tehfran.

Into this environment, the barge *Hercules* deployed for her first operation in the northern Gulf. Paul Evancoe was assigned as the commander, and since his arrival in early September, the SEAL had worked tirelessly to outfit this first mobile sea base. His men filled twenty thousand sandbags and installed metal ballistic shields around the gun emplacements in the four corners. He had old crew quarters and drilling equipment removed and replaced by steel ammunition bunkers, an aircraft hangar, and a communications van. At one point forty welders worked twenty-four hours a day to transform the *Hercules* into an armed firebase bristling with weapons manned by 177 marines and special operators and a few intelligence linguists.[10] Meanwhile, work continued on the *Wimbrown*. Unfortunately, it would not be ready for operation until December.

The *Hercules* had a civilian crew of about thirty serving in such capacities as welders, cooks, and crane operators. Despite the secret nature of the sea bases, the civilian crew hired by Brown and Root were a motley group from Pakistan and the Philippines. Their background checks appeared sketchy to American counterintelligence officers, who worried that some might be Iranian spies or saboteurs.[11] Over the next year of the mobile sea bases' existence, however, other than to serve overly spicy curry to American special operators, all behaved properly and kept quiet.

Incredibly, as tugs towed the *Hercules* up to its station near Farsi Island on October 6, neither Evancoe nor Wikul knew anything about the near war between Iran and Saudi Arabia the preceding week.[12] For the first two days, they sent out their patrol boats looking for suspicious vessels. They found one, an Iranian dhow with an antenna sticking out of its cockpit, which appeared to be collecting intelligence on the barge. Both Wikul and Evancoe felt a growing sense of unease. With the nearest American ship, the frigate USS *Thach*, which provided air defense for the *Hercules*, twenty miles to the south, "we had the distinct feeling of being hung out to dry," Wikul said.[13]

On the evening of October 8, Wikul and Evancoe talked about their situation. Each had a strong suspicion that the Iranians intended to attack. Rather than just sit back and wait for the Iranians, they decided to put out a listening post to try to find out what the Iranians on Farsi Island were doing. After nightfall, they would send two patrol boats out with a small radar-absorbing Seafox. It would carry a couple of marine Farsi linguists with sophisticated eavesdropping equipment. As the patrol boats passed close to the Middle Shoals buoy marking shallow water, approximately fifteen miles west of Farsi, the Seafox would be dropped off, its radar signature blending into that of the buoy's.[14] From there, the marine linguists could listen in on the Iranian island and the Revolutionary Guard small boats. Similar tactics had proved successful with marine helicopters in other parts of the Gulf.[15]

After dark the operation got under way. Two blacked-out patrol boats left *Hercules* at nine p.m. with the small Seafox in tow and headed for the buoy only eight miles away. As insurance, Evancoe had three of the Little Birds fly ahead to scout out the buoy in front of the slower-moving patrol boats.[16] The lead helicopter, looking through its black-and-white infrared camera, noticed three boats already at the buoy. "That's strange," the pilot thought. "Our boats shouldn't be here yet." As he closed to within one hundred yards, he saw someone lean up in a small bass boat and man a heavy machine gun mounted on a tripod at the bow. As the American helicopter banked hard to the left, a string of tracker bullets whizzed past his canopy, missing the helicopter by mere feet.

Unbeknownst to the Americans, that very same night Mohsen Rezai decided to retry the Operation Hajj attack plan that had been thwarted by bad weather the week before. While the main flotilla assembled around some Iranian platforms in the northern Fereidoon oil field, that morning one of the larger cabin cruiser–type boats called a Boghammer and two smaller boats had departed Bushehr for Farsi Island. The group was commanded by a very forceful and competent young Revolutionary Guard officer named Mahdavi, who told his men, "You are headed on a great mission!"[17] Not all of the ten-man crew shared their commander's enthusiasm. They were a motley collection of conscripted landlubbers: one was a hulking illiterate farm boy, and another had deserted the army and traveled to Bushehr to visit a friend. The guards swept him off the street and threw him on the Boghammer to serve as their cook.[18]

After a brief stop at Farsi, where they waited for darkness and said their prayers, the three boats headed out shortly after sunset. The flotilla comprised the Boghammer with five men, including the officer in charge, and two small fiberglass fishing boats, each with a crew of three. All three men were armed with the traditional weapons of the Revolutionary Guard navy—a 107-mm multiple rocket launcher, heavy machine guns, and smaller-caliber weapons. But one Iranian on the Boghammer carried one of the American Stinger missiles, with orders to shoot any American helicopter he saw.[19] Mahdavi's mission was to prevent the Americans from interfering in the big attack on Saudi Arabia.

The three boats pulled up near the buoy and clustered together, the Iranian crews talking, relaxing, and smoking cigarettes as they prepared to bed down for the night. A man on one of the smaller boats heard the low whirl of a helicopter. He sprang to his gun and opened fire into the darkness in the general direction of the noise.

The lead Little Bird pulled out and vectored in the two attack variants trailing just behind. One unleashed two deadly fléchette rounds filled with tiny darts into the cluster of Revolutionary Guard boats. The American helo followed it up with a burst of machine-gun fire and explosive rockets. One of the fiberglass boats erupted in a massive fireball, blowing it in half and spreading burning gasoline across the water. The American pilot's wingman came in and unleashed on the remaining small boat and the Boghammer, leaving the former on fire. One crewman pushed the throttle full forward, and the Boghammer tried to pick up speed and maneuver to avoid being hit. The guard commander ordered it to circle back around and then slow to try to pick up survivors from the other two boats. The Little Birds closed in again and were greeted by the flash of a missile or rocket coming up from the Boghammer, which passed harmlessly by the helicopter. The Boghammer got up speed and tried to flee, maneuvering erratically. One of the Iranians grasped an Iranian flag and kneeled down on the cabin floor, praying for deliverance. A Little Bird launched his last rocket, which skipped off the water and hit the cabin cruiser squarely in the port side, igniting a fuel tank. The boat erupted in a massive fireball, instantly killing the man praying in the cabin as well as Mahdavi. The boat sank in less than thirty seconds.

Evancoe had immediately ordered general quarters at the first sight of tracer fire, clearly visible in the darkness eight miles away. As the marine security platoon manned their positions, the remaining patrol boat was lowered into the water, joining the other already serving as a local protection and reaction force. Marines and SEALs tossed grenades over the side in case Iranian frogmen might be lurking, ready to storm the *Hercules*. The commander launched the other two patrol boats, which took a position just north of the barge. Three additional Little Birds arrived as reinforcements.

The two U.S. patrol boats went to full speed and quickly arrived at the scene. Fire and debris littered the water. They pulled five Iranians out and discovered a sixth man terribly burned, clinging to the buoy. As they slowly searched for more survivors, Petty Officer James Kelz noticed a Styrofoam case floating in the water that looked like one that housed a battery for a Stinger missile. He dove over the side of the boat and swam out to retrieve the case. It proved to be electrifying evidence. Word quickly made it to the president that Iran had the most advanced surface-to-air missile in the American inventory.

With only one corpsman, Wikul established a makeshift aid station in the small office, its floor appropriately painted red. The medic frantically worked to save the six Iranians. One badly burned Iranian died shortly after arriving. Another more truculent Revolutionary Guard sailor muttered insults in Farsi at the Americans. He kept wiggling and seemingly trying to get up from his stretcher and kill them. One of the unsmiling SEALs leaned over and said, "How does it feel to be shot by the Great Satan?" Wikul realized that something more than hatred plagued the disgruntled Iranian. With a pistol trained on the patient, Wikul ordered the corpsman to turn him over, and when they removed his bunched-up shirt, a fountain of blood spurted out of a gaping bullet hole in the man's back. The corpsman tried to plug the wound, and they carried him up the ladder to the flight deck to an awaiting medical evacuation helicopter. Halfway up the ladder, the wounded sailor let out a gurgled gasp of air and "suddenly got very heavy," as one litter bearer recalled. Although this second Iranian died, the other four survived, and a marine helicopter flew them to a hospital on an awaiting warship.

Captain Frank Lugo immediately summoned Bernsen, who was in town having dinner with some Bahraini officials. Well to the south, an Iranian fired a missile from Rostam platform at a U.S. Navy helicopter operating from one of the frigates. The Middle East Force commander ordered the entire fleet to high alert.

While Evancoe tried to answer insistent questions from a nervous Middle East Force about the firefight at Middle Shoals buoy, the radar on the *Hercules* picked up forty small craft that appeared to be headed south toward the mobile sea base. To Wikul, it appeared to be part of a coordinated attack with the small boats at the buoy.[20]

Evancoe picked up the radio and called the commander of the two patrol boats, Lieutenant John Roark, standing in the path of the Iranian onslaught. "John, do you have the high-speed contacts?"

"Roger, Skipper. What are your orders?"

Evancoe calmly replied: "Turn and engage." And Roark did.[21]

Twenty miles to the south on the USS *Thach*, Captain Jerry O'Donnell was working out in the ship's weight room when a call came from the watch officer: "Captain, your presence is required in the CIC [combat information center]." He ran to the darkened room filled with radios and the glow of various radars. His own helicopter was aloft, using its radar to guide the Little Birds. O'Donnell had it return to his ship to pick up his corpsman and take him to the *Hercules* to help treat the wounded prisoners.[22]

His radar then detected the Iranian flotilla, only they were west, toward Saudi Arabia, and not coming from Iran. After relaying this back to Lugo on the *La Salle*, and without waiting for permission, O'Donnell ordered general quarters and then flank speed. As men ran to their battle stations and manned and loaded the automatic grenade launchers and machine guns, the frigate kicked up a rooster tail of white foam as it made thirty knots north to position the ship between the *Hercules* and the Iranian small boats. There they joined four patrol boats and six army Little Birds, all arrayed to do battle with Mohsen Rezai's Revolutionary Guard fleet.

Suddenly, the radar images started breaking up. Then they just disappeared. Although the images had been solid contacts, unlike any weather effect commonly witnessed, O'Donnell concluded they had all been a false echo, in part because they appeared right off the Saudi coast. While Evancoe and Wikul remained convinced of the Iranian presence, the captain of the *Thach* reported back to Bernsen that it had been a false echo.

But the two SEALs had been right. Operation Hajj was in full force, and the three Iranian flotillas off the Saudi coast were about to open fire. The boats had just landed Iranian commandos onto the Saudi beach when news of the disaster at Middle Shoals reached their makeshift headquarters in Bushehr. The ferocity and precision of the American attack stunned the Revolutionary Guard. With three boats sunk and seven sailors killed, and now faced with American helicopters and patrol boats headed toward them from the south, either Rezai or his deputy immediately concluded they had walked into an ambush. The Saudis and the Americans had been waiting for them. He recalled the entire force, which hastened back to Bushehr.

"No one realized how close a call we had that night," both Evancoe and Lugo recounted. By sheer serendipity for the United States, the unwitting commander of the *Hercules* had arrived just in time to thwart the largest Revolutionary Guard naval operation of the war. In war it is sometimes better to be lucky than good. On October 8, 1987, the American special operations forces were both. Unbeknownst to the anxious servicemen on board the *Hercules*, this marked the first and only time the Iranians would seriously challenge the barges for control over the northern Gulf.

In Bushehr, Mohsen Rezai and other senior officers immediately suspected that someone had tipped off the Americans. They had a traitor in their midst. Iranian counterintelligence agents looked to the handful of senior officers with access to the details of the Hajj plan. Already wise to the CIA's

Tehfran operation, the Ministry of Intelligence and Security focused on those who still harbored sympathy for the Americans. This included Captain Riahi.

Stung by two successive defeats, Iran decided to strike back at the chief culprit who had invited the Americans in: Kuwait. A week after the Middle Shoals shoot-out, the Liberian-registered tanker *Sungari* sat taking on a load of crude at Kuwait's main oil terminal just south of Kuwait City. A bright light, almost like a flare, appeared in the distance. It grew closer and larger. A massive Silkworm missile streaked in just above the waves. Its massive thousand-pound warhead slammed into the side of the *Sungari*, causing a fire but no casualties.

The next day, the reflagged tanker *Sea Isle City* approached the terminal to fill its own holds with Kuwaiti oil before the next convoy. The tanker's master did a slight deviation to look at the damage to the *Sungari* from the day before. He chose the wrong time to be a tourist. Another Silkworm missile lumbered in. Locking on to the *Sea Isle City*'s white superstructure, the missile plowed into the pilothouse and crew quarters. The blast permanently blinded the American captain and the Filipino lookout and wounded sixteen other crewmen.

Although Iranian president Ali Khamenei said that "Almighty God alone knew best where the missile came from," American intelligence quickly backtracked the missiles' paths and found that both originated from the Iranian-captured peninsula of al-Faw, Iraq.[23] Both Silkworms had actually been captured from the Iraqi military.

Rear Admiral Dennis Brooks commanded a newly established joint task force of all forces involved in the convoy operations. He decided to run this operation with little input from Bernsen. He hated the mobile sea base idea and disliked much of the surveillance scheme, including deploying the NSA assets down to the smaller ships. But Brooks knew what his boss, General Crist, wanted in the plan. With Washington unwilling to take stronger measures, the United States would move only to destroy the oil platforms that enabled the Revolutionary Guard to operate in the Gulf. Prime on Crist's mind was the one at Rostam. Rostam was actually three platforms—two only about a hundred yards apart and one to the north about two miles away, each resembling a square building and a three-level parking garage on stilts. They had facilitated the *Iran Ajr*'s mission and served as a major forward command post for the Iranian small boats. Strategically situated in the south-central Gulf along the convoy route, they provided the Iranian military with a steady stream of reports about U.S. ship movements in the Gulf.[24] While Crist ordered Brooks to give warning to the Iranians in order to avoid loss of life, any display of hostility would be met with American firepower, and he authorized Brooks to go into Iranian waters and airspace if necessary.[25]

At midafternoon on October 19, Brooks amassed four destroyers and two frigates off Rostam, set to begin the American answer to the Silkworm attack, code-named Operation Nimble Archer. Stationed off to the side was Jerry O'Donnell's USS *Thach* with Marc Thomas's SEALs embarked. Over the standard maritime radio channel the Iranians heard in English and Farsi: "Rashadt [Rostam] oil platform, this is U.S. Navy. You have twenty minutes to evacuate the platform."

The Iranians heeded the warning. Looking on from the bridge of the *Thach*, Thomas could clearly see Iranians scrabbling down the ladder from one platform and into a tethered tugboat. Forming a tight line of battle, separated by only one thousand yards, the five U.S. warships slowly steamed in a lazy racetrack, their guns lowered.[26]

"Commence fire." For the next hour, the American ships rained shell upon shell down on the platform proper and its nearby drilling rig. Most missed, falling over or under or simply passing harmlessly through the Erector Set–like construction of the oil platforms, but enough found their mark to obscure the target in smoke, blowing off the helicopter deck and severing one of the main support legs.[27]

From the bridge of the *Thach*, Marc Thomas watched the fireworks. In walked a slightly overweight chief with glasses, wearing his khaki uniform and a green steel-pot helmet. The chief was an avid reader of *Soldier of Fortune* magazine and had become friendly with Thomas, asking his opinion about fighting knives and guns described in the magazine. "We are really kicking their ass!" the chief said, pumping both fists into the air. After more than a thousand rounds had been fired, a cease-fire finally was ordered and the *Thach* with the SEALs closed in.

Thomas and his SEALs approached the two abject platforms just at sunset. One was completely engulfed in a tower of flames. A shell had ignited the gas coming up from beneath the ocean floor, and as it turned out, the safety valve to prevent such a blowout had been installed backward. Even two hundred yards away the heat was intense. As it was too dangerous to board,

Thomas's SEALs were directed to occupy the northern platform, which had not been shelled, to see if there was any useful intelligence.

With darkness setting in, Thomas approached the platforms cautiously. While it appeared abandoned, he could clearly see a twin-barrel antiaircraft gun. The SEALs fired a machine gun to clear out any Iranians remaining. The SEALs then clambered up the ladder from their boats and moved room to room clearing the three-story structure, which took more than two hours to complete. Hearing voices in one room, a SEAL tossed in a grenade. When they moved in with weapons drawn, they found the room empty: the voices were coming from the radio. The room proved another intelligence bonanza for the Americans. Reams of messages were stacked up, with some still churning out of the telex machine. Thomas's men scooped up all the documents, blew up any guns or radios, and headed back to the *Thach*. When all were safely back, some five hundred pounds of explosives sent one of the platforms into the sea. The other continued to burn until August 1988, when, after the war, repair crews finally got to turn off the flow of gas and oil. Middle East Force coined a name for it: "the flame of freedom."

Following the operation, the United States deployed an array of floating hexagonal radar reflectors around Kuwait's oil terminal and the barge. CENTCOM cajoled the Kuwaitis into deploying antiaircraft missiles on a northern island to shoot down any more missiles. The reflectors proved their worth in early November, when another Silkworm from al-Faw streaked in, only to hit the fabric reflector instead of a nearby tanker.

The spike in violence and the thwarted attack on the Saudi oil facilities opened the door for more American surveillance aircraft to keep tabs on the Iranians. As part of its covert air force, the CIA maintained a small paramilitary air wing housed near Williamsburg, Virginia. Operating under the Special Operations Group within the agency's Special Activities Division, it maintained ten specially configured fixed-wing planes and helicopters outfitted with the most advanced night-vision equipment and surveillance radar in the world, as well as forward-looking infrared radar and specially designed terrain-following radar, which permitted low-level flying in complete darkness. This included the small jelly bean–shaped Hughes/MD-500s, which were identical to the Little Birds of the U.S. Army's Task Force 160. In fact, army and agency aircraft had grown out of the same program, developed for the army. When funds dried up in 1971, the CIA quietly stepped in to finish the project. The army and CIA formed a joint aviation unit called Seaspray.

The unit soon broke into two different units, one "white," or openly acknowl-edged unit—TF-160 at Fort Campbell—with the other remaining a "black," or covert, unit.[28]

In September 1987, the director of CIA's operations, Tom Twetten, received a phone call from General Colin Powell. A graduate of Iowa State, now in his early fifties, Twetten was thin and fit with a shock of graying hair. He had the deserved reputation as a thoughtful, taciturn bureaucrat. That afternoon, Powell relayed a request from the Defense Department: "Would CIA be willing to provide some of their aircraft to use in the Gulf to support the escort operations?"

The CIA owned only a handful of these aircraft, and they were in high demand around the world. In recent years they had played a large role in America's secret war in Central America, but by 1987 this effort had largely ended. After mulling over Powell's request for a moment, Twetten said he did not see why not, but would take it up with the recently appointed new direc-tor, the popular and competent lawyer William Webster.[29] Around the same time, Howard Hart, now the director of the Special Activities Division and thus owner of the paramilitary aircraft, received a phone call on his secure phone from a navy admiral in Crowe's office. "Mr. Hart, we need to conduct operations in the Persian Gulf and we need a nighttime infrared capability. And we don't have anything. Do you?"

A bemused Hart thought, "This must be a joke." He said, "Admiral, you're my navy, and you're telling me you don't have anything that flies and can see at night?"

"No, we don't," the senior officer responded, adding that they were look-ing into obtaining it, but needed an interim capability as a stopgap measure.

Following a more formal letter asking for support coming from Wein-berger, drafted by the Joint Staff's J-3, Special Operations Directorate, Web-ster held a meeting with his top subordinates to discuss the request. All agreed without hesitation that the CIA should agree to the request and sup-port the military operation. Webster responded to Weinberger, agreeing to provide the aircraft, but with the caveat that they not fly within the "known threat ranges" of the Iranian weapons systems. This necessitated staying sev-eral nautical miles away from Iran's offshore platforms. Weinberger and Crowe both agreed to this stipulation, and while the skilled CIA pilots did not always adhere to this over the next year, it remained the rule on paper.[30]

Hart dispatched several CIA officers to Bahrain to meet with both

Bernsen and his intelligence officer, Commander Ziegler, to iron out tactical planning details with Middle East Force, a necessary precursor regardless of where they ended up in the Gulf.[31] The CIA agreed that its aircraft, while not falling under actual tactical control of Bernsen in the Gulf, would nevertheless take their direction from him and would provide their intelligence directly back to Middle East Force and Brooks's joint task force.

Prince Bandar phoned his father, the Saudi defense minister, and after a consultation with the king, Saudi Arabia agreed to allow the CIA planes to be based at a remote corner of the growing U.S. air base at Dhahran. On the night of October 14, a U.S. Air Force transport secretly landed at the Saudi airfield in Dhahran. It carried three CIA helicopters: two small Hughes/MD-500s and a larger Bell 212 helicopter for search and rescue. That night, a fourth plane joined them, a sleek Merlin twin-prop airplane configured with search and FLIR night-vision radars, as well as secure satellite communications back to Washington.

To maintain their independence and cover, they were housed in separate hangars well away from the seven-hundred-man military detachment supporting the P-3s and AWACS planes. The agency pilots operated under cover, refusing to acknowledge to their navy and air force counterparts for whom they worked, although it quickly became an open secret. As General Charles Horner recalled later, chuckling, "They would appear in the mess hall and the 'O' club and try to mingle with the other pilots as if they were just fellow military pilots, which most of them were, but it was something of a challenge with their longer hair and beards."[32]

While the CIA used its own connections with the Saudi intelligence service to smooth over any concerns and provide a cover story for its aircraft, the agency's arrival met with the same suspicion from some Saudi officials in the defense ministry as the arrival of the P-3s, all as part of an American ruse to get military access to the kingdom. Dissuading the Saudis of this concern was not helped by another American SR-71 spy flight just six days later, on October 20. While the sole focus of two air force pilots, Warren McKendree and Randy Shelhorse, was looking at the Iranian Silkworm missile sites around the Strait of Hormuz, the wide turning radius of their high-flying twin-engine Blackbird required them to briefly fly over part of the Saudi kingdom. For suspicion-minded Arabs, was Iran or Saudi Arabia the true target of this sudden rise in U.S. spy planes?[33]

Under the code word Eager Glacier, within three days of arrival the four aircraft flew their first mission. The Merlin aircraft especially were tailor-made to fill the vacuum of tracking the Iranians once the sun went down. Its equipment worked well and it could loiter much longer over the Gulf. The two CIA Little Birds worked equally well as their TF-160 cousins, their cockpits specially designed for flying with night-vision goggles.[34] The aircraft remained in the hangars during the day, flying only at night, trying to blend in with the normal air traffic over the Gulf before slipping off the main route and heading toward the Iranian side of the Gulf, often into the exclusion zone forbidden to U.S. military planes. There the Merlin loitered several hours every night, monitoring the movements of suspicious Iranian vessels. Specific attention was paid to the three main choke points through which the tankers had to transit: the Strait of Hormuz and the southern Gulf near Abu Musa; the central Gulf near the Iranian platforms at Rostam and Sassan just north of the United Arab Emirates; and in the north near Farsi Island and the Fereidoon oil fields.[35]

As agreed, the pilots took their direction from the joint task force's Middle East headquarters and provided their information back to their liaison officer on Brooks's staff, having first been quickly digested by a small cell of CIA intelligence analysts with direct communications links to the aircraft from their base in Dhahran. They tended to keep a wide berth of the Iranian platforms and ships, leading a few of the officers on scene to privately view them as being more risk averse than the TF-160 pilots, flying around trying to avoid Iranian machine guns and shoulder-fired missiles. Regardless, they flew virtually every night, often well into the Iranian side of the Gulf, tracking suspicious Iranian vessels and filling a niche capability not found in the U.S. military's inventory.

Working within the structured framework of the frequently inflexible and controlling U.S. military did not come naturally to these maverick CIA pilots. They flew where directed, but filing detailed flight plans of their itinerary with the Middle East Force staff felt awkward for those whose job was to remain unseen and inconspicuous.

"They never wanted to coordinate with anyone," recalled David Grieve.[36] On one occasion this nearly proved fatal. A U.S. frigate detected a small, unidentified aircraft coming directly toward it from the Iranian side of the Gulf. After trying to hail it on the radio, the frigate's crew checked with Middle East Force on the *La Salle*, which had no information on any friendly aircraft in the vicinity. After taking more aggressive options, such as locking on to it with its fire control radar, the U.S. warship requested permission to engage. Fortunately, it just did not seem to be flying the profile of a suicide plane, and the on-scene destroyer squadron commander, Captain Donald Dyer, ordered the crew not to engage. "It's probably one of ours," he thought.[37]

The next day the navy launched an investigation into the mysterious aircraft whose crew nearly met their maker. It turned out to be the CIA's Merlin aircraft. When accused of being rogue and a hazard, the agency pilots forcefully responded that their mission and area of operation had been assigned by the military Middle East Force, and they had in fact notified that same higher headquarters of their takeoff time. If the military command could not deconflict its flights with the ships it controlled plying the Gulf, "the problem was a fucked-up navy operations staff," one still irritated participant said ten years later. When the name-calling died down, both sides agreed to procedures to avoid another such close encounter. The Eager Glacier pilots agreed to file a formal flight plan before every mission through General Horner's air force command in Dhahran, although their mission objectives and their operations over Iranian territorial waters remained tightly held and off-limits to all but a few of the air force or navy staff officers in the Gulf.

On November 27, 1987, the CIA's Clair George sent a letter to Jonathan Howe, Crowe's executive assistant, inquiring about long-term intentions for supporting Earnest Will. Crist wanted the aircraft to remain until a suitable replacement could be found. "There is no single DOD platform which has the combination of capabilities the Merlin provides." Simply put, it was too valuable in providing real-time intelligence collection on Iranian Revolutionary Guard naval operations.[38] After the Pentagon examined some quick alternatives, such as leasing the aircraft from Langley—sans aircrew—or modifying a coast guard jet, both of which turned out to be too expensive and time-consuming, the CIA agreed to keep them there.[39]

On October 20, the first two MSOs, the old minesweepers, finally arrived in the Persian Gulf. Over the past six weeks, as they made their way from the East and West Coasts, a competition emerged as to which flotilla would arrive first. The West Coast won the race: the USS *Esteem*, commanded by a feisty, competitive Captain Robert McCabe, was the first to transit the Strait of Hormuz.[40] Hunting for mines was a slow, laborious process. The minesweepers moved slowly back and forth across the tanker routes. Each pass covered only a two-hundred-yard swath of water, and the Farsi mine danger area alone amounted to 140 square miles.[41] The crew topside suffered as temperatures reached 130 degrees. To help, the navy flew in ice vests in which frozen gel packs fit in pouches for those standing watch.[42] The Saudis agreed to allow the MSO crews to rest in a segregated dock area at the small port of Jubayl. Here they could get some relief from the confines of their wooden cells and barbeque in what the navy called "steel-beach picnics."

Everything looked like a mine. Old oil drums, cars, all the junk of the world dumped in the world's oceans appeared suspicious in the fuzzy glow of the sonar screen. Frank DeMasi's *Inflict* investigated ninety-two such contacts in a single day.[43] Ships loaded with sheep from Australia and bound for Kuwait became especially irritating. As they approached port, they dumped all the dead sheep over the side. The bloated carcasses turned turtle and the four black hooves bobbed just above the water and looked remarkably like the horns of an Iranian mine.

On November 19, Frank DeMasi's ship was operating around a dozen miles south from where the *Bridgeton* had hit its mine. It was late in the day and getting dark, and DeMasi was about to halt the search for the day. Suddenly, the sonar search radar operator announced, "Minelike contact bearing 020 range 450 yards." Slowing, the ship inched forward. As they closed to within eighty yards, the crew could clearly see a circular object with a chain going down to the ocean floor. "Jesus Christ, Captain," the seaman yelled, "this is a mine!"

As the minesweepers lacked a remotely operated vehicle, standard on the more sophisticated European minesweepers, which would have allowed them to view the mine with a camera and even place a countercharge on it, an explosive ordnance disposal (EOD) diver had to be sent to physically view the object and verify it was a mine. It was one of the smaller Iranian-made Myams laid specifically to catch the American minesweepers. As it was getting late, they decided to throw a buoy attached to a two-hundred-pound concrete block nearby to mark the location and come back the next morning.

At first light, the three-man explosives team puttered out to the marker in a Zodiac. One diver went over the side and, to his horror, saw a scrape mark down the side of the mine. The current had carried the weight and it had actually hit the mine. Had it struck one of the horns, there would have been nothing left of any of the men to send home for a funeral. The diver carefully placed a block of C-4 with a delayed timer on the side of the cylinder and returned to the boat, and the three men hastened back to the *Inflict*.

As DeMasi backed his ship away, his sonar discovered another mine just four hundred yards from the first. After the first mine detonated in a massive geyser of white water, the diver destroyed the other mine. DeMasi drew a line of bearing down the two mines and proceeded to search along the azimuth. In a few days DeMasi's crew had rolled up the entire mine line. Each time they blew up a mine, the elated crew painted a small mine on the bridge wing. In short order, the *Inflict* was adorned with ten such characters.

Meanwhile, the *Fearless*, searching the area to the north, discovered one of the larger M-08 mines dropped to catch the *Bridgeton* back in July. Following DeMasi's playbook, Captain Jack Ross rolled up and destroyed three neatly laid in a straight line.[44] DeMasi joined him and discovered five more mines. The Iranians aided their task by laying mines with sequential serial numbers. When the American divers noticed that they had skipped a number, they knew they had missed a mine in between.[45] By the end of the month, the aging MSOs had finished a remarkable operation and accounted for all twenty mines dropped by the Revolutionary Guard.

In addition to those planted on the Gulf floor, dozens of drifting mines presented a hazard to Gulf shipping. Many originated from the Iraqi and Iranian fields in the north and had broken away from their moorings, while the Iranians set others adrift hoping the currents would carry them to the waters of the Gulf Arabs. Around Christmas, one floater was spotted just outside Bahrain's main harbor. In the middle of a Bob Hope show, Middle East Force ordered Robert McCabe's ship out to sea to get rid of the mine. They found it just at sunset and decided to detonate it by shooting it with a rifle. Instead of exploding, the hollow case just filled with water and the mine sank to the bottom of the harbor, where it still remains, much to the considerable annoyance of the emir's government.[46]

Over the next several months, the hodgepodge of forces effectively cleared the mines and shut down Iran's Revolutionary Guard operation in the northern Persian Gulf. In December, the *Wimbrown* finally joined the *Hercules* as the SEALs and army pilots continued to refine their tactics. Operating in pairs and at night, except when investigating a specific contact, the patrols ranged from four to twelve hours. Occasionally, in an attempt to confuse the

Iranians, all four were sent out in a close diamond formation so as to appear as a large target to the Iranians on Farsi Island. When just outside the twelve-mile exclusion zone around the island, the boats would split apart at high speed, appearing to a thoroughly baffled Iranian radar operator as though the object had multiplied before his eyes. On one occasion, a Little Bird flew around the far side of Farsi and flew over the island just above the buildings. If the Iranians tried to pursue, Wikul sat waiting in an ambush with patrol boats and more Little Birds. After Middle Shoals, the Iranians showed little stomach to tangle with the Americans.

As a new year dawned, it appeared that the United States finally had the upper hand. A new American commander, Rear Admiral Tony Less, was headed to take charge in the Gulf, and the convoys went back and forth unmolested. Iran had not tried another mining since the loss of the *Iran Ajr*. The war with Iraq was turning against Iran, and leaders in Tehran grew increasingly desperate to try to curtail the Arab support for Saddam Hussein. But rather than calming down, the quasi-war between Iran and the United States was actually reaching its climax.

Seventeen

NO HIGHER HONOR

On a bright sunny late February day, General Crist joined Hal Bernsen for a ceremony on the fantail of the USS *La Salle*, tied up pierside in Bahrain. A strong wind blew the flags and flapped the awning covering the dignitaries from the Middle East sun. This was apropos, for a new American commander had arrived in the Gulf, Rear Admiral Tony Less. Less had a quick smile, a quicker wit, and a sharp temper. He had an effusive, sanguine personality that melded with common sense to make him a popular leader. He was a respected pilot with the navy and the former commander of the elite Blue Angels aerobatic flight team. The new commander knew a lot about what had transpired in the Gulf over the past few months. He'd commanded one of the carrier battle groups in August when Ace Lyons flew out with his Window of Opportunity plan. Crist, dressed in a high-collared white uniform, took to the podium: "Napoléon once said, 'Nothing is so important in war as undivided command.' One hundred fifty years later we are participating in a ceremony which bears witness to the truth of these words."

Admiral Less had arrived to relieve both Dennis Brooks and Harold Bernsen, consolidating both the joint task force and Middle East Force under one commander. Since the formation of the joint task force in September 1987, relations between Bernsen's and Brooks's staffs had become estranged, with the problem lying both in personalities and, more important, philosophical differences between the two navy commanders. Brooks had the difficult assignment of running an operation whose subordinate command was far more versed with the intricacies of the political and military concept of Earnest Will. Brooks disliked the idea of the mobile sea bases and delayed deploying the second barge *Wimbrown VII*.[1] He opposed the decentralized nature of the intelligence collection and viewed the use of the special operations forces as an overly aggressive posture toward Iran.[2] He believed that the best way to avoid clashes with Iran was to stay out of the Gulf, running heavily armed convoys when necessary. Otherwise, avoid confrontations. Unfortunately, this ran counter to the entire operational scheme. The end of Brooks came when Crowe grew irate following a phone call to Bernsen in which he learned that Brooks had refused to send a tanker to pick up free fuel offered by Kuwait as compensation to the Americans, apparently worried about the safety of sending a military tanker into the Gulf.[3] This decision by Brooks cost the U.S. government nearly five million dollars.[4]

While Brooks, having been fired, left the Gulf without fanfare, Bernsen received a proper send-off. In his address at the change of command, the CENTCOM commander lavished praise upon Bernsen: "I am sure that often in the privacy of his cabin, this calm, unflappable commander must have echoed the thoughts of General Joffre, the French hero of the first world war, who said: 'I don't know who won the Battle of the Marne, but if it had been lost, I know who would have lost it.'"[5]

By early 1988 the United States was firmly established in the Gulf. By the end of January, a total of thirty major convoys had made the three- to five-day transit from the Gulf of Oman to just south of Kuwaiti waters, or vice versa. While tension remained high, Iranian activity appeared to have tapered off. There still seemed no end in sight for the U.S. commitment, as critics of the reflagging operation continued to point out, but by the spring of 1988 events were finally coming to a head.[6]

On the afternoon of April 14, 1988, the American frigate USS *Samuel B. Roberts* steamed south toward the Strait of Hormuz, having just escorted two reflagged tankers—*Gas King* and *Rover*—to Kuwait, the twenty-fifth successful convoy of Earnest Will.[7] With a cloudless blue sky overhead and a light wind, the *Roberts* cruised at a brisk twenty-five knots as it headed to rendezvous with an oiler for some fuel before taking another Earnest Will convoy back north. She passed by the Shah Allum Shoal approximately fifty-five miles northeast of Qatar, an area of shallow water that forced the deep-draft tankers into a more constricted sea-lane. A mere two hours earlier, the French frigate *Dupleix* had passed through the area, reporting nothing of interest. The two navies exchanged officers, and occasionally food, back and forth for a pleasant change in the daily staple of the two ships patrolling the Gulf. Recently the *Roberts* and the *Dupleix* had held a combined mess night in the *Roberts's* wardroom, complete with some smuggled French wine, a welcome treat on board a dry U.S. Navy warship. More important, the two combatants looked out for each other; when an Iranian vessel loomed nearby, the *Roberts* noticed the French destroyer lying in the vicinity ready to provide assistance.[8]

The *Sammy B*, as her crew affectionately called her, was a newly commissioned *Oliver Hazard Perry*–class frigate, of the same class as the ill-fated USS *Stark*. It was the third ship to bear the name; the original *Samuel B. Roberts* had been sunk off Samar in the Battle of Leyte Gulf on October 25, 1944, with a loss of ninety crew. In his after-action report, the surviving captain, Robert Copeland, wrote: "In the face of this knowledge, the men zealously manned their stations wherever they might be, and fought and worked with such calmness, courage, and efficiency that no higher honor could be conceived than to command such a group of men." "No higher honor" stuck and became the motto of the next two ships. With a slender, 450-foot-long knife-shaped hull and boxy superstructure, the *Roberts* displaced more than four thousand tons and held a crew of 215 men. The navy had designed the frigate as an inexpensive solution to complete such unglamorous tasks as antisubmarine and convoy duties.

Commander Paul X. Rinn, forty-two, commanded the *Roberts*. Born in the Bronx, he had a rough-and-tumble upbringing, with a .22-caliber bullet hole in his leg to show for his youthful indiscretions. But he eventually turned himself around, graduated from a small Catholic college, Marist, in Poughkeepsie, New York, and in 1968 was commissioned as an ensign in the U.S. Navy. In 1972, during the waning days of the Vietnam War, Rinn found himself in a very unusual billet for a surface warfare naval officer. He worked as an adviser as part of the secret CIA war in Cambodia. Operating near the Laotian border building patrol bases along the Mekong River, he spent over two hundred days in combat areas being mortared and fired at along with a polyglot force of Navy SEALs and native levies. He ended up being the last U.S. naval officer out of Phnom Penh as the Khmer Rouge closed in and Cambodia became a killing field. The experience forever changed Rinn. Unlike many of his contemporaries who had never heard a shot fired, in anger or otherwise, Rinn learned what it took to lead men in combat and strove to instill in his subordinates the importance of training for the realities of modern war, anticipating the eventuality of going into harm's way.

Captain Rinn had the deserved reputation as an aggressive, cocky, in-your-face skipper. He spoke loudly and with confidence and had a temper dampened by a good-natured, sardonic sense of humor. In a service whose officers were largely engineers who acted more as technicians, Rinn was a bit of a novelty—he had charisma. It was contagious and engendered loyalty among his officers and crew.

The *Samuel B. Roberts* arrived in the Gulf on February 2, 1988, as part of Destroyer Squadron 22, commanded by a Red Man tobacco–chewing Captain Don Dyer. Over the next two months, the *Roberts* escorted five convoys entering the bizarre world of the Persian Gulf and the tanker war. On his first inbound transit through the Strait of Hormuz, Rinn nearly fired on two Iranian F-4 Phantoms coming from Bandar Abbas. At the last minute, both turned away, seconds before Rinn, standing over the shoulder of a seaman with his finger hovering above the launch button, intended to give the go-ahead. That night, he had another close encounter with the CIA's Eager Glacier aircraft flying out of Dhahran on its nightly patrol off the Iranian coast. Less's command informed him it was a friendly aircraft, but only a minute before the *Roberts* would have sent a missile skyward.

Rinn and the *Roberts* increasingly found themselves executing a new, more aggressive strategy against Iran. The new secretary of defense, Frank Carlucci, came to the Pentagon intent on making some changes to the U.S. operations in the Gulf. He was appalled at the specter of Iranians attacking unarmed merchant ships in plain sight of U.S. warships. He agreed with Joint Chiefs chairman Crowe that it was unseemly to have U.S. captains—bound by strict rules of engagement—unable to come to the aid of helpless seamen being gunned down by Iranian frigates and small boats. Admiral Crowe phoned General George Crist in Tampa late that January to direct him to up the ante on the Iranians. "Don't start a war," he said. "But, George, be aggressive and use radar, or this ship's presence—whatever you can do to break up their attacks." U.S. warships could not enter Iranian waters, but if they needed to push up into the Iranian exclusion zone, so be it.

It fell to Tony Less to implement the new strategy. "The Iranians are chicken shits," Less said. "When they see a ship coming over the horizon, they run for home." Less briefed the newly arrived ship skippers, including Rinn: "Guys, we're at war. Don't lose your ship, but you've got radars. . . . Stymie them, don't let them lay mines, don't let them attack ships." What followed was a series of intensifying confrontations between the two fleets, with the *Roberts* leading the charge.

The first encounter occurred near the Iranian island of Sirri. The *Roberts* detected the Iranian frigate *Sabalan* closing in for an attack on the unsuspecting Greek tanker *Tandis*. Rinn ordered "all ahead flank" as the *Roberts* rapidly closed on the Iranian ship. The British-built *Sabalan* was smaller than her American counterpart, only 311 feet in length and less than half the tonnage. But she represented the most formidable ship in the Iranian navy and was armed by a rapid-fire 114-mm turreted gun forward and three relatively small Sea Killer antiship missiles aft. The *Sabalan* was commanded by Abdollah Manavi, a regular navy officer with the dubious reputation of being one of the most cruel Iranian captains in the war. This odious skipper had earned the nickname "Captain Nasty" due to the ship's infamous reputation for deliberately attacking the crew quarters of neutral shipping. Even when his command in Bandar Abbas directed Captain Nasty not to attack a tanker, he often disregarded the order or openly lied to his superiors, seemingly delighting in aiming the ship's gunfire at the crewmen and their lifeboats. Then the *Sabalan* would transmit to the helpless tanker, "Have a nice day."[9]

Rinn brought his ship up on the *Sabalan's* stern, closing to within one mile. The crew of the Iranian vessel stared nervously back, pointing deck-mounted machine guns at the American ship. With the U.S. frigate on his stern, the Iranian captain turned hard to port and hit the accelerator. What followed was a strange minuet, with the *Sabalan* resembling a hare trying to elude a pursuing fox, turning rapidly to the left and right trying to throw off the pursuing U.S. ship and get into a position to bring her forward gun to bear while the *Roberts* matched her turn for turn. After several hours, the *Sabalan* had enough and headed north toward Iran. The *Roberts* did not pursue. That night an elated Rinn wrote his brother, "Crew on a high—captain's got balls!"[10]

The next few encounters between the two ships near Abu Musa Island nearly ended in bloodshed. While the *Sabalan* continued to back down from a confrontation, her sister ship, the *Sahand*, was not so docile. On one occasion, the *Roberts* and the *Sahand* spied each other on radar; each turned immediately and headed directly for the other. Closing at a combined speed of nearly sixty knots an hour in a deadly game of chicken, each locked on to the other with its fire control radar, as Rinn put a missile up on his forward mount, ready to send it screaming toward the *Sahand* should the Iranian open fire. Just before the two collided, the *Sahand* turned away.

Rinn continued to harass the Iranian ships near Abu Musa. On one occasion, he shadowed an Iranian ship all night despite some of the worst weather in the Gulf, with waves higher than the *Roberts*'s bridges, following the Iranian warship into the Iranian exclusion zone and breaking off pursuit only after daybreak. Less was pleased. While he admonished Rinn about being "too provocative," he admired the skipper of the *Samuel B. Roberts*. "He was one of the best captains I'd seen," Admiral Less later commented. The aggressive new strategy seemed to be working; Iranian attacks dropped off as the U.S. ships had the desired intimidating influence. U.S. intelligence monitoring Iranian communication at the 1st Naval District headquarters in Bandar Abbas noted the Iranians' growing concern at an inability to attack ships in the southern Gulf, one report remarking that the United States seemed intent on doing everything to "protect" Saddam Hussein's war machine.

One person who saw this cat-and-mouse game firsthand was an Associated Press reporter named Richard Pyle. Short, with black hair and a bit of a hangdog face, he possessed a quick wit and an attentive mind. Few reporters had as much combat experience as Pyle. He served briefly in the army before becoming a reporter, rising to become the AP bureau chief in Saigon for much of the Vietnam War. Here he learned firsthand the idiosyncrasies of the U.S. military, as well as the tragedy of war, brought home by the loss of four reporters and close friends in Laos, including famed reporter Larry Burrows. Pyle was the only American reporter continuously covering the ongoing Iran-Iraq War and the U.S. intervention, Earnest Will. He lived in Bahrain, where his wife attended the same small Catholic church as Tony Less and his wife. Pyle threw himself into the tanker reflagging story; he rode nearly every ship in the Gulf and served in virtually every press pool, including the very first with the *Bridgeton*.

Pyle watched the increased harassment with great interest, fully aware that the United States had escalated the operation and of the likelihood of more military confrontation. He rode on the *Roberts* with Rinn during his long night tracking the Iranian frigate. "I could not believe what this guy Rinn was doing. He must have scared the hell out of that Iranian ship!" In an interview with him in his stateroom, Rinn said, "We are going to follow him. He'll know we are there and we are going to make him think that we know where he is and what he is doing all the time. It's a psychological operation." Whether the Iranians were intimidated, however, was a different story.

As the United States tracked Iran's boats, the Iranian military was doing the same to the U.S. Navy. The Revolutionary Guard noticed a seam in the American surveillance scheme: the area in the south-central Gulf. In the summer of 1987, Bernsen had recommended stationing the *Guadalcanal* there to provide surveillance, but this had been denied. Less had tried to cover it by stationing warships and overflights of the P-3s operating from Saudi Arabia, but they could not be maintained continuously. Iran noticed an opening as the U.S. ships were pulled to the north and south on various duties, leaving a momentary window of opportunity. When Iranian forces on Rostam and Sassan confirmed the dearth of U.S. forces, they decided to act. For the first time in five months, Iran gambled with the invisible hand.

Following a meeting with senior military leaders in Tehran, on April 12 the Iranian ship *Charak* sailed from Bandar Abbas without fanfare. A small vessel at thirteen hundred tons and two hundred feet long, she had been designed as a lighter or support ship, with a wide, flat open area running from the bow back to the bridge and superstructure near the stern. She had a complement of around twenty, not counting a small fanatical Revolutionary Guard detachment. After a brief stop at Abu Musa Island for some last-minute instructions, *Charak* headed off west past the Iranian oil platforms manned by other Iranian guards: Sirri, Sassan, and Rostam. A four-engine, American-made Iranian P-3 flew the route that afternoon, providing some intelligence on U.S. ship positions, relaying it back to Abu Musa. On the night of April 13, the *Charak* discharged her duties. In a location where shoals forced the tanker route into a channel, the Iranian ship aligned herself with a navigation light on the horizon. Extinguishing her navigation lights, she sailed in the blackness. One officer had a stopwatch in his hand, while others methodically fused the black spherical objects arranged on top of the flat open deck hatch and carefully rolled them to the edge of a plank protruding off the side. Twelve mines fell over the side; unlike the *Iran Ajr*, the mines were arrayed in a circular pattern, designed to saturate the area and increase the chances of finding a target. Either that night or the next, the *Charak* or her sister, the *Souru*, undertook a similar mission some sixty miles to the southeast along an old Earnest Will tanker track that had not been used for several convoys.

O n the afternoon of April 14, Captain Rinn was down in his cabin and, in a good-natured way, berating his cook, Chief Petty Officer Kevin Ford, for having too much spinach on the menu. Ford was planning a steak and lobster dinner the next night, complete with a side dish of spinach. This vegetable choice had become a matter of some debate on the ship, and Rinn had been reading the numerous complaints dropped in the ship's suggestion box about an overabundance of spinach. "No more spinach, Ford!" Rinn exclaimed.

Suddenly, a pronounced shudder ran through the ship. The *Roberts* slowed down precipitously. Immediately the phone rang in his cabin. It was the officer of the day, Lieutenant Robert Firehammer, Jr.: "Sir, I think we're coming into a minefield."

The forward lookout was a young boatswain's mate named Bobby Gibson. He had been on the bow watch for about an hour, sitting in the bolted metal chair watching dolphins repeatedly dive before the *Roberts*'s wake, anticipating a beautiful sunset on a warm afternoon with a calm sea and light breeze. At 4:39 p.m., he saw what at first he thought were three dolphins— only these "weren't going back under water." Grabbing his binoculars, he could clearly see spikes sticking out from the black cylindrical objects, the sun glinting off their freshly painted metal skins. He immediately sounded the alarm.[11]

Rinn remained skeptical. The *Roberts*, as every other ship in the Gulf, had had its run-ins with a host of minelike objects: garbage bags, empty oil drums, dead sheep. This, he thought, would be one more piece of Persian Gulf trash. But as it warranted his presence on the bridge and was clearly a higher priority than spinach, he replied, "Okay, I'll be right up."

As Rinn arrived on the bridge, Firehammer explained that the forward lookout had spotted mines. Rinn grabbed some binoculars and took a look for himself, immediately spotting three dark objects floating on the surface, two directly in front of the ship and one only three hundred to four hundred yards off the starboard side of the ship. "Shit!" he exclaimed. "Those are mines!"

Rather than proceed, Rinn thought, perhaps the ship could simply retrace her steps, so to speak, and reverse engines and back out along the ship's wake, which remained clearly visible off to the horizon in the blue Gulf waters. "Having just sailed along that track," Rinn thought, "it should be free of mines." The captain got on the ship's intercom and said, "We've got mines in front of us. We are going to general quarters, but be quiet; I don't want all the noise. Check to see that condition zebra is set and then I want everyone who can be spared up above the main deck." This would ensure that all the doors and hatches below were secure, and if they did hit a mine, he wanted no unnecessary crewmen below deck. He then ordered the *Roberts*'s Lamps helicopter to get airborne immediately to serve as a spotter. With his executive officer, Lieutenant Commander John Eckelberry, looking on from the port bridge wing, Rinn posted lookouts on the four corners of the ship.

The *Roberts* slowly began retracing its path in a straight line, with Captain Rinn on the starboard bridge wing carefully monitoring the proceedings.[12] Ten, then fifteen minutes passed. "So far so good," Rinn thought to himself. But maneuvering a 4,000-ton, 450-foot-long ship backward along a straight line is easier said than done. She veered just slightly off her wake.

Suddenly the air was ripped by the loudest explosion Rinn or anyone else aboard had ever heard. The force of the explosion lifted the entire aft end of the ship out of the water some ten feet, forcing the bow nearly underwater. As the bow jerked back up, it catapulted Bobby Gibson, who did a complete somersault, landing in a sitting position all the way back at the missile launcher. The force of the blast sent Rinn and most of the crew sprawling on the deck, breaking Rinn's foot from the impact.

A mine had detonated on the ship's aft end, just between the 76-mm gun magazine and the torpedo magazine, blowing a twenty-two-foot hole into the port side and immediately sending two thousand tons of water pouring into the *Roberts*.[13] The force of the blast knocked the ship's two gas turbine engines from their mountings and hurled machinery upward with crushing force into the deck above. Two ten-thousand-gallon fuel oil tanks ruptured, sending fuel into one of the engines, which immediately ignited, shooting a huge fireball up through the smokestack, mushrooming some 150 feet in the air. The main engine room flooded immediately, and in minutes so did the space just aft.[14] Within minutes enough water to fill a tennis court some sixteen feet high had poured into the ship. Power began to fail as smoke and fire spread rapidly.[15]

As debris rained down from the explosion, the crewmen immediately responded and ran to their damage-control stations to deal with the crisis. The forward lookout, Bobby Gibson, leaped up and ran to his assigned station. He hooked up the fire hose before he started complaining that his back was hurting him—a natural feeling for someone with three broken vertebrae.

At this point Eckelberry walked up to Rinn and said, "Sir, you remember your last promotion?" "What the hell does that have to do with anything?" Rinn responded, with irritation in his voice. "Well," Eckelberry replied, "it looks like it will be just that!" Rinn could only chuckle at the attempt to maintain levity in the most dire of circumstances.

Heroes abounded on board the *Roberts* that day, including one unlikely seaman named Michael Tilley. Born in Missouri, he'd enlisted in the navy in 1984 and was assigned to the *Samuel B. Roberts* upon her commissioning. Petty Officer Tilley worked hard, but trouble seemed to follow him. Shortly after joining the crew, he was caught for underage drinking using a fake ID card. This led to his first captain's mast, involving a loss of pay and being placed on restriction. When the *Roberts* made a port visit in the Caribbean during her predeployment workup, Tilley and others went out to some of the local bars. Rather than wait in a long line for the bathroom, he decided to relieve himself behind a bush, which unfortunately stood in front of a large bay window of a posh local restaurant. Once again Tilley met Captain Rinn.

But Tilley appealed to Rinn's sense of humor. As Tilley worked down in the engineer spaces during the night shift, he dropped a note in the ship's suggestion box: "I never see the light of day. Can't you put a porthole in engineer spaces so I can see the sunlight?"

Rinn's executive officer and senior enlisted chief petty officer recommended getting rid of Tilley. When he appeared before Rinn for his third captain's mast, Tilley just threw himself at Rinn's mercy. "Sir, please don't throw me out," he pleaded. "The navy's all I got."[16] For a captain not known to tolerate discipline infractions, Rinn decided to let him stay, over the objections of his senior leadership. "After that," Rinn remarked, "Tilley busted his butt and kept his space near the engineering room immaculate."

When Captain Rinn had passed the word for the crew to come above decks and the *Roberts* proceeded to back out of the mine danger area, Tilley had stayed below in his work space. As he said to Rinn later, "You had given me so many breaks. I thought you needed me to stay down there." It was a decision that proved critical.

When the mine exploded, the resulting flooding and fire destroyed three of the *Roberts*'s four diesel engines required to keep power for the ship's pumps. The fourth had a cracked governor, and that knocked it off-line. As the crew fought to save the stricken ship, the lights began to flicker on and off as the power began to fail, finally going black as power ceased throughout the ship. Rinn knew that without power, he would lose his ship.

Trapped below deck, Tilley realized the predicament. He and two other sailors went down to check the diesel generators. One was damaged beyond repair, but the other seemed to be in good shape. With no power, the electric start button was useless. The only alternative was to execute what sailors refer to as a "suicide start." This is a manual start of the engine whereby high-pressure air is released straight into a start engine. Then, with the push of a button, the air is forced into the governor, somewhat akin to jump-starting a car by popping the clutch while the vehicle is rolling. It's earned its nickname because if it does not work, the engine will fly apart, showering the area with metal fragments. Tilley agreed to try the suicide start, and lowered himself into the confined room housing the generator. Complicating his work, the governor turned out to be cracked, forcing Tilley to climb onto the engine and manipulate it with a screwdriver. With a blast of air rushing by his face, the engine came to life. Amazingly, the jury-rigged process worked and the engine settled into its normal rhythm. With power, the crew had a fighting chance.[17] Suddenly, the lights came back on and desperately needed electricity surged throughout the ship. How or why, no one knew, but Rinn was thankful for this miracle.

In the main engine room, Chief Petty Officer Alex Perez had been climbing up a ladder from the keel area when the explosion hit, blowing the ladder off its frame and trapping him beneath deck plates just above the two engines in a rapidly flooding compartment. When a firefighting team arrived, they found him clinging to the grates, with water up to his chest. They immediately passed him a wrench to try to loosen the bolts that held the plates on. They were located underneath the plate itself, but despite his efforts, they would not budge. Finally one of the sailors climbed over some debris and lowered a battle lantern into the water.

"Can you see the light?" he asked Perez. "Yes." "Well, you got to swim to it or you're going to drown." Perez swam some twelve feet to where the battle lantern dangled in the water, and several sailors immediately grabbed him by both his hair and his shirt and pulled him to safety. Perez walked out and then collapsed with serious injuries. He was taken along with the other seriously injured to a makeshift aid station in the helicopter hangar.

At five thirty p.m.—some forty-five minutes after striking the mine—Rinn talked to Less with his second update: "Admiral, the ship is sinking at the rate of one foot every fifteen minutes. I've got five seriously wounded, perhaps more, progressive flooding, and uncontrolled fires." But, he reported, his 76-mm gun was back online and the ship could still fight.[18]

Less asked the tough question: "Considering your situation, what do you think about remaining with the ship? Have you considered abandoning ship?"

"I haven't thought about that at all," Rinn replied over the radio. "I have no desire to leave the ship. We'll stay with the ship and fight it. Right now, I think we can win this thing!" Privately, he thought, "We have no other choice. In a nutshell, we're in trouble." But the thought of his crew leaping into shark-infested waters seemed an even worse option.

"Roger," Less responded. "Do you have anything else to pass?"

"Roger," Rinn came back in a resolute tone. "No higher honor!"[19]

It was an amazing moment few listening in on the radio would forget. Anger mixed with pride as news of Rinn and his actions reached Admiral Trost.

B elow deck, the crew fought to save the ship. The forward bulkhead of the main engine room adjoined another compartment, which began to buckle as water cascaded in, threatening to short out the fire pumps. Sailors worked feverishly to shore up the collapsing bulkhead, using their clothes to plug holes and stop the flooding. Six men, including the cook, a radio operator, and regular deckhands, worked to stave off the flooding, shedding most of their clothing to stuff in the cracks in the aluminum wall. Rinn came down to assess the problem and immediately realized the gravity of the situation. If these men failed, the ship would be lost.

He gathered the men together, now clothed only in their underwear, and said, "Let me tell you—you have got to save this space. We've got two main spaces flooded, and the ship can't afford to lose a third. You have got to save that bulkhead, and if you don't, you're going to die right here."[20]

They all understood. "No problem, sir," Kevin Ford, the cook, answered. Someone then brought out a boom box and popped in a tape of the group Journey, and the men again set to work shoring up the bulkhead with wood support and patching holes with anything they could get their hands on. Rinn went back up topside. In his mind, Rinn had his doubts; he left the space privately believing that he would never see those men alive again.

As darkness fell at six thirty p.m., the first outside help arrived for the stricken frigate. A U.S. Marine CH-46 Sea Knight arrived from the *Trenton* to evacuate the wounded, including four who had to be rushed to Salmaniya Hospital in Bahrain. One, Petty Officer David Burbine, had burns over 70 percent of his body. Additional fire hoses and much-needed water arrived for the parched crewmen (the damage had knocked out the *Roberts*'s ability to make freshwater).[21] The helicopter returned, bringing in equipment and welders to help seal the cracks that had essentially split the ship in half. Her keel had been broken, and only the main deck held the *Samuel B. Roberts* together.[22]

By seven p.m. the fire had been extinguished in the main engineering spaces, but it raged in a space just above. As a precaution, Rinn ordered half the 76-mm ammunition and the missiles in the associated magazine emptied and thrown overboard. Unfortunately, one bright young sailor decided to throw a magnesium flare over the side right into the ammunition bobbing in the water next to the ship. Astounded and very much annoyed, Rinn asked him, "Why did you do that?"

The sailor answered innocently, "I wanted to mark where the ammunition was in the water. I thought you would want to know where it was."

Rinn just shook his head and mumbled, "This is not my day."

Below deck, the men rose to the challenge. Amazingly, through their Herculean efforts plugging holes, they kept the bulkhead shored up, staving off the loss of the space and their own certain deaths.

While the crew managed to stop the flooding, water continued to rise at an alarming rate. Standing on the flight deck, one could literally reach over and touch the water as the *Roberts* continued sinking. With water running over his shoes, Rinn concluded that the massive amount of water being pumped to fight the fire was the cause. The firefighting efforts were actually sinking the ship. "We are doing this to ourselves," he said. "We are sinking ourselves."

Captain Rinn walked up to the bridge and said, "Quartermaster, make an entry into the log. At 19:05, the captain orders the cessation of fighting all fires."[23]

His executive officer, Lieutenant Commander Eckelberry, went ballistic. He pulled Rinn out onto the bridge wing just in time to witness a large burst of flame shoot into the sky from the center of the ship. "Sir, have you gone crazy!"

"No," Rinn replied. "I'm not worried about the fire; it hasn't spread, and with the ammo gone, I don't think we are going to blow up. But I am worried about what is going on at the stern. We are sinking, and if it continues, we won't be able to save the ship."

With that came a reluctant "Aye, aye, sir," and the order was passed to stop putting water on the fire. Within thirty minutes the sinking stopped and the ship stabilized.

With the flooding mitigated, the next step was to put out a stubborn fire that seemed to be sloshing around on top of the firefighting foam somewhere above the engine room. Lieutenant Gordon Van Hook, the chief engineer, and Petty Officer Eduardo Segovia had, at considerable risk, gone below trying to pinpoint the fire's location. Van Hook suggested they remove the gas turbine engine ejection ports—huge metal plates weighing several tons each bolted onto the deck—as the fire seemed to be located underneath. Rinn reluctantly agreed. A team unscrewed the large bolts and, using crowbars, pried off the plate about three feet. Flames immediately shot out some twenty feet high like a torch. In a bit of grisly humor, Van Hook turned to Rinn and said, "Maybe that wasn't such a good idea!"[24]

Rinn cringed and said: "Now you tell me!"

But Van Hook's assessment had been right on. Fire hoses dumped foam into the hole and in about two minutes, with a puff of white smoke, the fire finally went out. The time was eleven fifty p.m., some six hours after the initial mine detonation.

A week or so later, with the *Roberts* laid up at a dry dock at Dubai, Captain Rinn received another note in the crew suggestion box from Mike Tilley: "Captain, with regard to the request for a porthole in the main engineering space, you've exceeded my wildest dreams."[25]

The day of the *Roberts* misfortune dawned unusually cold and blustery in Washington. Temperatures reached only to the high forties, with a strong breeze cutting through the morning commuters, who had been forced to break out their winter coats once again for this distinctly unspringlike day. That morning, the Middle East was not on the agenda for the country's leadership. Reagan was focused on pending talks with Congress regarding an upcoming trade bill and on his recent poll numbers. Others, including Colin Powell, William Crowe, and George Shultz, were immersed in preparation for an upcoming visit by the secretary of state to the Soviet Union to discuss the START arms-control agreement in advance of a summit between the superpowers. Shortly after hearing news of the *Roberts*'s misfortune, Crowe received a call from the Saudi ambassador, Prince Bandar. "I'm sorry to hear about your frigate," Bandar said in a consoling tone. He offered the use of Saudi facilities to repair the *Roberts*. The Saudi ambassador added, "Somebody should visit Farsi."

At the same time, some nine hundred miles south of Washington, General Crist met with his "board of directors" at his headquarters in Tampa to discuss possible retaliation against Iran. General Crist called Less to say that if he found the suspected Iranian ship, "I'll ask permission to sink her." But he was anticipating a call from the chairman or the secretary of defense, and he wanted to have several courses of action ready, from a single target to a large-scale retaliation. "The plan has to be flexible enough to respond to any Iranian escalation." The most obvious choices, once again, were the platforms that sat astride the convoy routes. But Crist wanted something bigger. He had advocated taking the three-square-mile chunk of rock and sand named Abu Musa Island. Strategically situated within the Gulf on the approach to the Strait of Hormuz, it was fast becoming a major hub for Revolutionary Guard Boghammer and small-boat attacks, which threatened to seriously undermine the entire American effort.[26]

But Crowe had his own idea of what they should do. "Get a ship!" he told Crist. Tehran had deliberately tried to sink a U.S. warship and had very nearly succeeded in doing so. The only response, he believed, was to put one of Iran's ships on the bottom of the ocean. To paraphrase a line from the movie *The Untouchables*: It was the Chicago rules. They put one of ours in the hospital; we were going to put one of theirs in the morgue.

Less too wanted to respond aggressively. He had a powerful armada with which to respond. Thirteen naval combatants sat within the Gulf or just outside, including two cruisers and the aircraft carrier USS *Enterprise* with its embarked carrier air wing of some sixty combat aircraft. Recently a force of four hundred marines arrived on the USS *Trenton* to conduct raids and attacks on Iranian islands and platforms. Two full SEAL platoons were on the two mobile sea bases.

Less proposed augmenting his navy air complement with B-52s from Guam or Diego Garcia, which would then fly in toward Bandar Abbas from over eastern Iran and bomb it from "behind," where Iranian air defenses were not arrayed.[27] He raised the idea of using Tomahawk cruise missiles to hit fixed targets such as the Iranian navy headquarters at Bandar Abbas.[28] Less called Rear Admiral Guy Zeller, commander of the carrier battle group in the Gulf of Oman, about possibly striking targets at Bandar Abbas, especially the naval headquarters and port facilities that enabled the Iranian navy to operate in the southern Gulf.[29] Zeller met with carrier wing commander Captain Bob Canepa, an experienced fighter pilot with one previous air wing command under his belt. He and his deputy, Commander Arthur "Bud" Langston, had considerable combat experience—Langston with two Distinguished Flying Crosses and more than 270 combat missions, many over North Vietnam.[30] The carrier crew knew well the targets in Iran. They had conducted twenty-seven exercises targeted at Iranian warships, hitting targets such as Silkworm sites around the Strait of Hormuz and even dropping air-deliverable mines as part of the long-standing CENTCOM contingency plans. Extensive planning had been done on ordnance selection, developing strike packages for over twenty different sets of targets around Bandar Abbas and all the way up to Bushehr.[31]

After receiving Zeller's input, on April 15, Less sent Crist a proposal to use aircraft to mine the entrance to Bandar Abbas Harbor, effectively bottling up the Iranian navy. Less also recommended destroying the naval district headquarters building in Bandar Abbas.[32] Meanwhile, U.S. forces would destroy three platforms—Rakhsh, Sirri, and Sassan—in the central and southern Gulf. The only apparent complicating factor was that Sirri remained an active oil producer, pumping 180,000 barrels per day.[33]

Early the next morning, the chiefs met in the Tank. Crowe explained to the assembled brass that there was a consensus within the administration to retaliate for the damage done to the *Roberts*, but beyond that members of the administration had very different ideas of just what exactly that should entail. With CENTCOM's proposal in hand, Crowe told them, "Crist wants heavy retaliation. Carlucci wants no loss of life on either side and a very restrained retaliation—little more than a couple of platforms." Crowe made known in no uncertain terms his own feelings that he wanted to sink an Iranian ship in response to the mining. One ship in particular raised the chairman's ire: the *Sabalan.* Reading reports over the past months of the tanker war, he grew increasingly irritated at the antics of Captain Manavi. As a sailor, he was appalled at the Iranian's deliberate targeting of crewmen, seeming to delight in killing as many as possible. Here was a ship and a skipper that deserved to be sent speedily to the bottom of the ocean.

Neither Carlucci nor Powell had much enthusiasm for a large attack against Iran, and both advocated moderation in the American military response. "No one had been killed," Powell cautioned during a meeting in the White House Situation Room. "We don't want to expand this conflict." He brought up the possibility of grave environmental damage to the Gulf should one of the Iranian platforms be destroyed and tens of thousands of gallons of oil spilled into the Gulf. Carlucci seemed to agree with his old NSC deputy, and expressed an almost obsessive concern with avoiding casualties, both American and Iranian. He insisted that any U.S. attack needed to be preceded by a warning, allowing enough time for the Iranians to abandon their ship or platform.

Normally cautious during such meetings, Admiral Crowe bucked his usual noncommittal stance and voiced strong objections to the line of reasoning being espoused by his boss and the general turned national security adviser. This time, he argued, they had gone too far, and a mere tit-for-tat response was not enough: "We have to let Tehran know that we are willing to exact a serious price," Crowe said, forcefully arguing to sink a ship. His logic eventually swayed both Powell and Carlucci, and the two agreed on adding a ship to the target list. No one, however, supported an attack on the Iranian mainland. The only condition in which they would attack Iran proper would be if the Iranians launched their Silkworm missiles against U.S. ships, at which time all bets would be off and the secretary of defense would authorize a very strong retaliation.

Afterward, Powell briefed Reagan. After some discussion, the president agreed to the recommendations to sink a ship and attack the Sirri and Sassan platforms, and if need be one other. Should the *Charak* venture out, or whichever ship had laid the mines, Crowe said they wanted to sink that as well, and Reagan agreed. With the decisions made, Reagan flew off that afternoon to Camp David in the hills of western Maryland for a weekend of horseback riding.

The meeting adjourned and Crowe's driver took him back across the river to the Pentagon. Once again, he called Crist in Tampa. "I just got back from the White House, and they want a combat ship." If the *Sabalan* was at sea, Captain Nasty would be sent to the bottom of the Gulf. To drive the point home in a conference call that evening with Crist, and Less, Crowe ended the conversation addressing Less directly: "Sink the *Sabalan*. Put her on the bottom."[34]

Less's force would form three surface action groups (SAGs), each comprising three warships. SAG B would attack the westernmost target, the Sassan platform. Commanded by Captain James Perkins of the navy, it comprised two destroyers plus a four-hundred-man marine raid force embarked upon the amphibious ship *Trenton*.[35] SAG C would attack the Sirri platform to the east of Sassan, commanded by Captain David Chandler in the aged cruiser USS *Wainwright*.[36] Due to her enhanced command and control suite, the *Wainwright* would also serve as the anti–air warfare commander, meaning that any aircraft from the *Enterprise* coming into the Gulf to strike a target had to check in with the ship before being cleared to attack any target inside the Strait of Hormuz. Finally, SAG D, commanded by Captain Don Dyer, comprising two destroyers and a frigate, would operate in the Strait of Hormuz. It was assigned to find and sink the *Sabalan*.[37]

To provide a cover for the impending attack, Less's joint task force and CENTCOM devised a deception plan to fool the Iranians into believing that the buildup of forces in the Gulf was merely part of a forthcoming Earnest Will convoy. U.S. intelligence suspected an Iranian mole within the Kuwaiti oil ministry. The United States relayed to the Kuwaitis a plan to go ahead with a large inbound convoy and to bring some more ships into the Gulf to support it, hoping this word would get back to Tehran to avert suspicion of the true nature of the force buildup. On April 17, three combatants detached from their carrier and entered the Persian Gulf, joining their respective surface action groups. Meanwhile, the *Enterprise* launched standard reconnaissance missions over the Strait of Hormuz and surface and air patrols in the Gulf of Oman, all routine prior to a convoy. Whether the Iranians bought the ruse, however, remained uncertain.[38]

Additionally, both CENTCOM and the State Department worked channels to get Saudi Arabian agreement for AWACS and tankers to air-refuel the navy aircraft over Oman, which had been included in an agreement signed the previous year, although Muscat's approval was not formally received until the operation was already under way.[39]

As U.S. forces positioned themselves, American officials were stunned when Iraq launched a massive offensive to retake the al-Faw Peninsula. Moving their forces at night, the Iraqi buildup had gone relatively unnoticed in CENTCOM. In an amazing coincidence, Iraqi forces attacked Iran on land as the United States attacked at sea.[40] Iraq launched a well-planned attack on the Iranian positions on al-Faw, labeled Ramadan Mubarak or Blessed Ramadan. Iraqi artillery opened with a short but intense barrage of a mix of explosive and chemical munitions. A rapidly dissipating, nonpersistent nerve agent was used on the Iranian frontline troops, while a longer-lasting blistering mustard gas was dropped on Iranian rear echelon forces. An estimated fifteen hundred 122-mm rockets filled with nerve agents fell in rapid succession on the hapless Iranian front lines.

While one brigade conducted an amphibious attack on the southern tip of al-Faw, flanking the Iranian positions, two Republican Guard divisions in chemical protective gear simultaneously struck the Iranian positions, supported by two regular army divisions. The Iraq air force finally proved its worth; it conducted three hundred sorties closely coordinated with the ground forces, bombing Iranian command and control, logistics, and reserve forces.

The Iraqi advance was both rapid and methodical. Once the lead Republican Guard units achieved the breakthrough, a third division passed through their lines and proceeded to seize the remainder of the peninsula. With a liberal use of chemical weapons, including deadly nerve-agent gas, it would take only thirty-six hours to overrun the ill-equipped Iranian defenders, who died by the hundreds, desperately injecting atropine to counter the effects of the nerve agent, leaving the empty injectors scattered around their trenches.[41] Never again would Iran threaten Basra or Saddam Hussein's survival.

The next day, the United States would launch its onslaught in the Persian Gulf in an operation called Praying Mantis.

Eighteen

GOOD-BYE, CAPTAIN NASTY

Reveille sounded shortly after four a.m. on April 18, 1988. Nerves and last-minute planning had kept most of the men up throughout the night. After a traditional breakfast of steak and eggs, the marines grabbed their weapons and gear and made their way down the flight deck, where they cued up to load on board four helicopters. At seven fifty-five a.m. the *Trenton* began broadcasting in English, Farsi, and Arabic: "Gas-oil separation platform Sirri, this is U.S. Navy Warship. You have five minutes to evacuate your platform. Any actions other than evacuation will result in immediate destruction."[1] The marines had arrived in February as part of Crist's desire to take islands and more platforms in case Washington allowed more aggressive actions against Iran. It was a compact force of four hundred men and eight helicopters embarked on one ship, the USS *Trenton*, commanded by Colonel William Rakow. Before arriving in the Persian Gulf, they spent nearly five months training for the mission, including working with the FBI and civilian oil companies in the Gulf of Mexico about how to attack oil platforms without causing an environmental disaster.

The *Trenton* and two other ships of Surface Action Group B, commanded by Captain James Perkins, sat five thousand yards away from the Sassan gas-oil separation platform, one of the larger ones operated by Iran. It comprised seven separate multileveled platforms, each a maze of pipes, ladders, wells, and equipment of every size and variety, all linked by catwalks running fifty feet above the water. Each served a different functional requirement, from crew billeting to pumping to one holding four large tanks containing deadly hydrogen sulfide gas, commonly referred to as sewer gas, an unpleasant natural by-product that is separated from the oil and natural gas as it is extracted.[2] After the brief reprieve from Captain Perkins for the Iranians to evacuate, the USS *Merrill* opened fire, sending seventy-pound shells hurtling toward Sassan, where they burst overhead in large puffs of black smoke raining red-hot metal down on the complex. In response, the defenders of Sassan came to life, and the twin-barrel antiaircraft gun on the southernmost platform returned fire with audible *pop-pop* sounds, sending large high-velocity rounds in the direction of the *Merrill*. All fell into the water well short of the warship. The navy shells pummeled the gun and the platform, and the gun went silent as its crew fled for the safety of the lower levels or, in the case of at least one Iranian, leaped into the water to avoid the deadly cascade.[3]

A Marine radio team monitoring Sassan's communication with Bandar Abbas learned that several Iranian marines—between three and six— remained on board to "interdict" the Americans in a last, desperate suicidal mission. Neither Perkins nor Rakow wanted to take any chances. After another fusillade, four attack helicopters fired antitank missiles into a multi-story structure that served as the workers' quarters. Then, banking hard, they came back raking the facility with 20-mm gunfire, starting a small fire on one of the catwalks. One of the missiles ignited the wood-framed structure, and soon flames engulfed the entire structure, burning furiously, sending black smoke high into the air.

With no more return fire, Rakow sent in the marines, who approached in two helicopters fast and low.[4] As the two attack Cobras peppered the target one last time with fire, the two twin-engine CH-46s popped their noses up slightly and came to a quick hover over their assigned platforms, immediately dropping a rope off their rear ramps, which marines began sliding down.[5] Within thirty seconds, each disgorged its passengers and quickly pulled away.[6] The marines immediately set about clearing their respective platforms, covering each other as they worked their way from top to bottom through a labyrinth of pipes and machinery. Captain Thomas Hastings, a smart, charismatic marine with a background in unconventional warfare, commanded the assault force.[7] Moving gingerly across the smashed and broken catwalks, they searched the remaining platforms. Finding no Iranians, alive or dead, the marines declared Sassan secured shortly after ten a.m. Then one marine climbed up a tall radio tower, the highest point on Sassan. He fastened the Stars and Stripes and, beneath Old Glory, a U.S. Marine Corps flag, to the wild cheers of those looking on below.[8] After a couple of hours, a marine sergeant set two timed fuses on thirteen hundred pounds of explosives placed around the seven platforms and flew back to the *Trenton*. Ten minutes later Sassan erupted in a massive explosion, briefly obscuring the oil facility in a brownish black cloud of smoke and debris.

While the marines stormed Sassan, other navy ships and embarked elite SEALs struck the Sirri oil facility. Much smaller, it comprised just three platforms connected by a long catwalk, with a small natural gas burn-off at one end. U.S. intelligence knew of at least one crew-served twin heavy antiaircraft gun and perhaps ten Revolutionary Guardsmen and twenty civilian workers.[9]

The senior commander for this group, SAG C, was David Chandler, captain of the large cruiser *Wainwright*; a Southerner, he had an easy manner and spoke with a slow drawl.[10] At six a.m., general quarters sounded on the *Wainwright*. The executive officer, Craig Vance, took position on the bridge while Captain Chandler took his seat in the combat information center (CIC). To his left sat Lieutenant Martin Drake, the ship's weapons officer, surrounded by the missile and main gun control consoles.[11] At seven fifty-five, with a haze hanging over the water, a sailor issued the same warnings to the Iranians on Sirri as had been given to Sassan, adding, in sardonic humor, Captain Nasty's famous line: "Have a nice day."[12]

Just before eight fifteen, Captain Chandler gave the order "batteries release." A rapid succession of deafening *boom-boom-boom*s followed. Within a minute, twenty-three shells burst around Sirri, sending the defenders running for cover from the rain of shrapnel.[13] Observers on the *Wainwright* could clearly see uniformed Iranians moving to man an antiaircraft gun. Chandler called off the SEALs and ordered the ships to open fire once again. The American warships opened up, and the first salvo from the *Wainwright* burst directly over the antiaircraft gun, killing two Iranians and wounding several others. One of the *Wainwright*'s next rounds exploded near Sirri's main gas separation tanks, sending a huge fireball mushrooming into the air, with the ensuing conflagration cooking off ammunition as heavy black smoke engulfed the main platform and fires spread down to consume the main platform's lower level.[14] Fatigue-clad soldiers leaped into the water while others were incinerated. As fires raged, setting off secondary explosions, Captain Chandler and senior SEALs agreed not to try to occupy the platform. Instead, the Americans dropped a life raft and medical kit to the Iranians in the water, six of whom managed to climb in. Sirri had been neutralized, but any intelligence had gone up in the flames.[15]

To the east, Captain Donald Dyer's three ships of SAG D hovered near Abu Musa Island. A big man, bald, ever quiet, and supremely self-confident, Dyer used the USS *Jack Williams* as his command ship, eager to put twenty years of training to work in his first combat operation. His mission was to find and sink the *Sabalan*, so Dyer monitored the intelligence traffic on the ship's location. About two a.m. that morning, Captain Nasty, Lieutenant Commander Abdollah Manavi, had radioed back to headquarters in Bandar Abbas that his ship needed to head back to port due to a broken freshwater condenser that prevented the ship from making palatable water. Dyer had his doubts about getting Captain Nasty. "We stirred up a hornet's nest with the *Roberts*, and they are not going to come out," he told his staff.[16]

At precisely eight a.m. Dyer's ships nevertheless headed north toward the Strait of Hormuz in search of her quarry. "General quarters!" sounded throughout the task force. The electronic *bong, bong, bong* sent the sailors scurrying to their battle stations, donning their white balaclavas, glove flash protectors, and olive-drab helmets. On board the command ship *Jack Williams*, crew hoisted a large battle ensign, and the Stars and Stripes snapped straight out in the strong wind. The three ships headed in a column north at nearly thirty knots, generating great white "rooster tails" off their bows as they cut through the calm, flat waters of the Gulf.[17] As Dyer's ships moved northward toward the strait, they detected nearly forty radar contacts ahead of them: fishing boats, dhows, and merchant ships all crowded the narrow strait. He ordered a helicopter aloft to scout ahead. An hour later, Dyer learned that the *Sabalan* was indeed in Bandar Abbas, straddled by two tankers, either, as some speculated, to protect herself from American Harpoon missiles or, more likely, to take on needed freshwater due to her mechanical problems.[18] Either way, as long as Captain Nasty stayed in port, he was safe from U.S. attack. A frustrated Dyer continued moving north in column, up into the traffic separation scheme, where, due to the narrows, ships are required to stay in a tight two-mile-wide lane either to the right or left depending on whether they are entering or leaving the Gulf.[19] The ships slowed and loitered before turning around and heading back south, retracing their steps.

Shortly after ten a.m., U.S. intelligence learned that the Iranian missile boat *Joshan*, about forty nautical miles north of Chandler's SAG C, had been ordered south to assist their forces at Sirri. The French-built missile boat had a crew of around thirty. Commanded by Captain Abbas Mallek, the *Joshan* served as an Iranian squadron flagship at Bushehr and was a near legendary boat in the Iranian navy, having executed some of the first attacks on Iraq at the outset of their war, including an attack on Baghdad's two offshore oil terminals, briefly knocking them out of action. The *Joshan* packed a powerful punch, in the form of the only remaining American-made Harpoon missile in the Iranian inventory. While no one could determine the missile's condition or whether it even functioned, its mere existence made American commanders nervous.

As news of the attack on Sirri reached Captain Amir Yeganeh, commander of the 1st Naval District in Bushehr, he immediately ordered Mallek to head south to reinforce Sirri. Mallek had just completed an escort of an Iranian tanker and was steaming leisurely back to her home port of Bushehr. Mallek, like his American counterparts, operated under a set of standing rules of engagement. In fact, the Iranian navy was even stricter than the United States', specifically prohibiting firing first at a U.S. warship. What exactly Mallek was supposed to do once he confronted U.S. warships at Sirri remained ambiguous, but he ordered his helm hard over, increased speed, and brought his ship on a southerly course toward Sirri and Chandler's three ships.

The *Joshan*'s communication with Bandar Abbas was dutifully reported to the *Wainwright*'s embarked intelligence detachment, whose officer in charge brought the flash message to Chandler in the CIC along with an intelligence packet about the *Joshan*, including a profile of her captain. Half an hour later, Chandler arrayed his three ships for the impending confrontation.[20] He formed his flotilla in a line abreast with the *Wainwright* to the west, the *Bagley* in the center, and the *Simpson* to the east, each separated by three nautical miles—close enough to maintain visual contact with each other but still provide a broad enough electronic triangulation to better fix the *Joshan*'s location. Heading northeast at twenty-five knots, the *Wainwright* began a broad weaving movement, zigzagging from side to side to make it harder to hit with an incoming missile.[21] Chandler ordered both the *Simpson* and the *Wainwright* to put a surface-to-air missile, a Standard Missile 1, or SM-1, up on the missile rails, but set for a surface-to-surface mode. The SM-1 did not pack a large warhead, but was a fast, accurate missile, capable of supersonic speeds. Chandler also sent a helicopter aloft to help locate the *Joshan*.[22] About half an hour later, the helicopter found the missile boat forty miles from the three U.S. warships and closing fast.

He relayed this back to Less, requesting further guidance. Amazingly, he received an unusual order directing him to "warn the *Joshan* away."[23] In an attempt to save Iranian lives, and perhaps unable to comprehend that any small patrol boat would single-handedly try to take on the full might of the U.S. Navy, Less directed Chandler to tell the Iranian patrol boat to keep her distance. He was caught in the strange condition of being between peace and war; this directive meant that he should try every means to warn the *Joshan* away. As Captain Chandler later said, "I would have shot him at thirty-five miles had I not been told to warn him away." The *Wainwright* raised the Iranian boat on the standard commercial frequency, and Captain Chandler grabbed the microphone: "Iranian patrol frigate," he began, giving the boat's location, direction, and speed, "this is United States Navy warship. Do not interfere with my actions. Remain clear or you will be destroyed."[24]

Mallek responded in his heavily accented but adequate English. "I am doing my duty," he said, adding that he was in international waters and "would commit no provocative acts." All the while the two forces closed at fifty miles an hour.[25]

Tension mounted both on board the *Wainwright* and up the chain of command. The *Wainwright*'s weapons officer, Marty Drake, could not understand why they did not fire. "Sir," he cautioned, "he's got the last remaining Harpoon." But Chandler still had it in his mind that he needed to warn her away, and he maintained this even when the *Joshan* locked on with its fire control radar.[26] Listening in over the net back on the *Coronado* and in Tampa, Less and Crist grew increasingly concerned. Less liked the idea of giving the Iranians a warning in hopes of sparing lives, but after repeated warnings he wondered why Chandler had not opened fire. General Crist turned to a senior staff officer sitting next to him and asked apprehensively, "Why doesn't he just blow him out of the water?"

Finally, with only thirteen miles separating the two forces—close enough for the *Joshan*'s captain to see the *Wainwright*'s mast peeking just above the horizon—Chandler issued his fourth and final warning to the *Joshan*: "Stop and abandon ship. I intend to sink you."[27]

With this Mallek decided to act. If the Americans were going to attack him, he would not take the first hit. He launched his one Harpoon missile. The U.S. helicopter pilot looking on shouted into his headset microphone, "I see a cloud of white smoke!"[28]

"Launch chaff!" Lieutenant Drake yelled. It was an unnecessary order, as the petty officer charged with the duty had already pushed the button, sending a plume of aluminum strips into the air. At the same time, the crew initiated electronic countermeasures to jam the *Joshan*'s radar.[29] Chandler immediately ordered his ships to open fire. The *Simpson* sent a missile streaking back, low and arrow-straight toward the *Joshan*, leaving a slight trail of white smoke. Onlookers standing on her bridge wings to watch the missile launch scrambled to get back in the ship as the missile left the rail with a deafening roar, coating some with a powdery residue.[30]

The Iranian Harpoon caught the *Wainwright* off guard. Her fire control radar had been set in surface-to-surface mode and, perhaps spoofed by all the chaff in the air, had difficulty switching to fixing onto the incoming missile. Drake tried to engage the missile with the ship's main self-defense system, the 20-mm antimissile weapon, but it would not engage as it was blocked by the captain's gig. In keeping with standard procedures, the *Wainwright*'s executive officer on the bridge ordered, "Turn to port!" to unmask her full complement of weapons.

To the amazement of everyone, Chandler countermanded the order, keeping the *Wainwright* with her bow essentially pointed straight toward the incoming missile. It was a gutsy call. Chandler surmised that, with his weapons out of position, it was better to keep a narrow profile toward the Harpoon, placing his faith in the ship's chaff and electronic countermeasures to throw off the missile's seeker.[31] The crew braced for impact, many instinctively bending over and putting their heads between their legs, mouths opened and legs crossed—just as they had been taught during training exercises.

With a rumble audible to Drake and the others inside the ship—something akin to a fast-moving train combined with the whoosh of a Fourth of July rocket—the Harpoon missile raced down the starboard side of the cruiser, sending a shudder throughout the ship as the watches topside reported an orange flash fly by the starboard side, barely one hundred feet from the *Wainwright*.[32] Captain Chandler's decision to keep his ship on a narrow profile had likely saved the ship. The U.S. Navy would not make another similar mistake. The *Joshan* received the full might of the American navy.

With the American countermissiles inbound, Mallek ordered the *Joshan* hard to starboard and fired off his own chaff to try to deflect the missile. It may have worked, and the Iranian later reported the first incoming missile missed the *Joshan*, impacting the water some seventy meters behind his ship. His luck would not last. The next missile found its mark, hitting the Iranian boat squarely, exploding in the boat's engine room, leaving the *Joshan* dead in the water. The blast severely injured Mallek, severing one of his legs. The next missile blew away superstructure, tossing Mallek and other crewmen overboard.[33] The *Wainwright* added a missile of her own, and it too slammed into the hapless patrol boat.[34] Following yet one more missile, the U.S. helicopter hovering nearby reported back to the *Wainwright*: "*Joshan* burning. All superstructure from the bridge to the aft end is on fire."[35] In keeping with the orders, the Americans steered clear, leaving it to the Iranian fishermen to rescue the *Joshan*'s survivors. In addition to losing his ship, Mallek later reported fifteen men—half his crew—had been killed in the duel with the Americans.

Well over three hours after the United States had attacked, the Iranian military began to stir, albeit in an uncoordinated and piecemeal manner. Iranian military commanders had little information about either U.S. intentions or locations. The Revolutionary Guard, the air force, and the navy did not cooperate with one another.

About the time the *Joshan* sank beneath the waves, five Iranian small boats stormed out from Abu Musa Island into the neighboring United Arab Emirates' Mubarak oil fields. They fired rocket-propelled grenades at the main production platform, starting a fire but inflicting no casualties. Next, they set their sights on the hundred-thousand-ton Hong Kong–registered tanker *York Marine*, used for oil storage by Dubai, spraying her with machine guns and rocket-propelled grenades, before turning their anger at the seven-hundred-ton American-owned supply boat *Willie Tide* and the small, U.S.-manned Panamanian portable drilling rig *Scan Bay*.[36] Their mission complete, the Iranian Boghammers returned to Abu Musa for their crews to eat, celebrate, and rearm.

Iranian jets took off out of the airfield at Bandar Abbas. The commander of Tactical Fighter Base 9, Colonel A. Zowghi, was outmatched. Only five of his eleven F-4 fighters could fly, and his entire command was distracted by grief, having lost a number of pilots and airmen in an accidental C-130 crash three days earlier. Zowghi held out little hope for his assignment; he knew the capabilities of the U.S. Navy, and if Washington wanted a fight, his pilots would do their duty, but he would be digging more graves.

The Iranian F-4s scrambled from Bandar Abbas and made several attempts to venture out over the Persian Gulf. Immediately detected, U.S. Tomcat fighters were vectored in to engage. The Iranian aircraft immediately turned back toward the Iranian mainland, not wishing to tangle with the U.S. fighters. This cat-and-mouse game repeated itself several times, but each time the Iranian pilots turned away or refused to leave the safety of the Iranian airspace.

Finally, one Iranian pilot decided to take his chances, and peeled off and headed out into the Gulf.[37] Chandler made two attempts to warn it away, but as it continued to close on his ship, Chandler opened fire with a surface-to-air missile. It appeared to miss, so Chandler immediately ordered another fired. No sooner had the second missile left the rail when the F-4 suddenly dropped altitude and its airspeed went from five hundred to two hundred knots as the *Wainwright* detected "bloom" on her radar, a clear indication of a missile detonation.[38] The first missile had in fact found its mark, blowing off part of one wing and peppering the fuselage with shrapnel. The second missile missed, but not by much, as the Iranian pilot later reported seeing the missile's impact in the water next to him. Amazingly, with one engine knocked out and his plane in tatters, the pilot regained control and managed to land his stricken aircraft at the Bandar Abbas airport, a credit to both a skilled pilot and the hearty construction of the American-built Phantom.[39]

In the headquarters of the 1st Naval District at Bandar Abbas, the full magnitude of the American attack finally hit the navy commander, Captain Amir Yeganeh. He decided to sortie the bulk of his fleet, including both the *Sahand* and the *Sabalan*, and possibly a third, older, World War II–era U.S.-built destroyer. Yeganeh directed the *Sahand* to attack the UAE-owned Saleh oil field, a largely automated complex consisting of eight platforms manned by only seven employees, which lay approximately halfway between the Mubarak oil fields where the Boghammers had run amok and the Strait of Hormuz.[40] Unfortunately for Yeganeh, his American opposite learned of his move and immediately passed this information down to Dyer's force and to the *Enterprise* battle group.

As ordered, at twelve thirty the *Sahand* got under way and headed out from Bandar Abbas, past an anchorage of rusting junk ships and nearby islands, and then out into the confined waters of the Strait of Hormuz. The *Sahand*'s commanding officer, Captain Shahrokhfar, displayed an uncharacteristic aggressiveness for his country's naval officers, and with orders to attack the economic interests of Iraq's supporters, his ship was the first to sortie. A U.S. aircraft picked up Shahrokhfar's ship as it passed Larak Island, making twenty-five knots as it headed for the Saleh oil field.[41]

Aboard the *Enterprise*, news of the Iranian fleet's leaving Bandar Abbas was met with relief and jubilation. The crews standing by all day in the ready room had endured several false starts that morning, and frustrated pilots began to lose hope that the Iranians would ever venture out. When they learned that an Iranian ship, likely the *Sahand* but perhaps her sister ship, the *Sabalan*, had been detected rounding Larak Island, Bud Langston got his jet and took off to try to find the Iranian frigate, as the steam catapult of the carrier's flight deck sent his A-6 aloft headed for the Strait of Hormuz.

Tony Less directed Dyer's force to establish a blocking position to protect the Saleh oil field from the impending Iranian onslaught. General quarters sounded and the crew rushed once again to their battle stations. Dyer turned his force around again, heading north, and arranged his three ships in a line abreast, with some five miles separating the warships. He put another helicopter up to help fix the location of the Iranian frigate.

Intelligence about the Iranians' movements came streaming in, allowing Admiral Less to again stay one step ahead to counter their moves. The navy had positioned a Farsi linguist on an EA-6B to eavesdrop on the Iranian Revolutionary Guards, who used rather unsophisticated and unencrypted handheld radios.[42] All this flowed back into an intelligence fusion cell on board the *Coronado*, where officers worked to piece together Iranian intentions. This revealed another impending Iranian Revolutionary Guard small-boat attack at the Mubarak oil field.

Four aircraft from the USS *Enterprise* were inside the Gulf. The flight consisted of two F-14 fighters for top cover and two A-6s—designated Lizard

503 and 507—each manned by two pilots and armed with an array of missiles and bombs. The lead pilot was Lieutenant Commander James Engler. With the call sign "Jingles" reflecting his love of piano playing, he lacked some of Bud Langston's combat experience, but had a deserved reputation as a bright officer and a competent flight lead; he was also one of the air group's more experienced officers. His wingman in Lizard 507 was Lieutenant Paul Webb, call sign "Jack" for his no-nonsense, "just the facts, ma'am" personality. Dyer requested that Engler and Webb come down toward Abu Musa Island to look for Iranian Boghammers who had fired on the UAE oil field.[43]

The rules of engagement, however, did not allow for preemptive action; U.S. forces were allowed to respond only in self-defense. Less requested permission to engage the Iranian boats. In turn the request went to the White House and National Security Adviser Colin Powell. He had already called the president once, having awakened him at five in the morning to report the successful taking of Sirri and Sassan. Otherwise, Reagan remained remarkably disengaged from the process, leaving it up to Powell to monitor the war. The action requested, however, could not be approved by anyone but the president. "Let me check," Powell replied. He picked up another secure phone and called Reagan in the Oval Office. After Powell briefly explained the situation, Reagan responded without hesitating, "Do it." The entire process took ten minutes.[44]

The timing could not have been better for the Americans. Engler could clearly see four white streaks highlighted on the blue water below, headed directly toward a nearby UAE oil platform. Engler dove down at four hundred knots and set his sights on the lead of the four Boghammers, the one closest to the platform. He released two Mk-20 Rockeyes, the clamshell-shaped canisters each holding 247 dart-shaped bomblets designed to detonate on impact.[45] Banking hard, he looked back and could clearly see the Rockeyes descending all around the Boghammer, but none found its mark. The Boghammer jerked to and fro at fifty miles an hour in a desperate bid to throw off the Americans, the Iranian occupants looking up anxiously at the two American planes circling above. Lieutenant Webb tried hitting the small, fast-moving speedboat with a five-hundred-pound laser-guided bomb. A near impossibility: it landed close, but behind the Iranian speedboat, sending up a tower of white water but failing to damage the boat. Now it was Engler's turn again; he came in low and dropped his remaining three Rockeyes. This time at least one of the bomblets found its mark, and as the A-6 pulled away, the Boghammer sank, carrying its occupants down to the bottom of the Persian Gulf.[46]

Meanwhile, Bud Langston's aircraft arrived over the Strait of Hormuz looking for the Iranian frigates headed south out of Bandar Abbas.[47] As he described it, "It was one of those milk-bowl days, where you could see straight down but visibility was obscured looking off in the distance." Looking down, Langston saw the unmistakable white wake of a ship. He relayed back, with "90 percent assurance," that he'd located an Iranian frigate, five nautical miles southwest of Larak Island headed due south at twenty-five knots.[48]

To prevent any mistake of attacking the wrong ship, Langston put the A-6 down in a steep dive and came up behind the frigate. Flying fast just above the wave tops, he blew down the side of the ship. He could clearly see a large number 7 painted near her bow, meaning it was in fact the *Sahand*. As the A-6 streaked by, Langston clearly saw large-caliber tracer fire from the frigate's 35-mm gun and two shoulder-fired missiles launched off the stern in his general direction.

Langston pulled the aircraft up into a steep climb and banked away. He called back to the carrier, "I've got positive ID on them!"

"How do you know?" he was asked.

"Because they fired on me!"

Langston swung out about fifteen miles from the *Sahand* and armed his Harpoon missile. In keeping with Defense Secretary Carlucci's requirement to warn the Iranians before opening fire, over the open international distress frequency Langston broadcast, "Iranian ship that just fired on U.S. Navy A-6, you have five minutes to abandon ship." Whether the Iranians heard him is not known, but Langston received no response and the *Sahand* continued heading south. Langston put his Intruder into a shallow dive and launched his Harpoon antiship missiles. The missile dropped down, skimming just above the water and rapidly covering the distance to the Iranian frigate.

Captain Shahrokhfar never stood a chance. The sleek missile slammed into the starboard side near the bridge, igniting an inferno inside and sending black smoke billowing into the clear blue sky. Then Langston added his five-hundred-pound laser-guided bomb, which hit amidships on the frigate.

Back on the carrier, seven more jets launched all headed toward the *Sahand*. Unfortunately, none of the aircraft bothered to check in with any of the surface ships. Dyer had no idea that *Enterprise* had launched any aircraft. One of the inbound jets was not displaying the proper identification friend or foe, or IFF, which sends a coded message denoting it as a friendly aircraft. As the plane rounded the strait and headed into the Gulf, it looked to Dyer's ships menacingly like an Iranian aircraft out of Bandar Abbas.

The captain of the USS *Joseph Strauss* requested permission to engage. Her skipper was an aggressive officer named Samuel Anderson, a forty-four-year-old mustached Hawaiian who bore a resemblance to the actor Edward James Olmos. Since taking command in June 1986, he'd earned both admiration and head shakes of amazed disbelief from his superiors. Reputedly, on one occasion when the ship pulled into Sydney Harbor on a port visit, it ran over a Greenpeace sailboat. Anderson proudly painted a sailboat with a slash through it on the bridge wing. These and similar actions earned him the nickname "Slamming Sammy" by an admiring crew.[49]

Something about the plane just did not look right to Dyer, and he held Anderson off for the moment. On board the *Wainwright*, Chandler too had his doubts about this inbound aircraft that appeared as a blip on his radar screen; he suspected it might be from the *Enterprise.* After consulting with Dyer, he decided to hold off Slamming Sammy as well. A short time later, the aircraft's IFF was finally detected, and everyone breathed a sigh of relief knowing they had narrowly avoided shooting down one of their own aircraft.[50]

Dyer too decided to finish off the *Sahand*. With his three ships in a line abreast some twenty miles south of the burning Iranian ship, he ordered the *Joseph Strauss* to put a Harpoon of her own into the *Sahand*. The U.S. destroyer slowed to five knots and fell out of formation, as Anderson turned the ship broadside to unmask his weapons and obtain a firing solution. Crewmen on the other two ships and the press pool on the *Jack Williams* poured out onto the upper decks to catch a glimpse of the impending launch. As a CNN camera crew recorded for posterity and the evening news, the *Strauss* sent her missile streaking skyward, momentarily covering the ship in a white cloud of exhaust. It impacted thirty seconds later, blowing a large hole in the *Sahand*'s starboard side.

Two minutes later, the *Enterprise* aircraft began dropping bombs on the hapless Iranian ship. Another missile hit the ship, followed by Langston's adding two thousand-pound bombs, one of which hit the ship squarely.[51] But the punishment inflicted upon the *Sahand* had only just begun. Her captain, wounded with shrapnel and a fractured leg, ordered the crew to abandon ship. They scrambled down into bright orange life rafts floating nearby as over the next fifteen minutes bombs rained down on the *Sahand.* The unguided "dumb" bombs had as many near misses as hits, leading the *Sahand*'s captain later to accuse the U.S. pilots of deliberately targeting the survivors in the life rafts. While these charges were without merit, one can only imagine the terror experienced by captain and crew as they floated helplessly with the water erupting in massive explosions all around.[52]

The *Sahand* was wrecked; it listed heavily to starboard and fires raged from end to end. Pilots detected hot spots along her hull, indicating uncontrolled fires within. Smoke poured out from large gaping holes and fissures in the hull and deck, which had been perforated by the U.S. bombs.[53]

As the aircraft landed back on the carrier, the ground crew and the ship's complement ecstatically cheered their arrival. "It was like the final scene from the movie *Top Gun*," Langston thought.[54]

In the northern Gulf, protecting the two mobile sea bases fell to the USS *Gary*.[55] The *Gary* and the two barges spent most of the day at general quarters, but while fighting raged to the south, the northern Gulf had been quiet thus far. Suddenly she detected a Silkworm missile launch on al-Faw some 120 miles away. Shortly thereafter, her radar detected the inbound missile. The *Gary* went to full speed, turning hard to unmask her weapons, firing off chaff and decoy flares; she began firing her 76-mm gun in the direction of the missile, still showing on the radar screen.[56] Witnesses saw an object pass by the *Gary*, perhaps through the chaff bloom, then impact about one mile astern of the frigate.[57]

In the *Jack Williams*'s darkened CIC, Dyer listened intently to radio reports from the USS *Gary* of the Silkworm missile headed toward the U.S. frigate, mindful of the fact that his own ships remained within the Iranian Silkworm envelope at Qeshm Island. Suddenly his ships detected an incoming Silkworm missile. Simultaneously, a report came in from one of the U.S. aircraft of an incoming missile. Dyer ordered the three ships to fire chaff and head at flank speed south in an attempt to get out of the range of the Iranian missiles. The ships accelerated repeatedly, sending rockets aloft that exploded with the sound of firecrackers in white puffs, seeding the skies with magnetic strips.

A minute later, the lookouts on the deck of the *Jack Williams* suddenly got everyone's attention: "Missile inbound, port quarter!" With the late afternoon sun low on the horizon, casting a golden glow over the calm blue water, the embarked CNN camera panned around to the port side and captured a bright glow low in the near distance. One of the embarked Stinger missile teams briefly locked on to the inbound missile, but could not hold the target. Lookouts topside ducked down, shouting a few expletives as the missile streaked by aft of the ship's stern. Witnesses reported it striking a platform in the distance, clearly visible in the golden light of the setting sun.

At this moment, Dyer's ships detected radar emissions from an Iranian four-engine C-130 twenty-five miles away. Fearing the aircraft might provide targeting data on U.S. ships for the Silkworm sites, Dyer ordered Captain Anderson to engage the Iranian aircraft. Just as the *Jack Williams* dodged its missile, Anderson wheeled his ship about to close the distance with the Iranian C aircraft. The *Joseph Strauss* sent five surface-to-air missiles in quick succession streaking into the sky toward the Iranian airplane. One missile malfunctioned and deviated from its flight path. Anderson ordered it destroyed in flight, filling the blue sky with long white streaks as its pieces rained down on the Gulf waters below. But each thrust by Anderson was parried by a lumbering four-engine aircraft whose skilled pilot managed to keep his aircraft just beyond death's grasp.

"Enough of this bullshit," Dyer said, as he ordered one of the F-14s to close and take care of the problem. The C-130's pilot evidently decided not to push his luck and exited the Gulf, likely flying back over the Iranian mainland.

Having sunk the *Sahand* and dispatched the Boghammers, Engler's and Webb's planes topped off with fuel from an air force tanker over Oman and went looking for some reported Boghammers, which turned out to be only fishing boats. Dyer requested that they head up near Larak Island to look for the *Sabalan*. Looking through the black-and-white images displayed on his aircraft's radar, he and his wingman investigated an endless string of contacts, from junked vessels to fishing dhows that pervaded the Gulf waters southeast of Qeshm Island.

At four thirty p.m., Captain Nasty finally came out to fight. Engler and

Webb immediately closed in to attack.[58] The *Sabalan* saw the approaching American aircraft and fired a surface-to-air missile (likely a shoulder-launched SA-7) at Engler's A-6. It never came close, but Webb radioed back that they had been fired upon. Each A-6 still carried a Harpoon surface-to-surface missile. However, Larak Island silhouetted the *Sabalan*, and Engler feared that the Harpoon might not track with this background clutter, leading to the missile's inadvertently hitting the Iranian mainland. He reluctantly decided against using his Harpoons—a decision he would later lament. This left Engler with a single five-hundred-pound laser-guided bomb with which to dispatch the Iranian frigate.[59]

Engler pushed his yoke forward and put his plane into a steep dive. His bombardier, Lieutenant Mark Herath, released their one laser-guided bomb, which went straight down the *Sabalan*'s smokestack. The bomb exploded deep inside the ship's engineering spaces, giving the appearance of the ship "belching," followed by plumes of heavy black smoke and a large oil slick on the surrounding water. The *Sabalan*'s captain, Abdollah Manavi, radioed over the international radio channel in heavily accented English, his voice near hysterical, "I'm sinking! I'm sinking! Send help!" For a man who had deliberately inflicted so much misery upon defenseless merchant seamen, it seemed fitting.

With the *Sabalan* dead in the water and no other effective ordnance, Engler and Webb reluctantly headed back to the carrier. Back on the *Enterprise*, the crew began spinning up another strike package to finish off the *Sabalan* and to address a new intelligence report of a third Iranian frigate getting under way at Bandar Abbas. The flight deck hurriedly began bringing up more munitions, and two more aircraft were readied. With the main target of Operation Praying Mantis now immobilized, the U.S. commanders itched to finish her off. Less called Zeller and asked how long before they could get aircraft back up to finish off the *Sabalan*. Zeller responded that it would take time, perhaps an hour. As the *Sabalan* had been attacked out of "self-defense," this long delay stretched the intent of the rules of engagement. General Crist picked up the open phone and talked to Crowe. "It would be nice to sink her," he told Crowe, "but it's hard to say it's self-defense at this point."

Secretary of Defense Frank Carlucci had left the Pentagon for a morning swim in the small pool of the dingy labyrinth of the Pentagon gym. A brigadier general came down to grab him, and Carlucci quickly arrived back in command center.

Crowe updated him on the situation. "We've got the *Sabalan* dead in the water and planes circling overhead. What do you recommend?"

Carlucci replied, "Well, what do you think?" Crowe, who had pushed to specifically target the *Sabalan*, responded, "Mr. Secretary, I think we've shed enough blood today." Carlucci, who had always wanted to keep casualties to a minimum, nodded his head. "I agree with you. Tell the planes not to attack."[60] A tug and then the Iranian lighter *Chiroo* took the *Sabalan* under tow back to Bandar Abbas, and removed her many casualties.

Just before sunset, Less picked up the radio and called Rakow over on the *Trenton*, ordering him to dispatch two of his Cobras over to the *Wainwright* to provide Chandler with some helicopter gunships in case the Iranians staged a small-boat attack during the night. Rakow and his air officer Lieutenant Colonel Larry Outlaw strenuously objected. His pilots, he argued, had been flying for nearly twelve hours; most had not slept the night before. They were exhausted. But the order stood, and Outlaw dispatched his executive officer and one of his best pilots, Lieutenant Colonel David Dunkelberger, along with Captains Stephen C. Leslie and Kenneth W. Hill.

The two sleek gray Cobra helicopters arrived over the flight deck of the *Wainwright* well after sunset. Dunkelberger was lowest on fuel so he went in first, landing on the small aft flight deck. As his rotor came to a gradual stop, the crew moved it into the aircraft hangar to make room for his partner, dogging down the Cobra with hooks and metal wire.

The *Wainwright*'s radar suddenly detected a ship directly off the bow some fifteen miles distant. It appeared to be the Iranian logistics ship *Larak*, certainly capable of laying mines or other mischief. Chandler asked if Leslie and Hill would investigate. The Cobra moved swiftly away, the distinctive *whop-whop* sound of its rotors fading away into darkness. Suddenly, a brief voice from one of the pilots broke in over the radio net: "Radar lock on!" Whether it was Iranian or American remains unclear, but Leslie banked his Cobra hard, taking it down low to the water in a sudden maneuver intended to evade an inbound missile. But on night-vision goggles, depth perception flattens; over water, the horizon blurs with the water in a green hue. Even the most experienced Army Special Forces pilot found it challenging, and neither Leslie nor Hill was up to that level of night flying experience. The fast-moving twin-blade Cobra slammed into the ocean, killing both pilots instantly.

As night settled in over the Gulf, Less ordered the three surface action groups south, away from the Iranians into a more defensive stance. Crist called Crowe to provide him an update. Numerous small boats manned by the Revolutionary Guard seemed to be poised to attack the next day. He added, "I think tomorrow may be a tough day."[61]

But the Iranians did not attack. April 18 proved costly to Iran, with nearly sixty Iranians killed and more than one hundred wounded. In the two days following Praying Mantis, tension remained high, but Iran kept its remaining boats safely in harbor and the Revolutionary Guard showed little interest in tangling again with the United States. On April 20, four Iranian boats from Bushehr closed on the two northern mobile sea bases, but they turned away and headed back toward Farsi.

The navy commissioned a team to look at the Silkworm missile firing. While the team suspected that Iran had fired one in the northern Gulf as Iraqi forces were overrunning the battery, the analysts found no evidence of any missile having been fired in the southern Gulf at Dyer's forces. The Silkworm reconstruction team summed it up as radar anomalies, false reporting, and errant missiles from Sammy Anderson's attack on the C-130. When asked about the lack of evidence of Silkworms being fired at his ships, Dyer quipped, "Well, whatever it was, it was big and fast and came from Iran."

Shortly after the fighting, General Crist wrote to the secretary of defense: "The proof of the planning was in the pudding, and we dined rather well on the 18th." Praying Mantis was an unqualified success for the United States. In addition to the material damage done, it greatly reduced the Iranian navy as a major threat to tanker traffic. Attacks by Revolutionary Guards in speedboats ceased for the next month. The combination of the disaster of Praying Mantis and the ease of the Iraqi recapture of al-Faw stunned Tehran. The Revolutionary Guards defending al-Faw had not simply been defeated; they had collapsed. An examination of their positions after the battle revealed that many had fled from the moment of the first Iraqi assault. Hashemi Rafsanjani said afterward that Iran could not stand up to both the United States and Iraq, and time was no longer on the side of Iran. Iran later accused the United

States of ferrying Iraqi troops to al-Faw; though it was untrue, Tehran believed it.[62]

After the fight, Less met with the emir of Bahrain. "The Iranians don't understand anything but power," the royal leader told him. "Next time give it to them one thousand times harder!" As it turned out, Iran would not need another beating. The ayatollah was about to fold.

Nineteen

THE TERRIBLE
CLIMAX

Conspiracy theories abound in the Middle East in part because there frequently *are* so many conspiracies. To leaders sitting in Tehran, the seemingly combined American and Iraqi offensives on al-Faw and in the Persian Gulf reinforced their long-held opinion of collusion between their two enemies. The accurate Iraqi attack and newfound proficiency of Saddam Hussein's army all showed the handiwork of the Great Satan. American spies appeared everywhere. Iran had uncovered the CIA's paramilitary schemes, and a spy in their military had compromised the punitive attack on Saudi Arabia. New American-led efforts had made it increasingly difficult for Iran to purchase weapons and spare parts for its American-made equipment. Heavily in debt and its economy in shambles, Iran had been pushed to the breaking point by the combined force of Iraq and America. The war was nearing a tragic climax, and neither side would emerge unscathed.

The Pentagon's own intelligence organization is housed in a massive gray building-block-shaped structure at Bolling Air Force Base, across the Potomac River from the Pentagon. The Defense Intelligence Agency reports to the secretary of defense and focuses its intelligence collection on foreign military forces, working in tandem with its sometime rival at Langley. In the mid-1980s, Colonel Walter Patrick Lang headed the DIA's Middle East and South Asia section. An Army Special Forces officer who served two tours in Vietnam, Lang transitioned to become a foreign-area officer, studying the Middle East and becoming the first Arabic studies professor at West Point. A skilled intelligence officer, he eventually rose to become the first director of the Defense Human Intelligence Service, which controlled all the Pentagon's own spies. Pat Lang was an opinionated contrarian, especially regarding the Middle East. Acquaintances viewed him as too cynical to be a true Arabist. A frequent critic of Israeli actions, he had no great regard for Iran either, having found the Iranian students he met around the commons while in graduate school at the University of Utah to be pushy and arrogant—a view he held of the Islamic Republic's leadership too.

The Iran-Iraq War consumed much of Lang's time as defense intelligence officer for the Middle East, and he found himself frequently called upon to brief senior officials on the ebb and flow of the war. At the direction of Caspar Weinberger's powerful assistant secretary, Richard Armitage, these briefings included the close confidant of many administrations, Saudi ambassador to Washington Prince Bandar bin Sultan. For his first meeting with Bandar, Lang traveled to the Saudi's sprawling home off Chain Bridge Road along the Potomac, lugging a case of large classified maps of front lines. The two men spread the maps out across the floor of Bandar's study, poring over them for the next three hours and carefully discussing the blue and red symbols that represented the armies of Iraq and Iran.[1]

Bandar liked the presentations and discussions so much that he asked Armitage if Lang could give the same talk to Jordan's King Hussein. Armitage agreed, and Lang quickly found himself on a plane to Amman.

The king arrived a few minutes late. He had been out riding and appeared dressed in jeans, checkered shirt, snakeskin cowboy boots, and a belt with a large silver rodeo buckle in the shape of Texas. They cleared off a large marble coffee table, and Lang laid out satellite photos and maps and provided a detailed talk on the current military situation along the Iran-Iraq front lines.

At the end of his formal presentation, King Hussein asked, "Is there anything the Iraqis could do better—something they could fix?"

"Well, yes, Your Majesty, there is." Pointing down to the map, he fingered two Iraqi units near Basra. "One has its front line on the riverbank and the other is deployed half a kilometer back. They are not tied in together at all. If Iranian patrols discover this gap, they could exploit it and drive right between the two divisions."

"How could they make such a mistake?" asked the king.

"I don't know, but it needs to be corrected right away."

King Hussein turned to the chief of Jordanian intelligence and asked in Arabic, "Can you fly to Baghdad and brief our brothers about this?" Quickly realizing that Lang understood Arabic, a sheepish King Hussein asked if they could take the map and brief the Iraqis on their ill-disposed army.

"Sir, my map is your map," answered Lang. That afternoon a team of Jordanian officers arrived in Baghdad with Lang's map, and by the time Lang arrived back in Washington, the Iraqis had moved their forces to close the vulnerable hole in their front line.

In early 1988, spurred on by Jordan, Kuwait, and Saudi Arabia, the White House renewed its help for Iraq. The DIA focused on helping the Iraqi air force. Lang established a dozen-man cell, replete with satellite imagery interpreters and air force targeting officers, near the director's office at the DIA building at Bolling Air Force Base. Lang's deputy was Major Rick Francona, a Middle East air force specialist fluent in Arabic. Francona became the point man for working with the Iraqis. Lang's team focused on the key operational targets behind the Iranian front lines whose destruction would upend Iran's ability to launch major offensive operations. These targets included division and corps headquarters, supply dumps, railroad bridges, boatyards where the Revolutionary Guard stored landing craft, and troop cantonments. The Iranians had no real appreciation for modern airpower. They carelessly built large supply bases far forward to support their attacks; most sat out in the open, without adequate protection and virtually undefended from air, or even artillery, attacks. Destroying these would scuttle any Iranian offensive before it began. Within days they had put together twenty target packages, each with multiple individual targets, to pass on to Baghdad. Each one consisted of beautiful hand drawings made from the satellite photographs, plus maps with the locations of nearby Iranian antiaircraft weapons.[2]

After receiving approval from both nations' joint chiefs, Lang and Francona flew into Kuwait and drove up to the Iraq border, where the U.S. defense attaché in Baghdad, Colonel David Lemon, and a major in Iraqi intelligence greeted them. The Iraqi major greeted them warmly. "My orders are to take you anywhere you want to go on the way to Baghdad." Lang decided to test his sincerity: "Okay, I want to see the Iranian front lines around Basra."

The group drove straight up to Basra, ending at the riverbank near the Sheraton Hotel. Lang climbed up a nearby berm to get a better view and could clearly see the Iranian trenches in the near distance. After a couple of minutes the Iraqi major came up beside him. "Sir, the Iranians have seen you by now. May I suggest you get back down unless you want to die right here." It was sage advice. As they drove off, their vehicle was straddled by six Iranian artillery shells, exploding uncomfortably close. The Iraqi driver froze in panic, his eyes as wide as saucers and hands clutching the steering wheel in a death grip. Colonel Lemon reached across and grabbed the steering wheel and jammed his foot down on the accelerator. They pulled away just in time to avoid the next six incoming salvos. They arrived at the al-Rashid Hotel in Baghdad, and both Francona and Lang headed straight for the bar.

Lang and Francona met with a collection of Iraqi generals and colonels and briefed their proposed targets. As Lang expected, they were ecstatic. "We were greeted like long-lost brothers, or as the cavalry arrived to save the fort." Lang told them, "We are going to give these intelligence packages to you. We can give you feedback after each strike and tell you whether you destroyed it or need to hit it again, but it's up to you to prosecute these targets—we're not going to do it for you. You need to knock them out by yourself."[3]

The very next day the Iraqi air force began bombing the first of the twenty target sets, with the DIA back in Washington looking at the imagery following each strike to see what effect the Iraqis had achieved. Despite its large, modern air force and the United States giving the grid coordinates of the Iranian targets down to the meter, the Iraqi pilots displayed greater concern for self-preservation than for military effectiveness, often dropping their bombs from too high an altitude or simply not even approaching the target. As Richard Armitage later observed with open disdain, "They weren't very good." But with the DIA providing a steady stream of intelligence updates, the Iraqi pilots went back again and again, bombing the Iranians until they obliterated the bridge or troop cantonment, killing hundreds of soldiers and seriously disrupting Iran's ability to mount any sort of large-scale attack.

Lang and Francona developed a good rapport with the Iraqis, exchanging ideas for new Iranian military nodes to bomb. By the time the war ended, in August 1988, the Iraqi air force had attacked thirty-five different target arrays provided by the United States. America's proxy war against Iran proved a remarkable success.

The defense secretary did not authorize Lang to help the Iraqi army, but when asked his military opinion by an Iraqi general, Lang gave it to him. On numerous visits to Baghdad or down to the front as a guest of one of the Iraqi Republican Guard divisions, over a hot cup of sweet tea, a senior Iraqi general would lay a map of the front line on the table in front of the army colonel. "We are looking at attacking here. What do you think of that?" Lang offered suggestions, such as attacking the Iranians from an exposed flank rather than head-on. The Iraqis invariably took his advice, and while it did not decide the war, the Iraqi Republican Guard battered the Iranian army in a series of tactical victories. Both Lang and Francona became minor celebrities in Iraq, including being invited as guests of honor of Saddam's elite Hammurabi division.

Saddam Hussein was justifiably pleased with the American intelligence support. In payment, the Iraqis provided American intelligence officers access to dissect the latest Soviet tanks and missiles, and Francona was invited on a tour of captured Iranian trenches where the evidence of Iraqi chemical weapons littered the ground in the form of atropine injectors used by desperate Iranians to stave off the horrific effects of nerve gas. The U.S. Army analysts produced a detailed report on the artillery piece, classified with the highly unusual caveat: "Secret/Not Releasable to Foreign Countries except Iraq."[4] In honor of the United States, Saddam Hussein named a new Republican Guard mechanized division the Tawakalna Division, short for *Tawakalna ala Allah*, or "In God We Trust," the motto of the United States. The division would be destroyed by American airpower three years later during Operation Desert Storm.

Saddam increased the pressure on Iran in his normal brutal way. Iraq rained dozens of missiles down on Iranian cities, sending at least two hundred screaming down into Tehran, including eleven in one day. Each missile cut a swath of destruction, killing or wounding scores of civilians. By the end of the war, these attacks had killed or injured twelve thousand civilians. The randomness of the destruction played on the population's fears as the notoriously inaccurate Scud missiles hit schools, apartment buildings, commuters headed home from work. One Iranian living in the United States received a letter telling him that the nice old lady down the block who used to bake cookies was killed when her house took a direct hit from an Iraqi missile. Civilians stayed away from downtown and government buildings. A massive exodus of frightened people fled from the city to the countryside. In April and May 1988 protests began as people started questioning the continuation of the war. This led to clashes between police and rock-throwing students. One of the demonstrations occurred following a Scud hit on a hotel that killed more than one hundred people who had been celebrating a wedding. Protesters started criticizing Khomeini himself, which was unprecedented even after eight years of war.

R obocruiser had arrived. The USS *Vincennes* was the most sophisticated ship in the U.S. Navy. The *Ticonderoga*-class cruiser had been commissioned just three years earlier at a cost of more than $1 billion. With a crew of about four hundred, she bristled with modern weapons, including two 5-inch guns and an array of antiair and antiship missiles. But the *Vincennes's* real worth lay in her radar. Outfitted with the latest Aegis combat system and combined with the ship's radar, weapons, and command suite, the warship could track and engage dozens of surface or air targets simultaneously. As early as September 1987, the Pentagon pushed to station such an advanced cruiser in the Persian Gulf to monitor Iranian activity in the congested Strait of Hormuz. The chief of naval operations, Admiral Carl Trost, had balked at sending such a ship to the Gulf, telling Colin Powell, "Why would you want to put a diamond in a pigsty?"[5] But Weinberger had countered, "What other war do you have going on?" He and his successor, Frank Carlucci, finally ordered the deployment, and USS *Vincennes* arrived in the Gulf a month after the April clash of Operation Praying Mantis.

The commanding officer of the cruiser *Vincennes*, Captain William Rogers, was not afraid to sail into harm's way. When his draft deferment ended in the mid-1960s, he joined the navy, attending officer candidate school in Newport, Rhode Island. He had two great loves: his wife and the navy. Self-confident and aggressive, he wanted to prove the mettle of his ship and its advanced Aegis system in combat. When the outgoing officers of the *Wainwright* offered to brief his crew on the air picture in the Gulf, "Aegis will sort it out" was the dismissive refrain from the *Vincennes's* officers. In keeping with its role to control the surveillance of the Strait of Hormuz, Rogers's ship took station inside the Gulf but well away from the Revolutionary Guard attacks. Disrupting their attacks and escorting the convoys fell to the smaller frigates and destroyers. This role did not sit well with Rogers. He wanted to take a more active role in the aggressive shadowing operations that Admiral Tony Less had initiated. Rogers wrote numerous messages to Less urging him to aggressively use the *Vincennes* against the Iranians—to "go into harm's way for which she was intended," as he said in one message.[6] Commander David Carlson, captain of the USS *Sides*, which was frequently located near the *Vincennes*, commented of the ship's behavior: "My impression was clearly that an atmosphere of restraint was not her long suit."[7] Soon, sailors around the Gulf took to calling the *Vincennes* "Robocruiser" for her similarity to the popular futuristic movie *Robocop*, in which a half man, half machine cleaned up the streets of a crime-plagued city.

On April 29, 1988, President Reagan ordered U.S. forces to broaden the protection of vessels in the Gulf. This marked a major change in the rules of engagement in the Gulf and muddled the clear distinction about belligerency. U.S. warships were now free to take any action necessary to end an Iranian attack in progress, including using deadly force, but they could not retaliate for an attack that had previously occurred. The Iranians had to be caught in the act. Anticipating reporters' questions about whether this constituted an expansion of the mission or a tilt in U.S. neutrality, during a press conference announcing the change Carlucci responded in his prepared statement: "We are not the policemen of the Gulf, nor do we wish to be." The truth was somewhat different.[8]

In June, Iranian military activity increased again in the Gulf. The Iraqis continued to press the land offensive and intensified their air attacks on Iranian oil facilities and shipping in the northern Persian Gulf.[9] As expected, the Iranians retaliated by attacking shipping around the Strait of Hormuz. Even the Iranian air force came back to life. It shifted two or three F-14s from Bushehr to a joint military-civilian airfield at Bandar Abbas.[10] While the F-14 had been designed as a fighter jet, Iran had shown a proclivity to improvise, and Less's intelligence section worried that Iran might have been able to outfit the fighters to drop bombs.[11] On July 2, the USS *Halsey* warned away two potentially hostile Iranian aircraft near the Strait of Hormuz.[12]

On July 2, the USS *Elmer Montgomery* received a distress message from the Danish ship *Karama Maersk*, outbound from Saudi Arabia. In accordance with the new rules laid out by Washington, the *Montgomery* moved to intervene and observed at least three Revolutionary Guard boats shooting at the Danish ship.[13] The U.S. vessel fired several warning shots at the Iranian speedboats, which promptly broke off their attack.

The next morning, several more Revolutionary Guards challenged a Pakistani merchant ship. Less agreed to allow the *Vincennes* helicopter to investigate, but on his own volition Rogers moved his ship nearly fifty miles north of his assigned station to join the *Montgomery*. When the destroyer flotilla commander learned about this, he ordered Rogers to return to his designated station south of Abu Musa Island. But the helicopter remained, shadowing a group of Revolutionary Guard boats loitering off Qeshm Island and well within Iran's territorial waters. With the *Vincennes*'s helicopter buzzing overhead, one of the guard boats fired off about ten rounds in front of the helicopter—a not uncommon way for the Iranians to warn away military or civilian helicopters when they approached too close.

"We are taking fire!" the pilot radioed back to the ship.

With this pretext, Rogers immediately turned his ship about and, along with the *Montgomery*, headed back north at more than thirty knots to where the Iranian boats lay. In doing so, and in violation of the standing rules of avoiding Iran's war exclusion zone, he crossed into Iranian waters, a fact dutifully recorded by a military combat camera team that happened to be on the *Vincennes*'s bridge.[14]

As the two ships closed on the Iranian small boats, two of them turned toward the approaching American warships; the others, according to Rogers, acted erratically and appeared to be maneuvering to attack him. Rogers requested permission to open fire. He described the Iranians as in attack profile and having fired on his helicopter. Neither Less nor his command had any idea that *Vincennes* was in Iranian waters, but approved the request, believing the ship was under attack.

The Iranian Revolutionary Guard commander at Bandar Abbas was a young firebrand named Ali Fadavi. Bright and circumspect, like many guard officers he had been a student transformed by war into a military commander, and he'd moved quickly up through the ranks. An avid supporter of the revolution, he believed the new Iranian fleet of small boats and mining vessels was a more effective strategy to deal with the Americans than the large ships of the regular navy. As the senior Revolutionary Guard commander in Bandar Abbas, Fadavi had orchestrated a number of attacks from there on shipping headed to and from the Gulf Arabs who supported Iraq. Following the drubbing the regular navy had taken in April following the attack on the *Roberts*, Fadavi's mosquito fleet remained the only force capable of continuing the tanker war. The new aggressive American posture complicated his operations, so the guards lurked just across the exclusion zone border and quickly struck passing tankers before the Americans arrived. But now the Americans had taken their cat-and-mouse game to a new level and entered Iranian waters intent on a fight.

As the American ships closed in, one Revolutionary Guard boat moved down to reconnoiter the *Vincennes*; it passed along the side of the large cruiser, its small crew crouched low as the two sides stared at each other. When the other Iranian boats maneuvered to spread out, two boats headed toward the U.S. warships. Rogers characterized this as a hostile act to Less's command, and he received permission to defend his ship from an attack entirely of the American captain's own making.

At 9:43 a.m., the two American ships opened fire. Shells splashed down around the Iranian boats, which maneuvered to and fro firing their machine guns wildly in the direction of the Americans.[15] Nearly one hundred shells were fired, and several hit home. Two Revolutionary Guard speedboats caught fire and sank, while a third was damaged by a near miss.

At 9:47, Iran Air Flight 655 took off from Bandar Abbas destined for Dubai. Mohsen Rezaian held the yoke of the Airbus A300, painted in the blue and white livery of Iran Air. An experienced pilot, he had flown this short, thirty-minute route many times, a regularly scheduled flight every Sunday and Tuesday.[16] On this day, a passenger with a visa problem had delayed the flight, and Iran Air 655 took off twenty-seven minutes late. After being cleared by the tower in Bandar Abbas and being advised to make sure his civilian transponder was set to mode 3, which broadcast his plane as a civilian airliner, Rezaian lifted off and headed southwest on a straight line to Dubai. Rezaian began his steady ascent up to fourteen thousand feet approximately three to four miles off the center line, but well within the twenty-mile-wide air corridor. Neither he nor the air traffic control tower knew that the flight path would take his Airbus directly over the *Vincennes* and the skirmish under way in the Gulf.

The *Vincennes* radar detected the jet taking off from Bandar Abbas. A sailor manning the radar initially received a military aircraft reading (mode 2) on his sensors, likely from an Iranian F-14 sitting on the tarmac at Bandar Abbas. As the Iranian Airbus took off, he mistakenly kept the cursor on the plane at Bandar Abbas and not on the one taking off. This confirmed in his mind that the two were synonymous. Even when the ship's system started tracking the Airbus's civilian transponder, the ship's anti–air warfare coordinator, Lieutenant Commander Scott Lustig, took the initial signal at face value, since Iranian military jets often transmitted using both military and civilian modes. Lustig was an affable man, liked by Rogers and the reporters who came on board with the media pools, but he had never seen the stress of combat, and his reaction to the stress of the ongoing surface fight in the Gulf was noticeable. A petty officer working for Lustig consulted the scheduled flights; he found none for that time and apparently never considered that planes do not always take off as scheduled.[17]

In moving north into Iranian waters, Rogers had placed his ship directly in the flight path of the Iranian jet. Lustig passed along to Captain Rogers, now engaged in a fight of his making, that an F-14 had taken off from Bandar Abbas headed in their direction.

At that moment, a shell casing jammed the forward gun on the *Vincennes*. Rogers ordered the ship's rudder hard over to spin the ship around so his aft gun could be brought to bear on one of Fadavi's boats. The *Vincennes* heeled over. Books, coffee mugs, and papers went flying across the darkened room of the combat center where Rogers sat controlling the fight. In the chaos and tension of their windowless environment, men grappled with their first experience of combat. Not all performed well. With an ongoing surface engagement and a possible Iranian aircraft closing in, an increasingly hysterical Lustig became convinced that the Iranians were conducting a coordinated air-sea attack.

David Carlson on the USS *Sides* watched the same aircraft take off from Bandar Abbas. Stationed to the northeast of the *Vincennes*, he saw the designation of the aircraft as an F-14. When it failed to heed any verbal warnings, Carlson ordered it painted with his missile's radar, a signal any combat jet would immediately recognize as a threat. When the jet did not alter its course or speed but continued its straight, gradual ascent without emitting any characteristic electronic signatures of an F-14, Carlson concluded it had to be a civilian airliner. Unfortunately, he never passed this along to Rogers, falsely concluding that the *Vincennes*'s much more sophisticated systems had to show something his didn't. Carlson would regret his hesitancy.

As the Iranian Airbus continued to close on the *Vincennes* at 360 knots, more warnings were broadcast, but no response came from the aircraft. Rogers asked again about the unidentified plane, using its computer-generated target number, 4474.

"TN 4474 is descending. Speed 450 knots!" said a petty officer monitoring the screen. This proved yet another blunder by the *Vincennes* crew. During an update of the radar picture by the Aegis system, the computer had renamed the Airbus TN 4131, from the radar track of the USS *Sides*. Unknown to Rogers, the old number had been reassigned by the Aegis computer to a U.S. jet descending to an aircraft carrier in the middle of the Gulf of Oman. When Rogers asked the question, the petty officer gave the right answer, but for the wrong plane. A quick look at the radar by anyone in the information center would have immediately shown that the plane in question continued to ascend, had not accelerated, and had emitted no weapons radars. But no one bothered. Groupthink took hold in the darkened command center. It all fit: an F-14 from Bandar Abbas had taken off to support the Revolutionary Guard and was now diving down to attack the *Vincennes*.

On the Airbus, Rezaian was busy talking to the tower at Bandar Abbas and preparing to report passing a waypoint, and he coped with demands of the cockpit during a short flight. Even if his radio *had* been set to monitor the *Vincennes's* warning over the distress frequency, there was no way he could have known that the warnings were intended for him.

At ten miles out, with Lustig panicking, Captain Rogers had to make a decision. The aircraft was not responding to the repeated warnings.[18] Having instigated the fight with the speedboats, Captain Rogers now found himself in a larger engagement than he had bargained for. At approximately 9:54, less than ten minutes after he'd fired his first shells at Fadavi's boats, Rogers reached above his head and turned the key granting permission to fire. A light flashed on the console of the missile operator sitting behind Rogers.

"Do I have a take order on TN 4131?" he asked.

"Yes, take," an officer said.

Two missiles blasted off, leaving a trail of white smoke as they streaked toward the airliner. One hit the Iranian Airbus's wing, the other its tail. The airplane broke apart as the force of the air stripped the clothes from its passengers, sending their nude bodies raining down on the blue waters of the Persian Gulf. All 290 souls on Iran Air 655 perished.

"That was dead-on! A direct hit!" shouted a sailor on the *Vincennes's* bridge looking at the radar. The crew cheered before being told to quiet down by the officer on watch. Soon Dubai airport started inquiring about a plane overdue, and Rogers noted that Iranian helicopters and even Fadavi's small boats had broken off and were headed on a rescue mission over to where the plane had gone down.

With the information being fed by Lustig and his officers, Rogers had made the correct decision to fire. He had been told it was an Iranian military jet closing in on his ship. Yet it had been Rogers's own actions that created the situation whereby he had no choice or time to reevaluate the approaching aircraft. Still, Captain Rogers remained undaunted. In the family gram sent out by his ship after the incident, it said, "Two burning and the rest turning. *Vincennes* operating in its natural environment." It was an oddly boastful statement considering what had just happened.

The navy and the U.S. government closed ranks behind Rogers and the *Vincennes*. To Admiral Crowe, the principle at stake was supporting a captain who'd adhered to the rules of engagement and who had not taken the first hit like the *Stark*. "It was important that captains knew that we would back them up if they used force to defend their ships," he explained in an interview.[19] In a press conference after the incident, Crowe said the *Vincennes* had been in international waters the entire time—a lie the United States clung to until a *Newsweek* article in 1992 exposed the truth. The official investigation by Rear Admiral William Fogarty accurately described the details of what had happened, but the U.S. government had carefully redacted key details that showed the *Vincennes* had violated the standing orders and instigated the fight. The investigation did not recommend disciplinary action against anyone on the *Vincennes* and concluded: "Based on the information used by the CO [commanding officer] in making his decision, the short time frame available to him in which to make his decision, and his personal belief that his ship and the USS *Montgomery* were being threatened, he acted in a prudent manner."[20] In the heat of combat and in the short time available for decisions to be made, mistakes were made, but not with malice. Essentially, the tragedy was a function of the fog of war.

The U.S. Navy handed out medals. Captain Rogers received a Legion of Merit medal, a high-level award usually given to a commander following a successful command, not to one who could be viewed as having been responsible for the death of 290 innocents.[21] Lustig received a comparable medal and went on to get promoted.

Commander Carlson of the *Sides* held a different view of events than that of the official investigation: "The helicopter drew fire because it was a nuisance to the IRGC [Revolutionary Guard] boats. The *Vincennes* saw an opportunity for action, and pressed hard for Commander Middle East Force to give permission to fire. Deescalation went out the window. Equipment failed. The fog [of war] rolled in."[22]

Iran took its grievances to the United Nations Security Council. Iran's foreign minister, Ali Akbar Velayati, gave an impassioned speech in which he produced transcripts of the plane's flight recorder, leaving little doubt the plane had been a civilian airliner. While agreeing to pay restitution to the families of the victims, the U.S. delegation, led by Vice President George Bush, said Iran was the real culprit in the tragedy. Bush launched a vigorous defense before the world body, one of half-truths and obfuscations, including an assertion that the Iran Airbus had been well off the flight path—in truth, it had been well inside the designated air corridor.[23] The United Nations refused to condemn America's actions. Even within the Muslim world, there was little outcry. Only Syria publicly supported Iran. The Islamic Republic had become so isolated that the deaths of 290 civilians failed to move the international community.

On July 12, the Iraqi 4th Corps and Republican Guard attacked along an eighty-mile front and in five hours shattered all remaining opposition in the south. Their advance continued until they'd penetrated some forty miles inside Iran.[24] The intelligence provided by the CIA and DIA were key in Iraq's eventual victory. The resources of American intelligence closed opportunities for the adaptive Revolutionary Guard. "It bolstered the Iraqi military's confidence," Pat Lang said. Whether Saddam Hussein ever really stood in danger of losing remains debatable, but the American intelligence assistance greatly mitigated the chances of any Iranian breakthrough. The DIA's targeting allowed the Iraqi air force to knock out the key pillars underpinning the Iranian military. The steady stream of intelligence and poststrike analysis by Lang's team turned a lackluster Iraqi air force into a killing machine.

Iranian leaders believed the shoot-down of the Iranian Airbus had been intended to send a message to end the war. Serious discussions began about finally ending the war out of fear the United States would take even more drastic action against Iran. A few days after the Iran Air incident, a secret meeting was held between the Ayatollah Khomeini, parliament speaker Rafsanjani, Prime Minister Mousavi, and Revolutionary Guard commander Mohsen Rezai. Rezai stated that the Revolutionary Guard could continue the struggle for years, but the others saw things differently. They convinced Iran's spiritual leader that the choice was "between ending the war now, or continuing it and facing the eventual destruction of the Islamic Republic."[25] They added that the regime was isolated and confronting an American-Iraqi coalition that would stop at nothing to defeat Iran, including using chemical weapons and shooting down helpless civilians. They had no ability to replace their battlefield losses, the economy was in shambles, and the very survival of the regime was at stake. Iraqi missiles rained down on Tehran, creating near panic in the streets. Lacking the same missile capability, Iran was helpless to respond. Large demonstrations had occurred in major cities across the country. Khomeini agreed there was no choice but to accept UN Security Council Resolution 598 and end the war with Iraq. The last official attack against a Kuwait-bound ship occurred on July 15, when two Iranian gunboats attacked the Liberian-registered ship *Sea Victory* with rocket-propelled grenades.[26]

On July 20, in a statement read on Tehran radio, the Ayatollah Khomeini said he personally had made the difficult decision to accept UN Resolution 598 and end the eight-year war with Iraq—a decision he said "was more deadly than taking poison."[27] The ayatollah's statement followed a July 18 letter to the United Nations by Iranian president Seyed Ali Khamenei, in which he said the war against Iraq had now reached "unprecedented dimensions, bringing other countries into the war and even engulfing innocent civilians."[28] Khamenei went on to say that the shooting down of the Iranian Airbus had pushed Iran into accepting a cease-fire, in the interest of sparing Iranian civilians continued suffering at the hands of the revolution's enemies. On August 20, the cease-fire went into effect and the Gulf grew quiet for the first time in nearly eight years.

On a windy day in November 1988, the command of Central Command passed from General George Crist to army General H. Norman Schwarzkopf. The new commander was a large, imposing officer with an explosive temper but a skilled military planner and combat veteran. As the cease-fire held, the United States began to withdraw forces. On September 11, the *Vincennes* left with little fanfare and without replacement. Eight days later, Eager Glacier ended and the CIA aircraft at Dhahran were sent back to the United States.[29] Saudi Arabia briefly considered taking over the two mobile sea bases, but with the war over, it decided not to. On July 11, 1989, the secretary of defense approved standing down the *Hercules*, and it was towed to Bahrain, where sailors removed U.S. equipment and turned it back over to Brown and

Root. CENTCOM wanted to resist the temptation to rapidly draw down American forces, a move that would alarm the Gulf states about the U.S. commitment to the region.[30] On October 2, 1989, President George H. W. Bush signed National Security Directive 26. This presidential directive designated the Persian Gulf as an area vital to U.S. national interests. The directive noted that the United States had achieved an "unprecedented level" of cooperation with the Gulf states since the operation had begun, and that this should be broadened by continued joint military exercises, planning, and arrangements to pre-position U.S. equipment in the area. Immediate termination of Earnest Will could jeopardize this newfound influence. As a result, Bush directed that any change in forces in the Gulf be taken only after an interagency review with input from political, military, and intelligence agencies.

In December, the newly appointed chairman of the Joint Chiefs of Staff, General Colin L. Powell, ordered a review of U.S. force structure and the continuation of the Earnest Will mission. Powell urged caution, concerned about the perception of a decreased American commitment to the Gulf. But the Joint Staff proposed U.S. forces should be withdrawn down to a baseline force of one flagship and five combatants, or one warship over pre–Earnest Will levels. Schwarzkopf strongly disagreed with these numbers. Schwarzkopf pointed out that Kuwait continued to provide the U.S. Navy with $6 million every month in free fuel—a bonus that would end with the convoy mission. The United States, he argued, was actually making a profit by continuing the current arrangements, and it "is probably the only military operation in the world operating at a net profit."[31]

In conversations with Powell, however, Schwarzkopf finally conceded, saying he could live with five combatants. Secretary of Defense Richard B. Cheney accepted Powell's recommendation to reduce forces in the Gulf. The last minesweeper deployed to the Gulf for the convoys finally returned in April 1990, nearly three years after their arduous journey to the Persian Gulf. They would return to the Gulf a mere four months later, when America's former ally Saddam Hussein created another new crisis centered around Kuwait.

The final act of the Reagan Iranian saga turned into one of the biggest disasters in the history of American intelligence. Around 1985, a new director arrived to run Tehfran, Stephen Richter. Slight, with dark hair, the Washington, D.C., native had graduated from the Naval Academy in 1963.

His entry in the school's yearbook, the *Lucky Bag*, noted that "he considers himself one of the best shower singers in the world." After his obligation to the navy, he joined the CIA's clandestine service, although he continued to proudly wear his large, bulbous Annapolis ring.

Richter and his boss, Tom Twetten, agreed that the rationale for BQ Tug was gone. There seemed little reason to maintain two dozen men staged to conduct sabotage and attacks against a Red Army now bogged down in Afghanistan. The operation seemed to continue more for the steady payments from the Defense Department than out of any operational necessity. Richter's predecessor at Tehfran had proposed the idea of converting the Tuggers into standard spies. Although they had been recruited to carry out paramilitary operations and were neither positioned nor trained for espionage, Richter pushed the idea, with Twetten's approval. It raised no alarms up the chain.

"The U.S. government was never serious about it," said retired CIA officer Jack Devine of the Iranian desk. "You have peoples' lives on the line and the government's not really committed to the operation. That gets people killed."

At this point, the decision to merge the BQ Tug assets with the other spies exacerbated the CIA's emerging catastrophe. All communications with the Iranian agents, now including the Tuggers, were handled through a few post office boxes in Frankfurt. The reason was either laziness or incompetence, but it was easier to use an address close to Tehfran rather than a variety of different addresses that would require a case officer to travel to pick up the communiqués. Compounding this error, every return letter written to those American agents in Iran was written by one person, frequently writing the letters in English, not Farsi. On at least one occasion, all the letters were simultaneously mailed to around twenty agents. Each was mailed from Frankfurt, written by the same hand, with the same return addresses in Frankfurt.[32]

Iranian authorities were already wise to the BQ Tug effort when several years earlier, one perspective CIA recruit had reported the contact with American intelligence officers to security officials.

Alerted by the failed recruitment, Iranian agents employed countless workers to painstakingly screen all incoming mail. They could not possibly have overlooked the unusual cluster of letters from Frankfurt, with some likely destined for suspected BQ Tug agents.[33]

In 1987, Stephen Richter became alarmed and immediately ordered Reza

Kahlili and the other agents to use different return addresses in other countries. But the damage had already been done. When combined with the letters to Frankfurt and the merging of the BQ Tug operation, these gross errors handed Iranian intelligence America's entire spy network within the country.

Captain Touradj Riahi's own actions had raised suspicions as well. The man who compromised Iran's attack on Saudia Arabia took an enormous risk in 1987 by traveling with his wife and daughter to visit his son in Honolulu. During that vacation, he apparently met with his CIA handlers for a debriefing. Captain Riahi also made a memorable visit to Pearl Harbor. In a photograph from that day, a smiling Touradj Riahi holds his beloved daughter with blue skies and the stark white USS *Arizona* memorial in the background. The fact that Pearl Harbor also housed the American fleet, then aggressively confronting Captain Riahi's own Iranian navy in a quasi-war for control over the Persian Gulf, did not escape the notice of his minders back in Tehran.

The MOIS had been prepared to take action a year earlier, but delayed in hopes of catching an even bigger prize: a particular American CIA officer operating in nonofficial cover, or NOC. In late 1987, Iran intelligence read a letter communiqué from Tehfran to one of the Iranian agents saying there would be a "new communication system for Iran." Although the message was ambiguous, the Iranians concluded it referenced an undercover CIA operative, and they hoped to capture this very valuable American spy. Iranian counterintelligence officers believed the NOC was due to arrive under the guise of a foreign businessman. Without any public ties to the U.S. government, many NOCs spend their entire CIA careers pretending to be private citizens and never even visit CIA headquarters. It is hazardous duty. Without embassy cover, NOCs lack diplomatic immunity and, if caught, could face a death sentence.[34] The NOC, however, never arrived. Whether the Iranian conclusion was correct is not clear, but after the first BQ Tug arrests, Langley may have concluded the risk was too great to travel to Tehran.[35]

In 1988, an Iranian hit team targeted the CIA officers doing the recruitment in Istanbul. To flush them out, Philip Giraldi, outfitted with a bulletproof vest, went out the front door of the consulate, past the usual crowd of Iranians clustered around its entrance waiting for visas, and walked down the street, trailed by three Turkish surveillance teams. Two Iranian men emerged out of the crowd and followed him. After walking about a block, the Turks descended on them with guns drawn. They threw the two Iranians to the ground, removing a concealed pistol from one of the MOIS agents.[36]

In September 1988, the Iranian intelligence service struck. Former BQ Tug agents were the easiest to track down. Many were simple peasants, and a visit to a dark holding cell with menacing interrogators proved sufficient to get them to talk. When one talked, the MOIS would quickly roll up his entire team. When coercion failed, they would be pinned to a cot and beaten on the soles of their feet with a wire rod. Months of solitary confinement in dark cells, the monotony broken only by beatings, waterboarding, and electric shocks, loosened the tongues of those who continued to withhold information.[37]

In February 1989, Captain Riahi's eight-year-old daughter bounded home from school. She put in her favorite video, *Cinderella*, only to discover that the VCR was broken, prompting an emotional outburst when her mother arrived home from shopping. Just then, four men arrived at the front door. Serious and unsmiling, they demanded entry and began methodically searching the house while the captain's wife and daughter waited nervously in the living room.

A couple of hours later, Captain Riahi arrived home, tired after an hour-long bus commute from his office. Two security officers greeted him and coolly ordered him to accompany them. As his wife began to cry, he gave his daughter a kiss and said a quick good-bye before being placed in the backseat of an unmarked car and whisked away.

Iran finally went public about the spy network on April 21, 1989, when Hashemi Rafsanjani, the speaker of the Iranian parliament and future president, announced at Friday prayers that "several dens of espionage" had been uncovered. He was repeatedly interrupted by a large crowd chanting, "American spies must be executed!"

"God's decree will be carried out!" Rafsanjani responded.[38]

On April 26, the information minister held a press conference and released the names of sixteen men in custody, including Captain Riahi and air force colonel Masoud Babaii. Noting that the CIA recruited its "hirelings" mainly from those seeking visas to America, he described this tactic as Satan-like, exploiting the weak elements in a man to force a betrayal.[39] Over the next few months, Iranian news reported forty men arrested. A few were paraded before the cameras in daily news conferences to confess their crimes. When questioned about the allegations, the White House press secretary denied any knowledge.

Iran's public pronouncement was the first Langley knew of the spy network's compromise. Philip Giraldi, who had just left Iran operations to work counterterrorism, recalled first reading of it in the *International Herald Tribune*. He stormed into Richter's office demanding to know what had happened, but Richter never answered him. Then widows, or soon to be widows, of the spies suddenly began arriving at the American consulate in Istanbul and the embassy in Ankara pleading for help. The new deputy chief at Tehran, Gary Schroen (who would be instrumental in the CIA's paramilitary operations in Afghanistan after 9/11), and Reuel Gerecht scrambled to obtain American visas for the women and their children. Captain Riahi's wife and daughter were flown out of Tehran to Istanbul, and then on to Vienna and the United States, where the CIA settled them in the United States.

A month later, in May 1989, Iranian state television began a four-part miniseries about the CIA spy ring entitled *Top Secret*. Part documentary and part propaganda, the docudrama included tantalizing details about the long history of the CIA's meddling in the country and of America's desire to oust the Islamic regime. Attracting large audiences, the show included interviews with the men arrested, describing their training and even the use of invisible ink to communicate with their American handlers. One episode included confessions of a British businessman, Roger Cooper, who had been arrested in 1985 and accused of spying for the British government. He had been given the unusual sentence of death plus ten years.[40] The series repeatedly warned Iranians not to fall for the CIA's lies: "The only promises of the spies and the intelligence organizations to their agents and contacts which are realized are betrayal of self, treachery against the homeland, regret, and sorrow," cautioned the announcer.[41]

For Touradj Riahi's wife and family, this was not a TV show but a very real unfolding tragedy. His captors kept Captain Riahi in an isolated cell in the notorious Evin Prison in Tehran. Once a small facility managed by Savak under the shah, the prison now swelled with several thousand political prisoners—leftists, separatists, and pro-Iraqis. Many would be killed in an orgy of executions ordered by Ayatollah Khomeini that July. Using sleep deprivation and occasional fists to the face and body, Riahi's interrogators repeatedly questioned him to learn what information he had passed on to the Americans and to get him to confess his crimes publicly.

He proved a tough man to break. While admitting to having passed war plans to the Americans, he refused to admit to treason. He was tried before a military special war tribunal, a proceeding videotaped by the authorities. Standing in the docket, he repeatedly denied being unfaithful to his country. "I remain loyal to Iran," he said, implying that the current Islamist government was not. Not surprisingly, the testimony never aired on Iranian television.

The guards allowed his family to visit a few times. On one occasion, his wife and other relatives hoped to get the authorities to release him for just one day, on March 21, the Iranian new year. Arriving at the prison, the captain's wife prompted her young daughter to ask that her father be freed for the day. The request was denied, but they were granted a brief visit in a basement room.

Captain Riahi looked thin and haggard. He did not discuss his plight, but complained that he spent most of his days in a dark, windowless cell. Occasionally, a guard would take pity on him and allowed some light to read either the Koran or a religious and social treatise written by Ayatollah Khomeini, both common items in Iranian jails.

In early November 1990, Iran prepared to mark the tenth anniversary of the November 4 seizure of the U.S. embassy—now a holiday called the National Day of Confronting Global Arrogance. The government planned a massive demonstration in front of the former American embassy. Inside the old chancellery building, the intelligence ministry opened an exhibit displaying sixty-eight volumes of classified American documents, painstakingly pieced together after having been shredded by the embassy staff before the takeover, as well as pictures and models of the helicopters used in the abortive American rescue raid, and pieces from the Iran Air plane shot down by the U.S. cruiser *Vincennes* the year before. Loudspeakers serenaded visitors with the confessions of the recently captured American spies.

On the evening before the official anniversary, Iranian television began another series with more of the spies on display. They included the air force colonel who had agreed to work for the CIA for two years in return for asylum. Appearing weary and gaunt, he began sobbing as he warned Iranians "not to become entrapped in the spider's web of espionage services, because their golden dreams will become a hellish nightmare." That evening, Captain Riahi was allowed to briefly speak to his wife, explaining that he was being moved to another cell. This was an ominous indication for those in Iranian jails.

The next morning, hundreds of thousands of Iranians gathered in front of the old American embassy celebrating the takeover a decade earlier, carrying signs of the Ayatollah Khomeini while the streets echoed with the roar of "Death to America!" Prominent government officials spoke, lashing out against the Islamic Republic's enemies.[42]

Riahi's jailors had allowed him one last call to his family. He spoke with a younger cousin, but neither his wife nor his daughter was at home. It would be the last anyone heard from Touradj Riahi.[43]

The Iranian government used the anniversary of the seizure of the embassy to send a clear message to Washington about the fate of its spies. Riahi and three other naval officers were escorted to the gallows at Evin Prison. The executioners first placed the noose around Commodore Kanoush Hakimi, who had revealed Iran's sensitive arms purchases from China. Riahi was next to drop through the trapdoor, then, finally, two other junior officers who had also spied for the CIA.[44] The next day, the captain's family learned his fate when Tehran television announced the executions of four traitors.[45]

Over the next year, Iranian authorities executed more than fifty men, including some convicted of spying for Iraq and Israel.[46] A number of the BQ Tug agents who had more menial roles in the CIA paramilitary scheme were given minimal prison terms or allowed to serve their sentences in internal exile—they were not imprisoned but forbidden to leave their hometowns without permission.[47]

The CIA never held any officials accountable for the deaths of twenty agents in one of the worst blunders in the agency's history. Despite procedural weaknesses at Tehran detailed in the CIA's internal investigation, the senior leadership at Langley decided not to reprimand anyone or so much as derail a single career. Langley viewed BQ Tug as a sideshow. The investigation, as one CIA case officer remembered, had little consequence. "One moment you could find copies of this counterintelligence report and the next moment they were all gone," he said.

Giraldi never got over the debacle and the needless deaths of the men he'd recruited. "We eat people alive, spit them out, and then don't give a shit about them afterwards," he recalled bitterly. "At the end of the day, what did we accomplish? Twenty guys got killed, and some people got promoted." He decided to put in his retirement papers.

As the decade ended, Cold War concerns gave way to new challenges. The CIA found itself in much the same position as ten years earlier, with an intelligence network in tatters and with William Casey's ambition of bringing Iran back into the Western fold frustrated. Looking forward, it would be local potentates—rather than the Red Army—that threatened American interests. Saddam Hussein's Pyrrhic victory left Iraq devastated but with the largest Arab army. Iran was bloodied but unbowed. After Iran-Contra, Washington politicians remained skittish about trying to thaw relations with Tehran; however, the Islamic Republic remained a natural balance to Iraq. There remained one important outstanding issue: the American hostages in Lebanon. But with a new, pragmatic Iranian president, there was hope that the two nations could leave their animosity back in the 1980s.

Twenty

GOODWILL BEGETS GOODWILL

O n Sunday, February 4, 1990, President George H. W. Bush returned from a weekend at the presidential retreat at Camp David
in the mountains of western Maryland. After changing into more
formal clothes, he attended a concert in the White House and then retired for
the evening. Around nine forty p.m., a call came through the White House
switchboard. On the other end reportedly was an aide to Iranian president
Hashemi Rafsanjani calling Bush from Tehran. Bush's close friend and
national security adviser General Brent Scowcroft took the call. The man on
the other end sounded believable, so Scowcroft agreed to another call the next
evening between the two presidents.

For the past year, President Bush had been working to get the remaining
hostages in Lebanon released. Bush wanted a rapprochement with Iran. He
believed it served as a buffer against Iraq and the Soviet Union, and the hostages remained the major stumbling block between the two countries.[1] In his
inaugural address the previous January, he extended a major olive branch to
the Iranians to try to get them released. "Assistance can be shown here, and
will be long remembered. Goodwill begets goodwill. Good faith can be a
spiral that endlessly moves on." He continued on, hoping to modify Iranian
worries about working with America. "Great nations like great men must

keep their word. When America says something, America means it, whether a treaty or an agreement or a vow made on marble steps."

A lot had changed in Iran over the past couple of years. The Iran-Iraq War had ended. Ayatollah Khomeini had passed on to the house not made with hands, replaced by Ayatollah Seyed Ali Khamenei, a cleric of no particular renown. Rafsanjani now served as the new president. A pragmatist who had supported the arms-for-hostages exchange earlier, Rafsanjani ran construction companies in Iran and had a good head for business. Quick and clever, he appreciated mammon as much as the imam. He understood the importance of the private sector and wanted to limit the size of the government in the economy. Rafsanjani had an open mind regarding relations with other countries, including the United States. He worried that the constant mantra of "Down with America" was both naive and counterproductive. "What does this mean?" he once said mockingly to an adviser. He worried that the Americans would misunderstand the meaning—it meant a rejection of American policies, not the nation, its culture, or its people.[2] Rafsanjani sent out feelers to the State Department indicating the Iranian president wanted better relations with the West and to get past the animosity of the last decade.

The next evening, Bush picked up the phone in his second-floor office. While long-serving policy officials Richard Haass and Sandy Charles listened in from the Situation Room, through a State Department interpreter the American president spoke for twenty-nine minutes with a man in Tehran claiming to be Rafsanjani.[3] The caller said Iran wanted to improve relations and was prepared to release the American hostages in Lebanon. He supported the effort by United Nations secretary general Javier Pérez de Cuéllar to achieve that end. Before hanging up, he added that he, Rafsanjani, wanted to make a public announcement about the release so the world would know that Iran had taken the first step to improve relations.

Unfortunately, President Bush had not spoken to President Rafsanjani. After hanging up, Bush spoke with a CIA officer in Falls Church about the origin of the call, and after a flurry of talks with his advisers and with de Cuéllar in New York, Bush learned he had been duped. The caller had been an Iranian opposed to any rapprochement with the United States. He apparently intended to publicly embarrass Rafsanjani.

The incident served as a disturbing indicator of the state of relations between the United States and Iran. Not only were the two sides not talking, but they struggled to even figure out how. Both sides preferred to talk through intermediaries, which provided a level of deniability. Despite the rhetoric, neither country wanted to be the first to publicly extend the hand. The United States remained ignorant of Iran, so much so that the president of the United States could not even differentiate between an official call from a head of state and a prank caller.

The American hostages held by Hezbollah in Lebanon colored the new president's thinking regarding Iran. The arms-for-hostages fiasco continued to reverberate. The issue had been a major political club used by the Democrats during the 1988 election. It culminated in a testy exchange in January 1988 when CBS News anchor Dan Rather badgered Bush about his support for Reagan's arms transfers to Iran. "You made us hypocrites before the world," Rather said.

Bush responded vigorously, citing the details of the capture and torture of the CIA station chief, William Buckley. "If I erred, it was on the side of getting those hostages out!"

Hostage taking remained a lucrative practice in Lebanon. In 1987, ABC reporter Charles Glass had arrived to do research for a book. An Iranian Revolutionary Guard officer who'd learned of his planned visit to Sidon drove to a Hezbollah agent's house in the southern suburbs of Beirut. The Lebanese moved quickly and snatched Glass near the airport. For once, the CIA had good information, including the license plate of one of the cars to be used, but simply could not get to Glass in time.[4] That same year, Marine Colonel Richard Higgins, a member of the UN security mission in Lebanon, was captured while driving along the coast to meet with a Shia Amal leader. His captor, Mustafa Dirani, headed a small group called Believers' Resistance, which sympathized with Hezbollah.

The following year, Imad Mugniyah orchestrated another effort to get the seventeen Dawa Party members released from Kuwait. This time, Iran showed less enthusiasm for its ally's actions. On April 5, eight hijackers seized Kuwait Airways Flight 422 as it neared Kuwait City on a flight from Bangkok. They took control of the Boeing 747 and forced the plane down in Iran. An embarrassed Iranian government ordered them to leave and threatened to send in commandos to storm the plane. The jet then headed for Beirut, where Iranian pressure resulted in the denial of landing rights. So the aircraft set down in Cyprus. When Kuwait refused to release the captives, the hijackers executed two passengers. When the jumbo jet took off for its next destination, Algeria, the hijackers told the tower that they had "donned death shrouds and renamed the jetliner the 'Plane of the Great Martyrs.'"

On takeoff from Cyprus, when the air traffic controller referred to the jet as "Kuwait 422," a hijacker snapped back, "No! Plane of Martyrs!" The controller responded, "Sorry, Plane of Martyrs."[5] After sixteen days, with the assistance of the Iranian government, the hijackers surrendered.

While both Rafsanjani and Bush wanted to end the hostage quandary, without diplomatic relations the two sides were forced like schoolchildren to pass messages back and forth via intermediaries. The State Department's assistant secretary for Near Eastern affairs, John Kelly, regularly received messages from Tehran, or those reporting to speak for its government. The Iranians wanted to meet with an American emissary anywhere in Europe, as long as the meeting remained a secret. His standard reply to these feelers: "We would be happy to, but not in the shadows."[6] Iran consistently refused. Having been burned by the Iranian arms sales, Rafsanjani wanted to retain plausible deniability for domestic reasons. He did not want to be viewed as the one needing to talk with the Great Satan.

Washington continued to reach out to Iran. One of the Iranian president's close aides was an American-educated engineer who served as the editor for the *Tehran Times*, Hossein Mousavian. As he heard visiting dignitaries reciting a similar message from the Americans, he started keeping a log of each communication. He noted over forty messages to the Iranian president via foreign ministers and heads of state, all asking for Iran's assistance in releasing those held in Lebanon. In every case they came with the same refrain: it's time the two countries move forward; "goodwill leads to goodwill."[7]

The Bush administration approached the United Nations to broker the release of the hostages in Lebanon. President Bush called Secretary General de Cuéllar and asked if he could meet with National Security Adviser Brent Scowcroft. De Cuéllar agreed, and the two men met at a home in the Hamptons on Long Island. Scowcroft passed along a message from Bush: the president was prepared to take a series of reciprocal actions to ease tensions and free the hostages. The basis of this was the president's inaugural address and the notion of goodwill meeting with goodwill. Scowcroft asked de Cuéllar to deliver the message directly to Rafsanjani.

The UN secretary general tasked a trusted aide to work the discussions between the Americans and the Iranians. Italian diplomat Giandomenico Picco served as a special envoy to de Cuéllar and was no stranger in Tehran. He'd first arrived there in 1983, and over the years the tall, sophisticated public servant had earned the respect of Iranian leaders, especially Rafsanjani. He played a key role in negotiating the final agreement on the cease-fire that finally ended the slaughter of the Iran-Iraq War. He had also had some experience in working the hostage issue, as two UN employees were among those held in Beirut.

On August 17, 1989, Rafsanjani met with the Pakistani foreign minister. In response to the American mantra, Rafsanjani agreed to work to obtain the release of the hostages in exchange for some demonstration by the United States that it accepted the Islamic Republic. Rafsanjani was keen to put the war behind him. Iran needed Western investment to rebuild its shattered economy. The Lebanese hostages had outlived their utility.

On August 25, Picco arrived in Tehran for his first meeting with President Rafsanjani. Javad Zarif, a young Iranian diplomat destined to play a larger role in talks with the Americans, drove him to the presidential palace. Picco met the Iranian president in his office, a room Picco described as one of "overpowering whiteness, accentuated by the afternoon light flooding the room through huge windows."[8] As Zarif translated, the UN envoy described the sincerity of President Bush's offer of "goodwill begets goodwill." However, in light of Iran-Contra, Bush could participate only in a tit-for-tat exchange. If Rafsanjani secured the hostages' release, the American president would reciprocate in kind.

Rafsanjani flashed with anger. He wanted action, not words, from the Americans. Regarding those holding the hostages, the Iranian president replied, "These people are not easy to find. They do not have an address." Israel had just seized a prominent sheik in Lebanon, and Hezbollah wanted him back before releasing any Westerners.[9] It would be a long and difficult task, Picco thought.

In November 1989, President Bush took a few steps to demonstrate his sincerity. The president disposed of an escrow account held by the Bank of England from the 1981 Algiers Accords to settle claims stemming from the hostage crisis. This returned $567 million to Iran. President Bush allowed an Iranian interests section in the Pakistani embassy in Washington. While the U.S. government limited its size to a staff of only forty-five and its function to travel services, it marked a major milestone. Thousands of Iranians living in the United States could now apply for a visa to travel back to the homeland. Last, following the 1988 bombing of Pan Am Flight 103 over Scotland, Bush refused to act against Iran when early press reports and members of Congress such as Benjamin Gilman raised suspicions of Iranian culpability. Evidence would later point to Moammar Gaddafi as the culprit.[10]

However, Bush continued intelligence sharing with Iraq. As emerged during the 1991 confirmation hearing for Robert Gates as CIA director, the president had authorized limited intelligence passed to Iraq relating to Iranian military dispositions. Just three months before the Iraqi invasion of Kuwait, with CENTCOM commander General Schwarzkopf already planning for a possible conflict with Iraq, the CIA gave Iraq information out of concern that ending the intelligence exchange might close off access to the Iraqi military.[11] Iran knew of this continued intelligence sharing through a double agent in the Iraqi intelligence service. It only fueled suspicion among hard-liners in Iran over America's true intentions with respect to the Islamic Republic.

Iran soon became a sideshow for the United States in the Persian Gulf. At two a.m. on August 2, 1990, Captain (later vice admiral) Kevin Cosgriff's frigate had just dropped off a Kuwaiti tanker as part of the Earnest Will convoy missions that continued out of inertia more than necessity. Thin, intelligent, and businesslike, he had several deployments in the Gulf under his belt. But that night would be like no other. His radar and radio lit up with images of war. Waves of Iraqi aircraft bombed Kuwait. Helicopters landed Iraqi special forces along the coast, while columns of Iraqi tanks poured into the tiny emirate. As the Kuwaiti air force and navy scrambled to get out of the way, Cosgriff radioed back to the Middle East Force asking for instructions. "Wait out," came the reply.

"That was not what I wanted to hear when a war is breaking out all around me," Cosgriff said. The American ship made its way south away from Kuwait, with a trail of tankers following in Cosgriff's wake looking for protection. It would be the last convoy operation of Earnest Will.[12] Operations Desert Shield and, soon thereafter, Desert Storm were about to begin.

During the eight-month crisis, Iran and the United States maintained an uneasy understanding. Iran viewed this new Middle East crisis as both an opportunity and a challenge. Rafsanjani rejected a dubious offer by Saddam

Hussein to support Iraq in exchange for major concessions after the war. Instead, he supported the UN sanctions against Iraq. Leaders in Tehran united behind removing Saddam Hussein, but with some unease as the prospect of a prolonged American military presence would threaten their long-term goal of regional dominance.

The United States simply wanted Iran to accept the United Nations resolutions and stay out of the way. No one in the Bush administration expected the war would lead to a breakthrough. "Our policy that normal relations can be reestablished only after Iran helps obtain the release of American hostages without bargaining or blackmail remains valid," stated a Deputies Committee meeting paper penned by Robert Gates.[13]

During the Gulf War, the United States maintained regular, indirect contact with Iran through Swiss intermediaries. The U.S. government passed as many as three démarches a week to Iran during the 1990–1991 Gulf crisis. This included information about U.S. deployments to Saudi Arabia and the buildup of naval forces in the Gulf to avoid raising alarm in Tehran about American intentions. The United States asked Iran not to take action should American aircraft stray into Iran's airspace. While Iran did not reply, it tacitly agreed: in the few instances when a coalition jet strayed into Iranian airspace, the Iranian military took no action. Just before the hundred-hour ground war began, Iran relayed through the Swiss that an American helicopter had attacked several Iranian patrol boats, chasing them up into the mouth of a river. But Iran's protest was muted. It did little more than demand "prevention of such provocative acts" while reassuring the United States of Iran's neutrality.[14] The report proved unfounded.

On several occasions, the State Department received information that an American citizen trapped in Kuwait planned to flee to Iran. The United States relayed this to Tehran, and the Islamic Republic cooperated in safeguarding the American's passage to freedom.[15]

The war did, however, help Picco and the efforts to free the hostages. The Iraqi invasion set free the "Dawa Seventeen" in Kuwait and all had quickly made their way into Iran. Held since their bombing rampage in 1983, their release had been a major fixation by Hezbollah in Lebanon. In April 1991, Picco pressed again to secure the hostages. He traveled to Damascus, where he met with the Iranian ambassador and Syrian military officers before flying on to Beirut. Thirty minutes after arriving, he received a call from the Iranian embassy confirming that he had a meeting with Sheik Fadlallah at his

home in south Beirut. Traveling alone at night, a nervous Picco met the Lebanese spiritual leader, who greeted him with a warm smile. During the ensuing discussions, the Lebanese threw his support behind the UN effort to free
the hostages. While not a decision maker within Hezbollah, Fadlallah agreed
to work with Picco in securing the release of all hostages held in Lebanon and
Israel.

On August 10, 1991, Picco found himself back in Beirut to meet with
the hostage takers. Iran had arranged the meeting, but when Picco met with
the Iranian ambassador at his embassy, the UN representative asked if the
ambassador was going to accompany him. "Oh, no, Mr. Picco. I don't know
these people. It's going to be between you and them!"[16]

At the instruction of the Iranians, Picco left the embassy and started
walking down the street. All was quiet, with only one other person on the
sidewalk. After ten minutes of this unnerving stroll, a Mercedes drove up
next to him and an occupant pulled him into the backseat. The abductors
drove a now hooded Picco around, eventually stopping at a building in south
Beirut. They ushered him into a room with all the walls covered in white
sheets. Two masked men came in to greet him. After verifying that Picco
came at the behest of the UN secretary general, the two were joined by
a third masked man. He appeared more confident and had a commanding presence, and introduced himself as Abdullah. He was likely Imad
Mugniyah.

The mood lightened and they got down to business discussing the various hostages and how to arrange a swap of everyone held in the region. At the
end of the conversation, the captors offered to let Picco see one of the hostages. Picco insisted on taking one with him as a sign of good faith. After
some back-and-forth haggling, they produced Edward Tracy, an American
who had traveled to Lebanon to sell Bibles. After five years in captivity, Tracy's sanity had become questionable. He could not remember his name and
claimed that he ate cordon bleu three times a day.

But this small step started a chain that eventually led to the release of all
the Western hostages. Over the next months, Picco flew from New York to
Cyprus, Beirut, and Damascus, meeting repeatedly with Zarif and Scowcroft
to secure all the hostages' freedom. Iran threw the weight of its diplomatic
effort behind the talks. But as Picco understood, the real broker was the
masked Abdullah. After an intricate series of releases of prisoners in Israel
and Lebanon, on December 4, 1991, Picco completed his mission. The reporter

Terry Anderson was the last American hostage freed, and later in the month Hezbollah turned over the bodies of CIA station chief William Buckley and Colonel Richard Higgins.[17]

With Rafsanjani having upheld his end of the unwritten bargain, he now wanted reciprocity. But when it came time for the United States to respond with its own goodwill gesture, the Bush administration reneged.

On the morning of April 7, 1992, Picco flew down to Washington to meet with Scowcroft. The national security adviser had shown signs of back-pedaling on his earlier commitments, but now with Picco in his office, Scowcroft came to the point quickly: "There will be no goodwill to beget goodwill." He then accused Iran of continuing to carry out terrorism, most recently the bombing in March of the Israeli embassy in Buenos Aires, which Iran had carried out in response to the Israeli killing of the Hezbollah leader. Scowcroft added to the litany of Iranian offenses the brutal murder of Higgins and the killing in August 1991 of former Iranian prime minister Shapour Bakhtiar by three Iranian agents who'd entered his house in Paris and stabbed him and an assistant with a kitchen knife.[18] Scowcroft had been leery of Iranian regional aspirations. Keeping an Iraqi balance against Iran had been an important rationale in his mind for not removing Saddam Hussein during Desert Storm.[19] Iranian support for the spontaneous Shia uprising at the end of the war only reinforced his concerns about expanding Iranian influence. After the war, Bush and Scowcroft deliberately excluded Iran from the regional peace conference in Madrid, a slight that Rafsanjani never forgot. Now, with all the hostages out, Scowcroft felt no need to honor the American side of the deal. It was a bitter blow of duplicity to the Iranian president.

Picco had the unfortunate task of breaking the news to Rafsanjani. Meeting in the president's white-decorated office, Picco looked into his eyes and said he had come with news of broken promises. No goodwill gesture would be forthcoming from the Americans.

Rafsanjani's eyes narrowed. "We have taken many political risks in our cooperation with you. Not everybody was in favor of such cooperation. You understand, Mr. Picco, that you are putting me in a very difficult position." The Iranian president then added, "I think it is best if you leave Tehran very, very quickly. The news of what you told me will travel fast to other quarters, and they may decide not to let you go."[20]

———

U ndaunted, Rafsanjani tried another initiative through the Germans. Beginning in 1990, Iran's ambassador to Germany, Hossein Mousavian, passed to Washington a list of four issues that divided the two nations: terrorism, the Middle East peace process, weapons of mass destruction, and human rights. He relayed that Rafsanjani was prepared to establish a joint working group to resolve these issues as a means to pave the way for a rapprochement. The Germans came back to the Iranian ambassador with the message that the Americans were not interested in the proposal.

Rafsanjani never forgave the Americans. He could overcome American support for Saddam Hussein as a by-product of war. But he had hoped to bring about change in the postwar world. "It was the first strategic mistake by the United States after the war," said Hossein Mousavian. Hard-liners in Tehran like Mohsen Rezai seized on the American rebuff as proof that the United States was not serious about better relations. The United States needed a new enemy after the Cold War, he argued, to justify its imperialistic ambitions. Iran served that purpose.[21]

Years later, Richard Haass, who worked with Scowcroft on Iranian policy, met the Iranian foreign minister at a conference. When the Iranian heard his name, he replied, "Ah, yes. Mr. Goodwill Begets Goodwill."[22]

I n 1993, a new political wind blew into Washington. Unlike the man he'd defeated for the presidency, William Jefferson Clinton arrived in the White House with no foreign policy experience. Perpetually late for any occasion, Clinton was a career politician—both glib and charismatic. He possessed an uncanny ability to remember people's faces—even those he had met briefly months earlier on the campaign trail—that charmed many prospective supporters along his way to the highest office in the land. A quick study, he impressed many senior officers, even those who disagreed with his policies. The marine commandant during Clinton's second term, General Charles Krulak, a born-again Christian and a staunch Republican, respected President Clinton both for his willingness to ask for advice and his quick grasp of the complexities of modern military operations.

Clinton shared a common trait with other politicians who have occupied the Oval Office: a conviction in his own power of persuasion to solve foreign policy challenges. Clinton believed that he could sit down with any leader, no matter how disreputable, and resolve disagreements. In an interview with *New York Times* reporters a week before his inauguration, Clinton responded to a question about future relations with Saddam Hussein. "I think that if he were sitting here on the couch I would further the change in his behavior," he said, later adding, "I always tell everybody, 'I'm a Baptist; I believe in death-bed conversions.' If he wants a different relationship with the United States and with the United Nations, all he has to do is change his behavior."[23]

Clinton's Middle East agenda did not center on either Iran or Iraq. Iran remained devastated from its eight-year war with Iraq. Desert Storm had neutered the Iraqi dictator, and although still an irritant to the sole remaining superpower, he posed no threat to his neighbors. The U.S. military maintained tens of thousands of troops in the Persian Gulf region, keeping both countries in check and safeguarding Pax Americana.

The new national security adviser, a puckish Anthony Lake, cautioned against trying to engage Tehran. His Republican predecessors had failed miserably in their search for the elusive Iranian moderate. Iran refused to moderate its anti-American stance or curb its support for terrorists, so why waste time trying to talk with an implacable antagonist?[24] President Clinton focused on forging a peace between the Palestinians and Israelis rather than refighting his predecessor's wars.

Clinton threw his efforts behind peace negotiations that had been jump-started by President Bush after Desert Storm. He achieved a public breakthrough in 1993 with an agreement, forged during secret meetings in Oslo between Palestinian and Israeli diplomats, that led to the dramatic handshake between Yasser Arafat and Yitzhak Rabin on the South Lawn of the White House.

Martin Indyk shepherded the Clinton administration's new Middle East policy. The London-born, Australian-educated forty-two-year-old Indyk arrived at the White House as the NSC's senior director for Near Eastern and South Asian affairs, having served as the research director for the pro-Israel lobbyist organization American Israel Public Affairs Committee (AIPAC). Before joining the administration, he had served as the first director of the Washington Institute for Near East Policy, a think tank sympathetic to Israel, whose intellectual rigor had earned grudging respect even from the rival Arabist policy wonks inside the Beltway. Indyk played a critical role in all of

Clinton's Middle East initiatives: he was an ardent supporter of the peace process and of building strategic alliances with moderate Arabs.

Shortly after taking office, Indyk headed a policy review for the president on both Iran and Iraq. It reconfirmed Bush's policy of containing Saddam Hussein and included a new finding by President Clinton for the CIA to try to overthrow the Iraqi leader. However, Iran posed a different set of challenges. While the pragmatic Iranian president, Rafsanjani, had made overtures for better relations, Indyk believed the Iranian government showed no real signs of moderating its behavior.

"A consensus quickly emerged that Iran was the archetype of a hostile rogue regime—the most important state sponsor of militant Islamic terrorism," wrote Indyk.[25] Iran's support for Hezbollah, its fatwa to kill author Salman Rushdie for his book *The Satanic Verses*, its assassination of a former prime minister in Paris, its desire for nuclear weapons, and its regional ambitions all supported the diagnosis of Iranian recalcitrance.

Indyk never viewed overthrowing the Islamic Republic as a realistic option. "The revolution had succeeded in conferring on the clerical regime a legitimacy that nobody in Iran seemed willing or able to challenge," Indyk wrote in his memoirs. The regime had legitimacy with the Iranian population, and there appeared to be no appreciable opposition inside the country.[26] If there had been a robust opposition, no one in Washington would have known. The CIA was still recovering from the exposure of its entire spy network just four years earlier and had few new assets positioned within the country. The agency's best information came from interviewing Iranian exiles living in Los Angeles, many of whom traveled regularly to visit family still in the old country.

Sanctions and isolation seemed the only logical way forward to Indyk. The United States would maintain its sanctions against Iran while pressuring other nations to join in Washington's embargo. Eventually, Indyk and the president hoped, the Islamic Republic would realize the tremendous economic cost of its nefarious actions and would moderate its behavior, perhaps leading to a rapprochement.

The Israeli view of Iran dovetailed with Washington's objectives. Indyk and the president's special envoy for the Middle East, Dennis Ross, shared a similar view of Israel and the peace process. "We were both strong believers in the strategic importance of the U.S.-Israeli relationship, convinced that

Israeli deterrence and the possibility of peace depended on never allowing a wedge to be driven between America and Israel," Ross wrote in a 2004 book about the peace process.[27] Both men fervently believed that peace between Israel and its Arab neighbors would promote American security, bringing stability and economic development to the region. The more we succeeded in brokering comprehensive Arab-Israeli peace, the more isolated Iraq and Iran would become; the more effective we were in containing the destabilizing activities of these two rogue regimes, the easier it would be for Israel's Arab neighbors to make peace with the Jewish state, Indyk explained. "It was a neat and logical design."[28]

Indyk used his old think tank, the Washington Institute for Near East Policy, as the forum to publicly reveal the results of his policy review as part of a wide-ranging speech describing the new American strategy for the Middle East. On May 18, 1993, at the institute's annual Soref Symposium held at a Washington hotel, Indyk described the strategy as "dual containment."[29]

"Our approach begins with the concept of independence between the eastern and western halves of the region." The two were symbiotic, Indyk said. Containing Iran and Iraq would free the Arabs and Israelis to make peace. Then a unified Middle East would help strengthen the containment of Iraq and Iran.[30]

"Iran is fishing in troubled waters across the Arab world, actively seeking to subvert friendly governments." Indyk singled out Iran's attempts to scuttle the peace process through its support of Hamas and Hezbollah, and accused Tehran of pursuing nuclear weapons and "seeking an ability to dominate the Gulf by military means." To counter this, the United States would continue economic sanctions and pressure Europe and Asia to agree to both economic and military restrictions on trading with Tehran.

"If we fail in our efforts to modify Iranian behavior, five years from now Iran will be much more capable of posing a real threat to Israel, to the Arab world, and to Western interests," Indyk warned.[31]

Harsh rhetoric by senior officials accompanied the new administration's Iranian strategy. In a series of talks around Washington, the prim secretary of state, Warren M. Christopher, called Iran an "international outlaw" for its support of terrorism and its opposition to the peace process. Anthony Lake penned a confrontational article in *Foreign Affairs* that supported dual containment and advocated a strategy in which the United States would transform rogue regimes.[32]

Iran's nascent nuclear program caused much tub-thumping in Washington. Israeli foreign minister Shimon Peres predicted that Iran would possess the bomb by 1999, and said that "you can't deter a fanatical terrorist state with nuclear weapons." At the same Washington Institute conference, Republican Paul Wolfowitz echoed concerns similar to those of Indyk: "The Iranians are embarked on a long-term program to acquire nuclear weapons." He added direly, "This problem is not yet with us in its nuclear form, but, if nothing else changes, it will be with us somewhere in the next five to ten years."[33]

Many in official Washington shared Peres's expectation of an Iranian bomb within a decade. During his confirmation hearing as the new chairman of the Joint Chiefs of Staff in 1993, Army General John Shalikashvili told the senators that Iran could produce a nuclear weapon in eight to ten years, or between 2001 and 2003. His statement reflected current CIA predictions and was supported by a recent intelligence community estimate.[34]

The new Iranian supreme leader, Ayatollah Ali Khamenei, had fewer reservations than Khomeini regarding the atom. The uncovering of Iraq's clandestine nuclear weapons program after Desert Storm and the seemingly permanent American military presence in the region no doubt contributed to Tehran's decision to hasten its nuclear research.[35] In 1991, Iran resumed its nuclear power program, looking for European and Chinese assistance. Tehran signed an agreement with China for construction of a power plant, and in 1995, after more than a year's negotiations, it signed another agreement with Russia to complete the Bushehr nuclear power plant. But none of this constituted proof of a nuclear weapons program, and a 1992 inspection by the International Atomic Energy Agency (IAEA) found no evidence of a clandestine program.

While the CIA suspected Iran's motives, intelligence remained scanty, and U.S. assessments of Iran's nuclear progress proved well off the mark. In 2002, when the U.S. government had predicted Iran would have the know-how to produce a weapon, the CIA was predicting Iran was yet another eight to ten years away from a nuclear weapon.

If the dire predictions about Iran's nuclear program were inflated, those concerning Iran's opposition to the Arab-Israeli peace process were deadly accurate. Iran viewed peace between Israel and the Arabs as a grave threat. It promised to unite both of Iran's foes and leave the Persian country isolated, just as the Clinton administration predicted. While President Rafsanjani still hoped for a rapprochement with Washington, as onetime candidate for the Iranian presidency Hooshang Amirahmadi observed, "No Iranian government would allow their two enemies to unite or that alliance to develop."[36]

The Iranian government viewed dual containment and the peace process as aimed squarely at overthrowing the Islamic Republic. Leaders in Tehran tended to see all American actions in the region through their own lens, and every new deployment of American forces in the Gulf was aimed at them. With thirty thousand American troops in the Gulf, as Middle East scholar and former CIA analyst Ken Pollack noted, "The radicals—and much of the Iranian populace—saw it as further proof of the malevolent designs and single-minded focus of the United States on Iran."[37]

The tension escalated. Israeli aircraft attacked a Hezbollah training base, killing dozens of recruits and several Iranian advisers. Hezbollah and Iran bombed a Jewish community center in Buenos Aires on July 18, 1994, killing eighty-five and wounding hundreds more. Iran began cultivating Palestinian rejectionist groups, principally Hamas. A religious fundamentalist group with loose ties to the Muslim Brotherhood in Egypt, Hamas had emerged during the Palestinian uprising in 1987 with a little help from Israel, which hoped it would undermine Arafat's power. While the fundamentalists acknowledged and respected Yasser Arafat, they strongly objected to peace with Israel as an abandonment of Palestinian claims to their pre-1948 homeland. It was an unlikely union between Shia Iran and Sunni Hamas. Iran had never cared much for the Palestinian cause, and Hamas remained a local group focused solely on its problems with the Israelis. But as Martin Indyk said, the east and west halves of the Middle East were joined, only now by Iran too.

One of those dispatched by Hamas to Tehran to solidify relations was a twenty-seven-year-old chemical engineer, Osama Hamdan. The son of a refugee living in Gaza, with a close-clipped beard and a kind but forlorn expression, Hamdan arrived in Tehran in 1992 first as the deputy and then as the principal Hamas representative to Iran. He spent six years going back and forth from his home near Beirut to Iran as one of the main negotiators helping to foster Iranian political support for Hamas. Like many Arabs living in exile among the Persians, he found the Iranians supercilious. He played a key role in cultivating Iranian support for Hamas, convincing Iran of advantages to supporting them at the expense of Arafat's Fatah Party. With a polished manner and fluency in English, Hamdan developed the persona of a rock star as he made the rounds of the posh hotels of the Gulf Arab cities. He contributed to developing legitimacy for Hamas among the Arab governments, whose natural tendency remained hostile to Islamist groups. As a security precaution, Hamas separated its political wing in Iran from the military, with Hamdan working the diplomatic side apart from other Hamas operatives arranging for weapons and explosives. Even so, Hamdan maintained a detailed, although passive, knowledge of their activities.[38]

Osama Hamdan held no illusions that Iran really cared about the Palestinian plight. He viewed it as a marriage of convenience. The ideological and religious ties that bound Hezbollah to Iran did not exist with Hamas.[39]

Support for Hamas afforded Tehran the means to strike at the Israelis and expand their influence beyond Lebanon. For Hamas, Hamdan noted, "Iran provides us the means to resist. If more countries supported our cause, no one would care about Iran, including us."[40]

Over the next two decades, Iran provided both weapons and explosives to Hamas. The covert operatives of Iran's Revolutionary Guard, the Quds Force, developed an intricate network to flow arms to Hamas. Iranian ships sailed with secret stashes of weapons in their holds through the Red Sea, where the weapons were transferred to Sudanese smugglers paid by Iranian Quds Force officers. Traveling by convoys, they worked their way up through Sudan and Egypt, from which they would be carried into Gaza and the West Bank disguised in bags of concrete or other innocuous items. This allowed the group to wage a terrorist campaign in Israel that seriously undermined the peace talks and ushered in a hard-line Likud government that had as little interest in reconciliation as Hamas. Meanwhile, the Revolutionary Guard nurtured its relations with the Sudanese, to the point that by 2008 discussions were under way to establish a Revolutionary Guard naval base in Sudan that would position Iranian naval forces to threaten the other great maritime choke point in the Middle East besides the Strait of Hormuz: the Suez Canal.

While Washington remained slow to grasp the reality, the strident American policy behind dual containment and Iran's bloody response to the peace process had started a chain reaction that quickly found the two countries on the path to war again. Neither side understood how its actions were being perceived by the other. Miscalculation threatened to exacerbate the growing crisis.

The combination of the Iran-Iraq War and the swift American victory over Iraq during Operation Desert Storm influenced Iran's military thinking. In the spring of 1991, military officers met in Tehran to discuss future requirements in light of both the recent war in Iraq and their own recent confrontation with the U.S. Navy. Although the attendees devoted much of the meeting to lengthy soliloquies about their heroic efforts during the Iran-Iraq War in fighting off the powers of global arrogance, the generals and admirals drew important lessons looking at the recent past. The naval officers concluded that their strategy against the United States had been sound, but they lacked the means to properly implement it. One lone missile from the *Joshan* had nearly knocked out the largest U.S. warship in the Persian Gulf. More small boats and missiles, they surmised, would have made the battle a costly one for the American navy.

The Revolutionary Guard believed that large conventional ships only played to the strength of the Americans. The ease with which the U.S. Navy dispatched the *Sahand* and the *Sabalan* provided graphic proof of the vulnerability of their capital ships. What had worked had been their attacks with small boats and mines. While these grew out of necessity, Iran had uncovered an asymmetrical means to strike back at the superior Americans. The Iranian navy opted for small boats and stealth to counter the United States. While fiscal shortfalls coupled with reluctance by the navy and air force to wean themselves from American hardware prevented any quick modernization, Iran concluded that improving its own military technology based on its new doctrine was important to competing with the U.S. military.[41]

Iran nearly doubled its arms purchases from 1990 to 1993. The Revolutionary Guard purchased one hundred Chinese bottom-influence mines. Its inventory of mines—many the same as those laid during the 1980s—grew to more than five thousand. At the end of the Iran-Iraq War, Iran had no working antiship missiles in its inventory. While it tried to hide this by displaying nonfunctioning missiles at military parades, overcoming this shortage became a major effort. In 1995, the country acquired Chinese C-802 antiship cruise missiles, essentially the Chinese variant of the Exocet that Iraq had used so effectively against Iranian merchants during the tanker war. The following year, Iran purchased fast Chinese-built missile boats to carry this new missile. All of them went into the Revolutionary Guard's inventory. In the next war with the U.S. Navy, Iran would not be caught with just one lone missile and some speedboats to send against an American cruiser. Iran would send a swarm of boats, outfitted with rockets, machine guns, missiles, and torpedoes, all designed to overwhelm the ship's defenses.

Iran embarked on a massive ballistic missile program. Iran's helplessness to prevent Iraq from punishing it at will dramatically affected the new supreme leader. Iran spent millions of dollars researching and building hundreds of its own missiles. Each generation grew more accurate with a longer range. The program's backbone was a series of Shahab missiles capable of sending a twenty-two-hundred-pound warhead as far as Israel. Iranian defense minister Ali Shamkhani frequently characterized Iran's strategy as one of "strategic deterrence," aimed at both Iraq and Israel based largely upon Iran's inability to respond to Iraq's missile attacks in 1988.

Iran dug two huge tunnels under more than one hundred meters of dirt and rock to safeguard its stockpile of missiles from American precision-guided missiles. As a backup, the Revolutionary Guard built more than six hundred reinforced concrete bunkers, ringing the Strait of Hormuz, all designed to house Iranian mines or newly acquired antiship missiles. Spreading their facilities out made it difficult for the Americans to knock them out by air strikes.

Inside the Pentagon, Iran's nuclear program and its weapons buildup indicated a new challenge to American preeminence in the Persian Gulf. A 1994 military assessment warned that Tehran now had the "ability to threaten shipping from virtually any location along the Iranian littoral." Although the United States remained flushed with victory against Iraq, with a massive air force presence over Iraq, Iran had come back on the Pentagon's radar as the next threat to American hegemony over the Persian Gulf. For the first time since 1988, CENTCOM dusted off its military plans for Iran, only this time the plans would not be directed against an invading Soviet army, but would outline the overthrow of the Islamic Republic.

Twenty-One

WAR OR PEACE

In 1995, the United States and Iran appeared headed for war. The CENT-COM commander, Army General James Henry Binford "Binnie" Peay, had decided to hector Iran with a series of amphibious exercises around the Persian Gulf. For a week in September 1994, two thousand marines from the 15th Marine Expeditionary Unit conducted an amphibious landing in Oman. A substantial contingent of elite army and navy special operations forces joined the marines, in addition to warplanes from an aircraft carrier. When this exercise finished, the marines quickly moved to the United Arab Emirates and conducted another exercise, labeled Iron Magic, which consisted of a series of quick amphibious raids duplicating a landing on one of the Iranian-held islands such as Abu Musa. CENTCOM had hoped it would have a deterrent effect on Iranian leaders. It backfired.[1]

Tehran viewed this mock operation as a rehearsal for an impending American attack. When one of Tehran's spies in the Gulf passed on spurious information that supported this assumption, General Mohsen Rezai of the Revolutionary Guard hastily convened a meeting in Tehran. He warned that the United States was preparing to take back the Gulf islands for the Arabs, perhaps as a prelude to invading and overthrowing the Islamic Republic. Iran began a massive buildup of military forces on the Persian Gulf islands, transforming them into virtual fortresses, building concrete bunkers with tanks and artillery and endless ribbons of trenches. On Abu Musa alone, Iran stationed four thousand troops armed with surface-to-air and antiship missiles. A move intended to intimidate Iran raised tensions to the boiling point.

On March 1, the chairman of the Joint Chiefs of Staff, General John Shalikashvili, sounded the alarm in Washington. During a breakfast with reporters, the Polish-born army officer bluntly responded to a question about the Iranian buildup on the islands near the Strait of Hormuz. "The other day they started putting missiles on their launchers, which they have not done before," he said worriedly in a pronounced accent, adding that it raised concerns about Tehran's ability to disrupt the world's oil supplies.[2]

President Clinton publicly downplayed the Iranian actions: "There is no undue cause for concern at this moment," Clinton told reporters after cable news outlets had repeatedly replayed Joint Chiefs chairman Shalikashvili's comments. Conveniently absent was any mention of the American actions that had precipitated the Iranian military buildup.

Defense Secretary William Perry quietly told the military to prepare a new war plan for Iran. The only military plan existing at CENTCOM was a holdover from Earnest Will, a long-standing requirement to keep the sea-lanes of the Persian Gulf open for commercial shipping. In a personal message for the CENTCOM commander, Shalikashvili directed him to expand this limited plan to include defending the Gulf Arabs from Iranian missile attack and to plan for air strikes on Iran proper.[3]

Iranian president Rafsanjani tried to defuse tensions and improve relations between the two countries. With the approval of the supreme leader, Rafsanjani awarded a $1 billion contract to the American oil company Conoco to develop one of his country's underwater oil fields near Sirri Island. When news of the deal reached Washington, both the State Department and the CIA supported it. The diplomats believed it could help defuse tensions while the spies hoped it would permit better access to information inside Iran.

But that year a new Republican-controlled Congress swept into office. The Conoco deal galvanized those Republicans sympathetic to Israel and hostile to the Clinton administration. New legislation made its way through both houses designed to close down trade between the United States and Iran, which amounted to nearly $4 billion annually, and kill the Conoco agreement. Clinton quickly acquiesced. In the spring of 1995, he signed two executive orders that quashed the Conoco agreement and drastically limited trade with Iran. The State Department stepped up its efforts with Russia and Europe to drastically curtail selling Iran anything conceivably used by Iran's military or nuclear program.

Initially, Rafsanjani's response to the Americans' actions was muted. In a meeting with Russian reporters, he said the United States was the only loser with its trade embargo. He did not countenance the fears of some Iranian leaders as to American intentions to overthrow the Islamic Republic. "I do not tend to see at present any threat against the revolution and the political system internally or externally." Rafsanjani added that a goodwill gesture by the United States would beget the same from Iran.[4]

But then the new speaker of the House, Newt Gingrich, a plump Georgian intellect and not one to shy away from the press, openly advocated overthrowing the Iranian regime. He argued that Clinton's dual containment lacked any stick with which to beat the intransigent mullahs.[5] While the Clinton administration immediately rejected the feasibility of overthrowing the Iranian government, Gingrich pushed through a very public $18 million plus-up for the CIA's covert action budget for Iran. The agency did have a very modest program designed to get truthful information about the United States into Iran, but Gingrich's additional funding added little to this nascent espionage effort. The money did not lead to an effort to destabilize the Iranian government. Langley set its sights low, conducting small operations such as the "Great Books" program, which sought to smuggle classics of Western literature into the country.[6] While this guaranteed that students at Tehran University would have access to Kafka and Alexis de Tocqueville's *Democracy in America*, it had no impact on Iranian behavior. Gingrich's public announcement of the funding guaranteed that any slim chances for a covert operation were now nonexistent. The speaker certainly knew this, but the debate itself sufficed, in his view. The mere discussion of a covert action against Iran served the same purpose as if there were an actual program.

Gingrich's CIA funding enraged the Iranians. CIA meddling in their internal affairs remained a sore point. Many assumed the CIA conducted such activities, but now they had a prominent American politician publicly pronouncing just such operations. While $18 million was small by American standards, it represented a significant percentage of Iran's covert budget.

"They saw it as an American declaration of covert war against them. The

U.S. was not going to invade, but was going to do everything else," said NSC official and former CIA officer Ken Pollack.[7]

Deputy foreign minister Javad Zarif, a pragmatic diplomat who actually favored better relations with Washington, condemned the United States for violating international law and the 1981 Algiers Accords, which led to the release of the embassy hostages and whereby President Carter pledged "not to intervene, directly or indirectly, politically or militarily, in Iran's internal affairs."[8] The supreme leader chimed in with his own condemnation of Washington. Addressing a graduation ceremony of newly minted army officers, Ayatollah Khamenei blasted America's actions: "So long as beloved Iran continues to shine as an Islamic country among the other countries of the world, it remains the target of terrorist moves and shameless action of the enemies of Islam—that is to say, the CIA organization of America, Zionist agencies, and their evil-minded allies."[9]

Publicly, the Iranian parliament quickly approved its own $20 million to counter the CIA covert action—a plan that had as much chance of succeeding as Gingrich's own idea. The Iranian government rounded up and hanged five men accused of being spies for both Iraq and the United States. In June 1996, Iran arrested three more men suspected as being CIA agents.[10]

Iran excelled at covert war, and its intelligence services responded in their traditional way. The tiny Gulf state of Bahrain became its first target. Iran believed it had a base of support in Bahrain, with its majority population of disenfranchised Shia living under an autocratic Sunni emir. Iran flew several of its Bahraini agents to Lebanon for training and returned them as part of a sleeper cell called Hezbollah-Bahrain, which Tehran had formed three years earlier. In June 1996, Bahraini security forces uncovered an Iranian-led plot to overthrow the emir. In a meeting at the White House, the Bahraini ambassador presented the Americans with hard evidence, including photos of weapons caches and Revolutionary Guard documents outlining the operation. Police rounded up twenty-nine conspirators, with others fleeing to Iran.[11]

Iran had inspired a similar cell in Saudi Arabia from the Shia in the country's eastern area. It had begun this recruitment drive in 1988, possibly in response to Saudi Arabia's support for the U.S. military escort of Kuwaiti tankers.

The leader of Saudi Hezbollah's military wing was Ahmed al-Mughassil.

A slight man with a black goatee, he was devout both to his religious beliefs and in his hatred for the Saudi monarchy. Living chiefly in Beirut, al-Mughassil developed close ties with Hezbollah's older Lebanese wing. He funneled Saudi militants through Syria to Lebanon, where they received weapons and bomb-making training.

A shadowy compartment of Iran's Quds Force called Department 6000, headed by Brigadier General Ahmad Sharifi, managed the Saudi cell. Sharifi kept close tabs on al-Mughassil's operations. He and his officers suggested U.S. bases and buildings for surveillance, even calling them on the phone to inquire about their progress and providing additional "targets" for Saudi Hezbollah to explore. To finance its operation, the Quds Force met with al-Mughassil in Beirut, frequently paying the Saudi with stacks of American hundred-dollar bills.[12]

Syria became an important way station between Saudi Hezbollah and Iran. The Iranian embassy provided funding and logistical support for al-Mughassil's operations. Iranian Quds Force officers frequently met their Saudi operatives at the Sayyida Zeinab shrine in southern Damascus. An imposing structure with a large courtyard and cloaked with brilliant blue tile and a shimmering gold dome, it is believed to be the burial location of Ali's daughter and the granddaughter of the Prophet Muhammad. Thousands of Iranian pilgrims arrived there every year, making it easy for Quds Force officers to move in and out undetected. The Iranians met their Saudi operatives in quiet corners of a chamber and kept a lookout for new candidates to recruit.

As early as 1993, al-Mughassil's men began monitoring American installations, with their reports making their way back to Department 6000. While no attacks were in the offing, the Quds Force viewed this as prudent planning. Early on, the U.S. embassy in Riyadh drew their attention, and Saudi Hezbollah watched the comings and goings of its employees, including staking out a fish market frequented by Americans. In late 1994, at the request of General Sharifi, Iran passed a list of American facilities within the Saudi kingdom that they wanted al-Mughassil's men to keep under surveillance. One of the targets listed was a housing complex for the American air force called Khobar Towers, which was initially built in 1979 for Bedouins, who refused to live there. The Saudis kept it to support the U.S. military, as it was located near the important air base at Dhahran in the Shia province of eastern Saudi Arabia. Khobar Towers was made up of high-rise apartment buildings, including two eight-story T-shaped buildings on the north end. After Desert Storm, some two thousand Americans called Khobar Towers home, at least during their deployments supporting operations over the skies of Iraq.

Following the cancellation of the Conoco deal and the new American trade embargo, likely on the orders of supreme leader Ayatollah Khamenei, both the Iranian intelligence service, MOIS, and the Revolutionary Guard Quds Force stepped up their surveillance of U.S. military bases in the Middle East looking for prospective targets. In a meeting in his Beirut apartment, Ahmed al-Mughassil explained to one of his men—in Lebanon for rifle training at a Hezbollah range—that the goal would be to drive the Americans from Saudi Arabia. But it was clear that the when and where would be dictated by Iran. By mid-1995 al-Mughassil and the Iranians had settled on the sprawling complex of Khobar Towers as their target. Following the public plus-up for the CIA, the Quds Force leadership issued the order to carry out the attack in the spring of 1996.[13]

Saudi security officials uncovered part of the Iranian operations when a bomb-sniffing dog at a border customs checkpoint reacted to one car that turned out to be carrying over eighty pounds of plastic explosives. After brutal interrogation, the driver admitted he had come from Lebanon, and he intended to bomb the American barracks at Khobar Towers. He gave up the names of three accomplices, including one Lebanese Hezbollah adviser inside the kingdom. Convinced that it had nipped the terrorist attack in the bud, a complacent Saudi government never informed the Americans of the threat.[14]

Ahmed al-Mughassil assembled a small cell of fifteen members to execute the attack. They purchased a large tanker truck and hid it in a remote farm some twenty minutes' drive from Dhahran. The men stashed five thousand pounds of plastic explosives, secretly ferreted in from Lebanon, in fifty-kilogram sacks, burying them in caches around the desert. They hid the more delicate items, such as detonators, in old coffee cans. Over the next three weeks they converted the truck into a massive rolling bomb.[15]

In early June, a fair-skinned, fair-haired Lebanese man with green eyes arrived at the remote farm. An explosives expert, he had been sent by Lebanese Hezbollah to double-check on the construction of the truck bomb. The mystery man spent a week working at the farm, staying at the home of one of the conspirators. His expertise ensured that the attack did not end in a fizzle. He returned to Lebanon, where he briefed both Hezbollah and Iranians from Department 6000 on the likely success of the "project."

On the evening of June 25, six of the men, including al-Mughassil, met at the farm. They prayed and made their final preparations. A small caravan of vehicles departed for the twenty-minute drive to Khobar Towers, with al-Mughassil driving the explosives-laden tanker truck.

When Saudi guards turned al-Mughassil away from the main gate, he quickly switched to plan B. One terrorist driving a small Datsun had entered a large parking lot adjacent to the north side of Khobar Towers. The driver flashed his lights, giving the signal to al-Mughassil that the coast was clear. The tanker truck lumbered into the parking lot and stopped next to a chain-link fence that separated the public parking from the American compound. Barely eighty feet away stood Building 131—an eight-story apartment building housing airmen chiefly from the 4404th Composite Wing. Ahmed al-Mughassil set the timer, and he and his side rider leaped from the truck's cab, ran to a waiting white Chevrolet Caprice, and sped off into the darkness. It was just before ten p.m.

The day so far had passed unremarkably for those living at Khobar Towers. The dedication of a new aerobics room at the base gym had been the day's highlight; the base commander had cut the ribbon to open the new facility with much fanfare. Officers lounged about watching the old Dustin Hoffman movie *Marathon Man* while others did household chores or had already turned in for an early flight mission the next morning.

From the top of the roof of Building 131, three air force security officers watched the tanker truck park next to the fence line. Staff Sergeant Alfredo Guerrero immediately realized the danger when he saw the white Caprice speed off. The officers began running down the passages pounding on doors: "Get the hell out of the building. We have a situation with a fuel truck. You need to get out of the building now!"[16] In four minutes the airmen cleared the top three floors of Building 131. Then they ran out of time.[17]

The tanker truck exploded with the force of twenty thousand pounds of TNT. It blew a thirty-five-foot crater and sheared off the entire north face of Building 131 as a massive concussion wave followed by a heavy brown dust cloud rolled over the compound.

"It felt like I was being sandblasted," recalled Tech Sergeant George Burgess, who was cleaning out his refrigerator on the first floor of Building 131—closest to the blast. "It was like I was just in the stream of a sandblaster.

Then it stopped and it was like dead silence. Then you could hear water start-ing to run."

Large picture windows disintegrated. Shards of glass sliced through humans who a moment earlier had been sitting quietly reading or watching television. Hundreds of yards away, in quick succession, the concussion shat-tered every newly installed mirror in the renovated gym.

One airman happened to test his alarm clock the moment the bomb went off. "I hit my snooze button and . . . that's when everything blew up. It was like I'd pushed a button and everything blew up." The force of the blast threw him across the room. "I could see that the walls were gone and every-thing was gone. And I realized that it was something more than just my alarm clock going off."[18] When the dust settled, 19 Americans lay dead, with 372 more injured.

The day after the attack, Richard Clarke, who headed counterterrorism at the White House, told the national security adviser, Anthony Lake, that Iran's Quds Force had been behind the bombing. He was the only one in Washington with that firm of a conviction. Neither the CIA nor CENTCOM had any hard evidence of Iran's culpability, and would not for months.

The FBI led the investigation. The bureau's director, Louis Freeh, a vet-eran federal prosecutor, doggedly pursued the perpetrators. Unfortunately, Saudi authorities proved less than cooperative. Freeh grew irritated at the Saudi intransigence, writing a letter to Prince Bandar, who wielded influence as ambassador in yet another American administration. "Mr. Ambassador, the only way to move the investigation forward and arrest the terrorists who committed this heinous act is for our two countries to cooperate fully and effectively."[19]

Initially, Bandar doubted Tehran's involvement. "For Iran to officially sanction an attack in the Saudi kingdom would be very serious—a grave turn of events," the prince told Freeh during one meeting at his home. Due largely to the personal intervention of Prince Bandar, FBI agents gradually gained access, first to the crime scene and eventually to the evidence. However, it took until September 1998 for FBI agents to gain access to suspects held in a Saudi jail. By the spring of 1997, evidence of Iran's culpability had mounted. Two terrorists arrested in Syria and Canada had confessed, and Saudi intelli-gence uncovered further evidence of Iranian involvement. American commu-nications intercepts confirmed the knowledge at the highest levels of the Iranian government and the approval of the supreme leader.[20]

Iran denied any involvement. The two nations had been secretly working to mend relations. The Iranian president tasked his trusted adviser Hossein Mousavian to head the Iranian delegation to talk with the Saudis. The first meeting occurred at the Saudi prince's oceanside villa near Casablanca. Three more meetings followed in Jeddah, successfully concluding a large framework, including security guarantees, just three months before the attack. "This was a major strategic initiative," recalled Mousavian. "Why would Iran risk it by attacking Khobar?"[21] It would not be the first time, however, the left and right hands of the Iranian government were not in sync.

Two months later, contract security guards noticed individuals conducting surveillance on the large American logistics base west of Kuwait City called Camp Doha. It looked eerily similar to what had preceded the Khobar Towers attack, with the suspicious men especially interested in the location of living quarters of American service personnel. U.S. Army counterintelligence officers suspected they were Iranian agents, scoping out the base for a reprisal attack should the United States retaliate for Khobar Towers.

In September, a stocky, dark-haired marine arrived as the deputy chief in Tampa: Anthony "Tony" Zinni. A year later he moved up to take over as the new CENTCOM commander, in charge of all U.S. military forces in the Middle East.

Known by the call sign "the Godfather," he was a graduate of Villanova University and the jungles of Vietnam. Politically a moderate Democrat, in his youth Zinni had campaigned for Jack Kennedy. He was charismatic and possessed an innate gift for public speaking, mixing humor with thoughtful analysis. He proved equally popular at CENTCOM. The long-serving command historian observed that "Zinni was the only commander the staff was actually *sorry* to see retire."[22]

Iran kept Tony Zinni awake at night. Following the imposition of American trade restrictions in the spring of 1995, Iranian Revolutionary Guard small boats stepped up their harassment of American warships transiting the Persian Gulf. They repeatedly approached at high speeds, conducting mock attacks on American warships. "It was clearly orchestrated and planned," said Zinni.[23]

One incident was typical. On May 1, 1997, the American destroyer USS *Paul F. Foster* was steaming in the northern Gulf enforcing UN sanctions against Iraq by interdicting oil smuggling. An Iranian fast boat suddenly appeared in the distance. The boat headed straight for the American warship, turning away at the last minute, speeding past the alarmed American sailors at less than fifty yards. While the ship's captain did not open fire, Zinni worried that other skippers would show less restraint.

"This outward hostility by the Revolutionary Guard might cause a spark and ignite a conflict," Zinni wrote in a message after the incident. "Eventually some captain would open fire on an Iranian boat—who might have intended to bump him—but the ship's skipper doesn't know that the Iranian boat isn't packed with explosives. Then we have a serious problem."[24] The State Department sent a warning through the Swiss to Tehran to rein in the guard, but it had no effect.

The Revolutionary Guard actions came from zealotry as much as national policies. Guard officers were expected to act with both initiative and aggressiveness. Those who showed these characteristics received promotions, and officers frequently pushed the envelope with the Americans. In the case of the *Paul F. Foster*, the likely cause was mammon. An irate Revolutionary Guard officer profiting from the illicit Iraqi trade objected to the U.S. warship interfering with his side business. However, the Iranian government encouraged these provocative actions, determined to maintain pressure on the U.S. military through harassment and terrorism.

Defense Secretary William Cohen ordered Zinni to develop a new military plan. "The goal of any military strike should be to impose such a steep cost that the Iranian regime will be loath to contemplate an attack on American personnel ever again," Ken Pollack said in a talk before a Washington think tank, reflecting the administration's views.[25] CENTCOM came back in the late summer with a hasty plan code-named Iron Lightning. American aircraft and cruise missiles would knock out key Revolutionary Guard bases, including their naval bases at Bandar Abbas and their headquarters in downtown Tehran. Zinni offered other options, including bombing Hezbollah targets in Lebanon. Iron Lightning would be quick and punishing, he told the secretary.

In late 1997, Zinni began a new war plan for Iran. Unlike Iron Lightning, which had been hastily conceived in response to Iranian terrorism, this new Iranian plan required two years of intensive work to complete. Zinni's plan would take the conflict with Iran to its logical conclusion: overthrowing the Islamic Republic.

"Gentlemen, we are going to assume that Iran responds with all of its capabilities," he told the small, close-hold staff charged with the Iranian war plan. "I want you to take it full circle—from the start of a conflict to what it would take for regime change."

Several months later, Zinni flew up to Washington to brief his preliminary findings in the Tank. "There was sticker shock," he said, recalling the reactions of Secretary Cohen and the Joint Chiefs. "They thought it would be like Iraq, where we could take down the regime in nineteen days. This was far from the case with Iran."[26]

Ironically, the United States faced many of the same natural obstacles that CENTCOM had hoped to use a decade earlier to thwart a Soviet invasion. U.S. forces would have to advance across the formidable Zagros Mountains along the same narrow roads, tunnels, and bridges that General Robert Kingston had intended to use to beat the Red Army.

Zinni predicted the Persian population would unite behind their government, making a protracted military campaign unavoidable. The war would spread throughout the Persian Gulf. Iran would strike at the Gulf Arabs providing bases for Americans. There would be massive protests in the Arab streets, destabilizing these same pro-American countries. "You can't underestimate the propaganda value of another attack on an Islamic country," Zinni said in a 2010 interview.

Zinni's plan involved several army and marine divisions pushing north from the Gulf with the aim of taking Tehran. NSC counterterrorism chief Richard Clarke privately referred to this scheme as "the Eisenhower option."[27] To remove the regime, Zinni told the secretary of defense, would require at least half a million American troops and three years of combat. The military option for regime change in Iran was not realistic.

Instead, Zinni recommended that the United States forge a military coalition against Iran. "It would never rise to the level of NATO," Zinni said. "Complete integration was a bridge too far, but the U.S. could serve behind the scenes in a supporting role as the glue that tied the disparate militaries together." Secretary of Defense Cohen liked the idea.

Zinni began with baby steps. He got the Gulf Arabs to agree to use their military forces to clean up hazardous material left over from Desert Storm and to search for naval mines still lingering in the northern Persian Gulf. CENTCOM then spearheaded a planning conference that ended in an agreement to combine efforts to contain an oil spill.

Zinni next set his sights on building a Gulf-wide air defense system. The idea, pushed by CENTCOM a decade earlier, had languished with the end of the Iran-Iraq War. With the upsurge in Iranian truculence, the Gulf states agreed to buy new antiair defenses and to cooperate in a loose early-warning system that would allow American aircraft to respond to an air attack on any one of the six Gulf countries. CENTCOM organized some exercises to respond to an Iranian attack. The enemy in the scenarios was never mentioned, "but everyone knew the enemy was Iran," said Zinni.

While the White House weighed military options for responding to the Khobar Towers bombing, Clinton approved a CIA counterattack. Iran's MOIS had been complicit in the bombing in Saudi Arabia, so the CIA set out to disrupt the spy service's worldwide operations. In Operation Sapphire, CIA officers began openly approaching known MOIS agents and asking if they would work for American intelligence. They spoke to the agents at parties and in cafés, publicly soliciting them without concern for who might overhear the conversation. Just being seen talking with a known CIA officer created suspicion in the minds of the MOIS leadership. On several occasions in European capitals, the CIA officers simply walked up to the Iranian spies' homes and knocked on their doors, telling the startled occupants that the Americans knew where they lived.[28] These "cold pitches" created havoc within the Iranian spy operations. If the MOIS agent reported the contact, he immediately came under scrutiny on why a CIA officer had been to his house. If he did not report it and his superiors learned of it, his fate would be worse. Unsure of who might be working with the Americans, the Iranians simply sacked their agents. Some MOIS officers retired, but others found themselves in the hangman's noose, falsely charged with cavorting with the CIA. As George Tenet, the director of the CIA, later wrote, "It couldn't happen to a nastier bunch of people."[29]

Just as the two nations appeared headed to war, however, the brewing conflict terminated. The catalyst was the election of a new Iranian president, Mohammad Khatami. On May 23, 1997, Khatami stunned the Iranian hierarchy by garnering 70 percent of the vote in the presidential elections. He easily trounced the candidate backed by the supreme leader and the commander of the Revolutionary Guard, performing well even in the Tehran neighborhoods populated by the guard's officers.

A mild, bookish man, Khatami had been an early supporter of the revolution. Although a respected cleric, he had not served in any significant positions; at the time of the election, he ran Iran's national library. But Khatami tapped the growing discontent in Iranian society. With 30 percent unemployment and an even higher inflation rate, the Iranian people clamored for change.[30]

Khatami pushed for economic reform and political liberalization. Independent proreform newspapers sprang up across the country. He advocated that there could be more than a single interpretation of Islam, with a more contemporary reading of the Koran. This made the conservatives within the Iranian government nervous. "Whoever said I have a new reading of Islam should be slapped in the mouth," said one mullah to his congregation.[31]

President Khatami's reforms extended to foreign policy. His goal was to break Iran's isolation with the West. He called for a "dialogue of nations" as a remedy to the divide between the West and Islam. He reestablished good relations with Europe by vowing not to carry out Khomeini's fatwa to kill Salman Rushdie for *The Satanic Verses*. In January 1998, Khatami moved to improve relations with the United States, and he granted an interview to Iranian-born CNN reporter Christiane Amanpour.

The Iranian president expressed regret for the takeover of the U.S. embassy, adding that "the events of those days must be viewed within the context of the revolutionary fervor." While listing the American affronts to his nation, including the downing of the Iran Air flight and the recent CIA funding, he said Iran harbored no malice toward the United States. Khatami rejected terrorism as incompatible with the Koran. "Terrorism should be condemned in all its forms and manifestations," Khatami told the American reporter.[32]

Khatami went beyond words. He halted the MOIS's extrajudicial killings of dissidents. When several of his liberal supporters were killed in Tehran, he opened an investigation that uncovered a secret committee under the auspices of the MOIS and the Revolutionary Guard charged by the supreme leader's office to eliminate potential enemies of the revolution. As these killings had been done without the supreme leader's knowledge, Khatami sacked the head of the MOIS.[33]

While he wanted reform, President Khatami was not a revolutionary. He was a part of the political elite and had no interest in overthrowing the Islamic Republic. In July 1999, students from Tehran University took to the streets following the killing of several students in their dormitories by security forces during protests against legislation passed to curb the burgeoning open press. Khatami refused to back the protestors, accusing them of undermining his reforms. He sat by as the Revolutionary Guard moved in, arresting a thousand protestors.

The election of Khatami created a buzz inside the Beltway. A month after the election, the Washington Institute for Near East Policy—the same venue where Martin Indyk had argued for dual containment—hosted a discussion with two prominent foreign policy officials about the election's implications. Zalmay Khalilzad expressed caution; he was not convinced that Khatami could overcome hard-liners' opposition to implementing any dramatic shift. But former Reagan assistant secretary of state Richard Murphy urged the U.S. government to engage in a new "critical dialogue" with Iran. He recommended opening direct talks on Iran's nuclear program, holding out the prospect of returning billions of dollars of frozen assets remaining from the days of the shah.[34] The United States refused to take these steps until Iran renounced terrorism and its weapons of mass destruction program.[35]

On a Saturday morning in October 1997, Indyk received a phone call from Deputy Secretary of State Strobridge Talbott. Indyk had recently returned to Washington from a few years as the American ambassador to Israel and had the Iran portfolio as the assistant secretary of state for Near Eastern affairs. The two men went for a walk, along a dirt path of Washington's Rock Creek Park, as Indyk recalled. Talbott wanted Indyk's opinion of Khatami and whether he marked an opening for better relations. Indyk remained skeptical: he cited Iran's continued pursuit of nuclear weapons and its role in the Khobar Towers bombing. But Talbott showed more optimism: "If Khatami is able to moderate Iran's behavior," he told Indyk, "it will change everything."[36]

But the political landscape was littered with those trying for a rapprochement with Tehran, so despite the apparent opening, President Clinton proceeded with caution. The new secretary of state, Madeleine Albright, sent a message to Khatami via the Swiss embassy in Tehran proposing a meeting between senior officials.[37] Although Iran never responded, the United States decided to include the Mujahideen-e Khalq, the Iraq-based, anti-Iranian government terrorist organization, on the State Department's list of foreign terrorist organizations. Clinton relaxed visa restrictions, allowing more Iranians to travel to the United States, and refused to impose sanctions on the French oil company Total for developing the Iranian Sirri oil field originally awarded to Conoco.

The election of President Khatami changed the discussion regarding military retaliation for the Khobar Towers bombing. With the renouncement of terrorism and the replacement of one of the instigators of the terrorist attack—the head of MOIS—by the new Iranian president, the wisdom of retaliating for Khatami's predecessor's crime was called into question. Attacking Iran at this point would simply have undercut Khatami and the reform movement and ended any chance for improved relations between the two nations. Clinton shelved the military response.[38] Once again, Iran had killed American service personnel and the U.S. government chose not to respond.

The election of Mohammad Khatami changed the dynamics in the waters of the Persian Gulf too. The harassment of U.S. warships transiting the Persian Gulf ceased. Late on the morning of September 19, 1999, the American cruiser USS *Lake Erie* intercepted a Belize-flagged merchant ship suspected of smuggling Iraqi crude. The U.S. warship stopped the ship just three miles from Iranian waters, but in an area claimed by Tehran.[39] It was just the sort of incident that would have threatened to escalate in the past. But this time Tehran simply lodged a complaint with the United Nations. The Revolutionary Guard never displayed the professional attitude of the Iranian navy, but it was clear that Khatami had reined in the bellicose excesses of the guard commanders. The tension in the Gulf decreased precipitously.

Clinton continued to feel out the Iranians. At the 1998 U.S.-Iranian World Cup game in France, a prerecorded message by the president aired just before kickoff. "As we cheer today's game between American and Iranian athletes, I hope it can be another step toward ending the estrangement between our two nations," Clinton said to the worldwide audience.[40]

The next spring Clinton took a gamble by offering another olive branch to Iran. In April, during a Millennium Evening dinner at the White House, President Clinton gave a lengthy off-the-cuff response directed squarely at Khatami during questions and answers. "Iran, because of its enormous geopolitical importance over time, has been the subject of quite a lot of abuse from various Western nations. And I think sometimes it's quite important to tell people, 'Look, you have the right to be angry at something my country or my culture did.'"[41]

"It was not quite an apology," wrote Ken Pollack, "but it was closer than any American president had ever come . . . just what the hard-liners had been demanding since 1979."[42]

At the same time, Indyk and Bruce Riedel, a senior CIA official working on the NSC, approached Oman requesting that the country deliver a message to President Khatami regarding the Khobar Towers attack. Their goal was to put Iran on notice in hopes that the new regime would take action that would allow both sides to move beyond the incident.

The United States had conclusive evidence of Iran's Revolutionary Guard's involvement in the bombing, they said. The United States sought better relations with Iran, but Iran must end its terrorist activities and provide assurances that those responsible for the killing of the nineteen Americans would be brought to justice.

Oman's foreign minister delivered the message, and Khatami read the démarche carefully. After he accused the United States of even bigger terrorist actions, the Iranian president promised to look into the accusation. Weeks went by before Iran responded to the U.S. démarche via the Omani foreign ministry. The response was typically Persian. While the Iranian government denied any involvement, the message added that no such action would happen again, and the Islamic Republic harbored no ill will to the United States. According to Indyk, the United States took this to mean that nothing would be done to those who carried out the attack, but no further attacks would be forthcoming.

In 2000, liberals and reformers backing Khatami won another whopping 73 percent in parliamentary elections. Thus far, American overtures toward Iran had yielded nothing. Iranian response remained muted. Concern grew that the hard-liners in Tehran, including the supreme leader, were maneuvering to rein in Khatami and squelch any rapprochement. Back-channel talks with Iranians and intelligence confirmed both Khatami's and the reform movement's strength; perhaps a more overt offer from Washington would strengthen Khatami's hand.

The administration chose a meeting of the American Iranian Council in Washington, D.C., to get its message to Khatami. The organization's president, Hooshang Amirahmadi, had lived for two decades in the United States and taught at Rutgers University. Animated and confident, he maintained a close rapport with the Iranian reform movement as well as with Khatami's government. He lobbied for closer ties between the two nations. If Khatami wanted to listen, Amirahmadi's group would be the best megaphone.

On March 17, 1999, Secretary of State Madeleine Albright stepped up to the podium as a keynote speaker before a day of panel discussions, including one to honor Christiane Amanpour.

"Spring is the season of hope and renewal; of planting the seeds for new crops," said Albright to a riveted audience. "And my hope is that in both Iran and the United States, we can plant the seeds now for a new and better relationship in years to come." She expressed regret for past American misdeeds, including tolerating the shah's repression, and indicated Washington's willingness to meet with Iranian officials without preconditions.[43]

Ayatollah Khamenei responded a week later during a speech before Shia pilgrims at a holy shrine. "The confessions of American crimes are of no use to the Iranian nation," he said dismissively. As for talks with Washington, the supreme leader called the idea "deceitful," intended to "set the stage for more enmities and to regain its former interests in Iran."[44]

Clinton decided to throw a Hail Mary and try to use his considerable interpersonal skills to talk directly to Khatami. Both presidents were scheduled to speak at the United Nations General Assembly. After Clinton spoke, he agreed to stay and listen to all of Khatami's speech in the hopes that the two would bump into each other afterward on the assembly floor. It was an unscripted gamble, but Clinton was desperate to start the thaw before he left office. After Khatami's talk, Clinton loitered around the assembly hoping to meet Khatami. But the Iranian president's advisers worried about an unscripted meeting at such a senior level, and Khatami did not have the supreme leader's blessing to meet with Clinton. So he had his aides spirit him out a different way to make sure he would not meet the American president. Clinton's last overture had flopped.

In three years Iran and the United States had swerved from open hostility to hopeful accommodation. The election of President Khatami portended an end to twenty years of hostilities. A pragmatic Bill Clinton repeatedly tried to seize the opportunity, starting with modest steps at easing trade and travel restrictions and leading to increasingly bolder initiatives designed to extend a hand of friendship to Iran. While Khatami may have wanted to reciprocate, the hard-liners controlling the other apparatuses of power—the parliament, Guardian Council, Revolutionary Guard, and supreme leader—all conspired to undermine his policy. Khatami served two full terms, but each year his authority and independence eroded, and he was unable to grasp Clinton's extended hand. In the end, Khatami proved to be no revolutionary. He was not willing to run against the will of the very government he had spent his professional life supporting.

"In the end, rapprochement failed because Iran was unwilling to move forward," said Ken Pollack. "But the Clinton administration's attempt was the right thing to do. The animosity remained because the other side wanted it."

The outgoing Clinton administration recommended that the two nations should be talking to each other, despite the disagreements and without pre-conditions. "Iran has a critical role in questions of regional stability and security, and cannot be ignored," wrote Edward Walker, the outgoing director for Near Eastern affairs at State, in a memo for the new administration.[45] But President Bush would make his own decisions.

Twenty-Two

AN ATROCITY

I nitially, senior military officers welcomed the new Bush administration. The breadth of experience coming in with the Republicans impressed many in uniform. "It appeared to me to be an extraordinary group of talent," said Marine Lieutenant General Greg Newbold, then head of operations for the Joint Staff, of the new Bush national security team. Tall and thin, with a forthright, monotone persona, Newbold applauded the return of Colin Powell and Richard Armitage to run the State Department and the respected former defense secretary Dick Cheney as vice president. They seemed to be harbingers of a remarkable team at the helm, guiding the foreign policy of the United States into the new millennium. Although the chairman, General Hugh Shelton, and the other Joint Chiefs respected President Clinton, he was not overly popular with the officer corps due to his moral lapses and evasion of the Vietnam War. During the campaign, George W. Bush called for a stronger military that would not squander its power on nation building: "Our military is meant to fight and win war," Governor Bush said during the second presidential debate with Vice President Al Gore.[1] Few within the uniformed services seemed to notice the fact that many of those coming in with the Republican administration—including the new president—had shown the same penchant as Clinton for avoiding their generation's war in Southeast Asia.

The new secretary of defense hit the Pentagon like a whirling dervish. With slicked-back hair and rimless glasses, at seventy-four Donald Rumsfeld was the oldest man ever to run the Defense Department, but he possessed the energy and drive of a man half his age. Rumsfeld was a tenacious bureaucratic infighter; his management style was to take charge and force everyone else out of his way, even if he really didn't have the faintest idea of what to do. Rumsfeld also shared a widespread suspicion within the new Republican administration of the loyalty of the military leadership, all of which had been appointed by the Democrats. General Shelton spent months trying to convince Rumsfeld that he was beyond partisan politics and would support him as much as he had his predecessor.

One of the top items in the new secretary of defense's in-box carried over from the end of the Clinton administration: a military plan to attack Iran. On October 12, 2000, the American destroyer USS *Cole* sat moored, refueling, off the port of Aden, Yemen. A small white boat approached the anchored ship. The two men aboard waved at the U.S. sailors and then detonated hundreds of pounds of explosives hidden in the boat's hull. The explosion blew a forty-foot hole in the *Cole*'s port side, killing seventeen sailors and wounding thirty-nine in the worst attack on an American warship since the Iraqi attack on the USS *Stark* thirteen years earlier. President Clinton ordered the military to dust off the Iron Lightning plan developed after the Khobar Towers incident and to explore Iran's role in the bombing. Newbold worked with the new CENTCOM commander, General Tommy Franks, to flesh out a broad range of military options designed to both retaliate and deter Tehran from undertaking any future terrorist attacks. These ranged from a massive week-long bombardment by aircraft and missiles against military sites in downtown Tehran, including destroying Iran's oil export facilities, to such—in the parlance of the Pentagon—"nonkinetic actions" as working with the Treasury Department to disrupt Iran's financial system.[2] Myriad other possible missions, including a renewed CIA targeting of Iranian intelligence officers and covert operations supporting the Iranian opposition, were suggested. "They were unconventional and imaginative and punitive," said Newbold of their proposals.[3]

While the evidence soon pointed to al-Qaeda and Osama bin Laden as the culprits behind the *Cole* attack, Newbold remained suspicious about Iran's involvement.[4] Just four years after Iran's deadly attack in Saudi Arabia, the *Cole* seemed to fit into a pattern of Iranian-sponsored strikes at the American military.

Five days after Bush's inauguration, CIA Director George Tenet briefed the new president on the terrorist threat, including Iran.[5] The next day, Rumsfeld demanded an update on the military plans, including those for Iran. Newbold laid out both the contingency plan developed under Clinton to retaliate for the *Cole* and the much larger Iranian military plan approved under Anthony Zinni to remove the regime. The latter resembled the old plans dating back to the days of General Paul X. Kelley and the rapid deployment force. It called for half a million men invading Iran from the east and west and converging on Tehran in two giant pincers.

Rumsfeld hated both ideas. He lambasted CENTCOM's invasion plan as unrealistic and a Cold War relic that relied on masses of men, tanks, and artillery and failed to adjust force levels based on new technology. The Iran briefing reinforced in the secretary's mind the idea that military planning lacked any imagination. He ordered Newbold to come up with a new plan to respond to Iranian terrorism with a range of military options against Iranian "centers of gravity" and to prevent responses that threatened U.S. forces or access to the Strait of Hormuz. And yesterday was not soon enough for the impatient new defense secretary.

In less than a week, Newbold was standing again in front of Rumsfeld with a revised plan. Cruise missiles and aircraft would strike Iranian Revolutionary Guard Quds Force training camps near Tehran; this could be expanded to other targets, such as the Quds Force or the MOIS headquarters buildings. CENTCOM commander Tommy Franks added an option similar to those schemes developed when the United States last squared off against Iran in the 1980s. At the time, CENTCOM called them the invisible hand in reverse, which were a series of nonattributable American operations against Iran. Franks proposed a similar concept. Navy SEALs would secretly infiltrate Iranian harbors and blow up high-value targets such as the three Iranian submarines or Revolutionary Guard missile boats. This would send the Iranian government an unmistakable message about the consequences of terrorism. But keeping the fight in the shadows, Newbold stressed, would lessen the likelihood of escalation as the U.S. government maintained the illusion, at least publicly, of deniability.

A gruff Rumsfeld listened and interrupted. He finally cut Newbold off with his own idea. He ordered CENTCOM to prepare to execute Franks's "invisible hand in reverse," as well as a large three- to four-day bombing campaign designed to destroy not only terrorist targets, but all of Iran's ballistic missiles and naval and air bases. The alert order went out to Franks the next day labeled as a top secret special category message, with the code name Polo Step.[6]

But Donald Rumsfeld had no intention of actually attacking Iran or, for that matter, the perpetrators of the *Cole* attack, including Osama bin Laden lurking in Afghanistan. The Bush administration had little interest in military action to avenge terrorist attacks that happened under Bill Clinton. As former NSC counterterrorism official Roger Cressey observed, "It didn't happen on their watch. It was the forgotten attack."[7] But Rumsfeld had shrewdly used the Iran military plan to send a strong signal to the Pentagon. He intended to shake up the Defense Department and force the generals and the civilian bureaucracy to mold to his will. He pushed out longtime civil servants, replacing them with political appointees well down into the lower levels of the department. He cut the Joint Staff by 15 percent, moving many of the billets up into his own office. He personally approved every promotion to three-star general. He incessantly questioned the status quo and peppered subordinates with short memos called "snowflakes," raising questions and demanding answers on issues great and small. He berated or "challenged" the generals to think "outside the box," and demanded answers from the military in days, or sometimes hours, even to enormously complex problems.

One of the Bush administration's first acts in developing a new policy toward Iran came from the new head of the State Department's policy planning staff, Richard Haass, who produced a paper on a list of topics for possible negotiations with Iran. It listed the significant areas of disagreement— that is, Iran's support for Hezbollah and its nuclear program—but also areas where the two nations could work together, such as counternarcotics. Haass shared this with Condoleezza Rice and Colin Powell and advocated engagement with Iran rather than isolation.[8] The Joint Staff also prepared a paper recommending trying to build on the Clinton opening to President Khatami. Although the Iranian government continued to pursue weapons of mass destruction and ballistic missiles, the military offered an optimistic assessment of the reformers and of Khatami's ultimate success: "With 25 million reformers and 5 million conservatives, change is simply a matter of time," wrote a military Middle East analyst.[9] The military agreed with Haass and recommended engaging Iran along areas of common interest, including Iraq, while pressing them to renounce terrorism and their missile programs.

The idea found no support within the administration. Many senior officials believed the Iran government teetered on the brink of overthrow. "Any U.S. diplomatic initiative would be tantamount to throwing a rope to a drowning man," Haass recalled. The new civilian defense team flatly rejected the Joint Staff's views. Early engagement with Iran never gained traction. "Iran was at the bottom of the list of regional concerns," Ken Pollack noted.[10]

Rumsfeld took a different course. Although he believed that Iran would eventually obtain a nuclear weapon, he did not view it as an immediate crisis.[11] Instead he called for a comprehensive review of U.S. policy toward Iraq. Rumsfeld had served as Reagan's Middle East envoy when the United States played a balancing act between Iran and Iraq. "I wondered if the right combination of blandishments and pressures might lead or compel Saddam Hussein toward an improved arrangement with America," Rumsfeld wrote in his memoirs. He advocated a throwback to the days when Iraq served as a bulwark to contain Iran. "While a long shot," he wrote, "it was not out of the question."[12]

Iraq also galvanized the conservative intellectuals filling the political appointee positions within the Pentagon. This included Rumsfeld's number two, a rumpled ideologue named Paul Wolfowitz. Collectively known as neoconservatives, or "neocons," they were a loose grouping of like-minded men who sprang from the political left and merged with the anti-Soviet hawks of the Cold War. They argued for a unilateralist foreign policy centered upon America's moral superiority and her willingness to use military force as an instrument to confront the world's evils. They were not shy about using force to remake the globe in an image pleasing to America.[13]

Wolfowitz viewed Saddam Hussein as the principal threat to American security. A polite, likable, soft-spoken man, Wolfowitz exemplified the absentminded professor, possessing a quick mind and exhibiting perpetual personal disorganization. He had first raised the Iraqi threat thirty years earlier when he headed a 1979 limited contingency study for Secretary Harold Brown. Wolfowitz viewed Iraq through the lens of the Holocaust and the Jewish experience during the Second World War. Saddam Hussein and his Baath Party represented the modern face of fascism. In a 2004 memo after the U.S. invasion, in response to proposed reconciliation with former Baath officials, Wolfowitz killed the idea, scrawling in the margin, "They are Nazis!"[14]

During the Republican exile between George H. W. Bush and George W. Bush, the neocons pushed for the overthrow of the Iraqi regime using covert action and armed exiles backed by American airpower.[15] Now back in power, they pressed for using U.S. military muscle to establish safe havens in which free-Iraq forces could muster to overthrow the Iraqi government.

President Bush's national security adviser, Condi Rice, had a close rapport with the president, having served to educate the neophyte candidate on foreign policy. A bright policy wonk and Russia expert, she was more than just an adviser, becoming a close friend to the president and First Lady. Her frequent contact with them gave her both the insight and access needed for an effective national security adviser. But the president used her as his personal foreign policy adviser and not as the heavy hand to coordinate and implement his policy goals.[16] Instead, Rice worked to build consensus decisions within the National Security Council. When senior officials differed, rather than raising these differences to the president for his decision, Rice sent it back to senior officials for them to try and hash out the issue once again. On contentious policy issues, endless discussions never led to a decision on which course to take. This made for a feeble national security adviser and a dysfunctional national security process.

George W. Bush was chiefly responsible for this inertia. By his own admission, the swaggering Texan was not introspective. He showed little interest in second-guessing his policy decrees.[17] Bush fashioned himself as a decisive captain and titled his memoirs *Decision Points*, in which he discusses a series of case studies, all of which show the self-described "decider" confidently making the important decisions of his presidency, guided by his religious faith and the righteousness of the cause. In actuality, Bush avoided making stark choices. Detractors and admirers alike who worked in the White House agreed that the president wanted his subordinates to form a consensus on foreign policy and then present the decider with a single course of action. The problem with this managerial style occurred when his subordinates could not come to an agreement. In other administrations, such as that of President Reagan, the national security adviser simply forwarded both views with a cover sheet on which the president would check either choice A or B, sign it, and everyone knew, unequivocally, how the commander in chief had ruled. "This never happened in the Bush administration," lamented a midlevel NSC official. Instead, the president ordered his national security adviser back to hash out the issue again, in spite of the fact that it would never have been brought to the Oval Office had his advisers been able to form a collective decision.[18]

On June 1, 2001, Condi Rice chaired a meeting with Rumsfeld, Powell, and Cheney on Iraq. The Pentagon urged quick action, and was supported by the equally hawkish vice president. They argued that time was not on Washington's side. Saddam Hussein had kicked out UN inspectors three years earlier and, unchecked, "Saddam could possess nuclear and other weapons of mass destruction," a Defense Department point paper warned.[19]

In the heat of the Washington summer, the Bush inner circle met twice more to examine regime change in Iraq. Secretary of State Colin Powell advocated for targeted or smart sanctions, and not military action, to keep Saddam Hussein in his box. The outgoing chairman of the Joint Chiefs, Hugh Shelton, agreed. The U.S. military's air campaign had reduced the Iraqi military to a hollow shell—a brutal dictatorship but no threat to its neighbors, he argued. Rice offered no strong opinions either for or against the Pentagon's recommendations. But Shelton grew concerned that those advocating military action had begun to sway others in the interagency debate.

The one person in the administration fixated on Iran, perhaps more so than Iraq, was John Bolton, the new undersecretary of state for arms control and international security. With his shock of graying hair and a white walrus mustache, Bolton advocated a muscular foreign policy. Unlike the idealism of Wolfowitz, Bolton's views stemmed from the need for unilateral American action and hawkish Middle East views similar to those of Israel's Ariel Sharon. This placed him at odds with the more temperate Powell and Armitage running the State Department. But Powell accepted Bolton in part to deflect criticism by the more hawkish people in the administration. Armitage suspected he had been placed deliberately by the vice president to keep an eye on the powerful top diplomat, and referred to Bolton as one of the "bats." "When the day ended and the sun went down, they left their caves and flew back to report to the White House," Armitage said.

Bolton viewed Iran as a serious threat. Iran's unrelenting nuclear program presented the gravest of challenges, and he sympathized with the Israeli worries of the existential threat of a nuclear-armed Iran. In his portfolio of arms control, he pushed the administration to pressure Russia to halt its aid to Iran's nuclear and missile program, especially completing the twenty-year-old fledgling reactor at Bushehr.[20]

George Bush showed little interest in either Iraq or Iran. During the transition, Newbold briefed President-elect Bush on the current air operations over Iraq enforcing the no-fly zones. Bush asked only one question: how much money the Iraqi no-fly zones operation cost. Iran did not even come up in conversation.[21] As the heat of summer began to wane, the decider had yet to engage on Iraq. How he would have finally come down between smart sanctions or action remains speculative and would have been the great foreign policy debate of his first term. A terrorist attack by al-Qaeda ended the debate.

September 11, 2001, was a typical late summer day in Washington. A brilliant sunny blue sky superimposed itself over the white monuments and imposing granite buildings built with socialist grandeur during the 1920s. With Labor Day over and the kids back at school, hordes of government workers clogged the Beltway and the other highways running into Washington. While Cheney and Rumsfeld worked in their respective offices on opposite sides of the Potomac River, much of the government's senior leadership was scattered across the globe: the president in Florida, Hugh Shelton on his way to Hungary, other senior defense officials scattered about Russia and Europe.

That morning, nineteen Middle Eastern men boarded four jets in Boston, Washington, and Newark. Air traffic controllers soon noticed someone had turned off the transponder of American Airlines Flight 11, a 767 bound from Boston to the West Coast. The aircraft did an abrupt course change, turning back east. At the controls was Muhammad Atta, the ringleader of the band of Muslim anarchists and supporters of the Saudi zealot Osama bin Laden. Flying fast and low across the Manhattan skyline and chanting "Allahu akbar"—God is great—Atta flew the large passenger jet straight into the side of one of the two tallest buildings in the world and a symbol of American capitalism.

When the first plane hit the World Trade Center, military officers monitoring the world hot spots in the dingy cubicle labyrinth of the highly secure

National Military Command Center learned of it from the television news. The NMCC was not the stuff of Hollywood. Rather than an impressive war room with high-tech electronic maps as described by fanciful writers, in reality it resembled more of an unkempt maze. A building within a building, it sat in the center of the Pentagon, easily accessible to the offices of the chairman and the secretary of defense, who could walk down the hall and enter from any number of guarded posts. At its heart was the current operations section. Here a host of officers toiled, monitoring crises around the globe in a large, narrow, open room that meandered back around large square pilings that supported the weight of the building. Off this room was a small office where a brigadier general sat twenty-four hours a day as the senior watch officer, and a small conference room, which served as the nerve center during a crisis, replete with phones arrayed around a large rectangular table and a video screen on the far wall. This was the station of the chairman, and frequently the secretary, during a crisis. Around corners and through other doors was the alert center, poised to launch America's nuclear arsenal, and a room housing the communications link with Moscow, installed shortly after the Cuban Missile Crisis to allow instant messages between the two countries.

At first, officers monitoring the plane crash in New York believed it might have been a civilian plane; a few even recalled the bomber that crashed into the Empire State Building during the Second World War. A call to the Federal Aviation Administration, however, dispelled this theory.

The Pentagon too was a target. Skimming over Arlington National Cemetery, another hijacked aircraft clipped a lamppost of a navy exchange gas station before its wing clipped a generator and it tumbled into the colossal five-story building. The jet's momentum carried it through three of the building's five expansive rings, finally depositing part of its landing gear in the center of an interior access road.

"There was a heat wave like haze extending from the back of the room up to the ceiling," described a defense civilian, Christine Morrison. "Before I could register or complete that thought, this force hit the room, instantly turning the office into an inferno hell. Everything was falling, flying, and on fire, and there was no escaping it."[22]

In a small conference room next to the desk of the senior watch officer at the NMCC, Rumsfeld and Joint Chiefs vice chairman General Richard Myers monitored the attacks on New York and the Pentagon and prepared for whatever else might come. It was a stifling environment; two dozen men crammed into the small conference room. Designed to be self-contained in the event of a nuclear war, the NMCC had been sealed shut, closing the two sets of airtight doors to prevent smoke from entering the sensitive area. Within a couple of hours the oxygen ran short and the doors were reopened until the choking smoke forced them closed again.

With the smoke thick in the corridors of the Pentagon, at two forty p.m. Rumsfeld met with Stephen Cambone, deputy to the undersecretary of defense for planning, Douglas Feith. They discussed what information they had about who had been behind the attack, and the secretary brainstormed about the military response. Iraq immediately came out of Rumsfeld's mouth. Cambone jotted in his notebook, "Hit SH [Saddam Hussein] at same time—not only UBL [Usama bin Laden]."[23]

"The events of September 11 make it clear that we can simply no longer tolerate networks of state support for terrorism—particularly not those which are pursuing weapons of mass destruction—whether or not they were involved in this tragedy," Wolfowitz wrote in one of a series of memos to Rumsfeld immediately after the attack. "If there is even a 10% chance that Saddam Hussein was behind Tuesday's horrors, a maximum priority has to be put on eliminating that threat."[24]

Not surprisingly, Wolfowitz wanted to start with Iraq. Iraq was assumed to have weapons of mass destruction and had shown a willingness to use them. He now couched it as a key component in the new global war on terrorism. "We can't find all the snakes in the swamp . . . unless we drain the swamp," he wrote to Rumsfeld. Wolfowitz raised doubts about al-Qaeda's being responsible. He went so far as to suggest to the defense secretary that another country might have staged the attack to look as though 9/11 had been carried out by Osama bin Laden. "One could also imagine why someone would want it to appear that way even if they were, for example, Iraqis or Iranians or Syrians."[25]

A few days after the terrorist attack, Newbold walked into Feith's office with a rough plan to strike al-Qaeda targets in Afghanistan. Feith looked disdainfully at the marine general. "What are you planning that for?" he said. "Iraq is the target."[26]

Newbold was aghast. "Iraq had not attacked the United States." In 2002, Newbold retired in protest. Before leaving the Pentagon, he handed the chairman a scathing letter outlining the folly of the coming war with Iraq.

The weekend following the 9/11 attacks, Bush convened his foreign policy team at Camp David in Maryland. The discussions centered on the coming war in Afghanistan and how the United States could avoid repeating the errors of earlier empires. Wolfowitz made a pitch for attacking Iraq rather than Afghanistan.[27] Going after al-Qaeda and the Taliban in Afghanistan was more akin to a police action, explained Doug Feith, reflecting the views of many of the civilian appointees at the Pentagon. By striking at Iraq, you addressed the larger problem of state sponsors of terrorism, and that was "thinking strategically."[28] Bush rejected the argument, but Wolfowitz had laid down the marker for what would follow Afghanistan.

Douglas Feith was charged with developing defense policy for Secretary Rumsfeld. Thin with thick black hair, he was viewed by many officers as an arrogant ideologue. But Feith had a lawyerly precision. He drove subordinates crazy, proofreading their reports and criticizing comma placement even with time-sensitive briefings, but he proved adept at fleshing out Rumsfeld's and Wolfowitz's ideas.

The defense secretary wanted to put the "global" in the war on terrorism. He looked for a way of demonstrating unilateral American action, the ability to strike anywhere in the world to root out America's enemies. He wanted an aggressive, offensive military strategy. Richard Perle, the head of the influential Defense Policy Board, an advisory panel for the secretary, agreed. He advocated a series of successive campaigns, including Iraq, Syria, and Iran. The U.S. military would defeat one, withdraw quickly to avoid a lengthy occupation that would drain public support and resources, and then swiftly move to attack the next country. This appealed to Rumsfeld.

In the aftermath of 9/11, Feith and Joint Chiefs vice chairman General Peter Pace developed a matrix of the global terrorist network as part of regular meetings on building a "global war on terrorism" campaign. One objective behind their efforts was to ensure that the nexus of weapons of mass destruction and terrorists did not occur. While some countries linked to terrorists, such as Syria and Libya, might be coerced into giving up their weapons, others, such as Iraq, Feith and Pace believed, were beyond compelling with diplomatic or economic tools. "For over ten years, every reasonable means had been tried short of military force against Saddam Hussein," said Feith. Iran fell into a different category, Feith believed. "The United States had not tried to pressure the Iranians in a meaningful way using economic and political tools. Military force was not a serious alternative in 2001 and 2002."[29]

American intelligence aided the design by playing a double game on linkage between 9/11 and state sponsors of terrorism. On October 18, CIA Director George Tenet passed a report to Rumsfeld speculating as to which countries might have a motive to conduct terrorist attacks against the United States, focusing on Libya, Iran, and Iraq. Both Rumsfeld and Wolfowitz seized on this think piece as additional ammunition in their crusade to attack Iraq. When CIA analysts continued to come up short in proving this nexus, the Defense Department established the Office of Special Plans under Feith's oversight. Headed by a taciturn policy insider, Abe Shulsky, its mission was to look for links between al-Qaeda and Iraq that the intelligence community had missed. The fact that Shulsky's group did not find the link either did not dissuade the Bush Defense Department. An October 21, 2001, memo edited by senior defense officials Peter Rodman, Doug Feith, and Donald Rumsfeld summed up their views succinctly: "The absence of evidence is not necessarily evidence of absence."

The hijackers who plowed their planes into the World Trade Center in New York and the Pentagon on September 11, 2001, caused Bush administration policy to congeal as ideology merged with power politics. Both Armitage and Powell quickly fell in line. Vice President Dick Cheney believed in power politics and executive authority. He fixated on the weapons of mass destruction argument. "If a terrorist group acquired a nuclear or chemical device," he told a staffer, "they would certainly use it and create far greater damage than on September 11." Believing that a higher power had placed him as president during this critical moment in history, George Bush embraced Wolfowitz's goals for the war. He viewed the coming war against terrorism with a Wilsonian grandeur. The terrorist attacks now presented the opportunity to remake the Middle East based upon American values of the rights of individuals and not the whim of oligarchy.

Atrocity" is how Tehran's *Iran News* described the slaughter. Some Iranian officials believed that the United States had created al-Qaeda as a tool against the Islamic Republic. Conspiratorial-minded officials remained skeptical that such an operation could be conducted without the American government's knowledge. But the magnitude of the attack as well as the culprits stunned the Iranian government and its populace.[30] "My deep sympathy goes out to the American nation," said President Mohammad Khatami.

"Terrorism is condemned and the world public should identify its roots and its dimensions and should take fundamental steps to eliminate it." Mourners held a spontaneous candlelight vigil as thousands of people took to the streets of north Tehran chanting, "Death to terrorists." Iranian soccer fans observed a minute of silence before a match with Bahrain. Even Supreme Leader Ayatollah Ali Khamenei condemned the attacks: "Mass killing is wrong, whether it's in Hiroshima, Bosnia, New York, or Washington."[31] During Friday prayers at Qom, Ayatollah Ibrahim Amini said that the Iranian people grieved with the relatives of those killed, and the traditional slogan "Death to America" was absent from the crowds' mantras.[32]

Tehran had mixed emotions about the new administration. President Khatami desperately wanted to improve Iran's economy. He needed this for political survival, but also to show detractors within the government the tangible benefits from better relations with the West.[33] Bush's family ties to the oil industry appeared to be a good omen. Rafsanjani believed that pressure from American oil companies might lead to a lifting of the sanctions. Although his father's assignment as CIA director caused some unease within the Iranian government, many within the Iranian business community hoped the Republicans would be more sympathetic to lifting the sanctions in order to make money for American companies.

If the terrorist attack changed the focus of the U.S. government, it portended a change regarding Iran too. The traditional American antagonist suddenly loomed as a potential ally. "The Iranians seemed shocked by the scale of the attack," said Richard Armitage. Iran showed no enthusiasm for al-Qaeda or its Sunni-based objectives.

The perpetrators of 9/11 were harbored by a fiercely anti-Shia, anti-Iranian Afghan tribal alliance, the Taliban. Iran supported the main opposition group, the Northern Alliance, with close ties to the legendary Afghan resistance fighter who opposed both the Soviets and the Taliban, Ahmad Massoud. In 1998, Iran threatened to invade Afghanistan following the killing of eight Iranian diplomats by Taliban forces when they stormed the city of Mazar-e Sharif in northern Afghanistan. As a result, Iran increased its support for the Northern Alliance and the anti-Taliban forces. In the first half of 1999 alone, thirty-three cargo planes with 380 metric tons of small arms, ammo, and fuel arrived from the eastern Iranian air base of Mashhad to Tajikistan for transport to the Northern Alliance.

Since the late 1990s, the United Nations had sponsored meetings in Geneva with Afghanistan's neighbors plus the United States and others with an interest in Central Asia to resolve the myriad problems caused by the Afghan civil war and the Taliban's victory. Iran housed two million Afghan refugees. Afghan opium made its way through Iran's porous border bound for Iranian cities as well as the streets of Europe. The seventh floor of the Department of State paid little attention to these discussions, which fell under the auspices of the department's bureau that handled India and Pakistan rather than the Middle East. But the venue placed American and Iranian diplomats in the same room, and after September 11 the State Department saw this informal venue as a means of reaching out to Iran to leverage its access and cooperation with the Northern Alliance in the forthcoming American attack on the Taliban.

"The Iranians had the contacts to help us in Afghanistan, and appeared to be willing to use their influence in a constructive way," said Flynt Leverett, a CIA officer serving as the director for Middle East affairs at the National Security Council.[34]

Secretary Powell dispatched Ryan Crocker to meet with the Iranians in Geneva. As cover, the Italians and Germany were included to avoid the appearance of direct talks. But in fact, it would be the first face-to-face discussions between the two nations since 1986, during the arms-for-hostages debacle of the Reagan administration.

Discreet and experienced, and fluent in both Arabic and Farsi, Crocker served in some of the most demanding posts of the Middle East. In April 1983, he suffered superficial injuries from flying glass when an Iranian surrogate detonated a car packed with explosives in front of the U.S. embassy in Beirut. He headed the State Department's Iraq task force following Saddam's invasion of Kuwait, before returning to Lebanon in 1990 as the ambassador. This would be the first of six ambassadorial appointments in the region, including Iraq in 2007 during the height of the violence following the U.S. invasion and Afghanistan during the surge there under President Obama. Crocker knew something about Iran. His first posting as a Foreign Service officer in 1972 was to the American consulate at Khorramshahr in southwestern Iran. A captive of the student protests on American university campuses at the time, Crocker arrived convinced that a leftist revolution would send the shah's reactionary, authoritarian regime to the "dustbin of history." He spent two years traveling the countryside, talking to students and labor organizers trying to prove this thesis. "I could not have identified a politicized mullah if I tripped over one. I had no idea of what Khomeini was writing in Najaf," Crocker recalled, lamenting his own naïveté. With the shah's overthrow, Crocker realized the inherent problem of looking at another society through one's own lens. "I learned the important lesson that you need to check your intellectual baggage at the door when you arrive in someone else's complex society, and Iran is an incredibly complex country."

Not everyone in the U.S. government agreed about the wisdom of talking to Iran. When Paul Wolfowitz heard of the Crocker mission, he wanted it shut down. John Bolton concurred, seeing it as a reward for bad behavior and distrusting anything coming out of the mouth of an Iranian official. One of the most strident opponents was William Luti, deputy assistant secretary of defense for Near Eastern and South Asian affairs. A retired navy captain who rose to prominence as Newt Gingrich's military assistant, he'd earned a doctorate from Tufts University with his dissertation on Operation Earnest Will and the escort of Kuwaiti tankers during the 1980s, in which he'd opposed the joint operation led by CENTCOM. "He is an extremely bright guy and a good friend," said Tony Less, a commander during the tanker war, "but he is very right wing."[35]

Luti was excitable regarding Iran.[36] He openly advocated regime change rather than what he saw as fruitless talks with a duplicitous nation. Luti had Larry Franklin, a civilian staffer who shared his views, draw up a set of counterpoints against engagement with Iran. "Iran is a hostile nation," Franklin began in an eight-point diatribe against the Islamic Republic. "Iran mouthed words of condemnation for the September 11 attacks, but actions speak otherwise." It violated its international obligations, was duplicitous, and actually worked to undermine the Afghan government and fragment the country. "Iran must cease illegal programs and halt its terrorist ways."[37]

But Powell and Armitage stood firm, and for once Rice herself interjected, concurring that meeting with the Iranians about Afghanistan could be useful. As long as the discussions remained at a low level and did not stray into other areas of U.S.-Iranian relations, the Pentagon acquiesced and raised no strong objections, other than to razz Crocker with a few good-natured jabs for "talking with the enemy" when he departed on a junket with Rumsfeld in Cairo in order to meet with the Iranians.[38]

Crocker supported meeting with the Iranians. "I generally believe in talking to anyone who will talk to you," he said. "Maybe you will persuade them; maybe you'll neutralize them; maybe you can just mess with their mind."[39]

The Iranian delegation consisted of three individuals. In an echo of McFarlane, North, and Cave's talks fifteen years earlier, all the Iranians had strong connections to the Revolutionary Guard commander, Major General Yahya Rahim Safavi, and to the supreme leader. One was a deputy foreign minister and an experienced hand in international political organizations, another a Revolutionary Guard general who had served as Iran's liaison to the Afghan Northern Alliance. The third man was the most intriguing to the Americans: former Iranian ambassador to Afghanistan and Bosnia-Herzegovina Mohammad Taherian. His career blurred the distinction between diplomat and military officer. During the 1980s, as ambassador in Kabul, he had secretly funneled arms to the mujahideen, when the Reagan administration was engaged in the same activity. A decade later, as ambassador to Bosnia in the midst of the Balkan civil war, he had funneled Iranian military aid to the Muslims, an operation that included deploying two hundred to three hundred Revolutionary Guardsmen to Central Europe to fight for Bosnia. He had also held private meetings with the CIA on opposing the Serbs during his time in Sarajevo, a fact he informed Crocker's delegation of during one of their lengthy chats.[40]

From the outset the discussions showed promise. During the breakout sessions during the first meeting in Geneva, the Iranians made it clear that they wanted to support the United States in Afghanistan. "They were in favor of swift and decisive action, military action by the United States against the Taliban," recalled Crocker. A couple of days before the United States launched its attack on Afghanistan, Crocker was having a theoretical discussion with the Iranians on the makeup of the future Afghan government. One of the Iranians rose to his feet and threw some papers on the floor: "None of this matters if we don't get on with the war!"

A short time later, the Revolutionary Guard general produced a map and pointed out all the Taliban troop locations. "Here's where you need to concentrate your bombings," he advised. Crocker immediately passed this back to Washington.

The Iranians repeatedly stressed that the two countries needed to work together. "We have more in common than differences," they said. They shared the same adversaries—Saddam Hussein and the Taliban—and needed to end thirty years of estrangement and build a new relationship. "The sweep of history and the geopolitics of the Middle East made Iran and the United States natural allies," Crocker recalled one saying. Crocker remained uncertain whether the Iranians believed this or if anyone in Tehran shared the same opinion.

The two parties met roughly once a month, bouncing between Geneva and Paris. The Germans and Italians dropped out, leaving the Americans and Iranians alone for hours, meeting in hotel lobbies, Crocker's suite, and at the United Nations special representative for Afghanistan Lakhdar Brahimi's plush apartment overlooking the Luxemburg Gardens on the Left Bank of the French capital. The discussions were always cordial and professional. Crocker's instructions from the State Department were not specific; as they were informal talks, no one back in Washington paid too close attention. With this freedom, Crocker and his Iranian counterparts held long, freewheeling conversations that meandered into a wide array of contentious issues, from history, Lebanon, and Iraq to terrorism.

The Americans and Iranians quickly came to common agreement on the need to stabilize Afghanistan and for mutual cooperation on the formation of a post-Taliban government. Militarily, Iran offered the use of its airfields and ports to support the campaign in Afghanistan. While this offer was rejected, the United States did accept an Iranian offer to provide sanctuary for downed American pilots. U.S. airmen were told that if they had to bail out, they should do it over Iran and the Iranian air force would provide search and rescue units to retrieve them.

As the discussions progressed, the Iranian delegation proposed expanding the talks. The State Department prepared a comprehensive package of carrots and sticks designed to take advantage of a strategic opening with Iran. The goal would be a normalization of relations between the two antagonists. Armitage viewed this as prudent planning, but he remained doubtful that Iran would acquiesce to the U.S. demands: ending support for Hezbollah and terrorism and respecting democratic principles.

In November, President Khatami arrived in New York for the opening of the United Nations General Assembly, which had been delayed due to the havoc caused by the collapse of the World Trade Center. The Iranians had two requests. Khatami wanted to go to Ground Zero—the site of the Twin

Towers—and light a candle and pay his respects. Second, the Iranians recommended bringing additional Revolutionary Guard officers to expand the security dialogue beyond those in Geneva.

The U.S. government refused both requests. A visit by the president of a terrorist nation would not only insult the memory of those killed, a senior Bush administration official wrote; it threatened to undermine the monolithic nature of the war on terrorism, which lumped Iran, Iraq, and Syria all into the same nefarious category.

Newt Gingrich summed the concern up neatly during lunch with Doug Feith and Peter Rodman less than two weeks after the September 11 attacks. The United States needed to maintain a consistent message that the war on terrorism was a broad campaign and did not distinguish the policy rationale behind each terrorist actor. "We confuse Americans, allies, and our enemies when we speak of Iran joining the coalition against terrorism," the unofficial minister without a portfolio declared.[41]

But the success of Crocker's meetings set the stage for the next major diplomatic leap in Afghanistan: the Bonn conference in December 2001. In late fall, Powell appointed Ambassador James Dobbins as the American representative for the Afghan opposition. Although Dobbins was planning on retiring after three decades as an American diplomat, he had unique experience in nation building in the Balkans. Dobbins was tasked to work with the United Nations–supervised negotiations with Afghanistan's neighbors, including Iran, to structure a new post-Taliban government and constitution.

Few within the government objected to Dobbins's effort. As the United Nations had invited all of Afghanistan's neighbors, including Iran, it made no sense not to attend a forum in which the United States needed to exert influence, just to avoid the Iranians. "That would have been the policy equivalent of cutting off our nose to spite our face," recalled Feith.[42]

Dobbins's discussions remained autonomous from Crocker's meetings in Geneva. While each knew of the other's meetings, the coordination between the two centered back in Washington with Marc Grossman, the number three man at the State Department.[43] Unlike Crocker's limited, secretive meetings, Dobbins wanted a broader-based delegation from within the U.S. government. The White House dispatched Afghan-born Zalmay Khalilzad to Dobbins's team. Although an administration hawk on Iran, Khalilzad was fluent in Farsi and had a solid grasp of the intricacies of Afghanistan and generally supported Dobbins's goals.

Meeting in a sprawling guesthouse called the Petersberg, a holdover from the days when the small German town served as the West German capital, Dobbins led the American delegation—including Luti, who had been sent along to keep an eye on Dobbins—to the UN-sponsored conference to formulate a new government for Afghanistan.

Javad Zarif headed the Iranian delegation. Prematurely gray, Zarif looked older than his forty-one years. Educated at San Francisco State with his doctorate from the University of Denver, he was a sensible, savvy diplomat. Quick-witted and erudite, Zarif deftly navigated the greenrooms of the Western news media, providing a public face of a seemingly rational Iranian government. As a pragmatist, he was distrusted by hard-liners in Tehran, and the supreme leader tended to prefer diplomats from the Revolutionary Guard, such as those meeting Crocker. But Zarif had the backing of Khatami and was a powerful player in Iranian diplomacy.

The Iranians remained supportive of the dialogue with the United States. Both the hard-line supreme leader and the reformist president Khatami supported the opening, although for different reasons. Khatami viewed this as an opportunity to revive his reform movement and strengthen his power in Iran. Ayatollah Khamenei feared the Islamic Republic was next in America's crosshairs in its war on terrorism. While the United States had two separate tracks with Dobbins and Crocker, Iran tended to shuttle the same individuals between the two Americans. Not surprisingly, the Iranians' talking points were consistent regardless of which American they happened to be having tea with that day. Both Dobbins and Crocker reported back that Iran wanted to cooperate in Afghanistan.

The evening before the conference convened, Dobbins received a call from the Iranians asking to meet at their hotel. Fearing Luti would try to derail the talks, Dobbins deliberately excluded him and took Khalilzad to meet with Zarif. Khalilzad proved a valuable sidekick both for his language abilities and for his sage advice during the talks with the Iranians. Zarif and Dobbins spent an hour together comparing notes. Both sides agreed on the core issues: the Northern Alliance should provide the nucleus of a new government and Hamid Karzai was an acceptable candidate for the new president.[44]

When Dobbins briefed his American team the next morning on what had been discussed, another hard-liner in Luti's party, Harold Rhode, who worked for the Defense Department's Office of Net Assessment and frequently

Navy SEALs seize the Iranian oil platform Rostam following shelling by American warships, October 19, 1987. The attack was in retaliation for an Iranian missile attack that damaged a U.S. flagged oil tanker. (*U.S. Special Operations Command*)

An American helicopter and surface minesweepers search for Iranian mines in the Persian Gulf, December 1987. Iran laid nearly one hundred mines in international waters, threatening to disrupt the entire world's economy. (*Department of Defense*)

National Security Adviser Colin Powell updates President Reagan on the morning of April 18, 1988, about the military retaliation against Iran for the mining that nearly sank the frigate *Samuel B. Roberts. (Reagan Library)*

Iranian oil platform Sassan burns following an attack by the U.S. Navy and Marines. The large complex served as a base for Iranian operations against American convoys. *(Department of Defense)*

The Iranian warship *Sahand* before and after being hit by nearly twenty bombs and missiles by U.S. naval ships and aircraft, killing almost a third of the crew. *(U.S. Navy)*

The American air force housing complex, Khobar Towers, following a bombing by Iranian surrogates, June 1996. *(Department of Defense)*

The commander of U.S. Central Command, General Anthony Zinni, developed new set of military plans against Iran following the bombing of Khobar Towers and increased harassment of American warships in the Persian Gulf by the Iranian Revolutionary Guards. *(Department of Defense)*

President George W. Bush meets with his foreign policy team in the secretary of defense's office during the invasion of Iraq, March 25, 2003. Their war plans failed to take into account the impact Saddam Hussein's removal would have on the larger Persian neighbor. *(Getty Images)*

Iranian Revolutionary Guard boats interdict U.S. boats trying to move up the Shatt al-Arab, April 3, 2003. The Iranians were supporting a massive influx of Iranian and surrogate forces moving into Iraq during the American-led invasion of Iraq. *(Author's collection)*

U.s. troops raid a compound used by Iranian-backed militias in Iraq, 2007. *(Department of Defense)*

Soldiers uncover a cache of explosive formed projectiles (EFPs) in Iraq. Iran's Quds Force provided these deadly devices, which killed and wounded several thousand American troops, to their Iraqi allies. *(Department of Defense)*

Chairman of the Joint Chiefs Richard Meyers (*left*) and Central Command commander John Abizaid (*right*) testify before Congress. Both men grappled with growing Iranian influence in Iraq and increased covert military activities across the Middle East. *(Department of Defense)*

U.S. ambassador to Iraq Ryan Crocker (*left*), Iranian ambassador Hassan Kazemi Qomi (*right*), and Iraqi prime minister Nouri al-Maliki (*top center*) meet in the Iraqi prime minister's office in Baghdad on May 28, 2007. It was one of the few face-to-face meetings between Iran and the United States in thirty years but failed to resolve the two nations' differences. (*Associated Press*)

Iranian nuclear scientist Shahram Amiri with his son after his arrival at Tehran airport, July 15, 2010. He defected to the United States, where he provided valuable information about Iran's nuclear program, only to return to Iran claiming he had been kidnapped. (*Associated Press*)

Iranian president Mahmoud Ahmadinejad (*center*) tours the uranium-enriching centrifuges at the Natanz nuclear facility, April 8, 2008. (*Associated Press*)

January 13, 2012: Iranians carry the flag-draped coffin of Mostafa Ahmadi Roshan, the director of the Natanz uranium enrichment facility in central Iran, who was killed when two assailants on a motorcycle attached a magnetic bomb to his car in Tehran. He was the victim of an assassination campaign against Iran's nuclear program that Iran blamed on Israel and the United States. (*Associated Press*)

General James Mattis (*left*) confers with Defense Secretary Robert Gates in Amman, Jordan, March 25, 2011. A thoughtful tactician and warrior, Mattis is the latest American military commander to confront Iran in an increasingly tense situation in the Persian Gulf. *(Department of Defense)*

An Iranian antiship missile is launched during an exercise near the Strait of Hormuz. Iran has developed an unorthodox military force capable of inflicting significant damage to the U.S. Navy in the event of a new war in the Persian Gulf. *(Fars News Agency/Department of Defense)*

did special tasks for Wolfowitz, "became agitated," as Dobbins put it mildly in describing the scene. Luti and Rhode strenuously objected to the talks, rejecting the very idea of any limited convergence of interests between the United States and Iran. To Dobbins's relief, both men left Bonn the following day.[45]

Dobbins and Zarif proceeded to hammer out the framework for a new Afghan government. The two men met every morning at ten o'clock for coffee, with the Italians and Germans coming along to provide the fig leaf of multilateral talks. During one of these meetings over tea and cookies, Zarif brought to Dobbins's attention a major omission in the draft of the final agreement: "The text makes no mention of democratic elections," Zarif said in his flawless English. "Don't you think the new Afghan government should be committed to holding democratic elections?"

Dobbins agreed, somewhat embarrassed that the U.S. delegation had not noticed the absence of this obvious basic tenet of American policy and that the Iranians had.

"Further," Zarif continued, taking obvious pleasure in stealing the customary American themes, "the draft makes no mention of terrorism. Should we not insist that the new Afghan government be committed to cooperating with the international community to combat terrorism?"[46]

The irony of this was not lost on Dobbins. Despite America's castigation of Iran as a totalitarian, fundamentalist, and terrorist regime, the country opposed both al-Qaeda and the Taliban and was more democratic than many of Washington's Arab allies in the Middle East, including the two stalwarts, Egypt and Saudi Arabia. It exposed a major flaw in the Bush administration's evolving war on terrorism: by lumping Iran, Iraq, the Taliban, and al-Qaeda all in the same monolithic camp, the United States lost the opportunity to exploit the natural divisions and open hostility that existed among those grouped under this broad tent of terrorism.

After more than two weeks, the conference concluded. In the final hours, Zarif and the Iranians played a critical role in uniting the disparate Afghan warlords. Zarif's personal intervention overcame a final hurdle to the apportionment of the ministry positions among the ethnic groups, which had threatened to derail the entire accord. Both Iran and the United States coalesced behind the new president, Hamid Karzai, a pro-American Afghan who had arrived in Kabul on the backs of American special operations forces.

The following month, Dobbins met again with the Iranians during a fund drive for Afghanistan held in Tokyo. Accompanied by Treasury Secretary Paul O'Neill, the United States pledged only about 5 percent of the $5 billion total to support reconstruction in Afghanistan, a paltry sum that irritated Dobbins and attested to the Bush administration's disinterest in nation building in Afghanistan. By contrast, Iran offered $540 million, twice as much as Washington. Iran understood what the Bush administration did not: with money went influence over allocation of reconstruction funds and influence in the new government. Over the coming years, Iran followed this up with tens of millions of dollars in additional aid, plus a steady stream of bags of cash given directly to Karzai to ensure Iranian influence over the new government. In January 2002, the Iranians sent technicians to restore radio and television service and provided over a billion dollars in assistance. Tehran established regular commercial airline flights into Kabul, greatly expanded exports of commercial goods into the country, and was a leading supplier of humanitarian aid.

While at the conference, former UN high commissioner for refugees Sadako Ogata passed a note to Secretary O'Neill from the Iranians. They were proposing once again to open a formal dialogue with the United States to discuss all issues dividing the two nations. Dobbins and O'Neill dutifully reported this back to Rice and the State Department. "No one evinced any interest," Dobbins recalled.[47]

Just before the Tokyo summit, the Revolutionary Guard had aided the administration hawks opposed to any dialogue when they tried to smuggle a ship full of weapons to the Palestinians, then in the midst of their second intifada. Some fifty tons of arms were loaded by a lighter from Qeshm Island onto the ship *Karine A*. Israeli commandos intercepted the ship in the Red Sea. It seems unlikely that hard-liners in Tehran were hoping to scuttle the talks with the United States; the Revolutionary Guard operation appears to have been more on autopilot, planned well ahead of time. Israel paraded the crates of Iranian-made explosives and rockets before the press. Immediately, during interagency meetings at the White House, both Peter Rodman and Bill Luti touted this as evidence of Iranian support for terrorism and argued that regime change and not accommodation should be administration policy. "It showed once again you could not trust Iran and you cannot change a leopard's spots," said one former Bush defense official who urged overthrowing the Iranian regime.

D espite the apparent harmony on Afghanistan, suspicion about al-Qaeda's presence in Iran reinforced hard-line views inside the U.S. government. As a sidebar to Crocker's talks in Geneva, James Pavitt, the CIA's deputy director for operations, met separately with another Iranian delegation, composed of MOIS agents.[48] Pavitt raised concerns about al-Qaeda fleeing across the Afghan border into Iran. The CIA estimated that some five hundred al-Qaeda suspects and their families were in Iran, including Osama bin Laden's eldest son, Saad, and one of his daughters. The Iranians responded to Pavitt that they did not have enough forces to guard their expansive and lawless border with Afghanistan and that many undesirables crossed into Iran. But they claimed to have arrested many al-Qaeda members and placed others under house arrest. The CIA passed the names of several high-value al-Qaeda members suspected of being in Iran, requesting that they be turned over to the United States. Iran viewed these al-Qaeda captives as important for its own security. They provided valuable insight into the organization that Tehran viewed as a threat to its own security. Holding them also provided insurance against al-Qaeda attacks against Iran. The several hundred al-Qaeda captives and their families were held in varying degrees of confinement, from prison to limited free movements under the supervision of security officials.[49] The Iranians refused to give up anyone from the bin Laden family, but did turn over one highly sought al-Qaeda affiliate to Karzai's government in Kabul. In return, Iran requested information on those Taliban members responsible for the killing of their diplomats in 1998. Unfortunately, Crocker responded, the United States had no specific information on the culprits and none were in American custody.

To placate the Americans, Javad Zarif flew to New York. He carried photocopies of the passports of more than two hundred al-Qaeda and Taliban fighters held by Iranian authorities, as well as a flowchart of who each of them was and how that fit into the larger network. In return, Zarif requested America's help in repatriating some of these captives to Saudi Arabia and Egypt, with whom Washington had better diplomatic relations than did Tehran. One of those in custody was a renegade Afghan who opposed both the Taliban and the United States with equal fervor, Gulbuddin Hekmatyar. Zarif agreed to keep Hekmatyar, a brutal cutthroat, under arrest, as long as the United States did not then accuse Iran of harboring terrorists.

Despite these overtures, the U.S. government remained suspicious that Iran knew far more about other al-Qaeda members in its country. "The Iranians were trying to give us the limited modified hangout," said Armitage, referring to a quote by Richard Nixon during Watergate. "Give a little ankle and let them think we are showing them everything."[50]

One of those the CIA suspected of being in Iran was Abu Musab al-Zarqawi. The Jordanian had been bankrolled by Osama bin Laden to form his own militia near Herat in western Afghanistan. A cutthroat, al-Zarqawi later participated in beheading hostages and in organizing suicide bombings against U.S. forces in Iraq, until American special operators dropped a laser-guided bomb on him in 2006.

Rumors of al-Zarqawi's presence in Iran persisted in intelligence circles, which nearly led to a secret raid into Iran to kill him in 2002. The U.S. government learned of an upcoming meeting with al-Zarqawi and other al-Qaeda operatives about obtaining chemical or biological weapons. The meeting was to occur near the northern Iranian city of Chalus, in a house only three kilometers from the Caspian Sea. Navy SEALs developed an imaginative plan. A small team would be air-dropped into the water off the coast, and then make its way across the beach to the suspected al-Qaeda meeting house. Once in position, the SEALs would call in an air strike and drop a thousand-pound smart bomb on top of al-Zarqawi.

Joint Chiefs chair Richard Myers briefed President Bush that it would be a "high-risk" operation. Iranian military forces were nearby, and the SEALs had serious intelligence gaps—lacking both photographs of the attendees and an agent on the ground to update them on the actual time of the meeting. Myers cautioned against the mission, unless they obtained some rock-solid intelligence that spelled out when al-Zarqawi would be at the safe house. The daring raid had captivated the president, and the hawkish Dick Cheney liked the idea of striking simultaneously at both Iran and al-Qaeda. But President Bush reluctantly agreed with the chairman's concerns that the risks outweighed the gains. It was a wise decision by Bush. While detractors in the administration used Iran's failure to produce al-Zarqawi as evidence of Tehran's obstinacy, the man in question was never even in Iran, but in a remote, ungoverned area of Iraq.[51]

Despite the setbacks of the *Karine A* and detractors within the government, the United States and the Islamic Republic had sustained their most important diplomatic contact in two decades. The shock of terrorism on a grand scale allowed the two rivals to find common ground in remaking the political landscape of a troublesome Afghanistan. Meanwhile, the quick rout of the Taliban and its al-Qaeda parasites meant that Iraq came up next in the queue, even if the decider had not yet ruled on the next war. In early December, CENTCOM commander Tommy Franks flew to Bush's ranch in Crawford, Texas. After getting a tour of the large spread, Franks updated the president on the invasion plan for Iraq. While Dobbins had hoped his talks would serve as the catalyst for a permanent thaw with Iran, years of suspicion would not be easily overcome. With the neocon grand design about to come to fruition, Iran would not be a partner; instead, it would be part of the nefarious lineup of the "axis of evil."

Twenty-Three

AN AXIS OF EVIL

George W. Bush strode up to the podium for the customary State of the Union speech. In just four short months since September 11, 2001, U.S. troops and Afghan allies had driven the Taliban from power. On that night of January 29, 2002, the president swaggered with self-confidence. His popularity stood at 85 percent in the polls, and the nationalist fervor of the moment swept up even the most partisan Democrat. The American flag on the lapel had become a mandatory fashion accessory. Twenty-two years earlier, President Carter had stood at the same lectern and delivered one of his most important foreign policy addresses, in which he promised to use the might of the American military to defend access to Persian Gulf oil. Now, in arguably an even more pivotal moment in history, George Bush laid down his marker for Middle East security.

"As we gather tonight, our nation is at war, our economy is in recession, and the civilized world faces unprecedented dangers. Yet the state of our union has never been stronger," Bush opened to thunderous applause. As the president moved into the meat of his address, he singled out three nations—North Korea, Iraq, and Iran—for closer scrutiny. "States like these, and their terrorist allies, constitute an axis of evil, arming to threaten the peace of the world. By seeking weapons of mass destruction, these regimes pose a grave and growing danger." As for Tehran's trespasses, the president said they were aggressively pursuing weapons of mass destruction and exporting terrorism, while "an unelected few repress the Iranian people's hope for freedom."

In what became known as the "axis of evil" speech, the memorable line itself had been originally penned by speechwriter David Frum. It had originally been intended to be a few lines warning of the danger of Saddam Hussein, but Frum liked the term "axis" as a throwback to the great crusade of the Second World War. North Korea and Iran were more of an afterthought, as they were both state sponsors of terrorism and you could not have an axis of just one country. As Frum noted, State of the Union speeches were akin to a moon launch, drawing in all the resources of the executive branch.[1] The White House routed the speech through all the departments for their review and input, and the "axis of evil" line garnered little attention, with neither Condoleezza Rice nor Richard Armitage even recalling the line. The only senior official who objected was Richard Myers.[2] The affable and accommodating air force pilot rarely rose in opposition, but he believed the line counterproductive in the larger war on terrorism. But the president liked it. So in spite of Iran's help in stabilizing Afghanistan and the ongoing talks between the two nations, the line stayed.

Iranian leaders greeted President Bush's "axis of evil" speech with indignation. "Those comments stunned everyone in the government," said Hossein Mousavian, a close adviser to the Iranian president. Bush's remarks reinforced suspicions about talking with the Americans. The supreme leader called Bush's remarks indicative of "a person thirsty for human blood." Meanwhile, former president and head of the powerful Expediency Council Hashemi Rafsanjani seized on the "unelected few" remark with a jab at Bush's own problems winning the popular vote in 2000: "It is interesting that this prodemocracy claim is made by somebody who has been elected with less than 25 percent of the popular vote under a court intervention."[3] The deputy foreign affairs minister sent a letter to the United Nations secretary general denouncing the speech, accusing the United States of missing the opportunity to develop a global response to end the roots of terrorism, with Washington's "egoistic, unilateral and simplistic policy, which merely uses threats of brute force against what America one-sidedly considers to be terrorism."[4]

Iran's response did not stop with words. Iran immediately withdrew from the promising talks with Ryan Crocker. A humiliated Javad Zarif believed the United States had betrayed Iran's good-faith overtures. In retribution, in

February Iran released the wanted Taliban commander Gulbuddin Hekmatyar, who immediately went back to his old ways and became a significant thorn in the American side by organizing resistance to the U.S.-backed government in Afghanistan.[5] Iran launched a propaganda campaign using radio to foment anti-American sentiments in western Afghanistan, which helped undermine the Karzai government Tehran had helped to install. And it increased its military support for longtime ally Ismail Khan, who had sold Iran American Stinger missiles during the tanker war.

Like many military officers, Chairman of the Joint Chiefs of Staff Richard Myers had worked in Iran during the heady days of the shah. In 1976, he'd traveled to the desert to help the Iranian air force build an electronic warfare range to train its pilots on countering enemy air defenses. Myers noted that most of the passengers on the flight to Tehran were defense contractors headed there to sell the shah even more weapons. "I didn't have any revelations about the shah's overthrow three years later," Myers said. But as he watched all the high-tech salesmen disembark carrying their briefcases, he thought, "Is this sustainable?"[6]

Myers had a likable, easygoing persona, and a passion for Harley motorcycles. Detractors called him the "pliable chairman," and over his four years as the senior military officer, he raised few objections to the unfolding Bush military policies. Myers shied away from politics; he practiced a "salute smartly and carry out orders" work ethic. Rumsfeld was a demanding boss, but as Myers recalled, he never tried to stifle the chairman's views in front of the president.

But the Iran policy, or lack of it, frustrated Myers. The "axis of evil" line typified the problems within the administration in the chairman's mind. "There were attempts to address Iran strategically," Myers said, "but at the NSC level, it always became too sensitive or not the right time." Myers suspected there might be something going on behind the scenes, perhaps a backdoor strategy that he was not privy to; in reality, however, the Bush administration had developed no Iran strategy.[7]

Iran typified the entire NSC process, said John Bolton: "It reflected a breakdown in the national security decision-making function. Understanding the president's managerial style, Condi did not want to present disagreements to the president. When you are not willing to air disagreements before the president, you get mush as a policy."[8]

On January 6, 2002, Condoleezza Rice sent out a set of draft talking points on Iranian policy as part of an effort to publish a new national security decision directive, essentially a government-wide order dictating U.S. policy. Rice took a positive view of talking to Iran. While cautioning that Iran's continued refusal to turn over members of al-Qaeda prevented any major improvement in relations, as one of the first bullets on the memorandum stated, "We are prepared to discuss practical issues related to Iraq that would be of mutual interest to both Iran and the United States." Rice advocated exchanging information regarding Iraq's weapons of mass destruction (WMD) programs and humanitarian assistance. The United States had no intention of staying in Iraq permanently and understood that Iran, having been on the receiving end of Iraqi chemical weapons, had an interest in the elimination of that threat. If Iran provided its own intelligence on Saddam's illicit weapons programs, the United States would respond by offering ways to help protect the Iranian populace should Iraq strike at Iranian cities with missiles loaded with chemical warheads. Iran could allow humanitarian assistance to move into Iraq from across its border and establish refugee camps should a chemical attack on U.S. forces cause a mass exodus by terrified civilians.

General Myers agreed with Rice. He piped up that they could use the Geneva channel to deconflict the military operations with the Iranian military and to avoid an inadvertent conflict, especially near the Iraq-Iran border. If Iran provided search and rescue for downed American pilots, that too would be useful, the chairman added. But the normally reticent chairman wanted those responsible for Khobar Towers brought to justice as part of any strategy with Iran. For the air force general, the attack on the airmen's barracks by Iranian surrogates was personal. Scrawling a note on a routing sheet for his plans officer, Lieutenant General George Casey, he stated: "I think any Iran policy should acknowledge that Iran had a direct hand in the Khobar Towers bombing. This seems to be forgotten."[9]

Rice's attitude immediately set off alarms within the Pentagon. The tenor of the draft seemed to "undercut our policy of rejection of the Iranian regime's legitimacy," wrote Peter Rodman on a draft of the talking points. "We don't want stories in the press about reconciliation."[10] Rodman believed that there might be some merit in learning what Iran knew about Iraq's WMD program, but this intelligence should not come at the expense of minimizing the Iranian threat in any post Iraq War plans. His deputy, Bill Luti, agreed. Iran viewed a free Iraq as a threat, he wrote. While recognizing Iran's own experience on the receiving end of Iraq's chemical weapons, the United States viewed Iran's nuclear and chemical programs as equally dangerous. The United States should not consider the Iranians in any postwar role, and the only communications with their government should be to tell them not to interfere in Iraq after the U.S. invasion and to keep such terrorist surrogates as Hezbollah in check, or else.

On this issue, Secretary Rumsfeld shared his views only with the vice president. On January 9, Peter Rodman forwarded a memo with Rumsfeld's views to Cheney's office in order to synchronize the two offices as part of a coordinated effort to steer the Geneva talks with Iran from a dialogue to an ultimatum against Iran. In a principals meeting in late January, both the vice president and Rumsfeld echoed the same refrains: the United States should not duplicate the Afghan model with Iraq, and any attempt by the Iranian military or intelligence service to "penetrate Iraq" or "exploit pro-Iranian assets inside Iraq" should be construed as a hostile act toward the United States.

The civilians surrounding the secretary of defense and the vice president remained convinced that the Iranian regime was ripe for overthrow. Most advocated supporting domestic opponents to foment civilian unrest. It was a hard-line policy designed to spark a revolt that would overthrow the regime. In a January 2002 NSC briefing led by Donald Rumsfeld entitled "Global War on Terrorism: The Way Ahead," the secretary stridently recommended against any rapprochement with the regime. Instead, he recommended supporting internal democratic opposition movements, the argument being that the clerical regime was teetering—it was corrupt and despised by the Iranian youth. With the right amount of support, Iranian opposition groups inside and outside would bring the government down. "Collapse of the Iranian clerical regime would deflate Islamist militancy worldwide," Rumsfeld argued, without offering any substantial proof, before adding that this would help defeat al-Qaeda—even though the terrorist organization had nothing to do with Iran and was not even Shia.

Within both the CIA and the State Department many Iran analysts objected to the Defense Department's characterization of Iran's government.

"It was ridiculous," said one senior State Department official. "There was dissatisfaction, as reflected by Khatami's victories, but this did not translate into support behind an American-led revolt."

Over the next few months, Rice tried to shepherd the national security planning document through the government and get it in front of the president. On May 21, Rice, Powell, Rumsfeld, Tenet, and Myers met to go over an NSC paper and address the vice president's and defense secretary's concerns. All present agreed on the broad goals: get Iran to stop its nuclear and missile weapons programs, cut ties with Hezbollah, become a Western democracy, and generally acquiesce to American desires in the Middle East. But they remained split on how to move forward in a strategy to achieve these goals. The main "land mine," as an air force lieutenant colonel described it, in pursuing any constructive dialogue was the civilian hawks in the Defense Department. "OSD [Office of the Secretary of Defense] takes a strong position on regime change and sees very little value in continuing any engagement with Iran," a Pentagon memo bluntly stated.

Paul Wolfowitz, who rarely came to White House meetings, took an active role in steering Rice's document away from reconciliation to antagonism. With the backing of the vice president, the document's verbiage became more strident with each successive draft. Passages praising President Khatami for restraining extremist elements disappeared, replaced with a rejection of the reform movement as not bringing about "meaningful democratic changes or moderation in policies inimical to U.S. interests." Recent Iranian arrests and turnover of al-Qaeda suspects or support for the Bonn agreement were not enough. Nothing short of Iran's capitulation to American demands would satisfy the hawks. Iran even needed to support the recent Arab League's peace proposal for Israel and Palestine, which not even the right-wing Likud Party in Israel embraced. But lacking this, Iran could not reenter the community of nations.

Rather than engagement, Rumsfeld's office pressed for overthrowing the Islamic Republic by supporting internal and external opposition groups and proposed forming an Iranian National Congress to organize the opposition groups.[11] The United States would install a secular, democratic government. Iran was a terrorist organization, Feith and Wolfowitz argued during meetings. It was intent on undermining American interests and destroying Israel. They placed no confidence in Khatami or his reform movement to bring about any meaningful change in Iranian behavior. The Pentagon's civilians pressed that any references to constructive cooperation on Iran's interests in Afghanistan be struck from memos. "Clear possibility," one officer working in the Pentagon wrote in February 2002, "that OSD would propose Iran as the next target in the war on terrorism."

Donald Rumsfeld wanted language stating that overthrowing the regime would be American policy. On August 19, 2002, in a letter to Bush, he proposed dealing with two thorns in the American side: "I believe that the situations in Iran and North Korea are sufficiently interesting and unsettled that fashioning a major U.S. government effort, for the most part confidential, to undermine the current regimes and encourage regime change from within is worth consideration."

Powell, who along with Myers had been deliberately left off Rumsfeld's memo to the president, learned of Rumsfeld's end run. Both he and Myers went to Rice to voice their rejection of arming any opposition groups within Iran. Powell had no confidence that any opposition group had the strength to challenge the current oligarchy. But more important, a scheme to overthrow the Iranian government violated the two-decades-old Algiers Accords, signed in 1981 as a precondition for release of the American hostages, in which the United States pledged "that it is and from now on will be the policy of the United States not to intervene, directly or indirectly, politically or militarily, in Iran's internal affairs."[12]

Condi Rice and Attorney General John Ashcroft agreed with Powell's view. The final draft included this line: "The United States should not at this time provide overt or covert support to opposition groups or call for regime change."

When Peter Rodman saw this, he raised the alarm back with Rumsfeld. This ties our hands in foreign policy, he told the secretary. "The Algiers Accords are not a binding obligation. The U.S. has in any case the right of self-defense. This is a red herring."[13]

"Good!" Rumsfeld wrote in response to Rodman. The secretary recommended that they delete any reference to language that opposed regime change or mentioned obligations signed by President Carter.

As for the recent overtures from President Khatami, Vice President Cheney pushed to insert language in the draft national security document that flatly rejected them. "The United States should not at this point respond to overtures from the current regime but will continue to meet with the

Iranian Government representatives in multilateral settings when it serves U.S. interests."[14]

Whether regime change should be American policy brought Iran policy to a halt. "We were at loggerheads," Richard Armitage said, "and the president, who has put himself up as the great decider, would never decide."[15] After months of debate and discussion, Rice shelved the national security document. It would be another five years before the administration tried again to formulate a cohesive strategy to deal with this antagonist.

The Pentagon's views were heavily influenced by Ahmed Chalabi, the head of a group of Iraqi exiles funded by the U.S. government called the Iraqi National Congress. Founded in 1992, the INC, as it became known, served as an umbrella organization for those opposed to Saddam Hussein, and its contacts within Iraq proved useful for open-source information. Chalabi told the willing listeners in the administration, including an admiring Vice President Cheney, that removal of Saddam Hussein by U.S. forces would put tremendous pressure on the Iranian government. "The U.S. could even build military bases in Iraq to pressure Iran," said Richard Armitage, recalling a quote by Chalabi.[16]

The fact that Chalabi lived in Tehran and that a number of his key advisers were known by the CIA to be on the payroll of Iranian intelligence—with suspicions even pointing to Chalabi—should have given his advocates pause to consider his assessment of the situation. Of particular concern was the INC's chief of intelligence and close confidant to Chalabi, Aras Habib, whom the CIA and British intelligence believed to be an Iranian MOIS agent. The agency warned senior defense officials and Congress about the penetration of the INC by Iranian intelligence. It raised this as well to Rumsfeld's newly appointed intelligence director, Stephen Cambone, who met several times with Aras Habib. But senior Bush officials discounted much of this, in part due to profound distrust of the CIA and its information on Iraq. A Defense Department inspector general report later concluded that about one-third of the information provided by Chalabi and the INC proved accurate and actionable, and in 2002, the State Department withdrew its funding of the INC. But Chalabi retained supporters in Rumsfeld's office, and funding continued through the DIA at $340,000 a month.

Chalabi never denied his involvement with Iran. Many Iraqi opposition groups were based in Iran and had been so for more than two decades. When questioned about his ties to Iran by an American intelligence officer in October 2002, Chalabi dismissed this criticism. "This relationship is normal and necessary," he said. It did not alarm senior officials in the Pentagon either. Feith, for one, always assumed that the foreign spy services had penetrated the exile groups. So long as Chalabi and the INC supported the goals of overthrowing Saddam Hussein, their manipulation by Iranian intelligence did not matter to those determined to invade Iraq.

The Defense Department expanded its work with the INC in developing the Free Iraqi Forces. Spearheaded by Bill Luti, this idea had captivated the neocons during the Clinton administration, when Wolfowitz and Newt Gingrich had proposed using the army of Iraqi exiles to serve as the vanguard for a "liberation" of the country and establishing a safe zone in southern Iraq backed by American airpower. Now in power, the neocons in the Defense Department and Chalabi moved ahead with the plan. The INC provided nearly five thousand names of "volunteers" to serve in the army. The U.S. military built a camp in Hungary to train the exiles. The entire concept proved a canard. DIA quickly ascertained that most of those on the list either did not exist or were duplicate names. At a cost to the American taxpayer of more than $90 million, fewer than one hundred Iraqis ever showed up at the camp, and of these, only seventy completed the training program—more than $1 million per recruit.

The Defense Department also opened an old wound from the Reagan administration. In early November 2001, Michael Ledeen arrived at the White House to meet with an old acquaintance, Deputy National Security Adviser Stephen Hadley. Since his fall from grace twenty years earlier as one of the chief instigators behind the Iranian arms sales that led to Iran-Contra, Ledeen had continued his fixation on Iran. In the intervening years, he had switched sides, along with the Israeli government, and now advocated regime change rather than rapprochement. He worked at the hawkish American Enterprise Institute and continued peddling information about Iran to anyone willing to listen; after 2001, he found a number of willing ears among his former think tank colleagues now in senior positions in the new Bush administration. Ledeen told Hadley that he was in contact with Iranians who possessed exceptional information regarding Iran's links to terrorism. While he did not vouch for its accuracy, Ledeen thought it important enough to bring it to the U.S. government's attention. The one caveat, however, was that his sources had a deep distrust of the CIA and would not work with Langley. The better conduit would be through the Defense Department, and Ledeen suggested that Harold Rhode and Larry Franklin, both of whom shared a similar view of the Islamic Republic and were fluent in Farsi, meet with the Iranians.[17]

What Ledeen omitted telling Hadley was that his chief Iranian conduit was none other than Manucher Ghorbanifar, his old partner in Ronald Reagan's worst political nightmare. The smooth Iranian had undergone the same political metamorphosis as had his friend Michael Ledeen, and he now offered to arrange a meeting between American officials and senior Iranian officials who had information about the political situation in Iran as well as its support to terrorist organizations, including "plans to kill Americans in Afghanistan." With a twenty-five-year-old reputation as a fabricator and a burn notice by the agency still hanging over Ghorbanifar, it is not surprising he did not want to meet with CIA officers.

Hadley agreed with Ledeen's proposal. On November 7, he called Wolfowitz and requested that the Defense Department handle the meeting. He emphasized to Wolfowitz that the meeting had to remain "very close hold" due to the Iranians' distrust of the CIA.

Hadley then phoned both George Tenet and Richard Armitage: "Do you mind—the Defense Department believes they have some sources in Italy with information on terrorism. Do you mind if they go to Rome and interview them?" Both men agreed without giving it too much thought. While this lay more in his purview, Tenet did not wish to be seen as parochial just two months after 9/11. Hadley failed to mention to either that the information came from Michael Ledeen, which would have elicited a howl of protest from Armitage, who still vividly recalled the Iran-Contra scandal from his days as a senior defense official under Caspar Weinberger.[18]

Rhode and Franklin broke away from the Crocker talks in Bonn over Afghanistan and flew to Rome. On December 10, they met in an apartment in Rome arranged by Ledeen using his contacts with Italian intelligence. Ghorbanifar brought two Iranians with him: one was an exile living in Morocco who claimed to be a former Revolutionary Guard officer, and the other self-reported to be a high-ranking official with Iranian intelligence. The CIA later determined that the latter was an information peddler who sold his memory to the highest bidder. For the next three days, Ghorbanifar and the two Iranians regaled the two American officials with stories on just about anything the U.S. government would have wanted to know. They described the political and economic conditions within Iran, growing discontent within the populace, Iran's relationship with the Palestinians, its illicit weapons, and of course, Saddam Hussein. One of their more sensational items was a description of Iranian hit teams dispatched to kill U.S. troops in Afghanistan. When Franklin asked for more details on the hit teams, the Iranian claiming to be in the intelligence service provided names and a photograph that he claimed to be one of the team members.[19]

But Ghorbanifar had his own ideas of where these talks should lead. Late one night in the hotel bar, he outlined his plan for overthrowing the Iranian government on a cocktail napkin. He suggested executing a series of operations designed to create havoc and general unhappiness with the Iranian government. He would begin with a simultaneous disruption of traffic intersections all around Tehran, which would create panic and paralyze the city. Not surprisingly, Ghorbanifar wanted the United States to pay for his caper, with an initial payment of $5 million as seed money and another $20 million once he had snarled Tehran's already congested traffic.

As the meetings in Rome continued, on December 12 Ledeen had breakfast with the American ambassador, Melvin Sembler. Ledeen bragged that he was in Rome meeting with two Iranians under the auspices of the Department of Defense. Although Sembler remained friendly with Ledeen, this clandestine meeting in his country without his or the CIA station chief's knowledge alarmed the ambassador. It looked like the beginnings of a covert action, and he knew of no presidential finding authorizing any such operation. Sembler began making inquiries, but it would take until February before the role of Ghorbanifar became known to senior officials in Langley and Foggy Bottom.

Ghorbanifar's plan was too much even for those within the Defense Department who agreed with regime change. Franklin recommended to his boss, Bill Luti, against Ghorbanifar's war on Tehran's commuters. Luti's boss, Peter Rodman, raised eyes at the $25 million price tag floated by the Iranian exile. But Franklin claimed that the information provided "saved American lives," which Luti touted as justification for keeping the channel open. Rodman recommended to Wolfowitz that they should continue meeting with Ghorbanifar and the two Iranians for the intelligence value, but it should be carried on through normal intelligence channels by the DIA, which would keep the CIA out of the picture.

On February 9, with the full measure of Ghorbanifar's role now known, both the CIA and State Department raised strong objections. A visibly irate Richard Armitage called Hadley: "If Ghorbanifar sets one foot in an embassy, he'll be arrested," he said sternly. "This is the man who almost single-handedly brought down the president's father, and you are responsible for having him feed us misinformation again. We knew then and we know now that he is an Iranian agent!"[20] Hadley reluctantly agreed to shut the talks down.

But Ledeen retained friends within the Defense Department and continued to find the doors open in the Pentagon to relay his dubious information derived from Ghorbanifar. He contacted the vice president's office about enriched uranium buried in Iraq that had been moved to Iran. On August 6, he met with senior Pentagon intelligence officials on the location of once buried uranium.[21] It turned out to be spurious. As late as 2003, Rhode met again with Ghorbanifar in Paris on returning from a trip to Turkey, but nothing came from the meeting. Powell had won this round.

As momentum built for invading Iraq, some within the military questioned why Iran should not be the next target in the global war on terrorism. In April 2002, Tom Milton, an army colonel working Iraq policy in the Pentagon, built on these ideas by floating a think piece entitled "Getting to Baghdad through Tehran." Echoing some of Newbold's views, he argued that moderate Arab support was vital for success in the war on terrorism, but Arab support for the American policy on Iraq was limited: "They do not see Iraq as a major regional threat." The better strategy would be to shift the focus to Iran, which posed a greater danger and had a much longer track record of using terrorism. Overthrowing the regime in Iran, the officer believed, would unite the Arabs behind the United States and actually undercut Saddam Hussein, leading to his demise as well.

Others in uniform agreed. In a memo for Abe Shulsky, another colonel contended "the most urgent threat is arguably Iran." Iran had "direct links to terrorism worldwide and directly supported Hezbollah. . . . From a WOT [war on terrorism] perspective, Iran is the most urgent."

The civilians within the secretary of defense's office did not necessarily disagree with these officers' logic, but Iran posed a far different challenge than Iraq.[22] In the days after 9/11, Feith's subordinates drafted PowerPoint briefings that lumped Iran in as part of the war on terrorism. But as Abe Shulsky later noted, "Iran was a much more difficult country militarily than Iraq, a harder target. With Khatami still in office and a vibrant opposition movement, the United States had other means to bring about regime change in Iran short of war." Shulsky and Richard Perle both worried that attacking Iran would bog down the war on terrorism. An invasion of the massive country of seventy million people would require all U.S. military resources and end any follow-on operations, while invading Iraq permitted the United States to "maintain momentum" in the war.[23] It was best to grab the low-hanging fruit of Iraq—or even Syria—before tangling with Iran.

Even hard-liners like Luti shied away from sending tanks and troops into Iran. Covert means to overthrow the government offered a better alternative, he argued, especially since the Iranian people already clamored for change. Besides, removing Saddam Hussein would have a "salutary effect" on Iran.[24] The Iranian government was fragile and unpopular; change could come from within. "The establishment of a representative government in Iraq would invigorate anticlerical forces in Iran," Feith wrote in May 2002, in a memo entitled "Strategic Timing."

"We understood that removing Saddam would have major impact on Iran," Feith said. While it could open the door to greater Iranian influence, an alternative scenario also seemed possible to the Pentagon's civilian leadership. Empowering the Shia in Iraq could have a significant impact on Iran. The sight of Iraqi Shia electing their own leaders might have a subversive effect on Iranians who could question why they did not have the same opportunity. Further, a free Iraq could provide an alternative voice to the world's Shia. There was no way to know whether Saddam's removal would eventually end up helping or hurting the Iranian regime's interests. "It was not inevitable that overthrowing Saddam would over time strengthen the Iranian regime's hand in Iraq," said Feith.[25]

Feith's office drafted another paper that circulated around the Pentagon, entitled "What Happens When We Succeed?" It asked other government agencies to examine the effects of overthrowing Saddam Hussein, speculating that it might lead to a transformation of the Arab world, including revolution in Iran. These other agencies agreed. At a minimum, it would put Iran on the defensive and might lead them to cease their nuclear and missile programs.

The military, however, remained divided, especially between the colonels and the generals. A June 2002 paper prepared under the auspices of the chairman's strategy and policy office predicted that overthrowing the Iraqi regime would have little impact on Iranian behavior, especially its support for terrorism or its ballistic missile program. At best, an invasion of Iraq would put Tehran on the defensive and lead to "temporarily" halting overt support for external groups. At worse, it might fuel Iranian paranoia, for Tehran already believed that the United States wanted to encircle and overthrow the regime.[26]

One midlevel air force officer, Tom Billick, viewed overthrowing Saddam as an opportunity for Tehran. In a March 1, 2002, paper on possible Iranian reactions to a U.S. invasion of Iraq, Billick wrote, "Iran's rhetoric in response to U.S. action against Iraq will be harsh. However, Iran will quietly view the removal of Saddam's regime as an opportunity to influence post-Saddam Iraq. Iran could actually increase in strength and influence with the removal of their chief rival."[27]

But both Joint Chiefs chair Myers and his deputy, Peter Pace, supported or at least went along with the Pentagon civilians. "The Iraqis were not Persians," Myers explained. "They are nationalistic, and I did not think they would come under Iran's sway."[28] Pace agreed with another paper churned out from his staff: "Bottom line: a successful campaign to disarm Iraq of WMD, remove Saddam's regime and replace it with a broad-based representative government will fundamentally change the geo-political landscape in the region." Iran would see this as a direct threat to the clerical power in Tehran. This direct military and diplomatic pressure could compel or coerce Tehran to change its policies of support for terrorism and weapons of mass destruction.

Even retired CENTCOM commander Tony Zinni agreed with Pace. No friend of either Feith or the neocons, Zinni believed that Iran would be scared to death should Iraq become closely aligned with the United States.[29]

The idea of going after Iran as the third installment in the war on terrorism appealed to some civilians in the Pentagon. Bill Luti made repeated pronouncements about taking down the Iranian government. Larry Franklin, who shared his boss's view, called Iran a "hostile regime that harbors, finances, and exports terror even while oppressing Iranian people's hopes for freedom." He strongly advocated for Iran as the next target after Iraq.

Despite conspiracy theories of secret plans to invade Iran, neither

CENTCOM nor the Joint Staff nor Bill Luti's office prepared for any such attack following the invasion of Iraq.[30] While some in the Pentagon harbored those opinions, point papers are not military plans. Had the war in Iraq gone well, Iran or Syria may well have come to the forefront for military planners. But Washington could handle only one war at a time. Rumsfeld was too seasoned to think you could just tick off countries. As the Middle East political landscape changed after Saddam, the Iranian calculus would change too, and the administration would reevaluate its options. The lead-up to invading Iraq consumed all the officials' energy, and after the invasion the insurgency sucked all the adventurism out of the pursuit.

The only serious discussion about Iran occurred right after a January 2003 briefing for President Bush by Tenet and Rumsfeld. Responding to the optimistic assessments from Feith's staff, Rumsfeld asked General Myers to look into what could be done if success in Iraq had a "cascade effect" and destabilized Iran. The chairman sent a warning order directing General Tommy Franks at CENTCOM to develop "proactive, as well as reactive, options" that would bring about regime change in Iran. With typical Rumsfeld impatience, Franks had only thirty days to come back with a plan, including military targets in Iran that the United States could attack to help foster the downfall of the Islamic Republic.

"This is bullshit," General Franks told General Myers over the phone in his usual colorful way. The intelligence did not support the premise and his staff was already stretched with one war in Afghanistan and planning for another in Iraq. Myers agreed. He convinced Rumsfeld to hold off issuing the order to Franks, at least until after Iraq.

In all the back-and-forth deliberations about the impact on Iran of an American invasion of Iraq, no one bothered to test the theories. For an American military that prides itself on its planning prowess, surprisingly little had been done beyond the initial drive up to Baghdad. The opening gambit, as the marines called the march to Baghdad, was rehearsed for nearly a year; what happened after reaching Baghdad received little more attention than a massive CENTCOM PowerPoint presentation and two small staffs hastily assembled just before kickoff. But even that cursory swag had not been done regarding Iran. No Red Team was established to explore the ramifications of the removal of Iran's archrival. CENTCOM never war-gamed how Iran would react to another American invasion on its borders. The U.S. Navy's Fifth Fleet in Bahrain examined how to avoid an unintended skirmish with the Iranian navy in the northern Gulf, but beyond that senior officials merely opined and looked to peripheral issues.

Generals Pace, Myers, and Franks accepted the assumptions that invading Iraq would have a coercive effect on Iran. The closest the Pentagon came to interrogating this occurred just before the war began. A panel of experts met at the National Defense University in Washington, D.C., to look at the impact of Saddam's overthrow on the Gulf region. Middle East expert Judith Yaphe said that it would not convince Iran to change its behavior, and a long war and occupation of Iraq would undermine American goals.[31] But her views never resonated within the halls of power, and no one believed Iran would actually see the U.S. action as an opportunity to expand its influence.

For Iranian leaders, the prospect of the U.S. Army positioned in yet another adjacent country unsettled both reformers and hard-liners. Having suffered nearly a million casualties at the hands of invading Iraqis, Tehran viewed a friendly government in Baghdad as critical to its security. If the Americans removed their old archrival Saddam Hussein, the Iranians wanted to have a say in shaping the new government. They hoped to duplicate the cooperative spirit of Afghanistan in this new war on their western border and decided to reengage with the United States, despite having cut off talks following the "axis of evil" remark.

In September 2002, Javad Zarif arrived in New York as Iran's new ambassador to the United Nations. With the Iraq war drums beating ever louder in Washington, Zarif turned again to the president of the American Iranian Council, Hooshang Amirahmadi, who had continued to advocate rapprochement between his country of birth and his adoptive land. The month before the September 11 attacks, he had flown to California to meet with Reagan-era secretary of state George Shultz. Sitting out on Shultz's patio under the warm sun and with the wine flowing, the two men agreed that if Hooshang could get a senior Iran official to unequivocally declare a desire to normalize relations with the United States, Shultz would use his influence with the new national security adviser to get Washington to reciprocate. While the terrorist attacks changed Shultz's views, Amirahmadi remained committed to the idea.

In September, Zarif's house in New York took center stage for these back-channel talks. Amirahmadi brought five prominent former American diplomats, including Ambassadors Richard Murphy and Thomas Pickering, to meet with the Iranian ambassador. Zarif did most of the talking.

His government had neither rejected nor endorsed normalization with the United States. The supreme leader was not ideologically opposed to the idea, Zarif said, but he did not believe it served Iran's interests. "Distrust is so deep and thick in U.S.-Iran relations," the Iranian diplomat added. This included the American side, Zarif continued, where a strong anti-Iranian lobby prevailed due to the Israelis.

Before traveling to New York, the seasoned diplomat Tom Pickering met with William Burns, the deputy assistant secretary of state for Near Eastern affairs, at the department's headquarters in Washington. Burns said that the administration was prepared to normalize relations so long as Iran took concrete steps to halt its nuclear and ballistic missile programs and to end support to U.S.-designated terrorist organizations, such as Hezbollah and Hamas. Pickering passed this on to Zarif, saying that Iran needed to show the political will to do these things and to be prepared to discuss "substantive issues." Zarif agreed, but added that, for this to happen, the United States needed to show a degree of goodwill itself, which had been conspicuously absent thus far from the Bush administration.

The same group met again later that month for dinner at Zarif's residence. While staffers for two senators, Democrat Joseph Biden and Republican Chuck Hagel, joined Amirahmadi's delegation, Iran dramatically raised the meeting's profile by including its senior diplomat, foreign minister Dr. Kamal Kharrazi, a moderate within the Iranian government and firmly in the Khatami reformist camp. Over dinner, both sides talked about the need for improved relations, but all, especially Kharrazi, expressed extreme pessimism that it would ever happen. Finally, toward the end of the meal, Amirahmadi cut to the chase and bluntly asked the Iranian foreign minister: "Dr. Kharrazi, please tell us in the clearest possible language if Iran wishes to normalize relations with the U.S.?"

After a long pause, Kharrazi responded empathically, "Yes! We are ready to normalize relations." He added that his government was willing to discuss all the problems that exist between the two nations. The only caveat Kharrazi had for the bargain was for political cover at home: his government needed Washington to take the first step with a positive, public gesture. For the first time since 1979, a senior Iranian official had proclaimed Iran's willingness to end twenty years of hostility.

That evening, Amirahmadi, Kharrazi, and Zarif continued talking well into the morning hours about the next step. Amirahmadi agreed to sponsor a conference in which Burns and Kharrazi would meet, and the two men would issue joint statements about the need for better relations between the two nations.

Amirahmadi and Pickering met with Burns, Crocker, and the National Security Council's director for Iraq and Iran, Zalmay Khalilzad, who had carefully tracked both the Dobbins and the Crocker meetings. He had been considered to head the Crocker track, but a divided White House viewed Khalilzad as too high profile to meet with the Iranians at that time. While a hawk on Iran, he listened carefully as Amirahmadi recounted Kharrazi's statement about normalization and his proposed conference and joint declarations.

"Did the supreme leader approve this?" Khalilzad asked.

"No, but knowing Dr. Kharrazi, I do not believe he would have made any gesture of such magnitude without the knowledge and consent of the leader," Amirahmadi replied.

Khalilzad liked what he heard. "In principle, there is no problem with the proposal, but I need to consult with my superiors before I can give a definite answer."

Meanwhile, Zarif and Amirahmadi connived on a joint U.S.-Iran effort to overthrow Saddam Hussein. Both men agreed that they shared a common enemy in Iraq; the national interests of Iran and the United States were better served by cooperating as they had in Afghanistan. Iran agreed to aid the U.S. military by offering details about the Iraqi military and its weapons of mass destruction programs, permitting use of its airspace to strike Iraq, and providing humanitarian assistance in case of a refugee crisis. But the real goal went beyond just the war. Overthrowing Saddam Hussein merely served as the launching pad to grasp the brass ring: an end to two decades of hostility between Washington and Tehran.

"The idea was a grand bargain," Amirahmadi later said. In return for Iran's assistance, Washington would publicly advocate for normalized relations, and this would usher in negotiations that would address not only Iran's support for terrorism, but the end of two decades of punitive economic and financial sanctions against Iran.

Ryan Crocker soon became well acquainted with Ambassador Zarif and the ideas behind this grand bargain. In September 2002, Zarif arrived in

Paris and took over the meetings with Crocker. Unlike the earlier wide-ranging talks with the Revolutionary Guard officers, Zarif arrived with specific talking points to pass to Crocker. While this clearly represented a more formal, structured dialogue controlled by Iran's foreign minister, privately Crocker viewed Zarif's arrival as a downgrading of the talks on the part of Tehran. "This was not a channel that they attached the significance to as they had at the outset."[32] Zarif lacked the gravitas of his predecessors. More important to Crocker, as a Western-educated reformist, Zarif lacked a connection with the real power brokers in Tehran: the supreme leader and the Revolutionary Guard.

Over the next three meetings Zarif relayed to Crocker his government's desire to expand the talks beyond Afghanistan to include Iraq. His talking points tracked closely with the scheme drafted with Amirahmadi in New York, which he no doubt hoped was also relayed back to the State Department. Zarif began by expressing concern that, in the event of war, Iraq might launch chemical weapons at Iran. He discussed the ideas about working together with the United States in overthrowing Saddam Hussein. What had worked in Afghanistan, he told Crocker, could work again against another common foe.

Crocker dutifully relayed the Iraqi proposal back to Washington. Two days before Christmas, with most of official Washington on vacation, Bush's senior foreign policy team gathered in the White House Situation Room for a hasty meeting to discuss the proposal. They agreed that the NSC would draft a set of talking points for Crocker to relay to the Iranians and that the principals would reconvene after the new year to decide on how best to respond to the Iranian overture.

At the next meeting in Geneva, Zarif wanted to know what the United States would do about the MEK, the People's Mujahideen of Iran. This quasi-Islamic leftist guerrilla movement remained dedicated to overthrowing the shah and now the Islamic Republic, and Saddam Hussein gave the group sanctuary. It had conducted many terrorist attacks and was credited with the first improvised explosive device attacks in the Middle East, which nearly killed an American brigadier general in the 1970s. The U.S. government designated the MEK a terrorist organization in 1997; Iran worried the United States secretly wanted to use it to destabilize the Iranian regime.

"All you have to do is look at our stated policy; we don't support terrorists," Crocker responded.[33] But Zarif remained skeptical and listed public comments from influential neoconservatives that indicated the United States might use the MEK as a liberation force.

Iran's worries had merit. Within the secretary of defense's policy shop, some civilians did advocate using the MEK to strike at the Iranian regime, or at least to garner intelligence from inside Iran. Wolfowitz had even suggested this during a principals committee meeting. But in a rare show of resolve, Condi Rice quashed that idea. "If the United States stands for anything, it is against working with terrorists!"[34]

After several weeks of deliberation, the Bush administration again rejected the overtures from Zarif and Iran. An NSC document summed up the view everywhere but the State Department: "The United States should not at this point respond to overtures from the current regime, but will continue to meet with Iranian Government representatives in multilateral settings when it serves U.S. interests." The new envoy with Crocker, Zalmay Khalilzad, would be allowed to meet with Iran, but more as a means of issuing demands. He could discuss Afghanistan and getting Iran to turn over al-Qaeda operatives, or any topic "deemed to the advantage of the United States."[35]

On March 19, 2003, President Bush again took to the airwaves in a national address. This time speaking from his desk in the Oval Office, Bush opened with resolution: "My fellow citizens, at this hour, American and coalition forces are in the early stages of military operations to disarm Iraq, to free its people, and to defend the world from grave danger." Actually, the night before, U.S. Special Forces had infiltrated into southern and western Iraq, the vanguard of nearly two hundred thousand American and British troops. "Our nation enters this conflict reluctantly," Bush continued. "The people of the United States and our friends and allies will not live at the mercy of an outlaw regime that threatens the peace with weapons of mass murder."

After a year and a half of discussion, Wolfowitz had achieved his long-held goal. In less than three weeks, soldiers and marines entered Baghdad, toppling the Iraqi regime. The fact that virtually every rationale made by the United States for the war, especially Saddam's weapons of mass destruction program, turned out to be wrong did not faze those who advocated the conflict. In the pursuit of this myopic policy, the Bush administration had thrown away diplomatic openings made by Iran. Alarmed by the al-Qaeda attacks and fearful of America's response, Iran had extended its hand to cooperate in areas where the two nations' interests overlapped. Instead, the American government failed to develop any cohesive response or Iran strategy other than a policy that paid lip service to regime change in Tehran. In the end, this drift in American policy did nothing other than curtail rapprochement and eliminate Iran's archrival in Baghdad. If the postwar plan for Iraq turned out to be ill conceived, with too few troops and no occupation plan, so too was the regional security calculus used by the Bush administration for the Middle East. Those who pushed for war—aided by exiles as closely affiliated with Tehran as with Washington—opened the door for Iranian expansion.

But if the Americans were not going to talk, the Iranians had no qualms about fighting. The supreme leader had never been sanguine about prospects of talking with Washington. Rather than see American troops in Iraq as a threat to the Islamic Republic, Ayatollah Khamenei endorsed a Revolutionary Guard idea designed to take advantage of their contacts within the Shia majority in Iraq. America had presented an opportunity to achieve what Iran could not achieve in eight years of bloody slaughter in the 1980s. This time, much of the blood would be American.

Twenty-Four

DEFEAT OR VICTORY

For Captain Robert Harward, the first two weeks of Operation Iraqi Freedom had gone remarkably well. Even for an elite SEAL, he was a man of action. In his mid-forties and extremely fit, Harward was bald with a mysterious pronounced scar down the side of his face. He remained perpetually in motion, stopping only to fixate on someone with a hawklike gaze from his deep-set blue eyes. He was the senior commander of all the naval special warfare forces involved in the invasion of Iraq, and the March 20, 2003, opening night of the American onslaught had been one of the most complex operations ever undertaken by the SEALs. It entailed a simultaneous seizure of Iraq's two offshore oil platforms and the interconnected pipes and pumping stations on nearby al-Faw Peninsula—the mud spit of land that had been such a key and bloody battlefield during the Iran-Iraq War. U.S. intelligence had feared that Saddam would destroy this important center-piece of Iraq's economy either to deprive the Americans of it or to create an environmental disaster in the Persian Gulf by dumping millions of barrels of oil into the open ocean. After months of planning and rehearsing, the SEALs' operation had gone off perfectly. Without a single U.S. casualty and only sporadic resistance, they safeguarded all of Iraq's southern oil exports. After that, Harward dispatched his forces to search more than one hundred ships in the waterways off Kuwait and Iraq and sent reconnaissance teams and snipers to help the marines who, by early April, were already on the outskirts of Baghdad.

Few Americans had Harward's experience with Iran. The son of a naval officer who provided logistics support for the shah's navy, he'd lived for years in Tehran attending the American School. Here he became fluent in Farsi, and he frequently hitchhiked around the country. Harward went on to attend the Naval Academy, graduating in the last all-male class in 1979.

Harward had had an early brush with William Casey's efforts to build a spy ring in Iran. While a midshipman, Harward had befriended an Iranian midshipman named Saeed Ahmadi, who was from modest means: Ahmadi's father had been a postman in southern Tehran. Dark haired and a lover of disco, Saeed graduated from the Naval Academy with Harward. In the class yearbook, the *Lucky Bag*, a friend wrote affectionately in Saeed's entry: "May fair winds and following seas always be with you. Smile like a man."[1] But squalls and a historic storm blew in Iran in 1979. While his American class-mates headed off to begin their new careers, Saeed was ordered to return to Iran, with a veiled threat against his mother in Tehran if he refused.

As a recent arrival from the States with friends and classmates now in the American military, Saeed was an easy mark for CIA recruiters. One after-noon, then ensign Harward received a phone call from Iran.

"Your intelligence service contacted me and asked if I would work with them. Do you think I should?" Saeed asked, sounding excited.

Harward replied nervously, "I don't know what you should do, but, man, you shouldn't call me over this phone with something as sensitive as that." Saeed agreed; after some brief small talk, he hung up.

What transpired then between the young Iranian officer and the CIA remains a mystery. Whether he turned down the agency or simply failed to complete the CIA's formal indoctrination procedures is not clear, but Ahmadi never formally joined Casey's new stable of agents. Around the time of the CIA's overture, Ahmadi resigned his commission in the navy and joined the National Iranian Tanker Company. Unfortunately for American intelligence officers still hoping to recruit him, in 1984 an Iraqi missile struck his oil tanker as it shuttled a load of crude from the northern Persian Gulf oil fields. Saeed and two other sailors died instantly in the conflagration.

Harward learned of his friend's demise when a photograph by Australian journalist Michael Coyne appeared in the July 1985 *National Geographic* as part of a story about life in Iran under the ayatollah. Serendipitously, Coyne had visited the sprawling Behesht-e Zahra cemetery southwest of Tehran, where many of the country's soldiers and notables are laid to rest. Among the thousands of graves laid out in neat rows of headstones and white slabs, many adorned with photos of the young men who now inhabited this city of the dead, Coyne came across five women, all wearing black chadors and weeping around a fresh grave covered in flowers and fruit. He snapped a few shots of the mourners as one of the women held up a large photo of a young, clean-shaven naval officer. The image happened to be Saeed Ahmadi: either a strange coincidence or, as Harward suspected, a deliberate message from the shadowy world of spies.[2]

As the U.S. Army and Marines closed in on Saddam Hussein and Baghdad, Harward received a new tasking. The British army was cautiously closing in on the southern port city of Basra and wanted some of Harward's heavily armed small boats on the Shatt al-Arab waterway to help isolate the city and keep Iraqi forces from escaping to the far riverbank. Meanwhile, the senior naval commander in the Middle East, Vice Admiral Timothy Keating, worried that Iraqi suicide boats might launch out from the Shatt al-Arab and threaten his fleet. To achieve both ends, Harward intended to transport four of his riverine boats—essentially large camouflage-painted bass boats made of bullet-resistant Kevlar and bristling with machine guns—up to the mouth of the Shatt al-Arab and then sail them up to join the British near Basra. How Iran would react to this maneuver remained unknown, and at the time, no one seemed concerned except for Harward.

Before sending the boats up the Shatt al-Arab, Harward ordered a small surveillance team to al-Faw. Comprising eight SEALs in two vehicles each resembling a beefed-up dune buggy outfitted with a heavy machine gun, they established themselves at a good vantage point looking out over the water from an abandoned Iraqi army post. On the opposite bank they could clearly see three Iranian outposts, each a concrete pillbox mounted on stilts. The SEALs did not have long to wait to find out Iran's view of their presence. Three days after arriving, a small boat with armed Revolutionary Guardsmen closed to within thirty yards of the SEALs on the bank of the Iraqi side of the waterway. When the SEALs raised their weapons, the boat hastily headed back for Iran, raising a large Iranian flag in the process. At dusk, one of the

Iranian guard posts opened fire. While not terribly accurate, this harassment continued every night, with stray bullets and mortar rounds exploding in the vicinity of the SEALs' position. When Polish special operators relieved the SEALs, they received the same greeting from the Iranians. Several times, Iranian patrols crossed into Iraq, planting Iranian flags next to the road leading to the Polish position. None of this portended well for the next phase, moving the boats up to Basra.

As was described earlier, April 3, 2003, dawned bright and sunny in the northern Persian Gulf. Several miles from the mouth of the Shatt al-Arab, a massive gray-painted catamaran drifted, a crane slowly lowering the four American boats into the brown water. Known as the *Joint Venture*, the ship had been built in Australia as a high-speed ferry. Inside were extensive ramps capable of holding dozens of vehicles, and at its center sat an array of theater seating arranged around a bar, the beer now replaced with cases of bottled water and orange juice. The SEALs had converted this ship into a naval vessel and installed a sophisticated command center replete with radar, computers, and a large screen that showed unit locations in real time.

Harward jumped down into the lead boat. To try to demonstrate their benign intentions, he had an Italian flag turned sideways to resemble an Iranian flag draped over the starboard side of his boat facing the Iranian shore. With Harward at the bow as lookout, the four boats moved slowly in a lazy column up to the Shatt al-Arab and then, hopefully, up to join the British in Basra. The journey took time; the lead boat briefly ran aground as the most up-to-date U.S. charts proved to be woefully out-of-date, with the main channel having moved well to the east. A Farsi linguist with Harward raised an Iranian soldier on the radio. After he assured him that the United States would not enter Iranian waters, the Iranian soldier replied, "Good for you. Do you need any help?"

An hour later, as the four American boats turned into the Shatt al-Arab proper, a small blue-painted boat with three Revolutionary Guardsmen headed over and came next to the Americans. They were soon joined by two more boats, including one with a multiple-barrel rocket launcher affixed in its center. While the SEAL linguist explained their intention to stay in Iraqi waters, Harward ordered his flotilla to steer still farther west, away from Iran.

The situation suddenly escalated. A fast Swedish-built Boghammer speedboat outfitted with a twin-barrel machine gun on its bow came barreling over to join the other three Revolutionary Guard boats. With a rooster tail of white water, the Boghammer cut off Harward's boat, stopping in its path while the other Revolutionary Guard boats took up positions around the Americans from the front and side. The Iranians began removing the tarps covering their machine guns and the multiple rocket launcher, and then trained their weapons directly at the lead American boat.

Harward grabbed the radio handset and tried to talk to the senior Iranian on the Boghammer. A heavy-set bearded man dressed in the dark fatigues of the Iranian military, he repeatedly cut Harward off, warning the American to turn around or "face the consequences," before adding menacingly, "We will bomb and kill you!" As the SEALs jumped up to man their weapons, others listening on the nearby *Joint Venture* called for American airpower. Harward ordered no one to fire without his command and radioed back to his one-star commander asking for instructions. To Harward's dismay, he was told to turn around. Rather than risk a confrontation, the American commanders decided to leave. With no recourse but to obey his orders, he commanded his boats to turn around and head back to the *Joint Venture* at a leisurely pace so as not to appear to be retreating. Privately, Harward fumed. Despite being in Iraqi waters, the Iranians had forced the Americans to back down.

Over the next few days, Harward proposed a number of ideas to reassert American control over the Iraqi side of this key waterway. He suggested having his boats (which had to be airlifted to Basra in order to support the British) come down from the north backed up by SEAL snipers stationed in helicopters overhead and marine attack helicopters should the Revolutionary Guard try to resist.

"We are going to assert our right of passage," the commander of the naval force in the northern Gulf, Rear Admiral Barry Costello, told Harward, "but at a time and place of our choosing." But that promise was never fulfilled. Instead, the United States simply conceded control of the Iraqi frontier to Iran, remaining content to round up the few Saddam loyalists loitering in a derelict ship.

"We are going to regret letting them get away with this," Harward said when back on the *Joint Venture*.[3]

While Saddam Hussein had been Iran's long-term nemesis, the prospect of a U.S. invasion unsettled the supreme leader, Ayatollah Khamenei. As the likelihood of an American attack increased in the winter of 2002, Iran's Supreme Council for National Security met repeatedly to deliberate Iran's options. Iranian leaders had long suffered from a paranoid self-delusion that every action taken by the United States was secretly aimed at overthrowing the Islamic Republic. The debate in Tehran was bathed in this fearful light. But the leadership seemed as divided as officials in Washington. The majority of the council, including President Khatami and Mohsen Rezai, the former head of the Revolutionary Guard and a close confidant of the supreme leader's, argued that neutrality or even support for the Americans would demonstrate Iran's peaceful intentions and lessen the chances of an American attack. It might also take off some of the American pressure against their burgeoning nuclear program. Perhaps Iran could even cooperate in a way similar to that in Afghanistan, by allowing U.S. planes to skirt its airspace and rescuing any downed pilots.

Iran's military attaché in Bahrain relayed this message during a chance encounter with the American Fifth Fleet commander, Admiral Tim Keating. The Iranian effusively told a nearby officer, who in turn passed it on to the senior naval officer, that Iran would provide search and rescue for any American pilot who bailed out over their country.

Hard-liners—especially Major General Yahya Safavi, the commander of the Revolutionary Guard, and Major General Qassem Suleimani, the recently appointed commander of the Quds Force—argued that they needed to take the fight to the Americans. The United States intended to move against the Islamic Republic after Iraq. The massive American army deployed in Iraq would be turned against the Iranians to overthrow the revolution. They needed to mobilize their army to repel the invasion. Further, they needed to move immediately into Iraq after the United States attacked. They needed to position the Revolutionary Guard to strike back at the U.S. military and position resources to ensure that the new government would be favorably disposed to Tehran.

The supreme leader hedged his bets by supporting a talk-*and*-fight strategy. He approved continued talks with the Americans and declared that Iran would remain neutral and provide aid to coalition pilots who parachuted into Iran. But he also ordered army units to the borders and proclaimed that they would vigorously defend Iran's sovereignty. As soon as possible, MOIS and Quds Force operatives would move into Iraq to begin influencing the Shia population and working to ensure a pro-Iranian Shia government in Baghdad. Where feasible and without risking war, the Quds Force would create trouble for the Americans in order to prevent Iraq from becoming a staging

base against Iran. Iran's approach was very similar to that employed in Lebanon two decades earlier. It was a broad-based whole-of-government method
that leveraged the military as much as the political and economic forces to
advance its goals. Iran's ultimate objective would be uniting the disparate
Shia parties into a cohesive force to consolidate control over the new Iraqi
government—one sympathetic to Tehran.[4]

The legacy of the Iran-Iraq War and the Shia religious connections created a thick web between the two countries ripe for Tehran to exploit. Iran
supported a number of Iraqi exile groups. The Islamic Dawa Party, which
advocated creating an Islamic state in Iraq modeled after the Iranian Revolution, had long been used by Iran to conduct terrorist attacks against Saddam
Hussein and also against the U.S. embassy in Kuwait in 1983. Among their
ranks were prominent future Iraqi politicians, including the future prime
minister, Nouri al-Maliki.

The most potent force for Iran lay with the Islamic Supreme Council of
Iraq and its military wing, the Badr Corps. Its genesis went back to the 1970s,
when prominent Shia religious leaders, including Ayatollah Muhammad
Baqir al-Hakim and Ayatollah Muhammad Baqir al-Sadr, formed a militant
group of Iraqi exiles opposed to the secular Baath Party and Saddam Hussein.
Maintaining its headquarters in Tehran during the eight-year Iran-Iraq War,
the Badr Corps saw its membership grow with Iranian training and equipment to a division-size unit of nearly ten thousand fighters, all Iraqi Shia and
many deserters from the Iraq army.[5] While Baqir al-Hakim remained more of
a religious leader, his brother Abdul Aziz al-Hakim led these fighters as they
waged a mini civil war fighting for Iran against their own countrymen both
in the conventional battles of the Iran-Iraq War and in behind-the-lines guerrilla raids into Iraq.[6] Many of the corps' officers had close ties to Iranian intelligence, including its commander and future minister of transportation in the
post-Saddam Iraqi government, Hadi al-Amiri. The Iranian spy agency MOIS
built the Badr Corps' intelligence wing in 1989, and during the 1990s the
group infiltrated into Iraq and attacked the Iraqi military.

Although Iran exercised considerable influence with these organizations,
they were not puppets. Arab and Persian animosity runs deep. A haughty
Persian attitude made many of these Iraq exiles feel like second-class citizens
in Iran. In 2007, then ambassador Ryan Crocker recalled watching a speech
by the Iranian president in which Prime Minister Nouri al-Maliki needed a
translator. Crocker expressed surprise, telling al-Maliki that he thought he

might have learned Farsi during his long stays in Iran. The prime minister responded with disdain: "No. You don't know how bad it can be until you're an Arab forced to live with the Persians!"[7]

Iran's counterinvasion of Iraq followed shortly after the American attack. Iranian MOIS and Quds Force officers arrived in southern Iraq on the heels of U.S. tanks driving north to Baghdad. The Badr Corps led the vanguard of pro-Iranian forces. Some six thousand armed fighters poured hodgepodge into Iraq from Iran. The Badr Corps smuggled in heavy weapons provided by Iran hidden under tarps in commercial trucks. While some came across as armed bands, other individuals intermingled with the thousands of Iranian pilgrims traveling to visit the Shia holy sites in Karbala and Najaf. U.S. intelligence soon suspected that more than a thousand armed Badr Corps soldiers had taken up positions within Najaf proper. As the Iraqi army disintegrated, no one manned the border crossing and the Iranian forces simply walked or drove into Iraq and intermingled with Iranians headed to the holy cities.

Soon MOIS officers were present in all of Iraq. This included the Kurdish city of Arbil, where they established the Majran Tourist Company for Shia pilgrims traveling to Iraq, which also served as a front company for their spy operations. Following the fall of Baghdad, the MOIS operated out of several safe houses in Baghdad and spied on U.S. forces. These operations would not be uncovered until the summer of 2004, when U.S. forces raided one house in Baghdad and arrested four Iranian agents working for the MOIS, all of whom had targeted the U.S. military.

While the MOIS operated as a traditional spy service, the Quds Force operated as a blend of U.S. Special Forces and the Peace Corps. Just after the American attack, more than fifty Quds operatives, including three Iranian general officers, moved into southern Iraq. They came with money and expertise to open medical clinics, rebuild city services, and revitalize religious shrines. To facilitate their operations, the Quds Force established a new headquarters in Mehran, Iran, with two satellite offices in southern and northwestern Iran. From these bases, weapons as well as building supplies and medicine arrived to win hearts and minds—and outfit newly formed militias. They also carefully monitored American forces. *Time* magazine reporter Michael Ware claimed to have seen Quds Force reports from 2003 that logged U.S. troop movements in the city of al-Kut and claimed, "We are in control of the city."[8]

All this proved lucrative too. The Revolutionary Guard had increasingly become a business venture as well as military force. The guard owns export companies, financial institutions, and construction companies. Iranian Quds Force operatives opened up side businesses inside Iraq, making money as they fomented hate for the occupiers.

The Iraqi National Congress aided the Iranian effort. During the U.S. invasion, they passed along the locations of U.S. forces. In theory, this was to avoid any misunderstandings that might lead to a confrontation between the two countries, but it gave Iran the ability to move its agents into Iraq around U.S. forces who might be on the watch for Iranian subversives. U.S. intelligence suspected that Ahmed Chalabi had even told the Iranians that the Americans were reading their sensitive communications, an incredible compromise of some of the United States' most sensitive intelligence sources.[9]

The Bush administration found it convenient to ignore this. The silver-tongued Ahmed Chalabi, who maintained a home in Tehran and close ties to senior Iranian officials, continued preaching the gospel that the Defense Department and the White House wanted to hear: the virtues of a democratic Iraq; Baghdad as an ally in the war on terrorism and a bulwark against extremism, including in Iran; and even an Iraq ready to recognize Israel. The Iraqi exile had an American officer assigned to carry a secure phone for him to call back to Washington. On speed dial were two office numbers: Donald Rumsfeld's and Dick Cheney's.[10] When Chalabi flew into southern Iraq on an American transport aircraft following the U.S. invasion, his large ragtag entourage included many who'd come from Iran, including Badr Corps soldiers.

In Bush's State of the Union speech following the invasion, Chalabi was accorded a place of honor, sitting next to the First Lady in the gallery. The next day, during a White House meeting, with Bush still aglow from the heady congressional reception the night before, the president asked, "Who invited Chalabi to sit next to Laura?" No one sitting around the table answered, and the president did not press the subject. Richard Armitage, sitting in for Colin Powell, who was out of the country, shook his head. "The only person with that kind of clout in the administration was the vice president, and he sat there and never said a word."

In fact, rather than worry about Iranian influence, the United States embraced Iran's surrogates. On March 30, 2003, CENTCOM issued an edict for its troops to disarm any Badr Corps soldiers who appeared carrying weapons out in the street. It was not enforced. During the chaotic occupation of Baghdad, U.S. Marines operating in the sprawling Shia suburb of Sadr City (then called Saddam City) allowed Shia militias to remain armed. They roamed around the city rounding up Sunni and Baathist officials under the notion that they could tell the good guys from the bad. They certainly did. They rooted them out, killing many. In one instance, with marines nearby, a Sunni official was encased in tires and thrown alive into a burning building. When the on-scene marines learned of it, they treated it with little more interest than halting the pervasive looting throughout the city, the smoke from which cast a pall over the Iraqi capital.[10]

The Saudis and Kuwaitis raised the alarm over the influx of Iranians. Neither country showed much enthusiasm for the American invasion. Both feared the invasion would expand Shia influence and they believed it would remove a barrier to Iran by replacing the Sunni government with a Shia one. On April 13, Kuwaiti ruler Sheik Sabah al-Sabah expressed his anxiety about the increased turmoil in the Iraqi Shia community, urging the United States to provide security for the holy shrine in Najaf. If the United States failed to do this, Iran would step in and assume the prestigious role as the guarantor of safety of the key Shia shrines.[11] At the urging of the State Department, more American forces were moved to safeguard Najaf and Karbala. But Iran knew the language and culture far better than the well-intentioned American soldiers. While U.S. troops safeguarded Shia pilgrims, Iranian operatives moved among the populace and cultivated the emerging Shia groups.

Iran's sudden appearance in Iraq did not go unnoticed by the U.S. military. "We need to stop the Iranians from trying to influence Iraq," Rumsfeld wrote to Doug Feith in a May 1, 2003, "snowflake" memo. "Let's come up with a plan of four or five things to do, so we get some success. They need to know we are serious." After conferring with Joint Chiefs vice chairman Peter Pace, Feith responded with the now familiar line on Iran. They needed to sever any support for terrorist groups—as defined by the United States, dismantle the Quds Force, end its nuclear and missile programs, and support a Middle East peace process that maintains Israel as a Jewish state. Feith also suggested that the United States adopt a multifaceted approach similar to that of the Iranians. He recommended a list of different actions: closing down Iranian intelligence operatives and arresting the fifty to seventy-five Quds Force officers inside Iraq, providing security for senior Shia clerics, and developing a propaganda campaign that would highlight moderate Shia leaders and Iran's malign influence in Iraq. Feith also suggested the United States could expel the Badr Corps troops, although at nearly five thousand fighters, this would take considerable military muscle, and Feith offered no idea of where they would be expelled to.

Rumsfeld tasked both Joint Chiefs chair Richard Myers and CENTCOM commander Tommy Franks with countering Iran's growing influence. He liked the idea of targeting the Quds Force through arrests or harassment. But Rumsfeld ordered Franks to come up with a plan to arrest the four known Quds Force generals in Iraq. Franks agreed and tasked his special forces operators from Task Force 20, currently looking for the high-value men like Saddam and his two sons, to come up with a quick snatch of the four generals operating in Basra and Baghdad. CENTCOM issued a new directive to its commanders to detain by force any Badr Corps soldier found carrying a weapon or "engaging in conduct incompatible with good order and detrimental to creating a law abiding society."[12]

"I have no doubt that USCENTCOM forces will exercise their full authority when dealing with Badr Corps members," Myers wrote back to Rumsfeld.

American proconsul L. Paul Bremer too raised concerns about Iran and the Badr Corps with Rumsfeld in his first two weeks in Baghdad. "Iran is committing serious assets in Iraq, and it is time to move against what is a concentrated Iranian long-term strategy." Bremer recommended rolling up Iran's intelligence service and closing its embassy. He held a meeting with Abdul Aziz al-Hakim, the brother of the leader of the Islamic Supreme Council of Iraq (ISCI). Bremer told him that the U.S. government was concerned about Badr Corps activities and that the Iranians were up to no good in Iraq. Al-Hakim protested on both accounts, but listened.

Bremer postponed the planned June elections in Najaf in part to prevent the ISCI from winning the local elections through force of arms and intimidation. In an e-mail to Rumsfeld regarding Najaf, Bremer laid out his concerns: "Elements of the Tehran government are actively arming, training and directing militia in Iraq. To date these armed forces have not been directly involved in attacks on the Coalition. But they pose a longer term threat to law and order."[13]

Bremer asked the British commander to step up his forces along the border and raised the alarm with Rumsfeld that the Polish and Ukrainian forces arriving to relieve the U.S. Marines in southern Iraq were not up to the task of containing the Iranians.[14]

Bremer's comments about delaying the redeployment of the marines did not go down well with the Pentagon. In a note to the careerist and secretive army colonel who ran the chairman's Iraqi planning office, Kevin Bergner, Abe Shulsky commented on Bremer's meeting with Iraqi political leaders and his attempt to counter pro-Iranian elements in Najaf and Karbala: "Pretty strong language . . . definitely does not sound like he is on board with Polish-led MND [multinational division] taking over that sector."

Relations between Rumsfeld and Bremer had already turned sour, with Bremer's independent style aggravating the defense secretary. Going after the Badr Corps and Shia militias was a sensitive subject in the Pentagon, and Chalabi and the INC views held sway. The U.S. military could go after Saddam loyalists but not the Shia. In a phone conversation on May 20, Rumsfeld cautioned his four-star general that any dealings with Iran would be controlled by the National Security Council and the White House. "The NSC wants to be the center of gravity for all Iranian contacts," the secretary said. This included any dealings with the MEK. He ordered Franks not to take any action against Iranians inside Iraq without Rumsfeld's personal approval.

Harward also raised the alarm about Iran following his near shoot-out in early April. The SEAL commander had his intelligence section focus on the Iranian problem, and it quickly unmasked Iran's campaign to infiltrate forces into Iraq. The aggressive actions by the Revolutionary Guard small boats had been designed to try to prevent the Americans from interfering with one of their main routes into southern Iraq. One of Harward's intelligence officers was a direct-commission navy reserve lieutenant named Thomas Mahnken. The dark-haired Mahnken held a doctorate from Johns Hopkins School of Advanced International Studies, and when not in uniform he taught strategy at the Naval War College in scenic Newport, Rhode Island. He began analyzing the Iranian and Badr infiltration routes, termed "rat lines" by the SEALs. In short order, he uncovered several key routes following traditional smuggling trails leading into Basra and Baghdad. One of the key cities in the Iranians' movement into Iraq was Amarah, strategically situated on the Tigris River and only thirty miles from the Iranian border. With a population of some three hundred thousand, mostly Shia, the Badr Corps soldiers along with some troops from the Iranian Quds Force arrived in force and occupied the old Baath Party facilities, effectively taking control of the city. Based upon the information gleaned by Mahnken, Harward proposed deploying SEAL teams to interdict the Iranian rat lines. While Harward hoped to avoid an armed confrontation, the SEALs could at least detain Iranian agents and round up many of the weapons flowing in with the Badr Corps soldiers.

Harward met resistance from the United Kingdom too. With southern Iraq, including Amarah, in the British area of responsibility, the Queen's soldiers had to approve any operations by Harward's SEALs. Mahnken drove up to the headquarters of the British division near Basra to discuss options to counter the Iranians. Rather than support the Americans, Mahnken was told by the senior British intelligence officer that they were overreacting. The gunfire by Iranian soldiers had been directed at smugglers, and Iran was doing a good job of controlling its borders. Moreover, the British found no evidence of Badr Corps troops moving across the border. Mahnken tried to argue the point, but the British simply refused to accept his intelligence. "I believe you are overreacting; the Iranians are not a problem."[15]

Despite snowflakes and memos, in the end Rumsfeld's intent to counter Iranian influence ran contrary to the defense secretary's own desire to withdraw forces quickly. In an e-mail to his subordinate army commander Lieutenant General David McKiernan, Tommy Franks ordered him to "take as much risk getting out as you did getting in." Rumsfeld did not want the military tied down in a large occupation. "Recock" became the word of the day at CENTCOM. The United States would get out of Iraq and prepare for the next war in the global fight against terrorism, with rumors circulating that Syria was next. The U.S. military concurred. The short war of Desert Storm was the generals' model and no one in uniform wanted a long occupation. Franks was happy to leave the details of post-war Iraq to the Pentagon civilians. With Iranian influence growing and the security situation in chaos, rather than address the impending crisis and engage the British on the merits of the intelligence, American special operations troops packed up and left Iraq. Harward's ideas to counter the Iranians went to the shredder, and by mid-May the SEALs and Harward's command were back in California. Franks had taken a risk and left Iraq open for the Revolutionary Guard.

The early success in Iraq gave renewed impetus within the Bush administration for a strategy regarding Iran. Once again senior officials gathered around the table in the confined White House Situation Room to discuss what the U.S. policy should be toward Iran. On April 25, 2003, Condi Rice chaired a video teleconference with senior officials. The disembodied faces from across the globe all agreed that they should try to discredit the Iranian clerical rule, stop its nuclear program, and call for it to be a good neighbor to Iraq. But the group seemed no more united on how to achieve these ends than they had the previous October, when Rice shelved the idea of a presidential decision directive on Iranian policy. Over the ensuing six months, the national security adviser had not tried to force the issue with Bush either. Now, as Iran moved into the vacuum of post-Saddam Iraq, the U.S. government fretted and held more meetings.

Rice floated another paper outlining broad goals. The paper referred to "democratic transformation as opposed to regime change" as the American goal. The United States would maintain unrelenting pressure on Tehran to end its nuclear program and nefarious activities in Iraq, and held out the possibility of military action to rein in Iran. The U.S. presence in Afghanistan and Iraq would keep Iran on the defensive, the White House surmised.

The paper circulated among senior officials, and its lack of specificity made most everyone happy. In a June 25, 2003, principals meeting, Rice said the paper obviated the need for a more formal document and that she intended to give it as a memo to the president. "We should make it very clear that we will do anything to stop Iran from developing nuclear weapons, supporting terrorism, and disrupting our Iraq strategy."

Powell responded, "Student demonstrations indicate a desire for a better life, but we shouldn't push for regime change—we don't know what we'll get."

"I agree the paper lays out generally the right policy," Rumsfeld added. "But we should encourage the demonstrators, perhaps through IO [information operations]. We should tell the Iranian people the regime is harboring al-Qaeda personnel in order to embarrass the regime."

Rice added that the United States should encourage people-to-people exchanges, an idea Powell liked. Rumsfeld dissented. He suggested it would open the door to spies inside the United States and opined that talking with Iranian academics was a waste of effort. "We will be talking with people with no power," he said.

Toward the end of the meeting, Vice President Cheney added his opinion:

"I am not sure that the paper reflects the dangers and the opportunities in Iraq. We are not using our enhanced posture enough. It is not aggressive enough." Cheney objected to taking regime change off the table as an option. Further, he argued that the U.S. invasion and swift dispatch of Saddam Hussein presented an opportunity. Iran was nervous that it might be next. U.S. forces were poised on two sides of Iran, and Washington needed to leverage this to pressure Iran into acquiescing to America's wishes. Cheney had no use for talking to the Iranians, and this coercive window of opportunity would not stay open forever.

"We don't know what will happen if we have regime change. Need to be careful moving forward," Powell retorted.

"We can't just do nothing," Cheney threw back at Powell. "We need to determine targets, especially if they hit us. We need options to take advantage of this window."

Again, the administration was at an impasse. Rice refused to engage and shifted the subject to needing a diplomatic effort to isolate Iran, while Rumsfeld screeched about the need for actionable intelligence. Without any agreement, and lacking an unequivocal presidential edict, nothing happened. America's Iran policy drifted on an endless river of point papers and discussions.

However, the fact that the American military achieved in three weeks what Iran failed to do in eight years of war scared the supreme leader. Administration hard-liners like Cheney and Luti had been correct: American military force had successfully intimidated Iran. While continuing low-level enrichment of uranium, Iran halted its nuclear weapons program out of fear of provoking an American attack.[16] The supreme leader, hedging his policy bets, decided to again open a dialogue with the United States. Iranian leaders understood the divisions within the U.S. government and looked for a new channel beyond those in Geneva. Khalilzad had made it clear that the United States was unwilling to expand the talks beyond the narrowest focus as a one-way lecture on American demands. So the Iranians turned to the one recognized, official means of communicating with the United States: the twenty-year-old channel through the Swiss embassy. Perhaps this would get their message to senior officials disposed to talk.

On May 4, 2003, a mysterious two-page fax arrived at the U.S. State Department. Delivered by the Swiss foreign ministry, the document originated from its ambassador in Tehran, Tim Guldimann. On the second page, under the heading "Roadmap," the Iranians presented an astounding agenda, a way forward to address every issue of contention between the Islamic Republic and the United States. Breaking down U.S. and Iranian aims into a series of bullets, Iran agreed to full transparency for its nuclear program and agreed to halt its support for Hamas and to take actions that would lead to a demilitarization of Hezbollah. In return, the Iranians wanted the United States to stop trying to change their political system, to turn over MEK members, and to recognize "Iran's legitimate security interests in the region." They also wanted a public statement that Iran was not part of the axis of evil. To achieve these goals, the two nations would engage in a series of confidence-building measures, beginning with issuing joint statements on the need to meet with "mutual respect," moving to direct meetings and the establishment of working groups to hash out the details of a permanent arrangement that would end the thirty years of estrangement.[17]

Guldimann was a respected diplomat. When his five-year posting to Tehran ended, he moved up to a plum assignment as ambassador to Germany. His last few years in Iran had been marred by personal hardship. His wife had been diagnosed with cancer, requiring her to move to Hamburg, with Guldimann shuffling back and forth to visit her as she underwent lengthy but ultimately successful treatment.[18]

But the American State Department under Colin Powell had not been overly happy with Guldimann. Officials expected Guldimann, as the official conduit for démarches between the United States and Iran, to simply provide a messenger service without comment. Richard Armitage viewed him as too much a cheerleader for rapprochement, going beyond his mandate of simply relaying messages to actively working to resolve the diplomatic impasse. Those within the administration who opposed any talks with Iran, such as Elliott Abrams at the NSC and John Bolton at State, had even harsher words for Guldimann, recommending to the Swiss that he be fired.[19]

On April 21, Sadeq Kharrazi, Iran's ambassador to France and former deputy foreign minister, met with Guldimann, and the two discussed a draft road map for improving relations that the Iranian had developed. Kharrazi had clout within the Iranian government, with his sister married to the son of the supreme leader. Over the next two weeks, Kharrazi met several times with Ayatollah Khamenei to discuss the points in the proposed road map. The discussion remained a state secret, with only the supreme leader, President Khatami, and Kharrazi present at those meetings.

Ambassador Zarif, who now happened to be in Tehran for consultations and to see his family, reviewed the draft of the road map. He made numerous changes to the Microsoft Word document, his red tracked changes marking up the document, adding in the words "mutual respect" and the need for a democratically elected and fully representative government in Iraq. Zarif's input looked remarkably similar to those points he had discussed the previous fall with American Iranian Council president Hooshang Amirahmadi during their ultimately failed efforts to achieve a breakthrough in December 2002.[20]

Despite reservations, the supreme leader agreed with the opening. The Swiss represented the official means to communicate between Washington and Tehran. While a new round of talks was scheduled in Geneva, the Bush administration had refused to expand their scope beyond Afghanistan and subjects only of interest to the Americans. Kharrazi reassured the supreme leader that Guldimann could get to the highest levels of the U.S. State Department. Ayatollah Khamenei expressed some concerns, but commented that he concurred with 80 to 95 percent of the points laid out as far as U.S. and Iranian goals for the talks, deliberately remaining vague about the points on which he disagreed. "But everything can be negotiated," Khamenei said.[21]

On May 2, Kharrazi met with Guldimann. After Guldimann made some minor changes to the document, Kharrazi said, "If the Americans agree to have a discreet bilateral meeting on the basis of this road map, the meeting could be arranged very soon. In this meeting our remaining reservations could be discussed, as well as the U.S. would bring in their reservations on this paper. I am sure that these differences could be eliminated." If they agreed to the framework for talks, the next step, Kharrazi thought, would be a direct meeting between Secretary of State Powell and the Iranian foreign minister in Paris or Geneva with the supreme leader's blessing. Kharrazi continued, adding a historic statement: "We are ready to normalize relations."

Guldimann clearly approved of this new opening. "This is a golden opportunity; one day we must find a solution," the Swiss diplomat told Kharrazi. When asked if he believed that Armitage would represent the

United States at the first meeting, Guldimann correctly thought he would be too senior, but recommended that it mimic the ongoing meetings with Khalilzad and Zarif on terrorism with a similar-level group, perhaps with Kharrazi or even Zarif.

Guldimann sent the road map document with a cover letter describing his talks with Kharrazi through official channels back to the U.S. State Department. He followed it up with a quick visit to Washington, where he met with a powerful Republican, Congressman Bob Ney, a Farsi speaker known to advocate for talks with Iran. Guldimann provided a copy of the road map document to Ney and vouched for its authenticity. After meeting with the Swiss ambassador, Ney picked up the phone and called an old college friend at the White House, who happened to be the president's close political adviser Karl Rove. Rove assured Ney that the Iranian overture would get in front of the president.

The Guldimann fax with the Iranian road map circulated through the State Department. Assistant Secretary of State for Near Eastern Affairs Nicholas Burns brought it up to Armitage, who took it over to Powell. When Powell's chief of staff, Larry Wilkerson, read it, he immediately recognized many of the elements that Richard Haass had drafted at the beginning of the administration on the topics for negotiations. He claimed later that Haass's memo had been slipped to the Iranians during the Crocker meeting in Geneva. "They were responding to what we gave them," Wilkerson said.[22] Hillary Mann, who had worked with Ryan Crocker during the earlier talks with Zarif and the Revolutionary Guard, recommended testing Iran's sincerity. She drafted a memo and sent it to Richard Haass, who approved it and forwarded it up to the front office for Powell and Armitage. When the pugnacious John Bolton heard about it, he grew livid. "It was fantasy," he said. Bolton remained convinced that talking to Iran was fruitless. "They used diplomacy-stalling techniques. This was little more than a ruse to buy more time for their nefarious activities and nuclear weapons program."[23] He spoke to Powell and told him it was a bad idea to talk to the Iranians. Then he phoned the Swiss embassy and berated them for the excesses of their ambassador, who had exceeded his instructions in managing the official channel.

But Armitage remained skeptical about the provenance of this fax. "Guldimann was known to us as a very good person, but one who always looked on the brighter side of things. He seemed intent on bettering relations, and we had questions about where the Iranian message ended and the

Swiss message began."[24] Iran's willingness to abandon Hezbollah appeared too unrealistic. This memo seemed at odds, he told Powell, with what we had been hearing from the meetings in Geneva and our intelligence discussions. Armitage concluded "that Guldimann had gilded the lily."[25]

Powell passed the fax over to the White House for its review. With Armitage and Powell's disinclination, Condoleezza Rice dismissed it. Elliott Abrams and the vice president already steadfastly opposed any negotiations and seized upon Guldimann's tampering. Abe Shulsky, working for Doug Feith, dismissed the entire fax as just another probe, one of many from a very low-level functionary delivered in an obsequious manner.

But Armitage and Powell, unfortunately, had missed the true provenance of the road map. No one bothered to validate the Swiss ambassador's assertion that the supreme leader had blessed most points to be haggled. They never explored who had drafted the fax, and the input by Ambassador Zarif remained unknown in Washington. Had he known of Zarif's hand behind the memo, Armitage said in an interview, "Yes, I would have taken it far more seriously."[26]

Meanwhile, on May 3, Zalmay Khalilzad and Ryan Crocker met Zarif and Iran's Afghan ambassador, Mohammad Taherian, in Geneva, the first meeting of this group since the American invasion of Iraq. Khalilzad's instructions—prepared by the White House the night before, following consultation with senior officials in the State and Defense Departments—were direct and confrontational. While Zarif never mentioned the fax from the Swiss, his words matched its cooperative spirit. His government was not looking for a conflict with the United States, he said, and supported the idea of a representative, democratic government in Iraq that included all religious and ethnic groups. Neither the Iranians nor the United States should impose a government in Baghdad. He added that Iran did not believe an Islamic government was desirable for Iraq, nor would it work in the multiconfessional society. Zarif provided a litany of intelligence gathered on the Taliban—new bases being built, reports about secret Pakistani support for Taliban insurgent groups opposing the United States and the Karzai government—all of which proved correct. As Khalilzad wrote to Condoleezza Rice two days later, "The meeting was more useful than previous meetings. The Iranians presented a moderate and pragmatic vision for Iraq."

The American delegation surprised the Iranians too. Khalilzad reaffirmed that the United States would disarm the MEK and continue to treat it as a terrorist organization, which, as Khalilzad recalled, "took the wind out of their sails." Zarif had intended to give a lengthy lecture attacking the United States for harboring terrorists. When he heard the American position, he smiled, but added, "The way you treat the MEK is the way we will treat al-Qaeda."

Regarding al-Qaeda, Khalilzad pressed the Iranians to take immediate steps to thwart a planned attack. "There is absolutely reliable information that Iranian security forces have detained five members of al-Qaeda who have been operating in Iran. These same men have been planning a catastrophic attack in the Persian Gulf region. This attack will take place imminently," the American envoy said. The U.S. government wanted these men detained and any information gleaned turned over through the parallel talks between the CIA and Iranian intelligence. If Iran did not act, the United States would hold the Iranian government responsible for the attack.

Zarif responded that no Iranian officials harbored al-Qaeda. They would be punished, as the Iranian Supreme Council for National Security had declared the organization an enemy of Iran. But the Iranians looked surprised when Khalilzad rattled off the five names. Zarif replied that two of the men sought were already dead. An Iranian Revolutionary Guard general sitting with Zarif chimed in that just two weeks earlier their security forces had dismantled an al-Qaeda cell and arrested five men, plus more than forty family members.

Zarif asked for more information regarding the timing of the forthcoming attack, but the Americans either did not have any more details or refused to provide them to the Iranians. Zarif agreed to look into it, and the meeting adjourned with the two sides agreeing to meet later in May.

The planned attack occurred late in the night of May 12, 2003. Heavily armed militants and two suicide car bombers struck three different compounds linked to Western companies in the Saudi capital. One housed three hundred employees and family members of the Vinnell Corporation, a subsidiary of Northrop Grumman that had a contract to train the Saudi national guard. Gunmen opened fire, trying to kill the security guards and open the path for the suicide vehicles. They managed to force their way into two of the fortress compounds, where they detonated their bombs, causing massive damage and killing thirty-five, including seven Americans. Two days later Secretary Powell toured the devastation, a scene eerily reminiscent of Khobar Towers, with a ten-foot crater and the front of one building sheared off by the blast.

On May 15, the principals committee met, with Armitage standing in for his boss, who was still in Riyadh. A phone call between the perpetrators and an al-Qaeda member inside Iran suggested that terrorists inside Iran had planned the attack. While there was no evidence that Iran knew in advance about the attack, the United States put Tehran on notice, passing through the UN secretary general, the Swiss, and CIA channels that Washington would not tolerate any more such attacks and expected known al-Qaeda leaders to be turned over. There was no response from Tehran.

Awkwardly, as the United States looked to rebuild an Iraqi military force, Bremer found himself calling up Baqir al-Hakim, the leader of the Badr Corps, to incorporate his ten-thousand-man, Iranian-backed militia into the new Iraq military. Iran had pushed many of al-Hakim's soldiers into Iraq shortly after the U.S.-led invasion to begin building their control over the Shia population. Now the U.S. proconsul had invited them to help form the nucleus of a new army. Bremer was pleased with the idea. In his memoirs, he recounted meeting al-Hakim, trying to gain the leader's support for a new army: "'I promise you this, Sayyid,' I said, using his honorific title. 'The commander of the first battalion will be a Shiite.' The Coalition kept that promise." It, however, came with a price paid to Tehran.[27] While it would be a misnomer to call al-Hakim a puppet of Iran, his fondness for Tehran exceeded that for Washington.

In addition to infiltrating the army, Iranian agents or sympathizers infiltrated the new Iraqi police force. MOIS officers recruited several police officers to build a small spy ring focused on Kuwait to obtain information on U.S. forces in the emirate and on Kuwait's own military.

To try to contain the influx of Iranians, Feith suggested better control over the Iraqi border crossings. With the Iraqi forces having dissipated, the precipitous withdrawal of U.S. forces resulting from Secretary Rumsfeld's desire to pull forces out as quickly as possible left the borders entirely unguarded. For example, the U.S. Army's 5th Special Forces Group was supposed to be replaced by a cavalry regiment along the Syrian border. However, the special operators pulled out of Iraq before being relieved, leaving no Americans along the Syrian border. Likewise, U.S. Marines assigned to guard the Iranian border withdrew before establishing control over the border crossings, one of the tasks General Tony Zinni had prescribed during his development of the initial Iraq war plan in the 1990s.

An emboldened Iran even moved its own military checkpoints several kilometers inside Iraq along a significant section of the southern border near Basra. The Iranians ignored a British request to pull their forces back, so on July 17, 2003, the United States finally sent a démarche to Iran stating that this "forward movement of Iranian border posts is unacceptable." While Iran denied ever having moved into Iraq, it responded to the American threat and promptly dismantled the checkpoints and pulled back across the recognized border.[28]

As part of a campaign to influence the Iraqi populace, Iran began systematic broadcasts in Arabic with anticoalition themes sent into Iraq by fifty different radio and television stations. The broadcasts proved popular with Iraqis, in part because they had a polished Western format. CENTCOM developed a number of ideas to counter them, but all were hampered by the overall lack of an American policy toward Iran. With no approved national strategy, the authorities needed by the military never came from the secretary. Iranian broadcasts continued with a nascent American response. Opposition by the British government also restrained American efforts. The British military refused to discuss any overt jamming, let alone military strikes, and viewed the Iranian broadcasts to be inconsequential.[29]

Instead, the United States tried to influence the Iraqi media as a means to counter Iran. This included hiring individuals to plant stories in the Iraqi media that reflected well on the United States. In September 2003, the United States conducted a "thirty-day surge" to substantially increase the volume, type, and quality of media information, all of which reflected well on the American effort. Newspaper distribution increased from sixty thousand to three hundred thousand, and the United States hired a Dubai firm to provide popular pro-Western television programs. How effective these efforts were remained an open question, but at least there seemed to be an American response to Iran's media efforts.

On Friday, December 26, 2003, a massive earthquake struck Bam in south-central Iran. The calamity killed over twenty-five thousand and devastated the ancient city and surrounding villages. As international aid mobilized to provide relief, the following morning Richard Armitage met with President Bush and proposed offering the Iranians humanitarian aid. The president liked the idea. "Do it."

Armitage asked the State Department's command center to contact Javad Zarif, and it did so that afternoon. "Mr. Secretary, we've got Ambassador Zarif on the line. We're dropping."

"Good morning or good afternoon," said Zarif. The Iranian was in Tehran and had just walked in the door of his house.

Armitage offered American assistance, adding, "There is no political agenda. We are not going to play any games. This is strictly a humanitarian gesture."

"It's early in the morning here, and it won't be until tomorrow before I can get an answer for you," Zarif answered in his flawless English.

"I understand," replied Armitage. "The president instructed me to call you, and whenever you get an answer, just call me."

The next day, while Armitage watched football on his couch at home, he received a call back from Zarif. "We accept."

A mere two days after the earthquake, a gray-painted U.S. Air Force transport plane touched down in the airport at Kerman, Iran. Iranian soldiers came on board and helped the Americans off-load five pallets of medical supplies. Over the next few days, a mini airlift arrived in Iran, carrying tents, blankets, and an eighty-one-person hospital and search and rescue team. After two weeks and treating 727 patients, the Americans left Iran.[30]

Armitage hoped the Iranians would use the humanitarian opening to counter with a gesture of their own. Instead, once the U.S. aid workers left, Iran fell silent. "If they wanted an opening with the U.S., that was a good opportunity, and I hoped they would. But nothing more came from the Iranian government," Armitage later said.

By the beginning of 2004, Iran believed it had the upper hand. With the threat of a U.S. invasion receding, Iran had positioned its surrogate forces and operatives throughout the key areas of southern Iraq. It had cooperated with Bremer in forming a new Iraqi governing council with Abdul Aziz al-Hakim and other sympathizers as prominent members. The MOIS and Quds Force targeted recruitment of Iraqi government officials, and Iranian agents had even penetrated the Green Zone. Iranian-backed Shia clergy had assumed major roles in the holy cities. As the United States moved forward with Iraqi control over their government, pro-Iranian Iraqis continued to occupy key positions. The newly appointed Iraqi ambassador to Iran had long ties to Iranian intelligence and may have been a paid agent. The governing council that was formed in the summer of 2004 had the tacit approval of the Iranians through al-Hakim.[31] Iran's newly appointed ambassador to Iraq, Hassan Qomi, had served as the country's chargé d'affaires since December 2003 and was a classic diplomat and Revolutionary Guard officer. He had served as a Quds Force intelligence officer in Lebanon, and later as a diplomatic representative in the Iranian stronghold of Herat in Afghanistan. He was one of perhaps two dozen guard officers working undercover as diplomats in Iran's Baghdad embassy. Iranian Quds Force operatives were all over Iraq, undercover as reporters, tourists, pilgrims, and businessmen. Meanwhile, the growing Sunni insurgency played into Iran's hands. In a February 2004 interview, former president Hashemi Rafsanjani gloated, "[The United States is] stuck in the mud of Iraq, and they know that if Iran wanted to, it could make their problems even worse."

Twenty-Five

THE FREEDOM AGENDA

On a bright winter day with the National Mall covered in a dusting of snow, George Bush gave his second inaugural address. That fall, the president had comfortably won reelection, and after four years in the White House as a wartime president, Bush showed more confidence in himself and his core beliefs. The president wanted this inaugural address to be more than a litany of policy objectives. He wanted a grand statement about his vision, a Bush Doctrine, and he termed this "the freedom speech."

That day President Bush outlined a national manifest destiny to spread freedom and democracy. This was not only a historical calling of the United States, he argued, but it had become a security imperative: "For as long as whole regions of the world simmer in resentment and tyranny, prone to ideologies that feed hatred and excuse murder, violence will gather and multiply in destructive power." Only freedom and liberty would break this hatred. "America's vital interests and our deepest beliefs are now one," Bush said. The ultimate goal of his manifesto was nothing less than "ending tyranny in our world." The idea had fermented in the president's mind after 9/11 and in the lead-up to attacking Iraq. Free elections in Iraq had lit the spark, one that would sweep across the Middle East, and "one day this untamed fire of freedom will reach the darkest corners of our world," he said.[1]

While Bush never mentioned Iran in his inaugural address, the Islamic Republic would be the target of the new freedom campaign. The United States would throw its support behind democratic reformers inside Iran and those external activists advocating for the same reforms. Bush raised this directly the following month during the State of the Union address, on February 2, 2005. "And to the Iranian people, I say tonight: As you stand for your own liberty, America stands with you."[2]

President Bush's freedom agenda was grounded in both idealism and realism. His idealism sprang from his religious beliefs. "Freedom is a universal gift from the Almighty," Bush wrote in his memoirs.[3] But building on a widely accepted American political science theory that democracies don't fight each other, he believed that spreading freedom would strengthen American security. Bush frequently cited Japan to defend his view. Sixty years earlier, the current prime minister's father served in the imperial government while Bush's own father had been a navy pilot fighting that very regime. Now Prime Minister Junichiro Koizumi was a friend of the American president's and the Japanese government a staunch ally of the United States.

Neoconservatives both inside and outside the government embraced the president's words, especially at the influential conservative Washington think tank the American Enterprise Institute. Just after Bush's reelection, on November 10, 2004, Israeli minister and former Soviet dissident Natan Sharansky spoke there, along with conservative columnist Charles Krauthammer. The gathering highlighted Sharansky's new book, *The Case for Democracy*, in which the Israeli outlined America's new manifest destiny. The free world's—and especially America's—policy should be the expansion of democracy, he argued. As during the Cold War, individual liberty provided the best means to combat tyranny. Not surprisingly, Sharansky believed the main effort in the push for democracy should be in the Middle East, where authoritarian regimes predominated. Sharansky's thesis got him an invitation to the Oval Office, where Bush affirmed that the book encapsulated his views on foreign policy regarding the war in Iraq and the larger Middle East. "In *The Case for Democracy*," reported *Time*, "Bush found validation for his central theory about Iraq: give people liberty, and they will thrive."[4]

Implementing the new freedom agenda fell to a reshuffled foreign policy team as appointees great and small headed back to the private sector, replaced by new hires. While Dick Cheney and Donald Rumsfeld remained among the president's chief triumvirate, the third, Colin Powell (as well as his deputy, Richard Armitage), left the Department of State, replaced there by Condoleezza Rice. Stephen Hadley fleeted up to be national security adviser, with a new cast of more junior officials on the National Security Council. Two of the principal officials in the Defense Department, Paul Wolfowitz and Douglas Feith, headed to positions at the World Bank and academe, respectively, with the latter replaced by the conservative diplomat Eric Edelman, who had recently served as ambassador to Turkey and the vice president's national security adviser. William Luti headed over to the White House to run defense policy for Hadley; he was replaced at Defense by an abrasive retired army brigadier general, Mark Kimmitt, who had recently retired after a contentious tour at CENTCOM as a deputy to the chief planner.

The new secretary of state, Condi Rice, instantly became the most important person in American foreign policy. Overshadowed in the first term by bureaucratic heavyweights, like the president she had grown in both experience and self-confidence. With her close, personal rapport with Bush, Rice had the ear of the Oval Office, and everyone in Washington knew it or assumed it. "There was only one voice in American foreign policy in the second term," John Bolton said: "Secretary Rice."[5]

She too embraced Bush's freedom vision. In one of her first major speeches on the Middle East, before an audience at the American University in Cairo, Rice stated, "For sixty years, the United States pursued stability at the expense of democracy in the Middle East—and we achieved neither." In a haughty tone, she dismissed the foreign policies of nine previous presidents. She placed longtime authoritarian allies such as Saudi Arabia and Egypt on notice that a new wind of freedom was about to blow through the Middle East. "We should all look to a future when every government respects the will of its citizens—because the ideal of democracy is universal."[6] As for Iran, which had an electoral process far more vibrant than the stalwart American ally in whose country she delivered her lecture, the secretary dismissed its democratic process: "The appearance of elections does not mask the organized cruelty of Iran's theocratic state. The Iranian people are capable of liberty. They desire liberty. And they deserve liberty. The time has come for the unelected few to release their grip on the aspirations of the proud people of Iran."

The new team under Rice at Foggy Bottom grasped how woefully unprepared the Foreign Service had become regarding Iran. There had been no embassy in the country for nearly thirty years, and so no incentive or career track for the Foreign Service to focus on Iran. Few bothered studying Farsi, and the diplomats with any firsthand experience in Iran had grown gray and all but disappeared. The State Department had one Foreign Service officer, Henry Wooster, working part-time on Iran under the Bureau of Near Eastern Affairs. There was a handful of old-timers who had served in Iran, but the department had grown devoid of Iranian experts. "We have a problem," the new number three man at the State Department, Nicholas Burns, told Rice.

Nicholas Burns headed the Iran effort for Rice at the State Department. Thin, articulate, and polished, the career Foreign Service officer had recently served as the ambassador to NATO in Brussels, where he secured European support for the mission in Afghanistan. In one of her first assignments to Burns, Rice directed him to make Iran his priority, both developing a new policy and improving the department's expertise.

With Rice's support, Burns pressed to develop a career track for Iranian experts with the Foreign Service. To do this, he took a page from history. During the 1920s, when the United States did not have diplomatic relations with the Soviet Union, the State Department established Riga Station, where Russian-speaking officers sat and monitored events in the Soviet Union. When the United States finally opened a mission in the 1930s, these men formed the nucleus of the new diplomats in Moscow. Rice and Burns decided to take a similar action with Iran by establishing an Iranian regional presence office in the American consulate in Dubai, where Iranians could obtain visas and Farsi-speaking diplomats could be stationed and interact with the many Iranians who traveled to the relatively open and unrestrained emirate city. State officials built a supporting website to mimic similar ones by real embassies that provided information on the United States for Iranian citizens. Under the State Department's Bureau of Near Eastern Affairs, a new Office of Iranian Affairs was formed. If the U.S. government ever reopened an embassy in Iran, the Foreign Service officers manning this office would provide the vanguard of new American diplomats.[7]

Iran came to the forefront on Rice's first trip overseas as secretary of state in early February 2005. In his second term, President Bush was eager to repair the damage to American-European relations caused by the invasion of Iraq and Donald Rumsfeld's deriding referrals to Germany and France as "Old Europe." He traveled to Europe in what became known as the "olive branch" trip and met with both French and German leaders in Brussels and Mainz. Traveling with the president, Rice expected to hear about Iraq, as most of the Europeans, especially German chancellor Gerhard Schröder, had stridently opposed the U.S. invasion. Instead, Iran's nuclear program topped the Europeans' agenda. The Europeans wanted American backing for the ongoing "EU-3" (Germany, France, and the United Kingdom) talks about halting Iranian uranium enrichment.

The United States had not participated in the talks. Colin Powell had kept in close contact with the British foreign secretary, Jack Straw, and helped guide the discussions in ways acceptable to Washington, but the administration remained opposed to talking with Iran. "Iran is aggressively pursuing nuclear weapons under cover of an openly declared peaceful nuclear energy program," one 2003 NSC paper concluded. But the Bush White House offered no other avenue to redress the Iranian nuclear program. Now, with a new era of rapport across the Atlantic, the president agreed to support the European diplomatic effort to resolve the Iranian nuclear program peacefully. For the Germans, this new rhetoric by the U.S. government supporting their talks with the Iranians went a long way in repairing the damage over the Iraq invasion.

At the request of the Europeans, Rice extended a goodwill gesture to the Iranians. She agreed to drop the U.S. objections to Iran's application to the World Trade Organization and to allow the export of spare parts for American-made Iranian civilian airliners. While the secretary of state refused to take regime change off the public table, military action "is simply not on the agenda at this point," she said during a press conference.[8]

"I want you to lead this effort and work with the Europeans," Rice said to Burns in a meeting in her seventh-floor office. Burns remained skeptical about negotiating with Iran, but he threw his energy behind the public diplomacy drive envisioned by Rice to work to resolve the nuclear impasse. Just three weeks after his confirmation, Burns traveled to Europe and met with his German, French, and British counterparts actually negotiating with the Iranians. While there remained limits on what the United States would accept, Iran had to stop enrichment as the precondition. Burns offered additional carrots should Iran decide to cooperate, while pressing the European Union to curtail the transfer of technology needed by Tehran to build its nuclear program.

Iran's nuclear program had worried Washington for the past decade. U.S.

intelligence had suspected Iran's nuclear aspirations since the early 1990s. In General John Shalikashvili's 1993 confirmation hearings for chairman of the Joint Chiefs of Staff, he told the Senate that Iran would likely be able to produce a nuclear weapon in eight to ten years. This number kept shifting, so as late as 2004, the United States still predicted it would take eight to ten years.[9] In 2002, Iranian dissidents publicly exposed two unreported Iranian nuclear facilities: a heavy-water facility at Arak and a deep underground uranium enrichment complex at Natanz. While Iran had not been required to report these under the Nuclear Non-Proliferation Treaty, subsequent investigation by the International Atomic Energy Agency showed a pattern of obfuscation by the Iranians regarding their program. While Iran continued to maintain the peaceful purposes of its nuclear efforts, a contrite President Khatami agreed to suspend uranium enrichment in October 2003 and to allow more stringent inspections.

The nuclear program remained popular with the Iranian people. Clandestine polling by the State Department revealed that over 80 percent of the population agreed with the government's pursuit of peaceful nuclear power. And while the populace did not believe the government intended to produce a nuclear weapon, even on that there remained strong support. Many Iranians mouthed a common refrain: if Israel and Pakistan could have the bomb, then why not Iran?

After the Iran-Iraq War, Iran embarked on a "self-sufficiency jihad" to achieve energy independence. Ayatollah Khamenei added a vision of Iran as a leader in technology, which the nuclear program supported. Nuclear power would allow for great diversification of Iran's energy needs, especially as declining output from some of its oil fields fueled concern within the government about Iran's long-term export capacity. The new nuclear power plants would allow the country to keep up with electricity demand that grew at 8 to 9 percent each year. Iran relies on natural gas and oil for 85 percent of its power generation, and reducing this dependency would allow greater self-sufficiency. Lessons from the Iran-Iraq War heightened concerns about Iranian dependency on the West. Iranian officials wanted domestic enrichment capabilities so they would not have to rely on uranium sources from outside countries, which could conceivably withhold it from Iran in the event of a dispute.

However, the supreme leader never allowed the nuclear program to be publicly debated. Average Iranians cared more about jobs and improving their economic lot. If the nuclear program helped, they supported it. But if the cost imposed for pursuing nuclear enrichment through sanctions and isolation exceeded the benefit, there was far less certainty in Tehran of popular backing. Newspapers were quietly told the subject should be treated as a national security issue, with the press supporting the government's view that the West only wanted to keep Iran backward and dependent, depriving the country of its rights to the benefits of nuclear products.[10]

No one in the Bush administration had any doubt about the nature of Iran's program. U.S. intelligence concluded that Iran intended to have at least the technical expertise to produce nuclear weapons. The heavy-water reactor being built at Arak was similar to those used by other countries in their nuclear programs, and Iran's refusal to consider a European proposal for a light-water research reactor for medical and industrial material alarmed many. In mid-2004, a longtime CIA source passed along a laptop computer obtained from an Iranian; it contained reams of information from a team of Iranian engineers on designs for a compact nuclear warhead for an Iranian Shahab long-range missile. This included a compact sphere and detonators designed to trigger at two thousand feet above a target, viewed as a perfect altitude for a nuclear detonation.[11] Another intelligence report on Iran's long-range missile program indicated that Iran seemed bent on having the means to deploy such a nuclear warhead. But there remained differing views within the intelligence community about whether the supreme leader would actually decide to build the weapon or be content with the capability.

Events in Iran added to the heightened concerns in Washington. In February 2004, conservative candidates swept to power in Iranian parliamentary elections, chiefly due to the Guardian Council's disqualifying twenty-five hundred reformist candidates, including eighty sitting members. The supreme leader used his clerical influence with the vetting process to rule out the suitability of many liberal candidates. Khatami had only a year to go before term limits ushered in a new president, and the conservatives were determined not to repeat the mistake of 1997. This ended what little debate existed within the administration about Khatami's ability to make the real changes desired by Washington and provided further justification for those who had always opposed talking to Iran.

National Security Adviser Stephen Hadley tasked his deputy, Jack Dyer "J. D." Crouch, to supervise the new Iran strategy across the government. The balding longtime defense policy expert on nuclear weapons came over to the

White House as the number two man at the National Security Council, having served since 2001 in the Defense Department and as ambassador to Romania. On May 31, 2005, the NSC deputy's committee, chaired by Crouch, summed up the importance Iran now took in the administration: "The implementation of a robust Iran strategy should be a core foreign policy objective."

Putting flesh on the bones of President Bush's new vision inside the U.S. government fell to Elliott Abrams. Implicated in the Contra portion of the Iran-Contra scandal during the Reagan administration, Abrams remained unassuming, polite, and secretive. Politically, he came from the neoconservative wing of the Republican Party. A hawk, especially on Syria, he operated behind the scenes, where his experience in the White House made him a skilled operator in moving decisions through the labyrinth of government agencies. Hadley expanded Abrams's portfolio beyond just the Middle East, creating a new position for him as the deputy national security adviser for global democracy strategy. This entailed, according to the White House press statement, assisting "Mr. Hadley in work on the promotion of democracy and human rights, and will provide oversight to the NSC's directorate of Democracy, Human Rights, and International Organization Affairs." Now under Abrams's purview, the Middle East and the new democracy program were formally fused into a cohesive plan.

Before heading across the Potomac River to his new job at the White House, one of William Luti's last tasks was to oversee the drafting of a strategy paper designed to begin shaping the debate for the second term on Iran. A strident, occasionally fictional document, it accused Iran of cooperating with al-Qaeda in twenty separate acts of terrorism.[12] Although Luti never believed in talking to the Iranians, the first step, he argued, was to recognize that rapprochement had failed and negotiations with Iran served no purpose other than to provide Iran a method to talk and delay the will of the international community. The United States needed to highlight Tehran's ties to al-Qaeda and forcefully counter Iranian intelligence operations. Luti suggested repeating the Iraqi schemes by bringing together Iranian exiles into a collective opposition movement: an Iranian National Congress.

Abrams liked the paper. He massaged the ideas into an interagency plan to force Iran to end its support for terrorism as well as its ballistic missiles and weapons of mass destruction programs. Abrams agreed that the United States should also move forcefully against the Quds Force in the region. The

United States should declare it a terrorist organization and close down its operations in Iraq. He proposed more robust economic sanctions, combined with aggressive psychological operations to support opposition groups in Iran and to discredit the regime in the eyes of the world: "The failure and discrediting of this regime—a fount of modern Islamism—would help deflate and discredit extremist Islamist ideology and operational capability more broadly in the region. This should be one of the core objectives of the GWOT [global war on terrorism]," Abrams wrote.

Much of the rhetoric looked remarkably like the hawkish stands from earlier in the administration. "Recent Iranian elections have shown that Iran's leaders do not represent the Iranian people, and thus the regime has lost its legitimacy," one interagency paper from February 2005 stated. The United States intended to publicly discredit both Khatami and the clerical rule as being illegitimate, despite previous American statements and the worldwide recognition of the Islamic Republic as the rightful government of Iran.

Crouch shared both Abrams's and Luti's views that the government of Iran lacked legitimacy due to its support for terrorism and its failure to satisfy the desires of the Iranian people. Any official contact with the Islamic Republic only strengthened its claim to legitimacy and undercut the morale of dissidents and democrats within Iran. Within Crouch's staff, some argued that the Iranian government had become so unpopular that it appeared ripe for overthrow.

Over at the Defense Department, Abe Shulsky agreed with the tone. At the worker level, he continued playing his active role in shaping policy toward Iran and the war on terrorism. Shulsky wanted to support the reform movement within Iran and believed a window of opportunity presented itself in July 2004. Iran approached the fifth anniversary of the massive student protests that had rocked Tehran University in 1999. Following a small protest against shutting down a reformist newspaper, the Revolutionary Guard's thug force, the Basij, ran amok across the campus, dragging students by the hair from their dorm rooms and savagely beating them, killing one. This sparked the largest demonstrations in the country since the 1979 revolution and shook the confidence of the government. Shulsky proposed establishing a covert program to help support the students on the anniversary, anticipating widespread protests as Iranians were wont to do on such occasions. "The regime looked nervous," he said later. But this had conflicted with Colin Powell's views that the United States should remain open to working with the Iranian government of President Khatami and not subvert his position by providing aid to antigovernment forces. At loggerheads, the anniversary passed without protest or American support. Now with Powell gone and with new support in the White House for aiding Middle East democrats, Shulsky actively championed providing aid to Iranian opposition movements.

To support the White House deliberations, the CIA produced several different studies examining Iran's political strength. None expressed the optimism of those within the administration who advocated delegitimizing the Iranian government. The CIA concluded that the Iranian regime had grown more confident since the nervous days just after the U.S. invasion of Iraq. The hard-liners appeared ascendant, rolling back freedoms begun under President Khatami. The analysts saw no prodemocracy leader either inside or outside Iran capable of rallying the disaffected. A September 2005 report for Hadley concluded that the United States could sway the elite in Tehran University, but had little chance of influencing the average, largely conservative, citizen. The CIA remained skeptical that the supporters of American democracy—students, intellectuals, and old monarchists—had real influence with the average Iranian. The old shah supporters dominated the exile groups, and they appeared out of touch with current life inside Iran, having little influence with most citizens. Further, any taint of the foreign hand behind opposition groups could actually undercut support for those groups.

Unlike North Korea or the old Soviet Union, however, Iran was not a closed society. Its citizens traveled to the West. The Iranian diaspora, especially in the United States, maintained ties with family and friends inside the country. One State Department study found that many younger, better-educated Iranians had access to the Internet. Iranians loved blogs. A Harvard report found more than 700,000 Farsi blogs, mostly inside Iran, making Farsi the second-most-popular language to English in the "blogosphere."[13] According to one senior Bush official, the CIA did believe that the United States could aid human rights groups and Iranian democrats and help build a viable freedom movement; however, it would have to be carefully done in order to avoid the taint of being seen as interfering inside Iran, a long-standing concern of Iran's that could provide a rallying cry by the Islamic Republic to unite the populace. Polling of Iranian citizens consistently showed dissatisfaction with the government. Even under the popular reformist president Khatami, some six in ten described the economy as poor. A majority favored better relations with the West, including the United States.[14]

While the data of the State Department study also showed a nationalistic streak and widespread support for Islam, the disaffection within the younger population seemed ripe to exploit.

But the Bush administration had no appetite for attacking Iran. With the United States bogged down in wars in Iraq and Afghanistan, the president had little interest in embarking on another military adventure. While the president never took the military option to halt Iran's nuclear program off the table, he never seriously considered it. Condi Rice said as much during a 2007 trip to the Persian Gulf during which she met with the U.S. Navy's Fifth Fleet admiral. But the ambiguity about American intentions helped keep Iran guessing and aided the diplomatic efforts in Geneva, she said. While Newt Gingrich and others close to the administration continued advocating regime change, by force if necessary, Hadley wanted a new approach for Iran. His Middle East team at the NSC included a number of fresh faces, including a newly arrived academic from Princeton University, Michael Doran, as the director for near east and north Africa. "I always understood our goal as giving the president a third option, Doran said. "If the only two were war or a nuclear-armed Iran, then we had failed at our job.[15]

By mid-2005, Crouch had an outline of the new policy goals for Iran. Iran was critical to central tenets of the president's new foreign policy. "American security is advanced by the expansion of democracy and by the ending of support, active or passive, for terrorism." The United States sought "an Iran that does not possess or seek nuclear weapons, is a stable, democratic government, and fosters an environment inhospitable to terrorism."

Elliott Abrams cochaired a new interagency group with Elizabeth Cheney, the blond firebrand daughter of the vice president who worked as deputy assistant secretary of state for Near Eastern affairs. Cheney had no background on Iran or the Middle East, but that did not stop her from lecturing about the nature of Iranian society and its government to Foreign Service officers, including those few fluent in Farsi and those who had spent years studying the country. The Iran-Syria Working Group, as it was called, coordinated Iranian and Syrian policy across the U.S. government. Abrams wanted the State Department to lead the working group. He had personal experience from Iran-Contra in the pitfalls of running operations from the White House, and to avoid the perception of this as a planned invasion of Iran, the Pentagon willingly took a less overt role. The working group formed five separate subgroups with representatives from various agencies meeting regularly in a shabby conference room in the Old Executive Office Building or in a better-apportioned one at the State Department.

In late 2005, the president signed off on the Iran Action Plan, developed by the Cheney and Abrams group. It outlined a series of actions across the government to counter Iran and focused on sanctions, diplomacy, and a common message to highlight Iran's malign activities across the Middle East. A key goal of the Iran Action Plan would be to try to drive a wedge between the Iranian population and its government. On Halloween in 2005, Hadley laid out for the other principal officials a number of these actions to begin immediately. While the Treasury and State Departments moved to limit Iran's access to money and dual-use technology, the U.S. government would conduct a broad information operation campaign designed to promote freedom in Iran. This included welcoming dissidents to Washington, academic exchanges, supporting Iranian bloggers, and establishing Internet chat rooms to increase exchanges between Iranian and American students. "Expanding our contacts with/inside Iran would (1) enhance our ability to pursue prodemocracy programs in Iran; (2) help prevent misunderstandings and potential conflicts with Iran," Hadley wrote. President Bush liked the ideas. He hoped it would encourage a more open society and basic freedoms, which would eventually undermine the totalitarian character of the government. Five years into the administration, the Bush administration finally appeared to have a consensus on an Iranian strategy.

The State Department and Elizabeth Cheney led other efforts to support the freedom agenda. Elizabeth Cheney shepherded one of the important American efforts called the Democracy Project. It promoted American values with a strong dose of propaganda. One of its initial efforts was a media project that included a video teleconference with Iranian students and a speaker program to appeal to the Iranian diaspora, both of which highlighted the ills of the Islamic Republic. In 2005, the State Department spent $10 million to promote democracy and access to "unbiased" information.[16] This included $4 million in six different grants for Iran, the first such grants to promote democracy since 1979.[17] The following year the amount increased nearly twentyfold, to a whopping $75 million.

Deciding who would get this money fell to an affable man with a bearlike stature named David Denehy. He had served in the State Department before being detailed to the Defense Department, serving briefly in Iraq working for Paul Bremer.[18] He returned to the State Department and served as Liz Cheney's deputy, running the day-to-day meetings and the operations of the Iran-Syria Working Group. With so much money available, Iranian groups deluged Denehy with proposals, more than one hundred the first year. Some advocated parachuting arms to supposed resistance fighters and rehashed old schemes from the early 1980s to overthrow the regime. The old royalist exiles were the worst, and Denehy steered clear of them. These aging supporters of the shah amassed in Los Angeles and all wanted the State Department's largesse. None, however, really endorsed democracy, but favored a return to the monarch. As Denehy recalled, all wanted to be in charge of the effort and none wanted to cooperate with the others.[19]

Instead, the State Department concentrated on supporting groups inside Iran that advocated labor and human rights, freedom of speech, and more open and free participation in the political process. Denehy linked with private groups, especially in Europe, with established ties and lines of communication into civil society and the reform movements inside Iran. He developed relationships with nongovernmental organizations that could potentially partner or coordinate on reform efforts outside official U.S. government channels.[20] Some of these had standing ties with the U.S. State Department, including the conservative U.S. Foundation for the Defense of Democracies. The U.S. government provided grants to help start up such organizations as the Iran Human Rights Documentation Center at Yale University, which received $1.6 million to promote freedom, build alternative political organizations inside Iran, and campaign for human rights. As a supporting effort, Liz Cheney greatly expanded the State Department's International Information Program. U.S. consulates and embassies distributed e-journals, webcasts, CDs, and books in hopes of reaching Iranian citizens traveling to other Gulf countries.

Another effort centered on expanding the broadcasts of the Voice of America and Radio Free Europe/Radio Liberty's Farsi station, Radio Farda, into Iran. Officials worked with academics and Iranians in Los Angeles to develop better messages that would resonate with Iranians.[21] Despite the Voice of America charter's mandate to provide "accurate" and "objective" news, Liz Cheney and others within the administration wanted it to be more of a propaganda instrument, and took offense when the broadcasts seemed too sympathetic to Iran.

A low-level appointee and former student of Wolfowitz's working in Mark Kimmitt's Middle East office at the Defense Department wrote a report that was subsequently leaked. It was highly critical of Voice of America, saying that it "often invites guests who defend the Islamic Republic (of Iran)'s version of issues, [and] it consistently fails to maintain a balance by inviting informed guests who represent another perspective on the same issue."[22] As a counterweight, the shah's son, Reza Pahlavi, began appearing frequently. While certainly touting the proper anticlerical views, he remained popular only in the small circle of hard-core critics of the Islamic government around Washington, D.C. Inside Iran, the shah's son had no standing or support among the Iranian population. His appearances only undermined the American message.

The Iran freedom initiative did not sit well with everyone at the Department of State. Denehy steered the program between the two departmental organizations with a claim to the program: the Bureau of Democracy, Human Rights, and Labor and the Bureau of Near Eastern Affairs. Each had its own view about how to run the programs. The fallout from the Iraq War left bitter feelings by some diplomats against the neocons, and Denehy fell into that category. Other Foreign Service officers believed the effort would have little impact on the Iranian populace, who by and large still supported the Islamic Republic. Others agreed with former Bush official and now administration critic Hillary Mann: the Bush administration still wanted regime change, only now it was trying to achieve it through the guise of promoting democracy.

Iran correctly viewed all this as an attempt to overthrow the regime using "soft power." Iranian newspapers referred to this American scheme as a "spider's nest," a large web of subversion bankrolled by the United States that extended to anyone from the West who seemed intent on spreading liberal ideas. The government responded by clamping down and revamping its internal security plans. The Basij developed new military plans to deal with internal opposition and threw four Iranian Americans into prison, accusing them of spying. One, Haleh Esfandiari, a sixty-seven-year-old grandmother with dual citizenship and a scholar at Rand's Wilson Center for Middle East Public Policy, was arrested at the Tehran airport when she arrived for a family funeral. She spent 110 days in Evin Prison before posting over $300,000 in bail.[23]

In the end, whether any of this influenced the regime remained unclear. Nearly three-quarters of the Iranian population obtained their news on state-run media, and outside of the cities, few had Internet access. Both the BBC and Radio Farda remained popular, especially with students under thirty, but

Iran regularly jammed both broadcasts. The State Department's Bureau of International Information Programs had success with its Persian-language website. Launched under Powell in May 2003, it became a widely quoted source for information inside Iran, frequently used by the Iranian media.[24] The State Department continued to expand on its success during the second term. In 2004–2005, the Iranian government shut down more than fifty Internet service providers for not complying with orders to install Internet filters as it tried to block these foreign sources of disinformation. But Iranian censors showed an inattentiveness, and the U.S. efforts to circumvent their firewalls and the remarkable creativity of prodemocrats in circumventing government controls allowed for an exchange of information and ideas, at least among those few Iranians with regular access to computers.

I n August 2005, with term limits preventing Khatami from running, the Iranians elected Mahmoud Ahmadinejad as the sixth president of the Islamic Republic. Born in northern Iran as the middle child in a large brood to a sometime blacksmith and grocer, Ahmadinejad passed the demanding entrance exam for university and entered school just in time for the revolution. Like many students, he became an active supporter in overthrowing the shah, and then shared his generation's experience in war, serving in the Revolutionary Guard during the eight-year slugfest with Iraq. Ahmadinejad maintained his ties with the Revolutionary Guard. With this powerful base, he rose in the political ranks, eventually becoming mayor of Tehran before his elevation to the presidency.

The new president was a political secularist by Islamic Republic standards: his power base rested with conservatives in the guard rather than with the clergy or the supreme leader. Ahmadinejad was a populist. His unpolished rhetoric mixed social justice and revolutionary dogma in a manner that appealed to the poor and arcadian. He could be urbane. He understood the importance of pushing Iran's message in the West, and frequently traveled to Europe and even the United States, making himself available to the American press corps.

His election immediately added fodder for those calling for a hard line on Iran. Liz Cheney dismissed the entire election process, saying during one meeting that the regime simply picked and chose its presidents. Rumsfeld asked a similar question: had the election been rigged? Peter Rodman responded with reports about widespread voter fraud, but his examples supporting this looked minor, including a few women who were not allowed to vote based upon their inappropriate dress. More experienced Iran watchers found the process flawed but fair, other than the restrictions placed upon who could run for office by the Guardian Council.[25]

One of the new Iranian president's first actions was to restart the uranium enrichment program. While Iran had every right to enrich under the nonproliferation treaty, its track record of sleight of hand with its program caused alarm in Washington and the EU-3 to briefly break off talks with Iran. The new Iranian president's seemingly inane questioning of the Holocaust and his intentionally provocative statements about wiping Israel off the map worried many, and detractors cast the Iranian government as apocalyptical, intent on bringing about the Hidden Imam or Mahdi as a precursor to the day of judgment and the end of days.

"Mr. Ahmadinejad and the Iranian regime are genocidal," former CIA director James Woolsey said during a friendly Senate hearing in November 2005.[26] While more sober Iran experts countered that Ahmadinejad's religious beliefs had no more impact on his policies than Bush's as a born-again Christian waiting for the Second Coming, the hawkish, self-confident tone coming out of Tehran aroused the passions of those who had long called for overthrowing the regime. Newt Gingrich continued his decadelong mantra of removing the regime, now couched in the specter of Armageddon: "I think anything short of replacing the current government is basically irrelevant, and I think you should expect at some point in your lifetime to see a major war, and probably a nuclear war, if this government is not replaced." He advocated a mixture of sanctions, open support for Iranian dissidents, and veiled support for aiding Iranian ethnic groups opposed to the central Persian government.[27]

While the more extreme views of using force for regime change failed to gain ground in an administration bogged down in two land wars, U.S. officials accepted as truth a rumor that the first question asked every morning by Ahmadinejad during his version of the presidential daily briefing was: "Has there been a confirmed sighting of the Mahdi?"

In May 2006, Ahmadinejad sent a long, preachy letter to Bush that read as much as a religious discourse as it did substantive policy. But the letter had been approved by the supreme leader, and Ahmadinejad claimed he'd intended it to start a dialogue with Washington. Apparently, he believed that Bush, as a devout Christian, would respond positively to the Shia religious discourse that permeated the letter.[28]

The White House first learned of the letter by reading about it in the newspapers. While the administration remained unclear as to its intention, the last thing Bush's advisers wanted was to get into a discussion about religion, which would only add legitimacy to the Iranian president. Its public rather than private passage to the president struck Nicholas Burns as a publicity stunt and not a serious overture. "It provided the appearance of reaching out, but not in a meaningful way," he said, dismissing Ahmadinejad's overture.[29] Once again, the U.S. government refused to respond.

Shortly after the election of President Ahmadinejad, Hadley held a senior-level meeting to discuss its ramifications. The election had confirmed many preconceived views. His election appeared as a victory for hard-liners in a rigged election. It showed the lack of credibility the government had in the eyes of the Iranian population. The CIA representative pulled out a map that showed the variety of ethnic divisions within the country, and the discussion turned to the merits of exploiting these divisions. Non-Persians made up nearly 40 percent of Iran's seventy million people, and many, such as the Kurds in the northwest and the Baluchis in the southeast, had their own guerrilla movements fighting the central government. While the United States knew of other countries supporting these movements, such as Soldiers of God, or Jundallah, in Baluchistan, the prospect of their success had little appeal in official Washington. "The last thing we wanted was for Iran to break apart," said one former Bush official. "At the time, we were doing all we could to keep that disaster from happening in Iraq."[30]

Rice offered a measured response. "We need to take a longer-term strategy to weaken Iran's geostrategic position." She suggested increasing support for Lebanon as a way to undermine Hezbollah or "undercut some of Iran's terrorist friends," as Rice phrased it. This led to another set of actions supporting the Iran Action Plan "to strengthen the Lebanese government." Over the next couple of years, the U.S. government provided $885.5 million in economic and military assistance to Lebanon to undercut Hezbollah and Iran.[31] Not all of this assistance proved effective. In an effort to improve the quality of the anemic Lebanese police force, the United States provided dozens of Dodge Chargers to outfit the force with new police cars. Many ended up being sold on the black market and suddenly appeared all over the Lebanese streets, as young men enjoyed their muscle cars courtesy of the American taxpayer.

The Defense Department's Peter Rodman suggested duplicating the Iraqi National Congress by bringing together Iranian exiles and organizing them into a united front against Iran. He hoped it would promote a unity among reformers that would translate into action inside Iran. Others suggested duplicating the Free Iraqi Forces used in the American invasion of Iraq. That idea had failed. After spending $93 million, only one hundred men showed up for training in a camp in Hungary. But Luti believed the idea had failed because of opposition by the military, especially Tommy Franks, and not on its own merits. The Defense Department proposed approaching private groups and Iranian exiles to explore organizing them, perhaps even having the CIA organize a democratic movement inside Iran. If it had been done at the beginning of the administration, Luti believed, they would have been nearly a decade down the path to a peaceful revolution in Iran.

This met with skepticism outside of the civilians at the Pentagon and the White House. The Free Iraqi Forces and Chalabi's Iraqi National Congress were not seen with the same nostalgia in other quarters of the government, especially in light of their questionable ties to Iran and intelligence information on Iraqi weapons of mass destruction. The CIA had tried similar efforts during the early 1980s, when a large number of Iranians remained sympathetic to the United States, but it had failed to make any inroads in the military or the Iranian government. Rodman's idea died in deliberations of Abrams and Cheney's Iran steering group.

During the discussions about how to influence Iran, the idea of reopening an American consulate in Tehran emerged. On December 16, 2005, senior officials met at the Old Executive Office Building next to the White House to discuss the idea of establishing a consulate in Iran. J. D. Crouch presented a paper recommending a number of options, from opening a simple interests section in either the Swiss or the Polish (viewed as a more supportive ally, especially on Iraq) embassy to a larger consular office manned by U.S. Foreign Service officers. This direct presence in Tehran would provide a better venue to push the prodemocracy programs through easier access to visas for Iranian students and direct contacts with the Iranian population by American officials. It would allow poorer Iranians to reach the United States, as currently Iranians had to travel to Dubai or elsewhere to apply for an American visa.

Both CENTCOM commander John Abizaid and Chairman of the Joint Chiefs Peter Pace liked the idea, chiefly because they hoped it would lead to talks with the Iranian military and decrease the possibility of an unintended war in the Gulf. Michael Singh, who had the Iran portfolio at the NSC, agreed with the generals and pushed the idea of an interests section in Tehran. A pragmatist, Singh was under no illusions that this would lead to any thaw between the two nations. "It was more a means than a strategy," Singh said. But he believed it would allow for better insight into Iran and its opaque government, which would help the United States to craft a better strategy to counter the Islamic Republic. It would also show the world that Iran, not the United States, remained the obstacle to better relations.

The idea found few supporters. Dick Cheney opposed it, as did Elliott Abrams. Any diplomatic contact with Iran only afforded legitimacy to the mullahs. Hadley worried that it would appear to be a concession to Iran. After thirty years without an American diplomat in Tehran, it would send the wrong signal. Reestablishing diplomatic relations was a significant step, and the United States needed to receive some major concession in return for such a highly visible action; otherwise, it would look as though Washington had capitulated.[32] William Luti opposed it as well, although he conceded that it provided a means to getting the CIA back into Iran. John Limbert had reservations too. As a former embassy hostage and one of the few Persian experts left in the senior Foreign Service, he did not feel the United States should risk sending diplomats while Iran continued to glorify the embassy takeover with stamps and publicly sponsored rallies every November 4.[33] The idea died.

While the rhetoric inside the NSC shunned diplomacy with Tehran, the one woman who had the ear of the president viewed this differently. Having been the national security adviser, rather than impose the White House's view on the diplomats, she soon adopted their view of the need for engagement with Iran. On America's two main antagonists, Iran and North Korea, Rice turned to diplomacy to resolve the crises. This immediately clashed with the views of the vice president, who considered talks with those two countries a waste of time and endeavor. "Rice made concession after concession to the North Koreans and turned a blind eye to their misdeeds," Cheney penned in his memoirs.[34] While Abrams and others agreed with the vice president regarding Iran, Rice's close rapport with the president (and Hadley) allowed her to bypass the hierarchy and obtain Bush's approval without her ideas being vetted through Abrams and the NSC. "Cheney and Rice were at loggerheads," said one NSC official who worked Iran during the second term. "Cheney wanted to take a tougher line on Iran." This put the two most powerful advisers at odds, and again the Bush policy vacillated.

Secretary Rice hoped to improve the chances of diplomacy by reaching out to Iran's chief benefactors, China and Russia, and including them along with the three European countries in negotiations with Iran. The United States had tried appealing to Vladimir Putin during Bush's first term, John Bolton having succeeded in getting President Bush to raise the issue with President Putin in the spring of 2002. While Putin privately told Bush that he too viewed Iran as a security threat, his public statements and actions took just the opposite tact. Bolton pressed the International Atomic Energy Agency for action, but the process moved too slowly for Bolton, who blamed Powell for coddling the Europeans during the incessant negotiations, despite the uncovering of numerous instances of Iranian deceit that showed the true aim of their nuclear ambitions.[35] Rice renewed this effort in 2005, traveling to Moscow in October to attempt to sway Vladimir Putin as to the dangers of a nuclear-armed Iran. The IAEA found Iran to be in noncompliance with the nonproliferation treaty safeguards and referred the issue to the United Nations Security Council.

Nicholas Burns followed up with eleven trips to Europe, pushing a new UN resolution calling on Iran to cease enrichment. The United States launched a supporting public affairs campaign to undermine Tehran's case for its own enrichment capability and to highlight Iran's violations of the nonproliferation treaty and IAEA safeguards. John Bolton helped forge the policy by meeting with the head of the atomic agency to keep the pressure on Iran by curtailing technology transfers that would aid Iran's program and by aggressive nuclear inspections. Iran responded to the accusations with defiance and restarted uranium enrichment.

Over Easter weekend in April 2006, Condi Rice stayed in her apartment at the famed Watergate in Washington and crafted a two-page proposal for a new strategy regarding nuclear talks with Iran. Her recent trip to Europe had exposed divisions among the six nations involved in the negotiations, and crafty diplomacy by Iran had exploited these differences. Rice recommended a two-track strategy. On the one hand, the United States would offer bold incentives for Iran to give up the production of all nuclear fuel, while on the other hand simultaneously proposing stiff sanctions if it did not comply. As part of her plan, Rice raised the possibility of the United States playing its biggest card: actually sitting down and talking with Iran.[36] European Union foreign policy chief Javier Solana told Rice, "They want America. That's all they want—America."[37] As a carrot for ending their enrichment, the United States would do a dramatic turnabout in its delegitimacy stance and meet with the Iranians. The president remained intrigued but unconvinced.

On May 19, 2006, Rice attended an NSC meeting on the way forward. She proposed reengaging with the five Security Council members and Germany in offering a series of incentives in return for Iran's ceasing enrichment and giving up its designs for a nuclear weapon. The United States would pursue multiple tracks from talks to sanctions. If Iran agreed to stop enrichment, the United States would help by unfreezing some Iranian assets and placing any further sanctions on hold. More important, the United States would join talks directly with Iran on any issue, and Rice suggested relaying this directly to Ali Larijani, Tehran's chief negotiator and the head of Iran's national security body, through established Arab channels. For once, the gathering supported the idea. According to one source, even the vice president agreed, saying, "The offer might work, largely because it would force the choice back on Iran. When it failed, there would be no doubt Iran had scuttled it." Bush worried that it might be seen as a reward to Iran, especially when its actions in Iraq actively undermined the U.S. effort. But he did not want to be accused of not pursuing every option to resolve the nuclear standoff. This was the type of consensus decision Bush liked, and with Rice holding such sway with him, her opinion became first among equals.

In May, the president agreed. Rice publicly proclaimed that if Iran created the necessary conditions for negotiations by meeting its UN Security Council obligation to suspend all uranium enrichment and reprocessing activities, the United States would be willing to sit down to discuss the nuclear issue or anything else Iran wanted. She intimated that normalization of relations could follow. Rice's offer to meet the Iranians at any time and in any place if they suspended enrichment became a staple slogan in the secretary's press conferences.

Although Nicholas Burns believed the talks would fail, he thought that would not necessarily be the end of the discussions. "What we were looking for was a sustained engagement. It was not that we liked them—we opposed everything they were doing to us—but we had not had anything but episodic meetings for the past thirty years. If we could just get them to the table, we could get an idea of their bottom line and see if there was a deal to be made between the United States and Iran."[38]

In Vienna on June 1, 2006, all the permanent members of the Security Council plus Germany presented the proposal to Iran. In return for halting its uranium enrichment and transparency with its nuclear program, the United States would ease sanctions and permit the sale of a light-water reactor, with Europeans offering to help modernize Iran's oil and gas industry. The six nations even dangled the possibility that Iran could eventually be allowed to resume enrichment if it complied with all outstanding concerns and if it could be verified as a peaceful program.[39] Condi Rice added the biggest shift by agreeing to join the talks and sit down with Iran, a move that offered improved relations in other areas. But again, only after Iran had ceased enrichment.

Rice assumed Iran would accept the deal. Iran's chief negotiator, Ali Larijani, was an erudite man with a doctorate in Western philosophy. He had privately confided to Javier Solana that the terms were acceptable, and his public statements showed qualified support for the proposal. Even President Bush appeared upbeat. Speaking to reporters from his ranch, he repeated the offer to talk with Iran and said of Larijani's answer that it sounded "like a positive response to me."[40]

However, disagreements emerged in Tehran over whether to accept it. Larijani appeared to endorse it, only to back away. The opaque nature of the Iranian government made it difficult for U.S. officials to ascertain the deliberations in Tehran, "but it was clear there were disagreements in the Iranian government over accepting the proposal," recalled Nicholas Burns. When the Iranians asked for more time past the six weeks offered by the six parties, the United States accused them of trying to stall while continuing enrichment. The supreme leader objected to the dictatorial tone of the proposal: stop enrichment or else.

In the end, Iran turned down the offer. Rice had miscalculated. The big card of direct talks with the American government did not seem nearly so significant in Tehran. This was not 2003. Three years after the start of the Iraq War, Iran no longer feared an American invasion nor had much desire to talk with a government that had repeatedly rejected Iran's overtures. Iranian hard-liners took the U.S. insistence on halting enrichment as a precondition as an affront to their rights to have a nuclear program—illicit weapon programs notwithstanding.

So the Bush administration forged ahead with the stick. With the support of Russia and China, the United States ratcheted up the pressure. On December 26, 2006, the Security Council approved Resolution 1737, which banned supply of nuclear technology and froze the assets of organizations involved in Iran's nuclear program until Iran halted its enrichment. It also required countries to limit the travel of key Iranians designated as being involved in Iran's nuclear program. In March 2007, another Security Council measure banned arms sales and froze additional assets. Yet a third, Resolution 1803, passed unanimously in March 2008; it authorized inspections of cargoes bound to Iran suspected of carrying equipment for its nuclear program and squeezed Iranian banks by restricting transactions with Iran's Bank Melli and Bank Saderat. The United States succeeded in adding thirteen more individuals and twelve companies involved in building Iran's nuclear program, subjecting them to travel restrictions and freezing assets.

Using executive edicts, President Bush froze additional Iranian assets. Stuart Levey, who had been recommended by Abe Shulsky, headed the effort at the Treasury Department. He succeeded in ending the ability of Iranian banks to interchange with European banks. A serious blow to Iran financially, it isolated Tehran from the world's economy.

The Saudis helped the American effort. On September 5, 2006, Prince Bandar met with Treasury Secretary Henry Paulson. Bandar expressed Saudi support for efforts to cut off Iran financially and offered to head a tour of Europe to raise awareness of deceptive Iranian banking and business practices that aided its support for terrorism. The United States liked the idea, and on October 10 both Hadley and Rice met with Bandar and expressed American support, with the president adding his similar views during an Oval Office meeting on November 10. The Treasury Department passed Bandar a list of talking points and financial institutions with whom Bandar should meet to stress the importance of isolating both Syria and Iran. Bandar dutifully made the rounds, trying to convince the Europeans to cut off their financial dealings with Iran.

In December 2007, the U.S. intelligence community released a National

Intelligence Estimate (NIE) on Iran's nuclear program that deflated the efforts to hype the Iranian nuclear peril. The intelligence community judged "with high confidence that in the fall of 2003, Tehran had halted its nuclear weapons program." Assuming it would leak, Bush ordered portions of the NIE declassified. It created a sensation about the need to continue pressuring Iran, and any talk about a military option evaporated. Lost in the postleak hullabaloo about Iran ceasing its weapons program was the fact that Iran had run a covert program and stopped the nuclear warhead design only shortly after the U.S. invasion of Iraq. At the time, Iran feared attack and had approached the United States with its grand bargain that May. Nevertheless, when Bush traveled to Saudi Arabia in January 2008, he opened the meeting with King Abdullah, "Your Majesty, may I begin the meeting. I'm confident every one of you believes I wrote the NIE as a way to avoid taking action against Iran. You have to understand our system. The NIE was produced independently by our intelligence community. I am as angry about it as you are." Indeed, the Saudis and the other Gulf states were angry. Many suspected the United States had reached a secret accommodation with Iran.

"The NIE didn't just undermine diplomacy," Bush wrote. "It also tied my hands on the military side."[41] Talk of military strikes against Iran's facilities ended within the administration.

Iran answered with more centrifuges and expanded enrichment. In April 2008, President Ahmadinejad announced during a visit to Iran's main enrichment complex at Natanz that it had started installing six thousand centrifuges at the site, twice the number currently spinning uranium. Iran continued to proclaim the peaceful nature of its nuclear program. It stressed a fatwa against nuclear weapons issued by the supreme leader in 2005 and called for a nuclear-free Middle East. "We are willing to negotiate over controls, inspections, and international guarantees," Ayatollah Ali Khamenei said, but he viewed it as his country's right under the nonproliferation treaty to enrich uranium, and any effort to halt that impinged on its right to nuclear energy.

As the Bush administration neared its end, it tried a last, weak push to resolve the nuclear standoff with Iran. The six powers had offered a "freeze-for-freeze," with Iran agreeing not to expand its program in return for no additional sanctions, and included a package of new economic and political incentives in return for halting enrichment of uranium. The British had asked the United States to send an American diplomat to Tehran when they presented the latest offer to Iran, but the Americans balked.[42] Instead, on a Saturday in July 2008, William Burns, who had recently replaced Nicholas Burns (no relationship) as the undersecretary of state for political affairs, walked in during the ongoing talks at Geneva's city hall between Iran and the six nations that had been haggling with Iran for more than three years. While any meeting with the Americans and Iranians at the same table became a public spectacle, Burns never spoke privately with his Iranian counterpart. The U.S. delegation made it known that his presence was a onetime affair designed to show support for the talks and reiterated that further talks would be based upon the precondition that Iran stop uranium enrichment. Iran again rejected the precondition.

In the end, the United States failed to halt Iran's nuclear program. But the administration had taken long strides down the sanctions road, and these would bite deep into Iran over time. While the Bush administration's second term appeared more unified on Iran, in the end disagreements again plagued a coherent policy. Rice's views on a dual track of sanctions and diplomacy prevailed because of her personal relationship with the president and drowned out those calling for shunning Iran. These internal squabbles undermined a vibrant policy. Offering the stark contrast of freedom versus totalitarianism had worked well in undermining popular support for the Soviet Union in the Cold War. Rice and Bush set out a similar program designed to undermine the Iranian government through open information. But this contrasted with the hard-liners who desired to isolate Iran. They worried that allowing more Iranian students to come to the United States invited dangerous technology transfers and Iranian spies inside the United States. These attitudes undermined the basic intent of the freedom agenda. By refusing to talk to Iran, the United States operated blindly. American diplomats and intelligence analysts had minimal insight into the opinions of the Iranian people or its government and largely depended on third parties for information and insight into the country. In the end, American policy rested on prejudice and supposition more than fact.

But the one area where the facts proved incontrovertible and all the parties in the U.S. government should have agreed was Iraq. The American invasion opened the door for Iranian influence, and Iran moved to consolidate its power. While a nervous Iran had been willing to make an accommodation to

Twenty-Six

A Quasi-War

As Washington prepared for Christmas 2006, President Bush and Vice President Cheney traveled by motorcade the short distance over to the Pentagon. After the normal staged handshakes with some service personnel in the hallway, the two men sat down with the six members of the Joint Chiefs of Staff around the long table in a conference room that served as the temporary Tank, as long-awaited Pentagon renovations forced the men out of their usual haunts on the outer E ring. Stephen Hadley and Donald Rumsfeld joined them, as did the latter's designated successor, a levelheaded, sometimes ruthless, former CIA analyst and seasoned government official Robert Gates.

The affable chairman, Peter Pace, presented the president with a five-page document of PowerPoint slides titled "Joint Chiefs of Staff Military Advice—Predecisional—Close Hold." The briefing addressed a new military plan to win in Iraq. Tall and good looking, Pace had served six years in the top two positions within the military, where he used the talents that had earned him the nickname among his Annapolis classmates of "Perfect Peter" to get along with the prickly secretary of defense. He offered his advice only in private and had raised no discernable objections to the strategy toward Iran or in Iraq, even as the latter derailed under the pressure of religious strife and a growing insurgency.

Iraq had dominated much of these men's attention that fall. In the aftermath of the bombing of an important Shia shrine by Iraqi al-Qaeda, the security situation had deteriorated dramatically, and despite Rumsfeld's public claims to the contrary, it had descended into a full-scale religious civil war. The first line on the briefing summed up the situation as the chiefs viewed it: "We are not losing, but we are not yet winning—time is not on our side." Pace added his own comments to this: "at home, in the region, and in Iraq."

The normally reticent decider, President George W. Bush, understood the ramifications of failure, and for one of the first times, he fully engaged in the policy discussions, probing his divided advisers for answers. Army general David Petraeus, had requested additional troops for a surge that would support a new counterinsurgency strategy to win the war, yet the four-star generals in Washington, Tampa, and Baghdad all opposed the idea. Pace had asked for the meeting in the Tank for the service chiefs to air their views, but the senior officers and generals offered no new ideas—just an expansion of the current plan to increase training of the Iraqi army and put it in the lead. It was more a "crisis in perception, confidence, not violence," they said, and they recommended merely expanding the advisory effort to train the Iraqi army faster. "Now is not the time to surge U.S. combat forces, Mr. President," said U.S. Army chief of staff General Peter Schoomaker, who had been plucked out of retirement by Rumsfeld.[1]

"What's new?" Bush said. "We are doing much of this already. I have deep anxiety about Baghdad's security." The problem was that the Iraqi train was coming off the rails due to a lack of security, primarily in the Iraqi capital, and the president knew it.

Toward the end of the meeting, the talks turned to Iran's role in fomenting the violence. As the American problems mounted, Iran grew more emboldened. That year, Iran had dramatically increased its support for Shia militias and provided a new, sophisticated type of improvised explosive device that had killed 140 coalition soldiers.

"We are working on an execute order to neutralize their networks," Pace said. This would be part of an overarching military plan to counter Iran that included enhancing the Gulf Arab defense capabilities to respond to Iranian aggression. CENTCOM proposed two courses of action to deal with Iranians

inside Iraq. The first was a nonlethal option to harass and expose their operatives; the second would be a high-end option: to immediately begin arresting
Iranian agents inside Iraq and targeting their surrogate forces in the Middle
East. The chiefs cautioned against taking action that might escalate the crisis
and highlighted the risks of taking direct action without Iraqi prime minister Nouri al-Maliki's approval, but some in the room wanted decisive action.
As one participant wrote in his notes: "Kill Iranians in Iraq."

In the boldest decision of his presidency, Bush overruled the generals,
including Pace, and in January 2007 authorized sending in the de facto American reserve of five brigades—thirty thousand troops—to Iraq. And just two
days after the meeting in the Tank, the president also gave the go-ahead to
take military action against Iran. Amid the drama of the surge debate on
Iraq, the United States and Iran again appeared on a collision course to war.

The appointment in mid-2003 of a new CENTCOM commander, General
John Abizaid, portended a more informed approach to the Middle East
by the U.S. military. He relieved Tommy Franks in an unprecedentedly garish
ceremony at an indoor sports stadium in downtown Tampa. Franks had declined a request by the chairman to extend for an extra year to provide conti-
nuity on the war in Iraq in order to rest and pursue a lucrative book deal. A
Lebanese American, fluent in Arabic, Abizaid had served as the senior plans
officer for the chairman at the outset of the invasion of Iraq. In private discussions leading up to the U.S. invasion, Abizaid had cautioned that diminishing
Iraqi power might provide an opening for Iran, much in the same vein as the
United States worried about removing Saddam Hussein during Desert Storm
in 1991. During the war, Abizaid served as the forward deputy commander of
CENTCOM, where he was one of the few who cautioned against allowing the
unchecked looting and the open support for some of the Shia militias.

From the outset, Abizaid focused on Iran. He worried that the United
States lacked a strategic plan for the Middle East, with Washington entirely
focused on the war in Iraq. "We cannot lose sight of the growing role Iran is
playing across the region," he wrote to Rumsfeld shortly after taking over
CENTCOM.

Abizaid worried about an unintended conflict with Iran. On June 21,
2006, a U.S. Navy P-3 aircraft harassed an Iranian submarine by dropping

sonar buoys around it, and closed provocatively close again three days later. Tehran sent a diplomatic note to the United States protesting the incident. Since 2001, the United States had exchanged forty such démarches with Iran, each protesting the other country's actions, and while this seemed innocuous, if the Iranians mistook sonar buoys for bombs, there would be a shooting war in the Persian Gulf.

A more disturbing incident occurred toward the end of Abizaid's tenure. The water boundary between Iran and Iraq—haggled over in 1975—was a straight line from the mouth of the Shatt al-Arab. Over the years, the shifting sands had moved the boundary, and Iran and the coalition disagreed on the exact location of the international boundary. Since 2003, the Revolutionary Guard had increased its presence in the area, forming a new 3rd Naval District and establishing a surveillance post on a massive crane, leaning and heavily damaged from the Iran-Iraq War. U.S. sailors called it the sunken crane. On March 23, 2007, the HMS *Cornwall* dispatched a Royal Marines and sailor boarding party to search a suspected smuggler ship located near the disputed maritime border.

Alerted by the sunken crane, two Revolutionary Guard speedboats came across the waters. The senior Iranian commander was Captain Abol-Ghassem Amangah. Aggressive and ambitious, he quickly realized that the water was too shallow for the HMS *Cornwall* to come within ten miles. As his boats approached, most of the British personnel were searching the ship, leaving only a couple of sailors in the two Zodiacs. While the conversation was cordial at first, Amangah quickly accused the British of entering Iranian waters. Without any orders from his headquarters, the guard officer ordered his men to train their weapons on the British, and told the British to surrender and follow him to his base. After trying in vain to get support from their superiors and fearing loss of life, the Royal Navy lieutenant in charge ordered his detachment to surrender. The Iranians stepped into the British boats and took over the controls, driving them back to Amangah's base in Iran.

The commander of Fifth Fleet, Vice Admiral Kevin Cosgriff, learned of the incident while the Iranians were taking the British back to their base. An experienced surface warfare officer with multiple tours in the Gulf, he had commanded the last Earnest Will convoy just as the Iraqis invaded Kuwait. He dispatched surveillance assets to monitor the British captives and had his staff begin to develop some ideas about using force to get them back. But his British deputy waved him off. Her Majesty's government did not want to escalate the situation. So Cosgriff watched as the Iranian military flew the fourteen men and one woman to Tehran.[2]

The incident surprised Tehran as much as London. Amangah had had no orders to do what he did, but his seniors in the Revolutionary Guard liked that kind of initiative. President Ahmadinejad quickly took advantage of the gift. The British prisoners became a propaganda coup for the Iranian government, which paraded them before news cameras. After twelve days, Ahmadinejad ordered them released, sending them back in Iranian-made suits and carrying a bag of presents courtesy of the Islamic Republic. Captain Amangah was handsomely rewarded for his actions. President Ahmadinejad awarded him a medal, and he took command of a major Revolutionary Guard force, jumping over a number of more senior officers.

Abizaid and the Americans took notice. In keeping with Napoléon's maxim that "every soldier carries a marshal's baton in his pack," the incident provided a clear path to glory in the Revolutionary Guard. It would only serve to inspire more rogue and aggressive actions by the guard, Abizaid believed. "It provided every guard officer a model for how to get promoted," said one U.S. admiral.

The CENTCOM commander did not share all of the administration's views of Iran. He argued for a broader strategy to undercut Iran across the Middle East. He pressed for a new emphasis on Israeli-Palestinian peace to help improve America's position in the Middle East and suggested the United States could entice away Iran's only ally, Syria. After the overthrow of Saddam and before the insurgency took root, the United States held powerful bargaining power compared with a nervous al-Assad. It had a chance to cut a deal to curtail Syrian support for Hezbollah.

The army general repeatedly called for a meeting with the Iranians. "I did not want to talk to them because I wanted them to be our friends," he said after he retired. "I wanted to talk to them to avoid miscalculations that so often lead to conflict, much like the same way we had during the Cold War with the Soviet Union." He supported Richard Armitage in providing aid to the Iranians following the December 2003 Bam earthquake in hopes that the interaction between the American and Iranian soldiers and airmen might lead to a dialogue between the two militaries. General Abizaid proposed including Iranian officers in the International Military Education and Training programs sponsored by the Defense Security Cooperation Agency. These training programs emphasized democratic values and had been used for decades to influence military students on the virtues of the American way of life. Including Iranian officers, Abizaid surmised, would help break down the distrust of the United States. He also suggested cooperation on areas of mutual concern. Iran had a terrible heroin problem, with junkies littering Iranian parks high on cheap Afghan poppies. He suggested offering Iran nonlethal aid to control drug smugglers coming in from Afghanistan.[3]

These ideas did not sit well with the White House. Both the vice president's staff and Abrams opposed any dialogue with Iran, with Abrams seeing accommodation with Syria as naive.[4] Any assistance would only give legitimacy to the regime, and providing military training or assistance would only give them "unmatched" insight into U.S. military capabilities. Rumsfeld expressed concern about any military exchange programs, and none of Abizaid's Iranian openings ever got beyond point papers and discussions.

Abizaid and the administration did agree on the growing danger of Iran's ballistic missiles. Abizaid's concerns found support in the U.S. government. At the State Department, supporting CENTCOM's fell to another newly arrived appointee, John Hillen. With a goatee and short-cropped hair, the extroverted assistant secretary of state for political-military affairs had solid credentials both in foreign policy and in the military. He had received a bronze star during the epic tank battle of "73 Easting" with the Iraqi Republican Guard during Desert Storm. He then left the army and went on to earn his doctorate in international relations at Oxford University. Hillen proposed a new policy venture called the Gulf Security Dialogue. With the help of Egypt, Jordan, and Lebanon, Hillen wanted to get the Gulf Arabs engaged in working together in a common defense against Iran. He had no hope for a new Persian Gulf version of NATO, but just wanted to push forward in areas where they should be able to work together, such as missile defense.

Hillen worked closely with Peter Rodman at the Pentagon, and the two agreed on the policy framework underpinning the dialogue, which included deterring Iran, countering terrorism, and providing stability in the Middle East. The administration used this framework as a basis to significantly increase arms sales to the Gulf Arabs.

In May 2006, Hillen and Ryan Henry from the Pentagon traveled to all the Gulf countries to hawk the Gulf Security Dialogue and explore means of improving defense cooperation. Fear of Iran resonated in the Gulf. Peter Rodman even remarked that Arab-Israeli peace, which had always been a major topic of discussions, became a footnote. Hillen offered to facilitate greater cooperation with CENTCOM and among the other states. The United States offered to sell advanced Patriot missiles, new fighter aircraft, radar that could track missiles across the region, and even the brand-new Littoral Combat ship to the Gulf Arabs. Working through the U.S. military, they would integrate all this into a Persian Gulf–wide air defense system.

"The Gulf Security Dialogue mainly existed in the U.S. minds and in our memos," said one midlevel official in the NSC. While the Gulf states feared Iran, they still would not operate as a collective. They refused to share their air defense radar data with each other and only grudgingly agreed to train together at a new U.S. air-to-air combat center in the United Arab Emirates. Qatar and Oman had close economic ties to Iran and did not want to unduly antagonize leaders in Tehran. "The U.S. could never even mention Iran as the adversary," recalled one military officer. One Qatari official accused the United States of hyping the Iranian threat simply to sell more weapons. "Getting the Gulf states to do anything in consort is like herding cats," recalled one Defense official.

Hillen and Rodman tried to counter this trend by going back to an earlier policy playbook to get a multilateral impact through a series of bilateral agreements. "The idea was to forge a series of bilateral agreements between the U.S. and the Gulf Arabs that ended up being a de facto coalition, with the U.S. as the linchpin on which everything depended," recalled one Bush official. It was not ideal, but allowed the United States to lay the groundwork for more integration and cooperation in the future. It remained a work in progress, and over the coming years cooperation and coordination did improve, with hotlines installed between the militaries and some sharing of information. The United States increased its own missile defense system to provide a backbone to protect the Gulf states, with Abizaid approving sending three battalions of Patriot missiles to the Gulf.

Selling weapons to the Gulf Arabs has always drawn close scrutiny from Congress. Hillen and Abizaid worried about the political fight in improving the weapons of the Gulf Arabs. But President Bush had a better understanding of Congress. During a December 2006 meeting in the Roosevelt Room, Hillen mentioned that some of the systems they wanted to sell to the Arabs might be controversial. The president snapped, "Not if it's against Iran."

Iran had a dual-track policy regarding Iraq. In the long-term, Tehran wanted a stable but politically weak Iraq dominated by Shia coalitions. While the Bush administration continued issuing policy papers confidently proclaiming that Iran feared the emergence of a democratic Iraq, Tehran's diplomats actively supported the American democratic process, realizing it would guarantee a Shia majority in the government. In the short-term, however, the Iranians wanted a level of instability. Seeing the American military on their border as a grave threat, they wanted to bleed the Americans, make the cost of the occupation too high, and cause a chastened American government's ignominious withdrawal. They encouraged Abdul Aziz al-Hakim and others to participate in the political process, and before the 2005 elections provided pictures and posters supporting the Shia United Iraqi Alliance party. Iran provided al-Hakim's ISCI and Badr Corps more than $50 million a year and backed the American electoral process. Through their ambassador to the Court of St. James, Iran relayed its desire to work with Washington in free and fair elections in Iraq.[5] The Bush administration ignored the offer, continuing to assert that the specter of Shias voting in Iraq would undermine the totalitarian neighbor. However, a November 27, 2005, State Department report, leaked by WikiLeaks, warned, "Iran is gaining control of Iraq at many levels of government."[6]

Iran simultaneously increased its assistance to Shia militias opposed to the United States. The United States helped Iran in this when a U.S.-concocted plan to disarm militias integrated many of the Iranian-backed Badr Corps soldiers into the new Iraqi security forces.[7] In the spring of 2004 a young firebrand cleric, Muqtada al-Sadr, openly challenged the United States. The son of a prominent cleric killed by Saddam, al-Sadr possessed a family pedigree that appealed to many of the poor Shia, who flocked to his side. His militia force, the Mahdi Army or Jaysh al-Mahdi, grew in size and power with Iran's support. Although al-Sadr shared Ayatollah Khomeini's views of a pan-Shia movement, he remained independent and wary about Iranian meddling in his country. Iran supported him due to his widespread support from the populace. The head of Iran's Quds Force, Qassem Suleimani, despised him. Suleimani viewed al-Sadr as too reckless and thought his uncoordinated and independent actions only undermined Iran's goals in Iraq. But in April, as the crisis erupted, the Quds Force still provided al-Sadr's militia with medical supplies and three hundred rocket-propelled grenades. When the U.S. military crushed al-Sadr's uprising in August, Iran dispatched both diplomats and Quds Force officers to mediate the crisis and cajole al-Sadr back to supporting the American-established interim Iraqi governing body.

Supporting the Iraqi militias became one of the most important missions for the commander of the Quds Force, the secretive arm of the Revolutionary Guard. In his late forties, with salt-and-pepper hair and a matching beardary, Suleimani was an aggressive, hands-on leader. He had distinguished himself during the Iran-Iraq War and quickly rose to be one of the youngest division commanders in the Iranian military. He had a very close, trusting relationship with the supreme leader, who appointed him to head the Quds Force in 1998. Although a part of the guard, the Quds Force reported only to Ayatollah Khamenei. It was organized into regional commands called corps, each controlling operations under its area (for example, Lebanon or the Arabian Peninsula) under Suleimani's watchful eyes.[8] For Iraq, the responsible corps was Department 1000, or the Ramazan Corps, commanded by Colonel Ahmed Foruzandeh, which stood up in the early 1990s to try to subvert the Shia against Saddam Hussein. Foruzandeh had three subordinate headquarters, each close to the border. When inside Iraq, the Quds Force operated from a series of safe houses and front companies, and it had a presence everywhere but the Sunni-dominated western al-Anbar province. Suleimani took an active role in the operations in Iraq. He covertly traveled to Basra to meet with Iraqis and frequently stayed at a forward headquarters established in the Iranian border town of Mehran.[9]

In late 2004 and early 2005, Iran held a series of meetings in Tehran to support newly emerging pro-Iranian surrogate groups opposed to the United States. Lebanese Hezbollah operatives attended several of these, as Iran intended to use them to conduct military training inside Iraq, which would help minimize Iranian fingerprints on their operations. While Iran maintained its support for the Islamic Supreme Council and other large Shia parties involved in the government, Tehran cultivated at least eleven smaller rejectionist groups, several being splinter groups from al-Sadr's Mahdi movement. This included Abu Sajjal Gharawi, who served as a commander under al-Sadr only to fall out of favor after the cessation of attacks on the coalition. He had close ties with Quds Force officers, and they frequently met in a Basra safe house. Another was Abu Mustafa al-Sheibani, who had a network of perhaps three hundred men operating primarily in Baghdad's Sadr City. A dual Iranian-Iraqi citizen and former Revolutionary Guard officer, he maintained close ties with the Quds Force.[10]

To aid their surrogates, Quds Force operatives observed American forces and bases, meticulously noting convoy patterns and flight schedules. The large American air base at Balad and the U.S. embassy in the Green Zone were favorite bases for Quds Force surveillance teams. After a raid by U.S. forces in 2008, the Americans uncovered thousands of reports detailing Quds Force operations and attacks by their surrogates against coalition forces, as well as former Baathists, including retribution killings against Sunnis who had a hand in the massacre of the Shia during the 1991 uprising following Desert Storm. To aid them, the Quds Force recruited Iraqis—many of whom had fled to Iran during the Iran-Iraq War—living along the Kuwait border to provide additional information on troop movements. This supplemented information received by MOIS spies operating in Kuwait.

Iran decided to provide a new weapon to its Iraqi insurgents: enhanced formed projectiles, or EFPs. Improvised bombs made from explosives or old Iraqi munitions caused most American casualties in the war in Iraq, but these new weapons increased the lethality dramatically. Using a cylinder fabricated from commonly available metal or PVC pipe, the front end was encased with a concave copper or steel disk. When the explosive detonated, the force of the blast shaped the copper disk into a high-velocity molten-shaped slug—the poor man's sabot round. This slug easily penetrated armored vehicles and proved so accurate that insurgents could target specific seats in a vehicle. They usually aimed for the driver-side window to kill the driver and roll the vehicle, or targeted the front passenger seat where the officers usually sat.

These EFPs first appeared in Lebanon in the late 1990s, employed by Hezbollah against Israeli armored vehicles. Building them required precise manufacturing tools, which did not exist in Iraq but did in Iran, especially at an ammunition plant in northeastern Tehran in an area controlled by the Revolutionary Guard.

In July 2004, Quds Force officers met in a safe house in Basra with Mustafa al-Sheibani. Iran brought Lebanese Hezbollah trainers into both Iraq and Iran to teach al-Sheibani's men on the use and assembly of the EFPs, which would be manufactured in Iran from explosives produced at a plant in Esfahan, with other parts manufactured in the factory in Tehran. They agreed to ship the EFP components across the border disguised as food products, and with the aid of a Hezbollah agent, who provided the infrared triggers, they would be reassembled in Iraq. In the first nine months of 2005, this group alone conducted thirty-five EFP attacks against coalition forces in Iraq, killing seventeen soldiers and wounding thirty-six more. The EFPs proved especially lethal. Each attack left an average of two dead.

Iran expanded its distribution of EFPs. In May 2005, a Quds Force lieutenant colonel arrived in Basra to provide money and EFPs to several insurgent groups. In May, he met in al-Kut and paid one Shia leader 1.5 million Iraqi dinars to attack U.S. forces. The Iranians developed elaborate smuggling routes to get the EFPs into Iraq. One of the main routes was at a large border crossing near the Iranian city of Mehran, where Suleimani had his headquarters. The Iranian Quds Force built the EFP components in a clandestine lab, smuggling them across every month to Revolutionary Guard safe houses in An Numaniyah and Basra hidden in oil drums, cement bags, television sets, and food containers. There they could be reassembled by Iraqi insurgents. A U.S. intelligence report in the fall of 2006 noted that EFPs inflicted coalition casualties at a rate nearly six times higher than those inflicted by standard IEDs.

Iranian supporters in the army and police force aided the effort. For example, in late 2006 the former Badr Corps members in the security forces drove a truckload of EFPs to Baghdad, having been transported across the Iranian border and through Basra. They stored them in safe houses around the city and even in a Baghdad police station. Ever the entrepreneurs, some of these Shia sold the EFPs to their Sunni rivals, making handsome profits on this side business. When the U.S. military uncovered the network, analysts surmised that there may have been ninety EFPs prestaged in Baghdad.

Al-Sadr supporters traveled to Iran from Sadr City to receive training on the new EFP technology. Iran and the Jaysh al-Mahdi built a solid working relationship with both EFPs and weapons and explosives smuggled in from Syria on refrigerated trucks. As one American report noted: "The use of JAM [Jaysh al-Mahdi] operatives affords Iran plausible deniability as it continues to expand its influence in Shia populated areas of Iran." On January 16 and 18, 2006, Jaysh al-Mahdi fighters ambushed two British waterborne patrols on the Shatt al-Arab with antipersonnel mines and small-arms fire. They then shelled British positions with 240-mm rockets—some of the largest in the Iranian inventory.

Iran adopted a similar strategy to that used with Hezbollah in the early 1980s—provide training and equipment, but do not actually participate in attacks. While the more basic military training could be accomplished in Iraq, more advanced training designed to train the trainers—as the U.S. Special Forces described it—required traveling to Iran. Captured documents and Iraqi prisoners exposed an organized transportation network where buses and taxis took the select recruits and experienced militia members to the border. There, as one Iraqi described it, they were picked up in a variety of civilian vehicles and taken to safe houses in Mehran, being provided chocolate and biscuits along the way. After breakfast the next morning, the group headed to an airport, where tickets awaited them for a flight to Tehran.[11] The Lebanese group formed the new Unit 3800 to help the Iranians run their training camps.[12] At its height in 2008, it had between forty and sixty Lebanese running regular classes on EFPs and small-unit tactics in four small training camps scattered about Iran: in Tehran, Ahvaz, Elam, and Qom.

The United States was slow to address the Iranian EFP threat. Initially, so many intelligence personnel were tied up in the Iraqi Survey Group hunting for nonexistent weapons of mass destruction that they lacked the people to devote to Iranian weapons smuggling.[13] The U.S. forces in Iraq had their first breakthrough in unraveling the Iranian network in December 2004, when an Iraqi walked into one of the bases and provided details of the training he'd received in Iran and how the Quds Force smuggled the EFPs into Iraq. As the months passed, more information poured in and U.S. intelligence refined its knowledge of the Iranian hand behind the attacks. U.S. intelligence even identified two border crossings that the Iranians were using to smuggle in the lethal weapons.

When in 2005 Iran's hand behind the attacks became obvious, a debate ensued inside the Pentagon over whether the supreme leader had sanctioned the attacks or if they were being carried out by rogue elements within the Revolutionary Guard. In the aftermath of the intelligence failure on Iraq, relations soured between the civilians in the Defense Department and senior intelligence officials. A deep mistrust developed, with intelligence officials concerned that the neocons now wanted to start another war, using Iranian support for the Shia as a pretext. Intelligence officers downplayed the Iranian actions despite overwhelming evidence of Iran's government sanctioning the proxy war. In one meeting at the Pentagon in early 2005, a heated argument occurred after an intelligence analyst took pride in speaking "truth to power" by telling an incredulous civilian political appointee that the DIA had no proof that the Iranian government had sanctioned the attacks on the coalition forces.

The chairman, Peter Pace, agreed with the DIA analysis and offered a tepid response to the increase in Iranian-provided EFPs. In April 2005, he publicly said that the United States could not trace the EFP attacks to Iran. It was not true, but reflected, according to Abe Shulsky, the uncertainty at the Pentagon. Pace clung to this belief even as evidence mounted to Iran's involvement. In February 2007, he modified his views that while the EFPs came from Iran, there was no evidence that the supreme leader had authorized the attacks.[14]

Abe Shulsky completely rejected this view. On one occasion, he discussed the Iranian arms influx with a senior DIA analyst who echoed Pace, saying, "We don't have any evidence that the supreme leader is behind the attacks."

"What is it about this dog that doesn't bark?" Shulsky retorted, dumbfounded. "Are you telling me that these guys are out taking very risky operations with serious consequences and the supreme leader does not know about it? They work for him!"

When Pace uttered the words in 2007, the prevailing view within the intelligence community accorded with Shulsky's. Even senior analysts who distrusted the neocons found it incredible that the Quds Force would have orchestrated such a large campaign against the United States without the supreme leader's endorsement. But as more Americans died and the intelligence reports pointing to Iran piled up, the military leadership at the Pentagon remained lethargic. In one memo, a senior general in the Pentagon approved the convoluted logic that the Iranians were not making as much mischief as they could, so why stir things up by striking back, which might lead to a violent escalation. As long as Iran kept its support to a low level, some senior officers wanted to look the other way.

In early 2006, pro-Iranian militias ramped up their attacks. In February, army intelligence uncovered plans for a large-scale attack on an American base, Camp Bucca. Three Iranian Quds Force officers conducted surveillance of the base and met with Jaysh al-Mahdi fighters to plan the attack. With heavy weapons smuggled in from Iran just for the occasion, 120 Shia fighters would conduct a coordinated attack on the U.S. base. It would have been a major attack had it been executed. Additionally, Iran sent pallets of mortars and other munitions to Shia fighters. In March 2006 alone, U.S. forces estimated that Iran shipped 216 EFPs, half the number provided in all of 2005. Casualties correspondingly increased. In the first six months of 2006, sixty-seven soldiers died due to Iranian-supplied EFPs.

While the Joint Chiefs dawdled, pressure came from the military and civilian leaders in Iraq to do something about the Iranians. Leaks began appearing in American newspapers from officers in Iraq pointing to the growing danger of the EFP threat. The senior commander in Iraq, George Casey, and CENTCOM commander John Abizaid both raised this issue with Pace and Secretary Rumsfeld. The CENTCOM intelligence section in Tampa issued numerous reports about the growing influence of Iran among the Shia and about Quds Force operatives crossing the border.

Abizaid wanted to pressure the Iranians, but Iraqi prime minister al-Maliki always had a "red card that held sway. You could go after the Sunnis and al-Qaeda, but when it came to the Shia and the Iranians, the Iraqi government was much more reluctant, and Washington echoed that reluctance," he said.

On May 8, 2006, Abizaid sent Rumsfeld a three-page memo outlining his concerns about Iran. "Mr. Secretary, Iran, specifically the Islamic Guard Corps–Quds Force, is providing lethal support to Shia militants conducting attacks against coalition forces in Iraq. While there is no evidence Quds Force provides specific targeting guidance, I believe Iran is fully aware of EFP use against coalition targets." Abizaid proposed that a strongly worded démarche be sent to Iran, putting Tehran on notice that the United States would take action if these attacks did not cease. Alarmed, Rumsfeld forwarded Abizaid's letter and a draft démarche to Hadley and Rice.

In June, Bush met with his advisers at Camp David, and Hadley made sure the démarche and the EFP issue were discussed. A number of officials—from Cheney to Rodman—raised concerns that a démarche without action would have no effect on Iran. Rodman had recommended rolling up some of the Quds Forces in Iraq and then sending the démarche to show the seriousness of the United States. "Stern words without concrete action might risk sending the inadvertent signal to Iran that we are prepared to tolerate more of the same," Rodman wrote Rumsfeld.[15] Cheney agreed. "I don't see why we should tolerate Iran killing our soldiers," he said. The vice president suggested they consider a wider array of options, including a surgical strike at the EFP factories inside Iran, to signal American resolve.

Rice sided with Abizaid and the strong démarche, and this swayed the president, at least for a while. A note went out via the Swiss, stating, "The Iranian interference in Iraq is a blatant violation of the UN Charter. If Iran continues to support violent groups in Iraq, we will arrest and expel or detain any Iranians involved."

In the first week of July 2006, Zalmay Khalilzad, now the U.S. ambassador in Baghdad, returned to Washington and met with Rumsfeld. "The Iranians are doing harmful things in Iraq," he said. "The United States needs to make a decision as to what we are going to do about it and how we are going to pressure them." This prompted another snowflake memo from Rumsfeld to Pace: "Please think this through; get a team of people and let's get on it."[16] The following week Rumsfeld read an intelligence report that highlighted the Quds Force operations against the coalition in Iraq. An irritated defense secretary sent off another memo to the chairman: "I keep seeing this type of thing. If we're so darned smart, why don't we shut them down? I am really at my wits' end."[17]

Since the 2003 invasion, the Iraqi border had been a major problem for the United States. Iranian soldiers and smugglers routinely crossed it. As the Iranians increased their support for militias, tension grew with the Americans along the border. On the morning of September 7, 2006, a joint Iraqi-American vehicle patrol led by a lieutenant from the 5-73 Cavalry headed out on a reconnaissance looking for infiltration routes. The patrollers stopped when they observed two men running back to the Iranian side of the border. When Iranian soldiers appeared across the border, the Iraqis dismounted to start talking with the Iranians about resolving border issues, and soon the two sides were exchanging pictures of their families and having tea. While the American lieutenant tried in vain to convince his Iraqi allies to get moving again, two more Iranian trucks appeared and sixteen soldiers armed with AK-47s and rocket launchers dismounted and took up firing positions around the American patrol. The lieutenant tried unsuccessfully to get the Iraqis to end their meeting with the Iranians and see the gravity of the situation. So he ordered his four Humvees to back away. The Iranians opened fire.

The nineteen Americans immediately returned fire and maneuvered back out of the kill zone. A soldier manning a 50-caliber machine gun spotted one Iranian with a rocket-propelled grenade trying to get around to the back of the column. A few well-placed rounds hit the Iranian, literally blowing him apart. When the Americans had gotten back away from the border, mortar rounds rained down around them, but inflicted no casualties. Iran briefly seized the Iraqis, who had been captured still drinking tea.[18]

In November, an eight-man patrol from the 4th Infantry Division out inspecting Iraqi border posts came under fire from three Iranian soldiers clad in fatigues across the border. The Americans returned fire, killing one and wounding another before the sole survivor fled.[19]

During the intense discussions about the surge, the civilian leadership at the Pentagon carried the water for the soldiers in Iraq. Rumsfeld pressed Hadley on getting it on the agenda. In November, after reading another intelligence report, Rumsfeld pressed Pace yet again on doing something about the Iranian attacks in Iraq. "If we know so much about what Iran is doing in Iraq, why don't we do something about it?"[20] The pressure from generals and diplomats in Iraq and outrage by Rumsfeld finally forced action. In just two months—record speed by Washington standards—the various agencies agreed on a strategy. Along the way, the only push back came from the vice president's office. His foreign policy adviser, John Hannah, believed that Shia-backed militias did not represent a very significant threat. It was not a view shared by his boss.

On September 13, Hadley chaired a principals meeting. With Cheney's concurrence, they agreed to a multistep approach to counter Iran inside Iraq. This included a new information campaign to highlight Iran's activities and a directive for CENTCOM to develop a plan for a gradual escalation from non-lethal to lethal military operations to counter the Quds Force. In November, Abizaid came back with a proposal. The president and defense secretary gave the go-ahead following their meeting in the Tank on December 13. The authorizations were not as robust as Cheney wanted; there would be no killing of Quds Force except in self-defense, and American forces could not target Iranian operatives not actually engaged in supporting the militias.

The counteroffensive began less than a week later. The U.S. Special Operations Forces formed Task Force 88 (later changed to Task Force 17) to carry out neutralization of the Iranian Quds Force. Conducting what the military calls advanced force operations, they worked with Iraqi agents and began conducting their own intelligence gathering and surveillance on the Iranian operations inside Iraq and just across the border. Using national intelligence assets, the American task force soon developed a good picture of the Iranians and Iraqis involved in the attacks and the EFP rat lines coming in from Iran.

On the evening of December 20, American special forces planned to raid a suspected Iranian safe house in Baghdad. An intelligence source tipped them off to a suspicious vehicle leaving the ISCI headquarters building. The Americans formed a hasty roadblock and arrested four men. Three carrying Iranian diplomatic passports were suspected MOIS agents, and one happened to be the Iranian military attaché to Iran's embassy in Baghdad.

The next day, U.S. forces stormed the safe house and detained ten more men. While seven were Badr Corps officers and one was another MOIS agent, the United States had bagged two senior Iranian officers. "They were big fish," a former special operations forces officer recalled. One was a colonel and the operations chief for the Quds Force, and his accomplice happened to be Brigadier General Mohsen Chizari, the head of the Quds Force operations inside Iraq.[21]

Iran immediately sent a démarche to the United States demanding the release of its "diplomats." J. D. Crouch held a meeting at the White House, and the group decided to ignore the démarche. "Our actions will be our response."[22]

Prime Minister al-Maliki was livid. While the United States immediately released those holding diplomatic passports, the Iraqi prime minister called in the American chargé d'affaires and an army general and demanded the release of General Chizari for lack of evidence. The United States relented and handed General Chizari over to al-Maliki's national security adviser, who drove him to the Iranian border.

In the early morning hours of January 11, 2007, U.S. helicopters swooped down around a row house in downtown Arbil in northern Iraq. The building housed an Iranian consulate, but American intelligence suspected it really served as the Quds Force headquarters for Kurdish Iraq. U.S. forces also hoped to catch the soon-to-be commander of the Revolutionary Guard, Mohammad Jafari. Intelligence reported that this valuable prize had recently arrived in Arbil.[23] U.S. Special Operations Forces surrounded the building and used loudspeakers to call for those inside to surrender. Five guards standing outside immediately did, but those inside refused. The Americans stormed the building. While Jafari eluded them, they captured five Iranian Quds Force officers. The documents and laptops recovered proved a windfall for Americans in unraveling the EFP network. They incriminated the Quds Force in funneling weapons and support for those perpetrating the EFP attacks, including one in June 2006 that killed six American soldiers. Since none of the men had diplomatic passports, the United States threw them in prison at Camp Cropper near Baghdad. They remained in prison despite Iranian claims that they were "kidnapped diplomats" until 2010.

In February, the United States conducted yet another major raid. It arrested two senior Badr Corps officials, one of whom likely served with the Iranian Revolutionary Guard. U.S. troops rounded up four Iranian nationals posing as journalists who had documents showing that they were Quds Force officers.

U.S. intelligence received another windfall in February 2007. A senior Revolutionary Guard general, Ali Reza Asgari, defected while visiting Turkey. Asgari had worked for years in Lebanon aiding Hezbollah and had served in Khatami's government. He'd grown increasingly disillusioned with the government and apparently took the opportunity to leave while in Turkey.[24]

As the United States rolled up the Quds Force, the new defense secretary, Robert Gates, headed to the region to bolster support for the surge and the move against Iran. In January 2007, he met with Gulf leaders, who greeted him with the mantra that Iraqi prime minister Nouri al-Maliki was an Iranian pawn. The Saudi king showed the most hostility to Iran. He expressed concern to Gates that the United States was secretly talking to the Iranians and was going to privately cut a deal. Gates reassured the king this was not the case, pledging continued U.S. support and no secret deals. The Iranians have many problems, and in overplaying their hand in Iraq, he told the monarch, "they are punching above their weight."[25] On January 20, Gates back-briefed the NSC in the White House on his trip, telling Hadley and the others that the Gulf allies were nervous. "They mistrust Prime Minister Maliki and fear Shia dominance—which they equate with Iranian influence—in Iraq." All expressed support for the U.S. roll-up of the Quds Force. But "they all view Iran as the number one threat."

The U.S. Special Forces operations caught the Iranians by surprise. After nearly two years of attacks, Quds Force commander Qassem Suleimani seemed confounded by what had finally raised the ire of the Americans. The seizure of the five Quds Force officers in Arbil especially concerned him. They knew intimate details of Iranian operations in Iraq, and this clearly compromised his entire operation there. Shocked at the sudden fortitude of the Americans, Suleimani scaled back his operation and pulled many of Iran's Quds Forces out of Iraq due to concern that the Americans would seize them too.[26] But the Iranians remained determined to challenge the American surge and would not give up so easily in Iraq. The secretary of Iran's Supreme Council for National Security, Ali Larijani, privately confided to a Syrian official that Iran wanted to inflict much greater casualties. Iran began expanding its weapons flow, providing arms to any Shia group opposed to the coalition, especially al-Sadr's independent Jaysh al-Mahdi militia.

One of these groups decided to take a few Americans hostage to barter the release of the five Iranians captured at Arbil or other Shia militiamen captured by the Americans. Qais al-Khazali led a newly formed Iranian-backed group called Asa'ib Ahl al-Haq, or League of the Righteous. Thin with a cocky expression, he began his relationship with Iran in June 2003, when he and al-Sadr met in Tehran with Khamenei and Suleimani. He broke away from al-Sadr after al-Sadr joined the political process in Baghdad. After gaining approval during a secret meeting with a Quds Force officer and Lebanese Hezbollah, al-Khazali launched a daring operation against the Provincial Joint Coordination Center in Karbala, where nearly sixty U.S. Army soldiers lived and worked.

At five p.m. on January 20, five large black SUVs rolled into the fortified compound. Inside were between nine and twelve men, all dressed in American fatigues and helmets, with several speaking English. They mounted fake antennas to make the vehicles appear similar to those commonly used by the Americans. They easily fooled the Iraqi soldiers manning the guard post and made their way to the compound housing the American advisory team. In a hail of grenades and bullets, they stormed the office where the Americans were, likely aided by Iraqis inside the building. They killed one soldier and wounded three.[27]

The insurgents took four others captive, including two caught sitting in a vehicle, and then leaped into their SUVs and headed east at high speed. U.S. forces scrambled from across the area and closed in on the culprits. The Iraqi police found one dead soldier dumped on the side of the road. About four hours later, U.S. troops found the five SUVs abandoned on the road near a residential area. In the backseat of one, two soldiers had been executed, still handcuffed together. The final soldier lay dead outside the vehicle.

U.S. and British forces tracked down those responsible. The underling who commanded the force that killed the Americans at Karbala met his end a few months later, killed by American special forces. Coalition forces captured al-Khazali in Basra in March 2007, then rounded up his brother and a Lebanese Hezbollah adviser, Ali Musa Daqduq.

Daqduq was a twenty-year veteran of Hezbollah who had served as the commander of the leader's security detail. He arrived in Iraq in 2005 and worked with Iranian Quds Force officers to organize an Iraqi variant of Hezbollah. He made four trips to Iran, bringing several scores of Iraqis with him for paramilitary training. A disciplined soldier, when captured by the Americans he played deaf and mute for two months, garnering the nickname Hamid the Mute. He finally passed a note to his guards telling them that he could hear and talk; presumably enough time had passed to enable his accomplices to get away.[28]

While Iran's supreme leader denied any involvement, his surrogates at Asa'ib Ahl al-Haq responded by walking into a government building in Baghdad dressed as policemen and kidnapping five British contractors. They intended to use the hostages as barter to gain the release of their leader. The Iraqis executed four of the five, taking each out of his cell and shooting him in the back of the head. The Iraqi government finally brokered the deal in late 2009 that exchanged al-Khazali for the fifth British hostage, Peter Moore. The Iraqi militant then promptly fled to Iran.[29]

The administration looked at other ways to increase the pressure on Iran by going after the Revolutionary Guard. Hadley coordinated the broad U.S. campaign to expose the Quds Force, which included a wide-ranging set of nonlethal actions to expose the force, such as press conferences and selective leaks to reporters that highlighted its role in the use of EFPs. The United States exposed known Quds Force officers to Middle East governments and asked for them to be expelled.

President Bush executed one of the first salvos of this new scheme. On the morning of February 14, 2007, he held a press conference in the large, yellow-draped East Room of the White House. When asked by a reporter about Iran's implication with the EFPs, Bush responded with his well-prepared talking

points: "What we do know is that the Quds Force was instrumental in providing these deadly IEDs to networks inside of Iraq. We know that. And we also
know that the Quds Force is a part of the Iranian government. That's a known.
What we don't know is whether or not the head leaders of Iran ordered the
Quds Force to do what they did. But here's my point: either they knew or
didn't know, and what matters is, is that they're there."

The president then forcefully put the Iranian government on notice that
the United States intended to move against these networks: "If we find agents
who are moving these devices into Iraq, we will deal with them."[30]

On February 20, J. D. Crouch chaired a meeting with senior officials in
the Situation Room to recommend to the president a wide range of actions to
expose the Quds Force. The debate centered on whether to designate the
entire guard or just its covert Quds Force as a terrorist organization. While
no one disagreed about most of the plans, the military dissented about designating either group as a terrorist organization. Marine Lieutenant General
John Sattler attended the meeting for the Joint Staff. Friendly, positive, and
unflappable, the head of the Joint Staff's plans and policy office expressed the
concern of the chairman that designating military officers of another country
as "terrorist" could backfire, especially if it was reciprocated against American special forces officers, who frequently operated clandestinely and have
provided military assistance and training to insurgents. "The United States
has always carefully avoided declaring military officers engaged in activities
sanctioned by their government as terrorists to avoid the same being done to
us," Sattler pointed out.

The argument had merit, and over the next few months the idea of
declaring the entire Revolutionary Guard a terrorist organization diminished.
But the consensus remained for action against the Quds Force.

The main tools available to the U.S. government were spelled out in
Executive Orders such as 13224, which allowed the president to disrupt the
financing of those accused of supporting terrorism or nuclear proliferation.
Since the U.S. government already had comprehensive sanctions on Iran, the
use of these orders would be largely symbolic. In October 2007, the president
finally issued a carefully crafted order designed to target the pockets of a
few Revolutionary Guard leaders. Bush declared the Quds Force to be a supporter of terrorism and the larger Revolutionary Guard and the Iranian Ministry of Defense and Armed Forces Logistics as a proliferator of weapons of
mass destruction. The executive order singled out five senior guard generals,

including Qassem Suleimani, and nine guard-controlled companies. The Treasury Department then pressed for international compliance under UN Security Council Resolution 1737, which succeeded in severely hampering their ability to conduct business outside of Iran.

As the tension increased, the administration weighed taking military action against the Quds Force and its EFP-related facilities in Iran. Vice President Cheney led the call for more aggressive action. He again raised the idea of selective force against the Iranians during the spring of 2007.[31] "They are killing our troops. I don't see why we need to tolerate that," Cheney entreated in one principals meeting. Cheney suggested attacking the EFP factory at Mehran using Tomahawk cruise missiles, arguing that this limited action would send a strong signal to Iran. The chairman and the Joint Staff pushed back, saying that they needed to carefully examine the consequences of any strike on Iran, including possible escalation in the Gulf or increased surrogate attacks in Iraq. How far, Pace asked, would the United States be willing to go if Iran escalated the attacks by responding in Afghanistan or against the U.S. forces elsewhere in the Middle East or against the Gulf Arab states? But the vice president simply found it repugnant that Iranian operatives could kill American soldiers without any retribution. This only invited more attacks unless Iran saw a cost to be paid for its actions.[32]

The CENTCOM commander opposed striking Iran. General John Abizaid believed it would create even more problems, expanding a conflict with Iran at a time when the Sunni-based insurgency was at its height.[33]

The replacement for Abizaid at CENTCOM took things a step further. Admiral Joseph "Fox" Fallon came to Tampa from the four-star job at the Pacific Command, where he had impressed President Bush. He shared the navy's view that Iran did not pose a significant threat. CENTCOM had exaggerated the country's military capabilities. Self-assured in the extreme, Fallon put a halt to the planning begun by Abizaid. He believed CENTCOM needed to show more restraint and not expand a conflict that largely did not exist. He was not ignorant of the Iranian Quds Force activities and had authorized U.S. Special Operations Forces to move against some of its operations in Afghanistan, but Fallon offered no real prioritization of effort for the command and became mired in prerogatives. As one admiral commented, "Painting parking lines took on as much priority as Iran."

In case the order ever came, Fallon's naval commander developed a very surgical list of fewer than five discrete targets inside Iran. Using only stand-off cruise missiles, the navy could easily hit all the targets at once, with a minimal prospect for collateral damage. Whether they were the right targets to halt the Iranian EFP activity remained a question in his mind, however. "These buildings did not have signs on them that said 'Iranian EFP factory.'"[34]

While the U.S. government had not taken military action off the table to stop Iran's nuclear program, Fallon publicly called these sorts of "bellicose comments" unhelpful. This angered Vice President Cheney. In his memoirs, Cheney recounted comments made by a visiting diplomat that echoed his concerns: "If you guys are going to take the military option off the table, couldn't you at least have your secretary of state do it? When the CENTCOM commander does it, they take notice."[35]

According to Cheney, Defense Secretary Gates shared a similar view of the wisdom of military action against Iran. The vice president became incensed when Gates told the Saudi king that Bush would be "impeached if he took military action against Iran." This was not the news that either Dick Cheney or King Abdullah wanted to hear, and it "removed a key element of our leverage and convinced allies and enemies that we were less than serious about addressing the threat."[36]

But news of the deliberations over striking Iran leaked out. It created a frenzy in the media as articles appeared in *Time* and the *New Yorker*, among others, all reporting the United States was set to attack Iran and would use the excuse of Iraq to destroy its nuclear facilities. The recently established Office of Iranian Affairs at the State Department looked like a son of Shulsky's Office of Special Plans in the lead-up to the invasion of Iraq.[37] In truth, attacks on the nuclear sites were never seriously contemplated; the debate centered on a limited military response to Iranian-sponsored attacks inside Iraq. But this distinction failed to make it to the public debate, as detractors of the administration such as reporter Seymour Hersh touted the drumbeat of the next war. "Like a clock, Hersh is right twice a day," said Elliott Abrams dismissively.

America's aggressive actions in Iraq did bring Iran back to the bargaining table. Beginning in late 2006, Iran relayed through the Iraqi government a desire to talk with the Americans. Iran hoped to get more official recognition for its interests in Iraq and end the U.S. Special Forces onslaught on its agents. Whether to accept the offer to talk divided the administration. Rice thought Iran could help stabilize Iraq, as it had Afghanistan in 2001. Cheney expressed reservations about talking to Iran, seeing it as a reward for its bad behavior in Iraq. But Rice convinced the president to endorse this diplomatic effort, in tandem with Prime Minister al-Maliki, to broker an agreement, and Washington agreed to the talks. "The purpose is to try to make sure that the Iranians play a productive role in Iran," said a White House spokesman.[38]

For the Americans, the task of heading up the talks fell to Ryan Crocker, ambassador to Iraq and a veteran of Iran negotiations. Crocker had arrived at the embassy in Baghdad in March 2007. His first impression of the situation in Iraq was that it looked eerily like the Lebanon he had left in the 1980s, with Iran and Syria strategically collaborating against the United States. But Iraq was not like Lebanon. While al-Maliki remained friendly with Iran, he hated the country at the same time. "It was another example of the complexities of the Iran-Iraq War, where most of the fighting was done by Shia for a Sunni Arab regime against a Shia Persian one," Crocker observed.

Crocker knew of the discussions about military strikes against Iran but never viewed them as serious and would have opposed them. If the United States wanted to impact the regime, it could exploit the ethnic divisions by supporting the Kurds or Baluchis. "That would have really terrified the Iranians." Others outside the government, such as Michael Ledeen, thought the U.S. government never would approve that strategy. But Crocker fully backed the effort to round up the Quds Forces inside Iraq.

On May 28, 2007, Crocker met with his Iranian counterpart, Ambassador Hassan Kazemi Qomi, in Prime Minister al-Maliki's office. Al-Maliki introduced the two men, and they moved to a conference room. Al-Maliki sat at the head of the polished table as moderator, with Crocker and Qomi squaring off on opposite sides. Qomi had served in the Revolutionary Guard, and his appointment indicated the commanding role that the Quds Force and Suleimani played in Iraq.[39] Crocker held out little hope for the talks. They lacked the openness that marked his previous meetings in Geneva, and the Iranian ambassador operated under a tight rein. Any time Crocker raised an issue that was not on his talking points, Qomi asked for a break to call back to Tehran for instructions. Muddled American objectives undermined the talks too. The United States wanted to gain Iran's assistance in supporting the Iraqi government while chastising it for the Quds Force operations in Iraq. The two contradictory goals confused the Iranians. The Iranian ambassador raised the detention of the Quds Force fighters only one time, doing so in a lecture positing that "the totally unwarranted detention of these businesspeople was an indication of America's hostile attitude."

Crocker repeatedly tried to talk about Iran's unhelpful actions inside Iraq. "They need to cease," he said. But Qomi refused to accept the premise of Crocker's argument. Iran countered with a proposal to form a trilateral mechanism including Iran, Iraq, and the United States to coordinate security issues in Iraq. And Qomi offered Iranian support to rebuild the Iraqi military. Crocker agreed to forward the ideas to Washington, although he knew they would be a nonstarter at the White House. At the end of the meeting, both sides held separate press conferences and agreed the talks had been polite, but little else.[40]

On July 24, the two diplomats met again at al-Maliki's office. Iran sent its deputy national security chief—a Revolutionary Guard officer—who stayed in al-Maliki's offices one floor up, so when Qomi had a question, he paused the talks and scurried up to ask him. The unvarnished talks failed to produce any headway. While both sides professed support for a democratically elected government in Baghdad, each side accused the other of fomenting the violence in Iraq. Once again they adjourned without any progress. Both sides discussed a third round of talks, but the Iranian delegation kept shifting the date, agreeing to one one day and changing its mind the next. In the end, talks about talks faded away.[41] The failure of the talks frustrated al-Maliki. He confided to Crocker that Iran had not taken the talks seriously.

To try to undermine the Americans, the brother of the Revolutionary Guard commander, Salman Safavi, tried to work the American embassy in London. In August 2007, he participated in a group discussion and expressed the guard's interest in talking about security and the nuclear program. While he admitted that Iran had provided material aid to Shia in Iraq, he offered Iran's support to help in security. But he said that any American designation of the guard as a terrorist organization would preclude cooperation. This transparent ploy did not impress the Americans, and Safavi failed to haggle Iran's way out of further sanctions.[42]

As Secretary Gates had predicted, Iran overplayed its hand in Iraq. In the aftermath of the 2006 war between Hezbollah and Israel, in which the Iranian-backed militia performed well, a self-assured Quds Force decided to expand the distribution of weapons in Iraq in hopes of inflicting grievous losses on the United States.[43] The Iranian-backed Asa'ib Ahl al-Haq eagerly stepped up its attacks. Iran formed new special groups comprising four to ten men under the command of long-term Iranian agents, who frequently did Iran's bidding but just as frequently freelanced or operated as assassins for hire.[44] Iran miscalculated. As Iranian weapons flowed in, they fueled inter-Shia fighting. In 2007, fighting broke out in Karbala between rival Shia groups armed by Iran. Two Badr-affiliated governors were assassinated with Iranian-provided EFPs. Quds Force commander Suleimani stepped in to ease tensions. Al-Maliki appealed to the Iranians to halt the weapons flow and rein in al-Sadr's Jaysh al-Mahdi militia, which was frequently uncooperative with the Iraqi government. Iran denied providing weapons, but Suleimani ordered weapons provided only to select trusted groups.[45]

In March 2008, al-Maliki lost his patience with the lawlessness in Basra and sent ten thousand troops against al-Sadr. With no coordination with the Americans, the resulting battle turned into a stalemate until American and Iraqi reinforcements arrived and al-Maliki continued the offensive. His forces uncovered caches of newly arrived Iranian weapons; one stash alone had more than a thousand mortar rounds and thirty-three blocks of plastic explosives. A cease-fire occurred when Iran stepped in to broker a deal. During two days of meetings in Tehran, Suleimani negotiated a cease-fire between al-Sadr and al-Maliki. Crocker noted the irony of it all: Suleimani had been asked to "sort out the chaos that he has been instrumental in creating and perpetuating."[46]

But al-Maliki viewed Iranian actions as designed to undermine his government and pressed both Tehran and Washington to cut off funds for the Iranian-backed special groups. In October 2008, Iraqi forces engaged in a firefight with five likely Quds Force operatives who had recently infiltrated across the border, wounding two.[47] This hardly ended Iran's significant role behind the scenes in Iraq and in the government. But Iran's role in fueling the violence among the Shia had been exposed, forcing both Suleimani and the Iranian government to scale back their operations and temporarily cut funding for pro-Iranian political parties in Iraq.

The U.S. Special Operations Forces never fully shut down the Iranian networks. They killed Iraqi militia at the cyclic rate, seriously disrupted their operations, and destroyed their safe havens. Many fled to Iran. On September 20, 2007, the U.S. military rolled up another Quds Force officer during a raid at a hotel in the Kurdish region; the man had been involved in smuggling EFPs into Iraq. Suleimani ordered his officers to keep a lower profile and withdrew some back into Iran to avoid capture. But by the end of 2008, at the close of the Bush administration, they began trickling back into Iraq as the surge ended. U.S. soldiers continued to run across their handiwork, uncovering Iraqis trained in Iran as snipers and bomb makers.[48] But the ties that bound the neighboring Shia remained too strong. As the United States withdrew forces, Iran's surrogate network remained.

"I regret that I ended my presidency with the Iranian issue unresolved," President Bush wrote in his memoirs. "I did hand my successor an Iranian regime more isolated from the world and more heavily sanctioned than it had ever been." But he remained confident that his efforts would inspire Iranian dissidents and help "catalyze change."[49] The administration had provided a guide to continue the broad containment of Iran. While Iraq teetered between the two sides of the conflict, CENTCOM had positioned itself to deal with any eventuality. But the Bush policies to isolate Iran and "delegitimize" the regime had failed. The invasion of Iraq had placed Iran in a much stronger strategic position than it had been before with Saddam Hussein in power. Efforts at negotiations had proved equally fruitless. While the Iranians extended a halfhearted hand to cooperate in Iraq, they refused to entertain any talk about their killing of American soldiers. It fell to a new administration to pick up the pieces and continue to pursue peace or plan for war.

Twenty-Seven

AN EXTENDED HAND
AND A CLOSED FIST

On Wednesday, January 7, 2009, three former presidents of the United States joined the White House's current and forthcoming occupants in front of the president's imposing wooden desk. After a few remarks by President Bush, they adjourned for lunch. In less than two weeks, Barack Obama would be sworn in to join the world's most exclusive club. President Bush had organized the gathering as a show of national unity and support for the president-elect. As the two men warmly shook hands, Bush said, "We want you to succeed. Whether we are Democrat or Republican, we all care deeply about this country."

Bush had another, less public reason for wanting to meet with Obama. Before the formal gathering with the former commanders in chief, the two men met alone for thirty minutes, sitting next to each other in the Oval Office's blue-and-gold-striped upholstered chairs. Bush had avoided new foreign policy actions in his waning days as president that would commit Obama to courses that he might not support. But Bush wanted to talk with Obama in private about one exception: Iran.

"I have tried not to tie your hands," Bush began. "But regarding Iran, I have approved a number of actions that commit you to certain things, and I want you to be comfortable with them and to understand why we are doing them." Bush then proceeded to lay out the broad details of his programs aimed at delaying and undermining Iran's nuclear program, and he explained its various components, from military options to public messaging. Bush told Obama about some of the covert and overt operations under way, among them ones so close-hold that only a handful of senior officials were read into them. Many required time to play out, Bush said, and some of the more esoteric actions, such as those that lay in the world of cyber warfare or relied on other hidden tools available to the U.S. government, needed the new president's support in order to succeed. Bush was under no illusion that any of these efforts would halt Iran's nuclear program, but they might buy eighteen months to two years. This would give Obama and his administration enough space to get their feet on the ground and devise their own strategy for Iran and its nuclear ambitions. "I want to give you time and options," Bush said to Obama.

Obama listened intently. He knew many of these issues, having been briefed already by the vice chairman of the Joint Chiefs of Staff, Marine General James Cartwright. The president-elect confided the details of the conversation with his new national security adviser, another onetime marine general, James Jones. Bush had wanted to transcend the hyperpolitical environment of the time and pass the Iranian policy baton cleanly to the next runner in order to forge a consistent American policy in response to the threat from Tehran. While Barack Obama grasped the importance of Bush's words, the new president would decide for himself what to do regarding Iran.

From the outset, the Obama administration recognized that Iran would be one of its most important national security challenges. During the campaign, Barack Obama had been openly critical of Bush's Iran policy. During the primaries, Obama had stood out for his astute criticism that the invasion of Iraq had opened the door for greater Iranian influence in the Middle East. While he too called Iran a dangerous threat and a nuclear Iran unacceptable, candidate Obama argued that, as during the Cold War, the United States needed to have the strength of its convictions and talk to its adversaries. He called for a dialogue with Iran, proclaiming that he would sit down and meet with Iranian leaders without preconditions. "Demanding that a country meets all your conditions before you meet with them, that's not a strategy. It's just naive, wishful thinking," Obama had said.[1]

On the surface, the transition went well. President Bush and national security adviser Stephen Hadley had gone to great pains to brief the incoming national security team on Iranian policy. The fact that Robert Gates stayed on as secretary of defense and William Burns continued on at the State Department only further smoothed the transfer. But tensions almost inevitably accompany a change of parties and administrations, and this transition was no exception. The new deputy national security adviser, Tom Donilon, was a smart and aggressive lawyer, but he was a Democratic Party political operative and not a foreign policy professional. In his first meetings he repeatedly stressed that this had to be Obama's Iran policy and thus there was a need to eliminate any hint of "Bushism," even if the policy had not substantively changed. This grated on the senior generals and CIA officers present, who had to sit mum and remain nonpartisan.

Despite Bush's effort to bridge the two administrations, Obama and his appointees came to office concerned about Bush's use of covert action in the war on terrorism. CIA rendition operations and the prison at Guantánamo Bay had been hot political issues during the campaign. On his first full day in office, the president signed an order to close the prison in Cuba.[2] Under the rationale of better presidential oversight, in the first few weeks after the inaugural the White House conducted an exhaustive review of all the presidential findings, including those related to Iran. During this process the president canceled several that Donilon and he viewed as inappropriate or unworkable. All this frustrated Bush's appointed CIA director Michael Hayden and other career holdovers. They had been instrumental in developing these operations and now had to justify their earlier decisions while "educating" a new crop of senior appointees. Although Obama rejected a number of Bush's plans, he embraced covert operations and expanded their use. CIA drone attacks against al-Qaeda operatives in Yemen and Pakistan increased by three fold under the new president.[3]

While the National Security Adviser Jim Jones focused more on Europe, Iran fell into the portfolio of his deputy. Donilon preserved the Iranian small group that had been started by Stephen Hadley, and it continued to meet to discuss Iran three times a week without the nachos that Hadley frequently offered. But Donilon created a firestorm when he moved the small group to the larger White House Situation Room and invited ten people from the NSC staff to attend what had been a small, close-hold group. At the time, Donilon was not privy to the operational information relayed to Obama and

Jones by the outgoing Bush team and had no idea of just how sensitive the details were of efforts to thwart Iran's ambitions. General Cartwright and the CIA deputy director, Stephen R. Kappes, refused to brief such a large gathering about their operations against Iran.

"I am going to take this to the president!" said a furious Donilon to Cartwright.

"I welcome bringing this in front of the president," Cartwright answered sternly. "I am not going to discuss our sensitive operations in front of this large a group. It will leak out, and that will only limit your options in the future." Cartwright had earned Bush's respect for his calm and reasoned manner and would soon win Obama's. Donilon finally relented and agreed to hold off the most sensitive subjects for another forum, but he continued inviting twenty people to the Iranian small group meeting. The national security adviser believed that any strategy for Iran had to be a broad-based approach, one that incorporated all the agencies of the U.S. government. There was such a thing as being too secret. By keeping the details to only a handful of people, it would be impossible to bring in all tools available to pressure Iran into peacefully stopping its nuclear weapons program.

From the outset, Obama pressed for engagement with Iran. He personally believed the Bush administration had not seriously used diplomacy to address the tensions with the country. He wanted to test Iran's willingness to negotiate and resolve the differences that divided the two nations.[4] The president offered to talk without preconditions, including the requirement that Iran first halt its uranium enrichment. In a series of speeches around Washington think tanks, administration officials echoed a new slant: that what was unacceptable was a nuclear-*armed* Iran, not necessarily a nuclear-capable Iran. Just six days after his inauguration, President Obama appeared on Arab television and said that negative perceptions lay at the heart of Middle East quarrels. By implication, he was sending a message that Iran and the United States needed to get beyond the usual knee-jerk reaction that each side was inherently out to get the other.

In Tehran, the election of Barack Obama divided officials. Iranian news media became infatuated with the first African-American president and broadcast a steady stream of reports that the election represented a repudiation of Bush's policies and offered the prospect of better relations with the

United States. A number of Iranian diplomats expressed optimism about the prospects of better relations with the new American president. "The words of Obama were good," said one such foreign ministry official. President Mahmoud Ahmadinejad agreed. Just two days after the election, he took the extraordinary step of sending a congratulatory letter to Obama. "You are expected to make a fast and clear response to the demands for a fundamental change in U.S. domestic and foreign policy," he wrote. "Iran welcomes major, just and real changes in policies and behavior." The Iranian president's supporters, including the foreign ministry, praised Ahmadinejad's gesture as a constructive step toward ending thirty bitter years of estrangement.[5]

But hard-liners within the Iranian government lambasted their president. "Today becoming a politician in the United States is synonymous with bowing humbly before Zionism," wrote one commentator. These hard-liners countered that the Jewish lobby controlled both parties, so in spite of Obama's rhetoric, no American president would make any real substantive change in policy toward Iran. As proof, they pointed to the appointment of Dennis Ross as Obama's point man for Iran and the Middle East. Ross had recently come from the Washington Institute for Near East Policy, which Iranian leaders widely viewed as a key think tank for the Israeli-American axis. The powerful speaker of the Iranian parliament, Ali Larijani, said he was hopeful that Obama represented a real change, but thought it naive to think that the United States would make any substantive changes to its antagonistic policies, especially on the nuclear issue.[6]

As for the one man whose opinion counted most, the supreme leader, he remained silent. Ayatollah Khamenei had never been sanguine about accommodating Washington. Anti-Americanism remained a pillar of the revolution of whose flame he was the keeper. He had endorsed the openings ten years earlier, following 9/11, but after the Americans rebuffed his overture Khamenei had no urge to repeat the mistake. Still, he did not publicly condemn Ahmadinejad's letter to Obama. The only hint of his misgivings appeared in an editorial in a newspaper closely aligned with him, which implied that Ahmadinejad had "fallen for a mirage" in thinking Obama was different than Bush.[7]

The one point on which supporters and skeptics of Obama in Tehran both agreed was the need for the Americans to make a tangible gesture. Lifting some of the sanctions would be a good start. Iran would not respond to mere words.

The State Department drafted different responses for President Obama to Ahmadinejad's letter. When Obama took office, he refined the communiqué. At the outset, the administration had been bombarded by those purporting to represent the Iranian government or a moderate faction in Tehran. But Dennis Ross knew the disappointing history of using these intermediaries. Real decisions of this magnitude rested with only one man: the supreme leader. So Obama sent his response not to Ahmadinejad but to Khamenei. In the first of two letters to the Iranian spiritual leader, Obama suggested direct negotiations to resolve the nuclear impasse and offered the possibility of opening an American interests section in Tehran as well as cooperation in areas where the two nations overlapped, such as Iraq and Afghanistan. Obama received a reply to his first letter from the supreme leader's office. The polite but guarded response did not commit Iran to talks but highlighted Iran's own grievances with the United States, including the freezing of Iranian assets dating back to the shah.

Obama pressed forward. In March, he recorded a three-minute greeting for the Iranian new year, Nowruz. This was the first of what would become an annual Nowruz message by President Obama. "I would like to speak directly to the people and leaders of the Islamic Republic of Iran," he began, calling the nation by its postrevolutionary name in an effort to show that regime change was not his objective.[8] "We seek engagement that is honest and grounded in mutual respect." After praising Iran's rich heritage, Obama offered the country a seat at the community of nations and extended an offer for better relations. The American president closed with a bit of Farsi and a quote from the Persian poet Saadi: "The children of Adam are the limbs to each other, having been created of one essence."[9]

Iran refused to grasp the extended hand. Ahmadinejad expressed more optimism, praising the American president's words while telling reporters the United States needed to make fundamental changes in its behavior and take real steps to show goodwill. But the supreme leader remained unmoved. Following Obama's Nowruz video, the Ayatollah Khamenei dedicated much of his Friday sermon to responding to the Americans. He dismissed Obama's overtures as rhetorical and unsubstantive. "They say, 'Let us negotiate. Let us establish relations.' But they have only changed their slogan. Have you halted your oppressive sanctions? Have you given up your unconditional defense of the Zionist regime? Change must be real." As long as the United States continues its same policies, the ayatollah said, relations "will remain the same as thirty years ago."[10]

Obama continued trying, with another speech in June, this time at Cairo University. He called for a new beginning in the Middle East between Islam and the West. Regarding Iran, Obama admitted American mistakes, including overthrowing the democratically elected Iranian government in 1953; he highlighted Iranian errors too, such as the hostage taking during the 1980s. "Rather than remain trapped in the past, I've made it clear to Iran's leaders and people that my country is prepared to move forward. There will be many issues to discuss between our two countries, and we are willing to move forward without preconditions on the basis of mutual respect." However, the president drew a line with Iran's nuclear program. He acknowledged Iran's right to peaceful nuclear power, but not to nuclear weapons. "This is not simply about America's interests. It's about preventing a nuclear arms race in the Middle East that could lead this region and the world down a hugely dangerous path."

Iran remained recalcitrant. Its Supreme Council for National Security remained divided about whether this represented a real change in American policy that might work to Iran's advantage or just more empty words from an American government that remained bent on overthrowing the Islamic Republic. Unlike during the aftermath of 9/11, the supreme leader felt no need to respond to Obama. All the while, Iran's centrifuges continued spinning, enriching more uranium.

But American officials remained hopeful. Secretary of State Hillary Clinton briefly floated the idea of extending the U.S. nuclear umbrella to friendly states in the Middle East as a counter to an Iranian nuke. The administration's point man for Iran, Dennis Ross, an optimist by nature, wrote before coming into the administration, "It's not too late to stop Iran from getting the bomb. It's not clear the Supreme Leader, Ayatollah Ali Khamenei, would sacrifice anything to get nuclear weapons. In fact, history shows that his government responds to outside pressure, restricting its actions when it feels threatened and taking advantage when it judges it can."[11] But Ross already knew what many Iran neophytes now in the White House were just discovering: Iran was hard. Many officials wistfully hoped the entire issue would just go away.

A woman named Neda Agha-Soltan lay without moving in a street in Tehran, looking blankly up at the cameraman. Her black chador was flung up, exposing her Western jeans and running shoes. As two people frantically tried to attend to her, a stream of dark red blood suddenly poured from her mouth and nose. It was six thirty p.m. on June 20, 2009. The twenty-six-year-old aspiring musician, who worked in her parents' travel agency, had just exited a car to join demonstrations that had paralyzed Tehran for nearly a week following the disputed presidential elections. A gunshot had rung out; the shooter was either on a nearby rooftop or on a motorcycle just down the road. Neda had collapsed to the pavement. "I'm burning, I'm burning!" she had exclaimed before her eyes glazed over and the blood poured across her face. The death of this young woman on the street in Tehran caused a firestorm, as the video immediately appeared all over the Internet. She became the tragic human symbol of the largest demonstrations to roil Iran since 1979.

In the spring of 2009, President Ahmadinejad stood for reelection. In May, the twelve-man Guardian Council formally approved only 4 candidates from the 476 who had applied. In addition to the incumbent, the others were all powerful regime insiders: former Revolutionary Guard commander Mohsen Rezai; a former speaker of the parliament, Mehdi Karroubi; and an earlier supporter of the revolution and onetime prime minister, Mir-Hossein Mousavi, who had played a major role in the secret negotiations for arms during the Reagan administration. While they differed on domestic policy, none offered any course change regarding the United States, and all supported Iran's nuclear program.

For a week leading up to the elections, the candidates squared off in a series of one-on-one debates. On June 3, Ahmadinejad and Mousavi conducted a contentious debate. Mousavi accused Ahmadinejad of "superstition and adventurism." He said the president had cozied up to the Americans, and blasted him for his inane statements about the Holocaust; Mousavi said that "the American Israel Public Affairs Committee [AIPAC] members were very satisfied with Ahmadinejad's performance." The attacks caught the Iranian president off guard, but he defended his record, saying that he had improved Iran's position and accusing Mousavi of being involved in graft.[12]

On June 12, voters went to the polls. Although many ballots were cast in paper and not computerized, within a couple of hours of the polls closing, the government announced that Ahmadinejad had won reelection, capturing a whopping 62 percent of the votes and carrying every province but two. The president had won by a wide margin even in districts that he had lost in the previous election. Mousavi came in second, with just under 34 percent of the vote. While the voting patterns and quick announcement appeared highly irregular, it was difficult to prove outright fraud. Regardless, supporters of

the losing candidates cried foul. The next day hundreds of thousands of protesters poured into the streets, many wearing the color green, representing
Islam and Mousavi's party. The supreme leader ordered a partial recount, but
the results stood. Over the following days, the protests grew. Many computer-
savvy students used Facebook, Twitter, and other social media to organize
rallies and post videos of the upheavals to the outside world. Three days after
the elections, three million people poured out into the streets to protest the
results. "Where is my vote?!" they chanted.

The Iranian government responded with a deft use of force. Senior Revolutionary Guard officers wanted to crush the opposition, but the specter of
the last revolution hung over the crisis and the supreme leader worried about
the backlash if the security forces opened fire on the populace. The government initially allowed some protesters to vent anger, but as they continued in
defiance of the supreme leader's directive that they should cease, black-clad
Basij militia on motorcycles clubbed demonstrators while police, backed by
armed Revolutionary Guardsmen, occasionally shot protestors to establish
fear and panic. Neda Agha-Soltan fell into this unfortunate category. The
government selectively arrested relatives of the candidates and their chief supporters. Most were released from Evin Prison after a few days, but the action
had a chilling effect. Both Rezai and Karroubi fell in line and accepted the
election. But Mousavi held out. He was eventually placed under house arrest,
and to illustrate a point, security officials shot and killed his nephew during
a demonstration in December.

The Iranian government blamed the disturbances on Western intervention. It accused the U.S. soft-power operations by the CIA begun under Bush
of fomenting the disturbances. Iran expelled a number of British diplomats,
accusing them of aiding the Americans. Western journalists were ordered to
leave. The security services moved to shut down the media sites that allowed
information to flow inside and outside the country, and a series of "technical
glitches" shut down the Internet in Tehran on several occasions.

For President Obama, the crisis presented a conundrum. If the United
States came out strongly in favor of the demonstrators, it risked undermining
them by making them look as though they were lackeys of America. The
president wanted to avoid the perception of trying to stage a repeat of the
1953 coup—still a sore point with many Iranians. The information from
those protesting in the streets of Tehran steadfastly indicated that the protesters did not want American assistance. But the United States could not

simply ignore the repression of hundreds of thousands of people calling for free and fair elections.

The United States looked at various means to help the demonstrators, but the prevailing view during the nearly daily meetings in the Situation Room was that there was not much the United States could do to influence the events on the ground. "The uprising grew out of internal dynamics," said one retired general. "Our activities were not likely to influence many of the students."

The one area where the United States could aid the demonstrators was the Internet. The United States had the means to keep the Iranians from shutting down the social networking and blogging sites, like Twitter, that had become a prime means for demonstrators to organize and share information.[13] When Twitter announced a brief shutdown for server maintenance, the State Department successfully lobbied for the service to stay open to allow Iranians to continue communicating.[14] At the American government's request, Twitter took steps to try to actually increase connectivity for Ira-nians.

Congressional pressure grew. Bipartisan legislation threatened such draconian measures as the punishment of any country that sold refined petroleum products to Iran. Senior officials at both the State Department and the Pentagon cautioned that such harsh measures would lead to increased attacks by Iranian surrogates in Iraq and Afghanistan. Obama walked a tightrope, condemning Iran's actions while not escalating the crisis or closing the door to a negotiated settlement on the nuclear issue.

The protests spread to other Iranian cities, but the demonstrations largely remained localized among students in Tehran. Unlike 1979, the election did not galvanize the populace as a whole and remained chiefly a dispute among the ruling elite. The regime maintained strong support in rural areas. At one point both Karroubi and Mousavi considered calling for strikes in Tehran's bazaar, which had been critical to the downfall of the shah in 1979. Thirty years later, the bazaar remained one of the centers of power in Iran. Just the year before, merchants and traders had organized a successful general strike against a new value-added tax; it took only a few days before President Ahmadinejad reversed the decision and suspended the tax. But in the current crisis, the bazaar remained loyal or at least neutral. Without the merchants' support, a second Iranian revolution never got off the ground. While demonstrations continued into 2010, the enthusiasm of the students waned. When in February 2010 opposition leaders flooded the Internet, attempting to rally support for massive protests during the commemoration of the 1979 return of Ayatollah Khomeini from exile and the end of the shah's governance, a legal adviser for Mir-Hossein Mousavi said the turnout would shock the regime, but the event came and went without any significant demonstrations, as the city was ringed with police and Basij.

Despite the election disturbances, Obama still held out hope for a deal on the Iranian nuclear impasse. In August 2009, Iran allowed IAEA inspectors into its nearly completed Arak heavy-water reactor and allowed expanded monitoring of its Natanz facility, which produced all of Iran's enriched uranium. That fall, Iran asked the IAEA for help finding fuel for the small U.S.-built Tehran research reactor, which produced radioisotopes for medical use that treated about ten thousand patients a week. Supplies were slated to run out by the end of 2010. Working with the IAEA, the United States brokered an agreement for Iran to ship about 80 percent of its stockpile of low-enriched uranium to Russia, where it would be further enriched and eventually turned into fuel and sent back to Iran. The agreement was a concession by Washington in essentially acknowledging Iran's right to enrich its own uranium, even if it was turned into fuel rods elsewhere. At the same time, the United States surprised and embarrassed Iran by publicly exposing the existence of a secret nuclear facility being built at Qom.

Under the pressure, it seemed the two sides had achieved a breakthrough. Iran formally accepted the deal in principle, setting the stage for a face-to-face meeting between U.S. and Iranian negotiators. On October 1, the chief American diplomat, Undersecretary of State William Burns, met with Iranian negotiator Saeed Jalili. The two met for forty-five minutes during a break for lunch during the P-5 plus one talks in Geneva, with each side raising its concerns: the nuclear weapons program and human rights issues for the Americans; a worldwide ban on all nuclear weapons and access to peaceful nuclear energy for the Iranians. Afterward, Jalili called the discussions "good talks that will be a framework for better talks." It all appeared encouraging. Iranian president Ahmadinejad publicly backed the deal, calling it a step forward that paved the way for the future.[15]

President Obama expressed guarded optimism. "We're not interested in talking for the sake of talking. If Iran does not take steps in the near future to live up to its obligations, then the United States will not continue to negotiate indefinitely." In discussions with the Europeans, the president looked to the end of the year for progress on Iran; if this deal fell through, Obama would not abandon diplomacy, but he intended to turn to the stick of sanctions.

With so much at stake, Iran did an about-face and reneged on the deal. By constitutional design, the Iranian government was fractured into competing centers of power. Still reeling from the presidential election upheavals, the government simply could not make a decision on such a significant issue. The supreme leader distrusted the populist and secular Ahmadinejad and felt no inclination to accommodate the West. Ahmadinejad's other detractors within the regime were also not inclined to hand the president a victory, and they conspired to scuttle the agreement. As John Limbert, who headed the Iran portfolio at the State Department, commented about the collapse of the deal: "It was clear that serious divisions existed in Tehran. They could not come to an agreement among themselves."[16] One Iranian diplomat expressed the sentiment differently. "Just because the negotiation team agree to terms does not mean that the government will. But before we could decide in Tehran the Americans and Europeans were already pressing for sanctions. That was not the way one showed mutual respect."[17]

In his annual Nowruz speech the next spring, Obama began, "I said, last year, that the choice for a better future was in the hands of Iran's leaders. That remains true today." He then continued, "Faced with an extended hand, Iran's leaders have shown only a clenched fist."[18]

So Obama turned to the UN Security Council and took a page from his predecessor's book. On June 9, 2010, the council passed Resolution 1929, the fourth round of sanctions against Iran. These new sanctions targeted Iran's military by banning the sale of weapons to Iran and freezing the assets of the Revolutionary Guard, and targeted both individuals and institutions involved in developing Iran's ballistic missile program.

On December 6, 2010, the United States again sat down across the table from an Iranian delegation in Geneva. In preparation, the State Department had drawn up a list of items for discussion, including Iran's continued support of Shia militias attacking U.S. forces in Iraq. The United States would be prepared to discuss these and other issues of importance to Iran, provided the nuclear issue was first on the agenda.

However, the Iranian negotiator Saeed Jalili wanted to discuss everything but the nuclear issue. He proposed forming a series of working groups to explore the various issues dividing Iran and the West. William Burns countered that the United States would agree to support this only if Iran's nuclear program was addressed first. William Burns concluded that these working groups would offer the perception of cooperation, but would avoid making any actual decisions, which is what Iran wanted all along. The United States delivered a message to Jalili that Iran needed to take practical steps to build confidence in the peaceful nature of its nuclear program, or else the sanctions would continue. At the end of the talks, a State Department memo summed up the American view: "Iran's performance was disappointing and unconstructive."

While the president had not given up on diplomacy, he increasingly concluded he needed to rely on other options to curtail Iran's nuclear program. General Cartwright believed that, short of an invasion and occupation of Iran to overthrow the regime, Iran would not stop its nuclear program. He told this to President Obama in one of their first meetings on Iran. The president did not like the prospect, but he soon came to the same realization. Cartwright understood Iran's nuclear rationale. "They don't have much of a conventional military. The cheapest path they have to getting their sovereignty assured is a nuclear path," he said.[19]

Cartwright, the Joint Staff's point man for formulating Iran policy, met with Israeli officials to discuss a way forward against Iran. In Bush's second term, Israel and the United States had discussed joint operations to undermine Iran's program. Israeli officials proposed extreme measures such as assassinations of Iranian scientists and supporting armed opposition groups inside Iran. Washington completely rejected these schemes, but within the limits of American legality the two nations developed common plans to derail Iran's nuclear program as well as interdict arms transfers to Hezbollah and into Iraq. After a rough start between the Obama administration and Israel over Jewish settlements in Palestine, the two nations renewed efforts at cooperation to thwart Iran's mastery of nuclear enrichment even if the two allies had mismatched policies and were frequently at odds. As one 2009 memo noted, "For us, suspension of enrichment is a means to an end. For Israel, it looks to be an end in itself."

Other nations quietly agreed with the idea of a covert campaign to halt Iran's nuclear program. In January 2010, Volker Perthes, director of Germany's state-funded Institute for Security and International Affairs, told U.S. officials in Berlin that undercover operations would be "more effective than a military strike" in curtailing Iran's nuclear ambitions. In a memo leaked to the British media from WikiLeaks, he noted that "covert sabotage (unexplained explosions, accidents, computer hacking, etc.) would be more effective than a military strike whose effects in the region could be devastating."[20]

The role of cyber warfare took on a new importance. The U.S. military established a new four-star command called Cyber Command to carry out military operations in the computer battlefield. According to newspaper accounts, before leaving office, President George W. Bush had approved $300 million for projects aimed at delaying Iran's nuclear program. The *New York Times* reported that this included a joint effort with Israel at their Dimona nuclear site.[21] Israel already excelled at some aspects of cyber warfare, its efforts having begun as early as 1999, after an internal Israeli Red Team found massive vulnerabilities in its own networks. Israel launched a series of cyberattacks against Iran using malware. Iranian security officers caught one Iranian businessman, Ali Ashtari, whom they accused of trying to knowingly supply infected communications equipment at the behest of the Israelis. Ashtari was hanged at Evin Prison on November 17, 2008.

Beginning in 2010, a series of unexplained computer viruses found their way into Iran's nuclear facilities. The most significant was a carefully crafted bit of malware called Stuxnet. In June 2010, perhaps one-third of Iran's functioning uranium centrifuges at the Natanz enrichment facilities broke, seriously setting back Iran's program. The cause turned out to be a virus specifically designed to dramatically increase the speed of the centrifuges for short bursts while deceiving the safeguards into thinking they were still spinning at their regular speed. Security experts believed the evidence pointed to a joint U.S. and Israeli program, likely introduced into the Iranian computer system by an infected thumb drive brought into Iran's Bushehr facility. Privately, Iranian officials suspected a Russian technician as the culprit for the contaminated virus. Neither the United States nor Israel acknowledged the attack, although in a video played at the 2011 retirement ceremony of Israel's chief military officer, Lieutenant General Gabi Ashkenazi, the general claimed Stuxnet as an operational success on his watch as head of the Israeli armed forces.[22]

Tehran accused both countries of mounting these computer attacks as part of a soft campaign to overthrow the regime. According to Iranian officials, the CIA also began a program to allow dissidents to maintain access to the Internet. Iranian intelligence minister Heydar Moslehi dubbed this an "internet in a suitcase," apparently because it was a mobile system that amounted to a powerful router that when set up allowed the opposition to tap into the Internet, and even cell phone networks, while bypassing the security firewalls imposed by the Iranian government. An Iranian general said the design had been built in a fifth-floor office on L Street in Washington, financed by $2 million from the State Department, presumably from the funding approved by the Bush administration. To counter this soft-power attack, Iran formed its own cyber command, "equipped with state-of-the-art technology."[23]

If the U.S. government refused to engage in more lethal means, Israel and others were bound by no such restrictions. A series of bombings rocked Iranian oil pipelines and infrastructure. The terrorist group Jundallah stepped up its attacks on Iran. A string of bombings killed dozens of Revolutionary Guard officers, including a general, as well as numerous civilians. Iran, with some evidence, accused Israel of supporting the group. Starting on January 12, 2010, five attacks occurred against Iranian nuclear scientists in Tehran. Dr. Massoud Ali Mohammad, a fifty-year-old nuclear physicist who had backed the opposition candidates during the recent election, was killed when a remotely detonated bomb exploded as he left his home. Ten months later, prominent scientist Dr. Majid Shahriari and his wife were stuck in Tehran traffic on their morning commute. A motorcycle weaved its way between the cars and, with a faint click, attached a magnetic bomb to the driver's side of the car. Seconds later it exploded, killing the doctor and wounding his wife. Twenty minutes later, a Revolutionary Guard scientist, Fereydoon Abbasi, was the victim of an identical attack. He managed to roll out the passenger side just in time to avoid the bulk of the blast. In July 2011, thirty-five-year-old academic Darioush Rezaeinejad was shot and killed by motorcycle-mounted assassins. Iran authorities later arrested one of the alleged assailants responsible for Ali Mohammad's death, who prosecutors said had received training in Israel and agreed to carry out the attack for $120,000.[24]

Not all explosions could be attributed to Israel. On November 12, 2011, Iranian Revolutionary Guard officers gathered at a rocket range twenty-five miles from Tehran for the test of a newly designed rocket motor for a planned multistage ballistic missile. Supervising the test was Major General Hassan Moghaddam, the Werner von Braun of Iran's missile program. Iran's military did not always adhere to the best safety practices; it had had more than ten serious accidents in just the past couple of years at this facility. Suddenly, a massive explosion rocked the Iranian base. In overhead images of the facility, it looked like a tornado had swept through it. The blast leveled nearby buildings. In the worst accident of the Iranian missile program's history, Moghaddam died along with sixteen other officers and men.[25]

Regardless of the cause, the sheer number of explosions created a mood of uncertainty and paranoia within the Iranian government. The pervasive sense that outside forces were behind every accident worked to the Americans' and Israelis' advantage. It created paranoia that played havoc with Iran's nuclear and missile programs as scientists grew uncertain whether sabotage or design flaws set back their research.

Iran tried striking back at Israel with less than professional tradecraft. In February 2012, it tried a string of attacks against Israeli diplomats in Georgia, Thailand, and India. Security officials uncovered all but one. Duplicating the attacks on them, a motorcyclist attached a magnetic bomb on the car of the wife of the Israeli defense attaché in India, seriously wounding her. Indian police soon arrested a fifty-year-old Iranian journalist as one of the culprits. In Thailand, one of the bombs went off prematurely in the safe house. As the Iranian agents fled, one bloody operative tried to flag down a taxi, who not surprisingly refused to accept the passenger. When police arrived, the same Iranian threw a grenade at them, only to have it bounce back off a tree and blow off both his legs.

The CIA did not remain idle either. A number of presidential findings had been signed, going back to the Clinton years, to thwart Iran's nuclear program. In 1994, the U.S. military had executed an operation called Project Sapphire, in which thirty-one nuclear specialists and three massive C-5 transport aircraft landed in Kazakhstan to secure 1,320 pounds of highly enriched uranium that had been improperly stored; intelligence had indicated that Iranian agents were interested in buying it.[26]

In 2000, Langley hatched an idea to set back Iran's nuclear program by having a former Soviet nuclear scientist, who had defected and now worked for the Americans, pass doctored blueprints for a TBA 480 high-voltage block—the triggering device needed to detonate a nuclear weapon. Embedded into the design was a sophisticated design flaw, one that would take the Iranians down the wrong path, ending not in a brilliant blast of a man-made sun, but a puff of smoke.[27]

After briefing the Russian during a stay at a posh San Francisco hotel, the CIA turned him loose in Vienna. After stumbling around the city, he managed to find the Iranian delegation to the IAEA in an unmarked office in a five-story apartment building. After he dropped off the plans, American intelligence monitoring the building reported that a senior Iranian official suddenly changed plans and quickly returned to Tehran. Whether this Trojan horse operation proved effective remains unclear, but it seems likely it worked up to a point. At any rate, more than a decade later Iran still had not demonstrated any mastery of a triggering device.[28]

The CIA received a windfall in June 2009. Shahram Amiri was a young nuclear physicist with a wife and children who worked with radioactive isotopes at Malek-Ashtar University of Technology in Tehran, which had close links to Iran's nuclear program. How long he worked for the agency remains a matter of speculation—perhaps for several years, perhaps even providing input into the 2007 intelligence estimate on the Iranian nuclear program. For some reason, he came in from the cold or decided to defect while on a pilgrimage to Mecca. With the Saudis' assistance, the CIA spirited him in complete secrecy to the United States for extensive debriefings about Iran's covert nuclear weapons program. When he did not return, nervous Iranian authorities investigated, unsure of whether he had defected or been executed by Saudi Arabia or Israel. For his safety, the CIA secretly resettled him in Tucson, Arizona, well away from any Iranian communities.

After a year in exile, Amiri grew homesick. Against the advice of his handlers, he called home to talk to his son. Iranian authorities answered the phone. Now they knew he had defected to the United States. Amiri was told to recant his defection or else his family would pay the price. To placate his family's tormentors, he produced a video on his home computer saying he had been kidnapped and held against his will by the Americans. "During the eight months that I was kept in America, I was subject to the most severe tortures and psychological pressures by the American intelligence investigation groups," Amiri said. Iran released the video on state television.

The agency tried to do damage control and protect Amiri's family. It helped produce a slick video in which he recanted his story of abduction and reassured his family that he was safe in America, and released it on YouTube. "I am Iranian and I have not taken any steps against my homeland. I am not involved in weapons research and have no experience and knowledge in this field. I know that the government of the Islamic Republic of Iran will take care of and protect my family. I want them to know that I have never left them and have always loved them."[29]

Lonely and distraught, on July 13, 2010, Amiri showed up at the Iranian interests section at the Pakistani embassy near the vice president's home at the Naval Observatory in Washington, D.C. He asked to be returned to Iran.

Two days later, he arrived in Tehran, where after warmly embracing his seven-year-old son and his father, he held a press conference and claimed to have escaped from his CIA abductors, adding, "They offered me $50 million to cooperate with them and tell the media that I am a very important person in Iran's nuclear program. They wanted me to show a laptop on the TV and say we have obtained very important information on Iran's nuclear weapon program. But I promised myself not to tell [them] anything against my country." The Iranian Fars News Agency claimed Amiri had been a double agent the entire time, working for Iranian intelligence—a possibility that the CIA considered too.[30]

What happened to him after his return remains unclear. Iranian authorities wanted first to find out what had been compromised. Rather than throw him in prison, he received a hero's welcome that also helped the government save face. However, reports circulated in 2011 that he had been charged with espionage and imprisoned. If not executed, he is destined for a life in internal exile and house arrest.[31]

The spy game was not confined to Iran. In 2004, with Iranian assistance, Hezbollah established a counterintelligence unit called a spy combat unit.[32] The unit quickly grew in competence in its search for American and Israeli agents. Working with Lebanese government security officials, Hezbollah started using computers to search through phone call records looking for unusual calling patterns, such as short-duration calls between two prepaid cell phones.[33] In 2009, they claimed to have arrested a hundred Israeli agents. While this was likely a gross exaggeration, the new counterspy effort raised enough alarms in Langley to cause the Americans to reassess their own operations, and reportedly CIA officers were told to be especially careful about how they handled their agents in south Lebanon.[34]

In June 2011, Sheik Hassan Nasrallah disclosed during a television interview that Hezbollah had unmasked two CIA spies. These then led to a third man. Hezbollah's al-Manar news ran stories on TV using animation to describe the group's covert meetings with CIA officers at a prominent Pizza Hut in south Beirut, as well as a McDonald's and a Starbucks coffee shop. The Lebanese group listed the names of the chief of station and four other CIA case officers, plus nicknames for five other Americans accused of being CIA employees involved in spying in Lebanon. During his Friday sermon on June 24, 2011, Nasrallah summoned the often used Iranian line and called the American embassy in Beirut a "nest of spies."[35]

This drew a reaction from the American ambassador, a seasoned Foreign Service officer named Maura Connelly, who traveled to visit General Michel Aoun at his residence in the hills of East Beirut. Aoun, who had commanded the Lebanese army brigade during the 1983 engagement that had led to Bud McFarlane's famous "sky is falling" memo and direct American military intervention in the Lebanese Civil War, was now a coalition partner with his old adversary Hezbollah in the Lebanese government. Since American diplomats are prohibited from talking to Hezbollah, Ambassador Connelly went to Aoun to complain about Nasrallah's accusations against her embassy. "We view these accusations as an attempt to deflect attention away from internal tensions in Hezbollah," she said after the meeting. While it was generally the Lebanese leader who engaged in hyperbole, this time it was an American diplomat trying to deflect attention from the uncovering of U.S. agents in Lebanon.[36]

Just the previous month, in May 2011, Iran claimed to have arrested thirty suspected CIA agents, stating that the discovery of a secret Internet communication method used by the CIA had led to the uncovering of the traitors. But Iran defined spies broadly, and included journalists, academics, and officials in Iranian energy companies whose only "crime" was e-mailing colleagues in Europe or the United States. Iranian officials accused the United States of establishing special websites to communicate with its agents. An Iranian news website claimed that the MOIS had used a number of double agents to identify forty-two more CIA agents and revealed a program aimed at "misleading and entrapping Iranian youth and students," especially by telephone polling to ask their opinions.[37] It was indeed a broad definition of a Western spy.

Iran scored a lucky blow against the CIA when U.S. covert flights over the Islamic Republic were exposed. On December 4, 2011, Iranian troops stumbled upon a superstealthy U.S. Air Force RQ-170 Sentinel drone, operated by the CIA from an airfield in southwestern Afghanistan. Flying at fifty thousand feet, the bat-wing-shaped unmanned plane looked like a miniature B-2 Stealth bomber and carried sophisticated surveillance equipment. Designed to evade radar, it represented the most advanced drone in the American inventory. While 150 miles inside Iranian airspace, the CIA operator lost the satellite link that allowed him to control his drone, and the dune-colored plane came down largely intact to the sands of Iran's eastern desert. An Iranian military engineer claimed that Iran's electronic warfare forces had jammed the signal and had reconfigured the GPS coordinates to have it return not to home base near Kandahar, but to an air base in Iran.

U.S. officials talking on background to reporters denied this claim as an empty brag, while admitting that the drone had not accidently strayed over Iran. The CIA—not the air force—had been flying the drone and its covert mission had been to look for new Iranian nuclear sites. Since 2005, Iran has continually accused the United States of using drones to spy on its nuclear facilities. Normally, when a country is caught so flagrantly violating another state's territory, it apologizes or at least "expresses regret." But nothing is normal about relations between the United States and Iran. Instead of apologizing, President Obama had the temerity to ask for the drone's return. The chairman of the Joint Chiefs, General Martin Dempsey, never even denied American spying on Iran. Speaking to a CNN reporter, he flatly stated: "If you're asking are we gathering intelligence against Iran in a variety of means, the answer is, of course. It would be rather imprudent of us not to try to understand what a nation who has declared itself to be an adversary of the United States is doing.[38] Not surprisingly, Iran rejected the odd request. Tehran then complained about the intrusion to the UN Security Council.[39]

As tensions between Iran and the United States increased, the likelihood of military confrontation grew. Iran's ballistic missiles continued to worry CENTCOM planners. In remarks at Georgetown University Law Center on January 21, 2010, General Petraeus publicly stated that the United States had deployed eight Patriot missile batteries in the Gulf, deployed in Kuwait, the UAE, and Bahrain. Saudi Arabia, the UAE, and Kuwait had all decided to purchase more advanced missiles and radars.

Under President Obama efforts to build a missile defense array against Iran accelerated. As hopes of engagement faded, the administration moved to place additional pressure on Iran and prepare for war. The president ordered more forces to the Gulf to counter Iranian missiles. In February 2010, the Defense Department published a ballistic missile defense review study that continued to commit the United States to defend against Iranian missiles. During a March 2010 symposium in Abu Dhabi, the head of the Missile Defense Agency, Lieutenant General Patrick O'Reilly, outlined the overarching American strategy of a layered land and sea system that allowed the detection and engagement of Iranian missiles from across the Gulf and was capable of shooting down intercontinental missiles directed as far away as

Europe.[40] The United States deployed additional high-altitude Patriot batteries as well as Aegis radar ships outfitted with the Standard Missile 3, which had recently proved its ability to destroy high-altitude targets by shooting down a falling satellite. Secretary Gates ordered one of these cruisers to be permanently stationed inside the Persian Gulf.[41]

The United States sponsored the Integrated Air Defense Center for Excellence near the air force headquarters in Abu Dhabi, UAE. It was a state-of-the-art facility designed to simulate defending against a missile attack in order to develop common training and procedures across the Gulf militaries.[42] While Saudi Arabia objected to the center's being in the UAE rather than in its kingdom and initially refused to participate, in the early exercises all Arab planners privately acknowledged the need for better cooperation and were frank about both their shortfalls and their need to share information. While this did not translate into any immediate breakthrough in intermilitary cooperation, the admission alone was a major step forward in forging closer military ties with the United States and with each other.

CENTCOM also worried about continued Iranian mischief in Iraq. After the U.S. raids in 2006 and 2007, the supreme leader ordered Quds Force officers not to travel to Iraq. By 2009, however, Revolutionary Guard officers started reappearing in Iraq, now unhindered as U.S. forces no longer patrolled the cities. Quds Force commander Major General Qassem Suleimani wanted to hit the Americans as they left Iraq. "He wanted to kick us in the butt on the way out the door," said a senior U.S. military official during a speech at a Washington think tank. In June 2011, fifteen American soldiers died as a result of powerful new rocket-assisted munitions provided by the Quds Force to its Shia surrogates in Iraq, especially Kata'ib Hezbollah. The most deadly attack occurred on June 6, when one rocket killed six soldiers from the 1st Infantry Division at an air base near Baghdad.

In a manner similar to the debates in 2006, the generals were split on how to respond. A few strident voices advocated killing some of the Quds Force operatives inside Iraq, or at least rolling up some of their lucrative businesses in Oman and elsewhere. The senior commander in Iraq, General Lloyd Austin, cautioned against too harsh a response, worrying that Iran could dramatically increase the attacks on American forces. U.S. Special Forces did move to shut down the lucrative black-market business for the Revolutionary Guard of selling gasoline along the border with Afghanistan, an effort that had a significant impact on the guards' pocketbooks. Austin ordered military strikes targeted at the Iranian-backed militias inside Iraq. The United States sent a stern warning to Iran through the Russians and Chinese that the Americans would take further action if the attacks continued.

Iran continued to exert its influence in Iraq. Qassem Suleimani pushed to keep Iran's hand in the Iraqi political process. At the request of the Ayatollah Khamenei, Hezbollah dispatched a senior adviser to Iraq to lobby for Iran and to promote unity and closer ties with al-Sadr's group Jaysh al-Mahdi. With its Arab ally's assistance, Iran retained influence with the two main Shia parties, including al-Maliki's Dawa Party. During the 2010 elections in Iraq, which resulted in prolonged deadlock about who would lead the next government, Iran stepped in to influence the postelection jockeying, throwing its support behind the American-backed al-Maliki. After considerable cajoling by the supreme leader, Iran succeeded in herding the Iraqi Shia into a new coalition government.

Iranian Revolutionary Guard boats continued their harassment of U.S. warships in the Gulf, threatening a larger conflict between the two countries. As the guard operated with a decentralized command and rewarded commanders who took risks, Fifth Fleet commanders took seriously that any alteration could spiral out of control. A potentially serious incident occurred on January 6, 2008. Three American ships, led by the USS *Hopper*, were inbound through the Strait of Hormuz when five Revolutionary Guard speedboats approached. An Iranian on one of the boats raised the *Hopper*'s bridge on the radio. "I am coming at you," he announced, before adding in heavily accented English, "you will blow up in a couple of minutes." Another boat sped in front of the USS *Ingraham*, following behind the *Hopper*, and dropped several white objects in her path. The U.S. warship accelerated and turned to avoid them. When two other Iranian boats appeared to be making an inbound attack run, the skipper of the *Hopper* requested permission to open fire.

The *Hopper* had not undergone the normal training for a Persian Gulf deployment. Senior naval officers listening suspected the captain did not recognize the normal pestering by the immature Iranian sailors. The *Hopper* was ordered to hold its fire, and it turned out to be the correct decision. The objects dropped were only plastic boxes, and the guard boats soon lost interest in the Americans and headed off. When news of the near shoot-out broke in the press, the chairman of the Joint Chiefs, Admiral Michael Mullen, wanted to downplay the incident, concerned that it would only heighten tensions.

The U.S. Navy continued to operate with "disciplined restraint," as one senior naval commander in the Gulf, Vice Admiral Kevin Cosgriff, phrased it.[43]

Another serious incident occurred in April 2011. A Revolutionary Guard speedboat closed rapidly on the British warship HMS *York*. The ship sent verbal warnings and loud horn blasts to warn off the boat. When these failed, the captain ordered a heavy machine gun to fire in front of the boat; his next step would have been to fire into the boat. Fortunately, the guardsman piloting the boat stopped and raised his hands, and the crisis dissipated. But with tensions heightened, CENTCOM worried that this near incident could have easily led to a firefight.

To avoid this, in the spring of 2011 the U.S. Navy suggested establishing a hotline between the Fifth Fleet in Bahrain and the Revolutionary Guard commander at Bandar Abbas. If an incident at sea occurred, either side could quickly pick up the phone and talk to his counterpart and defuse a situation before it became a crisis. The new Fifth Fleet commander, Vice Admiral Mark Fox, was an experienced, charismatic aviator who had shot down an Iraqi MiG on the opening night of Desert Storm. While he supported the idea, he held out little hope that Iran would agree to it. When the U.S. government floated the idea to the Iranians, Fox's prediction proved correct. Iran refused to discuss the proposal. "The only reason for conflict in the Persian Gulf is the presence of the U.S. Navy," said the commander of the Iranian navy. "If they leave, there is no conflict." The idea of such a formal arrangement died.

Secretary Gates had not been pleased with CENTCOM. The commander, Admiral Michael Fallon, had stopped much of the theater planning efforts begun by Abizaid, concerned that it would only inflame tensions and lead to other wars, especially with Iran. Gates finally fired him for unflattering comments about the administration that appeared in a magazine. Into the vacuum a naval aviator named William Gortney offered up his own ideas, which captured the defense secretary's interest and quickly moved Gortney from one to three stars. A tough taskmaster known by the call sign Shortney (a hybrid reference to his height and last name), he was a self-confident pilot with years of experience flying over the Persian Gulf. As the new Fifth Fleet commander, Gortney believed the early hours of any conflict with Iran were critical. It would take time for reinforcements to arrive, and in a war, his fleet would have to fight with the ships and planes it had on hand.

Gortney called his new idea "the come as you are plan." It offered the first realistic view of the Iranian military in years. His staff devised a host of original ideas designed to kill small boats and take the fight to the Iranian navy. He would cede no water, but attack them anywhere from the northern Gulf to the Strait of Hormuz. Under his watch, Fifth Fleet experimented with forming surface task forces designed to hunt down Iranian boats. When Shortney left for a plum assignment in the Pentagon, his ideas remained a work in progress. But for the first time in two decades, the U.S. Navy had started to formulate a realistic scheme to grapple with Iran's unconventional military might.

During the course of Barack Obama's first three years in office, his policy had morphed from one of hopeful optimism and an extended hand of friendship to harsh sanctions and preparations for war. He had accused Bush of not seriously engaging Iran in diplomacy, but by 2011 he had adopted a policy nearly identical to that of his predecessor. While critics accused him of being naive in his initial approach, Obama's policy was more sophisticated than many realized. He knew the sticks of sanctions or military strikes were always there; what he did not know was whether Iran was seriously willing to sit down and discuss the differences that had divided the two nations for more than thirty years. As he discovered, the answer remained no. Any hope for an opening faded with the internal strife brought about by the Iranian presidential elections. As Nicholas Burns wrote in an op-ed praising Obama's attempt to extend the hand of friendship: "Because of it, the United States had significantly greater cordiality to take advantage of Iran's mendacity and to lead an international coalition toward comprehensive sanctions should talks fail."[44] With his overture rejected, Obama did just that.

EPILOGUE

For once, Abdul Reza Shahlai was nervous. The normally unflappable fifty-six-year-old Quds Force officer had seen his share of hazardous missions. He had served in Lebanon, Iraq, and now Yemen as one of the most competent and trusted of Qassem Suleimani's operators. He had given the final go-ahead for the 2007 attack on the training center in Karbala that killed five U.S. soldiers. He repeatedly displayed the initiative and resourcefulness needed by this independent special forces arm of the Revolutionary Guard. He now headed the Quds Force's small but growing effort to help train and equip a band of Shia tribesmen in North Yemen whose decadelong insurgency had become a thorn in the side of the Saudi government. But now his name was all over the Western media as having been implicated in a plot to kill the Saudi ambassador in Washington, D.C. The brash nature of the attack had surprised even Iran's most ardent detractors. Under President Obama, the U.S. military and the CIA had effectively forged an intelligence and killing team that had increased drone missile strikes fourfold against al-Qaeda in Pakistan and Yemen. Shahlai now feared that the next missile might be aimed at him. Suleimani reassured him that he would get him safely back to Iran.

Relations between Iran and Saudi Arabia had soured over the past decade. Iran held the kingdom (and its ally the United States) responsible for an upsurge in terrorist attacks by the separatist Baluchi group Jundallah, which had killed dozens of Revolutionary Guard soldiers and Iranian civilians over the past few years. Riyadh had sent troops into Bahrain to help crush the aspirations for equality of the majority Shia population there. The two countries had waged a proxy war in Yemen, with Iran backing a Shia Houthi faction. While Iran had no hand in starting the Houthi revolt, as the Saudis alleged, General Suleimani quickly seized on the insurrection to get Iran's foot into the Yemeni door and provide weapons and some training to the insurgents. Iran suspected Saudi money of keeping afloat the Mujahideen-e Khalq. When prominent Americans such as former Joint Chiefs chairman Peter Pace and Obama's first national security adviser, Jim Jones, publicly came out in favor of taking the MEK off the U.S. global terrorist list, it confirmed hard-liner suspicions that America was in cahoots with the MEK too.

The leaking of the U.S. State Department cables by WikiLeaks added fuel to the flames of Iran's animosity. Dozens of cables revealed the duplicity of the Gulf Arabs, especially Saudi Arabia. Despite their pronouncements of friendship to the Iranian foreign minister, they privately urged the United States to take a harsh stand against Iran, including military action. During a March 15, 2009, meeting with the White House's senior counterterrorism official, John Brennan, the Saudi king repeatedly stressed the dangers of Iran and its sway over Iraq and other Shia areas. "Iran's goal is to cause problems," the king said. "There is no doubt something unstable about them. May God prevent us from falling victim to their evil."[1]

The kingdom's ambassador to the United States, Adel al-Jubeir, was a particular target of Iran's ire. The slight, well-spoken ambassador was a favorite of the Saudi king's. Polished and fluent in English, al-Jubeir knew Washington and had projected a good image on American television in the aftermath of 9/11. During a meeting with General Petraeus in April 2008, he had referred to the Saudi king's approval of military action against Iran, speaking of the kingdom's desire to "cut off the head of the snake." When the cable appeared in the Western media, it infuriated many within the Iranian government. Killing the ambassador in return would send an unequivocal signal back to the Saudi king that the snake could strike back.

In 2010, in a manner similar to its planning of Khobar Towers, Iran began searching for soft targets to attack that afforded plausible deniability. Iranian operatives started looking at Saudi and Jewish targets in Turkey and the Caucasus, with some Iranians spotted looking at American-owned business buildings in Azerbaijan.[2] Saudi diplomats appeared on the target list. In May 2011, the Quds Force struck. Gunmen on motorcycles shot and killed the Saudi consul in Karachi, Pakistan, Hassan al-Kahatani, as he went to work.

It is a small world, and by happenstance, in March 2011, Abdul Reza Shahlai ran into his cousin, fifty-six-year-old Mansour Arbabsiar, who had recently returned to Tehran from the United States. The two had been friends as kids growing up in the city of Kermanshah, Iran, before Arbabsiar emigrated to Texas in the late 1970s. Although he was likable and friendly, life in America had not gone especially well for Arbabsiar. He attended Texas A&M University but failed to graduate. Settling in Corpus Christi and going by the name Jack, he tried his hand at a string of businesses. He opened the restaurant Gyros & Kabob inside the struggling Sunrise Mall, then the Stop and Buy store, and finally a used-car dealership.[3] All failed. His wife divorced him, took custody of their children, and filed a restraining order against him. In 2010, he moved back to Iran.

During the conversation with his cousin, Arbabsiar talked about his frequent trips to Mexico. He mentioned that he had once assisted a friend in smuggling her two sisters across the Mexican border and into the United States. While selling used cars, he frequently traveled across the border and had developed contacts with Mexican drug dealers.

Shahlai hatched an idea. Would Arbabsiar be willing to approach his drug dealer acquaintances and ask if they would help kill or kidnap the Saudi ambassador in Washington? It would send a strong signal to both the Americans and Saudis: if you kill our scientists in Tehran, we can kill the Saudi ambassador in Washington. Arbabsiar had no interest in defending the revolution; his god was mammon. Given the prospect of a considerable windfall profit for his efforts, he agreed to help his cousin.

This would be a risky operation for the Quds Force. In past bombings and assassinations, it had used trained surrogates and religiously aligned locals inside the target country. However, Iran had no network of sympathizers inside the United States to draw upon. Shahlai had little alternative if he wanted to strike in the U.S. capital. But he thought the risk looked minimal. Arbabsiar was a relative, not likely to betray him. He had a U.S. passport. He was clearly not an American double agent. By working through a Mexican drug cartel, the Quds Force thought it would be difficult to ever trace the scheme back to Iran.

The details of the plot remained closely held inside the Quds Force. It is not clear who had foreknowledge and whether Suleimani discussed the operation with Ayatollah Khamenei. But hard-liners such as the Quds Force commander continued whispering in the supreme leader's ear to strike back at the covert war being waged against them; this appeared to be a chance to accomplish that and to send a message to the American administration. Had the plan been vetted in a larger circle, someone might have questioned the wisdom of using a used-car salesman and rogue drug smugglers to undertake a significant terrorist attack inside the United States. But it wasn't. The scheme went forward.

Shahlai assigned his deputy, Colonel Gholam Shakuri, to handle Arbabsiar. An experienced Quds Force officer with a pronounced scar down his cheek, he gave Arbabsiar an envelope with $15,000 for expenses to fly back to Mexico and make the arrangements. Shahlai said they would use "Chevrolet" as the code word for the operation.[4]

In May, Arbabsiar made several trips to Mexico. He met with a man he believed to be a member of the ruthless Los Zetas drug gang. In fact, his contact worked for the U.S. Drug Enforcement Administration. He was a man who had been arrested in the United States on drug trafficking charges, and in return for having the charges dropped, he'd agreed to work for American law enforcement. In their first meeting, Arbabsiar asked the DEA informant if he knew anything about C-4 and explosives and confided to him the plot to kill the Saudi ambassador. The DEA informant agreed to undertake the mission, saying it required four men and would cost $1.5 million.

"You just want the main guy?" the informant asked.

"Yes, the ambassador," Arbabsiar answered.

The two met again on July 17. The DEA informant said his men had already conducted surveillance on the ambassador. He is protected by "eight to seven security people, but he eats regularly at a restaurant in Georgetown. I don't know what exactly your cousin want [sic] me to do."

Arbabsiar replied, "He wants you to kill this guy."

"There's gonna be like American people there, in the restaurant?" the informant responded.

"It doesn't matter how you do it," Arbabsiar replied. His cousin preferred that the ambassador be killed by himself, but "sometime [sic], you know, you have no choice."

By the end of the meeting, the two men had agreed to blow up Ambassador al-Jubeir while he ate at the swanky Georgetown restaurant Café Milano. As down payment, Shakuri had two deposits totaling $100,000 wired to a bank account provided by the informant.

On September 28, Arbabsiar flew back to Mexico to serve as collateral to the drug gang to ensure that they received the rest of the money after killing the Saudi diplomat. With FBI agents tailing him, Mexican authorities denied him entry, and federal agents moved in to arrest him upon his return to John F. Kennedy Airport in New York.

Once arrested, Arbabsiar confessed and agreed to help implicate the Quds Force. He made several calls to Colonel Shakuri in Tehran. On October 5, Arbabsiar said, "I wanted to tell you, the Chevrolet is ready, it's ready, uh, to be done. I should continue, right?"

"Yes, yes, yes," Shakuri answered. After discussing buying the car—code for carrying out the operation—the Quds Force officer continued, "Buy it, yes, buy all of it."

When the Justice Department announced the arrests and the details of the plot, Iran publicly scoffed at the allegations. Iran's foreign minister called it part of a "new propaganda campaign."[5] Privately, however, those who knew the details grew worried. Suleimani ordered a halt to many Quds operations and pulled back exposed operatives, as he had in 2007 when U.S. Special Operations forces came after him in Iraq. He then worked to get Shahlai back to the safety of Iran.

The exposure of the bomb plot came at a bad time for Iran. The country's only real ally in the Middle East and its key link to Hezbollah, Syria, had been rocked by the Arab Awakening, which had started in the spring of 2011 and had already swept several Middle East despots from power. Having successfully quashed its own protests in 2009, Iran dispatched Quds Force operatives and trainers to help Syrian president Bashar al-Assad retain power, but the situation remained precarious. What's more, the latest IAEA report, released in November 2011, sharply questioned Iran's claims that it did not have a covert nuclear weapons program. In light of the report and the foiled assassination, President Obama called for even tougher sanctions. When the United Kingdom agreed to the sanctions, the Iranians erred by taking a page from Iran's past. Civilian-clad Basij militia stormed the British embassy in Tehran. The mob ransacked the building, burning pictures of Queen Elizabeth and tossing diplomatic paperwork across the embassy grounds. The international backlash harshly condemned Iran. In retaliation, London closed the Iranian mission.

The Iranian government tried to conduct damage control following its string of setbacks. The government backtracked and pledged better security for Western embassies. The supreme leader approved sending Iranian intelligence minister Heydar Moslehi to Riyadh to meet with Saudi crown prince Nayef bin Abdul-Aziz al-Saud. Iran hoped to smooth relations, with Moslehi denying that his government had approved any assassination of the Saudi ambassador in Washington. The Saudis listened, but remained skeptical of anything said by the Islamic Republic.

In 2011, the media was again filled with reports about a possible Israeli strike on Iran's nuclear facilities. Every few years this story reared its head. In 2008, the Pentagon's DIA even issued a report stating that this was the "defining year" for any possible Israeli attack. The following year, Israeli defense minister Ehud Barak told Secretary Gates that 2009 was the year his forces would have to attack or else the "consequences would be too great." Both years came and went without any attack as Iran's enrichment program continued struggling. But with each story, leaders in Tehran took notice, and the Iranian military went on heightened alert. In the latest saber rattling, Iran threatened to retaliate by showering missiles on Israel's own nuclear facility. When Turkey announced it would host a new missile defense radar, Iran threatened to attack it too.

In the Pentagon, the prospect of being pulled into the conflict worried both Secretary Gates and his successor, Leon Panetta. Iran would assume the United States had been complicit in any attack and would retaliate against U.S. bases in the Persian Gulf. This would likely spark a regional war. Successive Pentagon officials spent considerable time getting the Israelis to think about the second and third order of effects of their attack. "They tended to default to the kinetic options and did not look at the long-term consequences," observed James Cartwright. But the Israelis viewed military action against

Iran in the same way they did attacks on such other intractable foes as Hamas or Hezbollah: it was mowing the grass. If it bought a year or so, that was good enough.

After Admiral Michael Fallon was replaced following an unflattering magazine article in 2008, CENTCOM had a string of remarkable commanders. This included the next chairman of the Joint Chiefs of Staff, General Martin Dempsey; the architect of the successful strategy that turned around Iraq, General David Petraeus; his deputy, a smart and humble marine general named John Allen, who headed the Iran planning effort before taking over as commander in Afghanistan; and straight-shooting warrior General James Mattis.

The appointment of Mattis got the Iranian military leaders' attention. He was arguably the finest combat marine to rise to four stars in a generation. He had commanded the battalion that first breached Iraq's defenses in Kuwait in 1991 and a decade later the marine division that swept into Baghdad in 2003. While not especially politic, he was as honest as his hair was gray, and he knew war. A true scholar of military history, he had a library of military works that famously ran into the thousands of books. His guidance to his commanders frequently incorporated historical anecdotes to help illustrate his points. During one meeting with subordinate commanders, Mattis spent five minutes reading an exchange of letters between General Douglas MacArthur and Admiral Chester Nimitz during the Second World War. The two had famously clashed over controlling the war in the Pacific, but in this dialogue MacArthur was asking for help in diverting the Japanese away from his landings in the Philippines. Nimitz replied with a laundry list of steps he would take to aid his sometime service rival in order to ensure success for the army's landings. While Mattis's history lesson went over the heads of a few less erudite officers, the lesson resonated with the majority of them: he intended his subordinates to take initiative and find ways to support each other during a war.

Defense Secretary Gates approved Mattis's choice for his deputy, a man who knew a great deal about Iran. Since his altercation with Revolutionary Guard speedboats in April 2003, now vice admiral Bob Harward had served on the National Security Council as the deputy commander at the premier special operations unit in Fort Bragg and had managed the detainee program in Afghanistan. He still possessed an understanding of the Persians that no other senior officer could match. The SEAL repeatedly surprised Iran experts at academic conferences by speaking to them in fluent Farsi.

Mattis viewed Iran as one of the most significant challenges for his command. As one official said in a speech before the conservative think tank, the Institute for the Study of War, CENTCOM had three countries on its mind: "Iran, Iran, and Iran." With the wars in Afghanistan and Iraq winding down, the United States intended to keep forty thousand service personnel stationed around the Gulf, chiefly to contain Iran.[6] As the ground wars died down, CENTCOM would revert to a posture akin to that during the tanker war, with the U.S. Navy safeguarding American interests.[7] Mattis started reading Persian history and toiling through Persian poetry to get a better sense of his potential adversary. No warmonger, Mattis preferred to talk with the Iranian generals rather than kill them. "I have the forces to squash the Iran military if I need to; but I've seen a lot of war and really don't want to kill young Iranian boys," he said bluntly, responding to a question during a conference at the Mayflower Hotel in Washington in the spring of 2011.

In 2012, relations between the United States and Iran had reached another nadir. The United States was now bent on more sanctions to bend Iran to the UN Security Council's and Washington's will. Rebuffed and wiser, President Obama ratcheted up the pressure, with the Treasury Department finding new, creative ways to close loopholes in sanctions and strangle Iranian commerce. Just before the new year, President Obama signed tough new sanctions against Iran. Imposed by a near unanimous Congress as a rider to the defense budget, for the first time, the United States targeted Iran's central bank, the means by which the country received payment for its oil exports. The twenty-seven nations of the European Union followed suit with a pronouncement that they intended to phase out all oil imports from Iran. Europe was the second leading importer after China of Iranian crude, taking 450,000 barrels of Iran's 2.6 million daily output.[8] Iran responded with bellicosity. The chief of Iran's regular navy, Admiral Habibollah Sayyari, warned that his country could easily close the Strait of Hormuz, through which one sixth of the world's oil flows. Sayyari, who came through the ranks of the Iranian naval special operations forces, was an aggressive combat veteran of the Iran-Iraq war and more akin to the Revolutionary Guard than his own naval service. In December 2011 and January 2012, both the regular navy and the Revolutionary Guard held large-scale and very public military exercises around the strait to demonstrate Iran's resolve.

Iranian authorities warned the U.S. Navy not to send another aircraft carrier through the gulf. "The Islamic Republic of Iran will not repeat its warning," said the head of Iran's army, General Ataollah Salehi.

President Obama and his national security adviser Tom Donilon were in no mood to back down from this blatant threat against the world's economy. Mattis was called back to Washington on a Sunday for two days of lengthy meetings at the White House, and the president publicly stated he would use force to keep the Strait of Hormuz open. In the end, Iran's threat proved hollow as American air craft carriers continued transiting without incident.

The crisis over Iran's nuclear program grew evermore ominous. In February 2012, the IAEA issued a scathing report about Iranian obfuscation. Inspectors were denied access to both scientists and Iran's secretive Parchin weapons facility. Israel continued to beat the war drums. That same month both the chairman of the Joint Chiefs, General Martin Dempsey, and National Security Adviser Tom Donilon led successive teams to Tel Aviv to try to talk Israel out of taking any immediate military action. They met with somber Israeli officials. Rather than spouting the usual talking points about Iran, the Americans found their counterparts far more serious and circumspect. Donilon's team returned to Washington convinced that Israel intended to strike Iran's nuclear facilities sooner rather than later.

On March 5, 2012, Prime Minister Binyamin Netanyahu met with President Obama in the Oval Office.[9] The two men already had a strained relationship, and the meeting did little to overcome their divisions, including those over Iran's nuclear ambitions. Obama stressed that there was no immediate need to attack Iran's facilities because all the intelligence pointed to the fact that the supreme leader had not even decided to produce a nuclear weapon. The tough Israeli pushed back, saying that they could not wait until Iran entered into a "zone of immunity." They had to strike now in order to prevent Iran from having the capability to develop nuclear bombs. Publicly, Obama tried to placate Israel's concerns. "My policy here is not going to be one of containment. My policy is prevention of Iran obtaining nuclear weapons," the president said before the meeting. He added, "When I say all options are on the table, I mean it."[10] Both sides agreed on tougher sanctions against Iran's central bank, aimed at curtailing their oil exports.

This growing international isolation and economic pressure only heightened Iran's paranoia that the real goal behind U.S. actions was the overthrow of the Islamic Republic. Anti-Americanism remained a pillar of the government's policies, and no real change in this regard was likely to occur while the revolutionary generation remained in power. The young men who took to the streets, overthrew the shah, and fought eight years of a bloody war with an Iraqi government backed by Washington now had gray in their beards, but their attitudes remained the same. Like the great Arab historian Ibn Khaldun, who wrote about the rise and fall of the great empires as repeated cycles in history, the supreme leader and his inner circle remained convinced that the West was declining and the next empire, Iran, was on the rise. The United States and its regional lackey, Israel, like the Soviets and communism before them, were going to collapse. The U.S. withdrawal from Iraq and Afghanistan showed that the United States was in retreat in the Middle East. While more realistic Iranian leaders like Javad Zarif understood that the reality was quite different, and Iran was never going to rival the United States in power, the fallout from the 2009 elections had marginalized many of these voices of reason.

While the 1979 revolution changed Iran's government, the Islamic Republic maintained the age-old Iranian goal of being recognized as a regional power. "We should be the greatest power in the region and play a role accordingly," said Hadi Nesanjani, who served in President Rafsanjani's cabinet. While the new government was loath to put it in these terms, deeper even than the Shia religious motivations is an ingrained sense of Persian historical entitlement. As a nation, the Iranians predate all others in the region, with a lineage tracing back to the Persian Empire founded by Cyrus the Great. A seat at the Middle East table is their natural right; it is the United States that stands in their path. Building this historical precedent, the Iranian Revolution had added a mission as the new defender of the downtrodden Shia across the Middle East and, by extension, all Muslims resisting the West and Israel. Starting in Lebanon, facilitated by the U.S. invasion of Iraq, and most recently in Yemen and Bahrain, Iran provided a steady stream of military and economic support to these movements. This puts Iran squarely at odds with both Israel and the Sunni governments backed by the United States.

The Iran problem is an enduring constant in American foreign policy. Over the decades, every administration has had its moments with Iran. The country has been too strategically important to ignore. Various administrations have tried to woo it back into the Western fold, or talk of replacing the Islamic Republic with one more to Washington's liking, but the results have been uniformly miserable. In the final analysis, Iran simply rejects any vision of the Middle East as imposed by the will of the United States. A famous quote by Ayatollah Khomeini puts it succinctly: "We will resist America until our last breath." Unfortunately, Washington has helped perpetuate the animosity. The United States has displayed a callous disregard for Iranian grievances and security concerns. Giving a medal to a ship's captain who just inadvertently killed 290 civilians and then wondering why Iran might harbor resentment is just the most obvious example of American obtuseness. An ill-conceived intervention in the Lebanese Civil War against the Shia, while at the same time backing Iraq, threatened the new Iranian government. Tehran's response, to level a building full of marines and to take American hostages, still colors American thinking, equally understandably. Washington invariably took the wrong course with Iran. When diplomatic openings appeared, hardliners refused to talk and advocated overthrowing the Islamic Republic. When Iran killed U.S. soldiers and marines in Lebanon and Iraq, successive administrations showed timidity when hard-liners called for retribution.

Glimmers of optimism invariably give way to the smell of cordite and talk of war. In 2012, the prospects for conflict peaked again. Seasoned, pragmatic Iran watchers called for tougher sanctions to punish Iranian intransigence regarding its nuclear program. But punishing Iran for its intransigence also hardens Iranian leaders and justifies in their minds the need for a nuclear program, both for increased self-sufficiency and as a deterrent against Western aggression. Within the U.S. administration, discussions in the White House Situation Room turned to the possibility of pressing for sanctions against Iran's central bank. As this is the means by which Iran receives payment for its oil exports, this would be a radical act, tantamount to an embargo of Iranian oil. "Iran could see it as a de facto act of war," said one senior Obama administration representative.

Unfortunately, now neither side has much desire to work to bridge their differences. Distrust permeates the relationship. Three decades of twilight war have hardened both sides. When someone within the fractured governing class in Tehran reached out to the American president, the United States was unwilling to accept anything but capitulation. When President Obama made a heartfelt opening, a smug Iranian leadership viewed it as a ruse or the gesture of a weak leader. Iran spurned him. Obama fell back on sanctions and CENTCOM; Iran fell back into its comfortable bed of terrorism and warmongering. Soon it may no longer be twilight; the light is dimming, and night may well be approaching at long last.

Acknowledgments

The burden of writing a book frequently falls on the writer's family. My wife, Heys, and my young son, Matthew, patiently endured the many days I spent ensconced in my study or away conducting research. My parents provided both their personal insights as well as continuous encouragement as this book morphed with each seemingly never-ending rewrite.

At last count, I interviewed well over four hundred individuals in the United States and overseas. They invited me into their homes and made room in busy schedules to share with me their recollections. Many sat for hours answering my questions and tolerated numerous follow-up questions and interviews. My chief regret is that so many of their fascinating stories could not be included in the final text. Several individuals deserve particular notice. The late Caspar Weinberger and William Odom offered their unique insights, and the former defense secretary's family graciously approved my request to review his papers. Richard Armitage always found time to answer my questions. Admiral James Lyons's memory and personal papers started me along many new and important paths to unraveling this history. Retired admirals Tony Less, Harold Bernsen, and John Poindexter kindly tolerated my frequent requests for interviews. Peter Wikul's and Marc Thomas's interviews filled in the details of some of the key military engagements against Iran during the late 1980s. My father, George Crist, offered up his papers and notebooks. The Islamic Republicc facilitated interviews with officials. Others who helped fill in key holes: James Parran, Anthony Zinni, John Abizaid, Hooshang Amirahmadi, Nazhatoon Riahi, George Cave, Jack Devine, Joseph Strasser, Richard Williams, Tim Weiner, Mark Perry, P. X. Kelley, Robert Harward, and Kevin Cosgriff. There were a number of others who provided invaluable assistance but need to remain anonymous. I am deeply grateful for their time and information.

The American public is fortunate to have the most accessible military archives in the world. The staffs at the Naval Historical Center, Air Force Historical Research Agency, Army Heritage and Education Command, U.S. Central Command, and U.S. Special Operations Command were extremely helpful in obtaining and, in the case of the navy's operational archives, declassifying many records. They allowed me to listen to hundreds of oral histories that provided recollections immediately after the events described. The staff at the old Marine Corps Historical Center at the Washington Navy Yard opened their extensive collections and declassified many documents and interviews too. The staffs at both the National Archives and Library of Congress were ever gracious and helpful. I am also indebted to the scholars at the Woodrow Wilson Center for Cold War Studies and the National Security Archive for breaking loose so many documents from the U.S. government.

I am also grateful to The Washington Institute for Near East Policy, especially Michael Eisenstadt, Michael Knights, and Patrick Clawson. They allowed me to use their facilities and opened their Rolodexes for six months while I wrote the Clinton and Bush chapters. Their collegiality and insights helped immeasurably in an accurate telling of this story.

I am indebted to several people who aided me in this book. Michael Gordon, a great reporter, encouraged the book and helped open doors. My agent, Andrew Wylie, saw the importance of the subject and applied his considerable talents to the project from the outset. Dr. John Shortal graciously allowed an extended absence from a demanding job to complete the book. My dissertation adviser, Peter Garretson, helped in the early stages of what would become this tome. Susan Carroll helped with copyediting. John Partin, the recently retired historian at Special Operations Command, aided this project immensely at various stages. His wealth of knowledge about the history of special operations forces is unsurpassed.

I could not have had a better team supporting me than the professionals at Penguin. My editor, Scott Moyers, offered sage advice that sharpens the manuscript and broadens its scope to encompass the birth of conflict between the United States and Iran. Emily Graff worked tirelessly to get maps and photos, all the while cheerfully incorporating many last-minute changes to the text. I am also indebted to production editor Noirin Lucas and copy editor Nicholas LoVecchio, as well as my publicist, Liz Calamari, who developed a great strategy to market the book.

This book required several years to write. With each iteration and new lead the story and accuracy improved. The murky world of writing contemporary history is not always straightforward. I have tried to be as thorough and evenhanded as possible, putting aside my own biases in telling this important story. Any errors are mine alone and the conclusions in no way represent the views of the U.S. government.

Notes

Research for this book began nearly twenty years ago as part of a dissertation on the Reagan administration. As time passed, I continued my research, interviewing more current participants and reading more material as it became available and declassified. Anyone who has written contemporary history understands the challenges of finding primary source documents. Before 1989, paper records were catalogued and frequently preserved at various archives; since the U.S. government started producing memos and messages in electronic format, preservation has been haphazard at best. Many still reside on computers with the originating agency and have never made it into any organized archives. Many more have been deleted. I have a stack of CENTCOM documents declassified in 1993 that simply don't exist anymore except in my files.

Many of the documents referenced were obtained through Freedom of Information Act and Mandatory Review Requests. I submitted some of these requests and benefited from other researchers' efforts. Both Donald Rumsfeld and Doug Feith declassified many documents related to the George W. Bush administration. Select documents and some oral histories held at the Naval Historical Center and the now defunct Marine Corps Historical Center at the Washington Naval Yard were reviewed and declassified at my request.

Fortunately, many people still keep notebooks and their own personal collection of key records. In researching the book, I interviewed hundreds of participants, many of whom served at the most senior levels of the U.S. government. This included off-the-record conversations with government officials, intelligence officers, and special forces operatives. I met with Iranian exiles and Revolutionary Guard defectors, and even family members of one

Iranian executed for spying. A number made their papers and diaries available for me to examine. Unfortunately, constraints on the length of the manuscript prohibited many of their often fascinating stories from being included in the final manuscript. They, however, provided the author with a far greater depth of understanding of thirty years of history of the U.S. and Iranian conflict.

Others provided unhindered access to their personal papers. This included: Lieutenant General William Odom, Admiral James Lyons, General George Crist, the family of Secretary of Defense Caspar Weinberger, and Captain Peter Wikul. The senior aide to the chairman of the Joint Chiefs of Staff, Admiral William Crowe, made available his own private diaries, in which he recorded daily meetings and significant conversations at the highest level of the U.S. government.

Iranian sources proved the most problematic, but I was able to interview a number of former and current Iranian diplomats and military officers, as well as read declassified intelligence documents. A number of former military and civilian intelligence officers shared their insight into Iranian actions. Iranian news media provided a wealth of information on both political and military issues. The Foreign Broadcast Information Service was invaluable in finding older Iranian new a sources.

There are several important archives that contain many linear feets' worth of records related to the U.S.-Iranian conflict. The Carter, Reagan, George H. W. Bush, and Clinton presidential libraries contain many of the most important records, although many of the documents still remain classified. Several service archives hold records of the military activities against Iran. These include: The Air Force History Office in Washington, D.C.; the archives and oral histories collection at the Air University, Maxwell Air Force Base, Montgomery, Alabama; the U.S. Marine Corps archives, personal papers, and oral histories at Quantico, Virginia; the vast collection of documents and oral histories at the Operational Archives, Ship's Histories, and Aviation History Branches at the Naval History and Heritage Command Center, Washington, D.C.; and the oral histories and personal papers held at the U.S. Army Military History Institute, Carlisle Barracks, Pennsylvania. The latter holds the collections of two CENTCOM commanders, generals Binford Peay and Robert Kingston. Both the U.S. Central Command and Special Operations Command historians provided access to some of their records. Several historians in the Joint History Office, Joint Staff shared their insights into U.S. foreign policy in the Middle East. The Library of Congress holds several important collections including those of Alexander Haig, Caspar Weinberger, and William Odom.

CHAPTER 1 "A LITTLE KING IN YOUR HEART"

1. Department of State memorandum, "The Huyser Mission in Iran: January 4 to February 4, 1979," February 1979.
2. Robert Huyser, *Mission to Tehran* (New York: Harper and Row, 1986), p. 1.
3. Jimmy Carter, Address to the Nation, "The Energy Problem," April 18, 1977, *Public Papers of the Presidents of the United States: President Jimmy Carter, 1977*, volume 1 (Washington, D.C.: Government Printing Office, 1977), pp. 656–62.
4. Department of State, *Foreign Relations of the United States, 1946*, volume 8, pp. 359–65.
5. There is considerable truth to the often cited quotation by American vice consul in Iran Robert Rossow, Jr.: "One may fairly say that the Cold War began on March 4, 1946." The agreement signed in 1942 following the Anglo-Soviet occupation of Iran stipulated that all foreign troops would leave Iran within six months after the end of hostilities. By late 1945, the Soviets had made no effort to withdraw their troops, and they were backing two communist independence movements: in Iranian-controlled Azerbaijan and in the Kurdish areas of western Iran. This stance coincided with intimidating forward posturing of Soviet forces against Turkey, both along their common border and on the border to the north with Bulgaria.

    On March 4, 1946, Rossow observed Soviet forces moving south from Tabriz, appearing to menace the Iranian capital of Tehran. An American army captain, Alexis Gagarine, who served as a military attaché to the shah's government, reported seeing a column of twenty-five Soviet tanks headed to Tehran. The following day, British prime minister Winston Churchill issued his famous Iron Curtain speech in Fulton, Missouri, although, arguably, his remarks reflected more upon circumstances in Eastern Europe than in northern Iran. The United States objected forcefully, but in measured terms, convinced that Moscow was unwilling to go to war over Iran. Later that month, an Iranian delegation headed by Iranian prime minister Ahmad Qavam arrived in Moscow for talks. After the Iranians agreed to a joint venture to explore for oil in northern Iran, with a slice for Moscow of any oil discovered, Joseph Stalin agreed to withdraw Soviet forces. In May, Soviet forces withdrew.

    The crisis alarmed Washington. In October 1949, the Truman administration adopted NSC 47/2, which would guide American policy in the Persian Gulf for the next four decades. In short, NSC 47/2 advocated three main courses of action: 1) promote Western ties with regional leaders, 2) prevent Soviet penetration in the region, and 3) ensure that regional disputes did not undercut the United States' ability to oppose Soviet aggression. American officials viewed the Persian Gulf, with its oil and warm-water ports, as too important to tolerate any Soviet penetration in the region.
6. Henry Kissinger, *White House Years* (Boston: Little, Brown, 1979), p. 1264.
7. Ambassador Theodore Eliot, Jr., Foreign Affairs Oral History Program, Association for Diplomatic Studies and Training, Arlington, Virginia, April 24, 1992.
8. Consul General Morris Draper, Foreign Affairs Oral History Program, Association for Diplomatic Studies and Training, February 27, 1991.
9. In support of this strategy, Cyrus Vance developed a strict criterion for U.S. arms sales to the Middle East, mandating that any new arms had to "uniquely strengthen the requester's ability to perform military function" and could not be achieved with less sophisticated weapons.
10. William Odom, "The Cold War Origins of the U.S. Central Command," *Journal of Cold War Studies*, Spring 2006, p. 61; Zbigniew Brzezinski, exit interview, February 20, 1981, Carter Library and Museum, at www.jimmycarter-library.org, accessed May 24, 2007.
11. Marilyn Berger, "Cyrus R. Vance, a Confidant of Presidents, Is Dead at 84," *New York Times*, January 13, 2002, www.nytimes.com/2002/01/13/world/cyrus-r-vance-a-confidant-of-presidents-is-dead-at-84.html?pagewanted=all, accessed March 23, 2009.
12. Overall, Vance abhorred the use of military force, despite, or perhaps because of, his own service as a junior officer on a destroyer during the Second World War. Having witnessed the Vietnam debacle unfolding on his watch at the Pentagon during the Lyndon Johnson administration, Vance was unenthusiastic about another similar scenario in the Middle East.
13. Harold Brown, quoted in Paul Starobin and Robert Leavitt, "Shaping the National Military Command Structure: Command Responsibilities for the Persian Gulf," Case Program, John F. Kennedy School of Government, Harvard University, 1985, p. 2. These differing views within the administration revealed themselves sharply with respect to arms sales to the shah and made for a schizophrenic Iranian policy. At the urging of Secretary Vance, the United States began reducing arms sales to the shah, in the process irritating the Iranian monarch by rescinding a pledge by President Ford to sell him advanced F-18 combat aircraft, a deal largely conceived between the shah and the plane's manufacturer before it had even progressed through the appropriate U.S. government offices. In August 1978, Vance blocked a proposal to sell Iran thirty-one additional F-4 Phantom fighters. However, both Secretary Brown and National Security Adviser Brzezinski persuaded President Carter to continue the flow of arms to Iran, with the

United States promising to provide Iran an astounding 648 artillery pieces to be delivered beginning in the early 1980s. Furthermore, the United States now agreed to replace the F-4 with more advanced F-16 fighters and to sell Iran highly advanced E-3 AWACS surveillance aircraft, which had only recently been deployed to NATO and European bases. The AWACS sale was later withdrawn after congressional opposition, joined by CIA Director Stansfield Turner, who testified that the sale posed a security risk if the Soviets induced one of the Iranian crews to defect.

14. Department of State, Bureau of Intelligence and Research, "The Future of Iran: Implications for the U.S.," January 28, 1977, pp. 1, 3.

15. Arthur Goldschmidt, Jr., *A Concise History of the Middle East* (Boulder, CO: Westview, 1996), p. 332.

16. Draft NIE, September 1978; Defense Intelligence Agency, "Assessment of the Political Situation in Iran," September 1978.

17. John Stempel memorandum for Ambassador Sullivan, "While You Were Away . . . The place really didn't turn to crap but it might have looked like it," August 22, 1978, p. 1.18.

18. Gordon Winkler, Foreign Affairs Oral History Program, Association for Diplomatic Studies and Training, March 23, 1989.

19. Department of State, Bureau of Intelligence and Research, "Iranian Dissidence on the Increase," January 29, 1978, p. 1.

20. Ambassador Sullivan message to Warren Christopher, "GOI Discernment of Dissident Political Action," April 25, 1978, pp. 1–3; Charles Naas message to State Department, "Uncertain Political Mood: Religious Developments, Tougher Royal Line on Demonstrators," August 1, 1978, p. 2.

21. Stempel memorandum, "While You Were Away," p. 2.

22. National Intelligence Officer for the Near East and South Asia memorandum for Director of Central Intelligence, "PRC Meeting on Iran, November 6, 1978," November 3, 1978, p. 2.

23. Ibid., p. 3.

24. Mohsen Sazegara, interview with author, May 2009.

25. Ibid.

26. Henry Precht, interviewed by Charles Stuart, Foreign Affairs Oral History Program, Association for Diplomatic Studies and Training, March 2000.

27. Consul General Charles McCaskill, Foreign Affairs Oral History Program, Association for Diplomatic Studies and Training, July 7, 1993.

28. Interview with retired CIA officer, August 15, 2007.

29. Central Intelligence Agency (hereafter CIA), Human Resources Committee, "Focus Iran Part II: Action Review," December 27, 1976, p. 3.

30. Interview with retired CIA officer.

31. CIA Human Resources Committee, "Focus Iran: Intelligence Committee Review of Request by Human Resources Committee for the United States Mission in Iran," November 4, 1976, p. 2.

32. Lawrence Altman, "Dr. Jean A. Bernard, 98, Dies; Found Cancer in Shah of Iran," *New York Times*, April 30, 2006.

33. Warren Christopher memorandum for President Carter, September 13, 1978, p. 2.

34. President Jimmy Carter letter to the shah of Iran, September 28, 1978.

35. Ambassador Sullivan message to Secretary of State, "Iran: Understanding the Shiite Islamic Movement" (031012Z), February 1978.

36. Sullivan message to Vance and Brzezinski, "Recommendations for President to Shah letter," August 29, 1978, pp. 1–2. Initially, Sullivan believed that the shah too recognized these realities. On August 29, 1978, Sullivan, who had just returned from an inopportune two-month vacation in the United States, wrote to Vance and Brzezinski: "In the few days that I have been back in Tehran, it has become clear to me that the shah has made a fundamental political decision to transform his authoritarian regime into a genuine democracy." Military and security officials, he wrote, were going along with it despite their trepidation regarding "The Great Beast, the people of Iran."

37. CIA, National Intelligence Daily, Situation Report: Iran, January 6, 1979; Henry Precht letter to William Sullivan, December 19, 1978, p. 1.

38. Stansfield Turner memorandum for the Deputy Director for National Foreign Assessment, "Meeting with Dr. Brzezinski," October 27, 1978.

39. CIA, "Prospects for a Military Government," November 1978, pp. 1–4.

40. William Sullivan message to Secretary of State, "Looking Ahead: The Military Option," November 2, 1978.

41. Steven Ward, *Immortal: A Military History of Iran and Its Armed Forces* (Washington, D.C.: Georgetown University Press, 2009), p. 214.

42. Precht interview, Association for Diplomatic Studies and Training.

43. Stanley Escudero, interview with author, October 5, 2006, and May 24, 2007.

44. Ibid.

45. Embassy Tehran message to Secretary of State, "Meeting with Ayatollah Shariat-Madari" (101740Z), January 1979, pp. 1–2.

46. CIA, intelligence memorandum, "Iran: Radicals in the Opposition," January 12, 1979, p. 1.

47. Henry Precht memorandum to Harold Saunders, "Seeking Stability in Iran," December 19, 1978.

48. George W. Ball, "Summary Memorandum for the President, Issues and Implications of the Iranian crisis," December 12, 1978. As the crisis deepened, the State Department ordered the evacuation of American dependents. U.S.

military transports flew out more than nine thousand dependents over the next few weeks, while the Pentagon began plans to evacuate between forty thousand and sixty thousand other American citizens living in the country. In his 1983 memoir *Power and Principle*, Brzezinski asserted that the State Department's order had hastened the collapse of the shah's regime by undermining confidence in his continued rule. But with oil exports stopped due to antigovernment strikes and massive demonstrations in every major city, the U.S. evacuation of its embassy dependents in Tehran had no more impact on the fall of the shah than the U.S. evacuation of its embassy in Saigon had on the demise of the South Vietnamese regime three years earlier. It merely reflected reality. Zbigniew Brzezinski, *Power and Principle: Memoirs of the National Security Adviser, 1977–1981* (New York: Farrar, Straus and Giroux, 1983).

49. Norb Garrett e-mail to author, April 16, 2010.

50. Paul Henze memorandum to Zbigniew Brzezinski, "Thoughts on Iran," November 9, 1978.

51. William Sullivan letter to John Golden, December 24, 1978, p. 1.

52. Huyser, *Mission to Tehran*, p. 18.

53. William Sullivan message to Cyrus Vance, "USG Policy Guidance," 101820Z, January 1979, pp. 1–2.

54. Huyser, *Mission to Tehran*, pp. 78, 99.

55. Brzezinski, *Power and Principle*, 376–78; Huyser, *Mission to Tehran*, pp. 48–63.

56. Said Zanganeh, interview with author, June 20, 2007.

57. The shah's navy took delivery of thirteen Harpoon missiles before the revolution curtailed further deliveries from the United States. Two recent Arab-Israeli wars had vividly demonstrated to the shah the power of the missile age. In October 1967, armed with just two Russian Styx missiles, a small Egyptian patrol boat had sent the destroyer *Eilat*—a ship more than ten times its size and the flagship of the Israeli navy—along with forty-seven of her crew to the bottom of the Mediterranean. Six years later, the Israelis exacted revenge. Six French-built patrol boats, outfitted with smaller—but no less lethal—Israeli-made Gabriel missiles and advanced electronic countermeasure systems, foiled incoming missiles and decimated the Syrian and Egyptian naval forces in a series of dramatic engagements in the eastern Mediterranean. The following year, 1974, Iran purchased twelve similar French-built Combattante II missile patrol boats. All were to be armed with the even more advanced American-made Harpoon surface-to-surface missile. See Abraham Rabinovich, *The Boats of Cherbourg: The Secret Israeli Operation That Revolutionized Naval Warfare* (New York: Seaver Books, 1988).

58. Bruce Laingen message to Secretary of State, "Meeting with PM Bazargan" (121002Z), August 1979; also American Embassy message to Secretary of State, "Meeting with Deputy Prime Minister Yazdi," undated.

59. Bruce Laingen, Foreign Affairs Oral History Program, Association for Diplomatic Studies and Training, 1992–1993.

60. General George Crist, USMC (Ret.), interview with author, February 22, 2007.

61. Admiral James Lyons, USN (Ret.), interview with author, November 6, 2006.

62. NSC memorandum,"Iran/Afghanistan," March 20, 1980, p. 5.

Chapter 2 A New Grand Strategy

1. Hamilton Jordan memorandum for President Carter, January 22, 1980.

2. Jimmy Carter, *White House Diary* (New York: Farrar, Straus and Giroux, 2010), January 23, 1980, pp. 394–95.

3. *Current Documents*, U.S. Department of State, 1983, p. 157; Jimmy Carter, "The State of the Union," January 23, 1980, Carter, *Public Papers*, p. 197.

4. See also "America Likes Its New Foreign Policy—Or Does It?" *Economist*, February 23, 1980, p. 45.

5. "Carter Takes Charge," *Time*, February 4, 1980, p. 12. On the night of his State of the Union speech, see Jimmy Carter, Presidential Daily Diary, entry for January 23, 1980, www.jimmycarterlibrary.gov/documents/diary/1980/; William Odom comments, "Interview with Zbigniew Brzezinski with Madeleine Albright, Leslie Denend, William Odom," February 18, 1982, Miller Center, University of Virginia, Carter Presidential Project, p. 52.

6. President Jimmy Carter Presidential Directive/NSC-18, "U.S. National Strategy," August 24, 1977, pp. 4–5.

7. Following a crisis in the Congo in December 1963, McNamara expanded the responsibilities of the Tampa-based command to include planning and executing of operations in sub-Saharan Africa and the Middle East. The U.S. military divides the globe up into large geographical commands, called unified commands, with responsibility for all U.S. forces regardless of service within their area. Strike Command, however, did not have a specific geographical area, but was given the mission of "providing a general reserve of combat-ready forces to reinforce other unified or specified commands. After considerable debate, the secretary of defense decided to expand the mission of STRICOM. On December 1, 1963, the new command's boundaries included the Red Sea and the Persian Gulf. Jay E. Hines, "From Desert One to Southern Watch: The Evolution of U.S. Central Command," *Joint Force Quarterly*, Spring 2000, p. 43; Lawrence R. Benson and Jay Hines, *The United States Military in North Africa and Southwest Asia Since World War II* (CENTCOM History Office, January 1988), p. 30; General George Crist, "CENTCOM: The Bastard Command," unpublished, 1989, p. 5.

8. As with the debate over STRICOM two years earlier, the chairman and army and air force chiefs of staff advocated having STRICOM assume the mission for controlling operations in Africa and the Middle East, deploying the U.S.-based forces in the event of a contingency. The navy and marine corps dissented. They wanted command responsibilities to remain the same, with Atlantic Command responsible for Africa and CINCNELM the Middle East. Not surprisingly, both of these were navy-dominated commands.

9. In a handy compromise, the Pentagon divided the Middle East between two four-star American commands: the army-dominated European Command and the navy-controlled Pacific Command, with the former having responsibility for the Middle East landmass while the latter covered Pakistan, the Indian Ocean, and the Gulf of Oman. Crist, "Bastard Command," p. 7; letter from Dr. John Partin, U.S. Special Operations Command to General George Crist, "Rapid Deployment Forces and Joint Command Arrangements for the Near East," October 11, 1989, p. 1. Dr. Partin had served as the Readiness Command historian in the early 1980s.

10. On July 27, 1978, the National Security Council looked to address the growing crisis in Afghanistan by strengthening CENTO, of which Pakistan was a member. This included a $5 million investment by the United States in new communications equipment. The overthrow of the shah and the end of CENTO killed the idea before it came to fruition.

11. When pressed, Jones suggested to Brown that they could deploy for a short time two carriers or a marine brigade. Report by the J-5 to the Joint Chiefs of Staff, memorandum for the Assistant Secretary of Defense (ISA), "U.S. Military Response to Minor Contingencies in the Persian Gulf," October 5, 1978, pp. 1–10.

12. Harold Brown, interview with author, August 25, 2008.

13. Brzezinski memorandum to President Carter, December 2, 1978, NSC Weekly Report No. 81, Jimmy Carter Library, Zbigniew Brzezinski Collection, Weekly Reports, Box 41, Weekly Reports 71–81 Folder.

14. Lieutenant General William Odom, USA (Ret.), interview with author, August 28, 2007.

15. Tim Weiner, "Robert Komer, 78, Figure in Vietnam, Dies," *New York Times*, April 12, 2000. Komer agreed with Brzezinski: "The Carter administration was very slow to awaken to the realities of the strategic vacuum in the Gulf." Robert Komer Oral History, Office of the Secretary of Defense History Office, March 25, 1981, p. 102.

16. Joint Chiefs of Staff memorandum for the Secretary of Defense, "U.S. Strategy and Defense Policy for the Middle East and the Persian Gulf," May 10, 1979, p. 1, Appendix A, pp. 1, 6, 13, 22; also mentioned in an earlier internal memorandum of the Joint Chiefs, "Review of U.S. Strategy Related to the Middle East and Persian Gulf," January 31, 1979, pp. 1–3.

17. General David Jones memorandum for Secretary Harold Brown, "Potential Joint/Combined Exercises in the Persian Gulf," June 18, 1979, pp. 1–2; CINCEUR message to Joint Chiefs of Staff, "Potential Exercises in Persian Gulf" (0111507Z), September 1979, pp. 1–3; Joint Chiefs of Staff memorandum for the Secretary of Defense, "U.S. Military Presence in the Middle East/Persian Gulf Region," November 23, 1979, Annex B, pp. 1–5, Annex C, pp. 1–2.

18. Only the chief of naval operations, Admiral Thomas Hayward—more proactive about the Middle East than most of his navy brethren—recommended anything substantive. He proposed forming a new Fifth Fleet for the Middle East and suggested that a carrier battle group be maintained on a permanent basis off the Iranian coast. Brown pressed the military to begin planning for the possible deployment of U.S. combat troops to the Persian Gulf. Brzezinski, *Power and Principle*, pp. 182–90.

19. The Joint Chiefs opposed the deployment in 1978, viewing Saudi motivations with suspicion. The deployment of these aircraft became complicated when Spain denied them landing rights on their flight from the United States to Saudi Arabia.

20. Brown interview.

21. Joint Chiefs of Staff message, "U.S. Military Presence in the Middle East/Persian Gulf Region" (071725Z), July 1979, p. 2; General David Jones memorandum for Secretary Harold Brown, "Potential Joint/Combined Exercises in the Persian Gulf," June 18, 1979, pp. 1–2; CINCEUR message to Joint Chiefs of Staff, "Potential Exercises in Persian Gulf" (0111507Z), September 1979, pp. 1–3; Joint Chiefs of Staff memorandum for the Secretary of Defense, "U.S. Military Presence in the Middle East/Persian Gulf Region," November 23, 1979, Annex B, pp. 1–5, Annex C, pp. 1–2.

22. Joint Chiefs of Staff message, "Middle East Exercises," September 7, 1979, pp. 1–2; Harold Brown memorandum for General David Jones, "Potential Joint/Combined Exercises in the Persian Gulf/Northwest Indian Ocean," May 25, 1979, p. 2.

23. A May 29, 1979, CIA report influenced the thinking of the national security adviser. "The departure of the Shah was a windfall for the Soviets," the CIA report stated. "While they have not benefited directly, the new regime's inherent weakness and its withdrawal from a regional security role have created power vacuums both with Iran and the area generally that they would like to exploit." Brzezinski latched onto this assessment and rejected Vance's views. CIA Intelligence Assessment, "Changes in the Middle East: Moscow's Perceptions and Options," May 29, 1979, p. iii; Olav Njolstad, "Shifting Priorities: The Persian Gulf in U.S. Strategic Planning in the Carter Years," *Cold War History* 4:3 (2004), p. 30.

24. Harold Brown memorandum for President Jimmy Carter, "U.S. Military Presence in the Middle East/Persian Gulf," July 11, 1979, pp. 1–3.

25. On November 15, 1979, General Jones relayed to the secretary of defense a rough force list that would be available to the new rapid force, from which forces could be tailored for various contingencies. This included three carrier battle groups, one corps-sized marine amphibious force, eight air force squadrons, and three army divisions (4th, 101st, and 82nd), including the elite XVIII Airborne Corps from Fort Bragg, the 194th Armored Brigade, and two battalions of Army Rangers. All told, 170,000 men were on tap for potential deployment under the rapid deployment force.

26. The four airfields were Masirah, Seeb, Thumrait, and Kasab. "Logistics Concept in Support of the Rapid Deployment Joint Task Force (RDJTF)," United States Readiness Command, J-4, Rapid Deployment Joint Task Force J-4, April 15, 1981, pp. A5–A6.

27. Joint Chiefs of Staff memorandum for the Chief of Staff, U.S. Army, "U.S. Access to Facilities in the Middle East/Persian Gulf Region," March 14, 1980, p. 1; Robert Komer memorandum for the Secretary of Defense, "Rear-Staging Areas in Egypt," March 7, 1980, pp. 1–3.

28. David Isenberg, "The Rapid Deployment Force: The Few, the Futile, the Expendable," Policy Analysis No. 44, CATO Institute, November 8, 1984, p. 9, www.cato.org/pubs/pas/pa044.html, accessed September 20, 2002. The ambassador to Jordan, a career Foreign Service officer named Nicholas Veliotes, secretly concluded an arrangement with the Jordanian king to establish a Jordanian counterpart to the U.S. rapid deployment force that could augment the American effort in the event of a war with the Soviets. The two countries conducted low-level military exercises and Jordan offered use of its bases as marshaling areas for the rapid deployment force. Ambassador Nicholas Veliotes, Foreign Affairs Oral History Program, Association for Diplomatic Studies and Training, January 29, 1990.

29. Brzezinski memorandum to President Jimmy Carter, July 31, 1979.

30. Harold Brown memorandum to General David Jones, November 10, 1979. Brzezinski's military aide William Odom later wrote that Carter contemplated just ordering its creation and dictating the command structure, but in the end the president let the Pentagon sort it out.

31. Secretary of Defense memorandum to Joint Chiefs of Staff, October 22, 1979.

32. General Paul X. Kelley, interview with author, May 13, 2009.

33. Two names—Army General Paul Gorman and P. X. Kelley—had been forwarded to Jones as possible commanders of the rapid deployment force. Gorman was well respected in the Pentagon and had the strong backing of the army chief of staff, Edward Meyer. But W. Graham Clayton, Jr., former secretary of the navy and now Brown's deputy, knew Kelley and liked the marines, and when Gorman's name came before Clayton, he suggested Kelley as an alternative choice. American Embassy Kabul message to Secretary of State, "Meeting with Soviet Diplomat," June 25, 1979, p. 3.

34. Robert H. Barrow memorandum for the Chairman, Joint Chiefs of Staff, "Rapid Deployment Forces," December 14, 1979, pp. 1–2, Personal Papers of General Robert H. Barrow, U.S. Marine Corps Archives, Gray Research Center, Quantico, VA.

35. Bright Star was an annual exercise until 1985, when, due to its size and the number of forces involved, the decision was made to hold it every two years.

36. The main Soviet attacks would come from the Transcaucasus and Turkistan toward Tehran along four main axes with a supporting attack from Turkistan and Afghanistan along the eastern Iranian axis to seize Mashhad and Zahedan.

37. The first was submitted for the Joint Chiefs' review on July, 31, 1980; it was modified over the coming year and resubmitted on February 13, 1981.

38. RDJTF OPLAN 1001-81, February 15, 1981, Annex C, pp. C1–C13.

39. The first plan was labeled 1001 but quickly three variants (1002, 1003, 1004) emerged, based upon the conditions that precipitated the invasion and if it coincided with a general war in Europe. COMRDJTF message to Joint Chiefs of Staff, "OPLAN 1001-81" (170350Z), June 1981, p. 1; CINCRED message to Joint Chiefs of Staff, "COMRDJTF OPLAN 1001-81" (132306Z), February 1981, p. 2.

40. The forces allocated to the Rapid Deployment Joint Task Force in 1981 included:

> Army
>> Third U.S. Army
>> XVIII Airborne Corps
>> 82nd Airborne Division
>> 101st Air Assault Division
>> 24th Infantry Division
>> 6th Cavalry Brigade
>> Two Ranger Battalions
>> One Special Forces Group
> Air Force
>> 17 tactical fighter squadrons
>> 2 tactical reconnaissance squadrons
>> 19 tactical airlift squadrons
> Marine Corps
>> 1st Marine Expeditionary Force
>> 1st Marine Division
>> 1st Marine Wing
>> 1st Marine Forces Service Support Command
> Navy
>> 3 carrier battle groups
>> 1 surface action group
>> Naval Special Warfare Group ONE

41. Joint Chiefs of Staff message to CINCRED, "Planning Guidance for Countering a Soviet Invasion of Iran" (262336Z), September 1980; Joint Chiefs of Staff message, "Planning Guidance for Countering a Soviet Invasion of Iran" (DTG 262336Z), September 1980, pp. 2–3; Department of the Army memorandum, "U.S. Strategy to Counter a Major Soviet Attack into Iran," April 25, 1981, pp. 3–4. In the various documents produced by the U.S. military and intelligence agencies, the number of Soviet divisions invading Iran varied considerably, ranging from seventeen to thirty.

42. For the Reagan administration, nuclear or strategic planning against the Soviets was an early priority. Iran remained an adjunct of the larger concepts. The new Weinberger Pentagon quickly set out three options for nuclear weapons against the Soviets. The first was designed to deter further Soviet attacks and limited the use of such attacks against Soviet military forces in Iran and Afghanistan only. Should that deterrent fail, the United States would escalate to a "geographical escalation" that entailed vaporizing Soviet military bases in neighboring countries, chiefly Ethiopia and South Yemen. The last escalation would attack Soviet military installations and combat units in the Soviet Transcaucasus districts.

43. The Brookings Institution, "The U.S. Nuclear Weapons Cost Study Project," www.brookings.edu/projects/archive/nucweapons/madm.aspx, accessed April 4, 2007.

44. Joint Chiefs of Staff message to Chief of Naval Operations, "CINCPAC Rules of Engagement for Patrol of the Arabian Gulf" (030133Z), March 1981.

45. Presidential Directive/NSC-63, "Persian Gulf Security Framework," January 15, 1981.

CHAPTER 3 BARBED-WIRE BOB

1. Allan Millett and Jack Shulimson, eds., *Commandants of the Marine Corps* (Annapolis: Naval Institute Press, 2004), p. 453.

2. John Poindexter, interview with author, March 8, 2008.

3. Joint Staff memorandum for the Secretary of Defense, "Facility Requirements in Support of Southwest Asia Strategy," February 3, 1982.

4. Richard Allen memorandum for Caspar Weinberger, "Iran Hostages and Related Issues," 1981.

5. Richard Allen memorandum on draft National Security Decision Directive toward Iran, "National Security Council Meeting," September 29, 1981, Weinberger Papers, Library of Congress, Box I:638, Folder Iran 2.

6. Caspar Weinberger, *In the Arena: A Memoir of the 20th Century* (Washington, D.C.: Regnery, 2001), pp. 287–88.

7. Caspar Weinberger, interviews with author, December 15, 1994, May 1, 1996, and September 2000.

8. General Volney Warner letter to Caspar Weinberger, January 20, 1980, Appendix B, Warner Oral History, Volney Warner Papers, U.S. Army Military History Institute, Carlisle, PA. Warner also advocated that Readiness Command be given responsibility for deploying forces to operations worldwide, using its subordinate, the rapid deployment force, as its headquarters for the Middle East.

9. Caspar Weinberger interview.

10. Lieutenant General Robert Kingston letter to Caspar Weinberger, November 2, 1982; Lieutenant Colonel Charles Seifert, USAF, memorandum to Weinberger, November 5, 1982, Weinberger Papers, Box I:713, Folder 1982 U.S. Commander Rapid Deployment Force.

11. Ronald Reagan memorandum to Caspar Weinberger, April 29, 1981; Richard Allen memorandum to Caspar Weinberger, "Middle East Command Arrangements," August 13, 1981; Ronald Reagan memorandum to Caspar Weinberger, May 17, 1982, Weinberger Papers, Box I:713, Folder U.S. Commander RDJTF 2.

12. Senator Stevens objected to the elimination of the global mission for the rapid deployment force and did not like a command solely dedicated to the Middle East. His objections opened the door for the navy to propose that the rapid deployment force should be, rather than a unified command, a "global strike force," which would not substantially alter its current mission.

13. In a sop to the navy, with the exception of the small flotilla operating in the Persian Gulf, the chiefs allowed the navy to be excluded from the new Middle East command. The Indian Ocean and the ships of the carrier battle groups operating there to support CENTCOM were excluded and remained under the control of the Pacific Fleet in Honolulu. They would be "in support" of CENTCOM, a nebulous concept that allowed the navy to remain independent of the new command's control but still nominally obligated to support its operations. This would cause no end of problems over the coming years. The navy formed a new combined task force, CTF-70, to support CENTCOM, but it operated under the operational control of the commander of the Pacific Fleet.

14. General Volney Warner letter to President Ronald Reagan, July 8, 1981, Appendix F, Warner Oral History.

15. General Volney Warner, USA (Ret.), interview with author, April 7, 2008.

16. The two men even discussed the possibility of a secret alliance between archenemies Israel and Syria to carve up Lebanon.

17. Ronald Reagan memorandum to Caspar Weinberger, April 29, 1981; Richard Allen memorandum to Caspar Weinberger, "Middle East Command Arrangements," August 13, 1981, Weinberger Papers, Box I:713, Folder U.S. Commander RDJTF 2.

18. Relations between the two countries were also already strained over the Israeli government's refusal to halt Jewish settlements on the Palestinian West Bank, which President Carter believed Prime Minister Menachem Begin had agreed to with the Camp David Accords between Israel and Egypt. While the Joint Chiefs of Staff did not see much utility in using Israel to defend the Persian Gulf, they did advocate using Israel to help maintain control over the western Mediterranean against Soviet submarines.

19. Ronald Reagan memorandum to Caspar Weinberger, May 17, 1982; Caspar Weinberger memorandum to Ronald Reagan, "Unified Command for Southwest Asia," June 23, 1982; Francis West, Jr., memorandum to Caspar Weinberger, "New Command for Southwest Asia," May 20, 1982, Weinberger Papers, Box I:713, Folder U.S. Commander RDJTF 2.

20. Henry Cunningham, "Delta Pioneer Dies," *Fayetteville Observer*, March 22, 2007.

21. Richard Shultz, Jr., *The Secret War Against Hanoi: Kennedy and Johnson's Use of Spies, Saboteurs, and Covert Warriors in North Vietnam* (New York: HarperCollins, 1999), p. 89.

22. Kingston had actually hoped to be appointed as the next deputy director of the CIA, which went instead to a civilian, John McMahon.

23. Major Caesar J. Civitella, USA (Ret.), interview with author, March 5, 2010.

24. William Williams and William Handy, interview with author at the reunion for the thirtieth anniversary of the Rapid Deployment Joint Task Force, March 4, 2010, Tampa, Florida.

25. CINCCENT message to Joint Chiefs of Staff, "Plans to Counter a Soviet Invasion of Iran" (021530), August 1983.

26. While keeping the original plans for a passive introduction of U.S. forces, CENTCOM built two slightly different new plans based upon the degree of basing and the forces prestaged for the invasion, available in nearby countries, designed to defeat Iranian forces first as well as the Red Army. For the first time, the planning reflected the challenges of countering the Soviets in a country fundamentally hostile to the United States. Should U.S. diplomacy fail to secure the Iranians' support, U.S. forces needed to be positioned in advance, "postured to enter Iran to counter a Soviet invasion, [as] interdicting the Soviet advance will be much more difficult." The new plans were labeled 1008 and 1009.

27. Joint Chiefs of Staff, "Study to Improve U.S. Special Operations Capability," March 18, 1981, pp. 1–20.

28. Kingston also wanted permission to use his special forces to strike deep into the Soviet Caucasus, even to try working with Muslim opponents of Moscow to foment a guerrilla movement within the Soviet Union. But that was a step too far for the White House, and the permission for other than rudimentary planning never came from the defense secretary.

29. Jeffrey Richelson, *The U.S. Intelligence Community* (New York: Ballinger, 1989), pp. 61–62; Steven Emerson, *Secret Warriors: Inside the Covert Military Operations of the Reagan Era* (New York: Putnam, 1988); Lieutenant General Philip Gast, USAF, J-3, memorandum for the Director, Defense Intelligence Agency, "Intelligence Capability," December 10, 1980, p. 1; "United States Army Intelligence Support Activity, 1987 Historical Report," U.S. Army Intelligence Support Activity, October 23, 1987, pp. 7–9; Deputy Secretary of Defense Frank Carlucci memorandum to Deputy Undersecretary for Policy, May 26, 1982; "Charter of U.S. Army Intelligence Support Activity," 1983; "Brief History of the Unit," 1986; National Security Archive, www.gwu.edu/~nsarchiv/NSAEBB/NSAEBB46, accessed July 4, 2007; www.specwarnet.net/americas/isa.htm.

30. Odom interview.

31. ISA was augmented by the Air Force Special Activities Center at Fort Belvoir and coordinated activities with the U.S. Navy's Office of Naval Intelligence, which conducted its own separate recruitment effort largely directed at Iranian naval officers.

32. Howard Hart, interview with author, June 26, 2007.

33. Odom interview.

34. Timothy Naftali, *Blind Spot: The Secret History of American Counterterrorism* (New York: Basic Books, 2005), p. 124.

CHAPTER 4 A DEN OF SPIES

1. Joseph Persico, *Casey: The Lives and Secrets of William J. Casey, from the OSS to the CIA* (New York: Viking, 1990), p. 71.

2. Ibid., p. 66.

3. Ibid., p. 83.

4. *Hearings on the Nomination of Robert Gates to Be Director of Central Intelligence*, volume 1, U.S. Senate, Select Committee on Intelligence, 102nd Congress, 1st Session, September 16–20, 1991, p. 475.

5. John Prados, *Safe for Democracy: The Secret Wars of the CIA* (Chicago: Ivan R. Dee, 2006), p. 500; Persico, *Casey*, p. 301.

6. It stated that events in Iran were no longer as chaotic as viewed in 1985, and as Fuller noted in congressional testimony, "Some of our concerns had not been borne out." *Hearings on the Nomination of Robert Gates to Be Director of Central Intelligence*, Executive Report 102-19, U.S. Senate, Select Committee on Intelligence, 102nd Congress, 1st Session, October 19, 1991, pp. 46–48.

7. Jack Devine, interview with author, March 25, 2008.

8. Richard Allen memorandum, "National Security Council Meeting, Draft NSDD on Iran," September 29, 1981.

9. Robert McFarlane, interview with author, March 23, 2008.

10. "Statement of the Honorable William Casey," November 21, 1986, in *Hearings on the Nomination of Robert Gates to Be Director of Central Intelligence*, volume 1, pp. 106–7.

11. Philip Giraldi, interview with author, June 15, 2010.

12. Tim Weiner, *Legacy of Ashes: The History of the CIA* (New York: Doubleday, 2007), pp. 425–26; Tim Weiner, telephone interview with author, May 29, 2007; "U.S. Spies' Statements on CIA Activities," Tehran Television Service in Persian, November 3, 1989, Foreign Broadcast Information Service (FBIS), November 7, 1989.

13. Giraldi interview.

14. Nazhatoon Riahi, interview with author, November 20, 2008.

15. Said Zanganeh, interview with author, November 18, 2007.

16. "U.S. Blunder Over Spies," Iranian News Agency, April 22, 1989, FBIS, April 24, 1989, p. 24; "Information Minister Names CIA Spies," Iranian News Agency, April 26, 1989, FBIS, April 27, 1989, pp. 43–50; "Text of News Conference," Tehran Television Service in Persian, April 26, 1989, FBIS, April 27, 1989; Zanganeh interview.

17. This included the captain of the Iranian flagship, the destroyer *Babr*.

18. Zanganeh interview.

19. Text of news conference by Minister of Intelligence and Security Hojjat ol-Eslam Reyshahri, April 26, 1989, FBIS, April 27, 1989, pp. 44–50.

20. Reza Kahlili, interview with author, July 10, 2010; Muhammad Sahimi, "Iran's Crumbling Judiciary," August 15, 2009, www.pbs.org/wgbh/pages/frontline/tehranbureau/2009/08/irans-crumbling-judiciary.html, accessed January 29, 2011.

21. "Tehran TV Details Covert Operations of Spies, Top Secret Program," episode titled "Covert Operations," Tehran Television Service, May 4, 1989, FBIS, May 8, 1989.

22. Kahlili interview.

23. "CIA Declassifies Oldest Documents in U.S. Government Collection," April 11, 2011, www.foia.cia.gov, accessed May 12, 2011.

24. Giraldi interview; Robert Wallace and H. Keith Melton, *Spycraft: The Secret History of the CIA's Spytechs from Communism to Al-Qaeda* (New York: Dutton, 2008), electronic version.

25. "More on Sermon on Spies," Tehran Domestic Service in Persian, April 21, 1989, FBIS, NES-89-076; Kahlili interview.

26. Kahlili interview.

27. CIA message to U.S. Embassy Tehran (102330Z), August 1979.

28. As early as August 1979, the CIA took interest in efforts by former Iranian military officers to organize opposition to the clerics in Tehran, with one of the first gatherings occurring in a London hotel room led by former Iranian air force general Hassan Toufanian. The Iranian government learned of the meeting after the embassy takeover, when students painstakingly pieced together the strips of the shredded message describing Toufanian's gathering. CIA message to U.S. Embassy Tehran (102330Z), August 1979.

29. Kenneth Timmerman, *Countdown to Crisis: The Coming Nuclear Showdown with Iran* (New York: Crown Forum, 2005), p. 215.

30. Prados, *Safe for Democracy*, p. 500; Richelson, *U.S. Intelligence Community*, pp. 355–56.

31. The 2001 American invasion of Afghanistan was a perfect example of this symbiotic relationship. CIA paramilitary operatives went in first, building upon their twenty-year ties with Afghan tribes, followed a few weeks later by soldiers from the 5th Special Forces Group, backed by the air force's own special operations forces and airpower. These special operations forces were then layering over the CIA effort, and the U.S. military succeeded in overthrowing al-Qaeda and its Taliban hosts weeks before the generals in the Pentagon thought possible. The Reagan administration came to Washington determined to strengthen America's military, including the elite special operations forces (SOF). The army's special forces—never popular with the conventional-minded armor and infantry generals—had atrophied after Vietnam. Their numbers were cut in half, their units ignominiously relegated to the national guard and reserves, where officers could receive the coveted "Special Forces" tab on their uniform not by passing a demanding screening process but by simply taking a correspondence course.

    After the failed Iranian rescue mission in 1980 and new civilian leadership, both Congress and the Defense Department forced the army as well as the navy and air force to renew these forgotten but choice men. The Joint Chiefs tried to placate the SOF supporters by forming the Joint Special Operations Agency within the Joint Staff. Intended to coordinate special ops training and operations across the military, it was largely inconsequential and purposely made so. Congress eventually forced the issue in 1987 with the establishment of Special Forces Command, which effectively took away training and funding for SOF from these three services. The marine corps opted not to participate in Special Operations Command until Secretary of Defense Donald Rumsfeld directed it in 2005. Department of Defense, Defense Resources Board–Directed Special Operations Review, "Special Operations Forces (SOF): Roles, Missions, and Organization," June 3, 1982.

32. This was a similar plan to what was employed in 2001 in Afghanistan. While that worked well, the CIA's record of success in these paramilitary operations has been mixed. "It is extraordinarily hard to foster antigovernment insurgencies in a totalitarian state," a retired CIA operations officer noted. "You need to develop a network of indigenous supporters, and trying to do that from outside a denied country using CIA resources or exiles rarely works." Under Casey in the 1980s, the CIA succeeded in fostering the anti-Sandinista rebels in Nicaragua and built a major resistance movement against the Soviets in Afghanistan. But going back to the 1950s, the CIA failed to organize any credible resistance to Soviet occupation in Ukraine and the Baltic states. The agency's most notable failure was in North Vietnam, where every CIA-led team of South Vietnamese was killed or captured, likely compromised by South Vietnamese double agents working for the communists.

33. "Spy Outlines Recruitment, Training, U.S. Plans," *Tehran Times* in English, September 14, 1989, FBIS, September 21, 1989.

34. Control of the critical location was very important to CENTCOM, which assigned one entire special forces battalion to the mission.

35. "CIA Spy Comments Further on Activities," Tehran Television Service, November 6, 1989, FBIS, NES-89-215, November 8, 1989, p. 57.

36. Hart interview.

37. Sazegara interview.

38. "Adventures with the CIA in Turkey: Interview with Philip Giraldi," Balkanalysis.com, July 30, 2006, www .balkanalysis.com/blog/2006/07/30/adventures-with-the-cia-in-turkey-interview-with-philip-giraldi, accessed July 5, 2007.

39. "CIA Spies," News Conference with Minister of Intelligence and Security Hojjat ol-Eslam Reyshahri, Tehran Television Service, April 26, 1989, FBIS, NES-89-080, April 27, 1989.

40. Kahlili interview.

CHAPTER 5 A FIG LEAF OF NEUTRALITY

1. Kevin Woods, Michael Pease, Mark Stout, Williamson Murray, and James Lacey, *Iraqi Perspectives Project: A View of Operation Iraqi Freedom from Saddam Hussein's Senior Leadership*, Department of Defense, Joint Forces Command, 2006, p. 7.

2. Saddam Hussein grew alarmed at reports of young Shia officers sabotaging aircraft and tanks in support of the Iranian Revolution. "Interview with Lieutenant General Raad Hamdani," in Kevin Woods, Williamson Murray, and Thomas Holaday, *Saddam's War: An Iraqi Military Perspective of the Iran-Iraq War*, McNair Paper 70 (Washington, D.C.: National Defense University, March 2009), p. 28.

3. Joint Staff, Contingency Planning Group, "Opportunities for U.S. Policy in the Wake of the Iranian Crisis," January 1980, p. 18.

4. Comments by George Cave, "Toward an International History of the Iran-Iraq War, 1980–1988: A Critical Oral History Workshop," Woodrow Wilson International Center for Scholars, Cold War International History Project, July 19, 2004; Cave interview.

5. Mohsen Sazegara, "Engaging Iran: Lessons from the Past," Washington Institute for Near East Policy, Policy Watch Focus 93, May 2009, p. 6.

6. Gary Sick e-mail to author, March 22, 2010.

7. Zbigniew Brzezinski memorandum for President Jimmy Carter, "NSC Weekly Report #122," December 21, 1979.

8. Rumors still persisted that Washington had secretly encouraged the Iraqi attack. In 1981 the new secretary of state, Alexander Haig, reported to President Ronald Reagan in a memo in April 1981 that Saudi foreign minister Crown Prince Fahd had confirmed that Carter had relayed a message through Fahd to Saddam Hussein giving the "green light to launch the war against Iran." While it's hard to completely discount Fahd's statement, it runs counter to the substantial catalog of declassified, once sensitive documents regarding Carter's views of the Iran-Iraq War. In hindsight, Haig's motive in the memo was self-conceit, intended to impress Reagan following his first trip as secretary of state to the Middle East. On the same trip, Haig also proclaimed that he had reached an agreement with Israel and the pro-Western Arabs on forging a common front to counter the Soviet Union. "It didn't happen," said Nicholas Veliotes, then assistant secretary of state for Near Eastern and South Asian Affairs. "So I cast great doubts on almost everything in this memo." Comments by Nicholas Veliotes, "Toward an International History of the Iran-Iraq War, 1980–1988: A Critical Oral History Workshop," Woodrow Wilson International Center for Scholars, Cold War International History Project, July 19, 2004.

9. Ward, *Immortal*, p. 242.

10. Ibid., pp. 253–54.

11. Sazegara interview.

12. Ward, *Immortal*, p. 226.

13. Ibid., p. 256.

14. Bing West memorandum to Caspar Weinberger, "Opening to Iraq," February 3, 1982, Weinberger Papers, Box I:683, Folder Iraq.

15. U.S. Interests Section Baghdad message to Secretary of State, "Meeting with Tariq Aziz" (231255Y), May 1981.

16. Lieutenant Colonel R. L. Hatchett memorandum for Director for Plans and Policy, Joint Staff, "Senior Interagency Group Meeting on Iran-Iraq," July 25, 1982.

17. L. Paul Bremer memorandum, "Discussion Paper for SIG Meeting, Interagency Group No. 2," July 23, 1982.

18. Sworn Statement by Howard Teicher, U.S. District Court, Southern District of Florida, case number 93-241-CRHIGHSMITH, January 31, 1995; Richard Murphy message to Donald Rumsfeld, "Follow-up Steps on Iraq-Iran" (120318Z), January 1984.

19. Philip Wilcox, Foreign Affairs Oral History Program, Association for Diplomatic Studies and Training, interviewed by Stuart Kennedy, April 27, 1988.

20. Robert Oakley, interview with author, December 12, 1994; William Taft IV, interview with author, August 16, 1996.

21. Richard Armitage, interviews with author, December 14, 1994, February 15, 2007, and March 4, 2008.

22. Zbigniew Brzezinski memorandum for President Jimmy Carter, "NSC Weekly Report #157," October 10, 1980.

23. In 1985, two KC-10 tankers were added to the three KC-135s, bringing a total of five air refuelers supporting the AWACS mission.

24. Brigadier General Wayne Schramm, USAF (Ret.), interview with author, May 26, 1995; Memorandum for General George Crist, "ELF-One Transition," November 1988. Also Colonel George Williams, USAF (Ret.), interview with author, December 13, 1994. The AWACS initially were under European Command, which in 1980 had responsibility for Saudi Arabia. It continued to be referred to by its initial name, European Liaison Force-One even after EUCOM relinquished control of the operation to CENTCOM. Six crews were on hand for the four AWACS, with each crew flying a mission every two days to provide continuous surveillance.

25. "ELF-One Fact Sheet," United States Air Force, February 1983, Operational Archives, Naval Historical Center, Washington, D.C., JTF/MEF records, Series 3, Box 10, Folder 5, ELF Exchange, p. 2.

26. Secretary of State message to U.S. Interests Section Baghdad, "De-Designation of Iraq as Supporter of International Terrorism" (272235Z), February 1982.

27. Kenneth Pollack, *The Persian Puzzle: The Conflict between Iran and America* (New York: Random House, 2004), p. 207.

28. Secretary of State message to U.S. Interests Section Baghdad, "U.S. Credit Possibilities with Iraq: Follow-up to February 14, 1983, Secretary Hamadi Meeting" (161515Z), March 1983; Secretary of State memorandum to Donald Gregg, "Eximbank Financing for Iraqi Export Pipeline," June 12, 1984.

29. Donald Rumsfeld message, "Rumsfeld One-on-One Meeting with Iraq Deputy Prime Minister and Foreign Minister Tariq Aziz" (211795Z), December 1983.

30. American Embassy London message to Secretary of State, "Rumsfeld Mission: December 20 Meeting with Iraqi President Saddam Hussein" (21165Z), December 1983.

31. Bruce Jentleson, *With Friends Like These: Reagan, Bush, and Saddam, 1982–1990* (New York: Norton, 1994), p. 45.

32. Robert McFarlane memorandum, "Iraqi Military Needs," May 7, 1984; Colonel John Stanford memorandum to Robert McFarlane, "Actions Taken in Response to Interagency Recommendations on Iraqi Military Needs," June 15, 1984; Walter Patrick Lang, interview with author, April 5, 2010.

33. Jordan became one of the prime conduits for military hardware heading to Iraq. In one deal alone, thirty-two thousand South Korean artillery shells arrived in Iraq by way of the Jordanian port of al-Aqabah. From 1984 to 1985, huge shipments of Soviet-built armored personnel carriers and French armored cars arrived destined for Iraq. A multilane highway was constructed from al-Aqabah to western Iraq, and eight thousand trucks traveled back and forth delivering their deadly cargo for the Iraqi war machine. King Hussein quietly allowed Iraqi aircraft to base out of western Jordan.

34. Bing West memorandum for the Secretary of Defense, "Sale of Helicopters to Iraq," January 1983; David Schneider and Jonathan Howe memorandum for Secretary George Shultz, "Easing Restrictions on Exports to Iraq," January 30, 1984.

35. Kenneth Timmerman, "Fanning the Flames: Guns, Greed and Geopolitics in the Gulf War," *Iran Brief*, 1988, pp. 1–10, www.iran.org/tib/krt/fanning_ch7.htm, accessed November 16, 2007.

36. Secretary of State message to American Embassy Amman, "Kittani Call on Under Secretary Eagleburger" (180139Z), March 1984.

37. Secretary of State message to American Embassy Tel Aviv, "Follow-up Steps on Iraq-Iran" (140318Z), January 1984, p. 2; Richard Murphy, interview with author, December 21, 1994; Richard Fairbanks, interviewed by Charles Kennedy, Foreign Affairs Oral History Program, Association for Diplomatic Studies and Training, April 19, 1989; John Stempel, interviewed by Kristin Hamblin Kennedy, Foreign Affairs Oral History Program, Association for Diplomatic Studies and Training, 1993.

38. "Iraqi Officer Cited on Cooperation with CIA in War with Iran," *Tehran Times*, March 11, 2002.

39. Ibid.

40. W. Patrick Lang, "The Land Between the Rivers," unpublished, April 2006, p. 21. Written as a supplement to his autobiographical file at the Virginia Military Institute archives.

41. Michael Dobbs, "U.S. Had Key Roll in Iraq Buildup," *Washington Post*, December 30, 2002, p. A1.

42. Comments by George Cave, William Eagleton, Nicholas Veliotes, and Steven Ward, "Toward an International History of the Iran-Iraq War, 1980–1988: A Critical Oral History Workshop," Woodrow Wilson International Center for Scholars, Cold War International History Project, pp. 263–65. At the height of the fighting, on March 23 the CIA issued a speculative report presenting the "worst-case scenario" on the prospects of an Iranian victory: "Iran is determined to replace Saddam's secular Baathist government with a radical fundamentalist Shia regime controlled by Tehran." With three-quarters of the Iraqi army being Shia, there was a distinct possibility of the army disintegrating—a prophetic prediction when one looks at the Iraqi army during the U.S. invasion of 2003. "An Iranian victory could lead fairly rapidly to Iranian hegemony over the entire Gulf—Kuwait and Bahrain would be especially vulnerable," the CIA report concluded. It went on for eight pages describing dire possibilities if the Iranians triumphed: massive disruptions in world oil supplies; spillover fighting in northern Kuwait; Saddam Hussein's retaliating by lifting all restraints, including hitting major Iranian cities with chemical weapons; massive airlift of new equipment from the Soviets to shore up their client, which would lead to a closer bond between Baghdad and Moscow. CIA, "Iran-Iraq: Consequences of an Iranian Breakthrough at Al Basra," March 23, 1984.

43. Thomas Twetten, interviews with author, June 20 and 28, 2007.

CHAPTER 6 SHARON'S GRAND DESIGN

1. John Boykin, *Cursed Is the Peacemaker: The American Diplomat versus the Israeli General, Beirut 1982* (Belmont, CA: Applegate Press, 2002), p. 43.

2. Peter Slevin and Mike Allen, "Bush: Sharon a Man of Peace," *Washington Post*, April 19, 2002, p. A1.

3. Veliotes memorandum to Bremer, "Telcon with Habib 10 July," July 10, 1982, cited in Boykin, *Cursed Is the Peacemaker*, p. 365; Ze'ev Schiff and Ehud Ya'ari, *Israel's Lebanon War* (New York: Simon and Schuster, 1984), pp. 31–108.

4. American intelligence first detected the Israeli buildup in December 1981, six months before Israel actually launched the attack. Noel Koch memorandum to Deputy Secretary of Defense, "Lebanon," February 1, 1982, Weinberger Papers, Box I:687, Folder 1982 Lebanon; Caspar Weinberger handwritten notes from meeting, September 9, 1981, Weinberger Papers; Bing West memorandum to Caspar Weinberger, "Invasion of Lebanon Next Moves," June 15, 1982.

5. L. Paul Bremer memorandum for William Clark, "Status Report on Lebanon Contingency Planning," February 12, 1982.

6. See "The Green Light," in *Foreign Policy* 50 (Spring 1983).

7. Veliotes interview, Association for Diplomatic Studies and Training.

8. Weinberger memorandum for the President, "POTUS Weekly Report," June 11, 1982.

9. Cited in Boykin, *Cursed Is the Peacemaker*, p. 65.

10. President Reagan letter to Menachem Begin, June 9, 1982.

11. Boykin, *Cursed Is the Peacemaker*, pp. 69–70.

12. Veliotes interview, Association for Diplomatic Studies and Training; Nathaniel Howell, interview with author, December 2, 1994. After the president appointed Philip Habib as his envoy to negotiate a cease-fire, Haig called him in during a meeting while in Paris and gave him instructions that contradicted the president's own desire to try to stop the war.

13. Department of State memorandum for William Clark, "Lebanon: Elements of a U.S. Strategy," June 5, 1982.

14. Ronald Reagan, diary entry for June 25, 1982, in Douglas Brinkley, ed., *The Reagan Diaries* (New York: HarperCollins, 2007), p. 91.

15. Reagan note, undated, Weinberger Papers. Reagan followed it up with an angry phone call on August 12. The Israeli prime minister finally bent to the American will. He ordered a cessation of artillery fire, and he called Reagan back pleading for their continued friendship. *Reagan Diaries*, entry for August 12, 1982, p. 98.

16. Cited in Boykin, *Cursed Is the Peacemaker*, p. 74.

17. The CIA initially suspected his motivation had been revenge for the killing of Tony Frangieh. Interview with retired CIA officer in 2009.

18. Comments by Colonel Robert Johnston and Colonel Mead, "Lebanon Briefing," December 1, 1982, Beirut Oral History Transcripts, U.S. Marine Corps Archives, Gray Research Center, Box 2, p. 31.

19. Report of the Commission of Inquiry into the Events at the Refugee Camps in Beirut, February 8, 1983, Israel Ministry of Foreign Affairs, www.mfa.gov.il, accessed February 12, 2011.

20. Rear Admiral Jonathan Howe, "Statement before the House Armed Services Committee," November 2, 1983, U.S. House of Representatives, Committee on Armed Services, 98th Congress, 1st Session; "Review of Adequacy of Security Arrangements for Marines in Lebanon and Plans for Improving That Security," House Armed Services Committee, Report No. 98-58, 1985, p. 96.

21. On October 19, 1982, President Gemayel traveled to Washington. The United States agreed to pay for thirty-five Israeli M-48 tanks for the Lebanese army, the first of some two hundred armored vehicles to be provided to that army.

22. Retired CIA officer e-mail to author, October 13, 2009.

23. Point paper, Headquarters Marine Corps, Deputy Chief of Staff, Plans, Policy, and Operations, "Attack on Marine Positions," August 10, 1983, U.S. Marine Corps Archives, Gray Research Center, Lebanon Papers, Disc 23.

24. David Martin and John Walcott, *Best Laid Plans: The Inside Story of America's War Against Terrorism* (New York: Harper and Row Publishers, 1988), p. 115.

25. "Agreement between the Government of Lebanon and the Government of Israel," May 17, 1983; Major General Andrew Cooley, USA, interviewed by Walter Poole, April 10, 1984.

26. Caspar Weinberger memorandum to William Clark, "Lebanon Initiative," July 28, 1983.

27. Colonel Timothy Geraghty, interviewed by Benis Frank, May 28, 1983, Beirut Oral History Transcripts, U.S. Marine Corps Archives, Gray Research Center, Box 2, pp. 5–6.

28. Timothy Geraghty e-mail to author, March 3, 2011.

29. Timothy Geraghty, *Peacekeepers at War: Beirut 1983—The Marine Commander Tells His Story* (Washington, D.C.: Potomac Press, 2009), p. 40; Colonel Jerry Walsh, USMC (Ret.), interview with author, June 18, 2010.

30. Colonel Timothy Geraghty, interviewed by Benis Frank, November 21, 1983, Beirut Oral History Transcripts, Marine Corps Archives, GRC, Box 2, pp. 6–7.

31. *Authorization Under the War Powers Resolution—Lebanon: Hearing and Markup before the Committee on Foreign Affairs*, U.S. House of Representatives, 98th Congress, 1st Session, 1983, pp. 2–7.

32. In May 1983 European Command looked to expand the marines' presence along the Sidon highway from Beirut to the Awali River. It was dependent upon the Israeli withdrawal, which did not happen until September. Lieutenant

Colonel William Solomon, "Beirut Lessons Learned," undated [1983], U.S. Marine Corps Archives, Gray Research Center, Box 1, Folder Chronology of Events.

33. Department of the Army, DAMO-SSM, "Lebanon Update," August 19, 1983; Walter Poole, "The Joint Chiefs of Staff and U.S. Involvement in Lebanon: July 1982–February 1984," Joint Secretariat, Joint Chiefs of Staff, May 1988.

34. Poole, "The Joint Chiefs of Staff and U.S. Involvement in Lebanon," p. 27.

35. Caspar Weinberger, *Fighting for Peace: Seven Critical Years in the Pentagon* (New York: Warner, 1990), p. 360.

36. Carl Stiner, interview with author, April 2009; McFarlane interview.

37. COMSIXTHFLEET message to CINCUSNAVEUR, "Deployment of FASTAB to Beirut" (0816Z), August 1983, GRC, Lebanon Papers, Disc 23.

38. U.S. Marine Corps, "Mass Casualty Report on Beirut, Lebanon," September 8, 1983, GRC, Lebanon Papers, Disc 26.

39. CTF Six One message to Commander, Sixth Fleet, "Joint Daily Intelligence Summary 095 for the Period 031800Z-041759Z" (05000Z), September 1983; CTF Six Two message to CTF Six One, "Update" (04117Z), September 1983, U.S. Marine Corps Archives, Gray Research Center, Lebanon Papers, Disc 26.

40. Tom Clancy, Carl Stiner, and Tony Koltz, *Shadow Warriors: Inside the Special Forces* (New York: Putnam's Sons, 2002), p. 238.

41. Martin and Walcott, *Best Laid Plans*, p. 121.

42. Weinberger Diaries, entry for September 11, 1983, Weinberger Papers.

43. Ronald Reagan memorandum addendum to NSDD, "On Lebanon of September 10," September 11, 1983, Weinberger Papers, Box I:729, Folder Lebanon 7.

44. CTF Six One message to COMSIXTHFLEET, "Employment of ANGLICO Team in Direct Support of the Lebanese Armed Forces" (131630Z), September 1983, GRC, Lebanon Papers, Disc 28; COMSIXTHFLEET message to CTF Six Zero, "Close Air Support for Defense of Suq al-Gharb" (191139Z), September 1983; CTF Six One message to COMSIXTHFLEET, "Concept of Operations in Support of Suq al-Gharb" (160517Z), September 1983, U.S. Marine Corps Archives, Gray Research Center, Lebanon Papers, Disc 29.

45. Geraghty, *Peacekeepers at War*, p. 65.

46. Ibid., pp. 62–63.

47. Geraghty interview with Frank, November 21, 1983, pp. 11–12. The United States had responded three days earlier. On September 16, several rounds from a Druze artillery battery landed near the U.S. embassy. The American naval gunfire responded by sending sixty 5-inch shells in the general direction of batteries in the Chouf Mountains. The next day, Stiner, who was not in the chain of command, canceled the order by calling in the rickety Lebanese air force instead of the 24th Marine Expeditionary Unit. Handwritten notes, "19 September After Action Report," September 19, 1983, U.S. Marine Corps Archives, Gray Research Center, Disc 29; CINCUSNAVEUR message, "Geopolitical Intelligence Highlights" (191820Z), September 1983; Summary and Conclusions, "Review of Adequacy of Security Arrangements," House Armed Services Committee; Clyde Mark, "Marine Security in Beirut: A Comparison of the House Armed Services Committee and the Long Commission Reports," Congressional Research Service, January 1984, p. 4.

Chapter 7 A Spectacular Action

1. Robert Baer, *The Devil We Know* (New York: Three Rivers, 2008), pp. 53–63; Ronen Bergman, *The Secret War with Iran: The 30-Year Clandestine Struggle Against the World's Most Dangerous Terrorist Power* (New York: Free Press, 2007), p. 59; David Hirst, *Beware of Small States: Lebanon, Battleground of the Middle East* (New York: Nation Books, 2010), p. 185.

2. Martin and Walcott, *Best Laid Plans*, p. 100.

3. Sayeed Ali is a pseudonym for a former Hezbollah fighter. The author interviewed him in a city in the southern United States in March 2010.

4. Naim Qassem, translated by Dalia Khalil, *Hizbullah: The Story from Within* (Beirut: Saqi, 2010), p. 58.

5. Geraghty, *Peacekeepers at War*, p. 9.

6. Ammar al-Musawi, head of international relations for Hezbollah, and Hussein Haidar, head of diplomatic and political contacts for Hezbollah, interviews with author, February 19, 2010, Beirut, Lebanon; also Hirst, *Beware of Small States*, p. 183.

7. Laingen interview, Association for Diplomatic Studies and Training.

8. Augustus Richard Norton, *Hezbollah* (Princeton: Princeton University Press, 2007), p. 33.

9. Sayeed Ali interview.

10. Baer, *The Devil We Know*, pp. 59–63.

11. Martin Kramer, "Hizbullah in Lebanon," *The Oxford Encyclopedia of the Modern Islamic World*, volume 2 (New York and Oxford: Oxford University Press, 1995), pp. 130–33.

12. Hani Abdallah, political and media adviser, Office of Religious Authority, Sayed Muhammad Hussein Fadlallah, interview with author, February 19, 2010, Beirut, Lebanon.

13. Fadlallah embraced modernity. Change, including new technology, is a part of God's design, he preached. He supported women's rights, considering women equal to men. He was not in a hurry to establish an Islamic state, believing it would evolve naturally over time. He maintained a large following among youth from all religious

sects. In his later years he established his own blog, where he answered all types of questions about life and religion, including such topics as whether it was permissible for a man to have anal intercourse with his wife.

14. Abdallah interview; al-Musawi interview; interview with a retired CIA officer.

15. Bergman, *Secret War with Iran*, pp. 63–64.

16. James Clarity, "Israelis Killed in Blast in Southern Lebanon," *New York Times*, November 12, 1982. Prime Minister Begin, who suffered a concurrent personal tragedy with the death of his wife of forty-three years, declared it a "new outrage perpetrated by the enemies of mankind."

17. Hirst, *Beware of Small States*, p. 183.

18. Israeli authorities believed it might have been caused by an accidental gas explosion and not a bomb.

19. Qassem, *Hizbullah*, pp. 169–70; Bergman, *Secret War with Iran*, p. 65.

20. "The Islamic Jihad," September 25, 1984, Weinberger Papers, Box I:779, Folder Lebanon 10.

21. Charles Allen, interview with author, October 7, 2009.

22. Baer, *The Devil We Know*, pp. 60–64.

23. Allen interview.

24. Osama Hamdan, interview with author.

25. Odom interview.

26. William Odom memorandum for Myers, "Middle East Trip Report, General Observations," April 4–14, 1983, Odom Papers, Library of Congress, Box 4, Folder 1983, memorandum notes.

27. Robert Baer, *See No Evil: The True Story of a Ground Soldier in the CIA's War on Terrorism* (New York: Three Rivers, 2002), pp. 65–67, 120.

28. Eric Haney, *Inside Delta Force: The Story of America's Elite Counterterrorism Unit* (New York: Delacorte, 2002), pp. 235–36.

29. *The U.S. Embassy Bombing in Beirut*, hearings, U.S. House of Representatives, Committee on Foreign Affairs, Subcommittee on Internal Operations and on Europe and the Middle East, 98th Congress, 1st Session, June 28, 1983.

30. Persico, *Casey*, p. 316.

31. CTF Six Two message, "Higher Alert Condition, Setting of" (081308Z), August 1983, U.S. Marine Corps Archives, Gray Research Center, Lebanon Papers, Disc 23.

32. Message, "Lebanon/MNF Iranian Ambassador Advises Attack Against U.S. Forces, Phalanges, and Lebanese Army," September 27, 1983.

33. The identity of the men who carried out the operation remains unclear. An American intelligence report from 1984, based upon interviews with Lebanese and Syrian intelligence officers, pointed the finger at a young Palestinian who had lost three family members in the Shatila and Sabra massacres. A Hezbollah source testifying in an American court in 2003 said the bomber who aimed at the marines was actually an Iranian, Ismail Ascari, who had been brought in specifically for the mission. Colonel Geraghty believed this man's story, which he said was confirmed by other sources. If so, it would have been a major deviation from every other Iranian-sponsored suicide attack. Iran preferred to stay in the shadows, using locals, and there was no shortage of willing men in Lebanon, so Iran did not need to export one. Iranians did not mind seeing young men sent to paradise; they were less enthusiastic about doing it themselves. See United States District Court for the District of Columbia, transcript of trial, *D. Peterson et al. vs. The Islamic Republic of Iran*, March 17–18, 2003.

The CIA later circulated a report that received considerable attention in Washington of a mysterious ceremony officiated by Sheik Fadlallah, perhaps involving smoking hashish, in which he blessed the bombers. While the grand ayatollah did not oppose suicide bombings against soldiers (civilians, he said, were a different matter), the report proved erroneous and was likely from an unreliable human source.

34. Lyons interview.

35. Lance Corporal Eddie DiFranco, testimony, November 13, 1983, *Review of Adequacy of Security Arrangements for Marines in Lebanon and Plans for Improving That Security*, U.S. House of Representatives, Committee on Armed Services, 98th Congress, 1st Session, pp. 307–26.

36. Eric Hammel, *The Root* (Orlando: Harcourt Brace Jovanovich, 1985), p. 293.

37. "Report of the DOD Commission on Beirut International Airport Terrorist Act," October 23, 1983, December 20, 1983, p. 99.

38. *Peterson vs. Islamic Republic of Iran*, p. 55.

39. Michael Petit, *Peacekeepers at War: A Marine's Account of the Beirut Catastrophe* (Winchester, MA: Faber and Faber, 1986), p. 172.

40. Geraghty interview with Frank, November 21, 1983, pp. 18–21.

41. Geraghty, *Peacekeepers at War*, p. 188.

CHAPTER 8 THE AMERICAN HAMLET

1. McFarlane interview; Robert Timberg, *The Nightingale's Song* (New York: Simon and Schuster, 1995), pp. 336–37.

2. Weinberger Diary and Appointment Folders, October 23, 1983, Weinberger Papers.

3. General Paul X. Kelley comments on draft manuscript of U.S. Marine Corps official history, Benis Frank, *U.S. Marines in Lebanon, 1982–1984*, June 23, 1986. Copy provided by Benis Frank.

4. President Ronald Reagan, "Address to the Nation on Events in Lebanon and Grenada," October 27, 1983, www .reagan.utexas.edu/archives/speeches/1983/83oct.htm, accessed April 22, 2011.

5. National Security Decision Directive 111, October 28, 1983.

6. Weinberger interview.

7. Poindexter interview.

8. *Peterson vs. Islamic Republic*, p. 146.

9. Gregory Vistica, *Fall from Glory: The Men Who Sank the U.S. Navy* (New York: Simon and Schuster, 1995), p. 116.

10. *Selected Works of General John W. Vessey, Jr.: Tenth Chairman of the Joint Chiefs of Staff, 22 June 1982–30 September 1985,* U.S. Department of Defense, Joint History Office, 2008, pp. 86–91.

11. Terence Smith, "At Least 39 Die as Truck Bomb Rips Israeli Post in Lebanon," *New York Times*, November 5, 1983; Thomas Friedman, "Israeli Jets Bomb Base of Suspects in Marine Attack," *New York Times*, November 17, 1983.

12. Notes for November 17, 1983, Weinberger Diary.

13. The phone log for the president revealed only two calls to the president after the NSC meeting: one from McFarlane and the other from the Tunisian ambassador. Phone call with archivist at the Reagan Library.

14. Weinberger, *Fighting for Peace*, pp. 161–62; notes for November 17, 1983, Weinberger Diary.

15. Thomas Friedman, "French Jets Raid Bases of Militia Linked to Attacks," *New York Times*, November 18, 1983; John Vinocur, "Questions Arise on French Raid in Lebanon," *New York Times*, November 22, 1983.

16. Alessandra Stanley, Bruce van Voorst, and Jack E. White, "An Officer and a Gentleman Comes Home: Lieut. Robert O. Goodman," *Time*, January 16, 1984.

17. Robert McFarlane memorandum to Ronald Reagan, "Long Commission Report," undated, Weinberger Papers.

18. Caspar Weinberger memorandum to Ronald Reagan, "Long Commission Report on October 23 Bombing," December 23, 1983.

19. Robin Wright, *Sacred Rage: The Wrath of Militant Islam* (New York: Touchstone, 2001), p. 89.

20. Richard Armitage memorandum to Caspar Weinberger, "External Security Force at American Embassy in Beirut," July 27, 1984.

21. *U.S. Intelligence and the September 20, 1984, Beirut Bombing*, U.S. House of Representatives, Permanent Select Committee on Intelligence, 98th Congress, 2nd Session, October 3, 1984.

22. Francis Clines, "Intelligence Cuts by Predecessors Had a Role in Blast, Reagan Says," *New York Times*, September 27, 1984.

23. McFarlane interview; Poindexter interview; Allen interview.

24. McFarlane e-mail to author; Brinkley, *Reagan Diaries*, pp. 267–68.

25. Bernard Gwertzman, "Shultz's Address Touches Off Stir in Administration," *New York Times*, October 27, 1984; "Shultz Says U.S. Should Use Force Against Terrorism," *New York Times*, October 26, 1984.

26. Nearly thirty years later, the Islamic Republic continued to raise the issue of the fate of the men at the United Nations, with Iran accusing the Phalange of selling the four hostages to Israel, where Tehran claimed they still languished in prison. When one of the diplomats, Ahmad Motevaselian's father, died in 2008, his funeral was attended by no less than President Mahmoud Ahmadinejad. "Ahmadinejad Attends Funeral of Iranian Kidnapped Diplomat's Father," website of the Presidency of the Islamic Republic of Iran, June 6, 2008, www.president.ir/en, accessed November 14, 2009.

27. Baer, *See No Evil*, p. 74; Ihsan Hijazi, "Iran Ties Help to Hostages to Fate of Its Nationals," *New York Times*, December 28, 1988.

28. Baer, *See No Evil*, p. 100.

29. Norton, *Hezbollah*, p. 42.

30. Allen interview.

31. Ambassador Robert Oakley, Foreign Affairs Oral History Program, Association for Diplomatic Studies and Training, July 7, 1992.

32. Ibid.

33. Duane Clarridge, *A Spy for All Seasons: My Life in the CIA* (New York: Scribner, 1997), p. 341.

34. According to Bob Woodward's book *Veil*, Casey met with the Saudi ambassador in his home in Virginia and the two agreed that the Saudi government would fund an assassination plot using Lebanese Phalange under the control of a former British Special Air Services operative. Israeli journalist Ronen Bergman reported that the CIA directly recruited three Phalange and provided them with the explosives, paying the men $100,000 to carry out the attack. The recollection of a retired CIA officer, interviewed in 2008, was something of a hybrid. The Saudis paid for the operation in order for the CIA to maintain deniability, with the operatives coming from a counterterrorist team recruited from Lebanese army intelligence. The officer maintained that the killing of Fadlallah was a rogue operation by Phalange trained by the United States. Bob Woodward, *Veil: The Secret Wars of the CIA 1981–1987* (New York: Simon and Schuster, 1987), pp. 395–97; Bergman, *Secret War with Iran*, pp. 72–73; Oakley Oral History; interview with retired CIA officer, Arlington Virginia, 2008.

CHAPTER 9 SLEEPY HOLLOW

1. Message for Major General Tixier, "Iranian Air Tactics" (211600Z), May 1984; statement of Colin Eglington, May 8, 1997, *Case Concerning Oil Platforms (Islamic Republic of Iran vs. The United States of America)*, International Court of

Justice, Counter-memorial and Counter-claim Submitted by the United States of America, Exhibit 31, Annex, Volume 2, June 23, 1997.

2. Christen Feyer Puntervold letter, "Re: Attacks Recorded Against Neutral Shipping During Hostilities Between Iran and Iraq in the Persian Gulf," Norwegian Shipowners' Association, January 6, 1989; Statement of Captain Christen Feyer Puntervold, *Case Concerning Oil Platforms*, Counter-memorial and Counter-claim, Exhibit 11, Annex, Volume 1, June 23, 1997.

3. While the United States did not accept the legality of the zone, it abided by it and avoided entering the Iranian exclusion zone. General Robert Herres letter to General George Crist, October 28, 1987.

4. Iran and Japan were in negotiations to renew a contract for daily oil shipments to Tokyo. This escalation may have been intended to discourage Japan from buying Iranian oil.

5. Martin Navias and E. R. Hooton, *Tanker Wars: The Assault on Merchant Shipping During the Iran-Iraq Crisis, 1980– 1988* (London: I. B. Tauris, 1996), pp. 74–76; Sreedhar and Kapil Kaul, *Tanker War: Aspects of Iran-Iraq War* (New Delhi, India: ABC Publishing House, 1989), pp. 89–90. A U.S. warship nearly found itself on the receiving end of an Iraqi missile when an Iraqi pilot failed to make the Farsi hook and turn east before releasing his Exocet. The missile struck a hapless tug only a few miles from an American warship steaming in the northern Gulf. The U.S. government warned Iraq to keep its aircraft at least five miles from American warships or risk being shot down, and Weinberger approved a change to the rules of engagement for the U.S. naval flotilla in the Gulf based in Bahrain, Middle East Force, that authorized the use of force against any ship laying mines in international waters or when faced with an approaching jet intent on launching a missile in their direction. At the outbreak of hostilities in September 1980, Defense Secretary Harold Brown had issued rules of engagement that required his approval for U.S. combatants to respond to any attack on neutral ships. If such authorization occurred, the American ships could not enter the territorial waters of either Iran or Iraq. Weinberger reaffirmed this guidance when he came to office. Assistant Secretary of Defense for International Security Affairs memorandum for the Secretary of Defense, "ROE for Protecting Third Country Shipping in the Persian Gulf," September 29, 1980, p. 2; Captain David Grieve, USN (Ret.), interviews with author, May 11, 1995, and August 14, 1995.

6. CIA message, "Iran-Iraq: Lull in the Gulf Anti-Shipping War," June 17, 1987.

7. Resolution 552, United Nations Security Council, Document S/RES/552, June 1, 1984.

8. Tom Cooper and Farzad Bishop, *Iran-Iraq War in the Air, 1980–1988* (Atglen, PA: Schiffer, 2000), p. 172.

9. Charles Horner, interview with the author, July 28, 1995; Anthony Cordesman and Abraham Wagner, *Lessons of Modern War: Volume III* (Boulder, CO: Westview, 1990), p. 214, footnote 7.

10. Caspar Weinberger memorandum to Robert McFarlane, "Crisis Planning Notice—Persian Gulf Situation," February 27, 1984.

11. Weinberger did concede that Iran might try to attack one of the five American warships stationed in the Persian Gulf. He ordered handheld Stinger missiles placed on the warships in case of a suicide plane, and the U.S. government issued a notice for planes and boats not to come within five miles of an American warship or risk being fired upon. The legal basis of these keep-out zones was dubious and likely violated international law of the right of freedom of navigation. Joint Chiefs of Staff message, "Notice for Persian Gulf, Strait of Hormuz, and Gulf of Oman" (210100Z), January 1984.

12. One that Tom Twetten, the head of CIA's clandestine service as director of operations, remembered involved establishing a logistics base in the Persian Gulf from which U.S. military transport aircraft would fly over Afghanistan and airdrop military equipment directly to the mujahideen. When challenged with the facts—that the Soviets had a large air force and would likely shoot the transports down, which could lead to World War III—Iklé thought for a moment and remarked, "Well, maybe that wouldn't be such a bad thing." Twetten interview; also interview with retired CIA officer.

13. Fred Iklé memorandum for Caspar Weinberger, "Iran-Iraq War and Gulf Threats," April 10, 1984.

14. Sandy Charles, "Talking Points for Breakfast Meeting with Secretary Shultz, April 11, 1984," April 10, 1984.

15. These were National Security Decision Directives 139 and 141.

16. General John Vessey memorandum to Weinberger, "Status of DOD Actions from NSDD 139," May 29, 1984.

17. Major General Samuel Swart, USAF (Ret.), interview with author, May 25, 1995.

18. Major General Donald Penzler, USA (Ret.), interview with author, December 14, 1994. While Penzler removed the deadweight, General Crist focused on building his intelligence capabilities. He tasked his able intelligence director, Army Brigadier General Cloyd Pfister, to build CENTCOM into "the premier source of intelligence" for the Middle East. Pfister worked to develop an independent intelligence capability primarily by bringing all the three-letter intelligence agencies—CIA, NSA, and DIA—into a coordinated "intelligence fusion" effort against both the Soviets and Iran. In June 1986, Crist directed Pfister to put together a closely held study group called the Afghan Fusion Cell. It brought together intelligence from all over the community to examine the Soviet military in Afghanistan with an eye to what this portended about that military should the two superpowers come to blows in Europe or the Middle East. By 1988, the group had produced nine monographs examining all aspects of military operations, including diverse topics ranging from the morale and motivation of the Soviet soldier to nighttime helicopter operations. Only the DIA remained lukewarm to CENTCOM's initiative. An entrenched bureaucracy resented the growing CENTCOM intelligence directorate and viewed it with suspicion, questioning its analysts' competence. General Crist, interview for "End of Tour Report," CENTCOM History Office, 1988, p. 11.

19. In April 1986, Crist wrote to Weinberger a pessimistic assessment of the progress of the war, noting that "more sophisticated operational techniques and brutal population repression are taking their toll on the Mujajedin [mujahideen] resistance."

20. George Crist interview with Department of Defense media pool, Gallant Eagle 86, August 10, 1986.

21. CENTCOM, "A Brief History of Russian and Soviet Expansion toward the South," June 30, 1985, p. v.

22. Crist interview; Armitage interview.

23. U.S. Marine Corps, *Lessons Learned: The Iran-Iraq War*, volume 1, Department of the Navy, 1990, pp. 17–19; Kenneth Pollack, *Arabs at War: Military Effectiveness, 1948–1991* (Lincoln: University of Nebraska Press, 2002), pp. 217–18.

24. General Council of British Shipping, *Iran/Iraq: The Situation in the Gulf, Guidance Notes for Shipping*, February 1988, pp. 70–73.

25. General George Crist message to Admiral William Crowe, "Increased Threat in the Persian Gulf" (242130Z), September 1986.

26. Bernard Gwertzman, "Iran's Navy Stops U.S. Ship in Search near Persian Gulf," *New York Times*, January 13, 1986.; also Bernard Gwertzman, "U.S. Says Halting of Vessels by Iran May Be Justified," *New York Times*, January 14, 1986.

27. Secretary of State message to American Embassy, Bern, "Message to Iran on Naval Seizures" (DTG 012225Z), February 1986, p. 1.

28. Chairman of the Joint Chiefs of Staff memorandum for the Secretary of Defense, "U.S. Démarche to Iran," October 1985, p. 1.

29. USCINCCENT message to Joint Chiefs of Staff, "MIDEASTFOR Operating Restrictions" (132130Z), January 1986; Middle East Force, *Command History, 1986*. Whereas previously two warships came each from the East Coast and West Coast, PACOM would be tasked to exclusively provide the additional combat augmentee. While remaining a part of the Pacific Fleet, this fifth combatant was under the operational control of Middle East Force. The first ship assigned was the USS *Jack Williams*, commanded by David Grieve. For both the ship and Grieve, this was just the beginning of a long affiliation with the Gulf.

30. CINCPAC message, "Promulgation of Visit and Search" (190432Z), March 1986. The Office of the Secretary of Defense guidance to CENTCOM emphasized that it was to monitor only U.S.-flagged ships and keep track of their locations, but this authority did not constitute an escort of those merchants. If it did, U.S. warships would have had to accompany the merchant ships throughout their transit and would have necessitated additional ships to be dispatched to Middle East Force; this was not well received by the navy, which complained that it was expensive and diverted ships away from the Pacific. Military Sealift Command ships were required to monitor the common U.S. military frequency of the Middle East Force ships; the U.S. commercial merchant ships maintained communication over the international distress frequency, channel 16. John Poindexter memorandum for Major General Colin Powell, "Visit and Search of U.S.-Flagged Vessels in the Persian Gulf," August 7, 1984.

31. CINCPAC message, "Visit and Search of U.S.-Flagged Vessels in the Persian Gulf" (DTG 290411Z), May 1985, pp. 3–4.

32. CENTCOM briefing, "Invoke Resolve Decision Brief," February 6, 1987, pp. 3–9.

33. In a somewhat controversial move, Crist recommended they knock out the main gas power plant at Bandar Abbas, which provided the power to run Iran's military operation, but also served as the main power source for the city.

34. Crist memorandum to Weinberger, "Central Command Update," undated [February 1986], pp. 1–2.

35. Secretary Weinberger approved the New Splendor initiative. "I applaud your efforts," he wrote Crist, "to develop campaign plans that also incorporate recent bilateral initiatives with a number of Gulf states and some rather significant intelligence enhancements as well. I wholly agree that each of these concerns is vital to the success and survivability of our CENTCOM forces." Secretary Weinberger letter to General Crist, February 2, 1987. CENTCOM also quietly obtained important support from most of the Gulf states. In the event of conflict with Iran, Oman granted permission to use their airfields. Bahrain, Saudi Arabia, and Oman had all agreed to allow CENTCOM to station F-16 attack aircraft in one of their countries should there be a protracted air war with Iran.

36. Crist interview, "End of Tour Report," p. 4.

37. Major General Cloyd Pfister, USA (Ret.), interview with author, November 22, 1994.

38. Pearson became particularly good friends with the Bahraini defense minister and crown prince, Sheik Salman bin Hamad bin Isa al-Khalifa, who was already favorably disposed to the United States.

39. Bahraini and U.S. planners focused on three likely Iranian scenarios: 1) an Iranian air attack on Bahrain proper; 2) naval or Revolutionary Guard attacks on shipping bound for the island; and 3) Iranian threat to close the Strait of Hormuz, in which Bahrain's primary role would be to provide basing for U.S. aircraft. Both sides hoped to deter Iranian aggression, conducting a number of highly visible joint exercises (the first began in January 1988) and expanded naval and air patrols around the island. A few years later, Pearson had the satisfaction of using Bahraini facilities when, during Desert Shield and Desert Storm, the Bahraini airfield Sheik Isa served as the main base for the marine air wing. Brigadier General Jeremiah Pearson memorandum for the Secretary of Defense, "U.S./Bahraini Military Planning Initiatives," October 27, 1987; Lieutenant Colonel Edward Robeson memorandum, "Agenda for New Splendor Update Briefing," June 10, 1987, pp. 1–2; Joint Chiefs of Staff information briefing, "New Splendor Planning Update," July 8, 1987, pp. 2–13.

40. Penzler interview.

41. Russell Violett, interview with author, November 13, 2007.

42. Admiral William Crowe, USN (Ret.), interview with author, April 11, 2001.

43. There are a large number of books and articles written about the Defense Reorganization Act of 1986 (the Goldwater-Nichols Act). The best was written by the chief staff writer of the legislation, James R. Locher III, *Victory on the Potomac* (College Station: Texas A&M University Press, 2002). Also James R. Locher III, "Taking Stock of Goldwater-Nichols," *Joint Force Quarterly*, Autumn 1986, pp. 10–16; Gordon Lederman, *Reorganizing the Joint Chiefs of Staff: The Goldwater-Nichols Act of 1986* (Westport, CT: Greenwood Press, 1999). The reorganization also established procedures for officer promotion that required a joint assignment before making general or admiral. This forced the services to send their quality officers to joint assignments such as Central Command.

44. Armitage interview.

CHAPTER 10 ARMS FOR THE AYATOLLAH

1. Weinberger interview.

2. McFarlane interview.

3. Soon to be deputy director of the CIA John McMahon noted that the Israelis had raised this to him in early 1980, when during a visit to Israel officials tried to convince McMahon of the advantages of selling weapons to Iran. In May 1982, for example, Defense Minister Ariel Sharon met with Secretary Shultz to discuss Iran and the two countries' differences over the war. Sharon freely admitted that Israel provided matériel as a means of maintaining its contacts with the Iranian military, as well as of keeping alive the prospect of influencing a post-Khomeini regime and of protecting Iranian Jews. At the same time, he tried to persuade the United States against encouraging arms being sent to Israel's archfoe Saddam Hussein. Of particular concern, Sharon said, was a recent massive arms sale of Egyptian T-62 tanks to Iraq, with the United States backfilling by providing newer U.S.-built M-60 tanks to Cairo. Following an hour of frank discussions, in the end this meeting, and others similar, concluded inconclusively, with both sides agreeing to disagree. American Embassy Paris message to Secretary of State, "Allegation in French Press of Israeli Sales of U.S. Arms to Iran" (191109Z), August 1983; American Embassy Tel Aviv message to Secretary of State, "Reports of Alleged U.S. Arms Supplies to Iraq via Egypt—Possible Items on the Agenda for MINDEF Sharon's Visit" (241534), May 1982; U.S. Department of State briefing memorandum, "Your Meeting with Israeli Defense Minister Ariel Sharon, Tuesday, 25 May," May 1982; Ambassador Samuel W. Lewis, Foreign Affairs Oral History Program, Association for Diplomatic Studies and Training, August 9, 1998.

4. Oliver North, "Special Project Re: Iran," December 5, 1985. John Poindexter said this as well during a meeting in the Oval Office on November 10, 1986.

5. The Reagan administration briefly flirted with the same idea at the beginning of the administration. On July 21, 1981, the State Department proposed encouraging third, other, countries to provide arms to Iran. The idea had originated with Secretary Alexander Haig. His rationale was similar to McFarlane's logic four years later: encouraging pro-Western states to provide weapons would lessen Iran's dependency on the Soviets and reduce the opportunity for Moscow to increase its influence. However, the Joint Chiefs stridently opposed the idea. In a memo for the secretary of state's special assistant, a youthful thirty-nine-year-old L. Paul Bremer, who would later be elevated to the senior U.S. official in Iraq following the invasion in 2003, the chairman wrote: "Rather than adding to the prospects for peace, increased supplies of arms may encourage Iran to intensify its military actions and continue to reject the negotiated settlement option." The military's opposition carried the day for the next four years. Lieutenant General Paul Gorman memorandum for L. Paul Bremer, "Arms Transfer Policy toward Iran," September 3, 1981.

6. CIA message, "Fabricator Notice—Manuchehr (Gorbanifar)," July 25, 1984, pp. 1–3, www.gwu.edu/~nsarchiv/NSAEBB/NSAEBB210/index.htm.

7. Michael Ledeen, *Perilous Statecraft: An Insider's Account of the Iran-Contra Affair* (New York: Charles Scribner's Sons, 1988), p. 120.

8. McFarlane contacted both Shultz and Weinberger. On Saturday, July 13, he called on a secure telephone to the defense secretary's home in McLean, Virginia. Weinberger was sitting in his garden going through some papers he had taken home to work on over the weekend. In the first of five phone calls to Weinberger—and one more to Powell—McFarlane relayed the Israeli proposal. Ayatollah Karoubi could attain the release of the seven U.S. citizens held hostage in Lebanon, but he wanted a hundred TOW missiles from Israel so he could show his supporters some positive result from their dealings with the West. Weinberger's reply to McFarlane remains a mystery, as he later denied any memory of the repeated phone calls from McFarlane. But Shultz, who was traveling to Australia, expressed cautious support for the Israeli proposal. "I agree with you that we should make a tentative show of interest without commitment. I do not think we could justify turning our backs on the prospect of gaining the release of the other seven hostages and perhaps developing an ability to renew ties with Iran under a more sensible regime—especially when presented to us through the prime minister of Israel." Later Bud McFarlane tried to exaggerate this initial positive response from Shultz as proof that the secretary of state initially supported the arms deal with Iran. In truth, Shultz advocated caution in his message back to McFarlane, but was not going to reject out of hand what might be a promising diplomatic opening, especially when he was halfway around the world in Canberra. But upon his return to Washington and once time afforded a fuller examination of the arms offer proposed by the Israelis, Shultz lined up with Weinberger in vehement opposition to the Iranian arms

scheme. While Weinberger denied any knowledge of the calls from McFarlane in his book *Fighting for Peace*, in 1991 the Office of the Independent Council found a note taken by the secretary mentioning the calls on July 13. See Weinberger, *Fighting for Peace*, p. 366; *Final Report of the Independent Council for Iran/Contra Matters* [hereafter referred to as Walsh Report], Part VIII, "Officers of the Department of Defense, *U.S. vs. Caspar Weinberger* and Related Investigations," footnote 9; George Shultz message to Robert McFarlane, "Reply to Backchannel No. 3" (142333Z), July 1985; *The Iran Contra Scandal: The Declassified History* (Washington D.C.: National Security Archive, 1993), p. 261.

9. Robert McFarlane, *Special Trust* (New York: Cadell and Davies, 1994), p. 27; Walsh Report, Chapter 1.

10. Weinberger interview; Weinberger, *Fighting for Peace*, pp. 368–69; McFarlane, *Special Trust*, pp. 32–33.

11. Attorney General Edwin Meese III, Grand Jury, November 20, 1987, p. 83.

12. McFarlane, *Special Trust*, p. 34.

13. They were delivered by the Pakistani foreign minister, Japanese foreign minister, and the deputy German foreign minister.

14. Poindexter interview.

15. But neither the CIA nor the DIA agreed. Both intelligence agencies concluded that no Soviet plane had overflown Iran. While complete fiction, Ghorbanifar's falsehood served to stimulate the Soviet suspicions of Casey and others of a similar vein in the administration about Moscow's intentions in Iran.

16. At the end of October, Ledeen met with Karoubi in Geneva. While multiple versions exist about what was discussed at this meeting, Ghorbanifar clearly reiterated the Iranian government's willingness to release all the remaining hostages in return for this batch of sophisticated American weaponry. Ledeen back-briefed both North and McFarlane. Oliver North's handwritten notes of the meeting remarked that Karoubi "wants to be U.S. ally—has support in Tehran." While Ledeen had become uncomfortable at the arms-for-hostages angle, he urged McFarlane to support the effort as an opening to the Iranian government.

17. Trita Parsi, *Treacherous Alliance: The Secret Dealings of Israel, Iran, and the U.S.* (New Haven, CT: Yale University Press, 2008), p. 118.

18. Clarridge, *Spy for All Seasons*, p. 309; Clarridge interview.

19. "Remarks Announcing the Resignation of Robert C. McFarlane as Assistant to the President for National Security Affairs and the Appointment of John M. Poindexter," December 4, 1985, *Public Papers of the Presidents of the United States: President Ronald Reagan, 1985*, p. 1440.

20. Weinberger Diary, December 7, 1985.

21. Instead Reagan decided to send McFarlane and North to London, where North was already meeting with Ghorbanifar and the Israelis. Meeting in a Victorian-era building in London's West End, McFarlane took an immediate dislike to Ghorbanifar, whom he later described as "kind of a north end of a southbound horse." "The United States," McFarlane began, "welcomes discussions with Iran and improvement of relations. We are interested in establishing contact with political figures committed to changing Iranian policy. Whenever you and your colleagues are ready for this, they should say so. But until that time, we have no interest in transferring more arms." Ghorbanifar exploded. He pounded his fist on a small wooden table. "What are you talking about?! Are you crazy? My contacts want change but they are too weak now for political talk with you. They must get strong and take power. If I take this back to my colleagues they will go mad. They might just say, 'To hell with the hostages! Let Hezbollah kill them!'" Kimche took a similar, albeit more measured, view. He expressed confidence that this would produce change within the Iranian leadership over time. "I think you're missing a big opportunity. These movements take time to consolidate; and these people are delivering to us important items, information, and we see signs from our intelligence that they're making headway." McFarlane flew back to debrief the president. As one of the principal architects of the arms sales to Iran, he left the London meeting convinced that Ghorbanifar was corrupt and duplicitous. His sole interest lay in acquiring weapons for the Iranian regime.

22. Ronald Reagan, "Finding Pursuant to Section 662 of the Foreign Assistance Act of 1961 as amended, Concerning Operations Undertaken by the Central Intelligence Agency," January 17, 1986, p. 1.

23. North memorandum to John Poindexter and Robert McFarlane, "Next Steps," December 9, 1986, *The Iran-Contra Scandal: The Declassified History*, pp. 280–82.

24. *Reagan Diaries*, entry for January 17, 1986, p. 384.

25. Charles Allen testimony, *Hearings on the Nomination of Robert Gates to Be Director of Central Intelligence*, volume 2, p. 4.

26. President's Special Review Board Interview of Robert Gates, Deputy Director of Central Intelligence, January 12, 1987; *Hearings on the Nomination of Robert Gates to Be Director of Central Intelligence*, U.S. Senate Select Committee on Intelligence, 1991, pp. 319–20.

27. Lang interview.

28. Ibid.

29. Allen interview.

30. Charles Allen, quoted in Weiner, *Legacy of Ashes*, p. 404; *Report of the Congressional Committees Investigating the Iran-Contra Affair*, p. 206.

31. Office of the Inspector General, Department of the Army, *Final Report of Investigation into the Facts and Circumstances Surrounding the Sale and Transfer of Missiles, Spare Parts, and Other Related Equipment to Selected Middle East Countries*, February 3, 1987, p. 6; Colin Powell, *My American Journey* (New York: Random House, 1995), p. 311.

32. North to McFarlane, February 27, 1986, *Joint Hearings before the House Select Committee to Investigate Covert Arms Transactions with Iran*, Appendix A, p. 1179.

33. Odom interview.

34. Walsh Report, Chapter 24, "The Investigation of State Department Officials: Shultz, Hill and Platt," www.fas.org/irp/offdocs/walsh/chap_24.htm, accessed December 12, 2010.

35. Armitage interview; William J. Crowe, *The Line of Fire: From Washington to the Gulf, the Politics and Battles of the New Military* (New York: Simon and Schuster, 1993), pp. 300–301.

36. Theodore Draper, *A Very Thin Line: The Iran-Contra Affairs* (New York: Hill and Wang, 1991), p. 314.

37. North e-mail to Poindexter, May 6, 1986, cited in *Report on the Congressional Committees Investigating the Iran-Contra Affair*, p. 231.

38. Rafsanjani's nephew Ali Hashemi Bahramani mentioned this to George Cave during a later meeting.

39. Notes by Oliver North, cited in Walsh Report, Chapter 1, "United States v. Robert C. McFarlane," fas.org/irp/offdocs/walsh; George Cave memorandum on the McFarlane mission to Tehran, May 30, 1986, National Security Archive Document Reader, pp. 295–96. According to the Bahramani, they looked to the embassy records and could find nothing about McFarlane, but did come across George Cave from his time in Iran a decade earlier. So they decided to meet with them.

40. McFarlane message to Poindexter, May 27, 1986, cited in *Report on the Congressional Committees Investigating the Iran-Contra Affair*, p. 238.

41. McFarlane message to Poindexter, *Joint Hearings before the House Select Committee to Investigate Covert Arms Transactions with Iran*, Appendix A, p. 1270, column 1.

42. Cave learned that, only that day, the Iranians had dispatched a delegation to Beirut to meet with their Hezbollah surrogates to discuss hostage release. With no advanced preparatory work, they simply could not react that fast to an issue as sensitive as working with Hezbollah to release their captives at the behest of the Americans.

43. *Reagan Diaries*, entry for May 28, 1986, p. 415.

44. North raised concern to Poindexter that if the United States did not respond to the release of Jenco, it could jeopardize the safety of the remaining hostages. North memorandum to Poindexter, July 29, 1986, cited in *Report on the Congressional Committees Investigating the Iran-Contra Affair*, p. 246.

45. The two sides differed on the Iran-Iraq War, particularly overthrowing Saddam Hussein. Bahramani agreed with North that his country wanted to live peaceably with its Iraqi neighbor. But he added that Iran needed some kind of victory. He stressed that the Iraqi president "must go" and inquired about the willingness of the United States to use its influence "to get rid of Saddam Hussein." North countered that he could make no such commitment, but the United States did not want to see Iran lose, nor did it want to see Iraq defeated to the degree that it might elicit Soviet intervention to prop up its client state.

46. *Report on the Congressional Committees Investigating the Iran-Contra Affair*, p. 253.

47. Ibid., p. 257.

48. Initially, the press credited Jacobsen's release to the efforts of the special envoy Archbishop of Canterbury, Terry Waite. See Ihsan A. Hijazi, "Anglican Envoy Renews Effort on Beirut Hostages," *New York Times*, November 1, 1986, http://select.nytimes.com/search/restricted/article?res=F50711FA38580C728CDDA8 0994DE484D81.

49. Bernard Weinraub, "Iran Says McFarlane and 4 Others Went to Tehran on a Secret Trip," *New York Times*, November 5, 1986.

50. President Reagan remarks on signing the Immigration Reform and Control Act of 1986, November 6, 1986, www.reagan.utexas.edu/archives/speeches/1986/86nov.htm.

51. Caspar Weinberger memorandum for the record, "Meeting on November 10, 1986, with the President, Vice President, Secretary Shultz, DCI Casey, Attorney General Meese, Donald Regan, Admiral Poindexter, and Al Keel, in the Oval Office," undated, p. 2, cited in *The Iran-Contra Scandal: The Declassified History*, pp. 315–17.

52. Walsh Report, p. 263.

53. "Message to Be Passed by Dunbar to Mehdi-Nejat," December 23, 1986; memorandum for Department of State, "Unscheduled Meeting with Iranian Official in Frankfurt," undated.

54. Caspar Weinberger memorandum for the Acting Assistant to the President for National Security Affairs, December 22, 1986; Richard Armitage memorandum for Caspar Weinberger, "Status of Discussions with Iran," December 22, 1986.

55. John Poindexter, "The Prudent Option in Iran," *Wall Street Journal*, November 24, 1986. A copy with President Reagan's comment provided by Admiral Poindexter.

CHAPTER 11 A RING ON THE AMERICAN FINGER

1. Weinberger Diary, entry for November 23, 1986.

2. *Reagan Diaries*, entry for November 24, 1986, p. 453.

3. Peter Burleigh, interview with author, December 16, 1994.

4. Oakley interview.

5. Richard Murphy, interview with author, December 21, 1994; *Report to the Majority Leader by Senator John Glenn and Senator John Warner*, U.S. Senate, Armed Services Committee, 100th Congress, 1st Session, June 17, 1987, p. 15.

6. Sandra Charles, interview with author, March 21, 1995.

7. Christopher Joyner, ed., *The Persian Gulf War: Lessons for Strategy, Law, and Diplomacy* (New York: Greenwood Press, 1990), p. 121.

8. Jordan's King Hussein was especially angry at the Americans in part because the last high-level briefing he received on Iran had been just days before the news broke of the secret arms deals. Murphy interview; Armitage interview; Crist, "End of Tour" interview.

9. General George Crist letter to Caspar Weinberger, April 3, 1987.

10. The first use of the Badger bomber to attack Iran was in August 1987, when one attacked shipping at Larak Island.

11. CENTCOM History Office, *Command History, 1987*, pp. ii–61; *National Security Policy Implications of United States Operations in the Persian Gulf: Report of the Defense Policy Panel and the Investigations Subcommittee to the Committee on Armed Services*, U.S. House of Representatives, Committee on Armed Services, 100th Congress, 1st Session, 1987, p. 8.

12. George Crist message to William Crowe, "Persian Gulf" (162000Z), December 1986.

13. CENTCOM, "Lessons Learned: Operation Earnest Will, July 1987–Present," slides 3L, 3R; Michel Heger and Yves Boyer, "U.S. and Iran Issues in the Gulf," *Case Concerning Oil Platforms (Islamic Republic of Iran vs. The United States of America)*, International Court of Justice, Corrigendum, tab B, pp. 8–17; Middle East Force, *Command History, 1986*, p. 2-3-3.

14. One other Harpoon was lost from the Iranian missile boat *Pekan* in November 1980. The head of the navy was a communist sympathizer and gave the coordinates to the Soviets, who then sent a salvage ship to recover the missile.

15. CINCCENT message, "Protection of U.S. Flagged Vessels" (270515Z), May 1987, pp. 1–4.

16. General Council of British Shipping, "Iran/Iraq: The Situation in the Gulf: Guidance Notes for Shipping," February 1988, pp. 30–40.

17. "Iran Promised to Leave Japanese Shipping Alone, Khuranari Says," *Kyodo News*, July 4, 1987.

18. *Case Concerning Oil Platforms (Islamic Republic of Iran vs. The United States of America)*, International Court of Justice, Counter-memorial and Counter-claim: Armed Forces of the Islamic Republic of Iran, 1st Naval District Fleet (Intelligence), "Instructions for Radar Stations," February 9, 1986, Exhibit 114; Armed Forces of the Islamic Republic of Iran, 1st Naval District Fleet (Intelligence), "Instructions for the Deployment of Observers on Oil Platforms in the Persian Gulf," October 1980, Exhibit 115; Archive of Incoming Messages, 1st Naval District, "Command Post to Rostam Oil Platform, 1986–1987," Exhibits 118–19.

19. *Case Concerning Oil Platforms*, Counter-memorial and Counter-claim, pp. 61–63.

20. General George B. Crist speech, "Cincs' Wargaming Conference," 1987, p. 9.

21. Message from CINCCENT to Joint Chiefs of Staff, "Protection of U.S. Flagged Vessels" (270515Z), May 1987, p. 2. Another source fixes the number of attacks directed at Kuwait from September 1986 to July 1987 at thirty out of forty-four attacks. See Janet G. Stein, "The Wrong Strategy in the Right Place," *International Security*, Winter 1987–1988, p. 148.

22. "War Risk Insurance," p. 1.

23. Ibid.

24. Anthony Quainton, interview with author, March 21, 1995; Burleigh interview. In the words of Richard Murphy, "Balancing the superpowers . . . has been an element in Kuwaiti policy over the years." U.S. Senate, Committee on Foreign Relations, *U.S. Policy in the Persian Gulf*, p. 30.

25. Howell interview.

26. Shawn Tully, "The Biggest Bosses 48. Ali Khalifa al-Sabah Kuwait Petroleum Dealmaker for a Dynasty," *Fortune*, August 3, 1987.

27. Charles interview.

28. In addition to the U.S. and Soviet request, Kuwait also asked Great Britain to reflag its tankers. Eventually two Kuwaiti tankers were reflagged and escorted by London.

29. "Chronology," Earnest Will Activation: Unclassified, p. 2. A detailed recap of Earnest Will compiled for General Crist by the staff of CENTCOM.

30. Memorandum for General George Crist, "U.S. Coast Guard Requirements," 1987.

31. American Embassy Kuwait cable to Secretary of State, "Kuwaiti Use of U.S. Flag Vessels" (131344Z), January 1987; Frank Carlucci, interview with author, March 20, 1995, Washington, D.C.

32. Secretary of State message (290850Z), January 1987, p. 1.

33. Quainton interview.

34. General George Crist, interview with author, Beaufort, South Carolina, February 5, 1993; also described in Michael Palmer, *Guardians of the Gulf* (New York: The Free Press, 1992), p. 123.

35. Weinberger interview.

36. Armitage interview.

37. Oakley interview.

38. On January 29, Shultz clarified the U.S. position in a message to Ali Khalifa, following it up with a phone call five days later. He stressed to the Kuwaitis that the onus for protecting their shipping remained with the Kuwaitis and the Gulf states themselves. Kuwait could register its ships in the United States, like any other country, but only if it met all the coast guard requirements. However, the U.S. military stood ready to provide any assistance needed

to protect the country from Iran, and he urged the Kuwaitis to become more involved with the contingency planning at CENTCOM. Joint Chiefs of Staff message to CINCCENT, "Kuwaiti Request for U.S. Flagged Vessels" (290850Z), January 1987; Secretary of State message, "Kuwait Request for U.S. Flag Vessels" (030010Z), February 1987.

39. Secretary of State message, "Kuwaiti Negotiations with U.S. and Soviets for Naval Protection" (050840Z), March 1987.

40. Weinberger, *Fighting for Peace*, p. 396; also Weinberger interview.

41. Sandy Charles memorandum for Caspar Weinberger, "Kuwait Request to the U.S. and Soviets to Protect Shipping," March 2, 1987.

42. Weinberger, *Fighting for Peace*, p. 397.

43. Secretary of State message, "Protecting Kuwait Shipping" (070909Z), March 1987; Joint Chiefs of Staff message to General Crist, "Protection of Kuwaiti Shipping" (071801Z), March 1987. At the same time Weinberger sent the letter to the Kuwaiti government, he sent a message to the ambassadors in the area informing them of the pending U.S. decision to escort all eleven Kuwaiti tankers. In return, he said, "We expect Kuwait to end its plan to complete agreement with the Soviet Union for protection of civilian vessels in the Gulf." If Kuwait decided to proceed with the agreement with the Soviets, Weinberger wrote: "We also want to be sure that if for some reason the Kuwaitis decide to proceed with the agreement with the USSR that we ensure that no other Gulf state give the Soviets access to refueling, repair or resupply facilities which would represent a significant advance for their position in the Gulf." Secretary of Defense message (070911Z), March 1987.

44. Secretary of State message (DTG 050710Z), March 1987, section 2, p. 1.

45. Personal message from General George Crist to Admiral William Crowe (DTG 101020Z), March 1987.

46. Rear Admrial Harold Bernsen, USN (Ret.), interviews with the author, August 10, 1995, and February 22, 2007; Rear Admiral Joseph Strasser, interview with the author, March 10, 2007.

47. Rear Admiral Harold Bernsen message to General George Crist, "Private Jewels" (110547Z), March 1987; message from Admiral Bernsen to General Crist (DTG 110547Z), March 1987.

48. Admiral William Crowe message to Secretary Caspar Weinberger, "Protecting Kuwaiti Shipping" (121330Z), March 1987; Crowe, *Line of Fire*, p. 178.

49. Swart interview.

50. The only contingency plan similar to this operation was Plan 1012. It focused on defending U.S. supply and lines of communications through the Gulf against a Soviet threat, and had very little bearing on the task at hand. Lieutenant General Robert Neal, USMC, interview with author, May 25, 1995.

51. Peter W. DeForth, "U.S. Naval Presence in the Persian Gulf: The Middle East Force since World War II," *Naval War College Review*, Summer 1975, p. 30.

52. Grieve interview.

53. U.S. Embassy Kuwait cable, "Recent Incidents Surrounding Kuwaiti Shias Trial," May 3, 1987.

54. The Silkworm is a relatively unsophisticated Chinese-made missile. It has a range of approximately ninety kilometers and carries a thousand-pound warhead. Launched along a programmed azimuth, it skims just above the water for a predetermined amount of time, at which point it turns on its radar and homes in on the first target it acquires. If the target moves or its position is off by more than three kilometers, there is no guarantee that the missile will hit the intended target. CIA, "Characteristics and Capabilities of the Silkworm," April 16, 1987; "Threat Activity: Iran."

55. Richard Norton-Taylor and William Raynor, "Jailed 'Go-Between' on UK-Iran Arms Deals Is Freed to Keep MI6 Secrets Out of Court," *Guardian*, February 6, 1999; Marie Colvin, "Secrets of the Silkworm Spy," *Sunday Times*, June 15, 1997, p. 15.

56. Weinberger interview.

57. CIA, "Iran Persian Gulf: Increased Threat to Shipping," February 27, 1987, and "Iran: Growing Threat to Persian Gulf Shipping," May 30, 1987.

58. CINCCENT, "Operation Private Jewels Commander's Estimate," March 1987; Bernsen interview; General Robert Herres message to Admiral William Crowe, "Private Jewels" (141845Z), March 1987.

CHAPTER 12 THE WAKE-UP CALL

1. Michael Vlahos, "The Stark Report," *U.S. Naval Institute Proceedings*, May 1988, p. 36.

2. Jeffrey L. Levinson and Randy L. Edwards, *Missile Inbound: The Attack on the* Stark *in the Persian Gulf* (Annapolis: Naval Institute Press, 1997), p. 12.

3. Crist interview; Bernsen interview.

4. Bernsen interview.

5. CINCCENT message, "Attack on USS *Stark* Chronology" (DTG 221500Z), May 1987, p. 2.

6. Ibid.

7. Rear Admiral Grant Sharp, *Formal Investigation into the Circumstances Surrounding the Attack on the USS* Stark *(FFG 31) on 17 May 1987*, Department of Defense, 1987 [hereafter referred to as Sharp Report], "Findings of Fact," Item 1.

8. Sharp Report, "Findings of Fact," Item 3.

9. The rules of engagement were based on two documents: CMEF Operations Order 400-85 from October 1, 1985, and Commander, Middle East Force, message of August 21, 1986.

10. Sharp Report, "Findings of Fact."

11. As the official investigation later stated: "The commanding officer failed fundamentally to appreciate the significance of the intelligence information provided to him regarding the recent trend in Iraqi ship attacks south of the 27°30´ north parallel, into the central Gulf." Sharp Report, "Opinions," Item 27.

12. Brindel believed they were in weapons "warning yellow," which allowed for much greater freedom for the *Stark*'s weapons to be fired. This, however, did not translate down to his officers and the CIC believed they were still in the restrictive condition "white" and placed the systems in a mode that prohibited any quick response.

13. Sharp Report, "Findings of Fact," Items 24, 25.

14. The broadcast was made over the narrow-band secure voice radio telephone circuit, or NBSV.

15. Greg McCannel, Lieutenant Commander, USN (Ret.), interview with author, March 22, 1995.

16. Sharp Report, "Findings of Fact," Item 51.

17. Ibid., "Opinions," Item 14.

18. Following the attack, the AWACS tried to vector in two Saudi F-15s to the Iraqi jet, but the Saudi pilots refused without orders from their commanders.

19. Interview with Ambassador Samuel Zachem, Oral History Collection, Operational Archives, Naval Historical Center, Washington, D.C., undated.

20. COMIDEASTFOR message, "Attack on USS *Stark*" (DTG 180208Z), May 1987, p. 1; Chief of Naval Operations message, "Personal For" (DTG 230140Z), May 1987, p. 1.

21. Levinson and Edwards, *Missile Inbound*, p. 33.

22. Interview with CWO3 Howard L. Geiger, USN, by Paul Stillwell, Operational Archives, Naval Historical Center, January 29, 1988.

23. Weinberger Diary, May 17, 1987; *Reagan Diaries*, p. 497.

24. Crist interview; Schramm interview.

25. Ten men were awarded the Navy and Marine Corps Medal of Heroism, including both Lieutenant Commander Gajan and Lieutenant Moncrief.

26. Sharp Report, "Opinions," Item 28.

27. General Crist had been passed a report, not through normal intelligence channels, that the attack was deliberate, in an attempt to draw the United States into the war. But he did not think it had much validity.

28. Lang interview.

29. *National Security Policy Implications of United States Operations in the Persian Gulf*, p. 81.

30. As Senator Pressler said in a congressional hearing in June, "Prior to that [the *Stark* incident], nobody was really paying much attention to the situation in the Persian Gulf. It is good that our attention has been drawn to it. U.S. Senate, Committee on Foreign Relations, *U.S. Policy in the Persian Gulf, May 29, June 16, October 23 and 28, 1987*, p. 32; also Charles interview.

31. Jacob Lamar, Steven Holmes, and Barrett Seaman, "Escort Service for the Gulf," *Time*, June 24, 1987.

32. Vice Chairman of the Joint Chiefs of Staff message, "Personal For General Crist" (DTG 222350Z), May 1987, p. 1.

33. "Admiral William Crowe Remarks to NSPG," undated [May or June 1987].

34. Weinberger Diary, May 22, 1987.

35. General Crist message to Admiral Bernsen, "Plan for Protection of Kuwaiti Shipping" (230130Z), May 1987.

36. Admiral Bernsen message to George Crist, "Increased Readiness in the Persian Gulf" (211510Z), May 1987. Bernsen believed the *Stark* tragedy was caused by errors made by the captain, not by inadequacies in the rules of engagement.

37. The incorporating of hostile intent into the inherent right of self-defense is always a tricky issue. Only the United States and Israel recognize this and regularly incorporate it into their military forces' rules of engagement. It defined a hostile act with the following examples: 1) Launching missiles or firing rockets at U.S. forces; 2) Conducting mine-laying operations to obstruct free navigation in international waters; 3) Attacking or interfering with friendly forces engaged in mine countermeasure operations; 4) An enemy aircraft, vessel, or land-based facility displayed hostile intent by threatening the imminent use of force against friendly forces. This would include electronically jamming U.S. forces or intending to lay mines in international waters.

38. Joint Chiefs of Staff message, "Peacetime Rules of Engagement—Northern Arabian Sea/Gulf of Oman/Strait of Hormuz/Persian Gulf" (3002035Z), June 1987.

39. USCINCCENT message to Joint Chiefs of Staff, "Protection of U.S. Flagged Vessels" (270515Z), May 1987.

40. CINCPACFLT memorandum for Joint Chiefs of Staff, "Status of TLAM/C Mission Planning," May 24, 1987.

41. Johns Hopkins University Applied Physics Laboratory, "USS *Missouri* BG in Strait of Hormuz," April 28, 1987, pp. 14–16; Commanders John Morgan and Harry Ulrich briefing, "*Missouri* Battleship Battle Group in Response to Provoked Anger," June 9, 1987.

42. U.S. warships would also monitor two additional frequencies that would not change monthly: a secondary UHF frequency of 243.0 MHz and an emergency VHF set at 121.5 MHz.

43. CINCCENT message, "Personal For Admiral Crowe: Joint Iraqi and United States Proposal for Avoiding Incidents" (DTG 032200Z), June 1987, pp. 1–2.

44. The Iraqi aircraft would respond by turning on its IFF transponder, change its course immediately by 90 degrees, and cease any radar emissions.

45. Admiral William Crowe memorandum to Secretary of Defense, September 3, 1987.

46. CENTCOM, "Weekly Update," August 30, 1987.

47. There were a few hiccups. In one case an Iraqi pilot's radio broke and his wingman could not speak English. The American defense attaché did not always receive the American convoy and ship locations in a timely manner. The Iraqi pilots were not always the most attentive. On November 26, 1987, an AWACS picked up three Iraqi Mirages headed south but could not raise them on the radio. The cruiser *Richmond K. Turner* maneuvered to unmask her weapons, and at twenty-eight miles locked on to the Iraqis with her fire control radar. Apparently unaware that this was from a U.S. warship, the Iraqis tried unsuccessfully to jam the cruiser. The *Richmond K. Turner* fired off its chaff and prepared to engage with missiles. When the Iraqi planes were only twenty miles from the cruiser, they finally established voice communication and the Iraqi aircraft immediately altered course just seconds before its flight would have come to an abrupt end. General George Crist to Caspar Weinberger, "CENTCOM Update," September and October 1987; Adam Siegel, "A Chronology of Events Related to Earnest Will Escort Operations," Center for Naval Analyses, June 1991, p. 30. Iraqi attacks necessitated an additional meeting in February 1988. That month, Baghdad increased the use of the large Soviet-built TC-16 Badger bomber armed with the C-601, the air-launched variant of the Silkworm missile. The existing deconfliction rules centered around the shorter-range Exocet did not suffice, with its range of one hundred kilometers. On February 12, a Badger fired a C-601 that accidentally hit the Danish-flagged tanker *Kate Maersk* north of Rostam, killing one sailor. Following this attack was another Badger strike that came within nine miles of the USS *Chandler* (DDG-996), then escorting an inbound convoy. The new procedures negotiated forbade Badgers from crossing south of 28 degrees north without positive communications with U.S. forces. These refinements worked reasonably well, balancing the U.S. desire to safeguard its ships while still allowing the Iraqi air force maximum flexibility to attack Iranian targets and freedom to fly over international waters, both of which the United States wanted to preserve.

48. Admiral Crowe memorandum to Secretary of Defense, "Fourth Endorsement on RADM Sharp Investigation of 12 June 87," September 3, 1987, p. 1.

49. Crowe interview; Admiral William Crowe, Oral History Interview with Colonel Charles Gross, Office of Air Force History, Bolling Air Force Base, July 16, 1991, pp. 16–18.

50. USCINCCENT message to Chairman of the Joint Chiefs of Staff, "Escort Regime" (27051Z), May 5, 1987, p. 3; USCENTCOM J-2, "Iranian Reactions to U.S. Escort Operations," May 1987, p. 1; Crist interview.

51. Ibid.

52. Pat Lang did not agree with the prevailing assessment by his organization. He contributed to a national intelligence estimate that was more circumspect about the Iranian mine threat, and the CIA was generally more concerned than other intelligence agencies. Lang interview.

CHAPTER 13 THE INVISIBLE HAND OF GOD

1. Five ships were damaged near the Suez Canal, including the American-owned (Panamanian-registered) *Big Orange XII*, while two more were attacked down near the Bab el Mandeb.

2. Juan Carlos Gumucio, "Iran Threatens to Block Persian Gulf Entrance," *Washington Post*, August 18, 1984, p. A1.

3. By far the most comprehensive account of this operation is Dr. Scott C. Truver, "Mines of August: An International Whodunit," *U.S. Naval Institute Proceedings*, May 1985.

4. Ibid., p. 102; comments by Major Rich Barry, USMC, "The Gulf of Suez Mining Crisis: Terrorism at Sea," U.S. Naval Institute Seminar, May 30, 1985, transcribed, p. 21.

5. The operation was code-named Operation Intense Look. Six other nations answered the Saudi and Egyptian request for assistance. The United Kingdom sent five mine-clearing vessels plus a support ship, arriving at the Egyptian port of Adabiyah on August 15. The French sent two mine-clearing vessels to Jeddah in response to Saudi Arabian requests. Later, in September, both the Italians and the Dutch sent two vessels. Ironically, one of the first countries to respond to the crisis was the Soviet Union, which had supplied Libya with the mines in the first place. Three mine-hunter vessels plus the helicopter cruiser *Leningrad* based in the port of Aden began looking for additional mines around the Bab el Mandeb.

6. Loren Jenkins, "Italian Ships Join Red Sea Mine Hunt," *Washington Post*, August 29, 1984, pp. A1, A20.

7. Comments by Dr. Scott Truver, "The Gulf of Suez Mining Crisis: Terrorism at Sea," U.S. Naval Institute Seminar, May 30, 1985, transcribed, pp. 32–33.

8. In February 1984 the Iranians mined Majnoon Islands, and two years later, in February 1986, the same unit mined the waters off the al-Faw Peninsula to support the Val Fajr VIII offensive. CENTCOM History Office, *Command History, 1988*, March 27, 1990, p. 76.

9. Quainton interview.

10. Ibid.

11. General Crist message to Admiral Crowe, "Mining in Northern Gulf" (11620Z), June 1987.

12. It comprised: a nine-man EOD detachment; a six-man area point search system team complete with precise navigation transponders and a sophisticated side-scanning sonar; and a three-man assistance team to provide expertise to the Kuwaiti military on countermining operations. The U.S. military operation was called Pneumatic Hammer. In addition to the team sent to Kuwait, on June 16 five RH-53D Sea Stallion helicopters along with their crews and maintenance personnel from Helicopter Mine Countermeasures Squadron 14 (HM-14) in Norfolk, Virginia, were placed on a seventy-two-hour alert for possible deployment to the Persian Gulf. As their use would amount

to a tenfold increase in the U.S. military presence in Kuwait, not to mention an overt and public commitment of U.S./Kuwaiti military cooperation, it remained an unacceptable option to the Kuwaiti government in all but the most dire of situations. Both CENTCOM and the Joint Chiefs of Staff agreed HM-14 would be sent only if there was evidence of widespread mining throughout the channel. Helicopter Mine Countermeasures Squadron 14, *Command History, 1987*, entry for June 16, 1987; General Herres message to General Crist, "Mining in Northern Persian Gulf: APF/MNM Assistance Team" (DTG 242120Z), June 1987, Earnest Will Activation, p. 1.

13. One mine was found by a Kuwaiti helicopter and subsequently destroyed by Kuwaiti divers. Office of the Chief of Naval Operations, memorandum for the Chief of Naval Operations, "Support of Middle East Force Operations—Sitrep 6," July 24, 1987, p. 1; Office of Naval Intelligence, "Iranian Mining Threat in the Persian Gulf," June 11, 1987, Operational Archives, Naval Historical Center, WB-7 Intelligence Files, Box 1, Series II.

14. Admiral Crowe message to General Crist, "Security of U.S. Military Forces in the Persian Gulf" (172330Z), July 1987.

15. Captain James Brodie, U.S. Coast Guard, memorandum, "Kuwaiti Tanker Reflagging," February 23, 1987.

16. "Reflagged Kuwaiti Tankers," Earnest Will Activation, p. 3; Colin Powell memorandum, "Reflagging," July 10, 1987; American Embassy Kuwait cable, "Confirmation of Reflagging Dates" (081039Z), July 1987. The eleven reflagged ships, their new redesignated names, and dates of reflagging were as follows:

Gas al-Minagish: *Gas Prince*, July 20, 1987
Al-Rekkah: *Bridgeton*, July 20, 1987
Umm al-Mardem: *Sea Island City*, August 6, 1987
Umm Casbah: *Ocean City*, August 6, 1987
Gas al-Burgan: *Gas King*, August 6, 1987
Umm Matrabah: *Chesapeake City*, August 11, 1987
Kaziham: *Townsend*, August 14, 1987
Gas al-Ahmadi: *Gas Princess*, August 16, 1987
Gas al-Kuwait: *Gas Queen*, August 18, 1987
Umm al-Aish: *Surf City*, August 23, 1987
Al-Funtas: *Middleton*, September 6, 1987

17. These two meetings were on July 2 and July 14, 1987.

18. Weinberger, *Fighting for Peace*, pp. 410–11.

19. Rear Admiral Joseph Strasser, notebook, entry for July 15, 1987.

20. Quainton interview. The flag raised had been flown over the U.S. Capitol and brought to the Gulf by a congressman from Kentucky who insisted he raise it on the first reflagged tanker. As this would have been completely unacceptable to Kuwait, Quainton defused the embarrassing political situation by raising the flag himself.

21. Quainton interview.

22. Admiral William Crowe message for General Crist, "Threat to Reflagged Ships at Khor Fakkan" (171605Z), July 1987.

23. The air force tanker support for the navy headquarters Strategic Air Command message, "Tanker Support for Earnest Will" (DTG 301804Z), June 1987, p. 2; CINCPAC message, "Earnest Will Tanking" (DTG 100001Z), July 1987, p. 1.

24. The mission was code-named Giant Scale III. This would be the first of four such missions during Earnest Will. Paul F. Crickmore, *Lockheed SR-71: The Secret Missions Exposed* (London: Osprey Aerospace, 1993), pp. 154–56; Pfister interview; "Giant Scale III/Earnest Will/Giant Express," Air Mobility Command Document, excerpts from an unspecified command history, undated, p. 2.

25. Alan Cowell, "Navy Enters the Gulf without Incident," *New York Times*, July 23, 1987.

26. Bernsen interview; Grieve interview.

27. Interview with Captain Frank C. Seitz, Jr., U.S. Merchant Marine, "SS *Bridgeton*: The First Convoy," *U.S. Naval Institute Proceedings*, May 1988, p. 52; COMIDEASTFOR message to CINCCENT, "After Action Report on Earnest Will Escort 770001, 22–24 July 1987" (310500Z), July 1987.

28. Bernsen interview; Strasser interview; Admiral William Crowe letter to the New York Yacht Club, March 27, 1987.

29. Harold Lee Wise, *Inside the Danger Zone: The U.S. Military in the Persian Gulf, 1987–1988* (Annapolis: Naval Institute Press, 2007), p. 72.

30. Rear Admiral Bernsen message to General Crist, "Iranian Mines" (240824Z), July 1987.

31. Foreign Broadcast Information Service, "Hashemi-Rafsanjani Political Sermon," July 24, 1987, *Case Concerning Oil Platforms*, Counter-memorial and Counter-claim, Exhibit 50, June 23, 1997, p. 2.

32. Alan Cowell, "A Kuwaiti Tanker under U.S. Escort Hits Mine in the Persian Gulf," *New York Times*, July 25, 1987.

33. The helicopters would use landing helicopter assault (LHA) and landing platform helicopter (LPH) ships, both designed to carry and launch helicopters. Chairman of the Joint Chiefs of Staff, Daily Schedule, July 24, 1987.

34. Joint Chiefs of Staff message to USCINCCENT, "Kuwaiti Mine Threat and Countermeasures" (14011Z), July 1987.

35. Caspar Weinberger letter to George Shultz, July 27, 1987.

36. Larry Martz et al., "Ollie Takes the Hill," *Newsweek*, July 20, 1987, p. 14.

37. Poindexter interview.

38. Ibid.

39. Siegel, "A Chronology of Events," p. 12; Bernsen interview.

40. Captain Jerry Manley, USN (Ret.), interview with author, August 17, 1996; Captain Robert McCabe, USN, interviews with author, May 10 and August 16, 1995; Grieve interviews; Captain Conway Ziegler, USN (Ret.), interview with author, June 15, 1995.

41. Bernsen interview; Captain Bruce van Belle, USN, interview with author, May 2, 1996.

42. Captain Frank DeMasi, interview with author, August 10, 1995.

43. Commander Steven Nerheim, USN, interview with author, August 11, 1995.

44. Edwin Simmons, "Mining at Wonsan and in the Persian Gulf," *Fortitudine*, Summer 1987, pp. 3–7.

45. Tamara Melia, *Damn the Torpedoes: A Short History of U.S. Naval Mine Countermeasures* (Washington, D.C.: Naval Historical Center, 1991), p. 76.

46. Commander Steven Nerheim, "Enabling the Enabling Force: A Naval Mine Countermeasure Force for the Twenty-First Century," Marine Corps War College Paper, Marine Corps University, May 1993.

47. Crowe notes; USS *Illusive* (MSO448), *Command History*, 1987, Ships History Branch, Naval Historical Center, p. 3. The actual deployment order came from the Joint Staff on August 14. General Robert Herres memorandum for Secretary William Taft, "Deployment of Ocean-Going Minesweepers to the Persian Gulf," August 20, 1987.

48. The six ships that deployed to the Gulf were:

     Atlantic Fleet: *Inflict, Fearless, Illusive*
     Pacific Fleet: *Esteem, Conquest, Enhance*

49. Manley interview; van Belle interview; Ellis Casteen, interviewed by Paul Stillwell, Unaccessioned Oral Interviews, Operational Archives, Naval Historical Center, January 15, 1988, p. 12.

50. DeMasi interview; Captain Steven Holmes, interviewed by Paul Stillwell, Unaccessioned Oral Interviews, Operational Archives, Naval Historical Center, January 15, 1988.

51. COMIDEASTFOR message, "MCM/AMCM Concept of Operations in Support of Earnest Will" (081315Z), August 1987.

CHAPTER 14 A WINDOW OF OPPORTUNITY

1. Crowe interview.

2. CINCPACFLT message to CINCPAC, "Window of Opportunity for Contingency Operations" (120410Z), August 1987.

3. Weinberger interview; Lyons interview; Armitage interview; Captian Kevin Healy, USN (Ret.), interview with author, 2006.

4. Vistica, *Fall from Glory*, p. 261.

5. Carlisle Trost, interview with author, December 9, 2006.

6. CINCPACFLT message, "Window of Opportunity for Contingency Operations," p. 1.

7. Admiral James Lyons letter to Admiral William Crowe, August 7, 1987.

8. Captain Morris Sinor, USN (Ret.), interview with author, May 12, 2007.

9. Lyons interview.

10. Transcript of phone conversation between Admiral Lyons and Vice Admiral Howe, August 5, 1987.

11. Admiral Ronald Hays, USN (Ret.), interview with author, August 6, 1996; Lyons interview; Strasser notebook, entry for August 14, 1987.

12. James Brewer, "Iran Warning as *Bridgeton* Begins Loading," *Lloyd's List*, August 1, 1987, p. 1.

13. Siegel, "A Chronology of Events," p. 13.

14. Crowe and Lyons conferred afterward and both supported the decision to jam the Silkworm site: "It is important for the on-scene command to take all prudent steps to defend against a successful Iranian fire of a Silkworm missile at U.S. forces or escorted ships," Crowe wrote.

15. Kahlili interview.

16. Reza Kahlili, *A Time to Betray* (New York: Threshold, 2010), pp. 252–53.

17. Strasser notebook.

18. Chief of Naval Operations message, "Persian Gulf Threat Alert" (032242Z), August 1987.

19. Alan Cowell, "Iran Warns It Has Extended Maneuvers in the Gulf," *New York Times*, August 7, 1987; Daily notebook of General George Crist, entry for August 7, 1987.

20. Ziegler interview; Admiral Crowe message for General Crist, "Threat to Reflagged Ships at Khor Fakkan" (081907Z), August 1987; Bernsen interview.

21. Ziegler interview; Bernsen interview. A brief description of this is also contained in *Case Concerning Oil Platforms*, Counter-memorial and Counter-claim, p. 25.

22. Ibid. This was confirmed by another conversation between the author and a U.S. naval officer.

23. This was a clear indication of the Iranian left hand not knowing what its right hand was doing. Tehran laid mines to catch the next U.S. convoy and the first vessel hit was a tanker loaded with its own oil.

24. Norman Hooke, *Modern Shipping Disasters, 1963–1987* (London: Lloyd's of London Press, 1989), p. 34.

25. *Lessons Learned*, p. 6.

26. United Kingdom Ministry of Defense, "Mine Clearance Operations off Funjahrah by HM Ships, 21 September 1987 to 25 October 1987," April 1997.

27. Trost interview; Ziegler interview. Lyons met briefly with the French task force commander and broadly explained his ideas to the admiral, but while the French wanted to cooperate with the United States, they remained unwilling to allow their forces to fall in under U.S. command.

28. "Iran Majlis Speaker on Oil Exports and Mine Production," Iranian News Agency in English, BBC Summary of World Broadcasts, August 16, 1987.

29. "Majlis Speaker's Prayers Sermon Views Gulf Events," sermon by Ali Akbar Hashemi Rafsanjani, Tehran Domestic Service, FBIS, August 21, 1987.

30. Department of State, "Message for the Government of Iran," August 31, 1987.

31. COMIDEASTFOR message to CJTFME, "3-87"(230030Z), November 1987, JTFME/MEF Operations Files, Operational Archives, Naval Historical Center, Series VI, Box 18, File 8, "Farsi Island Minefield," September 1987– January 1988," p. 1.

32. CINCPACFLT message for CINCPAC, "Rules of Engagement Cumulative Indicators" (050535Z), August 1987; CINCCENT message to Chairman of the Joint Chiefs of Staff, "Rules of Engagement Cumulative Indicators" (071730Z), August 1987.

33. Pfister interview; Secretary of State message to American Embassy Kuwait, "SR-71 Mission into the Persian Gulf" (080542Z), August 1987, p. 1.

34. Interview with retired navy admiral; also Vistica, *Fall from Glory*, p. 267.

35. COMSEVENTHFLT message to CINCPACFLT, "Reef Point Incident" (091625Z), August 1987, Lyons Papers, Operational Archives, Naval Historical Center.

36. There are discrepancies regarding this action. In *Fall from Glory*, p. 267, Vistica states that the pilots, Lieutenant Commander Robert Clement and Lieutenant Bill Ferran, fired three Sparrow missiles and confronted two Iranian F-4s of a total of six aircraft the Iranians had sent up that morning. The messages and after-action reports reviewed by the author indicate one F-4 and the likelihood that it was in fact a C-130. General Crist message to Admiral Crowe, "Message from COMIDEASTFOR" (1121100Z), August 1987; Vice Admiral Paul David Miller message to Admiral James Lyons, "F-14 Sparrow Engagement" (100030Z), August 1987, Lyons Papers, Operational Archives, Naval Historical Center. See also Cordesman and Wagner, *Lessons of Modern War*, volume 3, p. 303.

The author gave a talk at the Naval War College in April 2007. One of the students, who had been on the E-2 that tracked the F-4, came up to me afterward. He said there was no mistake that it had been an F-4, but that the Iranians also had a C-130 aloft conducting surveillance.

37. Rear Admiral Lyle Bull, USN (Ret.), interview with author, 2006.

38. Transcripts of phone conversations between Admiral Lyons and Admiral Crowe, and Admiral Lyons and Captain Strasser, August 8 and 9, 1987; Strasser notebook, entry for August 6 and 9.

39. CINCCENT message to Chairman of the Joint Chiefs of Staff, "Joint Task Force Headquarters" (140519Z), August 1987; Crist, "End of Tour" interview.

40. Crist interview.

41. Chairman of the Joint Chiefs of Staff, Daily Schedule, August 14, 1987; Weinberger Diary, August 14, 1987.

42. "I would never have chosen Brooks in a million years," lamented Lyons in an interview with the author. "A naval attack pilot who never went to Vietnam—that tells you everything you need to know."

43. Before retiring, Lyons tried to rally his supporters to counter the decision by Weinberger. He called Webb, but the navy secretary refused to take or return his calls. He talked to John Lehman, who contacted both Crowe and Weinberger to try and get them to reverse the decision, but to no avail. The former head of NSA and onetime CIA deputy under Casey, Admiral Bobby Ray Inman, came to Lyons's defense and called Trost. The two men disliked each other, and Trost refused to change his mind. In the end, Lyons found he had no supporters in Washington.

44. Tom Burgess, "Adm. Lyons Retires from Pacific Post," *San Diego Union*, October 1, 1987, p. A2.

45. Admiral William Crowe message to Admiral James Lyons (281915Z), September 1987.

CHAPTER 15 THE NIGHT STALKERS

1. Bernsen interview.

2. Message from Chief of Naval Operations, Office of Naval Intelligence, to Various Agencies, "Persian Gulf Threat Alert" (032242Z), August 1987, p. 2.

3. His critics believed he spent "too much valuable time on reconstructive intelligence analysis at the expense of analyzing the current tactical situation." Lieutenant Commander Peter Wikul, "Combat Action at Middle Shoals Light: A Case Study of Intelligence Support for Low-Intensity Conflict," Defense Intelligence College, December 10, 1989, p. 15.

4. COMIDEASTFOR "Personal For" message for General Crist, "MEF Force Levels" (062107Z), August 1987, p. 2.

5. Bernsen interview; Grieve interview; CENTCOM, "Lessons Learned," Draft Script Slides 16L and 16R.

6. Lieutenant Colonel James R. Pruden, CO HML-263, Oral History Collection, Marine Corps History Division, January 5, 1988. Additionally army personnel for Intelligence Support Activity with direction finding and frequency

locators were deployed, sending the information gathered back to the National Security Agency for further analysis.

7. Since 1985, CENTCOM prohibited ships from moving north of 27°30′—some thirty miles south of Farsi except as part of the convoy escort due to the hazards of the Iran-Iraq War.

8. Bernsen interview.

9. Ibid.

10. The individual Bernsen contacted did not wish to be identified.

11. CENTCOM History Office, *Command History 1987,* pp. iii–88; Commander Norman Carley, USN (Ret.), interview with author, June 28, 1995.

12. Bernsen interview; Lieutenant Commander Greg McCannel, USN (Ret.), interview with author, March 22, 1995.

13. COMIDEASTFOR message, "MEF Force Levels," p. 3.

14. Department of the Navy, Office of the Chief of Naval Operations, "Memorandum for the Chief of Naval Operations SITREP 12," September 24, 1987, p. 1; USS *Raleigh, Command History, 1987,* Ships History Branch, Naval Historical Center. In addition, the *Mount Vernon* arrived with four riverine patrol boats that proved worthless in the high seas of the Gulf.

15. His East Coast counterpart from Special Boat Squadron 2, Jack Gantley, arrived briefly on the *La Salle* as well, until the two determined that the mission would likely go on for a long time, and in late August Gantley headed back to the States with the intention of relieving Flanagan in a few months. Captain Jack Gantley, USN, interview with author, May 31, 1995.

16. The brotherhood of SEAL officers is a very small community and at times resembles a sewing circle with the abundance of internal gossip. During the course of my researching this book, few SEALs spoke highly of Flanagan, especially those who operated in the Gulf. However, among the "black shoes," or line officers, in Middle East Force, he receives credit most especially for the mobile sea base.

17. Rear Admiral Harold Bernsen interview with John Partin, May 10, 1989, U.S. Special Operations Command History Office, Tampa, FL; Trost interview. As a junior officer, Lugo served two tours in Vietnam as the commander of the USS *Antelope,* a large gunboat armed and packing a heavy punch, with a 76-mm gun among its weapons, for the brown-water world of the rivers and coastal waters off the Mekong Delta. He often operated off Sea Float, supporting the swift boats and SEALs engaging in countless skirmishes in the wet, murky world of the special operations forces in the delta. In one incident on Easter Sunday in 1971, Lugo's gunboat intercepted a trawler carrying ammunition for the Vietcong. After firing a warning shot across its bow, the North Vietnamese responded with a hail of gunfire. A running gun battle ensued, until a 40-mm round from the *Antelope* hit the trawler's embarked ammunition. "It erupted like a fireworks factory," Lugo later recalled, a dramatic image still indelibly ingrained in his brain decades later. Telephone interview with Captain Frank Lugo, USN (Ret.), December 10, 2006.

18. CINCCENT message to Joint Chiefs of Staff, "Arabian Gulf Sea Mobile Support Concept," August 1987, pp. 1–3.

19. Ibid., p. 4.

20. Howell interview.

21. A similar four-boat detachment arrived from Special Unit 11 in California. It was commanded by Evancoe's counterpart, Lieutenant Commander Bert Calland, who later commanded CENTCOM's special operations forces after 9/11.

22. The idea of using helicopters to support Earnest Will had come up even before the *Bridgeton* mining. COMUSNAVCENT message to CINCCENT, "Attack Helo Offensive Capability vs. High Speed Patrol Boat" (092046Z), July 1987, pp. 1–2.

23. Kenneth Finlayson, "Task Force 160 in Operation Urgent Fury," *Veritas: Journal of Army Special Operations History* 2:2 (2006), pp. 36–41.

24. Colonel Larry Outlaw, USMC, interview with author, August 9, 1995.

25. CINCCENT message to COMIDEASTFOR, "Helicopter Support for Earnest Will Operations" (261915Z), July 1987, p. 1.

26. Lieutenant Colonel Bryan "Doug" Brown interview with John Partin, June 28, 1989, pp. 2–3.

27. COMIDEASTFOR message to CINCCENT, "LAMPS Upgrades" (240900Z), July 1987, pp. 1–2; Penzler interview.

28. CINCCENT message, "Helicopter Support for Earnest Will Operations," pp. 1–2.

29. Armitage interview; Penzler interview.

30. While this capability is standard in today's military in Afghanistan and Iraq, it was, if not revolutionary, a major change in the way the United States used its intelligence, as there had always been the tendency for the intelligence agencies to resist allowing unanalyzed raw information from being sent down to tactical forces, without it first going through the wickets of the agencies' staff of analysts. Pfister interview.

31. See www.specwarnet.net/americas/isa.htm; Steven Emerson, *Secret Warriors: Inside the Covert Military Operations of the Reagan Era* (New York: Putnam, 1988).

32. Master Sergeant James Parran, USMC (Ret.), interview with author, 2006.

33. Colonel Wayne Long, USA (Ret.), interview, January 24, 2007.

34. Ibid.

35. Bernsen interview with Partin, p. 19.

36. CINCCENT message to COMIDEASTFOR, "Barge OICs" (15163Z), September 1987, p. 1.

37. Swart interview. Three years later, Moore would go on to command the marine air wing during Desert Storm. Biographical File, Major General Royal Moore, Jr., Marine Corps History Divison.

38. Lyons interview and his notes.

39. Weinberger interview; Armitage interview.

40. Bernsen interview.

41. Lugo emphasized that the Middle East Force viewed the threat largely as mines or terrorism. The threat from the Iranian air was minimal. The Iranians possessed fewer than twenty functioning aircraft in the north and these were consumed with fighting Iraq. Further, they had not attacked any ship with aircraft in nearly a year, and had shown no inclination to challenge the Fahd Line. The swimmer threat, he believed, was minimal and did not warrant the construction of cumbersome anti-swimmer nets. Lugo added, however, that the possibility existed of a bomb's being smuggled aboard with the incoming supplies from Brown and Root, and so security background checks needed to be done on the civilian employees, largely from the Philippines and Pakistan, to prevent a suicide terrorist from slipping into the crew. John Partin, *Special Operations Forces in Operation Earnest Will/Prime Chance I* (Tampa: Special Operations Command, April 1998), pp. 44–45.

42. Lugo interview.

43. CNO-OP 6B memorandum for the record, "Mobile Sea Base," CM-3-88 Document Collection, Marine Corps Historical Center, Folder USMC Ops in Persian Gulf, Folder #2, p. 1; Major, pp. 1–4; CINCCENT message to COMIDEASTFOR, "Barge OIC's" (151639Z), September 1987, p. 1.

44. General Royal Moore, "Personal For" message to Rear Admiral Fogarty, "Mobile Sea Basing Brief" (151820Z), September 1987.

45. Joint Chiefs of Staff, J-3 Decision paper, September 1987, CM-3-88 Document Collection, Marine Corps Historical Center.

46. Admiral Crowe "Personal For" message to General Crist, "Visit to CMEF" (172330Z), September 1987, pp. 3–8.

47. Parran interview; COMIDEASTFOR message, *"Iran Ajr"* (252035Z), September 1987.

48. This had led to speculation that Iran had advance information about the *La Salle*'s schedule.

49. Complete collections of teletype and paper-tape messages found on board the *Iran Ajr*, in *Case Concerning Oil Platforms*, Counter-memorial and Counter-claim, Exhibits 70–72, June 23, 1997.

50. Ziegler interview.

51. COMIDEASTFOR message, "Force Intelligence Advisory—175/87—Landing Craft Engagement" (221735Z), September 1987, Earnest Will Collection, Operational Archives, Naval Historical Center, Series VI, Box 10, Folder 9.

52. Grieve interview; Bernsen interview.

53. Captain Marc Thomas, USN (Ret.), interviews with author, August 15, 1995. Also again in 2007; Parran interview.

54. USS *Jarrett* message for COMIDEASTFOR, "SITREP" (212313Z), September 1987; COMIDEASTFOR message, "Force Intelligence Advisory—175/87—Landing Craft Engagement" (212245Z), September 1987, Earnest Will Collection, Operational Archives, Naval Historical Center, Series VI, Box 18, Folder 10.

55. Weinberger Diary, entry for September 21, 1987.

56. Thomas interview; Sergeant Gilbert Kerr, USMC Oral History, Marine Corps History Divison, January 5, 1988.

57. Bernsen interview with Partin.

58. Grieve interview; Lugo interview; COMIDEASTFOR message, "Iranian Landing Craft Capture Plan" (212315Z), September 1987.

59. Thomas interview. Combat photographers captured the entire assault on videotape. See *Persian Gulf Operations*, Defense Visual Information Center, March Air Force Base, Pin No. D5-208DM-002, Series Title DN-DEE-92-0009, Tape 5.

60. Thomas interview.

61. Parran interview.

62. Lieutenant Commander Paul Evancoe, USN (Ret.), interview with author, May 22, 1995; Commander Peter Wikul, interview with author, August 17, 1995.

63. Wikul interview.

64. Ibid.

65. "Excerpts from the Address to the General Assembly by the President of Iran," *New York Times*, September 23, 1987.

66. Most of the Iranians captured were very docile. Only a couple of officers showed any real hostility to the Americans. Lieutenant John M. Ickes, USN Oral History, January 28, 1988, Operational Archives, Naval Historical Center.

67. John Kifner, "United States Blows Up Captured Iranian Vessel," *New York Times*, September 26, 1987.

68. The location of the *Iran Ajr*'s sinking was 27°00′ north, 051°23′ east. COMIDEASTFOR message, "After Action Report for Sinking of *Iran Ajr*" (260030Z), September 1987; Evancoe interview.

CHAPTER 16 A VERY CLOSE CALL

1. CIA, "We Watched the Gulf," *Studies in Intelligence* 33:1 (Spring 1989), p. 6; Joint Chiefs of Staff message, "Planned Attack on Saudi Oil Facilities" (01150Z), October 1987, pp. 1–2; COMIDEASTFOR message, "Force Intel Advisory 187/87, Persian Gulf Threat Update" (271650Z), September 1987, Files Intelligence Notebook I, 1985–1987, JTFME/MEF Operations, Operations Archives, Naval Historical Center, Series VI, Box 18.

2. Michael Gordon and Bernard Trainor, *The General's War* (New York: Little, Brown, 1995), p. 38.

3. Strasser notebook, entry for September 29, 1987, Rear Admiral Strasser, USN (Ret.), interview with author, April 7, 2007.

4. Riahi interview.

5. CIA, "We Watched the Gulf"; Joint Chiefs of Staff message, "Planned Attack on Saudi Oil Facilities," pp. 1–2; COMIDEASTFOR message, "Force Intel Advisory 187/87."

6. General Crist daily notebook; Crowe, Daily Schedule, October 1, 1987. In May 1988 two additional P-3s were added, based with the others in Dhahran. *Command History, 1988*, pp. ii–121; Ambassador Edward Gnehm, interviews with author, May 16 and June 29, 1995.

7. USS *Guadalcanal, Command History, 1987*, entry for October 3, Ships History Branch, Naval Historical Center.

8. Penzler interview; Crist interview. Many believe that the AWACS radar while operating in maritime mode simply picked up wavelets and mistook them for small boats. As the radar has to be preset to pick up objects traveling at a certain speed, in this case twenty to twenty-five knots, it remains a distinct possibility that on October 3 the AWACS picked up the tops of waves in the water traveling at this speed. General Charles Horner and Colonel George Williams, both of whom were heavily involved with AWACS operations in the Gulf during this period, believe this was in fact the case. However, in light of what happened on October 8 and the additional intelligence indicators, the threat posed by massed Iranian boats was real. General Charles Horner, USAF (Ret.), interview with author, July 28, 1995; Colonel George Williams, USAF, interview with author, December 13, 1994.

9. Fariborz Haghshenass, "Iran's Asymmetric Naval Warfare," Washington Institute for Near East Policy, September 2008, p. 5.

10. Evancoe interview; Grieve interview; Lieutenant Colonel James R. Pruden, Oral History Collection, Marine Corps History Division, January 5, 1988. CENTCOM asked the chief of naval operations to dispatch a team from Naval Sea and Air Systems Commands to the Gulf to see the barges firsthand and come up with any additional recommendations. While NavSea established a twenty-four-hour crisis support cell to facilitate support for the barges, a survey team arrived in the Gulf on September 23. Many of its recommendations reiterated earlier concerns, especially ammo handling and HERO problems. One of the team's best ideas was for a redesign of the proposed helicopter hangar on the *Hercules*, which allowed for helicopters to be brought in for maintenance without tying down the main flight deck for operations. Additionally, it strongly recommended that a second helicopter deck be constructed on the *Wimbrown*. The current deck, thirty by thirty feet, while strong enough to support the small army helicopters, would not be strong enough to support the larger navy and marine helicopters.

Also from John W. Parton, *Special Operations Forces in Operation Earnest Will/Prime Chance I*, pp. 44–45. In case the Iranians directly challenged them, the barges would be reinforced with metal plating and sandbags while the marines manned a variety of weapons: .50-caliber machine guns, Mk-19 grenade launchers, a TOW missile, 81-mm mortars, and Stinger missiles. There was even discussion of placing a tank on board, but this was rejected as it would make the barge top-heavy. For protection, the barges would be moved randomly every few days among the Saudi islands and oil platforms. To prevent an attack on the barge, a layered defense was envisioned. The helicopters interdicted any target out to fifty nautical miles, while the Mk-IIIs covered the middle distances of ten to twenty miles, with the smaller Seafoxes and PBRs safeguarding the five miles around the barges. If all else failed, the marine security force would provide the final layer, manning the barges' machine guns, armed with pistols and M-16s to repel boarders if necessary. APP Comment on ComNavSpecWar Group One, Det. 12 (26170Z), September 1987; "Surveys in Support to Arabian Gulf Mobile Sea Bases," September 30, 1987.

11. Middle East Force/Joint Task Force Middle East, *Command History, 1988*, Enclosure 5, p. 7.

12. Interview with senior military officer.

13. Evancoe interview; Wikul interview.

14. Wikul interview.

15. Lieutenant Colonel Edward B. Cummings, USMC, interview with Mr. Benis Frank, January 4, 1988, and Captain Ernie L. Gillespie, OIC Det. 2d Radio Battalion, interview with Mr. Benis Frank, January 6, 1988, Marine Corps Oral History Collection, Marine Corps History Divsion.

16. Gillespie interview with Frank.

17. *Persian Gulf Operations*, Series Title DN-DEE-92-0009, Tape 4.

18. American Consulate message, "Partition of Iranian Detainees Observe/Interpreters Report" (181215Z), October 1987, Series IIII: JTFME Public Affairs, JTFME Iranian Gunboat Attack, October 1987–April 1988, Box 10, Operational Archives, Navy Historical Center.

19. It is not known if the Iranians realized the United States had deployed the mobile sea base. *Persian Gulf Operations*, Series Title DN-DEE-92-0009, Tape 4; American Consul message, "Partition of Iranian Detainees Observe/Interpreters Report."

20. Wikul interview.

21. Evancoe interview.

22. Captain Jerry O'Donnell, USN (Ret.), e-mails to author, April 27, May 1 and 2, 2001.

23. Sreedhar and Kaul, p. 61.

24. See "Archive of Incoming Messages, Rostam Oil Platform," *Case Concerning Oil Platforms*, Counter-memorial and Counter-claim, Exhibits 118–19, Annex, Volume 4.

25. CINCCENT message, "Execute Order—Operation Nimble Archer" (180350Z), October 1987.

26. CJTFME message, "Operation Nimble Archer After Action Report" (260958Z), October 1987; USS *Hoel* (DDG-13), *Command History, 1987*, p. 3.

27. The total number of rounds fired at the platform was 1,065. Chief of Naval Operations, "Arabian Gulf Lessons Learned Report: April–November 1987," p. 16.

28. Frédéric Lert, *Wings of the CIA* (Paris: Histoire and Collections, 1998), pp. 279–84; Wayne Mutza, *Loach: The Story of the H-6/Model 500 Helicopter* (Atglen, PA: Schiffer, 2005), pp. 71–75.

29. Twetten interview.

30. On October 5, 6, and 13, Admiral Crowe went to the Hill to brief relevant congressional subcommittees on both the Saudi decision to accept the CIA aircraft and the Eager Glacier program, describing how this capability added to the U.S. military. At least on this aspect of Earnest Will, Congress appeared satisfied and raised no objections. Admiral William Crowe, "Opening Statement," U.S. House of Representatives, Armed Services Committee, July 21, 1992, www.fas.org/news/iran/1992/920722-236124.htm, accessed September 1, 2005.

31. Hart interview.

32. Horner interview.

33. Penzler interview; Crist interview.

34. Lert, *Wings of the CIA*, pp. 279–80. Lert writes that the surveillance aircraft were Beechcraft King Air 100, very similar to the Merlin.

35. Grieve interview; CENTCOM, "Lessons Learned," Draft Script Slides 16L and 16R.

36. Grieve interview.

37. Rear Admiral Donald Dyer, USN, interview with author, December 19, 1994, Norfolk, Virginia.

38. General George Crist letter to Admiral William Crowe, "Eager Glacier," November 30, 1987.

39. CIA was adamant about maintaining its own search and rescue capability, in the event one of its aircraft crashed or was shot down. Howard Hart observed: "We have no protections, if we are shot down. It's not like an air force or navy pilot, which affords you some legal protections. What you are as a CIA pilot is a mercenary black spy who could be shot immediately. If a military pilot gets killed, it's an act of war; we get killed, nobody gives a shit—you're a filthy spy, so who cares."

40. USS *Esteem* (MSO-438), *Command History, 1988*, Ships History Branch, Naval Historical Center, p. 1. One of the MSOs, the *Conquest*, ran into the escort ship while conducting a replenishment operation at sea, thereby delaying her arrival until repairs were made.

41. The navy did not use the term "minefield." The Iranians laid mine lines and not large dense fields such as Iraq would lay during Desert Storm. Instead the navy called it a "mine danger area," as mines could be laid anywhere in a large geographical area. CTG 801.4 Message to USS *Conquest*, "Part II AGM MCM OPMEMO 1-5A (AG Minehunting Procedures)" (210701Z), March 1988, and "Arabian Gulf MCM OPMED 1-5A," March 21, 1988, JTFME/MEF Operations Files, Operational Archives, Naval Historical Center, Series VI, Box 18.

42. Van Belle interview.

43. DeMasi interview.

44. USS *Fearless* (MSO-442), *Command History, 1987*, Ships History Branch, Naval Historical Center, p. 3.

45. Van Belle interview.

46. Nerheim interview.

CHAPTER 17 NO HIGHER HONOR

1. Bernsen interview. In fact it took a direct order from Crowe to get the *Wimbrown* deployed near Farsi.

2. Major General James Record, USAF, interview with author, November 28, 1995, and January 29, 1996.

3. Bernsen interview.

4. The chairman ordered his assistant, Vice Admiral Jonathan Howe, to the Gulf for a fact-finding mission. After meeting with both Bernsen and Brooks, he recommended to Crowe that Brooks be relieved and the two commands merged under one hat. As Bernsen was due to rotate out anyway, it made sense to have Less replace both men, a decision with which Crist agreed. Vice Admiral Jonathan Howe, USN (Ret.), interview with author, August 8, 1996.

5. "Remarks by General George Crist at the Middle East Force Change of Command," Manama, Bahrain, February 27, 1988.

6. "JTFME/MEF Ops Officer Lessons Learned—Overarching," February 1989, JTFME/MEF Operations Files, Operations Archives, Naval Historical Center, Series VI, Box 21, Folder 8. Less made a number of changes to streamline the command and control over the operation. He implemented a more formal composite warfare commander concept structure for navy forces in the Gulf, which was the navy's standard way of operating a battle group. Under this system, Less delegated to specific commanders the control over certain functions, such as controlling air operations, surface ships (including the convoys), or countermine measures. Dyer interview.

7. CENTCOM, "Persian Gulf Escort Matrix—As of 13 June 1989," 1989. A recap of every escort convoy.

8. Captain Paul Rinn, USN (Ret.), interview with author, February 1, 2004.

9. Dyer interview.

10. Bradley Peniston, *No Higher Honor: Saving the USS* Samuel B. Roberts *in the Persian Gulf* (Annapolis: Naval Institute Press, 2006), p. 91.

11. Quoted in Chuck Mussi, "To See the Dawn: The Night-Long Battle to Save USS *Roberts,*" *All Hands,* August 1988, p. 4.

12. Rather than use the main propellers, Rinn ordered the ship's auxiliary propulsion units (APUs)—used to maneuver the ship in tight situations such as docking—lowered and set slightly off center and the rudder set hard left.

13. Oddly, many of the crew including Rinn initially thought it was the Lamps helicopter that had crashed and caused the explosion; this idea was just as quickly dispelled as it became immediately apparent that it was a mine.

14. This was the auxiliary machinery room 3 (AMR-3).

15. Kenneth A. Heine, "This Is No Drill: Saving the 'Sammy B.,'" *Surface Warfare Magazine,* July/August 1988.

16. Michael Tilley, interview with author, June 1, 2005; Rinn interview.

17. Tilley interview; Rinn interview.

18. Briefing, "USS *Samuel B. Roberts* (FFG-58) Mining Incident, 14 April 1988 Timeline," undated [hereafter referred to as *Samuel B. Roberts* Timeline briefing], provided to author by Captain Paul Rinn.

19. The original *Samuel B. Roberts* (DE-413) was sunk off Samar in the Battle of Leyte Gulf, October 25, 1944, with a loss of ninety crew.

20. Rinn interview.

21. CENTCOM, *Command History, 1988,* pp. iii–72; USS *Trenton, Command History, 1988,* Ships History, Naval Historical Center, Enclosure 1, p. 3; *Samuel B. Roberts* Timeline briefing.

22. Contingency Marine Air-Ground Task Force 2-88, "Command Chronology," November 23, 1987–February 29, 1988, Historical Overview Section, Archives Section, Marine Corps Historical Center, p. 10; Outlaw interview.

23. *Samuel B. Roberts* Timeline briefing.

24. Rinn interview; Mussi, "To See the Dawn," p. 10.

25. Rinn interview.

26. Ibid.

27. Captain Robert Canepa, USN (Ret.), interview with author, August 15, 2005.

28. Rear Admiral Guy Zeller, USN (Ret.), interview with author, April 10, 1995.

29. Zeller expressed some reservations against this action. "It ran too much risk of collateral damage," he cautioned, especially to a civilian hospital that sat near the naval headquarters building in Bandar Abbas. Zeller added that the complications that would surround the loss of an aircraft and a resulting POW situation outweighed any military benefit. Taking note of Zeller's concerns, Less nevertheless ordered him to come back with a list of targets for his aircraft. CENTCOM J-3, Joint Uniform Lessons Learned System (JULLS) Number 50343-51944, "Summary, Praying Mantis," August 23, 1988, p. 2 [hereafter JULLS Report]; Zeller interview; Vice Admiral Anthony Less, USN (Ret.), interviews with author, November 28, 1994, July 6, 2005, November 14, 2006, June 21 2007.

30. This was one of the first deployments of the senior, or "super," CAG concept. Conceived by Secretary of the Navy John Lehman as part of a wide range of changes to naval air following the debacle with the air strike in Lebanon in 1983, it elevated the CAG commander to a senior O-6 command on par with the carrier's captain, who would then serve as the advocate for strike warfare within the battle group command. To assist him, a senior commander/junior captain was assigned as the deputy CAG, whose primary role would be to oversee the execution of an attack mission. Rear Admiral Arthur (Bud) Langston, USN (Ret.), interview with author, July 12, 2005.

31. Chronology, "Battle Group Foxtrot War at Sea Exercises," undated [1988], provided to author by Captain James Engler, USN (Ret.); Langston interview.

32. The second option he proposed was to bomb Abu Musa Island with eight attack aircraft while simultaneously shelling both Farsi Island and the Forouzan oil platform with naval gunfire. CAG-11 Chronology, "Operation Praying Mantis, 18 April 1988," p. 1, provided to author by Captain Engler.

33. Less's own staff developed three courses of action for assaulting the platforms: 1) attack all three with naval gunfire only; 2) bombard all three, but board one with SEALs to look for intelligence while the marines provided support; or 3) attack two platforms simultaneously with marines taking one while the SEALs took another. Hans S. Pawlisch, "Operation Praying Mantis," *VFW,* January 1989, p. 35. Dr. Pawlisch was the command historian at CENTCOM.

34. Less interview.

35. The other two ships were the USS *Merrill* and the USS *Lynde McCormick.*

36. The frigates were the USS *Simpson* and USS *Bagley.*

37. If the *Sabalan* could not be found, he would destroy a third Iranian oil platform, Rakhsh. There was no SAG A. The joint task force had a communications circuit called Alpha, which was used to pass administrative traffic. In the planning sessions officers expressed concern about naming one of the surface action groups SAG A, fearing it would cause confusion at the height of combat operations. Vice Admiral James B. Perkins III, USN (Ret.), interview with author, August 9, 2005.

38. General George Crist, Persian Gulf Ops notebook, entry for April 16, 1988, in author's possession; letter from General George Crist to Secretary of Defense Frank Carlucci, May 20, 1988, p. 2; Zeller interview; "Operation Praying Mantis," *Surface Warfare,* November/December 1988, p. 17.

39. Crist interview.

40. Many have speculated whether the virtually simultaneous attacks by the United States and Iraq was really a coincidence. The July 13, 1992, *Newsweek* article by John Barry and Roger Charles speculated that the two nations conspired together, in a joint attack against Iran. However, General Crist firmly rejects these accusations, and says

that the Iraqi attack caught the United States "by surprise." The material I have seen supports General Crist's claim. Thus far there is no evidence that U.S. officials planned Praying Mantis before the *Samuel B. Roberts* struck the mine on April 14. As mentioned, discussions of a military strike on Iran did not commence in CENTCOM until forty-five minutes after the *Roberts* incident. By contrast, the Iraqis had planned their attack months in advance, carefully moving Revolutionary Guards and supplies at night so as to conceal their buildup from the Iranians. The United States had no way of knowing a U.S. vessel would strike a mine, thus providing an excuse for American military retaliation. It's more likely the Iraqis chose the seventeenth to attack because it was the first day of Ramadan, rather than out of any decision taken in conjunction with Washington.

41. Rick Francona, *Ally to Adversary: An Eyewitness Account of Iraq's Fall from Grace* (Annapolis: Naval Institute Press, 1999), pp. 23–24.

CHAPTER 18 GOOD-BYE, CAPTAIN NASTY

1. *Persian Gulf Operations*, Series Title T-1, 2, 3 (89-0003), Tape 3.
2. *Case Concerning Oil Platforms*, Memorial, Submitted by Islamic Republic of Iran, Volume 1, June 8, 1993, p. 47.
3. *Persian Gulf Operations*, Series Title T-1, 2, 3 (89-0003), Tapes 1, 2; James B. Perkins III, "The Surface View: Operation Praying Mantis," *U.S. Naval Institute Proceedings*, May 1989, p. 68.
4. Dunkelberger reported back, "Platform 1 is clear and Platform 2 is burning. Platform 2 is unusable; it is on fire." Outlaw and Brinkley quickly directed the CH-46 to insert the one assault force to the adjacent southern platform numbered 3. Thomas Hastings, USMC, interview with author, June 22, 1995; Outlaw interview; *Persian Gulf Operations*, Series Title T-1, 2, 3 (89-0003), Tapes 1, 2.
5. In all, the Cobras expended 15 TOW missiles, 140 2.75-inch rockets, and over 6,200 20-mm rounds.
6. As the marine helicopters were on their final approach into Sassan, the *Samuel B. Roberts's* Lamps helicopter suddenly detected an unknown patrol boat approaching at twenty-nine knots from the northwest. It was identified as a possible Boghammer, and concern grew as it closed to fourteen thousand yards and appeared to be armed with a Harpoon missile, possibly an Iranian missile boat. Fortunately, Perkins's force held its fire, for a closer examination revealed it to be a UAE patrol boat apparently unaware of the U.S. military operations under way at Sassan. The emirate boat quickly complied with warnings to stay clear of the area. A short time later, the U.S. ships detected an unidentified aircraft closing from due west. Ignoring repeated warnings to stay clear, two marine Cobras were sent to intercept. They discovered the culprit was a news helicopter from Dubai sent out to cover the action, not realizing how close it came to becoming part of the story.
7. While his senior Major Clyde Brinkley served as the overall raid force commander and embarked on board the UH-1 Huey command and control helicopter, Hastings would command the forces landing on Sassan. In Brinkley's helicopter sat Captain Vernon Scoggin of 2nd Air Naval Gunfire Liaison Company. It fell to his eyes and wits to control the naval gun predatory fires. Colonel William M. Rakow, "Marines in the Gulf—1988," *Marine Corps Gazette*, December 1988, p. 66.
8. *Persian Gulf Operations*, Series Title T-1, 2, 3 (89-0003), Tapes 1, 2.
9. Captain David Chandler, USN (Ret.), interview with author, August 12, 2005.
10. Ibid.
11. Ibid.
12. *Persian Gulf Operations*, Series Title T-1, 2, 3 (89-0003), Tape 3.
13. Unfortunately, the *Wainwright* did not transmit "rounds complete," which was the cue for SEALs to move in. This created a ten-minute delay as the UH-60 and embarked SEALs—already confused by the *Simpson's* unexpected participation in the bombardment—remained unsure if the ship's prep fire was over. CNSWTG, "After Action Report," p. 2.
14. Commander Norman Carley, USN (Ret.), interview with author, June 28, 1995; Rear Admiral Thomas Richards, USN, interview with author, August 11, 1995; also Middle East Force Naval Special Warfare Task Unit Atlantic message to CJTFME, "After Action Report at Sirri DTG" (072315), May 1988.
15. USS *Wainwright* message to CJTFME, "OPREP-3 Feeder After Action Report, Operation Praying Mantis" (190730Z), April 1988, p. 1. After the action, Richards and other SEALs voiced strong objections in their after-action reports and a series of "Personal For" messages about the "mishandled" operation, venting their irritation at just about every command in the Gulf. The force package for Sirri had been far too light, with at least a full SEAL platoon needed. The lack of an A-6 gunship supporting the insertion seriously risked the assault force. Command and control between the special operations force and the surface group was not "clearly delineated." Both Richards and May believed that after the first salvo by SAG C, the assault force should have been inserted immediately while the Iranians' "heads were down." But the lack of command and control between SAG C and the SEALs delayed their insertion, and the surface warfare officers did not fully comprehend the importance of timing the prep fires with this insertion of the SEALs. Ultimately, this poor coordination led to the "unnecessary" additional salvos that destroyed Sirri. In short, as Commander Richards's after-action report bluntly stated: "Planning was not done with SOF in mind. . . . JTFME staff were not fully versed in the use and limitations of Special Warfare assets. They treated the personnel boarding as an add-on requirement, not the primary focus." CNSWTG MEF message (20044), May 1988, "Praying Mantis After Action," p. 2; CNSWTG, "After Action Report," p. 2.
16. CINCCENT message to Joint Chiefs of Staff, "Update" (190900Z), April 1998, p. 3.

17. COMDESRON 22 message to CJTFME, "Operation Praying Mantis Post Mission Timeline" (210215Z), April 1988, p. 2; *Rear COMDESRON TWO TWO*, unclassified VHS tape of Persian Gulf Operations, Timeline 10-52, copy shown to author by Rear Admiral Dyer.

18. CT801.1 message to CINCCENT, "Praying Mantis OPREP-3 Feeder 002" (DTG 180645Z), April 1988, Naval Historical Center, Box 20, Folder 9 Praying Mantis Messages.

19. Dyer interview.

20. CJTFME message to USS *Wainwright*, "SAG Instruction" (DTG 180728Z), April 1988, JTFME/MEF General Attorney Files, JTFME/MEF Messages 1985 and January 20–April 19, 1988, Operations Archives, Naval Historical Center, Box 14, Series IV.

21. Chandler interview; Captain Martin Drake, USN, interview with author, September 1, 2005.

22. USS *Wainwright* message to JTFME, "Operation Praying Mantis" (241748Z), April 1988, Naval Historical Center, Box 20, Folder 9, pp. 2, 5; Perkins, "The Surface View."

23. Chandler interview; Drake interview.

24. JTFME message, "SAG C Summary of Operations, 18 April" (201223Z), April 1988, p. 2; USS *Wainwright* message to JTFME, "Operation Praying Mantis First Impressions/Chronology" (202320Z), April 1988; Craig Symonds, *Decision at Sea: Five Naval Battles That Shaped American History* (New York: Oxford University Press, 2005), p. 305.

25. Symonds, *Decision at Sea*, p. 305.

26. Drake interview.

27. USS *Wainwright* message to CJTFME, "Operation Praying Mantis First Impressions/Chronology" (DTG 202330Z), April 1988, Operations Archives, Naval Historical Center, Series VI, Box 20, Folder 9 Praying Mantis Messages.

28. Chandler interview.

29. USS *Wainwright* message to CTF 800, "SSM Engagement Data" (200246Z), April 1988, p. 1. At the time of the *Joshan*'s Harpoon launch, the *Wainwright* was in a broad weave and the starboard side was angled more toward the Iranian boat, thus her port chaff would not have been of any use.

30. Richards interview.

31. USS *Wainwright*, SSM Engagement message, p. 2.

32. The *Wainwright* did not detect the missile seeker of the Iranian Harpoon. U.S. experts later speculated that this may have been due to age and poor maintenance on the missile, which meant the missile never worked. Captain Chandler believed it was the electronic countermeasures that prevented the missile from hitting. Less interview; also CJTFME "Final Report," p. 2; CJTFME message, "Final Report, Operation Praying Mantis" (DTG 030855Z), June 1988, p. 2.

33. PTG *Joshan*, JTFME/MEF J-3, "Praying Mantis Brief," 1988.

34. USS *Wainwright*, *Command History, 1988*, entry for April 18.

35. USS *Wainwright* message (202330Z), April 1988, p. 2; USS *Wainwright* message to CJTFME, "After Action Report, Operation Praying Mantis" (181638), April 1988, p. 1.

36. American Embassy Abu Dhabi message to CJTFME, "Status of Americans in Mubarak Field" (181732Z), April 1988, p. 1; *Command History, 1988*, p. A6; Navias and Hooton, *Tanker Wars*, p. 171.

37. There are some discrepancies about the number of Iranian aircraft involved. Captain Chandler recalled three while others interviewed recalled that one or two had headed south from Bandar Abbas, with one turning toward SAG C. The final after-action report states that only one Iranian aircraft had ever headed south and ended up being engaged by the *Wainwright*. JULLS Report, p. 7.

38. JULLS Report, p. 7.

39. Initially there were indications of possibly two Iranian aircraft, one landing at Kish Island and the other at Bandar Abbas. Later U.S. officials determined that there had been only one Iranian jet, and it had landed at Bandar Abbas.

40. Message from COMDESRON 22 to CJTFME, "Operation Praying Mantis—Post Timeline 15" (DTG 210215Z), April 1988, April 20–22, 1988, Operations Archives, Naval Historical Center, Series VI, Box 20, File 11, Praying Mantis Messages; JTFME message to CINCCENT, "SPOT Report 021-88" (291950Z), April 1988, p. 1.

41. The *Sahand* was a sister ship of the *Sabalan*. The shah had bought four of these 1,250-ton warships from Great Britain in the early 1970s.

42. CTG 800.1 message, "Praying Mantis Ops—Summary of Lessons Learned," p. 1.

43. COMDESRON 22 message, "Timeline," p. 2.

44. The second F-14 ran short of fuel and had to break off to refuel with an air force tanker. Carlucci interview; Crist interview; Crowe interview; CAG 11, "Chronology," p. 3. The basic facts of this incident are undisputed and, from what the author can discern, were first revealed by the CBS correspondent David Martin. But there are different versions as to why they needed the president's permission to attack the Boghammers. Craig Symonds, in his book *Decision at Sea*, attributes this to ROE concern surrounding hot pursuit into Iranian territorial waters; see Symonds, pp. 311–12. The events happened quickly and were all done via telephone conversations. But the key ROE question clearly centered around a preemptive attack based upon a then closely guarded signals intelligence success in determining Iranian intentions.

45. The bomblet weighs 1.32 pounds and has a 0.4-pound shaped-charge warhead of high explosives, which produces up to 250,000 psi at the point of impact, allowing penetration of approximately 7.5 inches of armor. Rockeye is most efficiently used against area targets requiring penetration to kill.

46. Captain James Engler, USN (Ret.), interviews with author, July 16 and August 16, 2005.

47. Dyer interview.

48. Langston interview; CAG 11, "Chronology," p. 4.

49. George Burke, message posted to online forum, March 1, 2002, http://ussjosephstrauss.org/posted_messages .htm, accessed December 12, 2005; USS *Joseph Strauss* (DDG 16), *Annual Command History, 1988*, Enclosure 1, p. 2, Ships History Branch, Naval Historical Center.

50. Chandler interview; Dyer interview; CTG 800.1 message to CJTFME, "Praying Mantis Ops—Summary of Lessons Learned" (231800Z), April 1988, p. 4; JTFME/MEF J-3, "Praying Mantis Brief, Blue on Blue"; JULLS Report, "Praying Mantis," p. 7; COMDESRON, "Post Mission Timeline," p. 2. Following Praying Mantis, Joint Task Force Middle East looked at the cause of the near friendly-fire incident, but came to no real conclusions, as it faded quickly from memory except by those involved. It is quite clear that the A-7 did not properly check in with the surface forces, but from what can be determined, none of the War at Sea strike force did either. It certainly was not given authority by the *Wainwright* or SAG D. To the CAGs' credit, they reported trouble all day contacting the ships, and once they informed JTFME that they were launching the strike package to sink the *Sahand*, they operated under the assumption that this was their assigned mission and everyone knew it. The carrier had, perhaps, the best JOTS picture and had a clear idea of where the U.S. surface forces were located. Compounding the problem, the *Joseph Strauss* was not equipped to download the air tracks relayed by the E-2, and had to rely on its own organic systems to delineate the friendly-air picture.

51. Although prior planning between the air group and Dyer had been nonexistent for this ballet of destruction, it nevertheless was the first coordinated air-surface missile attack by the U.S. Navy, a much heralded subject in postengagement wrap-ups. CJTFME message to CINCCENT, "SITREP" (DTG 181245Z), April 1988; CJTFME message to CINCCENT, "SITREP" (DTG 181308Z), April 1988, p. 1; Dyer interview; Langston interview.

52. CTF 800.1 message to CJTFME, "Praying Mantis Ops, Chronological Report" (DTG 210600Z), April 1988, Operational Archives, Naval Historical Center, Series VI, Box 20, Folder 15, p. 4; CTG 800.1 message to CJTFME, "Ordnance Delivery Summary" (DTG 191845Z), April 1988, Operational Archives, Naval Historical Center, Series VI, Box 20, Folder 15, pp. 1–3; JTFME/MEF J-3, "Praying Mantis Brief: Ordnance Expenditure." The list of ordnance used on the *Sahand* is as follows:

AGM-84 Harpoon missile: 3
Mk-82 laser-guided bomb: 1
AGM-62 Walleye II: 2
Mk-83: 20
AGM-123 Skipper: 4

53. USS *Joseph Strauss* deck log, entry for Time 1601, April 18, 1988; Dyer interview. During my interview with Admiral Dyer, he showed the entire videotape taken by the Lamps and provided commentary. This was actually the second time the Lamps approached the *Sahand* for BDA. It closed with it following the first three Harpoons, but was quickly ordered away as the War at Sea strike package arrived.

54. During the day, a key support for the navy aircraft came from the air force's KC-10 refueling tankers of ELF-One. Just prior to H-hour, last-minute diplomacy by the U.S. government obtained overflight rights for U.S. support aircraft from Saudi Arabia, UAE, and, most important, Oman. After the attacks began, U.S. aircraft generally flew over Oman entering or exiting the Gulf, greatly shortening the flight route and avoiding the Iranian military's concentration around the Strait of Hormuz. At CENTCOM's request, the State Department obtained Omani permission for this later in the day, but Muscat had already agreed in all but formalities. Likewise, the UAE offered the United States blanket overflight clearance for two days. Over the course of the day, successive KC-10 tanker aircraft assumed a refueling track over Oman, south of the action but close enough to supply the SUCAPs within the Gulf. During the first twelve hours of Praying Mantis, the air force provided the navy with more than seven hundred thousand pounds of fuel. When the ELF-One stockpile of JP-5 aviation fuel at Dhahran ran short—used by the U.S. Navy because its higher flash point was safer on board ship—the Saudis volunteered an unlimited amount of Jet A-1 fuel to keep operations going.

The entire issue of fuel for the carrier aircraft became a headache for Admiral Less during Praying Mantis. When the JP-5 stocks ran low, JP-4 from the air force was made available for the KC-10s as well as the slightly safer commercial Jet A-1 from the Saudi government. But JP-4 had a lower flash point, and the navy had always been reluctant in peacetime to refuel aircraft with it due to the potential safety hazard on board the carrier. In the middle of the day, Less received a phone call from a fellow admiral on the navy staff. He immediately laid into Less, complaining that he had better not let the air force tankers refuel the aircraft with JP-4. "We can't have those fighters going back to the carrier with that; it's a safety hazard." In the middle of a fight, Less had little patience for this interruption. "You got to be shitting me that you're even making this call! Goddamnit, there are some people out there who stand a chance of getting blown out of the water or losing their life. This is war and all you can talk about is not putting JP-4 into those airplanes? We'll use JP-4 all day long if we have to, to keep airplanes up there! So you pump it over the side when you get back to the carrier and fill it up with JP-5 and get on with life." Less interview; General George Crist letter to Secretary of Defense Frank Carlucci, May 20, 1988, p. 3;

JULLS Report, p. 9. Over the two days of April 18–19, the air force passed over one million pounds of fuel to navy aircraft, much of it from Saudi stocks.

55. Dyer interview.

56. Captian Brian Davis, USMC, March 17, 1994; Crist interview.

57. Carley interview.

58. Message from CT801.1 to CINCCENT, "Praying Mantis OPREP-3 Feeder 002."

59. Engler interview; Zeller interview.

60. Crowe, *Line of Fire*, p. 202; Carlucci interview.

61. CINCCENT, "Update" (190900Z), April 1988, p. 4.

62. Oakley interview.

CHAPTER 19 THE TERRIBLE CLIMAX

1. Lang interview; Lang, "The Land Between the Rivers."

2. To avoid getting entangled with the Kurdish conundrum or Turkey, Lang excluded any Iranian targets near the Kurdish areas of northern Iraq and Iran and focused entirely on those facilitating Iranian attacks on the southern front between Basra and the Zagros Mountains. The Iraqis preferred working for the DIA, suspecting that the CIA had provided the intelligence that Oliver North had passed during the arms-for-hostages deal during 1986. See President's Special Review Board Interview of Robert Gates, *Hearings on the Nomination of Robert Gates to Be Director of Central Intelligence*, pp. 319–20.

3. Iraq also received satellite imagery from the French. While not as detailed as that provided by DIA and CIA, it allowed senior leadership of the Iraqi military to essentially confirm the information on Iranian forces provided by Washington. Author's interview with a former brigadier general in the Iraq military.

4. The gun was a 1,070-mm self-propelled gun mounted on a tank chassis, designed by North Korea to shell Seoul. Lang interview; Gnehm interviews.

5. Gnehm interviews; Armitage interview.

6. Taken from a message provided by a naval officer. The author has reviewed numerous messages that demonstrated Captain Rogers's aggressiveness.

7. Commander David Carlson, comments on article "The *Vincennes* Incident," *U.S. Naval Institute Proceedings*, September 1989, p. 88.

8. John Cushman, "U.S. Expands Protection in Gulf to Any Neutral Vessel Attacked," *New York Times*, April 30, 1988, p. A3.

9. Rear Admiral William Fogarty, *Formal Investigation into the Circumstances Surrounding the Downing of Iran Air Flight 655 on 3 July 1988*, Department of Defense, 1988 [hereafter Fogarty Report], p. 11.

10. William Crowe, "Second Endorsement of Rear Admiral Fogarty's ltr of 28 July 1988," Fogarty Report, p. 2.

11. Fogarty Report, pp. 14–15.

12. Ibid., p. 2.

13. Ibid., p. 12.

14. The Rules of Engagement issued by CENTCOM and approved by the Joint Chiefs allowed for U.S. warships to enter Iranian waters during an engagement or as part of a deception operation. The Iranian waters would not serve as a safehaven from which they could launch attacks at U.S. forces with impunity. However, short of protecting his ship, captains were prohibited from entering Iranian waters for both international law and to avoid being mistaken for an Iranian ship by the freewheeling Iraqi air force. The *Vincennes* helicopter clearly violated this prohibition, and Rogers the intent of the instructions by moving into Iranian waters to protect its helicopter from a fight he instigated.

15. There is no doubt that when the *Vincennes* fired on the Iranian airliner, it was in Iranian territorial waters. Admiral Crowe confirmed this on ABC's *Nightline* in 1992. General Crist supported this during the author's interview.

16. . Kristen Ann Dotterway, "System Analysis of Complex Dynamics Systems: The Case of the USS *Vincennes*," Naval Postgraduate School, June 1992, p. 13.

17. In CENTCOM's endorsement of the formal investigation, it stated that this initial IFF of an F-14 might have originated from an Iranian aircraft on the ground at Bandar Abbas.

18. The investigation speculated that the pilot of the Airbus may have been busy talking between the Bandar Abbas and Dubai airport controllers, and simply wasn't monitoring the proper frequency.

19. Crowe interview.

20. Fogarty Report, p. 41.

21. News briefing at the Pentagon by Secretary of Defense Frank Carlucci and Chairman of the Joint Chiefs of Staff Admiral William Crowe, August 19, 1988.

22. Carlson, comments on "The *Vincennes* Incident," p. 92.

23. Vice President George Bush, "The Persian Gulf Conflict and Iran Air 655," *Current Policy No. 1093*, U.S. Department of State, 1988, p. 1.

24. Stephen C. Pelletiere, *The Iran-Iraq War: Chaos in a Vacuum* (New York: Praeger, 1992), pp. 144–45.

25. John Bulloch and Harvey Morris, *Saddam's War: The Origins of the Kuwait Conflict and the International Response* (New York: Fabar and Faber, 1991), p. 248.

26. CENTCOM, *Command History, 1988*, pp. ii–102.

27. Robert Pear, "Radio Broadcast Shows Iran Leader Endorsed Decision for Truce," *New York Times*, July 21, 1988.

28. "Text of Iranian Letter to UN," *New York Times*, July 19, 1988.

29. CENTCOM, *Command History, 1988*, pp. ii–104.

30. CINCCENT message to Joint Chiefs of Staff, "Public Affairs—Earnest Will Support Forces" (151200Z), July 1989.

31. CINCCENT message to Chairman of the Joint Chiefs of Staff, "Earnest Will Review" (121225Z), December 1989, p. 2.

32. Weiner, Legacy of Ashes, p. 426; Weiner interview; Giraldi interview. Two other retired and one former CIA officers recalled the same events.

33. Interview with one former and two retired CIA officers in 2008; Giraldi interview; Greg Miller, "CIA Operation in Iran Failed When Spies Were Exposed," *Los Angeles Times*, February 12, 2005, p. A1.

34. For a description of nonofficial cover, see Ed Finn, "How Deep Is CIA Cover?" *Slate*, September 30, 2003, http://www.slate.com/articles/news_and_politics/explainer/2003/09/how_deep_is_cia_cover.html.

35. Interview with former CIA officer in 2008.

36. Giraldi interview.

37. For an example of typical punishments and of the arrest of another U.S. spy held at Evin, see Roger Cooper, *Death Plus Ten Years: My Life as the Ayatollah's Prisoner* (New York: HarperCollins, 1993), pp. 98, 224.

38. "Majlis Speaker Says U.S. Spy Networks Uncovered," Islamic Republic News Agency (IRNA), Tehran, April 21, 1989, FBIS, April 21, 1989, pp. 44–45.

39. "Information Minister Names CIA Spies," IRNA, April 26, 1989, FBIS, April 27, 1989, pp. 43–44; "Daily on Need to Eliminate Motives for Treason," IRNA, April 27, 1989, FBIS, April 27, 1989, p. 51.

40. Released in 1991, Cooper later wrote that his confession had been coerced through beatings and months of solitary confinement.

41. "Tehran TV Details Cover Operations of Spies," Tehran Television Service, May 4, 1989, FBIS, May 8, 1989, p. 57.

42. "Mohtashemi Speaks at Rally," IRNA, November 4, 1989, FBIS, NES-89-213, November 6, 1989.

43. In March the Iranian Flag of Freedom radio station reported his execution, along with fifty-nine other military officers. To his wife's relief, the report turned out to be false, and the family was allowed another visit a month later. See "60 Navy, Air Force Officers Said Executed," Flag of Freedom Radio, March 24, 1989, FBIS, March 27, 1989, p. 50.

44. Rear Admiral Frank Collins letter to James Woolsey, Director, Central Intelligence Agency, April 28, 1994.

45. "Information Ministry on CIA Agents Execution," Tehran Television Service, November 5, 1989, FBIS, NES-89-213, November 6, 1989.

46. "The CIA's Darkest Secrets," *US News & World Report*, July 4, 1994, pp. 34–44.

47. Weiner interview.

CHAPTER 20 GOODWILL BEGETS GOODWILL

1. Gordon and Trainor, *The General's War*, p. 10.

2. Hossein Mousavian, interview with author, October 7, 2011.

3. George H. W. Bush, Presidential Daily Diary, entries for February 4 and February 5, 1990, Bush Presidential Records, Bush Presidential Library, College Station, Texas, White House Office of Appointments and Scheduling, Box 29; George Lardner, "Bush Took Bogus Call on Hostages," *Washington Post*, March 9, 1990.

4. Baer, *See No Evil*, p. 115.

5. John Greenwald, Sam Allis, and David S. Jackson, "Terrorism Nightmare on Flight 422," *Time*, April 25, 1988.

6. John Kelly, interviewed by Thomas Stern, Foreign Affairs Oral History Program, Association for Diplomatic Studies and Training, December 12, 1994.

7. Mousavian interview.

8. Giandomenico Picco, *Man Without a Gun: One Diplomat's Secret Struggle to Free the Hostages, Fight Terrorism, and End a War* (New York: Times Books, 1999), p. 112.

9. The CIA also believed that Iran could not unilaterally order the release of the hostages but had to haggle with Hezbollah. CIA memorandum for Robert Oakley, "Iran and the U.S. Hostages in Lebanon," August 1, 1988.

10. Twetten interview; Allen interview; Benjamin Gilman et al. letter to the President, November 15, 1989; Assistant Secretary of State Janet Mullins letter to Congressman Benjamin Gilman, January 22, 1990, Bush Presidential Records, Bush Library, White House Office of Records Management. The former CENTCOM commander General George Crist also suspected Iran's involvement with the Pan Am bombing.

11. Statement by Representative Henry Gonzalez, Congressional Record, U.S. House, March 9, 1991, pp. 4699–703; J. Stapleton Roy memorandum for Brent Scowcroft, U.S. Department of State, "Iraqi Options Paper," May 16, 1990, in Congressional Record, U.S. House, March 9, 1991, p. 4703.

12. CINCCENT message to Joint Chiefs of Staff, "Termination of Operation Earnest Will" (172200Z), August 1990.

13. D.C. Discussion Paper, "Options for Iran," Bush Presidential Records, Bush Library, NSC, Robert Gates Files, Folder Notes, August 1990.

14. Diplomatic note from the Islamic Republic of Iran to the Competent U.S. Authority, translated by U.S. Interests Section, Swiss Embassy Tehran, February 23, 1991; Michael Carns memorandum for the Assistant Secretary of Defense (International Security Affairs), "Démarche to Iran," March 4, 1991.

15. Kelly interview with Stern.

16. Picco, *Man without a Gun,* p. 157.

17. Iran claimed that Marine Lieutenant Colonel William Higgins was killed in retaliation for the Israeli kidnapping of a Lebanese scholar. "I deeply regret the reported killing of the U.S. hostage but Israel should be blamed for the tragedy," said Majlis Foreign Affairs Commission official Sa'id Reja'i Khorsani, "Majlis Official Regrets Higgins Execution," *Tehran Times* in English, August 5, 1989, FBIS, August 10, 1989.

18. The killings of Iranian dissidents led many in the White House to conclude that the Iranians had merely exchanged hostage taking for assassinations. Bruce Riedel, interview with author, December 22, 2011.

19. George H. W. Bush and Brent Scowcroft, *A World Transformed* (New York: Vintage, 1999), pp. 383–84, 399, 432–33.

20. Picco, *Man Without a Gun,* p. 6.

21. Interview with former Iranian official; Mousavian interview.

22. Richard Haass, *War of Necessity, War of Choice: A Memoir of Two Iraq Wars* (New York: Simon and Schuster, 2009), p. 38.

23. "The New Presidency: Excerpts from an Interview with Clinton after the Air Strikes," *New York Times,* January 14, 1993. Under pressure from the media and his own advisers, President Clinton backtracked the next day on what many believed had been an offer to Saddam Hussein for better relations.

24. Pollack, *Persian Puzzle,* pp. 259–60.

25. Martin Indyk, *Innocent Abroad: An Intimate Account of American Peace Diplomacy in the Middle East* (New York: Simon and Schuster, 2009), p. 39.

26. Ibid.

27. Dennis Ross, *The Missing Peace: The Inside Story of the Fight for Middle East Peace* (New York: Farrar, Straus and Giroux, 2004), p. 105.

28. Indyk, *Innocent Abroad,* p. 43.

29. His words had been coordinated through the U.S. government and originally planned to be given by Anthony Lake, who canceled at the last minute because of a conflict. Remarks by Martin Indyk, "Challenges to U.S. Interests in the Middle East: Obstacles and Opportunities," Soref Symposium, May 18–19, 1993, Washington Institute for Near East Policy, pp. 1–8.

30. Ibid., p. 3.

31. Ibid., p. 6.

32. Anthony Lake, "Confronting Backlash States," *Foreign Affairs* 73:2 (March–April 1994).

33. Remarks by Paul Wolfowitz, "Challenges to U.S. Interests in the Middle East: Obstacles and Opportunities," Soref Symposium, May 18–19, 1993, Washington Institute for Near East Policy, p. 18.

34. General Shalikashvili, confirmation testimony, preparation book, volume 2, enclosure, "Potential Q&A," 1993; Elaine Sciolino, "CIA Says Iran Making Progress on Atom Arms," *New York Times,* November 30, 1992. Shalikashvili added that Iraq could also produce a nuclear weapon by the end of the decade if UN sanctions were lifted.

35. Greg Bruno, "Iran's Nuclear Program," Council on Foreign Relations, March 10, 2010, www.cfr.org/publica tion/16811/irans_nuclear_program.html, accessed October 8, 2010.

36. Hooshang Amirahmadi, interview with author, June 25, 2010.

37. Pollack, *Persian Puzzle,* p. 266.

38. Osama Hamdan, interview with author, February 16, 2010, Beirut, Lebanon.

39. Hamdan told the author this over dinner in a restaurant in Hezbollah-controlled south Beirut.

40. Hamdan interview.

41. Michael Eisenstadt, "Déjà Vu All Over Again? An Assessment of Iran's Military Buildup," Washington Institute for Near East Policy, McNair Paper 29: Iran's Strategic Intentions and Capabilities, April 1994, p. 12.

CHAPTER 21 WAR OR PEACE

1. 15th Marine Expeditionary Unit, *Command Chronology,* entry for July 1, December 31, 1995, Enclosure 1, pp. 2-6-2-7; Patrick Clawson, comments to author, January 14, 2010.

2. Eric Schmitt, "U.S. Is Wary as Iran Adds Troops in Gulf," *New York Times,* March 1, 1995.

3. Shalikashvili memorandum to Binford Peay, "Expanded Deliberate Planning Against Iran," October 5, 1995.

4. "Rafsanjani Answers Question on Regional Issues," Iranian News Agency in English, May 30, 1995.

5. Tim Weiner, "U.S. Plan to Change Iran Leaders Is an Open Secret Before It Begins," *New York Times,* January 25, 1996; Elaine Sciolino, "The Schooling of Gingrich, the Foreign Policy Novice," *New York Times,* July 18, 1995.

6. Pollack, *Persian Puzzle,* p. 274.

7. Kenneth Pollack, interview with author, March 2010. Pollack believes that hard-liners opposed to Rafsanjani seized on this issue as a way of scrapping any possible rapprochement between the United States and Iran.

8. Interview with Dr. Mohammad Javad Zarif, IRIB Television, Second Program Network in Persian, "Official Comments on U.S. Propaganda Campaign," FBIS, January 4, 1996; Algiers Accords, January 19, 1981.

9. "Khamene'i Assails U.S., Zionist Terrorist Moves," IRIB Television, First Program Network in Persian, FBIS, March 6, 1996.

10. All eight likely cooperated with Iraq during the Iran-Iraq War; however, it's highly unlikely they ever worked for American intelligence. "Five Sentenced to Death for Spying for U.S., Iraq," Voice of the Islamic Republic of Iran, FBIS, January 6, 1996; "Three People Arrested on Charges of Spying for the U.S.," AFP, FBIS, June 11, 1996.

11. Richard Clarke, *Against All Enemies: Inside America's War on Terror* (New York: Free Press, 2004), p. 112.

12. Indictment, *United States vs. Ahmed Al-Mughassil et al.*, U.S. District Court, Eastern District of Virginia, Alexandria Division, June 2001.

13. While many intelligence officers suspected that the supreme leader authorized the attack on Khobar Towers, to date, there has been no conclusive evidence that he did. While it is hard to imagine such an important action not having his blessing, the Quds Force is given wide latitude to undertake its operations. Riedel interview.

14. Both the DIA and the Air Force Office of Special Investigations had warned of possible terrorism in the region and had conducted a study that pointed out the vulnerabilities of Khobar Towers, especially the small perimeter that permitted civilian vehicles to get close to the barracks on the north side. Had they known about the plot uncovered by the Saudis, it might have galvanized officials to take action and averted the disaster that followed. Allen interview; Downing Report, August 30, 1996, Finding 18, p. 38; Lieutenant Colonel Robert Creamer and Lieutenant Colonel James Seat, "Khobar Towers: The Aftermath and Implications for Commanders," Air War College, Air University, April 1998, pp. 5–21.

15. *United States vs. Ahmed Al-Mughassil*, Criminal No. 01-228-A.

16. Perry Jamieson, *Khobar Towers: Tragedy and Response* (Washington, D.C.: U.S. Air Force History and Museums Program, 2008), p. 13.

17. Unfortunately, no one activated the basewide Giant voice with its audible alarm designed to alert everyone to danger. Downing Report, Finding 20, p. 46.

18. Staff Sergeant Eric Ziegler, cited in Jamieson, *Khobar Towers*, pp. 46–47.

19. Louis Freeh letter to Prince Bandar bin Sultan, July 11, 1996.

20. According to Richard Clarke, Bandar and others in the Saudi leadership welcomed a conflict with Iran, but were worried that Washington would start a war and not overthrow the Iranian regime based upon their experience in Desert Storm. Clarke, *Against All Enemies*, p. 117. On January 15, 2004, Paul Wolfowitz asked whether al-Qaeda had been behind Khobar Towers. The Joint Intelligence Task Force for Combating Terrorism responded to the deputy secretary "that no credible intelligence strand indicates Al-Qaeda involvement in Khobar Towers bombing. Intelligence has conclusively established Saudi Hezbollah and Lebanon Hezbollah's responsibility, with direction and oversight provided by the Iranian government."

21. Mousavian interview.

22. Jay Hines, interview with author, June 17, 2002.

23. There had always been some tension between the United States and Iran due to the latter's calculating its twelve-mile territorial waters differently than accepted conventions, giving Iran control over a few miles farther out into the Gulf. The U.S. Navy delighted in challenging these claims by steaming a frigate into the disputed water just to assert the right of "freedom of navigation." Frequently, Iran responded by dispatching some small boats to pester the American warship. CINCCENT message to Joint Staff, "Freedom of Navigation Program" (260959Z), April 1994.

24. Lieutenant General Anthony Zinni message for Vice Admiral Dennis Blair, "Maritime Incident between USS *Paul F. Foster* and Iranian Patrol Craft" (021912Z), May 1997.

25. Kenneth Pollack, "What If Iran Was Behind al-Khobar? Planning for a U.S. Response," Washington Institute for Near East Policy, Policy Watch 243, April 16, 1997.

26. General Anthony Zinni, USMC (Ret.), interview with author, August 26, 2010.

27. Clarke, *Against All Enemies*, pp. 119–20.

28. Riedel interview.

29. George Tenet, *At the Center of the Storm: My Years at the CIA* (New York: HarperCollins, 2007), p. 124.

30. Con Coughlin, *Khomeini's Ghost: The Iranian Revolution and the Rise of Militant Islam* (New York: HarperCollins, 2010), p. 279.

31. Cited in Said Amir Arjomand, *After Khomeini: Iran Under His Successors* (New York: Oxford University Press, 2009), p. 82.

32. "Transcript of Interview with Iranian President Mohammad Khatami," January 7, 1998, www.cnn.com/world/9801/07/iran/interview.html, accessed October 31, 2010.

33. Coughlin, *Khomeini's Ghost*, p. 282; Zinni interview.

34. Richard Murphy and Zalmay Khalilzad, "Iran after Khatami's Elections: Whither U.S. Containment Policy?" Washington Institute for Near East Policy, Policy Watch 256, June 20, 1997.

35. Deputy Assistant Secretary of Defense Joseph McMillan memorandum, "Iran: Domestic and Foreign Policy," February 3, 2001.

36. Indyk, *Innocent Abroad*, pp. 215–17.

37. Ibid., p. 219.

38. Pollack interview; Zinni interview.

39. Ambassador Hadi Nejad Hosseinian letter to the Secretary General, United Nations, S/1999/1274, enclosure, December 22, 1999; Secretary of State message to U.S. Mission, United Nations, "Response to Alleged Violations of Iranian Territorial Waters," undated.

40. Speech by President William Clinton, June 21, 1998, www.youtube.com/watch?v=PrsEhjm1DS0, accessed October 30, 2010.

41. President William Clinton, "Remarks at the Seventh Millennium Evening at the White House," April 12, 1999, *Public Papers of the Presidents of the United States: William Jefferson Clinton*, part I (Washington, D.C.: Government Printing Office, 2000), p. 545.

42. Pollack, *Persian Puzzle*, p. 323.

43. Secretary of State Madeleine K. Albright, "Remarks before the American-Iranian Council," March 17, 2000, Washington, D.C. The speech went exceedingly well except for one line by the secretary: "Despite the trend towards democracy, control over the military, judiciary, courts and police remains in unelected hands." Ken Pollack, a respected CIA analyst now working on the NSC staff, listened to the "unelected hands" line and cringed. He had lobbied hard to no avail to have it removed, believing that it would be seen in Tehran as questioning the legitimacy of the supreme leader.

44. "Iran: Khamenei on Albright's 'Deceitful' Remarks," Iranian News Agency, FBIS, March 25, 2000.

45. Assistant Secretary of State for Near East Affairs Edward Walker memorandum, "Iran Policy," February 16, 2001.

CHAPTER 22 AN ATROCITY

1. October 11, 2000, presidential debate, www.debates.org/index.php?page=october-11-2000-debate-transcript, accessed July 1, 2010.

2. CINCCENT briefing, "Assessment of Military Options to Iranian Sponsored Terrorism," January 2001.

3. Lieutenant General Greg Newbold, USMC (Ret.), interview with author, June 18, 2010.

4. On November 25, 2000, both Richard Clarke and National Security Adviser Sandy Berger wrote Clinton that the FBI and CIA believed that al-Qaeda had been behind the attacks. General Shelton remained uncertain about who had perpetrated the attack. *The 9/11 Commission Report: Final Report of the National Commission on Terrorist Attacks Upon the United States* (New York: Norton, 2004), pp. 194–95. The DIA had several unsubstantiated intelligence reports from human sources that pointed to Lebanese Hezbollah as having trained and provided the explosives to the perpetrators.

5. *9/11 Commission Report*, p. 201.

6. During the same briefing, Newbold described the military plans against al-Qaeda. Polo Step was also the name used by CENTCOM to protect Iraqi military plans. See General Tommy Franks autobiography *American Soldier* (New York: ReganBooks, 2004), p. 384.

7. Cited in Craig Whitlock, "Probe of USS *Cole* Bombing Unravels," *Washington Post*, May 4, 2008, p. A1.

8. Larry Wilkerson, interview with author, June 24, 2010; Haass, *War of Necessity*, p. 176.

9. Lieutenant Colonel Kim Olson, USAF memorandum, "Iran 101," February 1, 2001.

10. Pollack interview; Newbold interview.

11. Donald Rumsfeld memorandum to Condi Rice, "Iraq," July 27, 2001.

12. Donald Rumsfeld, *Known and Unknown* (New York: Sentinel, 2011), pp. 420–21.

13. Stefan Halper and Jonathan Clarke, *America Alone: The Neo-Conservatives and the Global Order* (Cambridge: Cambridge University Press, 2004), pp. 10–12.

14. David Rose, "Heads in the Sand," *Vanity Fair*, May 12, 2009.

15. "An Open Letter to President Clinton," Project for the New American Century, January 26, 1998, www.newamericancentury.org/iraqclintonletter.htm, accessed July 2006; Robert Kagan, "A Way to Oust Saddam," *Weekly Standard*, September 28, 1998; Richard Perle, "Rethinking the Middle East," speech before the American Enterprise Institute, October 14, 1998, www.aei.org/speech/16436, accessed August 3, 2010.

16. Frank Miller, interview with author, July 1, 2010. Five others who worked in senior positions within the Bush administration, who did not want to go on record, shared a similar view as Miller's.

17. During an interview with NBC's Matt Lauer promoting his book *Decision Points*, Bush echoed a frequent dismissive refrain about the judgment of history: "I'm gonna be dead, Matt, when they finally figure it out." President George Bush interview with Matt Lauer, NBC, November 8, 2010.

18. Interview with senior NSC official. Also see Peter Rodman, *Presidential Command: Power, Leadership, and the Making of Foreign Policy from Richard Nixon to George W. Bush* (New York: Knopf, 2009), pp. 249–50.

19. Office of the Secretary of Defense, "Department of Defense Position on Liberation Options," June 1, 2001.

20. John Bolton, interview with author, August 31, 2010.

21. Newbold interview.

22. Alfred Goldberg, Sarandis Papadopoulos, et al., *Pentagon 9/11*, Office of the Secretary of Defense, Historical Office, 2007, p. 35.

23. Stephen Cambone notebook, entry for September 11, 2001, redacted copy posted at www.tomflocco.com/Docs/Dsn/DodStaffNotes.htm, accessed August 17, 2010.

24. Paul Wolfowitz memorandum to Donald Rumsfeld, "Question of Identity of Hijackers," September 19, 2001.

25. Paul Wolfowitz memorandum to Donald Rumsfeld, "Preventing More Events," September 17, 2001; Paul Wolfowitz memorandum to Donald Rumsfeld, "How Certain Can We Be about the True Identity of the Hijackers," October 14, 2001.

26. Newbold interview.

27. Condoleezza Rice's testimony before the 9/11 Commission, April 8, 2004, at CBC News Online, www.cbc.ca/news/background/sep11/rice_transcript.html, accessed April 10, 2011.

28. Douglas Feith, interview with author, June 22, 2010.

29. Douglas Feith, *War and Decision: Inside the Pentagon at the Dawn of the War on Terrorism* (New York: Harper-Collins, 2008), pp. 229–34; Feith interview.

30. Interview with Iranian officials, February 9, 2011.

31. "Showdown with Iran," PBS *Frontline*, October 23, 2007.

32. "Text of Khatami Statement Condemning Attacks on U.S. Cities," Vision of the Islamic Republic of Iran Network 2, FBIS, September 11, 2001; "Qom Friday Prayers Leader Expresses Sympathy with Relatives of U.S. Victims," *Aftab-e-Yazd*, FBIS, September 22, 2001; "Iran Professor Urges Dropping of 'Death to America' Slogan," *Seda-ye Edalat*, FBIS, September 22, 2001; "Iran Denounces Massive Attacks on U.S., Expresses Sympathy with Victims," Iranian News Agency, FBIS, September 11, 2001.

33. In September 2000, Iran allowed foreign banks to operate in its free-trade zones and agreed to implement international standards for protection of intellectual property rights that computer companies wanted to safeguard their software from piracy.

34. Flynt Leverett, interview with author, March 16, 2010.

35. Less interview.

36. James Dobbins, interview with author, May 12, 2010.

37. Larry Franklin, "Talking Points on Iran," February 13, 2002.

38. Ryan Crocker, interview with author, May 2010.

39. Ibid.

40. Hillary Mann, interview with author, June 28, 2010.

41. Douglas Feith memorandum to Donald Rumsfeld, "Key Point from Newt Gingrich Breakfast," September 25, 2001.

42. Feith interview.

43. Crocker interview; Dobbins interview.

44. James Dobbins, *After the Taliban: Nation-Building in Afghanistan* (Washington, D.C.: Potomac Books, 2008), pp. 74–75.

45. Ibid.

46. Ibid., pp. 83–84.

47. Ibid., p. 121; Dobbins interview.

48. Armitage interview.

49. Interviews with Iranian officials and U.S. intelligence reports all support this view of Iran's relationship with al-Qaeda held inside the country.

50. Ibid.

51. Mann interview.

CHAPTER 23 AN AXIS OF EVIL

1. David Frum, interviewed by Linden MacIntyre, April 8, 2002, PBS *Frontline*, www.pbs.org/wgbh/pages/frontline/shows/tehran/interviews/frum.html, accessed April 22, 2011.

2. General Richard Myers, USAF (Ret.), interview with author, June 25, 2010.

3. "More on Khamene'i's Rejection of Bush Accusations," Iranian News Agency, January 31, 2002; "Rafsanjani Says U.S. Played 'Nursemaid to Evil,'" Iranian News Agency, January 30, 2002. President Bush actually captured just under 30 percent of the eligible vote, or 48 percent of those who decided to go to the polls.

4. "Iran's Kharrazi Answers Bush's Threats in Letter to UN Head," *Nowruz*, February 6, 2002.

5. Crocker interview.

6. Myers interview.

7. Ibid.

8. Bolton interview.

9. General Richard Myers memorandum, August 17, 2002.

10. Peter Rodman memorandum for Secretary of Defense, "Talking Point for Iran for Principals," January 2, 2003.

11. Lieutenant Colonel S. McPherson background paper for February 7, 2002, Principals Committee Meeting.

12. Algiers Accords, "Declaration of the Government of the Democratic and Popular Republic of Algeria," January 19, 1981, p. 1.

13. Peter Rodman memorandum for Donald Rumsfeld, "Iran National Security Presidential Directive," October 16, 2002.

14. Notes by participant on draft National Security Presidential Directive, "Iran Policy," October 8, 2002.

15. Armitage interview.

16. Ibid.

17. *Report on Intelligence Activities Relating to Iraq Conducted by the Policy Counterterrorism Evaluation Group and the Office of Special Plans within the Office of the Undersecretary of Defense for Policy*, U.S. Senate, Select Committee on Intelligence, 110th Congress, 2nd Session, June 2008. This provides a major overview of the Ledeen meetings and the talks with Ghorbanifar. Also Knut Royce and Timothy Phelps, "Arms Dealer in Talks with U.S. Officials about Iran," *Sydney Morning Herald*, August 9, 2003, www.smh.com.au/articles/2003/08/08/1060145871467.html, accessed

August 20, 2010. Ledeen had first approached Peter Rodman suggesting the defense officials meet with the Iranians, but Rodman declined the offer. So Ledeen moved up the chain to the number two national security adviser.

18. Tenet, *At the Center of the Storm*, pp. 311–14; Armitage interview.

19. Tenet, *At the Center of the Storm*, pp. 311–14.

20. Armitage interview.

21. Tenet, *At the Center of the Storm*, pp. 11–14.

22. While Iran and North Korea were long-standing targets of the neocons in the administration too, in the days just before and after 9/11 the principal focus at the White House had been stopping Russia from selling advanced weapons to Iran and debating whether to oppose the completion of the reactor at Bushehr. National Security Council, "Options Paper for Deputies, Russia-Iran Proliferation," November 8, 2001.

23. Office of Secretary of Defense, policy paper, "Current State of the War on Terrorism," May 25, 2002.

24. Ibid.

25. Feith interview.

26. Joint Staff J-5, information paper, "Leveraging Regime Change in Iraq to Support Continuation of War on Terror," June 11, 2002; "Possible Iranian Actions Including Likelihood of Military Responses to U.S. Actions Against Iraq," March 1, 2002.

27. Lieutenant Colonel Tom Billick paper, "Describe Possible Iranian Actions to U.S. Action Against Iraq," March 1, 2002.

28. Myers interview.

29. Zinni interview.

30. Myers interview.

31. Institute for National Strategic Studies memorandum for the record, "Regional Impact of Regime Change in Iraq," March 20, 2003.

32. Crocker interview.

33. Ibid.

34. Armitage interview.

35. Notes on draft National Security Presidential Directive, "Iran Policy," October 8, 2002.

Chapter 24 Defeat or Victory

1. Captain William Toti, interview with author, July 19, 2007; *Lucky Bag*, U.S. Naval Academy, 1979.

2. Michael Coyne, "Iran under the Ayatollah," *National Geographic*, July 1985, p. 120. One person interviewed remains convinced to this day that the photo had been planted in the magazine as a way to tell the Americans that one of their agents was dead, and the Iranians knew it. But a retired CIA agent who worked Iran believed that the Iranians would never have buried a known spy in with the martyrs at Behesht. Coyne was adamant that he was not deliberately guided to the grave and came upon it by happenstance.

3. Author's notes, April 4, 2003.

4. One of the best overviews of Iranian objectives in Iraq is Michael Eisenstadt, Michael Knights, and Ahmed Ali, "Iran's Influence in Iraq," Washington Institute for Near East Policy, Policy Focus 111, April 2011.

5. Interview with Iranian officials.

6. Michael Knights, interview with author, November 28, 2011.

7. Crocker interview.

8. Michael Ware, "Inside Iran's Secret War for Iraq," *Time*, August 15, 2005.

9. This eventually led to a raid on Chalabi's house in Baghdad, with the assistance of the U.S. military, in the spring of 2004. This infuriated his supporters in the Pentagon, who chastised Chairman Myers and the military commanders in Iraq and prohibited future actions against Chalabi without the defense secretary's concurrence. Tenet, *At the Center of the Storm*, p. 446; Matthew Aid, *The Secret Sentry: The Untold History of the National Security Agency* (New York: Bloomsbury, 2009), p. 270.

10. Author's notes in Baghdad, April 14, 2003.

11. Department of State message, "Kuwait Concerned about Iran's Power Play in Iraq," April 13, 2003.

12. CENTCOM Forward message to COMCJTF-7, "CFC Guidance Concerning the Badr Corps" (030218Z), June 2003. This was based upon guidance approved in late March 2003 that authorized future use of force against the Badr Corps.

13. Paul Bremer e-mail to Jaymie Durnan, "Message for SecDef," June 30, 2003.

14. L. Paul Bremer memorandum to Donald Rumsfeld, "Iran II," May 25, 2003.

15. Memorandum for the record, "Lieutenant Mahnken Meeting with 1st UK Division," G-2, April 23, 2003.

16. Mark Mazzetti, "U.S. Report Says Iran Halted Nuclear Weapons Program in 2003," *New York Times*, December 3, 2007.

17. Tim Guldimann, memorandum and "Roadmap," May 4, 2003.

18. Tim Guldimann, interview with author, 2011.

19. Elliott Abrams, interview with author, January 5, 2011; Bolton interview.

20. Ambassador Zarif draft of "Roadmap," May 1, 2003; Hooshang Amirahmadi, confidential memorandum, "The Chronology of the Grand Bargain," June 2004; Hooshang Amirahmadi e-mail to author, April 26, 2007.

21. Several years later, a clerical adviser to the supreme leader told Flynt Leverett and his wife, Hillary Mann, that the "road map proposal had been sanctioned by Ayatollah Khamenei," adding, "Today we would not be as generous." Leverett and Mann interviews.

22. Armitage interview.

23. Wilkerson interview. Crocker did not recall passing such a point to the Iranians.

24. Bolton interview.

25. Ibid.

26. Ibid.

27. L. Paul Bremer, *My Year in Iraq: The Struggle to Build a Future of Hope* (New York: Simon and Schuster, 2006), pp. 59, 274.

28. "Iran Denies It Has Moved Border Posts into Iraq," Reuters, July 10, 2003.

29. Michael Knights, "The Role of Broadcast Media in Influence Operations in Iraq," Washington Institute for Near East Policy, Policy Watch 758, May 19, 2003.

30. "Assistance for Iranian Earthquake Victims," U.S. Agency for International Development, January 15, 2004, www .usaid.gov/iran, accessed August 12, 2011.

31. Crocker interview.

CHAPTER 25 THE FREEDOM AGENDA

1. President George W. Bush Inaugural Address, "There Is No Justice Without Freedom," Federal News Service, *Washington Post*, January 21, 2005, p. A24.

2. Text of President Bush's 2005 State of the Union address, February 2, 2005.

3. George Bush, *Decision Points* (New York: Crown, 2010), p. 397.

4. John Dickerson, "What the President Reads," *Time*, January 10, 2005.

5. Bolton interview.

6. Department of State, "Remarks of Secretary of State Condoleezza Rice at the American University of Cairo," June 20, 2005.

7. Nicholas Burns, interview with author, September 1, 2011.

8. Steven Weisman, "Rice Gets Pledge from Schröder to Do More to Help Iraq," *New York Times*, February 5, 2005.

9. Statement by Senator Tom Coburn, *Iran: Tehran's Nuclear Recklessness and the U.S. Response—The Experts' Perspective*, hearings, U.S. Senate, Committee on Homeland Security and Governmental Affairs, Federal Financial Management, Government Information, and International Security Subcommittee, 109th Congress, 1st Session, November 15, 2005, p. 3.

10. Comments made at Brookings–U.S. Central Command Symposium, October 17–18, 2011, Doha, Qatar.

11. William Broad and David Sanger, "Relying on Computer, U.S. Seeks to Prove Iran's Nuclear Aims," *New York Times*, November 13, 2005.

12. "Iran Strategy," September 17, 2004.

13. Testimony of Carl Gershman, *The Role of Non-Governmental Organizations in the Development of Democracy*, hearings, U.S. Senate, Committee on Foreign Relations, 109th Congress, 2nd Session, June 8, 2006, p. 61; Sean Kenny, "The Revolution Will Be Blogged, *Salon*, March 6, 2006, http://www.salon.com/2006/03/06/iranian _bloggers/.

14. Department of State, "Iranians Widely Favor Economic Reform and Better Ties with the West," December 2000.

15. Michael Doran, interview with author, September 22, 2010.

16. Secretary of State Condoleezza Rice, "Prepared Remarks," testimony before the Senate Foreign Relations Committee, February 15, 2006.

17. "Responses of Barry Lowenkron to Questions Submitted by Senator Biden," *The Role of Non-Governmental Organizations in the Development of Democracy*, p. 85.

18. David Denehy interview, November 10, 2011.

19. Negar Azimi, "Hard Realities of Soft Power," *New York Times*, June 24, 2007.

20. Department of State, "Department Efforts to Promote Democracy in Iran," February 10, 2006.

21. Ibid.

22. Warren P. Strobel and William Douglas, "Pentagon Study Claims U.S. Broadcasts to Iran Aren't Tough Enough," McClatchy Newspapers, September 26, 2006, www.mcclatchydc.com/2006/09/26/v-print/14705/pentagon-study-claims-us-broadcasts.html.

23. The others were Kian Tajbakhsh, Ali Shakeri, and Nazi Azima.

24. Stuart Holliday memorandum to Colin Powell, "Persian Language Website," September 25, 2003.

25. Peter Rodman memorandum for the Secretary of Defense, "Iranian Election Questions," June 30, 2005.

26. James Woolsey testimony, *Iran: Tehran's Nuclear Recklessness and the U.S. Response*, p. 10.

27. Newt Gingrich testimony, *Iran: Tehran's Nuclear Recklessness and the U.S. Response*, pp. 17, 21.

28. This was the Iranian president's response in reply to a question that the author had passed during his September 2010 visit to the United Nations.

29. Burns interview.

30. A number of reports circulated in 2007 that the United States provided aid to Jundallah. See Brian Ross and Christopher Isham, "The Secret War Against Iran," ABC News, April 3, 2007; Seymour Hersh, "Preparing the Battlefield," *New Yorker*, July 7, 2007.

31. Robert Windrem, "U.S. Provides Millions in Lebanese Military Aid," NBC News, May 22, 2007, www.msnbc.msn.com/id/18809618/ns/nightly_news/t/us-provides-millions-lebanese-military-aid, accessed July 23, 2011.

32. Interview with former Bush administration State Deparment appointee, November 7, 2011.

33. John Limbert, interview with author, 2011.

34. Richard Cheney, *In My Time: A Personal and Political Memoir* (New York: Threshold, 2011), p. 474.

35. Bolton interview; John Bolton, *Surrender Is Not an Option: Defending America at the United Nations and Abroad* (New York: Threshold, 2007), pp. 130–64. In a March 24, 2003, memorandum to Stephen Hadley, Doug Feith wrote, "Iran is unlikely to abandon its nuclear weapons program and ambitions. Our long-term goal must be to press Russia to cancel all cooperation with Iran's nuclear program." Assistant Secretary of Defense for International Security J. D. Crouch summed up the U.S. government's view in a March 17, 2003, memorandum: "A Near-Term Strategy on Iran's Nuclear Program."

36. Helene Cooper and David E. Sanger, "A Talk at Lunch That Shifted the Stance on Iran," *New York Times*, June 3, 2006.

37. Condoleezza Rice, *No Higher Honor: A Memoir of My Years in Washington* (New York: Crown, 2011), p. 461.

38. Burns interview.

39. *Comprehensive Iran Sanctions, Accountability and Divestment Act of 2008: A Report to the Committee on Banking, Housing, and Urban Affairs*, Report 110-443, U.S. Senate, 110th Congress, 2nd Session, August 1, 2008, p. 3.

40. Nazila Fathi and Elaine Sciolino, "Iran Open to Incentives on Nuclear Talks, with a Hedge," *New York Times*, June 7, 2006.

41. Bush, *Decision Points*, p. 419.

42. Elaine Sciolino, "Nuclear Talks with Iran End in a Deadlock," *New York Times* July 20, 2008.

Chapter 26 A Quasi-War

1. Notes taken during the December 13, 2006, meeting and provided to the author. Another account of this meeting is in Bob Woodward, *The War Within: A Secret White House History, 2006–2008* (New York: Simon and Schuster, 2008), pp. 286–89.

2. Vice Admiral Kevin Cosgriff, interview with author, June 18, 2010.

3. General John Abizaid, interview with author, November 22, 2010. Major General Vern Findley memorandum, "USCENTCOM Recommendation on Low-Level Coordination with Armed Forces of Iran," 2006.

4. Abizaid interview; Abrams interview.

5. Mounir Elkhamri, "Iran's Contribution to the Civil War in Iraq," Jamestown Foundation, January 2007.

6. Michael Gordon and Andrew Lehren, "Leaked Reports Detail Iran's Aid for Iraqi Militias," *New York Times*, October 2010.

7. For an accurate and comprehensive overview of Iranians' activities in Iraq, see Joseph Felter and Brian Fishman, "Iranian Strategy in Iraq: Politics and 'Other Means,'" Combating Terrorism Center, West Point, October 13, 2008.

8. S. Azad, "The Qods Force—Godfather of Al Qaida?" *News Blaze*, September 7, 2007, http://newsblaze.com/story/20070907025952summ.nb/topstory.html, accessed November 27, 2009.

9. Michael Knights, Washington Institute for Near East Policy, interview with author, September 12, 2010.

10. Michael Ware, "Inside Iran's Secret War for Iraq," *Time*, August 15, 2005.

11. "Iranian Strategy in Iraq: Politics and 'Other Means,'" pp. 55–65; U.S. Army, "Intel Report: Investigation into Dbe Find on 10 Nov 05 Near Iranian Border," Serial No. HQ MND(SE) 202.1.2, November 2005, accessed at "Secret Dispatches from the War in Iraq," *New York Times*, www.nytimes.com/interactive/world/iraq-war-logs.html#report/D9E9E0BA-0273-46EE-A998-F2FBDA35951A.

12. "Hizballah External Security Organization," Government of Australia, November 8, 2010, www.nationalsecurity.gov.au/agd/www/nationalsecurity.nsf/AllDocs/7986D1536C0FFD5FCA256FCD001BE859?OpenDocument.

13. Myers interview.

14. "Top General Casts Doubt on Tehran's Link to Iraq Militias," CNN, February 13, 2007.

15. Peter Rodman memorandum to Donald Rumsfeld, "Démarche Iran," May 28, 2006.

16. Donald Rumsfeld memorandum to Eric Edelman, "Iran's Activities in Iraq," July 11, 2006.

17. Donald Rumsfeld memorandum for Peter Pace, "Intel Paper on Iraq," July 19, 2006.

18. "TF 5-73, Cross Border Complex Attk on 5-73 Cav Ivo Balad Ruz: 1 Iranian Army KIA," summary of incident along Iraq-Iran border on September 7, 2006, accessed at "Secret Dispatches from the War in Iraq," *New York Times*, www.nytimes.com/interactive/world/iraq-war-logs.html#report/A7868E9B-3E71-4CBE-93DF-EBEE44E49FD4.

19. MND-N Report, Event ID: 1202 Report Key, 672E9781, November 21, 2005.

20. Donald Rumsfeld memorandum to Peter Pace, "Acting on Intelligence," November 2006.

21. Robin Wright and Nancy Trejos, "Iranians Captured inside Iraq," *Washington Post*, January 12, 2007.

22. Mark Kimmitt e-mail to Eric Edelman, December 22, 2006.

23. Mohammad Jafari interview, PBS *Frontline*, August 2, 2007.

24. Dafna Linzer, "Former Iranian Defense Official Talks to Western Intelligence," *Washington Post*, March 8, 2007.

25. Secretary Robert Gates memorandum to President George Bush, "Trip Report," January 14–20, 2007.

26. Crocker interview.

27. "Karballa, PJCC, Direct Fire on 1-501 Pir Ivo Karbala: 3 CF WIA 5 CF KIA 1 Civ WIA, 201800," January 2007.

28. John Burns and Michael Gordon, "U.S. Says Iran Helped Iraqis Kill 5 GIs," *New York Times*, July 3, 2007.

29. John Leland and Jack Healy, "Briton Kidnapped in 2007 Is Freed in Iraq," *New York Times*, December 31, 2009; "Suspect in Deaths of 5 GIs Is Freed, Iraqi Official Says," *New York Times*, January 6, 2010.

30. Press Conference by President George W. Bush, February 14, 2007, http://georgewbush-whitehouse.archives .gov/news/releases/2007/02/20070214-2.html, accessed July 23, 2011.

31. Scott Carpenter, interview with author, June 14, 2010; "Fearing Escalation, Pentagon Fought Cheney Plan," Inter Press Service, June 6, 2010, http://ipsnews.net/news.asp?idnews=42696, accessed June 14, 2010.

32. Carpenter interview; also substantiated by interviews with three other former Bush officials and two military officers. Also see Helene Cooper, "In Bush Speech, Signs of Split on Iran Policy," *New York Times*, September 2007.

33. Abizaid interview.

34. Cosgriff interview.

35. Cheney, *In My Time*, pp. 477–78.

36. Ibid., p. 478.

37. Paul Krugman, "Scary Movie 2," *New York Times*, February 12, 2007, http://select.nytimes.com/2007/02/12/opinion/ 12krugman.html?_r=2.

38. Michael Slackman and Hassan Fattah, "Amid Friction, Plans for U.S.-Iran Talks on Iraq," *New York Times*, May 14, 2007.

39. Paul von Zielbauer, "U.S. Calls Iranian Official Part of Elite Force," *New York Times*, October 8, 2007.

40. "Remarks by Ambassador Ryan Crocker at the Press Availability after Meeting with Iranian Officials," U.S. Embassy Baghdad, May 28, 2007; "On-the-Record Briefing with U.S. Ambassador to Iraq Ryan C. Crocker on His Meeting with Iranian Officials," U.S. Embassy Baghdad, May 28, 2007; interview with former U.S. government employee.

41. Crocker interview.

42. U.S. Embassy London message to Secretary of State, "Iran: Brother of IRGC's Safavi Says a U.S. Terror Designation of IRGC Will Preclude Iraqi Security Cooperation" (170834Z), August 2007.

43. Knights interview.

44. Michael Knights, "Iran's Ongoing Proxy War in Iraq," Washington Institute for Near East Policy, Policy Watch 1492, March 16, 2009.

45. Michael Knights, "The Evolution of Iran's Special Groups in Iraq," CTC Sentinel, 2010.

46. U.S. Embassy Baghdad, "Analysis of May 12 16-point Sadr City Cease-Fire Agreement," May 14, 2008.

47. "MND-C, Friendly Action, Detain RPT 41 Fires BDE: 1UE, Report Key, 3144FC46," October 23, 2008, www. nytimes.com/interactive/world/iraq-war-logs.html#report/CBEA1920-423D-4561-50EF2C11 CE525E79, accessed at "Secret Dispatches from the War in Iraq," *New York Times*.

48. "MND-B EVENT 2, Friendly Action, Confiscation Rpt 2/B/2-30 In: 0 Inj/Dam," October 5, 2008, www .nytimes.com/interactive/world/iraq-war-logs.html#report/CBEA1920-423D-4561-50EF2C11CE525E79, accessed at "Secret Dispatches from the War in Iraq," *New York Times*.

49. Bush, *Decision Points*, p. 420.

Chapter 27   An Extended Hand and a Closed Fist

1. Michael Luo, "Obama Talk on Iranians Draws Fire from McCain," *New York Times*, May 20, 2008; transcript, presidential debate between Barack Obama and John McCain, September 26, 2008, Oxford, Mississippi.

2. President Obama would later have to reverse the decision to close Guantánamo Bay prison when he found no other suitable location to house the al-Qaeda prisoners.

3. "Mapping US Drone and Islamic Militant Attacks in Pakistan," *BBC,* July 22, 2010, http://www.bbc.co.uk/news/ world-south-asia-10648909, accessed March 22, 2011; "Obama has Increased Drone Attacks, *CBS News*, February 12, 2010, http://www.cbsnews.com/stories/2010/02/12/politics/main6201484.shtml, accessed March 22, 2011.

4. Dennis Ross, interview with author, January 6, 2012.

5. "Iran-U.S. Ties May Resume under Obama," Fars News Agency, November 11, 2008; "Obama May Bring Opportunity for Iran-U.S. Ties," Iranian News Agency in English, November 10, 2008; "Iranian FM Spokesman Says President's Letter to Obama Sign of Active Diplomacy," Fars News Agency, November 10, 2008.

6. "Larijani: It Is Presently Naive to Think Obama Will Take a New Way," Iranian Students' News Agency, November 9, 2008; Seyyed Hoseyn Alavi, "An Examination of the Real Strategy of the United States: The Great Satan behind the Mask of Obama," IRNA, November 5, 2008.

7. "Iranian Wrestle Over Policy Towards Obama," BBC Monitoring, November 10, 2008.

8. Ross interview.

9. President Barack Obama's Nowruz message, March 19, 2009.

10. "Iranian Leaders Call for Real Change after U.S. Nowruz Message," Open Source Center Analysis, March 23, 2009; "Tehran Welcomes U.S. Policy Change," Iranian News Service, April 7, 2009.

11. Dennis Ross, Op-ed, *Newsweek*, December 8, 2008.

12. "Presidential Debate," Visions of the Islamic Republic of Iran Network 3, June 3, 2009.

13. Twitter allows text-based posts of up to 140 characters.

14. MSNBC report, June 16, 2009.

15. "Iran's Ahmadinejad Calls Geneva Talks a 'Step Forward,'" AFP, October 7, 2009.

16. Limbert interview.

17. "Remarks of President Obama Marking Nowruz," March 20, 2010.

18. Interview with Iranian diplomat.

19. General James Cartwright, USMC (Ret.), interview with author, November 28, 2011.

20. Josh Halliday, "WikiLeaks: U.S. Advised to Sabotage Iran Nuclear Sites by German Think Tank," *Guardian*, January 18, 2011, www.guardian.co.uk/world/2011/jan/18/wikileaks-us-embassy-cable-iran-nuclear.

21. Ibid.

22. Christopher Williams, "Israeli Video Shows Stuxnet as One of Its Successes," *Telegraph*, February 15, 2011, www.telegraph.co.uk/news/worldnews/middleeast/israel/8326387/Israel-video-shows-Stuxnet-as-one-of-its-successes.html, accessed December 4, 2011.

23. "Iran to Boost Soft Power Through Establishing New Cyber Command," Fars News Agency, June 15, 2011; "Minister Says Iran Prepared to Defuse U.S. Internet in Suitcase Plot," Fars News Agency, June 29, 2011; "The Active Cyber War Front Against Iran," *Jam-e-Jam*, June 14, 2011.

24. Saeed Kamali Dehghan, "Man Pleads Guilty to Assassinating Iranian Nuclear Scientist," *Guardian*, August 23, 2011; David Sanger, "America's Deadly Dynamics with Iran," *New York Times*, November 5, 2011; "Is the Mossad Targeting Iran's Nuclear Scientists?" *Time*, November 30, 2011.

25. David Sanger and William Broad, "Explosion Seen as Big Setback to Iran's Missile Program, *New York Times*, December 4, 2011.

26. Jeffrey Richelson, *Spying on the Bomb: American Nuclear Intelligence from Nazi Germany to Iran and North Korea* (New York: Norton, 2006), p. 507.

27. James Risen, *State of War: The Secret History of the CIA and the Bush Administration* (New York: Free Press, 2006), pp. 194–212.

28. According to James Risen, the Russian had spotted the design flaws, and in an attempt to help the plan, he penned a letter to the Iranians essentially stating the blueprints were not perfect. By doing so, it tipped off the Iranians to look for the flaws. As much of the blueprints remained accurate, it could have actually aided Iran in designing the triggering device.

29. "Iran Scientist Shahram Amiri—Video Transcripts," BBC News, June 8, 2010, www.bbc.co.uk/news, accessed November 12, 2011.

30. Michael Shuster, "Covert War with Iran: A 'Wilderness of Mirrors,'" National Public Radio, May 11, 2011, www.npr.org/2011/05/10/136054851/covert-war-with-iran-a-wilderness-of-mirrors, accessed December 1, 2011; David Sanger, "A Defector Goes Home, but to What End?" *New York Times*, July 17, 2010.

31. Shuster, "Covert War with Iran."

32. Mark Duell, "'I Don't Think We'll Ever See Them Again': More Than a Dozen CIA Spies Captured in Iran and Lebanon Feared Executed," *Daily Mail*, www.dailymail.co.uk/news/article-2064286/CIA-spies-captured-Iran-Lebanon-Hezbollah-feared-executed.html, accessed November 21, 2011.

33. Robert Baer, "Did Hezbollah Beat the CIA at Its Own Techno-Surveillance Game?," *Time*, November 30, 2011, www.time.com, accessed December 1, 2011.

34. "Hizbollah Behind Unraveling of CIA Network," Associated Press, November 26, 2011; Ken Dilanian, "CIA Forced to Curb Spying in Lebanon," *Los Angeles Times*, November 20, 2011.

35. Nicholas Blanford, "Collapse of CIA Operations Benefits Iran," *Daily Star*, December 15, 2011; "Talk of the Hour," interview with Deputy Hasan Fadlallah, al-Manar, December 9, 2011; Jinan Jam'awi, "Beirut's Curse on the CIA from 1983 until 2011: Hezbollah Takes Advantage of the Sophisticated Techniques and the Agency's Folly," *al-Safir*, December 5, 2011; Scott Shane, "Hezbollah Station Identifies 10 Supposed CIA Officers," *New York Times*, December 13, 2011.

36. "Connelly Meets Aoun, Says Concerned Over Hezbollah Accusations," *Daily Star*, June 30, 2011; "Hezbollah Will Give Spy Probe Findings to State," *Daily Star*, June 28, 2011; "This Is How the Americans Recruit the Agents in Awkar and These Are Their Lebanese Targets," *al-Safir*.

37. "Second Intelligence Shock Inflicted by Iran as 12 Spies Arrested," *Raja News*, November 29, 2011. The minister of intelligence and security, Heydar Moslehi, accused one of these agents of being inside the government, a charge that was aimed more at discrediting President Ahmadinejad. Earlier, Ahmadinejad had tried to fire Moslehi, only to be overruled in a very public rebuke by the supreme leader. CIA spies have always been an easy scapegoat for Iranian officials.

38. General Martin Dempsey interview with Barbara Starr, Cable News Network, *The Situation Room*, December 20, 2011.

39. Scott Peterson, "Iran Hijacked U.S. Drone, Says Iranian Engineer," *Christian Science Monitor*, December 15, 2011; Bob Orr, "U.S. Official: Iran Does Have Our Drone," CBS News, December 8, 2011; Tim Lister, "Crashed Drone Was Looking at Iranian Nuclear Sites," CNN, December 15, 2011.
40. Lieutenant General Patrick O'Reilly, "Ballistic Missile Defense Overview for the International Air and Missile Defense Symposium," March 2010.
41. Comments by General David Petraeus at the Institute for the Study of War, January 22, 2010.
42. "Integrated Air and Missile Defense Center of Excellence: Information Briefing to 3rd Annual International Air and Missile Defense Symposium," March 2010; Lieutenant Colonel Ahmed al-Shehhi and Lieutenant Colonel Michael Tronolone briefing, "Integrated Air and Missile Defense Center," March 2010.
43. Cosgriff interview.
44. Nicholas Burns, "Obama's Opportunity in Iran," *Boston Globe*, October 1, 2009.

EPILOGUE

1. U.S. Embassy, Riyadh message, "Saudi King Says Talks with Iranian FM 'Heated,'" March (161418Z) 2009; cited in the *Jerusalem Post*, December 3, 2010.
2. Matthew Levitt, "Prepared Statement and Testimony," *Iranian Terror Operations on American Soil*, joint hearing, U.S. House of Representatives, Committee on Homeland Security, October 26, 2011, p. 6.
3. Justin Rohrlich and Donn Fresard, "So, How Does an Iranian Terror Suspect Pay the Bills?" *Minyanville*, October 11, 2011, www.minyanville.com/businessmarkets/articles/manssor-arbabsiar-mansour-arbabsiar-iranian-bomber/10/13/2011/id/37367, accessed December 3, 2011.
4. *United States vs. Manssor Arbabsiar*, Criminal Complaint, Southern District of New York, October 11, 2011; U.S. Department of the Treasury, "Announcement of Sanctions Against Five Individuals Tied to Iranian Plot to Assassinate the Saudi Arabian Ambassador to the United States," October 11, 2011.
5. Rich Gladstone, "Iran Scoffs at U.S. Account of Alleged Assassination Plot," *New York Times*, October 13, 2011.
6. Lara Jakes, "Iran FM Says U.S. Buildup Near Iraq Lacks Prudence," Associated Press, October 31, 2011.
7. Vice Admiral Mark Fox, interview with author, December 11, 2011.
8. "Europe Agrees to Ban Oil Imports from Iran as West Tightens Its Grip," *Moneynews.com*, January 4, 2012, http://www.moneynews.com/Markets/Europe-Ban-Oil-Iran/2012/01/04/id/423032, accessed January 7, 2012.
9. International Atomic Energy Agency, "Implementation of the NPT Safeguards Agreement and relevant provisions of Security Council resolutions in the Islamic Republic of Iran," February 24, 2012.
10. Mark Landler, "Obama Presses Netanyahu to Resist Strikes on Iran," *New York Times*, March 5, 2012.

Index